MW00936350

INTIMATE MEANDERINGS

Conversations Close to Our Hearts

By Morgan Zo-Callahan and Friends
Ken Ireland, editor
Elizabeth Russell, copy editor

iUniverse, Inc.
New York   Bloomington

Intimate Meanderings
Conversations Close to Our Hearts

iUniverse books may be ordered through booksellers or by contacting:

iUniverse
1663 Liberty Drive
Bloomington, IN 47403
www.iuniverse.com
1-800-Authors (1-800-288-4677)

ISBN: 978-1-4401-3658-0 (sc)
ISBN: 978-1-4401-3659-7 (e-book)

Printed in the United States of America

iUniverse rev. date: 6/2/2009

Contents

v

Part II

Appendix III

Foreword

Thank you for *Meanderings* and the invitation to write a foreword. Your book is the work of a midwife—bringing actions and concepts into existence, giving them life, new life. This is a noble tradition in the life of the mind.

The prefix *maia*, in Greek, is an address to an old woman or the word for a "good mother". The Greeks coined the phrase *gaia maia*, "Mother Earth." *Maieutikos*, the word for midwife, was used metaphorically for Socrates (Liddell-Scott's dictionary). *Maia* combined with *techne* becomes the art and science of midwifery. Socrates' method was called "maieutic" because he could elicit from others what was on their minds without their knowing it. You keep good company.

You blend the work of the academy, professional therapy, an activist life, Buddhist practice and spirituality. You yourself have a lot to say about death and dying, activism and Buddhism. Your interviews with such a diversity of people add more points of view, insights that are helpful and interesting. What appeals to me intellectually and emotionally about your book is that reading these pieces together creates a very new context to hold the experience of life. Spirituality, what you call meditation, is the glue that holds all the parts together. I feel that all your contributors are committed to integrate the fragments of what knowledge and methods we have acquired—in my case it is mainly scholarship—with real life experience. Taken as a whole, we accomplish that end much more successfully than we would as individuals. This is, as you might say, a real expression of inter-being.

Be well and keep meandering.

John Lounibos, Ph.D.

My Debt of Gratitude

I have a confession: my book, *Intimate Meanderings*, is not mine alone, but the work of many people's efforts, and the collaboration of many voices. Our book contains some reflections on Therapy, Meditation, Religion, Education for Older Adults, Hospice, Death; Community Organizing/Volunteering. The stories, essays, poems, therapies, spiritual "exercises," eulogies, and interviews present ideas for your consideration. Even if we disagree, I hope to pique your spiritual and literary curiosity about your own inner and outer journey.

"Meandering": (Greek *maiandros*): being, turning and winding with the Flow of Life; wandering toward an unknown destination, getting lost and finding yourself all over again; bodies of water moving—our human mostly water-bodies, rivers rushing, gurgling, dancing currents, interruptions, jam ups, changes of directions, rushing curvy waters, ascents and magnificent falls, placid clear, shimmering seas, tempestuous, ecstatically waving, brutal smashings against jagged silver stone, blue-gray serene waters. We're moving along, riding the Current of Life.

"Intimate": connected to my heart, as well as mind; personal, innermost; what we writers of *Meanderings* want to communicate *cor ad cor;* just honestly communicating/generating heart to heart sharing of deepest wants, desires, yearnings. Exploring the inner and inter-relational processes of obtaining a peace and joy within us.

I especially thank Ken Ireland for being my editor and a writer for this project. I call Ken "Big Dog," as he combines sweetness with incisive criticism of words that don't significantly affect our understanding and our hearts. Ken calls me "Mr. Glue" because I can stick a lot of us together who are following similar lines of thought, active co-conspirators to break down barriers among us, cordially and non-dogmatically. Thanks also to Elizabeth Russell for her meticulous work as copy editor as well as her writing. My appreciation goes to Robert Rahl for valuable proof-reading.

I'm grateful for the articles and consultations of Joyce Sin, "Ed", Doug McFerran, Gary Schouborg, John Lounibos, Bob Kaiser, Bob Brophy, Dan Berrigan, Paul Kelly, Harry Wu, Elizabeth Russell, Robert Rahl, Gene Bianchi, Rev. Sam Haycraft, Dr. Eng Moy, Dr. Nitin Trasi, Dilip Trasi, Rebecca Sheppard, Al Duffy, Don Foran, Dave W. Van Etten, Dan Peterson, S.J., Bhante Chao Chu, Ven. Dao Yuan and Rosemead Buddhist Monastery's Sunday Conversation group.

To friends, former students and mentors: Wendy; Lois, Mary, Javier, Java, Goyo & David Ferrer; Cecie McGrath & family; Tom McGrath (Rest in Peace); Dan & Katy Meyer; Belva; Melanie; Jack & Teresa Chang; Al Grana; Q; Jerry Shiga; Aura; Mariangela; Elizabeth; Stephanie; Gabriel; Louisette; Ken Rose; Joy; Rosemary; Johny; Linda; Holly & Danny; Jacky; Amy; Anh (Rest in Peace); Lon; Lily; Lena; Gina; Mercado Family; Alfonso Jimenez; Nancy; Dong Fang; Wen Li; Jackie; Helena; Sarah; Andrew Weil, M.D.; Harry, Ching Lee & Harrison Wu; Wail Haddadin; Ven. Bhante Chao Chu; Ven. Dao Yuan; Rev. Sean Thompson; Vinita, John Tarrant; Ven. Wendy Egyoku; Jim Yee; Joyce Sin; Lucky and Ira (Rest in Peace); Ven. Hui Cheng; Thomas; Rebecca; Rev. Sam, Emily & Kimmie Haycraft; Rev. Dhammaruchi; Huei Hsuen; Joel Sheldon; Jeff; Win May, Pamela; Peter Dibble; Shelley; Dr. Moy & Ivy (Rest In Peace); Master Adi Da (Rest in Eternal Love); William, Patricia; Ram Dass; César Chavez (Rest in Peace).

To companions: Gary Schouborg, Nini; Loretta Holstein; Bob Holstein (Rest in Peace); Don Cordero (Rest in the Music); Juanita Cordero; Pete Ferraro; Jim Donovan; John Lounibos; Bob Kramer; Kaiser; Doug McFerran; David Myers, S.J.; William & Donna O'Connell; Dick Pfaff; Larry & Myrna Romero; Dutch & Juanita Schultz; Jim Straukamp; Jim Brown; Zack Taylor; Tom Whaling; Robert Haslam; Neill & Carole Cooney; Mike Callahan; Rich & Kristi Berryessa; John Crillo; Dave & Mary

Ann Van Etten; David W. Van Etten; Joe & Kathy Mitchell; Shevlin de la Rosa; Tom Reidy; Tony Janda; Noel Brown; Bob Brophy; Paul Kelly; Lynn & Heidi Muth; Tom Zeko; Caspar Pedo; Dennis Mulvihill; Steve Olivo, S.J.; John & Melinda Aldrian; Michael Czerny, S.J.; Bill & Stacia Masterson; Mario Prietto, S.J.; Silvano Votto, S.J.; Pamela & Terry Sweeney; Jerry Brown; John Philip Mossi, S.J.; RRR; Andre; Leon Hooper, S.J.; Tom Reese, S.J.; Bill Muller, S.J.; Paul Locatelli, S.J.; Michael Moynihan, S.J.; Joe Fice, S.J.; Tom Reidy; Jim & Sue White; Mike & Ellen Johnson; Bob Semans; Ray & Cherla Leonardini; Ed; Ed Thylstrup, S.J.; Bill Bichsel, S.J.; Bro. Tom Marshall, S.J.; Dan Berrigan, S.J.; John Baumann, S.J.; Jack Donald, S.J.; Francis Rouleau, S.J. (Rest in Peace); Marcus Holly (Rest in Peace); Dave Ucker (Rest in Peace).

The working children of Veracruz; and the Veracruzanos: Julio; Hortensia; Paloma; Palomita; Oseas; Demetrio; Leon; Juan Manuel; Tere; Libertad; Rosy; Jose; Arturo; Chepis; Angelina; Octavio; Ana Grayeb; *la familia* Grayeb; Pepe & family; Teodulo Guzman, S.J.; Francisco Kitazawa.

The people, ideas, and programs of:
Alinsky Institute for Organizing – Chicago, Illinois

Baldwin Park Adult School – Baldwin Park, California

Dolores Mission – Boyle Heights (East Los Angeles), California

El Centro Community Mental Health Center – City of Commerce, California

El Monte-Rosemead Adult School – El Monte/ Rosemead, California

Matraca, A.C. – Xalapa, Veracruz, Mexico – http://www.matraca.org

Rosemead Buddhist Monastery – Rosemead, California

Sacred Heart Center – Los Gatos, California

Vivir Joven – Orizaba, Veracruz, Mexico – http://www.vivirjoven.org

There is, in fact, no spiritual life as such, separate from life itself. There is only one life....
—from J. Finley's *Merton's Palace of Nowhere.*

[H]ave patience with everything unresolved in your heart and try to love the questions themselves ... the point is to live everything .... Live the questions now ... live the way into the answer.
—Rainer Maria Rilke, *Letters to a Young Poet*

Theory is forever gray, but the tree of life is green.
—Goethe

With loving dedication and grateful blessing feelings to my students—who truly are my "teachers"—and to my family: my parents, Morgan & Helen Callahan (Rest in Peace), my sister Mary; Poppa Fu (Rest in Peace), Mamma Fu, Dori, Dave, Fay, John, George, Rosa, Evelyn; Allen, Sophy, Jeanelle; L.C., Christine, Joanne, Wayne & Maya; the Barber family: Aunt Mary (Rest in Peace), Russ, Annie, Einar, Tara, Inger, Bim, Joe, John, Rod & Barbara, Linda, Bill, Betsy, Bruce, Ellen, Katy, Morgan. To my birth mother, Vivianne duBouchet Lovell (Rest in Peace).

May we live our lives fully, with fun and unending curiosity. May we embrace the richness in differences. May our deepest yearnings flourish! Meandering. Wandering. Getting mesmerized, Waking up. Talking, Listening to others. Being "reconnected" to not quite knowing.

Morgan Zo-Callahan

Introduction

When Morgan asked me to edit *Intimate Meanderings*, I was quick to say yes. We first met eleven years ago when he dropped into a small meditation group that I had organized at the Central Y in San Francisco's Tenderloin. He had seen a flyer in the lobby; he had no idea that I had also been a Jesuit and that we already shared so much background and so many interests. Call it fate, good luck, or a random encounter in a chaotic universe, I would soon learn that Morgan grabs an opportunity—or in this case, me!—and makes the most of it.

It was Morgan who connected me with Bro. Tom Marshall S.J. who simply asked me, "How do you know all the Jesuits who practice Zen?" and thus began a long and fruitful friendship. It was Morgan who helped me find my way back to the *Exercises* of St. Ignatius so that when I was asked to lead them, I actually knew they were mine. It was Morgan who connected me with other Jesuits and ex-Jesuits who were continuing to live Ignatian ideals in their lives although their life experience had opened whole new vistas and possibilities beyond our Jesuit training.

This ability to meet a person and immediately begin connecting them into other worlds and relationships—there is no secret agenda in operation here—is part of who Morgan is. His gift is to be "the glue" in the network of people and their visions. In Malcolm Gladwell's terms (see his influential book, *The Tipping Point: How Little Things Can Make a Big Difference*), Morgan is also a Connector, a Maven—someone you can count on to gather the most interesting people for a dinner party or, because Morgan tells me that his days of putting together large dinner parties are now over, the planning meeting for a social, or better yet, a spiritual revolution. Even if we his friends do not know one another, once gathered together, the sparks of connection and synthesis fly. That magic also made my job as editor both interesting and a lot of fun.

A glance at the list of contributors shows our breadth and depth as well as diversity. We are men and women who range in age from recent college graduates to people approaching ninety. We are of European descent, as well as Asian, African, and Hispanic. We represent all walks of life. We are married, single, gay and straight. We have various religious practices although because of the network through which we came to know one another, we are mostly Roman Catholic, Buddhist, or non-affiliated believers. I would have to characterize the prevailing point of view as thoughtful skepticism mixed with dissent although there are some more conservative positions represented. Together we are determined that all voices not only be heard but most importantly, listened to attentively.

Particularly in the West, there seems to be an underlying unspoken presupposition that our understanding and communication with the Numinous follows the model of the way we speak to one another as humans. G_d spoke to Moses from a burning bush but the words are recorded in Hebrew and, from that point in time pondered and meditated upon as words, human utterance from a divine Source. In the same way, I think, we tend to imagine that Ignatius had a similar experience while he underwent his spiritual transformation: God spoke to him and told him what to do.

While that may be the end result, it obscures a more nuanced process, what Ignatius calls "Discernment." In *Meanderings*, there are many references to the prayer manual that was Ignatius' practical way to share his experience at Manresa. Though he showed clarity of purpose in his life that was truly inspired and unwavering, he also indicates that he didn't achieve this certainty in an instant of revelation. Rather the process involved every part of his being, his memory, his imagination, his deepest feelings and his will.

And it was not just his personal work on himself in solitude that produced the *Spiritual Exercises*. John Lounibos writes about the textual evidence that Ignatius may have heard of the spiritual instructions of Al-Ghazali, by way of the Sufis in Andalusia, on the other end of the Iberian Peninsula. This would not be the first time that Christians had "borrowed' from another monotheistic tradition. But more importantly, I think that this points to another conversation that cannot be overlooked: that mysticism is not just the result of humankind's direct experience of the Numinous, but is at least encouraged by the kinds of conversations that mystically inclined people have with each other. Some of what you will read in *Meanderings* is rooted in that ancient conversation. This much is obvious: we want to encourage the discussion of religious practice between Christians and those who practice in deeply rooted Buddhist traditions.

There are many kinds of writing in *Meanderings*. However, there is a thread that runs through all the words—they are meant to be shared among friends, to create the opportunity to open, deepen, and focus a conversation that is congenial, and to share insights that might otherwise be overlooked. Our intention is to encourage one another in spiritual practice and lead lives where the focus is not always on us. It is possible for believers to actually join in conversation with others, laying aside their particular belief structure and assuming more "objectivity" so that we can begin to speak across the religious cultures that divide us. Some modern scholars hold that this is the impossible dream—that belief, practice and scholarship are incompatible. This is an old argument that obviously none of us subscribe to, at least not without some qualification.

We have written essays, papers, and personal histories, both positive and negative, that need to be told and not forgotten—spiritual journeys that have a powerful impact. The poems are important; they are connected with spirituality in a deep sense. We wrote them for one another to capture emotional, inspirational moments in life that cannot be captured or held in ordinary language. There are several scholarly pieces because we honor the role of dedicated study in our practice. We also include the ongoing work of locating a spiritual dimension within modern psychological practice because that has been of interest to many.

Some of the "conversations" were originally done by Morgan for a small publication of the Rosemead Buddhist Monastery. These dialogues have been amplified during the process of putting the book together and contributors were able to review what they said in a specific time and place, to ask themselves if what they said still holds water or if they wanted to change an emphasis, elaborate, revise, or qualify. Some of these matters are continually in flux. That is their nature. As editor I have not censored or modified anyone's point of view.

Two of the conversations, though short, are deep tributes to people we can never forget: Rufina Amaya and Kennet Roshi. Their teaching went way beyond words that is very difficult to capture and express. How can I ask the reader to hear all that was not said? There, I think I just did.

The conversation regarding Muhammad and the followers of the Prophet will be with us for a long time and demands our attention. We feel that it has not been carefully enough examined in the public discussion, or the media, or the pulpit. We have included three very different articles regarding Islam, the story of a Jesuit who has immersed a community in Islamic practice, one scholar's work on a little known Sufi master, and an attempt to begin a conversation with Muslims that does not rest solely in the past. If left to hate mongers and xenophobes, any kind of inter-religious exchange will only produce more lack of understanding, distance, separation, and conflict. We see that there are several pieces missing in the current climate, the first is being honest with one another, and, almost as important, making sure that we get information as close to the original sources as possible and not rely on second or third hand commentaries and opinions. At least now most mainstream Americans have heard that there is a difference between the Sunnis and the Shia, but it is still difficult to grasp that for the most part, Islam has no familiar institutional structure. As people with some confidence in the religious sensibility that we share with other humans, as most of us are participants in the American democracy, and all of us conscious world citizens, we have to continue to become more sophisticated in our understanding of Islam.

The Resources are hybrids requiring a short explanation. This new "genre" does not fit any format that we are aware of. They are not bibliographies, nor indices, nor Web logs though they list books, Web sites, scholarly articles, DVDs and other links of possible interest. We hope they are more useful than the more revered bibliography that sat in the last pew for scholars or "when" we have more time. They are research logs that reflect very much how we did our own research. They read as a kind of document—we have attempted a kind of narrative form, but from time to time, when it felt appropriate, we used the time-honored form of bibliography. For example, you read and notice under the *Spiritual Exercises*, a book by Bernard Lonergan, *The Dynamism of Desire*, followed by a few remarks made by one of our contributors, and you say to yourself that sounds like a place I'd like to dive in and see what more I can learn. We want to support your own leaning process.

It is in the spirit of inquiry that I want to thank everyone who contributed. You have all been very generous with your time and effort. My work would have been impossible without the keen eye of Elizabeth Russell. I also want to especially thank Niels Swinkles who is a very astute reader.

I think that all the contributors would agree that there is nothing in *Meanderings* that comes close to being the final answer to any of the questions considered. Rather we hope that our offering is a thoughtful contribution to the ongoing exploration and conversation about questions that matter. It is our intention to deepen and spread the conversation.

And finally, as my work editing draws to an end, I notice

that mothers play a big part in *Meanderings*. We have included three stories of the impact of a mother's death. This was not planned. Morgan did not solicit them. It should no longer be a mystery to me, and yet I am always surprised that when we begin to speak from the heart, it opens a path back to the source of our human lives. And so I would like to dedicate my efforts and the work that I have done for Morgan's book to all our mothers anywhere and everywhere they may be.

Ken Ireland
San Francisco
March 20, 2008
Holy Thursday of the Christian year

Contributors

Rufina Amaya

Rufina survived the massacre of almost nine hundred people at El Mozote, El Salvador, on December 11, 1981. She died in March 2007 at the age of sixty-four. She is survived by her few remaining family members and a large host of men and women who admired and supported her.

Bearing witness! She bore a lot: the killings of nearly an entire village, including four of her children and her husband, by US trained government thugs, controlled by fear and ordered by paranoid leaders. The soldiers wrenched her two little babies from her arms. Ronald Reagan's administration trained and equipped the Salvadoran army whom he called "Freedom Fighters," and supported a government that Bishop Oscar Romero, at the cost of his own life, courageously denounced as perpetrators of gross violations of human rights and the murders of innocent people. As her response to this atrocity, she spoke to small groups about her Catholic faith and practice. She emanated a genuine aura of conviction, while remaining peaceful, utterly human and humble. May she rest in Ever-Abiding, Light-Bearing Peace.

Eugene C. Bianchi, Ph.D.

Eugene Bianchi is an Emeritus Professor of religion at Emory University. He recently completed a second novel, *The Children's Crusade*. He is currently working on *Coming To Be: A Spiritual Memoir*. His previous books include *The Bishop of San Francisco: Romance, Intrigue and Religion* (Authorhouse, 2005) and *Passionate Uncertainty: Inside the American Jesuits*, co-authored with Peter McDonough (University of California Press, 2002). He lives in Athens, Georgia, with his wife, Margaret (Peggy) Herrman.

Daniel Berrigan, S.J.

Dan grew up, one of six brothers, in Syracuse, New York. His dad was second-generation Irish-Catholic, a union man who left the Catholic Church, and his mom was German, a charitable woman known to feed the hungry during the Depression.

Paul Kelly tells this story about Dan: "In the 1970s, after his speech at University of New Hampshire and the congratulations had dwindled down, Father Dan Berrigan and I sat on a grassy mound outside the Athletic Center's massive hall, relieved that it was over, that the governor had not sent in the National Guard and the State Police to break it up. A woman beyond middle but not quite at elderly age, stalked right up, just below Dan's feet, but their eyes were on the same level because of the little hill we were using for a backrest. 'Your speech was fine, but your poetry is immoral.'

"Dan took the long piece of grass out of his mouth and said quietly, no smile, quite serious, 'Yes, I used the word penis in [one] poem.'

"The woman grew angry and made some insulting remark. Dan, never changing expression, neither warm nor cold, simply answering a question, said, 'Penis, the word used for part of the human anatomy. She left. And I knew I had just experienced another 'magic moment' in my life."

Some of Dan's works:

Prayer for the Morning Headlines: On the Sanctity of Life and Death, Apprentice House, 2007

The Raft Is Not the Shore: Conversations Toward a Buddhist/Christian Awareness, Orbis Books, 2000

And the Risen Bread: Poems 1954–97, New York, 1998: Fordham University Press

Hole in the Ground: A Parable for Peacemakers, Minneapolis, 1987: The Honeywell Project

Robert Brophy, Ph.D.

Bob Brophy is a native San Franciscan. After graduating from St. Ignatius High School in 1946, he entered the Jesuit Novitiate at Los Gatos. After the usual course of Jesuit training, Bob earned his Ph.D. in English, with a concentration American Literature, at University of North Carolina, Chapel Hill.

From 1965–68 he taught literature at the University of San Francisco, counseling students and directing liturgy. After tumultuous disagreements with the administration and community over justice and peace issues, he left the Jesuits in the fall of 1968. He married Mary Lou Berg that same year. They had four children, Charise, Christopher, Rachel, and Matthew. Bob and Mary Lou know the deep sorrow of losing their daughter, Charise Marie. May she Rest in Peace. Mary Lou and Bob have been divorced since the early 80s.

From 1968 until a 1996 retirement, Bob taught on the English faculty of California State University at Long Beach, lecturing also in American Studies, Religious Studies, and Comparative World Literature, in the last of which he still teaches "The Bible as Literature."

Bob has authored or edited seven books, the latest of which are *Robinson Jeffers: Dimensions of a Poet* (1995) and *William Everson: Remembrances and Tributes* (1995). He has been editor of *The Robinson Jeffers Newsletter, 1968–96*, and of *Jeffers Studies 1997–2002*, where he remains as senior editor. To indicate that he is still deeply immersed in Ignatian spirituality, here is his book recommendation at Christmas 2007: "my little Justice-Faith group, eight of us, yesterday finished discussing *The Call to Discernment in Troubled Times* by Dean Brackley, S.J. for the same purpose—pretty much Liberation Theology set to St. Ignatius' *Spiritual Exercises*."

Morgan Zo-Callahan

Morgan Zo Callahan was born in New York City, son of single

mom, Vivianne duBouchet Lovell, a reporter for the French press whom he never met but has never forgotten. He was adopted in 1949 by Morgan and Helen Callahan, and raised Catholic, "Irish" style. He was basically a happy boy, loving sports and nature above all. Early on, he also demonstrated interest in religious and psychological questions and activism. He loved hearing Gregorian chant at mass, but felt even at a young age that his religion could be oppressive, teaching more guilt and sin than love. He liked visiting with older adults very much. Early in life, he participated in writing campaigns regarding civil rights for African Americans and petitioning China to release political prisoners, especially Catholic priests. He loved walking alone in nature and playing basketball and baseball. He rooted fanatically for the New York Yankees and Yankee Stadium was his favorite cathedral (more than St. Patrick's), a source of awe and wonder and the unexpected showering of life and excitement that gathered all his youthful enthused attention.

After high school in 1962, he entered the Jesuits and remained for nine years, an invaluable time of learning and being introduced to the *Spiritual Exercises* of St. Ignatius and to Eastern philosophy by a Jesuit priest, Father James Healy. Morgan obtained an M.A. in Philosophy at Gonzaga University, spending some time at the Hoover Institute at Stanford University. He was trained as a community organizer at the Alinsky Institute in Chicago in 1970. After leaving the Jesuits, he joined the Jesuit Volunteer Corps for a year of community organizing in Xalapa, Veracruz, Mexico in 1971. Back from Mexico, he worked as a teacher and again volunteered with César Chavez. He began a wild spiritual experimentation with different religious traditions in 1973, including a five-year relationship with the spiritual master, Master Adi Da. During this period he met and conversed with spiritual teachers such as Suzuki Roshi, J. Krishnamurti, Alan

Watts, Ram Dass, Chogyam Trungpa, all the while keeping up a relationship with his Jesuit spiritual director.

He has known teaching to be his first and last calling since he was in high school; he continues to teach in a private high school (PSAT/SAT), in adult school (E.S.L.), and in hospitals-hospices ("Mental Fitness" for older adults).

He's presently interested in expanding his understanding about "the last things," hospice, death, dying, and living fully for older adults. He remains involved with two projects in Mexico. With admired African friend, Caspar Pedo, he's helping, along with Tom Zeko, to get books from the Loyola High L.A. family to Ger-liech Primary School, which Caspar and his friends built in the poorest area of Kenya, Nyanza Province.

Lic. Leticia Alba Cristales

Leticia worked for the Veracruz State Commission for Human Rights as the Director of Attention to Women, Vulnerable Groups and Victims. She was a supporter of Matraca and several groups who cared for those with AIDS/HIV; with abused women and children; with legal rights of very poor people. Leticia now has moved on to new challenges in her practice of the law.

Angelina Lopez Cuevas

Angelina and her husband, Jose, along with her daughter Gladis moved into Casa Matraca in 1998. Gladis, now thirteen years old, attends junior high school; Jose still works as a waiter; and Angelina continues to live with as many as ten girls, caring for them as her own children. Angelina is responsible for Casa Matraca's everyday management.

Ed, Ph.D.

Ed was born in San Francisco. He received a Ph.D. in

Philosophy in 1959. From 1963–68, he did post doctoral studies. From 1968 to 1994, he served as a Psychologist at a well-known and respected Medical Center. Since retiring, he volunteers as a docent at fine art museums.

Don Foran, Ph.D.

Don Foran, a former Jesuit priest, is professor of English and Philosophy at Centralia College in the state of Washington; he is also works part-time as a professor of Literature at Evergreen State College, one of the most innovative state colleges in the country. He taught at Gonzaga Prep in Spokane, WA, and chaired its English department in the 60s. After doctoral studies in English at University of Southern California, and postdoctoral work in theology and public policy at the Jesuit School of Theology at Berkeley, he taught at Seattle University and St. Martin's University.

He is currently president of the Washington Community and Technical Colleges Humanities Association. He has made numerous presentations for various professional and academic groups, including a paper about Utopian Communities in the Nineteenth Century for the Organization of American Historians in July 2006.

His students continue to delight and often astound him, and poetry and nonviolent action seem to him valuable resources in a fragile and beautiful world. "Sustainability must be our greatest common task and human dignity our most urgent concern."

He and his wife, Maggie, live in Olympia, WA. Their daughters are currently on the cusp of graduate school.

Rev. Sam Haycraft

Sam was born in the Central Valley town of Dinuba, California. His early years involved lots of attention to horses, and "Mountain Life."

The Korean War interrupted his college life in 1949; he enlisted in the United States Marine Corps and remained a Marine until 1953. After finishing college in 1954, he entered Hastings School of Law, San Francisco, and joined in discussion groups where Buddhism was a popular topic. That was when he made a personal choice to pursue the Teachings of the Buddha.

In 1963 Sam accepted an overseas assignment with the U.S. Department of Defense in Vietnam. He left government service, staying in Vietnam for private work. He remained in Vietnam for ten years. His interest in Buddhism intensified through exposure to Buddhism in an Asian environment, where, both in Cambodia and Vietnam, the protest against the US involvement in the war by Buddhist monks, came to international attention.

In 1995 he was ordained into the Order of Buddhist Ministers by Ven. Chao Chu. He's active in Buddhist studies at Rosemead Buddhist Monastery. Sam lives in Costa Mesa, California with his wife Emily and their daughter, Kimmie, who is a wonderful young woman, marathon runner, and golfer.

Jiyu-Kennett Roshi

Kennett Roshi (January 1, 1924–November 6, 1996) was the dharma heir of Koho Zenji for whom she had immense admiration and affection. She was his student at the Soto Zen Soji-ji monastery in Japan from 1962–68. She came to Northern California in 1971 and was Abbess of Mount Shasta Monastery, which she established, for 24 years until her death.

Her books include:

Zen is Eternal Life

How to Grow a Lotus Blossom

The Wild, White Goose

The Liturgy of the Order of Buddhist Contemplatives for the Laity

Collections of her lectures are published as *The Roar of the Tigress, Volumes I and II.*

Ken Ireland

Ken has been a student of Mahayana Buddhism for more than thirty years. He has practiced the major mediation traditions represented in the West, but he has spent most of his years on the cushion in Zen halls, the Hartford Street Zen Center under both Issan Dorsey and Philip Zenshin Whalen, in the Soto lineage, and working with Bob Aitken, John Tarrant and David Weinstein who are lineage holders in the Rinzai, or "koan," tradition as well as the Soto school.

In 1989, along the several others, Ken joined Issan in founding the Maitri AIDS Hospice, among the first Buddhist responses to the AIDS epidemic. He was Maitri's Executive Director though 1993. After that he became the Associate Director of the Spiritual Center for AIDS Services in Oakland. With his teacher's blessing, he has taught basic meditation as well as created and officiated at ceremonies to mark important life moments, birth and death, unions, commitments and adoptions. For five years, he was the practice leader at the Tender Zendo, a meditation group for the indigent and homeless in San Francisco's Tenderloin district.

Ken was a member of the Society of Jesus for ten years, and followed the normal training for ordination. In Berkeley he studied the Enneagram with Claudio Naranjo who introduced the modern version of this teaching to the West.

He currently lives in San Francisco, California where he is practicing, writing, as well as both examining and building connections between the meditation practices of Zen and the prayer life of Christians.

You can find some of his work online at Spiritually Incorrect and Buddha S.J. http://jesuskoan.blogspot.com

Robert Blair Kaiser

Robert Blair Kaiser was formally a Jesuit for ten years and has been informally so for many years. He has had a distinguished career as a religion reporter for *The New York Times, Time*, CBS. He is now a contributing editor in Rome for *Newsweek*. Among his books are: *Cardinal Mahony, Clerical Error* and *A Church in Search of Itself*, which is the source of his contribution to *Meanderings*. He is also wonderful raconteur as well as a thoughtful, loving critic of the Catholic Church. He calls his recent novel, *Cardinal Mahony*, a "scenario to help seventy-five million American Catholics see the possibilities—to help them understand how they can be Catholic—and aggressively American as well. And why they should…. Utopian? Yes."

Three newspaper editors nominated Kaiser for Pulitzer Prizes, and the book publisher E.P. Dutton nominated him for another Pulitzer for his exhaustive 634-page book on the assassination of Robert F. Kennedy, has been republished in 2008. Robert lives in Phoenix and Rome. His e-mail is rbkaiser@takebackourchurch.org.

Sophie Katz

Sophie was the mother of long-time Zen student, Joel Katz. She died during the great summer sesshin (Zen long retreat) in 2006. She lived in Quebec. Sophie has been published in several anthologies of minor Canadian women poets.

John Lounibos, Ph.D.

John writes: "My parents were both teachers. When I began the University of San Francisco in 1952, I switched majors from political science to philosophy that I loved. I attended lectures by Mortimer Adler. In 1954, after two years at USF, I joined the Jesuits. During my first seven years in the Jesuits I considered philosophy my major. At Gonzaga University in Spokane, Washington, John F. Kennedy greeted us on his presidential campaign. During my second year of teaching at Bellarmine High School in San Jose, California, Vatican II began and my academic interest shifted to theology. The death of JFK in 1963, the Vietnam War with its domestic protests, and the civil rights movement with MLK's and Robert Kennedy's assassinations in 1968 framed the social-political context for my theology studies. Daily mass, the *Spiritual Exercises* of St. Ignatius, spiritual advice and solid theological foundations shaped my spiritual life. A 1967 workshop by Carl Rogers and John Coulson, exponents of client-centered psychology, had an effect on the shape of my emotional life. I was ordained a priest in 1967. The next year I traveled to Europe with three companions to study German at the Goethe Institute, learn Italian in Florence and work as a civilian chaplain for the Third Infantry in Wurzburg, Germany. Eighteen months later I returned to the United States to begin my Ph.D. in theology at Fordham University. At Fordham I met Anne Marie Liston. We were released from our canonical obligations, married, and soon began parenting a son and a daughter.

"In 1971, I began full time teaching theology and religious studies to undergraduates at Dominican College, twenty minutes north of New York City. Over thirty-six years in the classroom, I prepared at least twenty-five different courses in philosophy, ethics, religious studies and theology for about six thousand students."

Doug McFerran

Doug McFerran entered the Society of Jesus in 1952 and left in 1962 at the end of the three-year teaching period called Regency. He taught at a military school in Brentwood before moving on to the community college system in 1966. He retired in 2003 but keeps a hand in education with several online courses, including a survey of world religions.

He has published several books on occult lore under the pseudonym of David Farren, as well as a study of Sinn Fein and the IRA under his own name. Most recently he edited a volume of recollections by former Jesuits entitled *Unexpected Company: Former Jesuits Tell Their Stories*. An early novel, *Mendaga's Morning*, which appeared in England in 1979, has now been republished and is also available through Amazon. com and other online booksellers.

He lives in the San Fernando Valley with Adrienne, his wife of twenty-five years. They have two grown children who live in the Bay Area.

Doctor Eng Moy, M. D.

Dr. Moy was born in Pyapon, Burma in 1942, the oldest of seven children—he has two younger brothers and four sisters. He went to Catholic school from kindergarten through high school. He graduated from the Institute of Medicine in 1967. His training took place in Rangoon General Hospital for one year. In 1970, Dr. Moy came to the United States, training in Baltimore for a year as a rotating intern. From 1971 to 1976, he trained as an anatomical and clinical pathologist. He was in the US Navy from 1976 to 1981 and honorably discharged as Commander in 1981. That year he bought a medical practice in Southern California where he continues to advise his patients to "eat well, exercise, and not to get angry."

He has a refreshing sense of humor and a practical, down-to-earth approach to Buddhism.

Robert R. Rahl

Morgan says this about Robert: "I remember Robert Rahl from Loyola High School days. He was, and is a marvel. We graduated together in 1962; he earned a classical diploma with honors. He was the smartest student I knew, handily conquering Greek. We worked together our junior year on the yearbook, *El Camino*; he became the Editor-in-Chief in our senior year. Over the years we've stayed in touch, but it is only recently that I discovered his brilliant, touching poems. They come from the period in the mid 1990s when he was dealing with the fallout from advanced prostate cancer. I find them full of light and tenderness, just like being with Bob."

Robert is a retired professor of humanities and technical consultant. He grows miniature roses and preternaturally hot peppers

Elizabeth Goodell Russell, Ed.D.

Elizabeth is an eighty-five year-old mother of five and stepmother of six who has twenty-three grandchildren and twenty great-grandchildren. She holds a B.A. and an M.A. in philosophy and a doctorate in education. She has lectured in the United States, India, and Turkey and currently lives in California. She is author of *Reading Under the Covers,* published by iUniverse in 2005, edited by Ken Ireland. Elizabeth writes: "I spent the first half of my life searching although, had you asked, I couldn't have told you for what I was searching. Perhaps it was for love, for an end to loneliness, for someone to listen, perhaps for answers to my questions about the meaning of it all. Sometimes that search seemed futile but I was always aware of an elusive something, just out of my grasp, something that every once in a while revealed itself momentarily and kept me searching."

Elizabeth's book is intended "to generate a conversation

that is missing in society today—a conversation about aging that views life as an opportunity not to be squandered, but to be cherished until the end." Elizabeth is the copy editor of *Meanderings*.

Gary Schouborg, Ph.D.

Morgan says, "A conversation with Gary is simultaneously an intellectual challenge and playful fun. He is my *hermano*, mentor, and dear friend. More than any other philosopher, Gary has shown me how valuable are subtle distinctions, patience, and rational, tolerant attention to what's being discussed. He encourages us all to pay attention to our experience, to add the balanced rational gift of incisive intellect to understand our complex, multi-variegated lives, and to extend that rationality to our philosophies and theologies.

"He is my principal source of information about classic movies and conversations about sports. We are unnervingly honest with each other, in a supportive way. Gary's quite like one of his heroes, Socrates, who set the stage, through attentive dialogue and insightful questions, for people to find within themselves answers to the questions they were really asking. Gary facilitates a dynamic that allows one to come to understand what is meaningful in one's life. I experience Gary as a giant teddy bear with bright lights and mischief in his eyes; he's extremely huggable, looking both to have a ball and a meaningful conversation."

Gary received his Ph.D. in philosophical psychology from the University of Texas at Austin. He has published articles about philosophy, psychology, religious studies, as well as corporate education manuals, and poetry. He is a partner of Performance Consulting, Walnut Creek, California, which provides both individual coaching and organization development.

He is currently constructing a naturalistic, developmental

theory of enlightenment as a sense of unconditional well-being. Some of his articles can be found at
http://www.performanceconsulting.org/gary/gary.htm

Correspondence should be addressed to Gary Schouborg, Performance Consulting, 1947 Everidge Court, Walnut Creek, CA 94597-2952. E-mail: gary@performanceconsulting.org.

Rebecca Shepard

Rebecca lives in Olympia, Washington, with her husband, Adam, and their, one-year old baby, Ella Sophia. She writes: "I find that my practice has helped me to become a strong, patient and compassionate mother, one that is totally devoted to raising our baby in a peaceful and happy environment. I can truly say that without meditation in our lives, this may not have been possible."

Rebecca started taking *Vipassana* Meditation courses taught by S.N. Goenka when she was in her mid-twenties, over ten years ago. She says that after her first Meditation course, she was hooked. She recounts how each course … would facilitate making her more aware of her actions, her feelings, intentions, how her mind and heart created her immediate world. "I served on a prison course at North Rehabilitation Center in Seattle, Washington. This really opened my eyes to seeing that there is a fine line between people in jail and people outside of jail.… [W]e are all victims and criminals to some extent. And *Vipassana* can change that. I have seen it change who I am. It's given me new life, a real life. Peeled off are the layers to expose who I really am."

Joyce C. Sin

Kept up late into the night by the sweltering Los Angeles heat on September 3, 2007, Joyce wrote a few words about her immersion into Buddhism.

"Ten years ago after I retired from my business, I wanted

to continue to enrich my life. I started reading some Chinese Buddhist classics, the first being the *Platform Sutra* of the sixth Patriarch. From the first page, I was drawn into his teachings completely, totally. What a profound, refreshing, and succinct path to liberation. I felt myself spiritually yielding. So I started my ten years' journey into seeking for the ultimate truth.

"Having a curious mind and being a voracious reader, I was led to various traditions of Buddhism. I had moments of ecstasy when I gained insights; the joy was so overwhelming that tears of gratitude fell ceaselessly. I also had periods of frustration when I would walk away in total puzzlement. Eventually those high and low periods all dissipated. I have gained the peace and tranquility of mind that I was looking for so passionately.

"Since the beginning of 2007, I've formed a non-profit organization to teach etiquette and good citizenship to new immigrants from China. Our mission is to promote good manners through integrating the practice of Eastern virtues such as loyalty, integrity, piety, and honesty with Western values such as altruism, aesthetics, cleanliness, consideration and compassion. Our goal is to encourage cultural sensitivity and raise awareness of both Eastern and Western traditions. We offer classes, discussions and demonstration at various learning levels in schools and club meetings to instill social confidence in daily life." Joyce's Web site is http://www.ewess.org. and can be reached at infor@ewess.org.

Dilip Trasi

Dilip commands an immense wealth of knowledge about Indian religion. He also possesses ample wisdom and comradeship. He hosts a conversation-list (mostly discussing Eastern thought) called *atmyadnyana*, and is a disciple of Sai Baba.

Morgan says: "Dilip has offered me many links to wonderful spiritual treatises and public dialogues, which have helped me to appreciate Indian religious philosophy. I've learned about the teaching of Nisargadatta from http://www.sankaracharya.org/i_am_that.php. I've also been able to read parts of *Jagatguru Adi Shankaracharya*, the four *Vedas*, eleven *Upanishads, Brahma Sutras, Mahabharata*, and Ramana Maharshi's *Who Am I*, which is my personal favorite."

Dilip designs and installs lighting for airways; he lives in Mumbai, India. He can be reached at: atmadnyana@yahoogroups.com.

Nitin Trasi, M.D.

Dr. Nitin Trasi is a gynecologist, with a post-graduate degree in the discipline from the University of Bombay (now Mumbai). Dr Trasi was born in Mumbai, India, to a traditional Hindu family. His mother, a devoutly religious woman, inculcated in him a love of religion and spirituality, while his physicist-mathematician father, instilled in him a scientific temperament. From childhood, he was fortunate to be in contact with several saints, but a long association with Sri Kamu Baba, a Sufi disciple of Sai Baba of Shirdi, primarily influenced him. He was also deeply impressed by the teachings and writings of several teachers past and present, including the Buddha, Jnaneshwar, Kabir, J Krishnamurti, Ramana Maharshi, Nisargadatta Maharaj, Anthony de Mello and Alan Watts.

Nitin combines serious studies of religion and philosophy, with profound personal insight. He is the author of several published articles on the psychology of spirituality and spiritual Awakening. He is also the author of *The Science of Enlightenment* (D.K.Printworld P Ltd, 1999), which presents a comprehensive explanation of spirituality, mysticism, and God, in scientific terms. The book was selected as a reference book by the Department of Education, Government of India.

In 2000, Dr Trasi was invited to present a paper on his

book at an International Conference at Bangalore, sponsored by UNESCO and several other international organizations. In 2001, Dr. Trasi was elected a Fellow of the World Academy of Art and Science. He currently works and practices in Australia.

David W. Van Etten

Dave is the youngest contributor to "Meanderings." His insights are valuable, not just for their freshness, but because he brings a discernment and love that is so heart felt that he gives real life to the Jesus Teachings. This is what he wrote by way of introduction:

"My mother was a Sister of Loretto and my dad was a Jesuit before they met at the University of San Francisco during the summer of 1967 where they were taking summer school classes. They left their religious orders, got married, and had a daughter—my sister, Mary Grace—and a son, me. My parents live in San Jose and run a home daycare center, affectionately called the Van Etten Zoo. My sister lives in San Jose with her husband, Andy Miller, and their two kids, Anna Marie and Jake; she works for the San Jose Sharks. I am finishing my last year of law school at Boalt Hall, the University of California at Berkeley. I continue to wrestle with the life lessons learned growing up at the Van Etten Zoo and the theological instincts I developed during my Jesuit education in college at Santa Clara University."

Harry Wu

Harry talks about his upbringing: *"My father was a banker and my mother had descended from a family of well-to-do landlords. My youth was one of peace and pleasure. Then in 1949 came the communist revolution, led by Mao. My life changed dramatically. During my teen-age years, my father lost all his properties. We had money problems. The government took over all the property in the country. We even had to sell my piano. You see, freedom is priceless. I had it. Then lost it. Then I finally got it back. You cannot understand what it means to have freedom unless you have lost it.*" (World People's Blog, November 16, 2005)

He is the author of three books. *Laogai: The Chinese Gulag*, published in 1991, is the first book to address the systematic abuses of the Chinese prison camps. *Bitter Winds*, published in 1994, is a memoir of his time in the camps. His latest book, *Troublemaker*, was published in 1996. It tells of his clandestine trips back into China to gather evidence about the Laogai and his detention by the Chinese government in the summer of 1995.

Harry has received awards from varying Human Rights groups around the world. He received honorary degrees from St. Louis University and the American University in Paris.

Harry lives in Virginia with his wife, Ching Mai and son, Harrison. His Web site: http://www.laogai.org.

Part I

Section One, The Art of Living Fully

Although the World is Full of Suffering:
Death, Dying, and Living Fully
Morgan Zo-Callahan

> *Although the world is full of suffering, it is also full of the overcoming of it.*
>
> —Helen Keller

> *This is what you do when you want to know God.*
> *You don't go looking for an object called God.*
> *You cultivate the awareness of love in an awake heart.*
> *You keep your heart awake to respond to God by love …*
> *This, a person can cultivate.*
>
> —Thomas Merton

I have been a participant and a seminar leader in an ongoing conversation about accompanying the dying and living aware of our own dying at the Rosemead Buddhist Monastery in southern California. This essay is drawn from my own reflections, notes, and the comments of other participants.

We begin each session by trying to create a loving and centered context, "right mind" in Buddhist terms, for the inquiry.

> *Our prayer is that we all be happy, free from worry, free from hatred. May we all develop hearts of loving kindness. We are alive!*
> *We begin by taking a few deep breaths to center ourselves, relax, be present and focused.*
> *Let's take a few minutes to forgive ourselves and release*

1

all unnecessary burdens of guilt, anger, jealousies, sadness, and worries.

Release any tense grudges we may be holding; forgive offenses against us, let hatred go and cultivate a compassion and loving kindness towards others and myself.

I acknowledge where I've hurt others, and myself and I try to see the thoughts that mobilized those behaviors. I release my "you should have's," "you're no-good's."

I forgive myself. I forgive you and thank you for in advance forgiving me for any way I might offend or mislead you.

I offer myself loving regard, appreciating myself, just as I am.

May we be happy and compassionate, in touch with what we love. May we be open to listen and hear.

We extend these wishes to family, friends, and to the whole world. May we all flourish, discover our heart's truest desires and live with renewed faith.

I bow to each of you and all of you with respect, reverence and gratitude for taking the chance that something is useful in this writing for the benefit of own lives and for its ending.

Several years ago, when I came to this temple and introduced myself to the abbot, Bhante Chao Chu, I told him that I was a Catholic who was also nourished spiritually by visiting the Vedanta Temple, that peaceful oasis above the Hollywood Freeway where there are images of Jesus, Buddha, Ramakrishna, Sarada, and Vivekenanda side by side in the shrine room. I shared with him how attractive the image of Buddha's serene face was for me. Bhante smiled broadly, nodding. He told me that he also goes to other temples from time to time for inspiration, and, then we laughed about how hung up people are about "their" religion. He said I was always welcome here. It's enlivening for me to sit quietly in this temple and from time to time talk about our lives. I would like to extend the same open welcome to everyone who is participating in this conversation.

We can talk with one another about this topic of birth, living and death if our conversation is in a loving context with an appreciation of each other, and of the wisdom and compassion found in all the great sacred traditions, as well as the intellectual rigor of what I will call "honest religious skepticism." My presentation may have a Buddhist flavor, but, no matter what our religion or lack thereof, we are all growing in wisdom, compassion, friendliness, and equanimity in relationship to the subject of dying and living fully.

We may bring perennial metaphysical questions into the conversation: "Is there a Personal or an Impersonal God?" "Is there an Uncreated, Unborn, Undying as Buddha declared?" "Is there an immortal soul?" "Is there Nirvana?" Perhaps we've concluded these are unanswerable questions. Certainly in the Pali *suttas* that we study here at Rosemead, the Buddha himself tended to steer his disciples in the direction of being more down to the earth, saying that very often metaphysical discussions about "imponderable subjects," such as whether the enlightened person experiences an eternal life after death, take away from the more important practices of ethical living, forgiveness, study, meditation, service. We can ask ourselves: what is the best way for us to live life completely, gracefully, with joy in losses and gains, in life and death? How do we prepare both spiritually and practically for our particular death?

Alan Watts once said: "To feel life is meaningless unless 'I' can be permanent is like having desperately fallen in love with an inch." We can end our suffering without having to answer metaphysical queries.

Someone once asked Bhante, "Does your temple belong to any particular branch of Buddhism? Bhante answered, "We respect many things people do in their respective Buddhist cultures, but the Buddha's teachings bow to no particular sect, tradition, ritual or culture." Of course, religion has myriad cultural expressions; we just don't need to absolutize or glamorize them. Cultures also have forms of magic—some call them superstitions—which we try to avoid (though I've found that magical thinking can be of help if used positively). There's no magic to being "holy" or truly "whole." True spiritual growth is rooted in our own selves, our own understanding, wisdom, loving-kindness. We enjoy and profit from inviting all faiths and traditions into the conversation.

We're all well aware of the Dalai Lama's urging respect for all religious traditions, that there are many paths to the common goal of liberation. In a public lecture I attended, he encouraged people to keep their own genuine religious traditions, while learning from Buddhism. If one did become a Buddhist, he or she should remember not to lose respect and appreciation for the good in their original religious training.

In much the same vein, Thich Nhat Hanh in a seminar a few years ago in Oakland called "A Taste for Diversity and Mindfulness," said he keeps an image of both Buddha and Jesus on his shrine, because, in his practice, as in mine, they are together. American Indians, Muslims, Catholics, Buddhists, Jews, Hindus, Christians discussed how, within each of our scriptural traditions, we can misuse interpretations, quotes to justify non-rational, non-compassionate actions toward other religions and toward other people different than ourselves and certainly unkindness and impatience towards ourselves. I was happy to see Islamic leaders protest the beheading of Daniel Berg in Iraq, saying it was hateful revenge of shameless political power of people who use scripture—"kill the infidel"—in a way that is contrary to true Islam.

A woman friend of mine, an activist, once showed me Buddhist scriptures that had been quoted to her to justify treating women as "second-class" citizens. We, Catholics living at the beginning of the twenty-first century, shudder at the scriptural justification once used to justify the Inquisition and the Crusades, as well as for slavery. The written words that exist in any tradition can be used to justify a particular, narrow, and in those cases I just mentioned, destructive worldview. Thich Nhat Hanh said: "God is neither small nor big. God has no beginning or end. God is not more or less beautiful. All the ideas that we use to describe the phenomenal world cannot be applied to God. So it's very wise not to say anything about God. To me the best theologian is the one who never speaks about God. Whether you call it Nirvana or Father; it's not important. What is important is that there is another dimension that should be touched."

Once a disciple of the Buddha was upset that some others wouldn't accept one of the Buddha's teachings. The Buddha wanted his disciple to understand his own anger, his own dualistic thinking (me against you), his preoccupation with the need to have absolute right and true doctrine. He asked: "Do you think that we are always 100 percent right and that group you are so mad about is 100 percent wrong?" The disciple calmed down and was blessed with insight.

Our spiritual efforts may allow us to develop some detachment, so that we don't give so much energy to the disturbing emotions that arise when facing death. The emotions of dread, fear, anger, sorrow, our habitual reactions and compulsions may not disappear, but they've lost mastery of our souls. In the movie "A Beautiful Mind," we see John Nash telling his delusional voices and hallucinations that he won't talk to them any more, that he feels the presence of their demand, but that he's not going to give them any more energy.

John Tarrant, a Zen teacher with whom I did two retreats, writes about the death of his own mother in relation to the koan, "The great way is not difficult if you just don't pick and choose." He said this isn't to prescribe some right way to live or think, but "to encourage us to make an ally of the unpredictability of the mind and to approach life more as a work of art."

John spoke how we might just automatically be compelled

to be happy at weddings and sad at funerals. Mindfulness is about meeting and being fully present in the moment, without being clinging or adverse to circumstances. Of course, we all do have personal preferences and intimate connections.

Here's what John writes about his mother's death: "My mom was extremely wasted.... I held her hand.... My father was trying to encourage Mum to stay in this world, to eat—for him, for life.... Mum was heedless, impatient, rude.... I noticed it was easy to think that my father should accept that my mother was dying and let her go. Acceptance, the last stage, and all that ... that my mother should bless Dad on her way out—why not? Or think that I should be able to help, oil the wheels. With any of these thoughts, the room became small and fearful ... a sense of strain, of needing to change others, of the hopelessness of that task, of picking and choosing ... wanting to change myself also led to this strain ... but when I wanted no one to be different, the room was large and at peace.... It even seemed that my father spoke out of love and my mom pushed him away out of love."

And finally I would like to note the urgency of the conversation. As best we can, we cannot put off dealing with the last things until they are upon us.

Whatever the tainted food was that Chunda inadvertently served as the Buddha's poisoning reminds us that death can rush in and stake its claim without notice ... our lives are so short so Buddha implored us to make haste, to pursue liberation 'as if there were fire in our hair.' Buddha took his last breaths under two stately Sal trees. Their falling red blossoms are said to have framed an intensely beautiful sunset. 'Ananada,' the Buddha asked quietly, 'do you really see it?'—Allan Hunt Badiner

■

My Mom's Dying

Rilke says that death is a great gift, but that few of us "open it." With the hope that I can begin to open it, both for myself and others, let me talk more personally about death, dying and fully living as grounds for reflection without any intention of dogmatism. We meander so personally, so differently. Can we face the naturalness of death? We welcome good-hearted gifts and even our deaths and the deaths of our loved ones can be good-hearted gifts, a final planting of the seeds of our so very unique and precious lives. Death has been for me the "great unwrapped gift" of mystery, fascination, fear and great yearning to touch what is eternal. I've been part of the dying of family, friends and of those I've known through hospice work. I'm humbled by the great change that is death and how unpredictable its circumstances are for others and for one's self.

Within an hour of the announcement of Challenger's seven astronauts' tragic demise, January 28, 1986, Mom told me she would only live for about three more months. She accepted the results of the biopsy gracefully—she understood "terminal" diagnosis—but she also felt humiliated and angry at the way she was told which she perceived as poor, insensitive hospital care.

I said to her: "Let's go home." My sister, Mary, with whom she lived, was eager to make her comfortable in a place she knew was home. A kind and efficient nurse, Felicia, stayed with Mom. All of her immediate needs were taken care of. Mary and Felicia would be with her during the days and I would visit after work into the cool evenings and on weekends. My mom loved being a "late-nighter." We always stayed up far after midnight, even if she'd drift off for short periods of time.

She lived for another fifty-four days. She died on March 24. My Dad had died nineteen years earlier on the 21st of

March. Mom had hoped to die on the anniversary of his death, which was also her birthday, for emotional reasons that we all can understand, but she lived three days longer. "Why does this dying have to take so damn long?" she moaned.

Loss is difficult and inevitable. While my mom was dying, I felt my attempts to manipulate myself emotionally and make death all right, but, in the face of death, there was a lonely emptiness and helplessness in my gut. At times, I was aware of my own hard heart as well as my generous side. It was a time of learning and letting go, of being aware and feeling my darker side as well as being light and attentive. All of us, even doctors, therapists, teachers, monks, priests, struggle with our "demons" and subtle preconceptions regarding death. I remember a Buddhist monk once telling me how he was unaffected by his mother's death, that he could easily just let her go. Yet, as he was speaking, he could not hold back the tears that were welling in his eyes. Perhaps he felt it was "proper" for a monk not to show any tears. We're human beings before any of our religious indoctrinations.

My mom's death was not my first experience of letting go of a loved one. I remember myself as an eight-year-old boy, late on a dark, starry night, touching the lifeless, cold arm and face of my grandma's corpse, as she lay in our downstairs living room. I was alone with her for a final time. "Grandma, I'll keep you company while you're going to heaven," I said to myself. I had the feeling somehow "she" was still subtly connected to her body as if her spirit had a faint but real presence while disconnecting from all association with bodily life. Though I was a bit afraid, I also sensed a peace and naturalness to her death. I went outside and looked up to the stars where I had a feeling of being engulfed by a spirit, a presence—that I called God—that was both wonderful and humbling. And such an unknowable Mystery.

The next day, my family gathered to perform the rituals of death: Mass and burial, food and drink, stories and memories, laughter and weeping. I saw how family members and friends react to death so differently. Some were inconsolable; others were accepting; some even argued. This was my first experience that letting go of a loved one leaves some deep effect, combustion burst from the inside to empower those still living to be nicer to each other and more wise. If we so choose. I would later learn that many religious traditions have similar periods of saying good-bye, even celebrations, and allowing the subtler energies of individual consciousness to enter into the greater stream of conscious life apart from one's body.

One of my mom's characteristics was that you couldn't fool her. Usually, she could see right through people, so any phony "solicitous" attitude on my part was quickly dropped. I felt like we were just together. I'd help naturally rather than in any preconceived ways. As hospice work taught me, listening and being oneself—at times just being there and not trying too hard—as well as being alert and of practical assistance, were the most helpful dispositions. I gave up trying to be the "strong" person in the family and "knowing all the answers." I stopped right away telling her not to smoke cigarettes that she'd continue to do until the end. "How I enjoy a good conversation and a smoke!"

One night, Mom had this incredible perplexed look on her face. She seemed confronted with a disconcerting puzzle. She was so lost. I spontaneously said, "Those are just experiences as you go deeper into the vastness. Relax. Let go. You're in the loving hands of your Source, God, your Destiny." I don't know how these words came out of my mouth. Mom started to breathe easily, letting go the tense contortions of her face.

Once I felt the vulnerability of my mom, lying there, alert, but helpless as a baby. We seemed at that moment specially connected in the fragility of our human condition. I felt comfortable, as never before, to ask Mom: "Is there anything bothering you? Do you have any worries?" No, she said everything's all right. However, the discomfort of her

9

body was intense at times. "It's difficult, Mom, isn't it?" She'd nod her head 'yes' and squeeze my hand tightly.

Another time, well past midnight, Mom told me—as she had only once before—how hard it was for her family during the Depression, a young daughter who had to work too soon. I guess that's why she had thousands of food coupons around. I asked her if she had any regrets about our relationship or held any grudges. She told me she learned to forgive, but that, of course, there were some regrets. She wanted me to be a lawyer, to be more of a traditional Catholic; yet she said she had to acknowledge my good heart and enthusiasm for my teaching, volunteering and for working in a mental health clinic which interested her. She said that I should follow my own lights, no matter what. I started to sob because I felt free from the feeling I had let her down, that I was a failure in her eyes. I lay my cheek against hers, an intimate touching that I never imagined with her, as if we were affectionately embracing each other, just the way we were, even if so different. Tears rolled down her cheeks. I had seldom seen her cry.

Mom would ask me to read her to sleep or tell her stories. I'd usually read for about twenty to thirty minutes. At times, she said to read for a longer time. She said: "Now I'm a little baby, and you're my mother." For my mom to say this was so surprising to me! I read St. John's gospel and St. Paul about the meaning of love. "Love is patient, is kind, is not puffed up.…" Mom enjoyed stories. She particularly loved this story I had read from the Jewish tradition of *tashlich*: One *tashlich*—the afternoon of the first day of Rosh Hashana, when everybody walks down to the river to symbolically throw their year's sins into the water—a congregant who was around sixty, started to weep. He had been unemployed for two years, and he was super uptight and profoundly resentful. No one would give much attention to his resume, he told anyone who asked, because he was over fifty; because our culture is so damn ageist.… He was throwing tiny bits of bread into the water like everyone, he related, and he was lamenting that is what society's done to him, just thrown him down a river, sold him out.... Yet suddenly he marveled at the words from the ceremony: "Cast your sins" the verse said, "into the depths of the sea." And he broke into tears, because he realized that he'd been throwing in everyone's sins but his own. His sin, he saw for the first time was this endless bitterness. And it was time to cast it into the sea, into the depths of the sea; so all resentment would truly be gone. "There's nothing to hold onto, right Mom?"

Once, my sister bought expensive French champagne for Mom. We partied with food, TV, and conversation. "Aren't we having a ball? It's just all so ridiculous." My sister soon retired to bed, but Mom and I watched late-night talk shows together. She said she was getting weary, and asked me to sing a Gregorian chant to help her relax and sleep. I recalled how when I was a young boy she took me to listen to the Holy Ghost Fathers chanting at Mass. *Kyrie Eleison … Kyrie Eleison … Kyrie Eleison….* She closed her eyes and fell asleep. The night felt so still, so expansive. I was full of energy as I drove home.

My mom and I seldom hugged warmly, but we shared an intellectual and conversational closeness. I had some fear in her presence, perhaps a feeling of being judged as unworthy, of not being as successful as she would have liked. These nights and early mornings melted away such attitudinal barriers that held us back from each other. She always expressed her love for me through conversation; I felt she enjoyed talking with me, which was very affirming and took the edge off my wanting to please her and her wanting to direct how my life should go. In conversation, somehow all our "issues" disappeared. We were both fellow explorers, delighters in just living, before all religions, all dogmatic ideologies. She had a marvelous capacity for stimulating and probing repartee. We recalled the rainy weekend afternoons when I was young, asking each other about our favorite things and talking about Huckleberry Finn and the daily newspaper. She'd say: "Did your Mickey Mantle, Jackie Robinson, Willie Mays hit any homeruns yesterday?" "Did you write any letters of protest about the civil rights movements?" "I hope you were respectful."

One evening she asked me to read a poem I wrote for her when I was in university. After finishing, she asked me to read it two more times. She became very animated. I felt it was an exercise of mutual respect and admiration, of somehow locating the inner goodness, expressed so uniquely in each of us.

Helen

Your face
was lovely white
in girlhood lace,
spring's delighting,
singing brown whippoorwills.
Your face
is snow-pearl deep
mosaic eyes embrace
as playful children
peeping through dancing yellow daffodils.

* * * * *

Is this life only a beginning, a journey leading to new life? I can never answer this question for sure.

My mom was confident she was going beyond the human existence into other dimensions of the conscious stream of light and life. She would be in a golden-lighted heaven with her husband, Morgan, and with Jesus. She was going to be dazzled in a beautiful, unspeakable rapture before the face of her God.

Mom told me how she appreciated her long life. As the Italian saying goes: "May death find you fully alive!"

"How do you describe a schizophrenic, Morgan?" she asked with her curious eyes. Well, I responded: "Confused. Disoriented. Fragmented. Hearing Voices. Here, then there, vacant, a mind disordered. Ideas disconnected. Intelligence and potency seemingly gone awry."

Mom replied: "Sometimes that's what it's like to be dying. It just came so fast, this dying."

Yes, like a thief in the night.

On Monday, March 24, 1986, I went to Mom's house and found a note on the door from my sister saying: "Mom's gone." She had been taken earlier to Hollywood Presbyterian Hospital where she died from metastatic lung cancer at 7:50 PM. She was eighty-one. I felt a part of myself also gone, but tears did not fall until her burial on April 1 at Holy Cross Cemetery, in Culver City, California. I still go at times to pray and "converse" with her at her gravesite, next to my father's.

■

Papa Fu Passes

This morning just before light, January 17, 2001, minutes to 6 AM, Papa Fu, my father-in-law, passed away. His family gathered around his deathbed, honoring a deeply felt belief that Papa's spirit would linger for some eight hours. We stayed talking to him and saying good-bye, adios, dear elegant long-limbed Chinese man, crying, touching him a last time, saying "I love you."

Some weeping, and certainly sadness, but Papa's serene face and the feeling of peace dominated. Happy that Papa wasn't suffering in the body, I bring two friends, Bhante and Ven. Dao Yuan, who are Buddhist monks, to be with Papa and comfort Ma and the family. I recall how Papa was so easy in his living, not bothering or making trouble for others. He was a gracious person, not "wanting to get something" from others. He seemed content and full within himself.

I would go visit with Papa after teaching, around 10 PM in the evening. At times, Papa would be breathing fitfully from a pipe in his throat, in beat with the Swoosh-Ahh-Swoosh-Ahh-Swoosh of a shiny new ventilator. I'd stand by his bed of tubes enmeshing his withered body. There are also moments of calm and acceptance, cradling his sweet dome in my palm, contemplating with him, holding and massaging his wrapped, slender hands, now needing restraints as he instinctively wanted to pull out the tubes invading his body. I'd put my face close to his and look into his loving eyes.

Papa enjoyed writing and reading, so I'd read some favorite texts out loud to him, sending feelings of well wishing to him, my desire that he be happy and tranquil. May his transitioning into the unknown Mystery be graceful, may he rest in a holy peace.

From Tilopa's *Song to Naropa*, I'd recite:

"White clouds that drift through the sky
changing shape constantly
having no root, no foundation, no dwelling
as changing patterns of thought
that float through the sky of mind.
When the formless expanse of awareness
comes clearly into view,
obsession with our thoughts
ceases easily and naturally.
Simply open into transparency
with relaxed, natural grace.
Allow the mind to be at peace
in brilliant wakefulness
This limitless radiance cannot be contained."

From St. Paul: "Love is patient; love is kind; love is not envious or boastful; it does not rejoice in wrongdoing, but rejoices in truth.... Love bears all things, believes all things, hopes all, endures all. Love never ends." Sacred words for Papa Fu, sacred person.

Death Too Is a Gift
The Grace of Hospice
Morgan Zo-Callahan

> *I slept and dreamt that life was joy*
> *I woke and saw that life was service*
> *I acted and behold! Service was joy.*
> —Rabindranath Tagore

A thousand years before the Common Era, there were healing sanctuaries in Greece, Egypt and Rome, sometimes attached to temples, for attending to the dying. The modern hospice movement developed in the 1950s, in England, to assist the terminally ill live the last part of their lives more harmoniously, free from impersonal institutional and technological dominance.

Dying can certainly be terrifying and frightening, and the individual is better served in a respectful atmosphere that eases the emotional, social, physical and spiritual stress. The most influential model of modern hospice care is St. Christopher's Hospice in Sydenham, England, founded in 1967 by Dr. Cicely Saunders. She was its medical director from 1967 to 1985. The wards and rooms at St. Christopher's are filled with photographs, personal items, flowers, and plants. Patients pursue familiar interests and pleasures. There's an acceptance of the naturalness of dying, with the opportunity of families, including children and pets, to be with the patient. As the proverb says: "What comes from the heart touches the heart." Cicely Saunders passed away at age eighty-seven in the hospice she founded. Hospices are now in more than ninety countries.

■

Elisabeth Kubler-Ross, M.D., a psychiatrist, came from Zurich to the United States in 1958. She passed away in 2004. Her writings are a great gift to those who work in hospice and to anyone interested in establishing one's inner process of accepting and understanding a little about death, in oneself and in relationship to serving the dying.

When Elisabeth first worked in New York, she was appalled that dying patients were too often shunned and even, at times, abused. "Nobody was honest with them."

She made it a point to sit with terminal patients, to listen. She wanted the patients to have the confidence to air their "inner-most concerns." Many hospice workers have told me that listening with patience and interest is the basis of all the services. Elisabeth wrote twenty books; perhaps she is most famous for her five stages of the dying process (which can be applied to other losses as well): denial, anger, bargaining, depression and acceptance. I find this useful, if it's not rigidly or dogmatically applied. I've found most helpful Elisabeth's advice that the dying need unconditional love.

Elisabeth was very generous about giving lectures and answering questions. I learned so much from small contacts with her. I realize how controversial she became in her exploring. Sometimes we get "spiritual egg" on our faces; we may appear ridiculous to others. I'm sure she would admit to going up mistaken paths, becoming overly dogmatic and quirky perhaps. We all are just such complicated, paradoxical mixtures of so-called good and bad, humans. Why want it to be any other way?

■

The hospice movement is now fairly widespread in the United States. It's a philosophy that enhances the quality of the dying person's life—not just a medical facility. Hospice is holistic, offering service to both the patient and the family. Whether at

17

home or in a hospice facility, the patient has reasonable control over pain control, treatments and environment. There's respect of privacy, with a communicated feeling of personal goodness and dignity, open communication, an opening to the spiritual needs of the individual as he or she defines them. The caregivers review and revise—if necessary—advance directives, as well as address financial and practical concerns of the patient and family.

■

In 2002, my friend, Ken Ireland, invited me to visit Maitri, a hospice for AIDS patients in San Francisco. Ken helped start this hospice with Issan Dorsey. I was impressed by the warmth and "at home" environment the staff and patients were creating together.

The very open and ample kitchen had a signed and framed photo of Elizabeth Taylor who had visited and encouraged the residents.

Golden light dappled the fresh green plants in the hallways and communal areas. I was reminded of Camus: "The great courage is *still* to gaze squarely at the light as it is at death."

■

I'm with a dying former student whose family has invited a few members of their church choir to go to the hospital to sing. She is barely aware of what's going on, but responds through her eyes—appreciative and soft—as the singing fills the room. She's holding her son's hand and slightly moving her lips to the melodies.

■

The National Center for Music Therapy in End-of-Life Care

is based at the State University of New York at New Paltz. Perhaps, for a patient whose breathing is very labored, skilled music therapists might sing fast, loud sounds that match the patient's. Then, there is a gradual slowing, softening of the music that calms the patient.

Also, there's a movement called "Threshold Choirs," which was started in the San Francisco Bay Area by Kate Munger. Choirs are invited into hospices, hospital rooms and homes where they sing to the dying, who may or may not be conscious.

"We walk not into the night; we walk up toward the stars," they might sing.

Kate confers with a patient or the family to make sure their music will be welcome. She tells the story of a nurse who wanted her group to sing for a man who was drifting in and out of consciousness. During the singing, the man opened his eyes suddenly and yelled: "Stop it! What the hell do you think you're doing here?"

We're always learning in hospice that good intentions are never enough. Kate says lullabies are requested the most.

■

It's always moving to see a dying person being able to forgive and let go of any held resentments, grudges. Many comment how "it's hard to forgive, but harder not to forgive." The forgiving person seems to soften and relax, somehow "empowered," whereas the person who is unforgiving and full of anger, appears hard and afflicted.

■

I visit a former teacher, Fr. "Pops" Silva, a Jesuit priest who is ninety-three years old and is in hospice. He tells me that he doesn't expect to live much longer; he still has that curious spirit and glint in his eyes. Even in his 80s, he was teaching that elegant bard of England, Shakespeare, in an Adult Program.

Pops is thoughtful, pensive. He's still savoring life, so lovable, full of simple devotion to God and interest in people. He's remembering sweet moments of his teaching life with me; he shows some annoyance at not quite remembering something. He says: "It's all going away."

He has this gigantic Shakespeare Concordance plunked regally on his mechanical bed. I muse how fortunate it is to share our beds with our loves. I give Pops and his wheels a push to late morning *misa,* and give him our final hug good-bye, as he dies four months later.

Not an Emergency, an Emergence

Hastening Death

Morgan Zo-Callahan

> *The best part of a good person's life, his little nameless, unremembered acts of kindness and of love.*
>
> —Wordsworth

> *Death, like birth, is not an emergency but an emergence. Death is akin to a flower opening.*
>
> —Stephen Levine

> *I believe life is a kind of Earth school, so even though assisted suicide meant you were getting out early, before the term ended, you were going to be leaving anyway, so who said it wasn't OK to take an incomplete in the course?*
>
> —Anne Lamott

One of my students was in the hospital as a terminal patient He had had two strokes, and was suffering terribly from bone cancer. Often, in his agony, he would say to me, "Can't you help me die now?" My instinctual feeling of empathy mixed with my personal ethical ideas. Just listening—being with him, even in awkward moments—was my response to him. He told me he wasn't asking for anything else but a sympathetic ear. He knew that assisted-suicide wasn't an option living in California.

He would say: "I wish I lived in Oregon." In lucid moments, he lamented what he called "paternalistic" medical practice. He told me how his doctor and he struggled over pain medication. "Isn't it just compassionate to give me, the patient, necessary medicine to help deal with my horrendous pain?"

He did find some solace in having drafted a Living Will

with the help of his family. He said he felt like "nothing was left undone that should be done."

■

In 1976, a court order had comatose Karen Ann Quinlan taken off a respirator, and in 1990, the parents of Nancy Cruzan went all the way to the Supreme Court to remove their daughter from life support. Now, through advance directives, there is more flexibility to accommodate patients' wishes. Of course, doctors and patients do not and should not have to go against their personal beliefs.

■

In the July 18, 2004 *Los Angeles Times* magazine, there was a story by Fred Dickey about an eighty-five year old Oregonian, Howard Wildfang, who was suffering from a lingering death of lung cancer.

He says he's decided to legally end his own life. In Oregon, "The Death With Dignity" Law (passed in 1994, in effect since 1998) states that with safeguards, any person professionally diagnosed with a terminal disease—within a probable six months—has the right to hurry along death. In the first eight years of the Oregon law, 240 people ingested lethal prescriptions.

Howard feels he doesn't only want to ease suffering for himself, but also to be part of social progress in our American culture. In California—with great protest from the Catholic Church and others—there is a similar bill being considered which would release doctors from liability in prescribing lethal doses of drugs. "Through his death, he sees another way he can serve that populist spirit by showing others that they can control their lives right up to the end."

Howard feels it's time for him to go, not to be forced

by technology to live longer than what he feels is natural. In Oregon, the assisted death law requires both two verbal requests (separated by fifteen days) and a written request signed by two witnesses. Two physicians must confirm the terminal diagnosis before the prescription is issued. The person must be judged as "capable" and be informed of alternatives, including pain control. The terminally ill person must take the drugs himself in Howard's case, it was to be ten grams of pentobarbital in a drinkable solution, about triple the amount necessary to kill an average adult.

Howard died seven days prior to the date he had planned on taking the final drug.

■

I visit a fellow Catholic—terminally ill—who is struggling with his conscience about how he would die. We discuss how Catholic teaching does not require one to take extraordinary measures to extend life. We say we'll do a "Discernment of Spirits" in the Ignatian sense.

The doctor says he does not have any reasonable chance to get better, so he doesn't want to be put on machines just to keep going. He seems peaceful with his decision not to have artificial procedures applied to him. "I won't take any extraordinary measures " he says; this is what I want and I'm happy to be conscious enough to choose this approach to my dying. I don't feel any obligation or desire to just prolong life as it is for me now."

■

Some doctors may not agree with physician-assisted suicide, but certainly they need not unnecessarily prolong life. A doctor might prescribe a powerful sedatives for severe pain which quickens death by deeply relaxing the person into a sleep from which he or she is unlikely to awaken.

Some people may choose to refuse nourishment as a way to die. Physicians report that dehydration and starvation in the terminally ill are relatively painless, part of a protective mechanism in the body. Patients die of dehydration rather than starvation, if they don't die from their illness first. The brain produces compounds, which create euphoria. The lungs breathe more intensely while the heartbeat slows and blood pressure drops. The kidneys release toxins that anesthetize the body; muscles shrink and the extremities turn cold.

Others have left instructions with their families or friends when to have life-support technology taken away. Doctors, with advance directives/family support, may remove the feeding tube-or stop intravenous feeding.

■

Living Wills/Advance directives

"Advance directive" is a term that covers living wills and health care proxies (durable health-care power of attorney). Some of our patients have a living will or an "advance directive" which prohibits the prolonging of one's life artificially should the person find himself in a terminal medical condition from which there is no reasonable expectation of recovery. It's put in words such as these: "I don't want to just be alive at all costs. If my death is imminent and cannot be avoided, and I've lost my ability to interact, in meaningful ways, with others, I do not want surgeries or resuscitation, nor life-support from ventilators, life-prolonging procedures such as feeding tubes, intensive care services.... I want to be sedated before being disconnected to a ventilator."

The Living Will defines the medical conditions—for example, a terminal illness; a permanent unconscious condition; a minimally conscious condition where there's an inability to express one's wishes. It tells whether and when to withhold or withdraw life-sustaining treatments, CPR, resuscitation, artificial administration of fluids and nutrition. You may also request sufficient palliative care with painkillers and sedatives.

Some, on the other hand, want to strongly affirm their desire for aggressive life-sustaining care. They do not want, for example, a feeding tube removed when their condition is apparently "hopeless." They affirm their "Right to Live."

Some people want to avoid having a conservator appointed for them and have set up a "revocable trust" (living trust), which designates someone to manage assets outside court jurisdiction, avoiding probate costs. Some—through a durable power of attorney—put a person in charge of finances. This doesn't have to be drawn up by an attorney but must be notarized.

For our own peace of mind, let's plan ahead of time. Ideally, we should write out our living will and go over it with our proxy so we'll be on the same page with our family, our intimates about our wishes.

Please refer to our Web site for "Death, Dying and Living Fully" which can be found at http://thelastthings.com. This is helpful to anyone who is looking for resources when faced with end of life decisions for themselves or someone close.

The Gift of Tears
May 15, 2007
Ken Ireland

I woke up this morning missing my mother who has been dead now for several years. Given the contentious quality of our relationship for most of our sixty years together, I am surprised that oftentimes I find tears in my eyes when I think of her. I still remember phone calls where she slammed down the receiver, our long periods of not speaking, her steely resolve that I was going to get straight somehow, by the force of her will, and marry (being her son, that locked us in absolute stalemate for almost twenty years), her cold punishment for my seemingly uncooperative nature.

In the few short years before she died, I got really lucky, or was blessed, when I was able to touch the pain these behaviors were covering. That alone took away their power to hurt, and allowed me to experience a kind of love that I could not have imagined. This is what I write about this Mother's Day morning.

There is a famous story in Zen about a monk who, by most standards applied to monks, was a failure. He worked away in the monastery of his teacher expecting nothing—and he got nothing; he sat long hours in meditation—nothing; he did rounds of begging—right, again only scraps; he got thrown out of the *dojo* every time he presented himself before his teacher to check out how he was doing because he didn't seem to be absorbing much. A hopeless case. So after many years of getting nowhere when his teacher died, convinced that realization was beyond his capabilities, he retired to a remote temple where he tended the teacher's grave. One day, the story continues, as he was raking the stones in the orderly Zen garden, (I like to imagine the ones you see in the fancy books with perfectly ordered lines in the rocks,) a small stone bounced off the garden wall with a bing! Just that sound, and in a tumble his mind gulped in all his training in a single instant and he understood. He got his life.

Even someone who has never practiced long days of meditation can understand the appeal of this monk's story. Everyone I know has some dilemma like this in his or her lives. For me my relationship with my mother was a huge conundrum.

I have flown to Tucson to be with my mother after her first serious heart episode. It is decided that she get a pacemaker, and that the doctor electrically jolt her heart and, hopefully, restore a normal rhythm. Then the elements of a really bad melodrama start to unfold, my father's disappearance for several days when he can't take any more, my mother brawling with her sister and a pretty buffed nursing attendant as she tries to put on her clothes to leave: she is going to go out into the street and hail a cab to take her home given that no one in her family seems willing to yield to her command and return her to a normal life. Eventually a really well trained and compassionate case manager is the voice of calm, and mother agrees to the procedure. The drama to follow can be a quick note in the margin: further refusal on the operating table; family crisis; harsh words exchanged in anger; the heart specialist looks like the fourteen-year-old prodigy, Doogie Howser M.D., on the TV (I'm not kidding. He really did look like a teenager). I started to laugh, "This kid is going to thread electrodes through the arteries to my mother's heart?" What is she going to think?" She thinks he's cute and refuses his treatment. Back to square one. That evening we will try again.

Before her surgery, she can have no food; even water is restricted. She can only have small ice shavings. I hold a plastic cup and gently spoon the ice shavings on her tongue. She chews, and sucks, and swallows with smiles. I hear the ice click against the side of the plastic cup as I scoop it up. I use every bit of all my long Zen training just to be with my mother for what might be her last moments of life: just her, just this spoonful, just this ice, just my breath and hers, just her pleasure in ice and water. It is very sweet and I feel like the good son. If nothing else about Zen, it does train you to be present in the moment. And that moment will have to be enough for this particular gay son after many long years of psychotherapy, feeling outcast and abused. Yes, I decide it will be enough.

The medical procedure goes as well as any scripted denouement on the Doogie Howser TV show. You couldn't hope for more: the patient gets well; the family crisis is temporarily resolved when the stubborn mother agrees to go to the nursing home; the father returns, shaken, humbled but unharmed, forgiven and loved; the gentle sister has taken over managing the mother's care. And I board Frontier Air for the return trip to San Francisco.

After the exchange of pleasantries, I discover that my seatmates are going to San Francisco to be reunited with their birth mother whom they have never met (how could I make this up?), and I tell them that I have been at my mother's sick bed. We are in flight. Staring out the window as we flew over the Rockies, across the desert and into the sky over Death Valley, I lapse into a brown study, and sit mesmerized by the wonder of the world. The flight attendant offers me a second Diet Coke with ice. My orphaned seatmates pass the offering across the seats. I take a big gulp and when I swirl the ice around the cup, it clinks against the edge. In an instant my mind tumbles and I am no longer "me" in a plane over Death Valley, but I am in my mother's life (I mean really, not some theoretical proposition), all of it, her hopes her pain her struggles her fear her birth her death, and I burst into tears and sob. My orphan seatmate understands something about finding mothers: she just reaches out and gently touches my arm, holding me connected to the breathing world as my mind flies away (did I thank her enough?). Any trace of resentment, regret, bitterness, or recrimination about the way my mother treated me at any time in our lives together evaporates. She is just my mother, and I am finally able to enter into the mystery and wonder of being a son.

The plane lands in San Francisco. I mumble good-bye to my seatmates whose mother that gave them birth is waiting at the gate. I wish them well and I walk back into my life, praying that everybody be lucky enough to find out who their mothers really are, to be able to step into their lives, and to cry when they are gone.

Drape All the Mirrors
A poem for my aunt
by Ken Ireland

For my aunt Judy Carroll in hospice care, noon May 13, 2007

I sit by the phone and wait for word that she has died,
    ready to cry.
But the news is still the same: she is resting comfortably.
If she has a lucid moment, yes,
I will tell her that her nephew in California loves her.

When we last spoke I was 10.
If that is how she remembers me, I will not complain
    or correct.
She only complained that the fall had blurred her eyes.
She could no longer call the pitch strike or ball.
Keep your eye on the ball, you are the best aunt in the world.
My last words.

It was just a spill a younger person could have walked off,
    but it shattered her back and pelvis.
Unable to speak, she pointed to the legal paper
    she had prepared.
The priest was called. He forgave, prayed and left.

An intern hauled out the tubes while my father stood
    expecting her last breath.
15 days later, nurses and doctors admire the body's desire
    to survive
while she lies waiting patiently for her hereafter now.

There is no looking back, no food, no water, no death.
I will drape the mirrors and exaggerate stories of no hitters.

Small Solitudes: Lonely Search for Meaning
A Poem by Sophie Katz

*Sophie wrote this poem in memory of her mother, Chaya Esther
Perelman, who died on November 22, 1947.*

My mother died. We opened up her bedside table
Just before the auction. Pills
For migraine, cough drops, a dusty comb,
Old pens that didn't work.
Scraps of cloth from old dresses,
A dozen paperbacks, high sounding titles
On poetry, metaphysics,
But mostly never read.
And papers
Hundreds of papers
Like leaves in an autumn storm,
and just as ragged.
Old bills with lines of poetry—
Her disembodied souls come into being
With no before or after.
Ten-cent notebooks
The home of daring thoughts on women's need
Before Friedan or Greer.
Health diary of the children, and in the back,
A list of topics that would someday make
Great articles,
Never to be written.
On an old paper bag
A bold title in spectacular green ink
—Law of Diminishing Returns: See
How this affects the senses and motivation and inflation!!
She's gone now. The scraps she left behind still fluttering,
Piercing reminder of her lonely search for meaning.

From *Reading Under the Covers*
Elizabeth Goodell Russell, Ed.D.

In this short excerpt from her book, Reading Under the Covers, *Elizabeth says, "The only thing that can be told about a life is a story, and telling that story is like recounting a series of incidents, more or less related to one another. Today, as I approach the end of my life, I know that I am someone other than that series of incidents." We hope that you may all find that "illusive something" in your own lives.*

Mother was barely recognizable under the network of wires and tubes. Her sparse gray hair was, in some spots, plastered to her head and, in others, spread out like a broken halo on the pillow. Her hands, still on the white sheet covering her frail body, were a life map of veins and bones thinly concealed by the delicate parchment of skin covering them. I stood at her bedside, tears slipping down my cheeks. As if sensing my presence she opened her eyes, and reached a hand out to me.

At 91, nearing death, Mother began a conversation we'd never had. She asked me, "Has it mattered that I have lived? Has my being alive made any difference? What's the point of it all?"

At first I fumbled for an answer, but then said, "Both Paul and I are grateful to you for giving us life." Knowing this was not what she wanted to hear, I realized that these were questions I couldn't answer for her, that she would have to find her own answers or go without finding them.

As I sat holding her hand, she seemed distraught, as if there were something she needed to say but couldn't. I waited and watched her struggle. When she spoke, her words were almost inaudible. "There's something I think you've wanted me to say, ever since you were a child. It's no easier today than it has ever been but I don't want to die without saying it."

There was a pause during which tears collected in her eyes and began slipping, almost reluctantly, down her cheeks.

Then she pulled me toward her, motioning for me to come closer so she could speak in my ear. In a voice barely more than a whisper, she haltingly said, "I love you, my little girl."

I had waited fifty years to hear those words. My mother had never said them to me before. I was sobbing as I put my head next to hers on the pillow. In an instant, the past—all the anger, the hurt, the things I hated in growing up—had disappeared. There was nothing left but my love for her and hers for me. She squeezed my hand and closed her eyes. Mother died a week later, having given me the greatest gift she could possibly have given.

The search had its origin in the mind and heart of a lonely but rebellious little girl who wondered but could not or would not accept the answers supplied by parents and church. From looking up at the sky at night and from listening to my Great Uncle Will read history, I knew I was part of something larger but when I spoke of it to my parents, they said I was being silly and that when I grew up I would understand. I stopped talking to them but kept the experience of wonder close to my heart.

I used to wonder what accidents of history had conspired to assemble the pieces of my life in such a way that I turned out as I have. I wondered how different my adult life would have been had I not gone to Europe in 1938 when Hitler began annexing Germany's neighbors or had not gone to school in North Carolina at a time when segregation was the rule or if I had married the boy next door instead of that stranger who came to town and swept me up in a passion I HAD never known.

The only thing that can be told about a life is a story, and telling that story is like recounting a series of incidents, more or less related to one another. Today, as I approach the end of my life, I know that I am someone other than that series of incidents. On rare occasions, Elizabeth disappears and there is nothing but an awareness of being at one with the whole of things and a momentary end to the loneliness and the separateness. If that is perplexing to read, take comfort in knowing that it was perplexing to write. My writing is an attempt to catch hold of that elusive something that hints at a waiting secret.

This story spans the major part of the twentieth century and is a journey through my life. It takes into account that all the challenges faced have contributed to the person I am today but only hinted at who I really am. I invite you to come with me on this journey—a journey shaped not only by the accidents of history but also by the moments of wondering, of being in the presence of that elusive something—a journey nearing its end but not over yet.

To purchase Elizabeth's book, amazon.com lists it or you can go to: http://www.theworldoftashatudor.com/cgi-bin/cellardoor/23764

Two Poems of Remembrance
Morgan Zo-Callahan

Prayer for Wilt
Loving Basketball & Wilt

Until my knees gave out, my favorite activity was to play basketball, especially at Venice Beach. I had so much fun, interesting competition and camaraderie playing at the public parks and at the beach. That's irreplaceable: playing hoops.

Sometimes after his retirement, Wilt Chamberlain would hang out and shoot hoops at Venice, laughing a lot, jostling, being "looked up to," yet connecting to us "common guys." I couldn't believe how tall he was! and how cool!

His lifetime stats include scoring sixty points or more, thirty-two times; he passed away on October 12, 1999.

So long
Big Dipper, You
so long
longing were you
reflecting
critical
inner warrior
against racism
against stereotyping
fit athlete
sweet pleasure to meet
legs still fleet
under blue, furry white skies
high fives
Venice Beach leisure.

Eternal rest
Eternal activity

Conscious Alive Circle of Life
passing to realms of Mystery
your spirit's next curiosity.
Bye elegant solitary man
human, hummin' man.

Thanks for sharing your glories, artiste
playing basketball
hoops
round ball like Earth
joy
the man in the boy
you, gracefully tall
quick wall with a finger roll
century of points: one game!

Scoring-exploring women too
loving
bragging
abusing
respecting
growing
glowing in the mirror above your bed.
You
disliking "hero" tag
people's person
learning kindness.

Ciao, Hasta la vista
to ineffable Unknown may you go
Continue
Passing through that wondrous Door
Go where you'll soar
like you danced down a shiny wooden floor.

Poem for Elias

> *One day I arrived at the Adult School to teach my class, and a weeping young woman told me that one of my students had died. Elias was so young, so enthusiastic, such a sharp, warm person. When I went home, I wrote this for his family, and for myself.*

Freshening up frustrating day
soft silvery rain,
pattering pain on my face, tears

under goldengreen lemon tree
dark now, teen boy-man, Elias,
dead so suddenly, beyond all fears.

How I clench my little life
as if I could survive *Señor Muerte*,
mind destroyer, thief on this dark night.

Consuming fire,
yet, a releaser of the soul;
Que descanse tu alma en Paz & Light.

Sure, the other night I could reach up,
hug happily kumquat kissing stars in the black galaxy,
breathing cool air, lost, away from damaged dreams.

I'll tell you, Elias,
you shared a precious smile,
gifting us, now Mother screams.

Makes me rain too, to say *adiós por ahora*.
Well, don't let us keep you here,
Fly away, sweet buddy.

"It's the Living that Counts!"
Eulogies
Morgan Zo-Callahan

The title is a quote from my mentor, Rev. Francis Rouleau, S.J. (1900–84)

To eulogize is a jewel of our humanity, to touch and open the heart, within intimate relationships—or perhaps even for a person you only knew and admired from some distance.

Joan Didion's book, The Year of Magical Thinking, *is an extended, insightful and emotional eulogy for her husband John Dunne who died December 30, 2003. "Grief when it comes, it is nothing we expect it to be." She was integrating his death, as much as possible, into her life without him. "Life changes fast. Life changes in an instant. You sit down for dinner and life as you know it ends".*

We survive after our loved ones are gone; yet, are they really ever gone? We go on both with and without them. There's an appreciative view of our lost loved ones and a spontaneous viewing of our own life, as it's unfolding at this time, contrasting, complementing the now passed-life of our loved ones.

■

Composition of Place: Vietnam Memorial, Washington, D.C., Monday, May 31, 1999

In honor of Dave Ucker, I came to Washington to rub his name onto to a white sheet of paper from the black V-shaped, black granite memorial just down from the stately Lincoln Memorial. The polished wall is engraved with the names of 58,195 men and women who died in the war or who were classified as missing in action. I started talking to Dave, telling him "I want to bring back the rubbing of your name to Los

Angeles, a small token of my appreciation for your being my dear high school friend." In high school I was closest to Jim White, Dave Ucker and Tom McGrath (Rest in Peace, Big Guy). Jim White's still very alive; but Dave and Tom are still living influences. Dave was killed in the war that tore our generation apart. He was a spirited, positive person, gifted in being able to bring people together in peace and with lots of fun.

Today, I'm lingering, remembering, praying, conversing in spirit with you, Dave Ucker, (later you'd change your name to O'Farrell, tired of the "fucker" jibes and charged by the flair of an extra "O" Irish syllable). Your name's etched in the shiny blocked unfolding tribute by architect, Maya Ying Lin. She submitted her design, which was selected from among the fourteen hundred other entries, when she was only twenty-one, just two years older than you when you died. I gaze at the two bronze sculptures that were added later, almost as an afterthought, Three Soldiers and The Vietnam Women's Memorial, three women, one attending a wounded soldier. I wonder how you died. Were you were alone? Did someone try to save you? Did a nurse attend to you?

So many years ago, but even now I cry my eyeballs out, right here outside with you, thinking of you, Dave, and your idealistic, loving smiling nature, your love for old cars, especially your turquoise '49 with its tall black stick shift, shiny knob on top, shiny like Maya's black monument. You were into debating, dramatics, yearbook, Pep Club, Dance, Track, Band, Rifle team. Oh man, I hate you, mother-ucker-fucking war, gobbling its power, its bleeding flesh, its rapes, its brutal commands to kill, its punitive goose-stepping, its weapons of mass people destruction, like grotesque giants wielding missiles, distorted, exaggerated dicks, to kill and subdue.

You know, Dave, you'd always say, "let's keep all of us together." You'd like the scientist Rupert Sheldrack who talks about "morphic resonance," how everything in our minds, negative-positive and in between, resonate with other people's minds; our "interiors" are not separate from other beings. So not with as much faith as you exuded, Dave, I'm sending blessing vibrations to victims—living or not—of today's wars. May all soldiers, all victims, all governments be at peace.

Can the peacemakers make a tiny drop of difference, can they be somehow multiplied? Remembering you is strong and immediate. Is there a place, Dave, where you don't die, where you, and all the rest of us, are together in our source? Last night very black clouds were swirling in front of a brightly illumined, fully round white, gray-tinged moon. For moments so densely dark, only a faint sure light could be revealed. Are the bitter clouds of Kosovo, Chiapas, Sierra Leone, Israel, Palestine, Iraq, the Congo, Uganda … only passing in that primordial, steady and eternal light? Life is always changing, living, dying. I'm grateful to remember you when we were teens together, with love, dear buddy Dave.

■

Roberto and Understanding Adoption

My dear amigo, Robert Holstein, passed away in January of 2003. He was a real activist, intensely interested in Ignatian spirituality. He lived his life fully. Once when speaking of the similarity of Jesus and Buddha, Bob remarked, "the commitment to compassion and the other is what I enjoy the most."

Bob said, "I meditate most every day, and am indebted to Ignatian spirituality. One thing for certain—my faith is not dependent upon a pope, a bishop or anyone else.… I would validate the presence of God in many of the spiritualities of the world from Native American to Buddhist—it makes no sense otherwise."

Bob adopted his five children, and we had some real heart-to-heart conversations, because I am adopted. "Please tell me honestly what it's like for you to be adopted," Bob asked me. He wanted to hear about adoptee's human rights projects and supported the ending of violations of adoptee's human rights as occurred and still occurs, especially for those of us born in the 40s and 50s. One basic right of the adoptee is to be able to get information about his or her birth parents if the adoptee desires to understand and have some feeling for heritage and genes. Although all of us are different in our needs for wholeness, we have to have to able to find out some basic information if we need it.

For the birth mother and father, as well as for the child today, the majority of adoption agencies treat adoption as a beautiful, deeply human transition, almost like a sacrament bringing people together. It's always been the intent of adoption agencies to serve the best interests of the child being adopted, but when I was given up, they caved in to hiding the child's illegitimate birth from the public, even if it meant denying the birth child full access to information about his or her heritage.

Bob wanted my opinion on issues such as whether the adopted child has the right to demand, even expect, a relationship with their birth parents and, perhaps, their siblings? No, I answered. I myself reached out to a brother and sister I discovered through accounts of services, obituaries, eulogies for my birth mother, Vivianne. But I had no regrets that my half brother and half sister did not respond. I welcome their freedom to do what's best for them, individually. If they'd like to meet me in the future, that would be fine, but I have no expectations. The important act for me was the invitation to my siblings to meet me. I don't feel any sense of rejection, just understanding that perhaps I also wouldn't be able to meet me, given their particular circumstances. I happily respect their decision, and I would never close my heart to them.

Does the child have the right to be recognized emotionally? Bob asked. Adoptees have the right to know their nationality, their blood, some circumstances relating to earliest years, why separation from the mother had to occur and, in most cases, realizing that the separation did not mean that we were not loved. In my own case, since I was five years old, I wanted some contact with my birth mother, but it wasn't to be. Bob listened to my stories of growing up as an adopted kid, and he told his stories about his adopted kids.

Bob Holstein made some good jokes with me about Irishmen and women and the Irish Catholicism we knew so well. He had great humor about the "sex-negative" "guilt-ridden" messages we were given in our youth. He came to see that women were treated shabbily in the Catholic Church. He said I was his favorite Black Irishman and he loved me. We'd assure ourselves not to take "self-psychoanalysis" too seriously. Not to take ourselves too seriously. A few times I got drunk with Robert. What fun we had; such laughter, stories, confessions of what was most intimate to each of us, sharing our life as it spills out before us so quickly and irreversibly.

I always was impressed that Bob could criticize and love the Catholic Church but always participate as a "Rebel," who didn't bow to dogmas or church pomposity. But one who still considered himself as integral to the church in its best sense, going to daily Mass, having a prayer and meditation life nourished by both the *Spiritual Exercises* and also by Buddhism. Bob would send me books on Buddhism, my favorite being *Peace in Every Step*, about walking meditation, by Thich Nhat Hanh. Bob Holstein wanted to reform, rather than to abandon the Catholic Church.

Bob told me that he felt adoption is closer to the reality we are stamped with than to ties of blood. "I can only observe—not live—in the intimate moments of my children's musings, be they night time or daydreams, but if they can get over the trauma of adoption (Why me? How could a mother abandon me? Who am I?), they will short-circuit the inevitable tearing of the umbilicus and find out that their relatedness is to the universe and all of humanity." He believed that the most basic bond was to the community of mankind—undefined by ties of blood. He felt Jesus was always alluding to this unconditional love and openness for all when he asked, "Who is my brother? Who is my sister, my mother, my father?" He would tell his children that they were freer than he was, since they could realize that their ties could only be of love, that they needn't be cajoled by clan or blood. "You always have the opportunity to choose."

Bob knew I was traveling to Southern Mexico, because I was involved in a couple of projects with working and/or homeless street children. He was very supportive. He invited me to start protesting again the School of the Americas, which, after studying the issues of the cause, I did for four years, at Fort Benning, Georgia.

Robert also invited me to a series of "consulting" discussions, in 2001, with Verbum Dei High School's president, Father William Wood, S.J., when the Jesuits began running the school in the Watts area of Los Angeles. The school once had a student body of around eight hundred boys. Now, starting anew, it has only 167 students, predominantly African American and Hispanic. Only fifteen of the boys are Catholic. Bob was a remarkable initiator of helpful brainstorming and ideas for fund-raising and opportunities to incorporate volunteers into the Verbum Dei family.

Bob: "I see tremendous power of our friends to do justice, to do for others—yes. I see opportunities for this power to be unleashed, but it is always in the context of a willing individual not a manipulated group." Bob was sincerely interested in being a part of organizing for the poor and promoting causes he truly believed in. Bob, *tan querido y una inspiracion*, heart-full, so human, vulnerable, and no-bull-shitting cantankerous call to "get off our asses" and do that "little part of service," suited just to the way our particular desires and yearnings attract us and to do joyfully what we really believe in and are convinced of for ourselves (no activist "bandwagons" jumped on, no "group-think").

Bob had just as hard a time as any of us in being open and fair with each other in all our differences. He could be tough—he wanted us all to help each other to help ourselves and not to be wasteful or over-loaded with authority and administration. He was generous with money, but careful and demanding of responsibility, accountability together with some wisdom and common sense.

He told us about how he decided to help Padre Orlando's project to build a community center: "Padre Orlando was not so inviting when we arrived forty-five minutes late in El Paisnal, thirty-five kilometers north of the border of the province of San Salvador. But after some 'real money'—we had planned on $100 but gave him $300," Bob said, "He loosened up and became much more warm and engaging. He is dreaming of building.... I had been waiting for someone in El Salvador who was poor. When he told us he received no more than nine *colones* for Sunday services due to the poverty of the parish, I knew he was our man.... He really cares for the poor."

Orlando had deep roots as a priest working for justice among the poor. His uncle, Father Rutilio Grande, had worked in the poor parish of Aguilares from 1973. It was a time of discrimination, poverty, and political violence, death squads, and "disappeared" people. Rutilio preached with great heart, that our one God abhorred the exploitation of people, whether poor or not, whether rich or not. He preached Jesus as present in the poor, and as present in politics, both religious and civic, advocating fairness and love among all our differences and being ourselves present to the spiritual life as it courses through us, in so many particular flavors and actions. Using the Bible as the base text for this effort, he waged a war against illiteracy.

On March 12, 1977 Father Rutilio was assassinated, along with two of his companions. The new archbishop, Monsignor

Oscar Arnulfo Romero was shocked. It was a turning point for the new bishop. When he was named archbishop, Romero said that the Church should stay out of politics, but now he pleaded for the rebels to lay down their arms and negotiate a meaningful peace treaty. He taught that a government is the servant of every strata of the community from rich to poor, not a power of destruction, and he embraced the poor—at every level of their lives, including the political. This call to champion their cause became self-evident, self-affirming and life giving.

Perhaps your spirit, Bob, will feel our love as a final embrace, *un fuerte abrazo y beso a ti. Tu*: twinkly, sparkling, lovable, dad, innovator, ass-kicker, hugger, encourager, partying, joking in foreign accents, gesticulating, cussing, loving Loretta, Mary, Matthew, Liz, Bobby, Chad, being embraced by Loretta, hard-working to obtain "living wages" for workers, "doing time" for radical protest against the School of Americas, speaking up for women's and gay rights and dignity, sinner and saint, broken and resurrected, fighting and being reconciled, inquiring about social justice, a rich man, chastising, learning, howling, story-telling, being undiplomatic, forgiving, wanting to reach out more profoundly, going to daily *misa*, exploring Eastern spirituality, being critical of "powers that be," fun and tears and living so heartily, philosophizing, connecting so many relationships, hosting, theologizing, getting-us-togethering, and, these last few years, even gentle.

Compas, my tears and prayers and weeping are drizzling on this skinny tree parchment to transpose to you a tiny heart-ode of appreciation to Roberto. Robert. Bob. Bobby. Berto, Holstein. How good-hearted you are; wise, not-so-wise, very human and humanistic, open more and more as your life evolved. I wish you a wonderful life in the heavens, where I'm sure you'll continue to raise hell—until we can understand what peace could be on this earth. May you be in Paradise, into your next Adventure. We will keep you in our hearts and recall your laughter, always.

> *The wan moon is sinking under the white wave and time is sinking with me, O!*
>
> —Robert Burns

■

Vivianne duBouchet Lovell

Dearest Bob, *hermano*:

Almost two years after your death, on October 3, 2004, my biological mom, Vivianne, passed away from Alzheimer's at age eighty-six. Because that event and what followed shed so much light on our conversation about adoption, I am writing this, as if you were still alive, to detail what it has meant to me.

Again another two plus years passed and on July 28, 2007, thanks to the Internet and the National Archives, three, 10 x 8½, black and white glossy photos of Vivianne duBouchet Lovell appeared in my mailbox. I see for the first time what my mother looked like. I wanted so much to see my mother who would look like me, who would still feel like she was connected to me, even after so many years.

I had yearned for a photograph of my mother, in particular a photo of her before I was given by her for a private adoption, an adoption facilitated and finalized on April 20, 1949. And here is a photo of Vivianne, a French foreign press correspondent, at the White House on August 14, 1945 (I know I was still living with her then). Viewing these three photos of mother, being with Harry Truman announcing the Japanese Surrender, and feeling, a part of this momentous time in U.S. history, I'm being healed in a most tangible way. Seeing Vivianne working, taking notes so intently stimulates me now to continue bringing some life and service into our cross-culturing, truly globally inter-connected world.

Peace at last. Eight days earlier, on August 6, Paul W. Tibbets Jr., and Robert A. Lewis, flew a four-engine propeller-driven B-29, the Enola Gay, named after Tibbets' mom, and bombardier Thomas Ferebee released the ninety-seven hundred pound "Little Boy," a slender, phallic, uranium bomb, on Hiroshima. Seventeen seconds after 8:15 AM, the biggest, most deadly explosion, fire, nuclear, destruction in history demolished 80 percent of the city, killed at least eighty thousand human beings immediately—radiation finished off many others later. Three days later, another atomic bomb destroyed Nagasaki, and forced Japan into unconditional surrender. No more slaughter, no more bombs, no more concentration camps, at least for now, and peace at last for me, no more burdens or resentments towards my own mother. Peaceful release from some of my inner war.

I contemplate with these three photos for hours over the next few days, allowing my emotions full play. I read all the information the Internet afforded me about Vivianne. I had been desperate to know—however little—about my birth mother. I make up a kind of "insight" meditation, paying full attention to the depth of my feelings, releasing any "clinging," letting go. It's just fine accepting the way things are—changing, non-separated from all else. Viewing the photos, venerating my relationship with my mother and letting go were necessary for me to settle emotionally with her.

The pain and hurt in my relationship to my birth mother dissolved by a kind of "composition of place" where, in my imagination, I placed my self with Vivianne as she was writing her notes, while Truman speaks. I "speak" with her; I wonder if my mother always wanted to be a writer, a journalist, just as I've always wanted to be a teacher and Tibbets a pilot. I'm with her.

I see Vivianne in Truman's office, pen and paper in hand

for her story. She's a beautiful woman, soft and tough and courageous. She has my eyes and nose, small mouth, nicely formed ears, small chin which shows emotional tension, slightly stooped shoulders, intelligent bright face, a little in awe, but seemingly very alert and attentive to her job and now standing right in front of the President of the United States. I feel proud of her. I sense her self-respect.

Perhaps the most important story of her life, she leans against the front part of the president's desk. She could reach out and touch Harry's lapel. She's pretty, her ample black hair pulled back, a sleeveless striped white dress; two bracelets, one dangling a gold medal, one thick with wide rectangular-gems. I like her sense for stylish fashion, along with the other well-dressed reporters and a handful of dignitaries in the room.

In two of the photos I count about forty-eight people. There are only twenty-eight people in one (some are only faces in the back) in the oval office. In this photo, I count twelve women in the room, including my mother. Two of the women are sitting comfortably, while one man seems uncomfortable pinned in a small stiff sofa, almost directly under FDR's elegant side-view portrait, sitting in this formal suit, with a white handkerchief showing in his left jacket pocket. On the other side of a door there's a photo of a glider plane. You can look out both windows and see some lawn, bushes, and the side of a white room in a small building with the window pushed out and open.

President Truman stands in front of his desk reading a statement, stately and confident in a tailored suit, gemmed ring on the middle finger of his left hand that holds the carefully scripted papers. This was an eagerly awaited moment.

Truman's looking down in two of the photos, reading notes. In one of the photos he's making eye contact with the reporters and with Vivianne. About half are looking down, writing and in one Vivianne is also looking down, writing notes; in another shot, also from the right side, she is looking directly at the president who is also looking up, notes now folded in his hands. It's interesting for me to see Vivianne from a side view.

Some big shots are sitting behind the president, one a military man; they're giving their attention to the announcement. One gentleman is standing, partially supported by the wall, with his hand on his hip, elbow extended … debonair. Harry—Give 'em hell, Harry—Truman gives me a feeling of reassurance. The buck stopped here that day. The framed painting of F.D.R. on the wall is almost resting on Truman's shoulder.

Truman's desk is an opportunity to explore some simple things. I see a telephone with a long coiled cord on the left side, plastic circular dialing, and a small round desk clock, encased tightly in black with three white stripes on the side. There's a fancy, brass-ornamented paper & pen holder decorated with a white horse seemingly walking out of its side, two pens at each end; a large leather holder for scissors or letter opener; binder with tabs, a notepad sticking out of its jacket; a large stack of type written papers on the desk from which the president is picking up and reading. There is a small framed picture of his daughter, Margaret, which shows how pretty she is, very open faced, large eyes, delicately sitting on a soft armchair in a fashionable dress and broad belt. Harry called Drew Pearson "a son of a bitch" for his unflattering comments about his dear daughter's singing. Behind the desk is a comfortable black leather swivel chair.

In my experience, for many sons and their mothers, this relationship is the most defining. I felt several emotions, feeling frustrated and empty, longing for my birth mother. For almost all my life, I tried to contact her (without any desire to impose myself in any way, but to learn about some fundamentals of who I am, my heredity, my life as a child). I wrote her some letters, which were never answered.

I feel the love between Vivianne and me. Yes, some

sadness, but an even deeper encompassing feeling of not being separate from my mother. I blamed her for giving me up for adoption. And I blamed myself. Why wasn't I good enough? Now Resolution just happens, "no longer holding on to something," graceful as if I opened my hand at the ocean and let sand fall out. This peaceful understanding was like a quick broad smile on the street, no big deal, but melting protected places inside. And it was some psychic load just slipping off my back, so I could easily stand up straight.

I no longer have the subtle feeling "my own mother didn't want me." Instead, I can be proud of both of us and happy for the little time when we were together, during my young, vulnerable time (now old age is presently running faster than me, making me more directly aware of nature's fragile birthing and dying). I understand her wanting the best for me in a world full of prejudices about single mothers in the 40s. She lived in her time, not ours. Being a correspondent in the White House is an amazing accomplishment for a woman of her times, but I cannot expect to break every barrier.

You might ask why I don't feel the same intensity about finding my birth father. I don't even as yet know his identity; though I finally learned that he and Vivianne were involved in a relationship, but not married, and that he died before I was adopted—most likely in World War II—leaving her as a single parent. I would like to know about him and will search, but my searching will be from an appreciative person. I'm disappointed that the earlier U.S. adoption system wouldn't give non-identifying information, but I never "longed" for my father. My adopted dad was a fine man, though I didn't get to be as close to him as I wanted as he passed away when I was in the first year of university. I've been blessed to be mentored by great men, strong and wise men who helped me understand manhood.

But at least I know, with great satisfaction, about my mother and my heritage. I also know some highlights in her life—career, marriage, children, and dedication to worthy causes for suffering children.

■

My Friend's Mom Passes Away

My friend, Gary, shared with some of us his final days with his mom. We were all nourished, able to understand more from his writing and our mutual electronic and telephonic "gathering" of friends. The tenderness in his account reflects some of my experiences in hospice, as well as remembering contrasting incidents where families were arguing and—sadly—bitter until the end.

Gary wrote: "My whole life has been a preparation for this evening's visit with my mother. She is now too tired to have thoughts that take her beyond the present. All she can do is rest with me now and give me a loving look that is a window to the heart of Being.

"There is nothing for me to do but look back at her with all my heart. We sat holding hands for an hour, talking occasionally about I don't remember what, and twice just quietly crying and holding each other.… I find her vulnerability heartbreaking. But, at least tonight, there was no more sense of vulnerability, only a sad and yet deeply gratifying sense that she is slowly, gradually escaping all her fears and worries.…

"She once mildly complained that she felt so very tired, too tired to do anything. I assured her that there was nothing she had to do, that she was being taken care of, and that she could enjoy her fatigue. She smiled as if she understood.…

"Until fairly recently, I resented being fated with her but more recently, I learned to accept her. Tonight, the particulars of our relationship dissolved into irrelevance. There was only mutual presence.… At 11 AM my mom died peacefully. They called me at 7 AM to say she was 'going down'; she was comfortable but breathing heavily and had three to four hours to live. But when I got there, they told me she could go within the next day or two. I asked if there was any chance she would gain consciousness and they said no, but that she could probably hear me, since hearing is the last thing to go, even though she could not respond.

"So I whispered in her ear that she was the best mom I could have hoped for, that her parents were coming for her and that she was wrapped in love.… Two days ago, when I visited, she didn't seem to know it was me until I got up to go and put my face inches from her to tell her I'd be 'back tomorrow.' She seemed to recognize me for the first time and held out her arms like a drowning woman. So that was our final hug.… "

The cuckoo's voice
is all the more intriguing
as I die.

—Keido (died c. 1750 at age thirty)

On May 27, 2005, I was honored to be gathered with my friend Gary and his sister Gayle and brother-in-law, Jim to pay our respects to his mother, Lucille Irene Nichols Schouborg (1912–2005).

"Lucille: Gary, Gayle, Jim and I are here to revere your life, to remember you with appreciation, to let you go gracefully to your parents, Gangi and Baby, into their embracing arms. As Gary whispered to you in your final hours: 'you are the best mom,' and your parents are with you; you are wrapped in love, dear Lucille, as we are bathed freely now in the Sun, only one, so amazingly, as you, of the four hundred billion stars in our galaxy, still riding, with wonder, on this speeding blue, white and brown Earth, where we shared your company and where now you are part of these grassy hills, always in our hearts and with trees, the ficus with its richly layered, deeply dark green leaves, our profound fondness for you; the magnolias, striking pearl, yellow, purple-flowering in spring, just as your colorful theatrical flair and enthusiasm; pines with slender elongated needles, elegant as you; eucalyptus evergreens, gummy, fragrant, 'Sweety' as Gary would call to you as he asked you to be careful going down the stairs of your home.

"May you now be ever peaceful in your home beyond our knowing, beyond our imaginations, as snowy clouds form and disappear so seamlessly.

"Gary told us two days before you died, he visited you and you didn't seemed to recognize him until he got up to leave and he put his face inches from you to say 'I'll be back tomorrow' and you were aware and held out your arms to him and hugged. To you, our final blessing hugs!"

Gary once shared concluding stanzas of Auden's "In Memory of W.B. Yeats" which remind us of how the suffering of your loss, Lucille, can be for us, life-enriching.

Follow poet, follow right
To the bottom of the night,
With your unconstraining voice
Still persuade us to rejoice;
With the farming of a verse
Make a vineyard of the curse,
Sing of human unsuccess
In a rapture of distress;
In the deserts of the heart
Let the healing fountain start,
In the prison of his days
Teach the free man how to praise.

Good-bye, Adios, Farewell, Dear Lucille, thank you for you. I send you a final ancient poem from an elderly, anonymous Buddhist nun at the end of her journey.

Though I am weak and tired now
And my youthful step long gone,
Leaning on this staff,
I climb to the mountain peak,
My cloak cast off,
My bowl overturned,
I sit here on this rock,
And over my spirit blows
The breath of liberty.

■

My First Guru: Father Francis A. Rouleau, S.J. (1900–84)

But oh! How far have I to go to find You in Whom I have already arrived.

—Thomas Merton

Francis Rouleau was a Jesuit priest and my spiritual counselor from the late 60s until his death in 1984. He would say to me: "Here we are arriving with each other at the level of the Heart," and, his personality reflected his own heart—he was a very open emotionally and sensitive with a wonderful smile and laughter. We could talk about anything, and even disagree, but mostly we held each other and our particular "worlds" with great esteem and affection. He would often say to me, "Let's lift each other up in the Lord, Jesus, the Heart," and this remains a wonderful description of how we related to one another.

He was born in Campbell, Minnesota, on January 23, 1900. A case of rheumatic fever, coupled with debilitating cardiac effect halted his plan to accept an appointment to the Naval Academy, in Annapolis. His sick bed became a kind of monastery—like Ignatius, and he decided to be a Jesuit. His suffering did not end there though as in later life he would be handicapped by severely active and painful Ankylosing Rheumatoid Spondylitis (spinal arthritis).

We had ongoing *cor ad cor* conversation about meditation, the *Spiritual Exercises*, sex, relationships, activism, theology, friendship, and his writing about the history of the Jesuits in China. We explored the Ignatian approach to "finding God in all things."

I always felt free to be myself, relaxed by Francis' quality of not being excessively judgmental. He didn't approve of my relatively free attitude about sexual love—for three or four years I just let the hippie 60s currents sweep me away. I actually loved that time of sexual experimentation. He couldn't understand how two of my homosexual friends could live in an open relationship, or how I might be making love to more than one woman at a time. His criticisms were never severe. He scolded me a few times for going through this promiscuous phase in my life. "You're being too selfish, he'd say … but let's discern more together, perhaps I'm missing something about this experimenting of yours." He'd tell me: "Don't forget; I'm of the old school." At other times, he'd squint a bit seriously through his wire glasses, as I'd tell him about one of the areas of my life that piqued his curiosity.

Once Francis surprised me when he said it was good that some Jesuit seminarians were falling in love as they were pursuing studies. It was, he felt, a natural thing for even a celibate to fall in love and then be open to learn what is love and be willing to choose wisely between a religious or lay life. You may feel it strange that a priest would discuss sex with me. He wanted to know how I felt about those still living in the Society of Jesus who were falling in love with women and sometimes with men and some were having sex. I was exploring living without Catholic sex-guilt trips and I felt free to share my wild stories. He also wanted to know my feelings about homosexuality; at that time, my best friend, Marcus Holly, was openly bi-sexual.

"Falling in love should teach such seminarians the nature of an authentic love of God and your self. Too often this love is rationalized abstractions, formalistic, a love smothered over with inner tensions, self-centeredness, petty motives, projection of the ego and something of a dichotomy in their lives. True love of God is the total out-going of self to another Person, a ravishment of the complete personality, the whole body-mind that we are ... not only of mind, but of the heart, the affectivity, our personality-bodiliness, explosive of one's whole being." (*Celestial Dragon*)

He would talk about his own loneliness at times. "Aloneness is often painful in my condition of a crippled body.... I pray to overcome self-pity and discouragement." Physically he was extremely afflicted with severe arthritis, but he studied and researched up to the day before he died. He said excessive self-pity takes away our sensitivity to the presence of God. A few times, Father Francis would talk about being at the end of his life and thinking about dying.

Francis always affirmed how we need to think for ourselves and check in with our own conscience and hearts, as the process is flowing on. "Realize God's love for yourself by cultivating a sincere interior life of contemplation." I told Francis he sounded like a Buddhist! Francis and I liked to talk about the psychology of our "selves," what made us tick, gave us some fire and motivated us to "love living" as he would say to me. Sometimes we just sat quietly. He made me feel our humanity was more important than our practice of religion or our theological conceptions, even life styles. He encouraged me to continue be interested in human rights. He wanted to know my stories of being at local meetings for human rights in China. My many stories about César Chavez' union movement delighted him. He loved stories of my travels in Mexico and

Central America. He told me his heart was that of a missionary who loved and respected the differences of all people.

And how Francis loved China! China's people welcomed him for thirty two years! He first went to China in 1923. When Japan attacked China, Francis was in Nanjing organizing a university student center. He fled Nanjing by train to get to Shanghai, two hundred miles away. Speeding through Wuxi, a Japanese bomber dropped a bomb on the crowded coach in front of Francis. Francis hid in a rice paddy with other passengers, before arriving in Shanghai. He engaged relief work for war refugees. To the end of his life he was in contact with former Chinese students. In his quiet, scholarly way, he was preaching deep respect for the inviolability of the human person; he spoke up against injustices in China. He was forgiving—but not forgetting or failing to speak up about human rights abuses in China. He was optimistic that the goodness and intelligence of the Chinese would more and more permeate political institutions.

When expelled from China, Francis had been through the Japanese invasion and then the Communists, time in Philippines and Rome and finally twenty-one years at Los Gatos, California where I would meet with him. In China, Francis was compiling a seven-volume work about the Jesuits in China, about such topics as the mass in the vernacular language. Francis was an active scholar in the field of Chinese missionary history. He would spend eight years in Rome pouring over archives, microfilming around fifty thousand pages, outlining some forty original historical studies.

One purpose of St. Ignatius' *Spiritual Exercises* is to learn to give up "inordinate attachments." Francis had that spiritual quality of non-attachment in its most passionate sense. He told me how some of his fellow Jesuit priests suffered in Chinese prisons. An excellent biography of Fr. Francis is *Celestial Dragon* by Barry Martinson (Taipei Ricci Institute, 1998). Father Francis would tell me about his writing a six-hundred-page story of Maillard de Tournon, papal legate, who went to China in 1707 to deliver the news that the pope was squashing Chinese Rites. This papal condemnation of the Chinese Rites prohibited Chinese Christians from integrating age-old sacred rites of honoring Confucius, honoring the ancestors. The Jesuits were wholeheartedly in favor of the Chinese Rites. Francis would talk about this as a legitimate instance in criticizing the papacy. But more importantly he said, it teaches the essentials and non-essentials of spiritual rites and rituals.

Francis was always a totally dedicated Jesuit, even faithful to his religious vows. Ed Mowrey tells this story about Francis' obedience as a Jesuit: "When the communists were arriving in Peking, his superior told him to take all of his work, thousands of pages of handwritten notes, hundreds of microfilms he had gathered from around the world working in eight different languages, etc., told him to take them all and throw them in the furnace and destroy them. He did it without question."

Francis died, early in the morning on February 21, 1984 at Sacred Heart Jesuit Center, Los Gatos, California. He was buried in the Santa Clara Mission Cemetery. I still marvel at the creative energy, love and wisdom he generated over the years. My appreciation and love for him continue to grow and open as I grow older myself.

■

My Dearest American Indian Amigo, Marcus Holly

I've been gifted with several "dearest" friends in my life, and I've had one extraordinary friend, Marcus Holly, now gone a quarter century.

Gone to where? I wonder. I continue to feel your presence, Marcus. My soul is still fed by your unique vision. I remember you so often, many of our stories together are still in my mind. Writing now, my tears for you are flowing unexpectedly. You see sometimes your memory takes me over when I least suspect it. You know how much you meant to me.

But how to express it? We cannot have a final conversation without uncovering some emotion buried in my heart. How can I let my heart flow in gratitude and communicate how special we were to each other?

Ken Ireland, whom you'd like very much and whom I'm happy to present to you now, gave me the best advice: just talk with you, Marcus, sharing what I would have shared with you about living life, let you know how much I've missed your advice and listening, and why I place your life and teaching among that of the great Indian medicine men and women.

May my words paint some scenes of our lives together, representing our enjoyment, how we learned together to be part of this living tapestry, even with all our differences.

I met you during your last year of high school in Santa Barbara, California, where you starred in basketball, 1963. We liked each other right away and from that moment I always felt we were close to each other. You were tall, cocky, handsome, and athletic. Sometimes you wore an outwardly hostile attitude towards the world, but there was always your shining heart underneath, waiting to come out. When your smile emerged, it animated your broad, large nosed face.

I started visiting with you at your home with your Dad and your fantastic step mom, Jean, whom I liked very much but lost contact with many years ago. Your Dad, may he rest in peace, suffered severe alcoholism. I remember once when he donned his Navy officer uniform and yelled, "I'm still a fucking somebody" over and over. But he was broken and wrecked, his white suit stained with red wine. You started to cry and I hugged you. Your Dad snapped out of his rant and, becoming tender and emotional, said he wanted us to know we were good people and that he loved us as sons. He said he was sorry for being so crazy. For those short minutes before he passed out, he was animated and involved. Then you picked him up in your large arms, laid him on his bed, kissing him, and whispered, "Have some good rest, you're my father and I love you."

Marcus, you said how healing that was for you, how healing it was when later you gave up hating your Father—and your self—for drinking lots of alcohol. I remember another time when your Dad was reeling drunk, you said out of the blue, "That's me." You taught me what fighting alcoholism is about. I did later see you become your Dad sometimes, where alcohol was strangling you and beckoning you to walk into many dark corners. Seven or eight tough years passed before you were healed of self-indulgence in alcohol and sex. You still loved alcohol and sex, but you changed your relationship of dependence on them. You encouraged me to experience that sex is great, to fully enjoy but to let our enjoyments go; at the same time we shared our pain as many gay friends were dying of AIDS. Once I visited to you and you were weeping because a friend died of AIDS, young and under the care of lesbian volunteers. How you cried uncontrollably, weeping for the truth of our suffering, the fragility of our existing on earth.

As I was finishing my first year in the Jesuit novitiate, I had no idea why you were given the ok to visit me. Maybe, unbeknownst to me, I was a recruiter for the Jesuits, as you would join me in the Society in 1965. And by 1970, we would both decide to leave the order. We had quite a year together in 1970, teaching and coaching basketball at Bellarmine High School in San Jose. We were happy to be paying back the Jesuits for giving us such a wonderful education. Though we hadn't signed our final papers of legal release from the Jesuits, we were already walking down new paths.

We visited Suzuki Roshi in San Francisco, whom you called your first Eastern teacher; we meditated, listened to talks and volunteered to work in the garden. We explored, experimented with "body" therapies. You wanted to know all about healing practices from the great traditions. You got me involved with organizing supplies, food for the American Indians who had claimed and occupied Alcatraz.

You announced you were bi-sexual and entered a secret world of wonder, sensuality, love between men as well as love between man and woman. And once you came on to me, but quickly accepted that I wasn't sexually into men. But that never stopped us from enjoying each other's company. We were comfortable hugging each other, crying with each other; giving each other massages. We both came to see how much the church was out of touch with human sexuality and we luckily fell out of the spell that the body and sexuality are bad. You would go to your parties and street scenes in San Francisco, cross-dressed, looking curiously feminine for such a strong man. Your stories allowed me into a fascinating world and encouraged me to "get out of my head" as you'd say with good humor.

After I worked in the Jesuit Volunteer Corps in Mexico for a year, we found ourselves together again, four years living in the community of Master Da from 1973 to 1976.

We hooted, danced and sang, listened to music we played too loud, talked long into the night, sat nude in the hot springs together under dark starry nights. That experimental time came so strongly upon us and then went poof, just like that, gone, just as you, my sweetest friend of all! Your young life extinguished. I'm without you, and it's never been the same.

I admire that you didn't care too much about the party line of any group or community, even though you lived in Master Da's community for many years more than I did. You felt all organizations—even mostly benign ones, are seduced by power over others. You said you'd have no problem leaving or staying in the community.

We each accepted each other's decisions in 1976: mine to leave the community so many years ago and yours to stay. We actually didn't feel there was that much difference, whether we were "in" or "out," a superficial barrier. Being friends never depended on being in or out of any community.

I am still listening to you with profound respect. I understand why your American Indian heritage was so important to you, so let's talk now about great American Indians and also about your activism on behalf of native peoples who are exploited by the dominant culture which you and I, Marcus, are a part. Can you tell us now what wisdom we can learn and apply to our be-here-now lives? You said the American Indian spirituality and rituals were the most simpatico to you, where you felt free to have visions and dance the ghost dance. What are you telling me today, dear friend? What kind of ghost dance can we engage? I'm listening along with anyone else who might be reading this.

We made trips to Indian reservations in Washington and to Arizona. You were the first to tell me the history of the American Indian, how they were forced off their lands, were killed, infected with smallpox blankets, the U.S. government's biological warfare against its native peoples.

I recall your dancing with Hopi Indians in Arizona, totally immersed in that profound world. We slept under dark golden skies, absorbed by the marvels of being alive. Thank you, God, for Marcus, I prayed, for bringing me to a land of wonder and revelation and healing.

Master Da asked you once at a party, "Marcus, do an Indian dance" which you did with your full heart. It was wild. Da was throwing firecrackers at you; we were all drinking and grooving with the music of your sacred dance which "came out of you" without hesitation. Fireworks and hooting and hollering were only part of the spontaneous theater. You said you felt the holiness of the event and absorption in your dance, even with "irreverent" carryings on.

Once we took peyote with Bubba and the community, after studying the sacramental use of peyote among the Indian people. We asked for preparation advice from Dr. Andy Weil who graciously shared his studies with us. When we took the peyote, we learned to keep some presence and space, even if hallucinations arose. Some felt revelatory insights; others felt connected with nature or meditative as we sat around a large fire in the woods. Those who feared peyote might cause panic for them chose not to participate. A very few had "bad trips" (over-anxiously feeling that they were going to die, feelings of panic, hysteria and the like).

We had eaten peyote on a reservation in Arizona a year earlier; we wanted to experience its psychedelic effects, but most of all to, as you said, Marcus, touch that Living Spirit, both immanent and somehow "beyond the beyond." The Indian ceremony was reverent and powerful. It was a one-time experience that was illuminating, and left me with no desire to repeat it. Yet the second time taking peyote with Bubba's commune was also very peaceful and grounding for me, no fireworks at all. Marcus, you danced through the entire night.

We each chewed, and ate about eight to twenty peyote buttons, a small cactus called lophophora williamsii. Some of us threw up (what a relief to get out the ugly tasting toxic parts!). Peak effects arose in about 2–4 hours but the experience lasted 10–12 hours. Vomiting was considered also a spiritual purification, dramatizing the release of our inner hatreds.

There were drumming, chants, prayers, as we sat around a fire all through the night; some of us were in a trance, allowing the Presence within to emerge, within the strong psychochemical effects of the peyote. Some were dancing, others sitting in meditation. We had prepared to ingest the peyote by three days of fasting, meditation, and allowing our bodies and our intentions to be healthy and further, to be open to the healings and spiritual consciousness that would arise, a feeling of unity with our Earth and with each other. Several of us felt some deeply meaningful, introspective spiritual experience. Others felt it was nothing special at all.

You taught me the healing rituals of the American Indian, the dancing, passing the pipe. You took me to some "sweat lodges" where we'd sit in a small structure made from a wooden frame covered with skins and blankets, canvas. A hole dug right in the middle, into which hot rocks catch water, create a healing steam. We linked our sweating with both physical and moral purifying. We felt this "sauna out in Nature" as spiritually renewing and physically rejuvenating.

You struggled like other Indian friends with alcohol, re-affirming what was so often said: that the Native American sacred substance, tobacco, has caused so many deaths to Christians and wine, a sacred substance for many Christians, has devastated many Native Americans. You showed me feathers and turquoise-silver jewelry you collected. Sometimes you wore large, round gold metal earrings and yellow-blue-red beads as a neckband.

Your two favorite Indians were the nineteenth century Lakota Crazy Horse and the Nez Perce Chief Joseph. You felt you looked like Chief Joseph, with your large expressive face. You loved them both for their resistance to the control of the whites, for their independence of spirit, for their heart, for being visionaries, for being both spiritual and being brave in war.

You spoke so often about Crazy Horse, one of the last great Indian leaders, who foresaw the end of the Indian way of living freely on the earth. You said, like Crazy Horse, you sought visions. Where is the Great Spirit leading me? Crazy Horse believed in cultivating one's healing powers. That inspired you to be a more genuine healer, to be a conduit for That which Truly Heals.

And finally, Marcus, we come to your own dying time. At the end of your life, you were committed to live a communal life with Master Da as your guru; that was your primary interest and fulfillment. Yet you had a very healthy attitude not to worry about communal politics and how we all get spirituality and power mixed up. You'd say "Who cares if we look good or not?" You took lightly the pronouncements, the repetitions of party lines in any group.

Three years before you died, when we were only seeing one another two or three times a year but very often talking on the phone, you started getting terrible headaches. Finally you were diagnosed with Cushing's Disease, an endocrinal disease, caused by high levels of cortisol in the blood. You developed cancer in your pituitary gland and you suffered a lot of pain. I remember when I gave you head, neck and shoulder massages, you told me the pain in your body made any strong massage aggravating. You became very bloated.

On our last visits together in San Francisco and Lake County, I would give you softer foot massages or hold your hand while we talked or sat quietly. I wish I could have given you my health. There were extended times when you felt fairly healthy but your headaches would come back, stronger and constantly until they became a cruel pounding in your head.

About four weeks before you died, I called you at the University of California Hospital in San Francisco where you had had some procedure. You assured me, "I'm preparing my dying in a sacred manner with the community, where my body will be washed, tended to, then iced for three days, with meditators present. Don't worry about me as I have excellent medical care. I won't die for six months or so. I've been sicker before. I love you, man." I said please always call me and to get better.

Who can say, Marcus, when any of us will die? When I asked you if you felt peaceful and you said, "Very," something in your voice, told me not to wait, to get to you, to help take care of you. I still feel guilty that I hushed that call behind your reassuring words and went back to work. Even so, your ever-forgiving heart melts away any concern I might have; our friendship always shines through!

Then Jean, your wonderful stepmother, called to tell me

you had died quite suddenly, much earlier than you expected, and just as you wanted, in the community. Jean was happy she was able to say good-bye on the third and final day of your funeral. Your body was covered in ice and beginning to decompose. Jean had a hard time seeing you; she wanted you in a wood and golden casket and with more friends around you. She said your face showed a slight smile and so she felt peaceful that this is the way you wanted to pass to other worlds. Jean liked that people were meditating in the room. But she felt she should have been able to participate more in your funeral and was surprised I wasn't there with you. You guys were always together she told me.

I told Jean the community hadn't told me of your death until after your funeral, though some had tried to reach me. She wanted me to tell her of our last conversation when you were in the hospital and how you had pre-planned this funeral. Jean and I spoke so long, about you, how we miss talking with you, being with you, sharing your abundant life, laughing and crying so much.

To you, *hermano* Marcus, I'm forever grateful. And it's true: you're always with me, with a sense of lightness and delight in you; I send my hugs and a kiss to you.

■

Maestro of the Stars: Don Alexander Cordero (16 January 1937- 9 December 2007)

> *For what are stars but asterisks*
> *To point a human life?*
>
> —Emily Dickinson

February 2, 2008, Santa Cruz, California

I'm going to talk as if you, Don, were sitting right next me which you were just a year ago.

You died in the presence of your devoted wife, Juanita, and your children, Maria, Angel, Rebecca, and Mimi, such a close family friend. You were embraced by the human touch of love and understanding, in an atmosphere that acknowledged the process of dying as eminently human, as sacred. You were continuing your spiritual practice and being with those you loved so much. You lived and died with exquisite dignity. My words, our words, are an offering to you: our reverence, our appreciation, our grateful good-byes.

Your sons Jonathon and Jose miss you so. I've been crying for you too, Don. Big round drops, wet emotions tumbling like yellow daisy petals, blown off by winds that come from nowhere, like memories of being with you. You would tell us—all of us—to go ahead, cry but not for too long, live, live, live, be alive, with the music. We too will someday have to leave the beautiful oceans, the tall redwoods, our wives, partners, husbands, children, friends.

So, we hear you, Don, singing to us: cherish your lives together, as you would our final, tender, kiss good-bye; tend to your precious lives.

I treasure your gorgeous, compassionate heart, Don, your ballsy being "out there" as a married Catholic priest. Your ability to keep going, when some were angered and threatened by your convictions. I admire you immensely, curly-headed creative embracer of life and people.

We're right now sending to you all the music you cherished in your life; music gracefully shaking the white snow-dressed mountains in Tibet you visited; in full crescendo, your orchestras, jazz, rock and roll, ethnic, mariachi, folk, classical songs and melodies of light, songs bearing gifts of confidence to our lonely souls, thrilling, resonating the natural beauty of the human spirit; you, that's you, Don, you are the beauty of the human spirit, you, contemplating the stars, jumping into the golden crystals lighting the sky, while infusing your body-mind-heart; dear Don, "done in" by the wonder and awe and just being, being so small as Don and yet so vast as the millions of lights, sparkling in faraway ever-receding black space.

You anguished too, as we did all together. What's happening? What's this all about?

You, gentle, a cool dude, non-aggressive, but fierce too, a steady activist for changes in education and church, counselor, a gracious counselor to me on a few occasions, such empathy and understanding in your advice! You, a teacher of Astronomy, a civil servant, elected member of the Mission College West Valley Board of Trustees (the first faculty member to do so no less); calm, energetic, frazzled yeah; all of it; appreciatively married to a woman Catholic priest, your beloved Juanita.

With a reflecting light for you, sweet Don, in her eyes, your Juanita said her first mass while celebrating your thirty-sixth wedding anniversary.

Don, a fool for your Lord, an extravagant giver, a Jesuit, an artiste of life, an enjoyer of laughter, scrumptious food and lively company, an hombre, a man; a conductor of life-giving liturgy, an innovator, a connector of people; attached so wholesomely to your wife and children and friends, you, curious to the Spirit, a wonderer about Buddha too, a singer of the Presence, an enthusiastic person's people person, all the way through, alive right until you died. You continue to affirm our shared sisterhood and brotherhood on this very occasion at the edge of ocean's shore.

You married your daughter, Rebecca, just before you had to leave us all, on your last Thanksgiving Day, grateful dad, priest for life, heart submitted to what you love so much.

Don, you are man of heart; your presence will be felt by so many of us for the rest of our own fading—but in your memory, colorful, involved, engaged—lives. A celebrator you are, *querido* Don; we celebrate your life! your life within us, and among us, fresh as the crashing silvery green waves gesticulating to salute you outside windows, framing seas.

Dying, you and Juanita read from *The Tibetan Book of*

Living and Dying. Your community anointed you with oil. You suffered terrible pain, in your bones; so, now, released like an unsuspecting fledgling into waiting blue and white skies; fly, soar, romp, as we honor you; go wild with the music-singing-dancing to the sounds of the heavens, jamming the nights away to welcome you, our Dearest *hermano* Don, to golden celestial company.

Three Poems
Don Foran, Ph.D.

Mountain Ash

I planted the spare stick fifteen years back
filling a space in our side yard
near where Corky, Marguerite's old pooch
now lies buried. It grew extravagantly
but only sprouted branches six years ago.
I see it now over my left shoulder, evening sunlight
striking the tree at a slant.
It's beautiful, forty-some feet high, leaves silhouetted
against the Northwest blue. It reminds me
of my oldest daughter, Amanda, swaying soulfully
to the ripples of her beloved bassoon,
and of my youngest daughter, Erin—tall like me,
skinny some say, but more graceful than I, and graced.
Maggie's bike helmet suddenly appears
in the driveway, and I shamble down to greet my wife,
the college counselor. The ash tree waves hello,
dancing, proud to be alive.

The River

I never know what's swimming toward me fast,
The questions students do or do not ask.
I flick my wrist: the fly rests where I've cast.

I make mistakes, I know. I've sometimes passed
Too quickly through a complex text or task;
I never know what's swimming toward me fast.

I've slipped on hidden shoals more slick than wax,

Or pulled the line before the hook was fast.
I flick my wrist, not knowing where to cast.

A shimmer in the swirling deep, some flash
Illuminates that dark, uncorks life's cask.
I never know what's swimming toward me fast.

And metaphorical mayflies sometimes hatch,
New theories surfacing, new worlds unmasked;
I flick my wrist, not knowing where to cast.

I've made mistakes I know; I've sometimes passed
An opportunity to revel or relax.
I never know what's swimming toward me fast;
I flick my wrist: the fly rests where I've cast.

The River was first published in *Crosscurrents*, the journal of
the Washington Community College Humanities Association
(WCCHA). October 20, 2007, page 66. Republished here
with their kind permission.

Cat Talk

They have it right, those cats:
Eat, sleep, cuddle, sleep some more.
They wonder why we fuss, plan, hurry, or watch football
When we could give them undivided attention, love.
Take Mickey, for example. We've been his people
Ten years now, enough time for him to know us,
Our quirks, our chatter, and our flaws.
I tell him, sometimes, what I'm grappling with,
What project looms, what back pain, what angst assails me.
He purrs, shifts himself on my lap
With studied nonchalance. He shimmies

Up the long body now invading his couch,
Plants himself at that perfect spot, my shoulder,
Just below my chin, the one place, he knows,
Where I cannot read my book.
He looks me in the eye and speaks:
"Quidquid recipitur ad modum recipientis
Recipitur," he says. Whatever is received is received
According to the mode of the one receiving it.
"That's plagiarism! I shout. He smiles –
Cats do smile – and licks, as always, my nearest ear.

Four Poems
Robert R. Rahl

Touch Hands

beginning and end
touch hands
exchange of gifts
in supple complement
strong and gentle
flowing firm
wildfire quickflash
long leisure lingering
fingering each the other
one another one
an other one
interchange in touch
nets tangling
letting go
untangling
trusting in between
letting go to leap
to fresh hold
energies radiant in
intersecting ripples
tingling glow
spreading everywhere at once
focusing there and here
diffusing everywhere
lives intertwining
pulses harmonizing
synchronizing
in delicate dynamic
of anything but homeostatic
balance

*Nigra sum sed formosa**

morning of all souls
día de los muertos
moon two days past full
Adam in the back
baking (this day) our daily bread
Our Lady of Guadalupe
shining on his back
black and very beautiful
horse-shoed with black roses
glowing turquoise ultraviolet
under the black light
radiating the racks of loaves

Adam of the Beautiful Woman
taking a smoke break
on the top rail of the back of the bus bench
under the too-full moon
thick black hair bandannaed
waist aproned in white
smoke curling past the moon
arms naked to the shoulder
dusted with white
swirls of black hair
gone back into the black light

Nigra sum sed formosa is Latin for "I am black but beautiful."

These are the opening words of the *Song of Songs*.

Spring Sunlight

this morning early
birds singing merry
spring sunlight softened
with tiniest droplets of floating rain
half an arc of rainbow
rising from the south
arching over the forest
where you are
shining from the gray-grey
layers and gradations
of cloud and mist
marking your presence
masking your presence
the rainbow
promising your presence
for the tiniest moment
then
like you
gone
dissolved into spring sunlight
and bright tears

Stardance

mysterious fairy beacon
tingling telegraphic current
invisible appeals, soft touches
little hands pulling and tugging
homing in on fragrance of delight
electric thrill of the far-known
riding rising warm air rafts
lifting deeper into promised meeting
skyriver stepping stones
warming with the warmth
delighting with the delight
letting go now catching
surfing the wind's soft shears
wild ecstasy shining
rivering stars deeper delight
tasting the light warmth of night

Section Two, The Group and the Classroom

Eight years ago I wrote my first book, a manual, *Notes of a Therapist, My View as a Mental Health Worker and Adult Special Education Teacher*, after I had worked as a recreational therapist at El Centro Mental Health Center in East Los Angeles. It was intended for other teachers and therapists; it contained lists of psychiatric drugs, an explanation of charting, a summary of the DSM presentation of mental illnesses and corresponding therapies. It also had a section on yoga and other alternative therapies for addictions. It was far less personal than *Intimate Meanderings*

After Dr. Andy Weil was kind enough to write a short plug for *Notes*, my colleagues and others bought half of the five hundred books that were printed over an eight-year period. The other half was given away. I still get questions about it today. I am including some of those notes here, as "My Mind Is Always Making Dates My Body Can't Keep."

I have included several other classroom notes and reflections to reflect my continuing work, plus a great introduction on the vocation of teaching by my friend Don Foran.

Love of Learning, Love of Learners
Teaching as Vocation
Don Foran, Ph.D.

I feel happy to introduce Don's piece on Teaching. It resonates with my heart. My first teaching job was from 1969–71 at Bellarmine High School in San Jose, California. And I've continued to teach, with gratitude that I make my living doing what's always attracted me. Don's writing wonderfully articulates "teaching as vocation." Teaching is mutual cultivation of our inner potential and abilities. The teacher draws out what is already in inchoate form within the student, with a respectful sensitivity to the individual student which Don exemplifies.

I've known Don for several years, especially re-engaging with him through an on-line discussion group. When I was editing the Buddhist journal, Common Sense, *Don contributed a wonderful poem, "Mountain Ash" which I've included in our book, along with other poems from Don. They communicate a lot about Don. For me, he is a poet, teacher and friend.*

The idea of being called to do something—*vocare* in Latin means "to call"—has a long and venerable history. Perhaps one of the most famous religious calls was that of Augustine. Everything in his past life seemed to argue against his becoming a priest and bishop. But he did. Thoreau felt called into the woods at Walden Pond, and he felt called out of them, he said, for the same reason he entered into them. He didn't tell us that reason; vocation is compelling, yet mysterious. I know something about vocation from experience. I entered a Jesuit novitiate when I was eighteen and left the religious order seventeen years later. My leaving was as much a vocation as my entering. I felt called in and then called out by the Spirit, but I'm not sure what that means. Most of what happens in our lives is pretty mysterious and the fact of choosing to do one thing rather than another is probably more important than the vocabulary we use to describe it.

One thing I am certain about: there was never any doubt in my mind that I have been called to teach. I cannot not teach. I'm hooked. My few forays into administration, social work, television production, and apartment management have certainly clarified my thinking about what I am called to do. I know, a teacher really does not stop teaching no matter what she does, but, in my case, despite my fondness for metaphor, I know that I am quintessentially a teacher. Like E. T., I am continually called home.

Parker Palmer, my favorite philosopher, or perhaps theologian, of education, has said that what is necessary in the classroom is "love of learning and love of learners." Yes,

I can recognize a fellow junkie when I see one. His words even suggest a further distinction: we are called both by the profession and by those we teach. We are called to co-discover the truth. Truth, Palmer tells us, is an ever-deepening conversation "about things that matter, conducted with passion and discipline." The tricky part of teaching is, of course, that the truth of things does not have a capital T. Truth is squidgy. The teacher can't afford to indoctrinate. He or she cannot lapse into monologue. Learners must be empowered to challenge the teacher's certain certainties as well as their own. Thus part of the teaching profession is the choosing and discarding of materials, texts, exercises, problems, those "conversation pieces" which stimulate the community of learners to be increasingly passionate and disciplined in their lives and their learning. A story like Ursula K. LeGuin's, "The Ones Who Walk Away From Omelas," or an essay like Peter Marin's, "Helping and Hating the Homeless," can engage the mind and heart of the learner, but so can a sonata, a pericope, a cell structure, a historical role-play, an ethics or psychological case study, a physics experiment, or a collaborative project which is threatening to fall apart. In education, as in life, as much or more can be gained from our failures as from our successes.

Teachers are, I believe, called to serve. They are the secular, though not necessarily secularist, priests and priestesses of society. Some are sadly self-promoting—just as some of their counterparts in religious ministry seem more honed on monetary enrichment than on empowering their charges to seek and find fulfillment in service to the truth. Yet, on the whole, teachers are, in my experience, more interested in the well-being of learners than in feathering their own nests.

The heart of the teaching profession is, of course, in the classrooms of cities, barrios, villages, everywhere on this still-green earth of ours. Women and men called to teach are exploring life and life's possibilities together. Just as a good parent does not hesitate to assist a sick or hurting child, the committed teacher does not forget to love the learner even when it would be easier to retreat to the office or seek refuge in research. As in religious vocation, teachers must often remind themselves what they are doing and for whom they are doing it. Every learner, however vulnerable, however irascible, however unattractive, receives far more than subject matter from our interactions.

Learners call us back to ourselves. They keep us alive. They force us to revise. They challenge our assumptions. They bring out the best in us and the worst in us. They make us aware of our shared humanity and the inter-dependence of our reciprocal teaching/learning.

We are called, and, whatever our energy, whatever our imagination, we will answer.

A Final Reflection

Question to Don: "If you had a crystal ball, what would you say about the future of education? How do you inspire a student to be a good citizen? You are an activist. Does your teaching include non-violent actions? Are education and actions against injustice and inequality related? And finally, what has happened to liberal education?"

DF: If I had a crystal ball, I see education becoming even more specialized in the future, but, paradoxically, I would predict that more interdisciplinary work would be done. I find my literature, ethics, and writing students very interested in sustainability. Our faculty are also collaborating more across disciplines. I'm in a statewide consortium of writing professors from four and two year colleges and universities who are creating fresh assignments and meeting to talk about what works best. Such rich collaboration is very exciting for those curious to become teachers.

I also suspect that despite students sometimes becoming addicted to video games, to consumerism, and to Facebook (all of which I find appalling developments), I also see more idealism, more interest in service and sacrifice. High tech may lead us inevitably to high touch. In our rich American diet, self-indulgence of all kinds, we are perhaps beginning to recognize deficiencies. Richard Louv's coining of the term "nature deficit disorder" is prophetic. Students are returning to Emerson, Thoreau, Aldo Leopold, Rachel Carson, E.O. Wilson, and others to find out what they've missed.

I strongly encouraged my students to take part in political caucuses in Washington State on Saturday Feb. 9, 2008, and I took some with me to the caucus I attended, (a couple were supporting candidates other than the person whom I personally endorse—Obama. That was fine.)

Do I involve students in the nonviolent direct action tradition? I must say that I have given several community and college lyceum talks recently on the history of nonviolence, have spoken at Martin Luther King Day events and brought King quotes into class often. Over the years, this has been my contribution. I haven't been in jail since 1973 (with Dorothy Day and César Chavez, and my only other civil disobedience action was at San Pedro harbor during the Indo-Pakistani war a long time ago). Virtually every student I have taught has been assigned and has appreciated Dr. King's "Letter from Birmingham Jail," and some have gone on to read the "Beyond Vietnam" speech from Riverside Church, and even done, occasionally, a research paper on non-cooperation a la Gandhi or Dorothy Day or Martin Luther King. Speaking of Gandhi, I put on a citywide Re-enactment of Gandhi's Salt March (with a contemporary theme of simplicity in an age of Peak Oil) with my friend Bernie Meyer, a Gandhi look-alike the summer before last. I involved four college students and three high school students in the planning, and, apart from Gandhi (Bernie), and I and Dr. Rudy Martin, the four other speakers at the end of the march were all students. About 350 people marched from the state capitol to the public market, then down to the banks of the Puget Sound where a "liturgy" of sorts took place.

I believe that students need, and crave, models of creative citizenship and social action. One of my most admirable students, Joseph Robinson, has educated the campus on Rachel Corrie's* death in Gaza and her courageous witness. He is spearheading an effort to add a plaque in her honor to our diversity clock tower. He is also a strong candidate to receive a full-ride to The Evergreen State College in Journalism. He has applied for the Rachel Corrie Scholarship, and I have written a letter of recommendation for him. Jody Peterson has been on three international medical emergency trips, and my daughters are both engaged in political action and missions of mercy.

"What has happened to liberal education?" It has contracted, but it has not gone away.

When students can read Walt Whitman, Lao Tzu, Emily Dickinson, Alice Walker, Albert Camus, when they are seduced into finding out that they have hearts of flesh, they are wonderfully idealistic even in this age of realism and—sadly—pre-emptive war. They are better able than I to be practical about their idealism. Some travel much more readily than I to assist victims of tsunami, flooding, forest fires, even genocide. Apart from liberal education, apart from professors insisting on the capacity for compassion, I would find little hope in the only world we have. Yes, there are horrors like depleted uranium in Afghanistan and Iraq producing leukemia in innocent children, but there are poets like David Smith-Ferri writing about such things. Late in their lives a Stanley Kunitz, who died at age one hundred, or Dan Berrigan, now in his eighties, work alongside others, write poetry, hold up a mirror to nature. We *must* too, to echo Phillip Sidney, look into our hearts and write.

*On Sunday, March 16, 2003, Rachel Corrie (1979–2003) was run over by a Caterpillar D9 bulldozer manned by the Israeli army in the Rafah Refugee Camp in the Gaza Strip. Corrie was a member of International Solidarity Movement, working with Palestinians and internationals to end Israeli occupation of Palestinian territory. She was speaking through a bullhorn to protest the demolition of Palestinian buildings and homes.

Always Making Dates in My Mind that My Body Can't Keep
A Recreation Therapist's Notes
Morgan Zo-Callahan

> *Love cures people—both the ones who give it and the
> ones who receive it.*
>
> —Dr. Karl Menninger

The following notes are excerpted from my first book, *Notes
of a Therapist, My View as a Mental Health Worker and Adult
Special Education Teacher.*

I'm happy to share what it was like going to therapy (and
the need behind seeking it) and also being a recreation and
physio-therapist doing group and individual therapy? Also I'd
like to encourage the reader to consider the meaning of giving
and receiving therapy in his or her particular conditions.
Consider as you read how you, the reader, can take better care of
yourself. You are a valuable treasure. For myself, I most benefit
from body based (including yoga) and movement therapies,
such as Feldenkrais, Alexander, along with conversations with a
psychologist/psychiatrist. I've benefited from some traditional
psychoanalytic insights. I suppose all our therapies include re-
processing our relationships to our parents, those early deep-
seated emotions our mothers and fathers planted. And how
perhaps, depending on our individual cases, understanding
how hurt and anger buried deep inside us affects our level
of maturity, our personal growth in our present living
circumstances.

Some of the psychiatrists at our Mental Health Program
were doing "transactional analytic" group therapies; I
participated in groups, and co-led them as well. As a team, we
would have workshops in transactional analysis. I did some
individual counseling and worked with intake information
and then ongoing charting of the progress and challenges and

needs of clients assigned to me. The medical caseworker was responsible for screening intakes and setting appointments for evaluations that were done in consultation with a team psychiatrist. If clients were not accepted, they were referred to alternative treatment facilities more apt to meet their needs. Evaluations were presented and discussed by the entire team. The unit leader assigned clients to one therapist (such as myself) to map an Individual Plan with the guidance and support of the psychiatrist and unit leader. The treatment plan included, most commonly, medications from the psychiatrist. For example, the client's week may include individual therapy, a group class in dance therapy, transactional analysis, making pottery, an outing to the ocean, going out to lunch with therapists and other clients.

Our program served as an alternative to hospitalization, and we, the therapists, had bi-weekly in-services; for example, a USC professor came to discuss dealing with sexual abuse and its effects for the victim; doctors came to present model programs for patients with challenging mental-emotional problems.

Along with an initially small group (it grew to much greater numbers), I helped organize a union for clerical and clinical staff when I was working at the clinic. The administration fought like hell to block the union. Organizers—including myself—were sometimes rowdy, and the administrators would at times be very threatening. There was a fairly long period of picketing, but the union prevailed and the staff had the chance to negotiate for better working conditions, more rights and professional salaries. There followed about a three-month period where administration and staff had to make a basic peace, and the initial hard feelings were smoothed by the more important task of running an effective mental health clinic.

Our Day Treatment Program provided services to the mentally ill (about 80 percent Hispanic), to minimize the need for in-hospital care (though some of our clients would go to inpatient care for periods of time). We provided support to some seriously challenged individuals, those suffering depression, schizophrenia, anxiety, panic disorder, and strong drug/alcohol addictions. Clients very often included Daily Life Skills together with therapy, in a supportive, welcoming, non-invasive, non-judgmental environment.

We opened from 9:00 AM to 3:00 PM for our clients and went to meetings, did in-takes, prepared classes and activities, meeting from 8:00 AM to 9:00 AM and from 3:00 PM to 5:00 PM Our team was composed of a team leader (who had a Ph.D. in Psychology), two Unit Leaders (one English speaking and one Spanish speaking), an R.N., a community mental health worker, a psych tech; a secretary, three part-time psychiatrists, three recreation therapists, and a medical caseworker.

* * * * *

Many of us binge to avoid dealing with a life crisis. I've certainly done it over the course of my life. I try to communicate to clients that, sure, it's great to enjoy celebrations, good food, drink and company. But what happens when we get into troublesome, addictive behavior around gambling, sex, alcohol, drugs, shopping, eating and the like? What are the consequences of the actions in our lives if we don't heal our addictions, including "situational" abuse of drugs? It's not the "things" that we become addicted to that are "wrong"; they can be fun, social, relaxing as an occasional-celebratory part of human life. It's our uncontrollable cravings that lead us "off the mark" to destruction, towards hurting others and ourselves seriously, creating an unhealthy balance and perspective. I'm sure a large number of us know someone who died from alcohol or drugs or whose lives were devastated by them. For two months in 1974 I was living with my wife, Wendy, in a very poor area of San Francisco. Sometimes I would walk upstairs to our apartment, past human beings, junkies shooting heroin into their veins. At times our eyes would meet and I felt such fear and desperation to deaden the pain of life and feel an opiate-bliss. Later I would get to know a few such people who were able to overcome their addiction and lead a happy life. I realized how I also drank too much to avoid feeling, to escape, to create a false courage. The "too much," with its underlying impulses, is what we're engaging with in therapy.

I've learned that it's enough for all of us, just being who we are naturally, without exaggerated chemical intoxicants, without mental-emotional toxins, just being honest and present to one's authentic, happy self. We can continue to learn to use nourishing foods, drinks, and medicines in non-addicting ways. Buddhists speak of not being caught in "craving" things—whether money, sex, food, drugs, power over others, revenge—and then further "clinging" onto them, "identifying" with the money, sex, power and so on. Psychologists and therapists use a model of health as a dynamic balance and also often conclude that it is the "craving" and "clinging" which most often throws us off balance.

Several of our clients arrive "smashed" from having fallen off various cliffs. They are pushed off course because they very often don't have the balance, flexibility, and emotional alertness to see obstacles they'd best avoid. The process of therapy helps them brush themselves off and get back into more interesting and healthy currents of life.

* * * * *

Our client said she stuffed herself so she wouldn't feel the pain and hurt she felt in an abusive relationship. She said she feels like a "bad mess of a person, a fucked-up rejected and self-rejecting mess." She often got drunk. Today, she says she understands, "all the way through her body-mind" that there's no way out of squarely facing problems. In therapy, she began to see the sense in abstaining from drink so she could get to the bottom of what was "driving her to drink." She says she never felt more like drinking, but with group and individual therapy, she got healthy in her body, in her mind, and in her spirit. She was encouraged by getting into exercise classes, enjoying the music and movement therapy.

She didn't want to feel condemned, judged by the therapist. In the group, we felt no need to judge each other. We were in mutual conversation, and she picked up immediately if we were being "condescending" or "patronizing" therapists. She communicated that denial, desperate distraction, and over-indulging prolonged the unresolved conflict. We facilitated an environment where she could "feel" and pinpoint what she wanted to avoid facing by over-eating, staying awake for exaggerated hours, over-sleeping, getting inebriated and passing out.

And most importantly, she really got into it! She wanted to heal. The first step is for the client to feel what's going on in his/her life that is hurtful, unproductive, what's killing the enthusiasm for living. Our client said she saw how she plays the spoiled baby "to get what she wants" and with her children how she becomes the judgmental, demeaning parent. She said she gave up screaming criticisms of her children. "I'm seeing my children as their own people for the first time; I'm giving up trying making them feel guilty and not good enough." Some of the therapy at the clinic includes family therapy, as a happy family is essential to the health of the individual.

* * * * *

She observes: "I say *yes* when I mean *no*. I'm afraid of being rejected; I already feel bad about myself." She's living in response to parental voices, which block her full life waiting to flourish. She's struggling with her emotional understanding of these voices which are insisting, "You're no good"; "Sex and body are bad"; "I'm not worthy of love and respect"; "I have to be a *good* girl." There are also tendencies to blame such as: "You're no good," "It's all your fault," or "Society's at fault."

We encourage a client to slow down in order to take a more relaxed and objective view of how she is living life at this time. She's evaluated by the therapeutic team and then offered therapies to heal some of the physical-emotional hurting, while concurrently, addressing most of her immediate needs. As the client does calm down, such belittling voices tend to fade into the background. As she progresses in the therapeutic process, what emerges? She experiences, often quite spontaneously, the life, intelligence, talent, heart she's yearning to express. Every client is so different. We say: "Welcome the difference that you discover for yourself; encourage peacefulness and tolerance in your particular living circumstances."

Our own confidence in basic human goodness, in our *own* basic goodness—however obscured—allows us to be patient. We're also aware that individuals can do evil deeds and have to be separated from the larger community, confined in a penal institution perhaps; but there's a potential, even for the so-called worst of us, to create one's environment—inner and outer—where we let the light shine from within us, that spark, which expresses itself in service and useful work, relationships and creativity, making us feel full, enjoying a certain tranquility that we are being and in touch with our deepest desires, that will lead and attract us to a genuine satisfaction. We therapists have seen ex-convicts who turn their lives around and use their past experiences to create a more-positive direction. These clients sometimes became our wisest teachers about life and the ability not to give up.

* * * * *

She came to the clinic full of murderous rage. Her husband had left her, dumped her and their three children. She was pissed off and out of control. Unlike some of the clients who suffer from inwardly repressed rages, she did not bear her agony silently. She didn't take her anger out on herself, at least consciously, but on the people in her life and the "representatives of the system." She was flailing and cussing. She was "in your face." I think it was good the clinic gave her the space and chance to safely vent her frustrations. Now we need to see if she can get down to more difficult therapeutic work—and healing. She's finding the anger management group very helpful.

* * * * *

I'm perplexed that my fellow therapist is so adamantly against psychiatric medication for depression, because I've seen— admitting a few cases of faulty evaluation and overly aggressive medical prescriptions—how some find relief in prescription anti-depression medication. Many clients have such depressive symptoms as not sleeping well, always being lethargic and without energy, inability to have some fun and pleasure. Some, who were predominantly subjective (just "in their own minds"), asocial, and withdrawn, with medication find simple, but satisfying enjoyment in ordinary social interaction, as well as take some pleasure just being in their bodies. Depression also certainly has its hereditary-biochemical influence.

* * * * *

We understand that depression is a serious illness; we can't write it off as a person just being lazy and negative. If we examine ourselves closely, we can feel the tendency to destroy ourselves that seems to lie just a bit more superficially above our deepest desire and ability to flourish.

Today we're doing art, exercise, and have an outing to the zoo. The group is also engaging in quiet times, the ability to concentrate on something engaging.

Our client said that his depression was both organic

and social. This is real insight. He feels a biological leaning to be "down." He wants to sleep a lot; he often "feels bad" and doesn't have much energy or focus. Sometimes he takes his anger out on himself by berating and hating himself. Yet he said it also is a social way of relating to his family, friends and the community. It's his way of saying to others: "I'm not happy; pay attention to me."

* * * * *

"I'm never going to forgive that degraded, sick bastard who raped me. He's not a human being."

It always enlightens, and amazes me when I see a rape victim go through the process—to me, quite mysterious and graceful—of forgiving the perpetrator. The victim gains my respect for navigating this difficult path. How is this woman finally able to forgive the man who violated her? Diogenes wrote: "Forgiveness is better than revenge." But it's not easy, she says, to do that "letting go," which is forgiving. "I'm not forgetting; I'm not being goody-goody. I'm giving up wanting to get revenge and hurt back. I even meditate, as well as talk to the counselor, so I can truly feel and observe the feelings going on within me. If there are still suppressed feelings, my forgiveness isn't integrated into my personality."

It's *not* easy to forgive if you've been raped, she tells me. It's a terrible trauma, a violation. Will our therapy be able to heal? Erin Prizzey says so poignantly: "I have been raped. It pollutes one's life. It is an experience that is contained within the boundaries of one's own life. In the end, one's life is larger. Assault by a stranger or within a relationship is very terrible. One is hurt, undermined, degraded, afraid. But one's life is larger."

* * * * *

Hans Küng, the Swiss-born Catholic theologian, once told psychiatrists in Washington D.C. that we can be "repressed from the expression of true religion." The psychiatrists agreed on a definition of religion as accessing "the ultimate reality." Küng suggested that some of our problems could be the result of spiritual trauma, the repression of deep spiritual feelings. So therapy should take religious phenomena as valid human expression. Learn to distinguish true from false religions: "True religiousness in whatever faith, functions not to enslave but to free, not to injure but to heal, not to destabilize but to stabilize."

* * * * *

Religion and spirituality are important to complement and fulfill my own personal therapy. Freud helped me to some insight into the powerful emotional-sexual subconscious relating to mother and father. Jung pinpointed the need for a spiritual life. He wrote that real therapy was based on the experience of "the overpowering psychic fact of God." Freud showed how important the unconscious and subconscious are and explored these "levels" under conditions that were free from conscious censorship like free associating, jokes, slips of the tongue, dreams.

After he left Freud's intimate circle in 1913, Jung explored psycho-spiritual themes. He felt that there was wholeness and integration beyond the great influence of drives and conflicts, which Freud had elucidated, and he wanted to achieve this state.

* * * * *

We understand that addiction means something, which can't be controlled. This man is a strong person, yet his addiction to heroin is such that he can only change *with the help of others*.

He admits his weakness and is willing to use the help he needs to overcome it, to make the effort to understand what's going on inside himself and in his life, to change his actions with insights into his personality, his patterns of thought and activity.

✓ He couldn't stop drinking tequila, and taking heroin until one day, his wife, kids, job, and self-respect were totally blown away by his tumultuous living. He manifested what is common with persons who have an addiction.

✓ He had to finish the whole bottle.

✓ And get some more.

✓ He was sneaky. Always around the corner "smoking'" or using the bathroom to "fix."

✓ He is compulsive. He *just does it* like he's being led by some over-dominating personality. The alcohol and heroin control him.

✓ Since he's in a gang, he's paranoid, fearful of physical violence to himself or his family if he doesn't do the gang's drugs to "be a part of the gang." He's afraid emotionally. He doesn't want to feel or be present with the therapists. Now he's able to sustain some eye contact. He's taking deep breaths, staying even with uncomfortable conversations.

✓ The drug is a pleasure, a kind of alluring and momentary euphoria, a boost of energy; yet it's also a form of slavery that causes self-hate and anger.

✓ He admitted his problem, first to himself and then to his intimates.

✓ He began to eat well, exercise, and use medications appropriately.

✓ He says: "I'm beginning to feel again."

✓ "I don't absolutize, make things as so black and white like 'I'm no good' or 'I'm the Greatest.'" He reduced the excessive "drama" he was acting out. He was getting in touch with himself, reflecting and making healthy life changes.

* * * * *

He feels he can't let go of certain pain and hurt in his life, some terrible losses—the inner anguish in life has extinguished the joy. He says he's stuck on what he doesn't have, rather than understanding and appreciating what he now does have. "I always want what I don't have." He defines therapy as "shifting his attitude."

Our client says he feels a change from being a resentful person to one who is grateful for life, even with all his problems and the challenges to free himself from his addictions. "Damn, a big chip fell off my shoulders. I'm *living* my life." I recall what Fra Giovanni said: "Life is so generous a giver, but we, judging its gifts by their covering, cast them away as ugly, or heavy or hard. Remove the covering and you will find beneath it a living splendor, woven of love, by wisdom, with power. Welcome it, grasp it, and you touch the angel's hand that brings it to you."

* * * * *

Do stressed social situations or occasions contribute to mental illness? Sure. How many abused, hurt, humiliated persons continue to feel "shell-shocked?" For example, some "illegal" immigrants have manifested some neurotic and even psychotic symptoms, being overwhelmed by fear of deportation and anxiety about surviving in a new culture with hostile elements. Some of these twelve million immigrants have been afraid for many years. I advocate a fair comprehensive immigrant bill for those living illegally in the United States, but contributing to its economy that allows for a thirteen-fifteen year path to citizenship a guest work program for those who want to come here to work when needed. I also advocate a secure border. People criticize President Bush—often, in my opinion correctly—but I hope his endorsement of an immigration plan, with some modification to acknowledge more the value of the manual laborer for our society, is eventually implemented. (Sadly as of 9/2008 this has not happened). The most important aspect is the "road of hope" for those immigrants who are here in the United States and contributing, so they can come out from the shadows and allowed into a process—not an immediate amnesty—of being a legal citizen. That means a lot to the dignity of worth-while, good immigrant persons, but also to us, the majority of U.S. citizens who welcome the immigrant and have the compassion and insight into how being poor is the principle motivation for "illegal immigration." There, but for the grace of God, go I.

* * * * *

Our client was fearful of his aging, less able, and having more ailments. This psychological fear of getting older is compounded by the social "scape-goating" and making the elderly obsolete.

Two cultural traits of Indo-Chinese students, which I admire, are that teenage girls would walk together holding hands, and secondly, that elderly people were always given the place of deference and attention. Soon the schoolgirls give up the custom of holding hands because of ridicule. But many continue the social practice of respecting their elders, which has been carried from their home country.

Once on a summer day, I was downtown and saw—a rare occurrence because of the care given most elderly Chinese by their families—an elderly Chinese woman eating out of a garbage bin on Main Street. I thought: "Everything is possible under this sun which is making all of us hot today." How fragile we are, how resilient too. I shared a few words with her;

she had the quality of a rugged peasant walking in the fields to pick up some vegetables.

Some of the elderly clients suffering depression are experimenting with nutrition, vitamins, natural herbs and also recreation therapy—having some fun, and not dwelling on problems, conditions that have seemed to hijack their lives. We've had wonderful parties, musical and artistic performances, excursions for cultural enlightenment, to malls, museums, zoos, and being out in Nature: the ocean, desert and mountains. Going to aquatic centers where we can be in soothing waters. We need that time to "re-create" ourselves with energy, interest, connectedness, and vitality.

* * * * *

My friends are faced with a decision about whether to institutionalize their Mongoloid, Downs-Syndrome child whom they love. At times, people cringe from seeing the child. They know that their child is not a monster. They choose to live with and nurture and enjoy their child, just as she is, even if different and genetically less gifted. They sense a real potential of exploration and life in their child. The dad says, "Accept the child as she is, a human being. Communicate acceptance to her with a million dollar smile."

* * * * *

We are in a group therapy-discussion about money. We identify the places where we feel money is controlling us; where we're feeling the emotional upsets in our relationships regarding money and what issues of power are involved. My experience is that most of us want to be "foggy" about money (even in the institutions of the great religions). We keep ourselves mentally unclear, in order to avoid a full, vital connection to all aspects of life. There's a deep emotional charge connected with money. A pointed mention of money hits people in the guts. So we're engaging the process of being honest in talking about ourselves, as well as listening to others, with full attention. We speak about how our lives have a cycle of inflow and outflow; we're learning how to respect those patterns of energy, when to withhold and when to let go, how to take and give energy which money represents. We talk about how we use our resources, how we handle debt and free ourselves from it. Usually we find we're happy if we're being generous, as well as enjoying ourselves.

* * * * *

The doctor tells us about his visit to New York's Mt. Sinai's psychiatric program for troubled babies. These infants suffer marked and extreme bouts of crying and passive listlessness. The mental health workers help the parent learn how to soothe and to stimulate the suffering child, and how to understand when to be tender and relaxing and when, through playful activities, to bring out active responses from the child. Mother and child are given therapy together, creating a more alive relationship.

* * * * *

Today in group therapy, we discuss and share feelings about how we can promote and encourage the inner process of experiencing the goodness, talent and joy within us and in *life* it self. We ask each other "what does it mean to take care of ourselves while we take care of each other?"

"Physician, heal yourself!"

We, therapists, discuss how our being aware and present with the client does more good than imposing "detached" "overly-intellectualized" treatment plans. Yes, some detachment is helpful, but we need to listen. Continue to encourage the client' deepest-most personal wants and needs. Our service is to stimulate a wide variety of interests for the clients through a holistic-humanistic environment, professional group-individual therapy; a variety of classes and seminars that attract the individual client. Art, exercise, excursions into the community, counseling sessions and group therapy, life-skills classes, art and movement therapy are now popular. This atmosphere, environment inspires relaxation, self-reflection, ability to use medicine appropriately; it's a haven to get perspective and health back.

* * * * *

We organize a union at work (early 80s) and it's not a friendly environment. There's picketing and nasty actions on both sides. We're convinced of our cause to improve the worker's lot. But there seems to be an inevitable tension between the union and the administrators. We can't let it get in the way of serving the clients. "Open" (even if not agreeing all the time) or contrasting "closed" roads of communication between worker and administrator can affect the therapists' front-line work with clients. We can't angrily mix our issues as a union with how we perform professionally. No matter what, we need to do our jobs, even though behind closed doors, we are often screaming at each other about the politics and power structure of our community mental health center.

We notice that some of us hide in our offices while clients wait for service. Sure, there's the usual paperwork or just needing a break, but we don't want to get into "job-refusal," fueled by the political resentment we feel at this time. The bosses right now are reluctant to allow a real input from the therapists or psychiatrists into how to work together in a creative, up to date, well-organized mental health business. Just as the boss must challenge the subordinate, we shouldn't fear expressing our concerns to the leaders. We're trying to act with mutual respect.

While some of us are kissing the bosses' asses (out of the fear of being fired or demoted for joining the union); many are openly joining the union leadership, organizing a contract for the therapists, office workers, nurses, and doctors in our mental health center in East Los Angeles. The administration has a hefty pay package and benefits (disproportionate to the pay scale of the clinical staff). What they pay themselves is fine, but let's be fair. We feel *both* staff and administration should receive a decent level of compensation. Now there are lots of bad and overly righteous feelings between the two "sides."

* * * * *

We never put our foot into the same river.

I think we can be a little more detached from our views, opinions, theologies, therapies, because our systems of thought can never capture the complexity of interaction in our living with each other. Our ideas *are* helpful for us to create meaning, but I'm sure we can agree that we can't let ideas, for example "liberal," "conservative," "union," "anti-union," preferences, and expectations get in the way of having an outstanding mental health clinic. And during the non-working hours, we continue organizing a union; but now we're fighting more fairly and with more mutual respect. The therapists and union organizers finally agree to be civil with each other at work. And we feel the different emotional "vibes" of the clinic being well run, welcoming, warm, and client-oriented. We do not allow our personal "hang ups" to get in the way of making a vibrant health center.

* * * * *

A few of the teenagers are suffering anorexia and/or bulimia. They tell us of a craving to "look good." We suggest that they consider a different way of measuring "goodness." After dramatic, difficult beginnings, they realize they're looking for love and acceptance like all of us. They're unhappy and want to get away from their families; they're confused and "uncomfortable" not measuring up to ingrained images of "what they are supposed to look like—some "idealized" thin, conventionally gorgeous woman. I value just being "me." I don't need to judge myself as unworthy. "Why do I have to convince others how equal and *good* I am?"

We limit our self-actualizing into a happy human being because of a self-image of how we, and others, are supposed to be. We don't allow ourselves to flower, be fully human and alive, interested and exploring.

* * * * *

He says he's "miserable" in his work, forced by his role as super-bread-winner to work 16-hour days. He drinks a lot, but "keeps it together." His wife castigates him, as never earning enough money, as a "failure." He wants to prove she's wrong, but he's in a vicious circle that's missing the real issues of power and mutually satisfying relationships. He's doing group breathing to ground himself. He's starting a healthier diet, rest and play times, energetic work hours. He's limiting his drinking and relating with his demanding wife by having nourishing times together with her. He's getting free from abusing alcohol by acknowledging he was using alcohol to find relief from something deep and unresolved in him. He's getting "to know himself."

* * * * *

The organism is a living co-ordination. Even one cell differentiates. So health is a balancing interaction of parts/

aspects. Therapy addresses imbalances within the person, including chemical imbalances, which the psychiatrist addresses. We try to heal the suffering involved when we "disown" any aspect of our being, even the so-called "unacceptable."

Many unhappy and non-functioning individuals come through the doors of our mental health center. Some feel the burden of obligations and commitments for which they have lost feeling. They can't "get free." Some are able to change and face personal challenge; some pull back from a decision or promise to follow their own heart rather than conventional pressure.

* * * * *

I'm at a seminar about rage and therapy for those who suffer rage and for those who have been abused. I recall the term from the 60s, "Black Rage," and a few visits with armed Black Power groups in Oakland, California. While I could sympathize with the Black expression of rage towards the profound insult of discrimination, I thought the emphasis on guns was only going to lead to more corruption and killings. I felt more in sympathy with the way of Dr. Martin Luther King, Jr.

We're asked to key into and acknowledge if we feel any rage against, women, homosexuals, ethnic groups, for example. We all seem to have our prejudices. We also can feel our violent tendencies, that terrible urge to hurt when feeling hurt, to destroy when feeling deprived, to want to establish ourselves as "superior." One of the presenters is a woman doctor who had been abused by her former husband. She brought pictures of herself with black and bruised eyes that the police took when she went to the police station after being struck by her husband. She told us how her husband's possessiveness and jealousies almost killed her. She described her own healing into self-respect and self-caring, as well as being a doctor dedicated to others. I felt she was very courageous and open. She said, with a wink: "I'm having fun being single."

"When man imprisons woman, he condemns himself to the life of a prison guard."—Anonymous

* * * * *

Fritz Perls said that our most important "unfinished situations" will always emerge when we seriously engage our own therapy. Therapy makes "conflicts" obvious and facilitates a natural process of completion. In the clinic, we ask people to act out, to move, to exercise, and be aware of bodily reactions (e.g. a "knot in the stomach," "a rigid neck"). They express feelings. Some feel a "catharsis" through such expression and by letting go of "buried parts" of the self that take up so much psychic energy. Therapy isn't a magic pill to make life's problems go away; rather its purpose is to rid one's self of burdensome tensions. It guides us to respond to our particular lives in balanced ways, to challenges that continue to arise. Our attitudes are of supreme importance.

* * * * *

A poignant episode of "The Twilight Zone" was the story of a father and his children at Mardi Gras. The father was soon to die and the children were excitedly looking forward to possessing the father's rich inheritance. At the Fat Tuesday party, the children's display their greed and envy as they jockey for position with Dad who was aware of their motivations, even though everyone had on a grotesque, gnarled mask. After the father died, the children could not remove their horrible masks—the true inner now on the outer for all to see. They had to live with faces molded by masks. Our therapy allows us to be whole, to radiate outwardly what's truly within our selves, and our masks melt when our hearts open.

Body, Breath, Movement, Mind: "Therapist, Heal Thyself!"

A Training for Physiotherapists and Movement Therapists

Morgan Zo-Callahan and Marcus Holly

San Francisco, 1979

I was asked to present some notes for the following three questions. Would you talk about your own growth, Morgan, facilitated by going to therapies such as Bioenergetics, Alexander Technique, Feldenkrais, Yoga? Also please tell us some examples of progress you've made or your clients have made in therapy? What is therapy in general and how can we take advantage of it for ourselves?

Marcus was asked: Would you give any practical tips about the essential guidelines for practitioners of the art/science of massage?

MZC: I was making a part-time salary as a physical therapist assistant, while teaching in Special Education. Also I was joining therapeutic groups to learn various physical-emotional techniques for my own healthy being. And sometimes I was asked to be an assistant facilitator with Marcus Holly, teaching techniques from Bioenergetics and Yoga. It was the age, along with the Spiritual Supermarket, of the Therapy-Supermarket and Noble Causes for Activists-Supermarket. I did a lot of shopping. With all my looking around, I'm learning how little I now know and how much "free water" and exaggerated claims are being sold to us in the "therapeutic world." But there's some wisdom and practical, down to earth help. Some of these "new" ancient techniques can be truly healing.

My tasks at work were usually delegated to me by the physical therapist such as having me do active and passive manual therapeutic exercises. My job included helping others stretch and breathe; applying heat, providing time in hot baths, saunas, steam rooms, Jacuzzis; doing some basic massage.

At times, I'd administer an electrical modality treatment of ultrasound or low level "shocks."

Very often I was "walking with" and supporting clients who had great difficulty in walking and lifting their arms. My job didn't mix any psychological interventions. I was just walking the person. The interaction with clients basically felt comfortable and healing in itself. We were friendly and professional with each other. We joked around as well as lament our physical difficulties.

We clinical teams generate a "healing" atmosphere/environment in the clinic of genuinely caring and intelligent staff, really being sensitive to the client's needs. The client and the therapist are in this together; there's a "give and take." It's never perfect; we do our best and keep our ears and hearts open.

In the late 70s, San Francisco was full of therapy groups-seminars which, in turn, were filled with us, therapists, and many from "helping professions" who also felt out of touch with our own feelings and what we wanted most deeply. What do I yearn for? How do I relate to myself? What are the parental programs within saying "My body's bad"; "I'm bad"? What's blocking my inner potential and the peace coming from understanding my own body, heart and mind?

* * * * *

I read William Reich, born in Austria in 1897, who spoke about knowing the inseparable relationship between body and mind. Body tensions influence emotion, energy and movement, and vice-versa. For example, every emotion is both a felt experience in the mind and an expressive movement-tension in the body. So chronic muscle tightness affects both our subjective mental states and the way our body moves.

We see how children stiffen and hold their breath when keeping surges of feeling under control. This "holding" is like clutching one's self for protection. I believe we all have this "protective-clinging" in varying degrees, perhaps mostly unconscious. We choose not to feel by chronically constricting breath and muscle groups. But the choice of cutting off our feeling limits our potential joyful expression of living abundantly. Only we, ourselves, can know the part of our personality that chooses to constrict breath and muscles and emotions. We can observe when it's unnecessary to tense up our bodies.

First, we just pay attention to our body, breathing, sensations, how we unnecessarily become rigid and tight. So we can naturally acknowledge we have some responsibility to change—however slowly—our habitual tightening of our bodies. We get a sense of humor at how ridiculous what we do to ourselves is. Feeling fully is in the living, involuntary movement of the organism. When I suppress my tears and pain, I tighten my mouth, lift up my shoulders, gag my throat, and suppress deep breathing. If I do it often enough, I turn my face into a mask.

* * * * *

We all, in varying degrees, numb ourselves from pain, anger, joy, sexuality, fuller love relationships. Reich's therapy aimed at encouraging the person to experience the self (some say "authentic self"), the whole organism, including voluntary and involuntary, superficial and profound levels of body-mind consciousness. Experience and feel!

Reich worked to undo the "contactlessness" of the person as manifested in the individual's energy, breathing and muscular armor.

Through therapy, many of us were seeing how there could be a restoration of the natural movement of the life force. Many of us were doing Yoga. Alexander Lowen wrote: "A body is forsaken when it becomes a source of pain and humiliation instead of pleasure and pride."

There are different ways of looking at a person's character and personality. The Reichian therapists are demonstrating for us that our character can be observed in the bodily attitude of each of us. We can experience in our own body where strong emotion is piled up within, let's say, in our shoulders, forming a tight ball around our necks, further "hanging us up" by hardened muscle mass. We can notice together how open we are to the generous flow of life. We breathe, move and emote to release the tensions in our body, allowing free expression of the previously "bound" energy we have inside. The first steps of therapy—adapted toward varying needs—is learning to breathe easily and deeply. Our clients are able to express emotional feelings by mobilizing and expressing them. If he or she needs to cry or be angry, then expression is allowed, short of violence.

* * * * *

Deep breathing produces respiratory waves throughout the body. This undulating movement is the foundation of the orgasm. The life of the body is within its involuntary aspect, not only in its rational, conceptual expression. I've had to face how I handle threatening situations by hardening myself. Some of this is necessary to survive, but as a chronic avoidance of feeling, it is like death. In my own therapy, I've observed a latent violence in myself which is being released, relaxing my "hung up" shoulders, my own emotional-physical hang ups which lift me off the earth. Therapy gives me a sense of being grounded and alive, not just in my head.

* * * * *

It's not enough just to talk about my anger. I need the

physical release of the muscular tensions that are making even cells rigid. I went to therapy to release and understand my violent impulses without hurting others or myself. I wanted to explore where such rage came from. The terrible problem with repressed violence is that it often comes out wildly and destructively. "I'm going to go off on you." Part of therapy is allowing the ability of the client to observe, really feel one's own feelings; to express; to be in touch with how our violent impulses are covering intimate yearnings.

My rage is only the smoke of the inner fire. Our particular "hang up" must be felt in the body. Then the client can allow the subconscious early conflicts to come into consciousness and be "re-related to" on a grounded, life-full level. Our conflicts become obvious to us and finally superfluous, even if they never go away entirely. In my opinion, our basic psychological tendencies won't go away, but we relate to them with some space and good humor. We have a feeling of our own inner worth and possibility, underneath even the most terrible of rages.

* * * * *

My own therapies and analysis have started from the ground up, from the expression of the body first of all. We all want to analyze our past repressions, our conflicts, but we are afraid to release suppressed violence.

This therapeutic release is necessary for some of us, in order that we can direct our natural aggressiveness towards pleasure, work and spiritual goals. Our aggression is the expression of our movement of the muscles of the body. A main muscle mass is upwards and downwards along the backbone. The energy going upwards and into the head, shoulders, and arms lead to such aggressive activities as looking, sucking, biting, reaching, vocalizing, kissing and so on. The downward flowing energy leads to aggressiveness in the lower body. The body, though one living entity, expresses a polarity of dynamic and circular movement. That's why we buzz and hum.

* * * * *

If the flow of life within a person is blocked, there is a pile-up of energy, too often angry energy, held in between the shoulder blades, a hump of unmoving life force. Literally, there is an unconscious posture of "fight or flight." There's a split between our brain and body. Perhaps I'm afraid, lonely, feeling as if my body isn't "charged" with good energy. I may feel that if I lose control there could be a terrible eruption of violence. Without confidence, my head hangs from lacking a supportive erect neck. I feel defeated and bad. Instead of a full emotional life, I feel an overwhelming sense of burden in my living.

She says she's "carrying rocks against her will." I observe her backbone muscles and the linear muscle line from shoulder blade to shoulder blade are rigid. There's tension that's limiting fluidity of motion. In her therapy, she's noticing for herself how she has "accumulated anger" expressed as knots in her neck. She's learning to both be in touch with her suppression of feeling and anger, going back to when she was a child. "No one paid attention to or was interested in my feelings."

* * * * *

We begin to see that "acting out" of violence destructively does no good for the community or for the person who is releasing suppressed tensions in negative ways. At the beginning for some of us, therapy provides the chance to vent, be physically expressive of anger without hurting others, or ourselves such as by slamming a tennis racket into a giant pillow. To scream out, to rant and rave in a protective, supported setting. When the animal that is man cannot breathe and be grounded, there's a tendency of energy to go upwards, a lifting up of the body from the neck and shoulders, breaking contact from the earth and creating a restrictive energy structure in the body.

Suppressed violence locked in chronic muscular tension in the upper body has to be released so the arms can more naturally reach out, take and give.

One of our clients is striking mattresses with his fists or a tennis racket. Such violence hurts no one and the exercise frees up his shoulders and neck from being in the defensive tension of an imminent danger.

A client going to therapy says she has "nice" personality which always wants to feel the tender, soft emotions that emanate from the front of the body, but not to feel the anger and rage felt in her back and shoulders. In counseling, she discovered that her passive personality blocks her ability to express positive aggression. She asked me to give her exercises that would help her feel more in her legs, to feel connected, with her "feet on the ground." Lying on a large mattress she kicks with her legs outstretched, doing this rhythmically and violently. Sometimes, she screams, "No, I won't."

* * * * *

However, we know the therapy has to move past this emotional releasing by substituting—in our daily lives—healthy expressions of both aggression and tenderness.

We see why we want to rage in the first place and we become simpler and more peaceful and balanced inside. We realize releasing our suppressed tensions and feeling does us no good now as we are letting go of the bad feeling that perhaps belonged to an earlier time and, perhaps, traumatic situation in our life. We just see that it's unnecessary to rave and rant anymore.

* * * * *

He said he abused his wife when he drank. He was keying into suppressed angry feelings against his parents who severely restricted his personal freedom and who were physically abusive. In therapy, he took the part of his wife and said: "I'm your dear wife and I love you. I'm not your parent." Our client wept for a long time, which reminded me of Zampano (Anthony Quinn, in the movie "La Strada") bawling uncontrollably on the beach, realizing his cruelty to the only woman who loved him. It was a crying that came from a dark, deep, distant yet powerful place. Our client began to see that genuine anger is a response to an actual restraint of freedom, not acting out or reaction to a suppressed reaction "waiting to explode." He eventually was able to forgive his parents and let most of it go. He could heal his emotional conflicts in the here and now.

Personality analysis can be very helpful along with body therapies. The person has felt in his or her body the chronic tension or hang-ups. The person often discovers latent violence within and begins to change through non-reactive and nakedly honest observation. "The truth will make you free." We see our hang-ups keep us from being grounded, natural, instinctual, breathing, alive, intelligent and loving.

* * * * *

The client is encouraged that he sees progress and is gaining insight into why he's "always pissed off" and "irritated." He recalls early in childhood how his mom was often yelling at him to control his "bottom part" by tensing up the pelvic musculature. The nerve to the anal sphincter is not fully functional until the child is about two and a half. The levator iliopsoas and the deep gluteal muscles are used to keep the bottom from falling out. If I let go, there will be a big mess. He felt the added rage of being forced to do what instinctively felt unnatural. Now as an adult, the client sees how his emotional "life-script" has restricted him, how he now can live without fear of what others may say or think since he now has the courage and energy to be himself. He could control himself. He was enjoying the unfolding of his liberated life-process.

* * * * *

Twelve suggestions to facilitate your massage therapies by Marcus Holly.

1. Experiment with herbal oils (e.g., Aloe Vera, Rosemary, Chamomile).

2. Experiment with clay powders for skin treatments; be aware of new and improved natural products.

3. Prepare the setting: quiet, feeling you won't be interrupted, sufficient warmth/air/proper therapy tables, correct use of devices and techniques. Give proper initial instructions such as advising the client to always say, "stop" if something is hurting or is overly uncomfortable.

4. Don't confuse the very different uses of massage just because many of us are comfortable and enjoying exchanging nude massages in this very open time in San Francisco. It's quite different giving your nursing home client a hand massage with lotion. We always respect the boundaries and conditions. We appreciate privacy and are non-invasive. We always ask for feedback. We emanate loving and respect to the client.

5. When receiving a massage, don't engage your own muscles when a limb is being lifted. Experience how you unnecessarily make muscle tensions and how you can inhibit this. Feel free to move your body such as

moving your head from one side to the other if your neck is getting stiff. Feel free to speak up if something is hurting or you need to be warmer or have a fan turned on, etc.

6.   Adapt to different massage techniques according to your purpose.

7.   Keep sensitive in your hands.

8.   Mold your hands to fit contours of the body.

9.   Maintain an evenness of speed and pressure.

10.   Use your weight as well as your muscle to apply pressure.

11.   Pay attention to your own posture and breathing; observe when you are "spacing out."

12.   Breathing out, apply added pressure; communicating healing energy and breathing in energize your own body-mind.

Teaching Those in the Venerable Years
Morgan Zo-Callahan

> *I feel caught in our cultural myth that aging is a failure,*
> *that if only I did it right I could avoid old age, even avoid*
> *death. What a peculiar notion! We have some ideas that*
> *as we age we are no longer sexy, vital, juicy. Sometimes*
> *when I walk into a room I feel as if I'm invisible, or even*
> *worse, an outcast.*

—Lee Lipp

> *I'm well aware of the fact that I'm old. By the way, I*
> *used to say "old," but now when I'm asked in interviews,*
> *"How old are you?" I reply, "Well, I grew up in China in*
> *a time when age was venerated, so I am eighty six years*
> *venerable."*

—Huston Smith

I've found that venerating the elderly grounds my teaching for older adults. It's an attitude of respect, attention, patience and love that makes my teaching rewarding and hopefully of some service. During the late 60s when it was not hip to trust anyone over thirty, I subtly discounted their exquisite value. Luckily, I soon learned to appreciate the wisdom and richness of the older generation while at the same time being able to think for myself.

As a young boy, I found older adults to be fascinating, somewhat mysterious and, when not playing sports or in school, I was very happy in their company. When I was in grammar school, I visited older neighbors who didn't seem to have younger people around them. One day I was walking past a large, but fairly run down home where Mrs. Davenport was pruning some bushes in her front yard. She lived alone and seemed to be a recluse. She also had the reputation of being a shrew, and instilled fear in the kids who sometimes played pranks on her. But on this particular occasion, she asked me if I would help her lift some trimmings into a wheelbarrow, which I did, while casting a suspicious eye on her, remembering some of the other kids saying that she was a *bona fide* witch. Apart from her unsmiling wizened face, I found nothing sinister about her. Her comments on plants, flowers, trees, squirrels, rabbits, muskrats, dogs and cats started to fascinate me. She never spoke about other people except saying that a group of "lousy boys" had thrown rocks at her dogs. After I finished, she invited me to enjoy freshly baked cookies. That began our friendship. I started visiting her, walking down the long driveway, knocking on her door and gaining entrance into magical conversations about topics new to me. I looked at her photo albums and inspected her "favorite contraptions." Once I opened a painted music box, inlaid with white-spotted black and orange butterflies—I marveled as the box released a melody that brought such delight to Mrs. Davenport, her face noticeably softened.

Now I find myself revering my older students, as naturally, as happily as greeting my family when they come home from a trip. It's a joy for me to be with older adults, learning and teaching. I am learning that our brains are elastic, that we can "stretch" our minds just as we stretch our bodies, even as we age. Neuroscientists call this ability of the brain to keep itself fit, "brain plasticity." The course I teach, through adult school, in convalescent hospitals is called "Mental Fitness."

In classes with our *venerable* seniors, we offer exercise (including simple Tai Chi), music and singing, arts-crafts, academics (history-geography; language arts; math), puzzles, lively questions and answers about trivia, video documentaries and educational movies. We create an atmosphere where my venerable students can stay mentally active, at a higher level for as long is possible.

* * * * *

Different animals are being brought into my class "Mental Fitness" at the convalescent hospital-hospice. We "therapists" and "teachers" call it therapy or education. It's just human. Of course some of the clients don't want to be close to any animal, yet many do and find it great fun and excitement, like having an instant "buddy." No judgments about being old. The furry ones make many clients feel relaxed, in what can be an alienating, colorless environment. Our 93-year-old client is happily playing with the fat kitty cat; so energizing for her. The animals are brightening the classroom today.

* * * * *

We discuss health and nutrition. We review studies—such as those by Dr. Andrew Weil—which recommend that seniors include plenty of antioxidant-rich vegetables and fruits, such as blueberries, and anti-inflammation vitamin C (found in citrus fruits, beans, oatmeal, enriched pastas, peas, wheat germ, rice bran) plus salmon, flax-seed oil, walnuts, supplements that provide these fatty acids). Dr. Weil cites studies from scientists at the University of Irvine (with mice) that show DHA (an omega-3 fatty acid) delays the development of protein "tangles" in brain cells and also reduces levels of beta amyloid. (Cf. *The Journal of Neuroscience*, April 18, 2007)

Research suggests that doing such activities as educational "trivia", learning a language or playing a musical instrument may help build reserve brain cells to fight against failing mental ability. We encourage each other to "use our wits." Many of our Southern California community colleges and adult schools offer "memory-enhancement" courses. We encourage stimulating the imagination, forming mental pictures to associate with information, using the force of our attention and memory, still learning and "connecting," and "re-connecting."

* * * * *

Some convalescent homes and senior adult programs have computers, with such programs as "Posit Brain Fitness." (Cf. http://www.positscience.com) Computers provide effective exercises to sharpen the minds of older adults. I did some of the sessions from a Brain Fitness Course from Posit Science where I and my fellow and sister seniors did different exercises to listen more attentively, to focus and concentrate, to improve our ability to process information and to remember progressively larger amounts of information. For example, we distinguish varying sounds; we remember details from stories. We are experiencing how our brains can change when we are paying attention, how we can improve the speed with which we process information and nudge our ability to communicate more effectively. I've done five different exercises: 1. "High or Low?" helps faster sound processing, so the brain can respond even to fast speech in conversation; 2. "Tell Us Apart" gives the brain practice to distinguish similar sounds so it can better interpret the spoken word while storing clear memories; 3. "Match It!" helps the brain remember better, as the brain processes sounds with more clarity; 4. "Sound Replay" stimulates the brain to remember information in the order it's presented; 5. "Listen and Do" exercises the short-term memory, which is critical in most cognitive tasks related to thinking.

"Dakim's [m] Power" is another computer-based program, which aids in slowing down memory degeneration by "matching" and "word" games, answering questions. Multiple level activities are available: for "high functioning," for "mild cognition impairment," and for those with "dementias." Seniors may review history or geography or watch clips from old movies where they are asked to remember setting, characters, and actions (http://www.dakim.com). Some of the hospitals and senior centers use the involving world of the Internet to look up information of interest, e-mail and chat.

* * * * *

Sadly, many of our students already suffer from the brain-clogging plaque (amyloid) and protein tangles of advanced Alzheimer's and other dementias that greatly limit memory and cognition, and may manifest in behavioral abnormalities. But even Alzheimer's doesn't exclude meaningful educational and social interaction. We continue to reassure, interact, creatively stimulate, listen, be with, teach and learn from. We have some fun and laughter together, even in this drastic—terribly sorrowful—situation of a slow, progressive diminishing of mental capacity.

Our students are often confused, disoriented, incoherent, alienated, angry, withdrawn, in slowly deteriorating conditions. Their words don't seem to express their thoughts. Some of our students appear "just out of it." We are aware of changing needs and must adapt, be responsive and understanding. It's messy sometimes; we accept all of it. These students are losing nerve cells that are associated with learning, judgment, and memory. The chemical acetylcholine—which is used by nerve cells to transmit messages—is decreasing dramatically.

One of my students greeted me each morning saying with a perplexed look: "I can't remember what I forgot to remember to tell you." Her daughter would visit her in class, but had to tell her each time that she was her daughter. She enjoyed going to class, especially singing and humming old songs; playing catch with a soft ball; listening to stories. However, there were times when she would sit with a blank expression on her face. J. Madeleine Nash writes: "Imagine your brain as a house filled with lights. Now imagine someone turning off the lights one by one. That's what Alzheimer's disease does. It turns off the lights so that the flow of ideas, emotions and memories from one room to the next slows and eventually ceases." (*Time* magazine, July 17, 2000) Though we cannot stop this process in our students, we do our best to accompany them, continuing to shine lights of caring on them.

* * * * *

Sites of Interest:

American Society on Aging http://www.asaging.org
Starting in 1954, this association has been committed to enhance the "knowledge and skills of those who seek to improve the quality of life of older adults and their families." A multidisciplinary group of professionals addresses the physical, emotional, social, economic, and spiritual aspects of aging. They publish three magazines: *Aging Today* (issues that professionals face today); *Generations,* a scholarly quarterly journal; *ASA Connection*, which updates relevant issues. Various seminars are offered online such as: "Comprehensive Geriatric Assessment"; "Planning and Coordinating Care for People with Alzheimer's"; "The Legal and Ethical Issues of Aging"; "The Role of Physical Activity in Reducing Falls: Best Practices for at Home and in the Community."

Alzheimer's Association http://www.alz.org
There is a search box to find any chapter of the Alzheimer's Association in the United States. It includes a 24-hour help line: 1-800-272-3900. Free book available: *Playbook for Alzheimer's Caregivers* by Frank Broyles, University of Arkansas.

This site also includes:

Informational Resources (e.g., "What is Alzheimer's?" "How to cope with Alzheimer's should you suffer it")
Programs for Caregivers, Families & Individuals with Alzheimer's
Information about the five drugs commonly used to treat Alzheimer's and other dementias Cholinesterase inhibitors: Aricept; Excelon; Razadyne Namenda and Cognex (used sparingly due to adverse side effects)
Variety of Relevant Articles
Message Boards/Live Chats
Help for locating Senior Housing Today there is a movement in the United States called "Aging in Place" where seniors stay in their homes and receive medical care as well. However, many seniors, especially with more advanced Alzheimer's, need to live in nursing facilities.
How to enroll in Medical Alert & Safe Return Program (to help a person with dementia who wanders away be reunited with the caregiver, via a pendant or bracelet with a 24-hour emergency response phone number & access to personal health records)

Alzheimer's Information Site (Fisher Center for Alzheimer's Research Foundation) http://www.alzinfo.org

Mission: Funds over eighty-five scientists in the United States with partnerships in 117 other countries
Directed by Nobel laureate, Dr. Paul Greengard at The Rockefeller University in New York City
Research & News
Publishes *Preserving Your Memory* magazine, with care giving tips and strategies for healthy living
Explains the seven stages of Alzheimer's: normal; normal forgetfulness with aging; mild cognitive impairment; mild Alzheimer's; moderate; moderately severe; severe.
Resource Locater for Continuing Care—thirty types of health care professionals available with a search by name, state, city or zip code (e.g., Elder Law Attorneys, NAELA; Geriatric Care Managers; Hospitals; Hospices; Long-term care ombudsmen; medical supplies; Medicare, Part A & B; Physicians; Rehabilitation hospitals; Skilled nursing facilities.)

We caregivers become more patient once we understand that this disease isn't something the patient can control.

American Association of Homes & Services for the Aging
http://www.aahsa.org

"Our fifty-seven hundred member organizations, many of whom have served their communities for generations, offer the continuum of aging services: adult day services, home health, community services, senior housing, assisted living residences, continuing care retirement communities and nursing homes."

Aim to make available affordable and ethical health & aging services
Advocacy, Policy & Government (for nursing home transparency and improvement)
Conferences; Learning opportunities; Newsroom, Online Communities, Publications & Research
Career Opportunities; Career Resources, including Web sites representing career specialties in the Aging Service field

Here are the Facts on Aging for the United States presented by the Association:

- By 2026, 65 year-olds and up will double to 71.5 million; among people turning 65 today, 69 percent will need some form of long-term health care

- 16,100 certified nursing homes (private rooms average $213 per day, $77,745 year; semi-private rooms, $189 per day, $68,985 per year)

- 39,500 assisted living facilities ($2,969 per month, $32,064 per year; with added fees for Alzheimer's, other dementias, $4,270 per month, $51,240 per year) (cf. Assisted Living Federation of America, http://www.alfa.org)

- 2,204 continuing care retirement communities ($2,672 per month, $32,064 per year; $60,000 to $120,000 buy in)

- 300,000 units of Section 202 affordable senior housing (average wait, 13.4 months)

- 40 percent of long-term care is from private funds
- Medicare covers rehabilitation services after an individual is discharged from a hospital; pays 19 percent of all long-term care spending
- Medicaid (for low-income individuals) pays 49 percent of all long term care spending

American Health Care Association http://www.ahcancal.org

A non-profit federation of affiliated state health organizations, together representing more than 10,000 non-profit and for-profit assisted living, nursing facilities, developmentally disabled and sub-acute care providers
The federation provides care for more than 1.5 million elderly and disabled individuals nationally
Based in Washington D.C., it advocates for changes to improve the standards of services in long-term health care

SNAP for seniors—Tool to Search for Senior Housing
http://www.snapforseniors.com

Senior housing available in one's location (with an explanation of the types of senior housing).
Assisted living & residential care; independent living & retirement communities; independent living & retirement communities; nursing care & rehabilitation; continuing care retirement communities (CCRC) & multi-level care facilities.

Resources: educational booklet; relocation services; glossary; government & non-profit agencies; health-related organizations; helpful links; placement/transition coordination; geriatric care management; legal assistance.
Home care & hospice.

UCLA Center on Aging http://www.aging.ucla.edu

Since 1991, the center has the "mission to enhance and extend productive and healthy life through preeminent research and education on aging."
Focused on Southern California, but its research and information may usefully be extended to all the United States
Promotes community education and life-long learning
Memory Training
Senior scholars; Annual research conference; Technology & Aging conference
Community meetings
Newsletters
Guided Autobiography
Lectures on Video (e.g., "Grandparents and their Children," "What you Need to know about Mood, Memory as you Age," "The Longevity Bible: Adding years to your life, the 8 Essentials"   I found Gary W. Small, M.D.'s online video "Memory Training Techniques" useful; Small is the author of *The Memory Bible*.

Small talks about four areas to improve one's memory: Reduce stress; Healthy diet (olive oil; omega-3 fats; anti-oxidant fruits and vegetables; reducing animal fat; choosing healthy carbohydrates); Physical exercise; Mental exercise.
Train but don't "strain" the brain
Three Memory techniques: Create the ability to relax (Small shows his audience a beautiful scene from nature and asks the audience to breathe deeply while releasing tensions from the top of body downwards (release tension in the forehead, neck, shoulders....) "Snap," Create a mental snapshot, a visual image of what you want to remember directly or by association; Decide in advance what you want to remember; Take your time to remember as our memory does slow down as we age.
Remembering names: Repeat in conversation; comment if the person reminds you of someone you know; ask the person to spell his or her name.
Referral to other sites: Medicare http://www.medicare.gov American Association of Retired Persons http://www.aarp.org National Institution on Aging http://www.nih.gov/nia Social Security http://www.ssa.gov UCLA Memory & Aging Research Center http://www.memory.ucla.edu

With Our Own Eyes, With Our Own Hearts

A Workshop on Stress for Those in Helping Professions
and An Invitation to Invoke Generosity and Gratitude
Morgan Zo-Callahan and Ken Ireland

> *Small is the number of people that see with their own
> eyes and feel with their own hearts.*
>
> —Albert Einstein

*Nothing remains the same for two consecutive moments.
Heraclitus said we can never bathe twice in the same
river. Confucius, while looking at a stream, said, "It is
always flowing, day and night." The Buddha implored
us not just to talk about impermanence, but also to use it
as an instrument to help us penetrate deeply into reality
and obtain liberating insight. We may be tempted to say
that because things are impermanent, there is suffering.
Without impermanence, life is not possible. How can we
transform our suffering if things are not impermanent?
How can our daughter grow up into a beautiful young
lady? How can the situation in the world improve? We
need impermanence for social justice and for hope.*

*If you suffer, it is not because things are impermanent.
It is because you believe things are permanent. When a
flower dies, you don't suffer much, because you understand
that flowers are impermanent. But you cannot accept the
impermanence of your beloved one, and you suffer deeply
when she passes away.*

*If you look deeply into impermanence, you will do
your best to make her happy right now. Aware of
impermanence, you become positive, loving and wise.
Impermanence is good news. Without impermanence,
nothing would be possible. With impermanence, every*

door is open for change. Impermanence is an instrument for our liberation.

—Thich Nhat Hanh

We're ready to believe—and we're continually taught—that we're in the world to take care of other people. But we'd be better health care providers if we'd also take care of ourselves. Learn to accept and express emotions.

—Diane Kjervik

This workshop is presented with three periods of a "Twenty-Minute Quiet Sitting." We have discussions about how to appreciate what we have in our lives, loves, work, rather than be putting all our energy and desire into what is "out there." We want our work lives to give us a lively enthusiasm about being in helping professions. We see how we can work together more happily, congenially, if we're balanced about giving and taking in our work situation. We don't want to feel we "work too hard" or "feel taken advantage of." We want to feel appreciated and given some leeway to work according our own style. We hear lots of complaints at work about people being unhappy, overwhelmed, stressed out to the max. One of our questions is: Does living with the spirit of generosity in giving and gratefulness when receiving, make for less stress-filled work ambiances? So we're both intellectually identifying the process of stress as well as suggesting practices for each other that may promote a softening of the stress inside the person and within the workplace. We're slowing down as well as conversing and studying Stress. We're taking meditation time to feel how we experience stress in our bodies and breathing. We can feel whatever personal conflicts we may have, any pent up resentments in our bellies, hearts, emotions, thinking. We're "accepting and expressing emotions."

So taking this break from work to reflect on our work, we're creating a fresh view of our lives and lives of others. Being appreciative just the way we are, the way it is for us at this moment in our lives gives us the energy to be generous helpers, nurses, teachers, doctors, social workers, therapists. All of us need "to step back" from the work environment from time to time, in order to regenerate the enthusiasm and joy in doing what one feels appreciative and thankful for doing. Then an intelligent generosity imbues the workplace. And most of us have experienced times when we worked in a harmonious and vibrant workplace. This time together helps us to touch again the congeniality of spirit in ourselves. We're happier when we can be friendly and supportive of each other at work.

If impermanence is such "good news," why is it that we "helpers, teachers, therapists, doctors, social workers" stress out so much with all the changes, which confront us daily: interruptions, confusions, demands, colleagues with personalities on the spectrum of very cordial to hostile? We find lots of stress in change; we don't yet have an attitude and a practice that allow us to release unnecessary stresses that grow inside us, as we work together, which means we have to deal with stress in our whole life. Our way of life must encourage this peaceful life. We've all seen dramatic actions in our schools and hospitals.

Our health is a result of psychophysical health, a balanced life, and a unified, not overly conflicted mind-emotion-body-spirit. Our life is healthy when stress does not radically upset our equilibrium. We're healthy when we don't hurt ourselves to accomplish our goals to help others. Therapists who are just always totally exhausted from work might check out if they are hurting themselves and to examine what need they may feel to want to be a "heroic" "super-dedicated" therapist? We've too often seen the helper as one who "has to go overboard" for his/her client, even to the detriment of one's own health. And maybe some of us are wasting our abilities, not practicing our profession with energy and kind attention to the degree we're capable. Maybe we'd be happier, healthier if we gave more of ourselves at work. We're asking what's a healthy balance that fits us personally, individually. None of us are so indispensable that we need to sacrifice our well-being. So "we love others as we love ourselves."

Stress happens. How can we deal with it? How can we eliminate exaggerated, unnecessary stress? How can each of us, in our own way, avoid burnout in ourselves and in others? All of us have seen some of our colleagues experience the life-squeezing extreme "burnout" from work.

What is "burnout"? A popular four-stage "psychological" definition was proposed by J. Edelwich and A. Brodsky in *Burn Out, Stages of Disillusionment in the Helping Professions* (Shawnee Press, 1980): enthusiasm, stagnation, frustration, apathy. Burnout is a process of "progressive loss of idealism, energy and purpose experienced by people in the helping professions as a result of conditions of their work."

All teachers and mental health providers face physical and emotional strain under the best of conditions. We face changes in responsibilities, hours; conflicts with superiors, co-workers, clients, students; work overload; lack of freedom to try new methods and often, little participation in decision-making. Sometimes we have great compassion but are not as wise, savvy, observant of what "truly helps" another. We realize sometimes we're trying too hard to help. Sometimes being patient is the greatest help.

Even "success" can cause us stress. There are many sources of our stress. It comes down to how we deal with it. We need to recognize that for ourselves, to feel within our own bodies, how we may have the inner resources to avoid "burnout." We analyze what seemingly takes away our feeling of being freely alive and happy. Sometimes I've found we helpers over-identify with our title (therapist, teacher, etc.) or some reputation we may have of being extra "nice" people, interpreted as a "push-over." We can be nice, as well as take care of ourselves and keep our boundaries, too. We can't be overly attached to wanting to be liked and accepted.

Stress is the way the body-mind responds to any change, challenge, be it positive or negative. In extreme negative stress, various bodily systems, "fight or flight" responses can be overwhelming. Physiologically, we have an "alarm reaction" (mobilizing energy to confront a challenge); "resistance" (using reserve energy); and finally "burnout" (extreme exhaustion and immobility).

What we perceive to be threatening activates the brain to stimulate adrenal glands to release adrenaline hormones into our system. It is a natural survival reaction, which is necessary for life-threatening situations, but is unhealthy if the source of negative stress is prolonged or left undefined. At first, we may be dedicated, committed to our work. We have lots of energy. However, over time, perhaps our hopes and expectations are not met. There's no momentum anymore; our zest and desire are gone. "I'm totally stressed out."

Our "enthusiasm" then has to be "put on" and is always then followed by an exhausting fatigue (not the "good" feeling of being tired after fulfilling work). We become less efficient and begin more escape activities. We worry too much about the inevitable "politics" at work. We feel stuck in a system; we don't feel appreciated. We lose some desire to serve our students and clients and may fall into the final stage of burnout that is apathy. "I don't give a damn anymore."

How do we cope with the stress in our work? The resolution of stress is in the balance of enthusiasm with discrimination; stagnation with creativity; frustration with communicative response/expression; and apathy with realistic caring.

Realistic caring is vital because clients/students greatly vary in their ability to realize potential. There's spiritual wisdom in not being overly attached to the results of our work, but rather to lovingly work and do the best we can without excessive worrying about results. Some people won't change, at least before "our eyes." It's satisfying to push both our own potential and that of our clients/students. However, just maintaining a present level of functioning is a success for some. Some need a low-key, low-pressure environment. At times, we just let the student/client "be" without an over-emphasis on what the student must "do."

We may feel an excessive personal responsibility for the care of others. Yet no one's indispensable. Just as some activists, monks, priests, helpers tend to do, we over-evaluate our service as an individual. That service is very significant and valuable, but a small part in a larger process of help in another's life.

Our professional duties are carried out through teamwork. Many factors contribute to the progress and setbacks in education and therapy. Our task is simple: informed service. We can't get overly involved with "being popular" and "praise and blame."

We need to help ourselves as well as help each other and our students. Some of us find exercise very helpful; some of us use meditation. I often tell my students to take and release two or three deep breaths. I try to practice taking ten deep breaths each day, just to release the stress I've built up. I also find it helpful to take a few breaths when I'm getting angry or upset. For those who would like, let's do the following exercise.

Breathing in through our noses, we fill our bellies as filling a balloon, allowing the breath then to fill our lungs, breathing to the number of counts comfortable for us; then holding, finally, releasing the breath, with mouths open, gently letting the stomach muscles squeeze out the breath, first in the belly and then in the lungs. Breathe in, hold, and let out breath as suits you personally. You can do this five to ten times, giving the exercise your full attention.

The process of "burnout" builds up in us. Sometimes, we are uptight and angry in the performance of our obligations.

We're, at times, "sick of it all." It can be a great error not to admit this and just feel it in our bodies so we can take "what's going on in us" into account. So we don't deny the negativity we may experience, but rather we find ways of re-perceiving our work. We find ways to get things "off our chests." We see our routine situations "in a new light" which can revitalize our ordinary duties. We acknowledge that this process of enthusiasm-stagnation-frustration-apathy is always going on to some degree. Part of the creativity in the art of living our lives is this management of stress. Doubt, fatigue, up-tightness come with the territory. Don't blame yourself or your clients/students. We still need to serve each other even if we're in a bad mood.

Observe but don't judge unnecessarily. Be kind to yourself. Our own total health is as important as that of our students. We can't change if we don't have a simple, considerate love of ourselves. If we are "stuck," we won't have the perspective to influence and model appropriate change for the student. We keep growing, learning, experiencing feeling as well as just thinking, eating and sleeping well. We laugh and have fun. We set goals consistent with our values and abilities. We organize our time while appreciating how everything is changing which allows us not to get overly identified with our "helping." We get support from both intimates and colleagues. We allow our work to be both professional and a work of art. We keep up to date and interested, while cultivating a rich personal life. We connect with the most curious and innovative in our particular fields.

Perhaps we aren't honest enough about our own overly "model" expectations to appear useful, important, powerful, helpful, needed, impressive. At times our self-esteem is riding upon misguided expectations.

Who cares past the gossip anyway? Let's accept the ambiguity of the "helping profession." It's paradoxical. Often we help when we least expect and, unfortunately, hinder when we're trying too hard to "help."

* * * * *

I'd like to end this with an invocation and visualization by Ken Ireland that can easily be adapted for us in the helping professions.

We celebrate and acknowledge two of the most human virtues, generosity and gratitude. They are really two aspects, two sides of the same coin—giving and receiving go together, accepting and giving everything away all over again. In this way we act to take care of our world— we create projects that make our love for one another as fellow human beings real.

Let us call upon the unseen powers of the universe, the mystery of Love itself, the divine, the protectors of our lives, to be present and bless us, bless our gatherings, our work together. The good news is that all of this is already present. Those forces are present in each of us, present in every act of generosity, present in projects that assist those who cannot help themselves, present when we provide love and comfort to fellow humans who are suffering, present when we create institutions to take care of our world.

Another aspect of generosity and gratitude is that we are not always aware that they are present. With your permission I'd like to invite you to practice a short meditation with me, a visualization that might allow us to be more aware that love is always present.

Please close your eyes, and feel your breath, enjoy your breath. Now think of someone in your life who exemplifies truly generous actions, a spirit that serves other people. It may be a parent, a teacher, a mentor, a colleague, a person whose work in their field has won your respect and admiration.

Who is this person for you? You might recall some specific actions, some interaction you had with them. There might be some feeling that remains very strong. Whether or not you have accurate recall, there are still some feelings just when you think of them. Take a few moments to see what bubbles up in your mind.

Now I'd like to suggest that the reason you can be sensitive to those qualities in the person you admire— his or her love, intention, drive, generosity— is that you possess these same qualities yourself. Please accept that. That is part of their generosity—showing you who you really are! Let that sink in for a few moments. We all share these human capacities; these virtues are part of being human.

Now open your eyes, look around you and silently acknowledge the love and generosity and the gratitude that is present right now.

May our hearts be open, may we be grateful to each other for all that we are, and all that we've done.

And now let's enjoy this life which comes to us through the generosity, the work and suffering of many beings and other forms of life.

Thank you very much. Generosity and gratitude are truly present.

Part II

My dear and loyal friend Don Foran sets the tone for the second part of Meanderings.

Who We Are
A Poem and Introduction to Activism and Volunteering
Don Foran, Ph.D.

If I could play that Dvorák, YoYo Ma,
Excruciating sadness yoked to joy,
I'd play it for all children of this raw
And dangerous world, the ones who most annoy
The very rich. I'd hold each note an hour
And place my quaking finger on the fret
Until my sweat ran free and sour;
Till tears flowed too, both mine and ours. I'd let
The world know that music with its charm
Redeems, somehow, much pain and many long
Long hidden wrongs, assuages grief and harm,
And sounds, at last, a plaintive, hopeful song.
Thus are we saved. You stir new mindfulness
Of who we really are and whom we bless.

Hooray for Jackie Robinson! Activism and Volunteering
Morgan Zo-Callahan

> *Compassion is not at all weak. It is the strength that*
> *arises out of seeing the true nature of suffering in the*
> *world. Compassion allows us to bear witness to that*
> *suffering, whether it is in others, or ourselves without*
> *fear; it allows us to name injustice without hesitation.*
> *And to act strongly, with all the skill at our disposal.*
> —Sharon Salzberg

> *Not being reactive is not being passive. It's not a kind of*
> *stupidity, holding back or being uninterested, removing*
> *oneself from the world. Real equanimity isn't indifference.*
> *It's the capacity to be present with your whole being and*
> *not add fuel to the fire.*
> —Jack Kornfield

In 1956, Autherine Lucy Foster would be the first African American to enroll at the University of Alabama. She was suspended, and then expelled three days later, because of hateful demonstrations against her. Thurgood Marshall of the NAACP Legal Defense Fund helped her sue the university. She won. It also was the year of the Montgomery, Alabama bus boycott. Rosa Parks was my hero. On May 23, 1956, I had my first taste of "activism" when I wrote this naive, but well-intentioned letter:

> *Dear Chairman Mao Tse-Tung,*
> *I am Morgan Callahan, a pupil in the sixth grade of St.*
> *Mary's School.*
> *In September of 1955, your government promised to release*
> *all Americans, and today thirteen are still in prison. I would like*

to see you carry out your promise. The names of the prisoners are listed on the back of this paper.

I have heard of the policy of leniency, which you profess toward violators of your law. It is my fond wish that you carry out this policy of leniency by applying it in full to these thirteen American prisoners by releasing them from prison and helping them to leave China and return to their homes.

(I imagined a face to each name; I wondered at their names and what it might tell me about their heritage. It was the first time I saw or used the word "Jesuit.")

McKinnon, Jr. Paul J., Lutheran Missionary, Baltimore, Maryland

Nham, Robert E., Altadena, California

McCarthy, Rev. Charles Joseph, Jesuit, San Francisco, California

Phillips, Rev. Thomas Leonard, Jesuit, Butte, Montana

Pinger, Bishop Ambrose Henry, Franciscan, Linsey, Nebraska

Redmond, Hugh Francis; Yonkers, New York

Wagner, Rev. John Paul, Franciscan, Pittsburgh, Penn.

Clifford, Rev. John William, Jesuit, San Francisco, California

Downey, John Thomas, New Britain, Connecticut

Fectian, Richard George, Lynn, Mass.

Gross, Rev. Fulgence, Franciscan, Omaha, Nebraska

Houle, Rev. Joseph Patrick, Maryknoll, Palmyra, New York

McCormack, Joseph, Maryknoll, Palmyra, New York

Sincerely yours,

Morgan Callahan

■

A year later on September 4, 1957, when I was thirteen years old, I read how the governor of Arkansas (with what I thought was an incredible name, Orval Faubus) and his National Guard prevented a fifteen-year-old, Elizabeth Eckford, from crossing a line to attend Central High School in Little Rock. I felt she was so courageous to try, because she was separated from the other black students who also would desegregate Central High and who wanted that day to enter their high school peacefully. The mob in front of Central High and the National Guard surrounded the terrified Elizabeth. There was a defiant refusal to welcome these students, just because of their skin color. A kind, white woman, Grace Lorch, escorted Elizabeth to a bus and safety.

I would read more about the Little Rock integration crisis that year; it was given a lot of press. For the first time I became aware of the depth of racial hatred in my country, but I felt some significant good-heartedness and efficient community organizing for civil rights by both blacks and whites. I was hopeful in the power of such bravery to initiate meaningful social change. I continued letter writing in support of Dr. Martin Luther King, Jr.'s amazing work and preaching. Within the white student Central High society, there were several acts of acceptance, as well as acts of harassment. Some students offered active support, but there seemed always to be some racial taunting going on. I felt that aligning myself with the supportive energy for African-American rights through writing letters was allowing me to fall a little more deeply into this monumental happening for change. I felt drawn as if in an inescapable whirlpool.

Carlotta Walls, Jefferson Thomas, Ernest Green, Gloria Ray, Melba Pattillo, Terrance Roberts, Minnijean Brown, Thelma Mothershed, and Elizabeth Eckford, were the nine students who were turned away that September 4. I applauded President Eisenhower who, after initially taking the stance of "wait and see," on September 25 sent in twelve hundred soldiers from 327th Airborne Battle Group of the 101st Army Airborne Division to escort the nine African-American students into the school. One of the girls, Minnijean Brown, later was kicked out of school when she dumped her bowl of chili on the head of a heckling, taunting student. The black cafeteria workers clapped at her shocking "retaliation." Imagine the release of some suffering of the workers who felt as "second class" citizens, that they "had to take it." Minnijean Brown was transferred to New Lincoln High School, in NYC. In 1958, Ernest Green would be the first black student, in a class of 602, to graduate from Central High. No one clapped for him as he walked across the stage with his diploma.

■

On September 10, 2007, Dave Van Etten, sent me an article from the *San Jose Mercury News* about the ongoing relationship between Melba Pattillo and Marty Sammon, one of the paratroopers sent by President Eisenhower to protect the nine black high school students. Marty had been Dave's teammate on the University of Santa Clara's boxing team. Marty and Melba sometimes get together to "share their time in history," when Melba was fifteen and Marty was twenty-three. Melba speaks of her appreciation of the soldiers who protected her for six weeks. Melba says: "I celebrate this man every day of my life." Melba is now sixty-five and the head of the Communications Department at Dominican University in San Rafael, California. Melba Pattillo recalled how she had talked to her grandmother about Mahatma's Gandhi's philosophy of non-violent resistance. She recounts saying at the time: "The troops are here. We are going to live; we're going to make it."

Marty volunteers as a boxing referee and even had a part in Clint Eastwood's film, *Million Dollar Baby*. He's also a stockbroker. Seventy-three years old, he said of the nine Little

Rock students: "I'm filled with enormous respect for those kids. None of them quit."

■

Because I woke up to activism during the African-American Civil Rights Movement, I would never feel righteous about the lack of human rights in other countries such as in China. There was an obvious lack of human rights for African Americans and other minorities in my own country.

A great hero for me was the gallant and dignified, yet tough, Jackie Robinson. I visited Ebbets Field in awe to watch him play with the Dodgers. My abiding memory of him: stealing-sliding across home plate in the 1955 World Series, with my beloved Yankee's catcher, Yogi Berra, going crazy. The Bums—to my dismay—finally won!

Jackie's inspiration was for an inclusive humanity. Now it's 2007, sixty years since Jackie bravely started playing ball professionally, breaking the "color barrier," despite vicious racist taunting and facing segregated hotels, restaurants, transportation, water fountains.

In the excellent book, *First Class Citizenship, The Civil Rights Letters of Jackie Robinson*, edited by Michael G. Long (Times Books, 2007), I read a letter that Jackie wrote to President Kennedy in June of 1963 after Medgar Evers was assassinated: "Utilize every federal facility to protect a man (Dr. Martin Luther King, Jr.) sorely needed for this era.… " Jackie was very concerned that there would also be attempts to assassinate Dr. King. He spoke out against racism whether by blacks or whites.

■

Human rights are both a local and a universal issue. An activist aligns his or her voice with others, against what is felt as abuse of human rights, in whatever country. A volunteer rolls up her sleeves and brings wise compassion (doesn't do for others what he or she could do for herself) to so many of the heart breaking "causes" facing us in our times.

One day, my niece, Jeanelle, was surprised when I said she was an activist because she volunteers with homeless people. We understand "volunteer," not in any condescending way, but as a mutually beneficial relationship. Jeanelle says she finds great joy in volunteering and learns a lot.

"Activism" was coined around 1915 to denote the doctrine or practice that emphasizes direct, vigorous action, for example mass protests in opposition to some law or societal norm, or a call for human rights, such as marching for civil rights, or picketing to organize a union. In a general sense, activism, including volunteerism, is involving oneself to help create change which might be social, environmental, political, communal.

We have only a very broad idea of who's an activist and who's a volunteer, and what is a genuine and efficacious expression for the activist and for the volunteer. I see what's happening in Myanmar, Tibet, in the Sudan as a mirror, reflecting, "What can we do to soften suffering in our world neighborhood?"

The volunteer and the activist promote change. I only distinguish volunteer from activist in that an activist may be paid. Some volunteers pick up trash on the beach; others, such as my friend Harry Wu, directly criticize and call for action against human rights abuses. The volunteer and the activist both promote change. I've been blessed to meet some incredible volunteers and activists who inspire me by their down to earth energetic and peaceful actions to lessen the tensions, violence, unfairness, and severe poverty in our world. My dear friends, Sue and Jim White, provide loving foster care to one baby at a time. They don't receive any salary. Jim exemplifies service with good humor and steadfastness. How I admire them! And to take affectionate care of babies, with the evident joy that communicates how nourishing it is both for the baby and for Sue and Jim. On the other hand, I have also met activists and volunteers who were in it for their own agendas, sometimes harming others rather than lifting them up. They are a definite minority.

Activism doesn't have to be related to religion, but it certainly can be, and in many cases is sparked by the same altruistic sentiments. I was touched by reading *Street Zen* about the life of Issan Dorsey, a wild gay man and Buddhist monk, who founded Maitri AIDS Hospice in San Francisco in 1989. He and several like-minded people, among them my editor Ken Ireland, used their Buddhist practice to create a direct and heart-felt way to reach out to the men and women in San Francisco whose lives were forever changed by the epidemic that swept through the gay community.

I think about other very practical, homely projects, like Dolores Mission's work with homeless men, opening up the church to them for three months—while they are getting back on their feet—for shelter, good meals, sleep, and the option to take classes, and in the same vein, the L.A. Catholic Worker's three day a week soup kitchen in downtown skid row. I think about projects that empower others such as http://www.kiva.org founded by Jessica and Matt Flannery; a foundation dedicated to providing micro-loans, as small as $25, to start a person towards making his or her own livelihood. I've seen in my travels that this is what so many of the poorest Latin Americans want—the dignity of providing for one's family. You can log on to this site and check out some people who want to start a business. It might be money to have a stand for selling peanut butter. In Xalapa, Veracruz, some charities have given the start up money for mobile selling stands, for around $40 per business. As the people pay back their loans, they establish credit, and they begin to establish a sound financial base for themselves and their families.

■

From 1969 to 1970, I learned specific organizing techniques at the Saul Alinsky Organizing Institute in Chicago. I was introduced to sensing the power of local communities, being united in a cause and the organizing necessary to direct that energy towards beneficial changes. Alinsky taught that an organizer has to get in touch with the community's social need; and work together to create concrete goals which address those real needs (such as housing, medical, landlord-tenant issues). That naturally unleashes great enthusiasm and "righteousness" in the community that lead to organizing "tactics" that bring change—the catalyst for community meetings, strategies, fundraising.

■

I also embrace activism as a "volunteer" to benefit the poor, severely handicapped, and other vulnerable brothers and sisters. It can be as humble as getting used clothes to the Salvation Army. You go, as Frederick Buechner says, "where your deep gladness meets the world's deep need."

Once when I was a sixth grader, coming back from playing in a Biddy League basketball game in Norwalk, Connecticut, I passed a disheveled lady sitting on a bench, on a hill overlooking the town's lights.

The moon was colorful and full on that chilly bright evening; she seemed full of a sad despair that touched me. As if for the first time, I felt empathy towards someone who was "down and out," wailing a sound of defeat.

I recalled that Jesus reached out to those suffering, to those often shunned by others.

I could only rush by this distraught lady, but my heart was opened to wanting to be a volunteer, to be of some comfort to others, less graced and fortunate than most of us, when I wouldn't be so afraid. Later I'd realize we all have our cycles of feeling "discarded" or being deeply lonely, of losing hope.

I imagined her praying for inspiration, for new life, for any hope, before the orange winter moon.

Tramp-Prayer to Selene

Chalk moon
changing into pleated skirts of kumquat gold,
bursting warmth, basking, swinging
orange gaiety, sashaying
above city fire-flakelets of light.

Dumped
crumpled
lady, torn apart,
sliced heart,
benching on icy goose-pimples.

Paint me, goddess Luna,
lips of gay rose-pink,
let me drink fresh blueberries
caress like Mother Mary
crashing heart, frozen black night.

■

American Indians occupying Alcatraz!—I was teaching high school boys in San Jose, Bellarmine High School when my buddy, Marcus Holly, asked if I'd help the organizing effort of getting clothes, blankets, food for Indian people who had "occupied" Alcatraz in the San Francisco Bay on November 9, 1969. The intention of the take-over was to make people aware of contemporary Indian people and how they are treated, how their history has been overlooked. My friend Marcus said "we've got to do this." The Native People were in Alcatraz for seventeen months, supported by donations and supplies coming from the Bay area.

The Indian activists fought among themselves ("being their own worst enemies" said one of the organizing leaders). On June 11, 1971, one of the leaders was arrested for stealing copper from Alcatraz, and it was over. But they had gotten some people thinking a bit about Indian Americans whom we've come to see as complex, full of nobility as well as showing treachery at times; that complexity is in us all, whatever our race.

■

By the end of April 2007, after two hundred and eighty of their neighbors' Chongquing, China properties have been leveled, Yang Wu, a martial artist, and his wife, Wu Ping, stand alone on a shaky dirt hill in their brick family home. It has been in the family since 1944 and completely re-built from the ground up in 1994. They've refused to give up to developers who want a mall and luxurious apartments. A huge, bulldozed pit surrounds them.

Wu Ping says: "People must live with dignity … if you are right, you must stand up for yourself and not allow your rights to be trampled."

A local court has ruled that the house must be vacated. Yang is hanging a protest banner while Wu Ping sadly says: "I am losing hope."

■

In May of 2007, peasants from counties in Guangxi province, protested against China's one-child policy, the forced sterilizations and mandatory abortions. Fortunately such coercive government action is much less common than in the late 70s and 80s.

■

In June of 2007, the Internet relayed a cry for help from four hundred fathers looking for their sons who were made slaves at brick kilns in Henan province. Some of the dads even went "undercover" to see for themselves the terrible working conditions at some kilns where the grueling day might start at 5 AM and end at midnight. Outraged Chinese citizens sparked the government to raid about eleven thousand kilns. More than five hundred, including some children, were gratefully released from the pernicious grip of forced labor. President Hu Jintao ordered a thorough investigation.

■

On October 2, 2000, thousands gathered at a park smelling of incense, on the Jumna River at Delhi where Mahatma Gandhi was cremated after he was assassinated on January 30, 1948. That day hymns were sung, verses from the *Gita*, the Koran and the Bible recited. Stories, poems, prayers for peace, people blend into each other. Cotton thread spun on small spinning wheels—as our ever-changing stream of life—recalled Gandhi's virtue of simplicity.

Mohandas Ghandi was born October 2, 1869. He is considered the father of modern non-violent activism. His first protest, or civil disobedience, was to manufacture salt from seawater, publicly breaking British law that Indians were only supposed to buy British salt. Salt water from tidal marshes was collected in pots. The sun then evaporated the water, leaving salt behind which was put on sale. "With this, I am shaking the foundations of the British Empire." Thus began a movement to bring political freedom to the Indian people.

India became independent seventeen years later.

■

In Rowland Heights, California, I listen to Chinese Falun Gong members, Bin Li, Jie Li, Hongwei Lu, Lingyun Zhao, Fengling Ge, talk about being in Chinese labor camps and prisons for practicing their beliefs. They speak out to put pressure on the Chinese government and Communist Party to stop persecuting Falun Gong members in China.

They ask for support. Bin Li with tears in her eyes recounts: "All of us were brainwashed. We were beaten, insulted so gradually you think, why are you here? At some point I thought I shouldn't exist in this universe." She says she's grateful to have come to the United States in 2004, with a visa as a visiting scholar.

Beijing has made some progress in human rights such as in reforming its death penalty system, acknowledging the sale of body organs from executed prisoners, giving more access to foreign journalists, but the PRC has a long way to go to measure up to a decent standard for protecting individual freedom and expression. This January 2008, the Rose Parade in Pasadena had a float representing China and the 2008 Beijing Summer Olympics. This was an opportunity for Falun Gong to protest human rights abuses in China, detentions, beatings, forced labor for members of the Falun Gong, also human rights violations against Christians and Tibetans. Awning (Jenny) Liu, who is a member of Caltech's Falun Gong Club, learned in mid-December that Chinese police had dragged her sixty-four year old mother from her home after seizing books about Falun Gong. The *Pasadena Weekly* reported (10/25/07) that Liu's mother was sentenced to thirty months in a labor and re-education camp without benefit of a public trial. At the Rose Parade, Chinese, Burmese, Falun Gong, and Tibetan supporters held up signs: "Free Tibet," and chanted, "Shame, shame, China, shame."

An AIDS activist who was previously banned from leaving China was recently allowed to receive an award in the United

States. Activists continue to ask for reform of the extensive use of detaining civil rights activists without trial. They advocate for the end of censoring the Internet.

Former student and friend, Dong Fang, just came back from China. He is interested in highlighting the need of the Chinese government to protect coal miners, to keep improving work safety in the coal mining industry that provides 70 percent of China's energy needs. Also there is a movement to provide a minimum wage. Government officials need to enforce new government policy; 60 percent of 5.5 million coal miners are rural immigrants who are more vulnerable to exploitation. In 2006, 4,746 miners lost their lives in accidents, gratefully down 20 percent from the previous year, but the numbers are still horrific for a civilized society.

■

I'm amazed at a woman activist in China, Xie Lihua, who works for women's rights in rural China, where women suffer three times the suicide rate of Chinese urban women. They are too often abused and treated as "lower" than their husbands, nervously beholden to their "masters." Xie Lihua for the last fourteen years has produced a magazine, *Rural Women* and founded The Cultural Development Center for Rural Women. She hopes to continue to end this "feudal ignorance." Her organization offers micro-loans for businesses, suicide prevention; literacy training, and involving women in the political process which, she says is improving slowly for women in China, but still has a long way to go. Her magazine discusses love, sex, being married, divorce, how to start a small business, and letters for a section she calls "The Emotional World of Rural Women." She tells women: "Your life is the equal of a man. They were not born unequal—society made them this way.... You are yours. You are not anybody else's. If there is no change, even though it is painful, then there is no progress." (*Los Angeles Times*, January 2, 2008) Three quarters of women in China live in the countryside.

■

I've listened to Chinese activists in California. I am struck by their stories of being in prison and in labor camps. I admire their bravery in speaking up.

What a stunning image, at the mid-April 1989 pro-democracy sit-in—a white-shirted student in central Beijing facing the army's tankers—alone—first walking to a column of five tanks, T-59s decorated with red stars and gold rays, then the young man sitting on a tank, chatting with the crew. Soon after we saw these images on TV, the authorities would start opening fire on the protesters in Tiananmen Square. An outraged Chinese soldier, Li Tiego, inspired me. I composed a poem for my Chinese students who are involved in activism.

Tiananmen

"I had been proud to be a soldier. When I saw these hooligans kill that girl I was disgusted with myself. Can those people be my comrades ever again?"—Li Tiego, after observing Chinese troops kick a twelve-year old girl to death, June 4, 1989

Instantaneously,
bloody square 440,000 meters
million people panorama stopped my mind.

My brains want to explode
All the putrid propaganda
blessed by Mao's broad hypnotic painted gaze,

blood spilling
from brothers' bellies
like slippery fish,

149

giving-taking revenge-orders,
before my living unbelieving eyes,
sacrilege of my shame.

O beautiful red-braided young sister,
black-water-falling, cascading hair,
Mai, Mai,
battered by bullies, kicking startled teeth.

Leader hiding behind shiny doors,
freshening up lines for home TV news,
as we kill our own selves,
I cry from green-oozing defeat.

My heart-cave, violated
I'm an agonized animal,
pacing like crazed Mother, tears, howls
calling "Mai Mai, little daughter."

Child, stomped,
hostile feet,
street-people crushing
feat of the power-coward,
in us all.

June 5, 2007, marked the eighteenth anniversary of the
Tiananmen massacre and I see a picture of thousands and
thousands of people in Hong Kong's Victoria Park holding
candles to remember the pro-democracy student movement.
Activists continue to ask for deeper political reform in China—
many using the 2008 Beijing Olympics as an opportunity
to shine some light on human rights abuses in China. Saul
Alinsky said a good activist uses the tactic of embarrassing,
let's say in this case, the government of China into living up
to their promises to abide by human rights and equality and

live harmoniously, despite different ethnic backgrounds and religions. China has persecuted many Christians or followers of Falun Gong. Our global moral consciousness can no longer tolerate such abuses, whether in China or in our own country. All of us have the right to be free. At the end of March 2008, Tibetan people are protesting; the Dalai Lama is calling for peaceful dialogue while at the same time asking that the Beijing Olympic Games go on.

■

On a sunny day in 2003, I visited Anna Carter in Watts. Only about 40 percent of the students finish high school here; Watts is also the location of Verbum Dei High School where the Jesuits recently started a program. Students work one day a week for businesses, both for learning and to make a reasonable tuition possible.

Anna is a lovely lady who wears flowers in her Afro. She is also called "the Seed Lady," who started the Watts Family Garden Club last year. It is full of youngsters playing and helping plant tomatoes, pansies, chamomile in the yard. She recently came back from Cuba where she learned farming techniques in urban environments. She was part of a delegation with the organizations, Food First and Institute for Food and Development Policy. They were studying using raised compost container beds in cities.

In the middle 90s, Anna was severely traumatized and injured by a high voltage electric shock; some Native American friends suggested she touch the roots of trees and work with soil to heal the electricity in her body. After three years of convalescing, she took a master gardening program through the University of California system. She found teaching others took her mind off her pain and self-pity.

She says she wants people in the community to see that they are themselves agents (seeds) of change, that they can empower themselves, feel good about themselves, feel self-respect, even in a rough environment. She offers classes in vegetarian cooking and gardening: "Wok with Me"; "The Value of a Seed"; "The Organic Greenhouse."

■

In March of 2001, I attend a peaceful protest against the Taliban's obliteration of ancient carvings and the remarkable, massive, two-thousand-year-old statues of the Buddha in Bamiyan, Afghanistan.

I ponder the story of the early twelfth century Turaskas, fanatical, murderous Muslims from Afghanistan, who entered India and destroyed all the Buddhist communities in their path of destruction. I think about the over-running of the great Buddhist monastic university, Nalanda, in India; and the beheading or burying alive of thousands of Buddhist monks. You can still view the ruins of Nalanda, once a walled city where students and teachers explored and plumbed the Buddhist philosophies of Hinayana, Mahayana, Madhyamika and Yogachara. Its reputation for open inquiry, discussion, debate and scholarship, attracted endowments from kingdoms of Ceylon (Sri Lanka), Java, Bengal, China, Sumatra, Mongolia, Japan, Korea, Turkestan. Hiuen-Tsiang, the seventh century Chinese pilgrim, wrote: "The whole establishment was of majestic appearance, with richly adorned towers and fairy-like turrets, the four-storied courts, their dragon-like projections and colored eaves, carved and ornamented pearl-red pillars, richly adorned balustrades, and roofs covered with tiles, reflecting light in a thousand shades."

Nalanda's extensive library—torched by the invaders—was said to have burned for months, devoured by fire and hatred. We humans have not managed to extinguish the fires of ill will in our own times.

■

During the Christmas vacation of 2003, I accompanied an Evangelical Christian church to Baja California, Mexico. This church travels twice a year to San Tecla which is home to a large ranch which attracts indigenous Oaxacans to travel north for a better salary of about $8.00 a day which is twice what they can get in Oaxaca, if work is even available. Some Oaxacans settle in Baja California, and others travel seasonally.

The church members and I arrived at the ranch early in the chilly morning to organize presents for children, clothes, food baskets for families; we've driven 2 ½ hours from the seaport of Ensenada, located on *Bahia de Todos Santos*, sixty miles south of Tijuana.

There's a rousing Christian service, with around 120 children sitting in front of the church's stage which features musicians, women preachers and singers, melodies with electric guitars and percussion beats. We weave and sway, swooning with Jesus. Alleluia!

Dios Es Amor is painted in large white letters on a brown cross. The sun is shining its bright yellow into the rocking church.

Children go to some small classes, while the adults receive bags of beans, rice, sugar, clothes, soap, shampoo. It's very cold outside; some of the shivering children still don't have shoes, so the church members make sure they are given sneakers. It's such a joy seeing a youngster receiving a gift, a quick beaming response, warming; generous volunteers realize they are receiving one of those small, fleeting satisfactions that feed our souls.

Seven of us take a quick dirt road truck ride to view the ocean, speeding past the tomato plants, which the Oaxacan Indians are covering with plastic to protect from the bitter cold sea winds. We stay on the hilly shore for thirty minutes, slipping on wet rocks, mostly grays, some ivory-colored blotched with rust, white and brown corrugated clam shells, delicate detached crab legs; waves spray salty water on me. I take a handful of ocean water to splash on my face.

I recall visiting Oaxaca with its fertile, vast plateaus, pretty valleys, the gorgeous Sierra Madre del Sur Mountain Range. Chiapas and Oaxaca have the largest Indian populations in Mexico, within which lie generous bounties of culture, handicrafts, folklore, spirituality. Oaxaca gave us Mexican President Benito Juarez, a Zapotec Indian. The Indians here in San Tecla, doing farm work, are descendants of the Mixtec or Zapotec.

Going home, we stop on the Tijuana border, on *las playas* of Tijuana. There are these tall black spotted, rusted steel pilings that form the *frontera*. We see some people put their heads through openings, perhaps longing for the "other side." As we cross the border, my friend, Margot Alvarado, shows us where, in '78, she and her three children crawled through a large drain into the United States. She was lucky, she says, to have been led by a "good" *coyote*.

■

Ah most precious children, children, little children! May you be well, be loved, safe and secure!

How tragic to know you've been enslaved, prostituted, made one of the worldwide three hundred thousand child soldiers who are perhaps only thirteen years old. In the summer of 2007, we hear how in Iraq children are used as boy soldiers, becoming killers and roadside bombers, being paid, for example, two or three hundred dollars to plant a bomb. Such money might support a family for two or three months.

UNICEF reports that children are used as spies, soldiers, messengers, cooks, porters, human land-mine detectors, suicide bombers, and prostitutes. For example, children make up an estimated 20 percent of Burma's three hundred fifty thousand soldiers. They are often drugged and abused. Some join because of poverty, abuse, discrimination, revenge; some are abducted, forced to join the armies.

Protect young children all over the world!

■

At the end of September 2005, I visited Padre Orlando Erazo who was in California from El Salvador. He wanted to show me some pictures to pass along to the *compañeros* who donated money to build a community center next to his parish church in El Paisnal.

Robert Holstein (Rest in Peace) visited with Padre Orlando in the spring of 2002 along with friends, Brophy, Straukamp, Baumann, Masterson. Orlando told me how Bob remains so close to his heart, even after just one meeting. They formed a human relationship that was more fundamental and meaningful than all religious or political association.

Orlando told me about the process of organizing this project that now offers a center with training in computers, classes in sewing, carpentry, masonry, electricity, as well as a meeting place for social events and general education. The multi-purpose room has a ping-pong table; there are posters warning of the dangers of drugs and alcohol abuse.

I view the pictures of the construction site, then bulldozers preparing the land and finally the building going up. The local people sold lunches and dinners to help raise money; teenagers played music and called out over loudspeakers to invite people to participate. It was a building for the people. Finally I see pictures of women cooking food and a truck with music and announcements for the people to come to the opening of the building.

Orlando speaks about "accompanying the poor, in the spirit of Jesus" in their journey to lead a full, happy life. Orlando's uncle, Padre Rutilio Grande, S.J., was killed by a death squad on March 12, 1977, the first of seven priests—working for social justice among the poor—killed in the next two years.

■

It's been nineteen years since I was in El Salvador to commemorate the fifth anniversary of the violent assassination on November 16, 1989 of six Jesuit Spanish priests, Ignacio Ellacuria, Amando Lopez, Joaquin Lopez, Ignacio Martin-Baro, Segundo Montes, Juan Ramon Moreno, and their housekeeper and her daughter, Elba and Celina Ramos.

I went to El Salvador to touch and be touched by the land and its people. El Salvador is a wonder, a display of hills, vegetation, city marketplaces, refreshing ocean, and great people—a wounded, but resilient people.

I also came to cry for brothers and sisters who have suffered, to try to understand and learn with reverence. And cry for myself, my own tolerance for violence. I asked many how could political power and government, conceived to serve the people and enrich all, become such destructive repression and death? As early as 1982 Joan Didion wrote: "Terror is the given of the place. Bodies turn up in the brush of vacant lots, in the garbage, thrown in ravines in the richest districts, in public restrooms; in bus stations.... Some are dropped in Lake Ilopango."

In the early morning, at the UCA University, around 2:30 AM, *los seis sacerdotes* were jerked from their beds and executed. There were about three hundred officers and enlisted men at the UCA campus on the night of the murders. The UCA had been bombed in April and July of '89. The death squad wrote "FMLN" over the walls to escape blame.

In January of 1990, eight men were arrested for the murders, six from the Atlcatl Battalion and two officers of the military academy. Two men were convicted—Col. Benavides of seven murders, Lieutenant Mendoza of the murder of Celina Ramos. They were sentenced for thirty years. The provincial of the Jesuits in El Salvador, Fr. Tojeira, officially asked for pardon for the two convicted men, because he stated those who ordered the attack were not brought to trial. Both men were set free.

The Jesuits had openly favored a peace accord among the political factions in the country. Some of the military wanted to continue to fuel the hateful polarities, especially propagating that the Jesuits were *only* supporting the *guerrillas*. The Jesuits, in fact, were imploring for the integration of the varied political and economic elements in Salvadoran society. Father Ellacuria and President Christiani, with all their ideological differences, were both talking about how they could unite energies to give reality to a peace accord. Many human rights groups say this is why far right elements killed Fr. Ellacuria and his friends.

The Jesuits favored agrarian reform and the end of political repression that stifled a sharing of power. Jesuits such as Rutilio Grande were speaking out for the poor, as well as for all elements in the society, political and economic. They were teaching principles of how to use and share, no matter what one's wealth or political belief might be. They spoke openly for social justice, human rights and against political terror.

I say a prayer at the memorial of the murdered Jesuit *padres* and for Elba and Celina Ramos who died with them. They were not the only ones killed by death squads. On March 24, 1980, after just three years as the archbishop of El Salvador, Oscar Arnulfo Romero was gunned down while saying Mass.

Now I see these pictures of bloody, mashed bodies. I am in anguish and want to feel the supremacy of the soul and inviolable spirit, but before me are these pictures of horror!

I later spent a few days visiting the UCA in the summer of '94. The peace accord was signed in 1992. I feel a relaxed environment here at the Jesuit university.

Politically, first steps of the peace process are being taken. There are pockets of healing and joy in piano, drums, guitars, and dance; there are the voices of students, visitors, faculty, workers, buildings going up, serious study, and a full library. I hear talks that encourage more political enlightenment and call for the end of repression and the opening of a multi-faceted society, imbued with knowledge and cherishing of human rights.

I met Ken Hauser, a volunteer from Virginia who has made several trips to El Salvador, bringing needed materials to the poor from the generosity of U.S. businesses. I run into an ecologist from Ireland who's working with farmers, organizing solutions to pollution and what he calls "the problems of natural resource exploitation." I visited Padre Vito Guarato who established a home for three hundred abandoned handicapped children, at *Casa de Piedra*.

I was welcomed in the home of a former student whose father—a "casualty" of the civil war—is now in prison. She says many of her friends no longer will speak to her. Yet she speaks so lovingly of her "disgraced" father ... how, when she was a little girl, they would dig for clams, lying buried, like gray fruit in the moist sands.

I marveled at the *Ruinas de el Tazumal* that gave me a glimpse of the reverberating hopes of the people I met on this trip. And later I wrote this poem at the UCA.

The Ruins of El Tazumal

My face battered
my body tight-fisted fear,
long enough, *Basta.*
Enough.
Stop.

Here's a story of Buddha
running quickly-gracefully, away,
just ahead of Angulimala,
garlanded with murder victims' severed fingers,
yelling, "Stop, monk!"

"I have stopped, Angulimala,
you stop too."

We—good, earthy people,
toil on sacred land,
where you can see for yourself
Las Ruinas de el Tazumal, hearts
echoing the *Pocomames* Indians*,*

Let's stop together on the top of the world.

Chalchuapa, Santa Ana.
Ah, mi tierra es muy agradable, very pleasing.
Let's climb up hewed steps, blue-sky walking,
Dancing our hands together,
upwards to unfathomable skies,

freely standing in peace
on top of ancient heights,
together on broad kind stone shoulders.

■

There always seems to be some question whether peaceful, even forceful, speaking up against injustice does any good. And I have to agree that peaceful protest isn't always enough. But I have confidence that it's a small but significant influence for change.

Isn't it important that many were not quiet about Pol Pot in Cambodia or about Rwanda or about the genocide now in 2007 in Sudan? President Clinton says the one regret of his presidency was that he hadn't done more to prevent Rwanda.

Nicholas Kristof wrote in the *New York Times* on April 17, 2007: "Americans often misunderstand genocide, assuming it is impossible to stop, because it is driven by millenniums of racial or ethnic hatreds. But historically, genocide has mostly been rooted in cool, calculated decisions by national leaders that the most convenient way to solve a problem or stay in power is to scapegoat and destroy a particular group. So it has been in most past genocides, and so it is again in Darfur."

Darfur—population of six million—is in its fourth year of conflict. Arab militiamen, the *janjaweed*, have killed, raped and terrorized mostly black African villagers. More than two hundred thousand civilians have died; 2.5 million are homeless. This atrocity is attracting both the hearts and intelligent organizing planning of several groups. See for example, http://www.savedarfur.org. If you were to put "Activism-Darfur" in the popular search machines you'd find hundreds of thousands of "bits" of information.

We should know that in 2004, Darfur's civilians suffered terror and murder by the Khartoum government and many rightly called for an African Union or United Nations intervention. No intervention happened and chaos reined in Darfur. There's plenty of blame; we can't over-simplify the good and bad guys. David Rieff (*Los Angeles Times*, October 7, 2007), writes we'd be mistaken to think there's only "an innocent victim (the Darfuris) and a group from whom they need to be saved (the Islamist government of Sudan and its murderous Janjaweed militia) … if, proverbially, the first casualty of war is truth, then the first casualty of activism is complexity…. If Save Darfur had said 'look, the situation in Darfur is very convoluted and, while the government of Sudan deserves the lion's share of the blame, the rebels are no prize either,' how many contributions would the group have received and how many volunteers would they have inspired? Precious few … now even factions are fighting one another while factions within the Janjaweed are doing the same. In other words, it's a war of all against all…. "

The most artistic and effective activists, just as creative people in all fields, are aware of "complexity" and the varying influences in the conditions, in which they want to be supportive and encouraging of peaceful ways to connect people and to create peaceful, non-violent living conditions for ordinary citizens. Activists are very right to mobilize for Darfur; but making changes will require addressing the causes among the various groups who are doing so much violence and first of all stop the violence effectively. David Rieff continues: " … the recent killing of the peacekeepers suggests that the template for understanding present-day conditions (rather than in 2004) as a case of innocent Africans being preyed on by Islamist Arabs no longer conforms to reality … but a crisis that involves innocent victims and evil victimizers is different from one in which there is evil enough to go around—which, as the headlines demonstrate, is actually going on in Darfur."

May all the people of Darfur find peace! May they be free from conflict!

Today (5/31/07) President Bush speaks up against the genocide; the global political community—many countries—are speaking up. Activists prod the process of peace making. In January of 2008 a UN peacekeeping force assumed responsibility from the African Union to bring some peace and stability to Darfur. There's more pressure on the Sudanese government to cooperate with the United Nations' effort. Groups such as Amnesty International USA are expanding the conversation with U.S. corporations with holdings in Sudan's oil industry to support the full deployment of the U.N. peacekeeping forces. Activists are lobbying with members of Congress to continue and increase the call for human rights in Darfur, as well as appeal for more funds for helicopters and resources for the UN soldiers. As of 2/22/08, only nine thousand police and troops are on the ground for the peacekeeping in Darfur. Twenty-six thousand troops have been authorized. Major powers need to act quickly to ensure an increase in soldiers. Darfur needs to be a top priority in

2008 to keep pressure on the Sudanese government to allow the UN peacekeeping mission to be effective.

There are usually three important aspects for the activist to analyze, in a case such as Sudan:

1. The peace-making process as a negotiated political solution, which gets all the vital sides involved.
2. Humanitarian aid: UN workers and volunteers donating direct services to the 2.5 refugees from Sudan.
3. Peacekeeping soldiers being allowed into Sudan at the authorized number and being protected from attacks from the *Janjaweed* militia and rebel soldiers.

Most of us can help a bit with humanitarian aid, which is very important. Presently, the nutrition and the health in the refugee camps are improving significantly. Many goods get through, but there is still a big problem with humanitarian aid (food and the trucks transporting the food) being stolen by armed rebels. In addition, the Sudanese government (President Bashir) makes it hard for humanitarian workers in Sudan.

Some activists are pushing the US government and international community to keep involved in putting an end to the "human rights" violations against the Sudanese. Very few of us will be peacekeeping forces or volunteers in the country, but we can support this three-fold effort.

∎

We activists are small cheese. No need to be dogmatic. Most issues, even going to a war, are "shaded," not black and white. Michael Oren of the Adelson Institute for Strategic Studies says, "Even the most justified wars have untold, negative consequences—World War II, for example, inaugurated the Cold War and communist control of Eastern Europe. The

American Revolution, it could be argued, prolonged slavery in the United States and set the stage for the Civil War. Israel's 1967 Six Day War was no exception … it resulted in a turbulent occupation of the West Bank and Gaza, and contributed to the rise of terror, though it saved Israel from destruction … opening opportunities for resolving the core issues of the Arab-Israeli conflict, for guaranteeing Israel's security and legitimacy and for achieving Palestinian independence."

So it's important to talk with each other to find mutual understanding that includes a respectful acceptance of other views.

■

On 12/30/2000, I write in my journal:

"5 PM Brrrr. Cold air, walking south down Maryland Parkway, Las Vegas. Can see the tall Stratosphere Casino, blinking red spear on top, rising up like a tiny torch to the vast openness, where one pretty bright star is accompanied by a tiny, twinkling light … four flashing planes bicycle leisurely by…. Sun's almost gone, lightly painting orange and pink on the endless blue dome, gray mountains topped by white furry clouds.

"I walk past a brick tower with a red neon lighted G, for Bishop Gorman H.S. and a light blue neon cross for the suffering and resurrected Jesus.

"I'm here for Millennium 2000, Religious Action for Nuclear Disarmament, four days of talks, activities and a demonstration at the Nevada Test Site and a vigil on the strip. It's sponsored by the Franciscans (Nevada Desert Experience), Pax Christi, L.A. Catholic Worker, Fellowship of Reconciliation, Buddhist Peace Fellowship.

"About 550 people show up. I'm so happy to see Dave Van Etten's friend, smiling, hugging Shirley Tung, a sure antidote to some serious faces with a 'cause.'

"I don't protest against nuclear power which has great promise for providing us energy; rather I feel we have the need—for peace among ourselves—to lessen the number (even eliminate if ever possible) the nuclear weapons in the world. Jonathan Schell gives a lecture; he's the author of *Fate of the Earth*, *The Gift of Time*, and Jan' 2000 *Harper's* magazine article, 'What We Have Forgotten about Nuclear Weapons.'

"Was the atom bomb the horrifying necessity to end the war as is the prevailing opinion? I can see how some might doubt this, examining documents such as the diaries of Truman and some voices in the military at the time to push harder for a diplomatic ending of the war.

"And seeing pictures from Japan after the bomb was dropped and in the years following: horror, annihilation, terrible physical and psychic effects. Yet, now, why do we need nuclear-biological-chemical weapons in post Cold War times?

"Liturgical dance and responses/prayers from Muslim, Jewish, Buddhist, Christian, Catholic, and Native American voices.

"And we shall beat our swords into ploughshares, and our spears into pruning shears ... and none shall be afraid.

"May all beings, being frightened, cease to be afraid, and may those bound, be free....

"The servants of God, Most Gracious, are those who walk on the earth in humility, and when we address them we say Peace.

"Manitou, Grandfather, we are here to mend the Hoop of Creation ... we seek your Peace in our souls; let your Peace flow through us into all four sacred directions. Make our hearts like those of children with spirits full of joy and excitement.

"Joyce Holladay (fifteen year editor of *Sojourner's* magazine, founding member of Witness for Peace in Nicaragua, worker with Reconciliation Commission in South Africa) spoke about her travels, with a response from representatives from five different religions.

"I think about poor workers, including many children, in southern Mexico and Central America who suffer from their environment, just as those in Japan suffered in the aftermath of the bombs. I went to talks and seminars, 'Human and Environmental Impact of the Bomb' (A Japanese delegation spoke to us about their heart-breaking stories and photographs); 'Impact on Aboriginal American Peoples'; 'Los Alamos'; 'Nuclear Waste.'

"New Year's Eve: Dan Berrigan recites his poem, *Some*, as he does, in slightly varying versions, at various activist events. I love Dan's poem very much—it seems to capture that hidden motivation that activists have to try to right wrongs and achieve justice."

You can read the poem yourself. It is on the next page.

Dan Berrigan has inspired me since the 60s. He's a genuine, thoughtful and courageous activist as well as a renowned poet, a friend and collaborator of Thomas Merton and Thich Nhat Hanh. He entered the Jesuits in 1939 when he was eighteen years old. I've conversed with Dan, listened to his poetry, pondered his words, so living, imaginative, affectionate, one-world embracing, challenging, inclusive, and insistent. I love his wry sense of humor. It is poetry from a gentle man.

For "outrageous" protesting activities and comments, Dan was once exiled from the archdiocese of New York. He's known loneliness, camaraderie, great appreciation and honors, bitter recriminations and condemnations. He has written more than fifty books, both poetry and prose. One of Dan's works is a play, The Trial of the Catonsville Nine; it explores the inner feelings of those who are actually doing civil disobedience, "calling power to account." Dan stressed that activists do not promote hate, or any sense of revenge or disdain for another human being.

He loves writing and he loves his Jesuit community, his home of cherishing, his family, including his beloved late brother Phil, and a wide circle of friends, admirers and supporters.

SOME
A Poem by Daniel Berrigan, S.J.

Some stood up once
and sat down.
Some walked a mile
and walked away.

Some stood up twice
and sat down.
I've had it!
they said.

Some walked 2 miles

and walked away.
It's too much!
they cried.

Some stood and stood and stood.
They were taken for fools
they were taken for being taken in.

Some walked and walked and walked.
They were asked, and
why do you stand?

Because of the heart, they said, and
because of the children, and
because of the bread.

Because
the cause
is the heart's beat
and the children born,
and the risen bread.

As Yellow Flowers to the Butterfly: de Brébeuf

Verses for *Jubilee 2000*
Morgan Zo-Callahan

> *People who go deeply enough into their own faith to be truly transformed by it are comfortable with that faith and feel no need to convince others of it.*
>
> —Clark Strand

Robert Blair Kaiser and Tim Smith's musical comedy, *Jubilee 2000*, tracks three bickering angels who lead the audience on a time-travel through two thousand years of Christian history. When Kaiser was writing the book, he asked if any *compañeros* or *compañeras* would like to write a few verses which Jean de Brébeuf, the sainted Jesuit missionary to the Huron in Canada, would lovingly sing back to Mohawk and Algonquin Indian saint, Kateri Tekakwitha. Bob Holstein asked me to give it a try, so, because I've always admired Brébeuf, I wrote a few lines to be sung by his character in play.

I recalled reading about Brébeuf, as one who reverenced, with all his humanity, the Huron and their culture, with the appreciation and admiration of the goodness of all people. He respected the people first and foremost. He spread Jesus by being like Jesus. Certainly, he wanted to share his faith in Jesus, as he knew it. But there didn't seem to be any insistence in his way of teaching. He would let those who were attracted to his Jesus come naturally. He didn't force his Catholicism on the Indian people. He didn't feel any prejudices (including wanting to change others) regarding the social conditions, the culture of the Indians. He felt all was just as valid as his French societal sensibilities. The Hurons were and continue to be a very amazing people.

Sadly, as well as running into such wonderfully unassuming and "down to earth" missionaries, I've encountered condescending missionaries of Protestant, Catholic, Muslim,

Hindu and Buddhist inclination. Not to mention self-proclaimed, abusive, arrogant gurus. It's a contradiction in the heart to "look down" on other religions, races, and cultural expressions. So that's why Brébeuf, and people such as Padre Kino and Bartolomé de las Casas (1474–1566), are refreshing examples as missionaries in the best sense, marvelous human beings. I've found Las Casas to be a great advocate and protector of Indians and black Africans, slaves of the Spaniards who were often treated with extreme cruelty. Over the course of his life, Las Casas traveled from Spain to Mexico, Peru, Guatemala, and Nicaragua and when he left the New World to return to Madrid at age seventy-three, he continued to speak out against slavery and the mistreatment of anyone. He openly took the side of the Indian's righteous complaints of human rights abuses. His life was full of severe opposition, but Las Casas never gave up. He put into the consciousness of the church that the rights of people must be respected and when violated, cannot be swept under the rug.

Brébeuf's life exemplifies a deep friendship with the Huron, realizing he's in love with the people who may be on the surface different. He experiences the Huron as full of life and wisdom. He's in awe of the people he's serving; he delights in them.

Brébeuf, a poet too, called "*Eton*," Healing Tree" by the Indians, wrote this pretty Christmas Carol in the Huron language:

It was in the moon of winter time
When all the birds had fled.
Mighty Gitchi-Manitou
Sent angel choirs instead.
In their golden light, the stars grew dim.

Wandering hunters heard the hymn.
Within a lodge of broken bark,

169

A tender babe was found.
Ragged tiny robes of rabbit skin
Enwrapped his shining beauty all around.

Hunter braves drew so intimately close.
Angels singing, ringing loud and high.

Children of the forest free,
O sons and daughters of Manitou,
A holy child of earth and heaven
Is born today for you.

Come, kneel before the radiant boy
Who brings beauty, peace and joy.
Jesus, your king is born
Jesus is born in *excelsis gloria*.

Brébeuf suggested some practical and sensitive instructions for Jesuits destined to work among the Huron: "You must love these Huron, ransomed by the blood of the Son of God; love them as brothers and sisters. You must never keep the Indians waiting at the time of embarking. Carry a tinderbox or piece of burning glass, or both, to make fire for them during the day for smoking, and in the evening when it is necessary to camp. Be the least troublesome to the Indians. Do not ask many questions; silence is truly golden. Bear with imperfections and be cheerful. Do not be ceremonious and do not begin to paddle unless you intend always to paddle." I've found these words inspirational for serving as a teacher to immigrant people, some also quite different in their backgrounds and cultures. Brébeuf impresses me as a man who really loved people truly as his brothers and sisters.

Here is my small poem. It was used in the performances of *Jubilee 2000* in Canada. Kateri Tekakwitha sings plaintively:

Rooted in the earth, the wisdom of creation
Blossomed in a lily, within an ancient nation:
Reverence for our Mother, Faith that's giving birth,
Nature is our teacher, the wisdom of the earth,
Setting things in order, putting Jesus first.

Listen to the hunger
Quench the deeper thirst
A lily is a healer,
Suffering as we go,
A sign of resurrection in the seasons of the soul.

Jean de Brébeuf responds, singing my imagined words:

Snow melting,
watering green spindly firs
like black morning birds, my soul stirs.

singing to orange-yellow Father Sun, shiny blue lakes
water-coloring mountains and sky.

Heart melting,
Embracing you, Huron People,
your original voices calling me Eton, 'Healing Tree.'

So you honor me.
Yet sweet Indian Sister, Native Brother,
it is I, I drawn to you,

as yellow flowers to the butterfly,
as yellow flowers to the butterfly.

Matraca
Visiting Southern Mexico's Street Children
Morgan Zo-Callahan

Matraca, for me, principally stands not as a cause or an appeal, but as a metaphor for my own conversation, self-inquiry and learning about poverty among the working street children in Veracruz and Chiapas where I've traveled for several years.

For me Matraca comes to mean: Help—Be of true service to others, both rich and poor.

Matraca also is an acronym for *Movimiento de Apoyo a Trabajadores de la Calle (Services for Working Street Children)* an organization based in Xalapa, Veracruz. *Matraca* means "noise-maker," a wooden toy that Mexican children use to celebrate and play. It makes a raucous, clacking noise. I imagine it represents children's lively expressions of spaciousness and glee when they are not being neglected or abused, free to explore and discover.

Hooray! Let loose! Spin, whirl that *matraca*! Dance. Laugh. Be free to grow, dear human flower. That's our *metta* for you, our heartfelt wish that you be well, happy, in circumstances where you can grow and blossom.

In Mexico, there are about one hundred eighty thousand children and adolescents who live in the streets; twenty thousand of them are less than five years old. Matraca, the organization, was started in 1991 by a Jesuit priest, David Fernández, and then directed by Juan Francisco Kitazawa, as part of the University of Veracruz community's outreach to these children. Its purpose is social, educative and formative assistance for child and adolescent workers, some living on the street. Director Octavio Diaz: "From the weakest we have learned that the hope for an ever-more just world is a task that we must all face together in order to create it; it's a gamble on brotherhood, on humanity; a gamble on love."

Xalapa signifies "sandy waters" in Nahuatl. It's in the

center of the state of Veracruz, ancestral land of the Olmecs, Totonacas, Chichimecas, Toltecas and Teochichimecas, the birthplace of Mexico's pre-Colombian cultures, still lightly whispering to us through ancient art. The lonely jagged peaks of Sierra Madre Oriental dominate the landscape of western Veracruz. Rolling green foothills unveil fields of flowers, rich coffee beans, *animalitos, gente genial....*

It was in the nearby gray-cool harbor of Veracruz that Hernán Cortez cast down his aggressive anchor in 1519, going on from there to conquer the Aztecs. Now the state of Veracruz is a 450-mile stretch, a multi-colored-blended tapestry of seven million people, most of them indigenous, with a mixture of Spaniards, Africans, Italians, Greeks, French and Cubans.

Some three thousand years ago, the Olmecs predominated here, a sophisticated race that created their own mathematics, their own religious myths and calendar, which was later adopted by the Aztecs and the Mayas. They were master carvers of giant basalt heads, nine to ten feet tall, nine to ten tons in weight, with large-lips and broad-noses and facial expressions that seem to express a faint disapproval.

Today at the port of Veracruz, at that magical moment of sunrise: barest light on hundreds of eager boats pushing into the sea, waters gradually illuminated by pinks and oranges, dabbled on oil-rig-shadowed silvery water, fresh *esperanzas* for an abundant catch.... And into the evening, lively marimba bands, *danzon, cervezas,* seafood, giggling-joyfully shrieking children, a beggar—lifted for a delicious moment from his squalor—mesmerized by rhythmic-sensual rounds of dancing in the sweating plaza.

The working kids in Xalapa pass hours in the streets selling gum, cleaning car windshields, flagging down taxis, begging—sometimes as clowns and jugglers. They spend a lot of time trying to stay one-step ahead of the *Seguridad Publica* whose officers try to get them out of the streets. Most of the children maintain a bond with their families. About 150 of Xalapa's three thousand working children have no home, no place to learn their ABCs, get their meals or any kind of medical care.

Street children, working kids, homeless young people here often sell their bodies to survive. According to government statistics, some sixteen thousand Mexican minors prostitute themselves; six of ten are boys. Some 60 percent of them are victims of sexual abuse; half of them have drug problems. Abusive pimps inject some of them with anabolic steroids to increase their sexual attractiveness. Ten percent are HIV positive. Five percent are teen moms.

It's Easter week, and I'm at Matraca's downtown facility of classrooms, offices, medical dispensary, kitchen, and showers. Young teens Omar, Miguel, and Juan talk to me about their lives on the streets. They play *futbol* and basketball with other children in Matraca's outside patio. One of the boys, drying off from a shower, pops his head out, hair over his eyes, like a seal emerging at sea-surface. Robert Colorado, hoping for tips, washes windshields at a nearby traffic intersection. He tells me how he and four other youngsters were recently detained for three days as a "traffic menace." I have a short talk with Angela Muñoz who works in an agrarian movement with indigenous people, helping farmers get access to water, tools and quality seeds. She says they want to be self-sufficient and how she admires the quiet dignity that informs their organizing together. I visit with Lara, a pretty, bright volunteer from Spain who for two years takes university students to assist and learn from outlying *barrios*. We check out the classrooms, offices, medical dispensary, kitchen, and showers for street youngsters.

Angelina tells me about the seven young girls and one six-year-old boy—all homeless—whom she lives with and cares for in Casa Matraca. Vanessa Torres describes going into the streets to support working children by providing snacks, art projects. Octavio tells me about working against a newly proposed law that will lower the penal age of young people from sixteen to fourteen in the state of Veracruz.

That night, Easter Saturday, *Sabado de Gloria, catedral, llena de gente*, lights from orange-flamed candles passed to each other, spreading blessing rays to everyone, even to the bent-to-the-ground *anciana*, who is selling *cositas* for pennies in the park across the cobbled street. Yes, I think, better to pass on wishes to create happiness, rather than "to curse the darkness."

Later, I say hi to two young sisters who sell and beg into the night. The older sister, age eight, recognizes me and takes my hand to see some assorted toys spread on blankets, all crafted by her indigenous family. She sways as a dancer in the dark, with red roses for sale in her arms. Her little sister, deep dark brown eyes expanded, listens to our conversation, quickly darting with an outreached hand to passers-by for a coin. Their vigilant mother is close by and comes over to greet me. She asks one of the boys to show me his juggling skills.

I'm at Casa Matraca, a home for abandoned or needy children just outside the city. It was originally given to the Jesuits, and is now owned by Matraca, a civil work, incorporated as a non-profit organization without religious affiliation. Angelina lovingly takes care of the children and is called "Mom." Some of the children previously just lived on the streets where they were robbed, beaten and sometimes forced into prostitution. Some lived in abusive families. Now they go to school and help in the house as well as receive medical and psychological counseling. Some will re-integrate with their families. In the evening, we have a birthday party for one of the girls. I see her crying because her mom who promised to come doesn't show up. "She never shows up." The children kiss her and sing *Las Mañanitas* to her and play the guitar and dance to Credence Clearwater and *cumbias* music. A party breaks out.

I go to visit families in the village of Miahuatlan. The huge church dominates, hovering over the small homes, its dome at one end and a three-tiered bell tower at the other. Seems like just older folks and children remain, with young adults fleeing to the cities or to *el sueño Americano*. About two hundred of the population of the four thousand in town have made it across the border to join the eleven million or so native-born Mexicans who live in the United States of America. Young people tell me they must leave because manufacturing, oil-producing, fishing, raising sugar-cane, beans, bananas, coffee doesn't employ enough or pay enough. Some *compañeros* have sent money for individual school tuitions (about $30 a year) and money for single moms with kids to buy *puestos* (about $40 for these small mobile stands to start a small selling business). A fourteen-year-old girl who suffers from slight cerebral palsy runs one of the mobile stands. She's wearing a pretty pink and white dress and says hello; a customer asks her to demonstrate that a lighter she's selling works properly, but she just can't quite manage. Spontaneously, seemingly out of nowhere, a swarthy young man sweeps the lighter out of her hand and elegantly flicks a flame to satisfy her nodding, approving customer.

In Orizaba, Veracruz, I visit the group, *Vivir Joven*, which runs a shelter and educational facility for working youth. The project was born from a group of mothers and fathers who went to meetings in the Cathedral of Orizaba. They help some poor indigenous families in *La Sierra de Zongolica*—a mountain area where many children suffer malnutrition. They also work with young people in the city streets of Orizaba and support some young abandoned and orphaned boys in a home-shelter named *Casa Hogar La Concordia*.

Only five kilometers from Orizaba, you find the entrance into la Sierra de Zongolica (ascending up to twenty-three hundred meters above sea level). It's composed of fifteen municipalities, 75 percent indigenous, who suffer a high rate of unemployment and low salaries (15-35 pesos a day). I meet some hardy workers who put in a day of 7:00 AM to 6:00 PM, cultivating corn and coffee.

Several families leave their land, for varying lengths of time, seeking better pay in the city of Orizaba. The children often beg in the streets and/or sell flowers, herbal teas, some crafts and wool products. *Vivir Joven* visits with street children, bringing food and support, with an open invitation to the services of its shelter.

A Heart-Breaking Evening

A sixteen-year-old boy I've known for several years is waiting outside of downtown Matraca to talk with me. He was abandoned, along with his sister, when he was eight. Over the years, he would take advantage of a few of the services at Matraca but liked finding his own places to sleep, his own ways to survive.

I always looked forward to being with him and, at times, his sister, learning about their lives, encouraging them to go to school, with available scholarships. He had struggled in previous years, often using cheap inhalants to warm himself. Guiding tourists (sometimes to prostitutes and drugs) would bring him tips. But this night he was disconsolate. He told me about his now seventeen-year-old sister, who—unknown to him—worked as a prostitute for a year, before committing suicide. "She despaired," he said bleakly.

Long into a blackest night, we sobbed together. Raging like mad wolves, we howled in the sleeping dark town. We wept and were silent. We sent our loving feelings and so many stories and smiles through tears, to a teenage girl who was killed by her own misery.

Chiapas

Matraca celebrated its tenth anniversary in 2001, highlighted by a visit from Bishop Samuel Ruiz, who had done so much to defend the human rights of the indigenous in Mexico and especially in Chiapas, Mexico's southernmost state. He is fluent in Tzotzil and Tzeltal, the region's two most important indigenous languages, and, *con gran gusto y respeto a todos,* he served for forty years in Chiapas before he resigned on his seventy-fifth birthday, on November 3, 1999. When I think of this friend of the poor, I'm reminded of Rumi: *I'm so small, I can barely be seen. How can this great love be inside me? Look at your eyes: they're small, but they see enormous things.*

Ideas of Mexican Revolution's social shaking, almost a hundred years ago, still stir in some leaders such as Samuel Ruiz: wanting the sharing of land, resources, dignified work; appreciation for indigenous culture-religion-customs; nurturing-educating children; changing from the exploitation of the poorest into an inclusive "fair-trading" giving and taking of goods and services.

Chiapas has a population of four million, and is a land of spectacular flowers, lakes, plants, rivers, hills, volcanoes, thick jungles, and forests producing mahogany and rosewood. Tourists come here to see the Mayan archaeological sites of Palenque, Bonampak, Izapa, Yaxchilan.

I meet with some indigenous Maya who are giving a presentation about their culture. They live in the forest, listening, appreciating, being fed by its life. They say we should stay open, in spite of our more "civilized" sensibilities (and with recognition of admirable progressive trends of city civilization); open to our bodies, the extension of which is our living environment. Our attention in modern day living is mostly absorbed away from natural settings.

The men—with Prince Valiant type haircuts—are dressed in white tunics, speaking through interpreters, of wanting to live "as the Earth does," accepting silences, being silent ourselves and not-knowing so absolutely, but reverencing what is Larger than we are, but of Which, an alive Totality, we are intimately a part. They ask us to join them in periods of silence. I think of Chuang-Tzu: *Where can I find a man who has forgotten words? I'd like to have a word with him.*

They speak of listening to variations, differences, natural

disaster, the routine and the spectacular. Politically and socially, they want interchange. They don't want to be absorbed by the popular culture, but to be a part of an inclusive emerging global economy. "We are connected to you, within the web of our forest life, with the ant, the pig, the sheep, the goat, the sun, the water, the wood, the fire, family, community, the corn and coffee." We are surely relative and relational, interconnected as the white-blue globe must appear to those riding in space.

On a cool, soft rainy evening I'm in *Parque Central de San Cristobal*, Chiapas. The Mexican Marine Corps, snappily uniformed, full orchestra and chorus, are singing their guts and hearts out: operatics and ballads of the Revolution such as "Adelita," a song praising the woman with long black hair to whom the revolutionary will return and, breathing liberty, make beautiful love. The park is packed, yet children still find space to jump as the choir's full voices shake a giant banner of two doves about to kiss, perched in the blue skies. *Todos a la Feria de la Primavera y de la Paz.* Peace. *Paz* to you. Violins, singing, tears touching so much pain and suffering and loves, joy of the aliveness of such emotion. *Dulces*, popcorn, steamed corn on the cob, dancing, waving, flirting. *Esperanza.* Hope for peace. For economic and political tranquility.

Luis Arriaga, lawyer and Jesuit scholastic, takes me to visit Acteal and *Las Abejas*, a peaceful group of Tzotzil Indians organized in 1992. We drive windy roads in a Nissan pickup, at times along pretty green forests, people scurrying with wood tied to their backs or pushing goats. *Las Abejas* community in Acteal are "displaced," peaceful revolutionaries, organizing for social justice, still a mourning community because of the massacre of forty-five of their members on December 22, 1997, an attack by paramilitaries who surrounded their community from 11:30 AM to 6:00 PM

Ernesto Paciencia (secretary of the Acteal community) shows me the makeshift chapel where so many, praying and fasting for peace were killed and the hilly gorges where people fled, a pregnant young woman stripped, violated, baby cut from her womb. Exactly forty-five bodies are buried in two layers in a concrete tomb, where Ernesto shows me pictures on the walls of the deceased, including his mother and sister. We sit quietly for several minutes. We embrace in our common fragility. We cannot hide our tears.

Pretty Zenaida, now holding hands so tenderly with *abuelita*, is one of the fifty children orphaned; she's blind from taking a bullet to the head.

Later we go to a wake, for the community's friend, Victoriano, in the mountains, our Nissan pickup sometimes sliding backwards, a donated coffin sticking out diagonally in the back. A few horses stare at us when we finally find a large community, some weeping around the corpse of their Victoriano, friend, relative, husband and father. He was fifty-two. Luis speaks the truth, with some irony when he says, "He died of poverty."

Many men wear white tunics. Three men play a cheerful melody: a violin, a guitar, and harp. The blanket-covered corpse is placed in the wooden coffin with some of Victoriano's belongings and a few *peso* coins. We smell unavoidable death and the life and humanity around it. As we leave, we are offered corn tortillas with beans, cooked over an open fire. They taste *muy rico,* as we stand eating, offering condolences, smoke in our faces.

Mexico City

Camping on cobblestone at the 1998 Congress For Indigenous, April 13–15. Such an inspiring happening, so invigorated being here! Fifty-six different ethnic groups are represented, co-mingling and peacefully marching for *derechos humanos.* I live with large groups on the *zócalo* for four days and three nights in open tents, on this *gran plaza* of *México Viejo,* risen from *Lago de Texcoco,* thousands of Indian peoples. Watching are heavily armed soldiers. They arrest some foreigners, so they can toss them out of the country.

Indigenous people are giving up being submissive Indians and demanding to be treated as equal human beings. There are marches and protests against economic oppression of Indian laborers and people. I hear other languages all around me: Tarahumara, Chol, Mixteco, Nahuatl, Zogue, Zapoteco. Banners fly, greens, reds, whites of Mexican flag: *Dignidad para los Indigenos and Nunca mas un México sin Nosotros.*

On the ruins of *El Templo Mayor*, the tall dusty crooked gray cathedral reflects light beams on the people, like reluctant blessings from a prudish grandmother. Inside the cathedral, I contemplate a painting of our Lady of Guadalupe and softly colored statues of St. Ignatius, Philip Neri, Dominic; Francis Assisi faces a black crucified Jesus, knees swayed and covered with a gold skirt.

It's late night, into the morning; I'm sleeping on blankets, so close, touching this plaza, sinking into this stone-blocked plaza, graced and warmed by hospitable indigenous, young and old. I'm visioning golden Aztec temples, enlightened, feathered priests dancing on tops of pyramids, supplicating a mystery. Now we're together, calling for a fresh—and non-violent—kind of human sacrifice to each other.

I am so enriched and nourished by my time with people and families of Southern Mexico: *tristezas, alegrias,* sharing ideas, hugs, laughter and crying, the sudden sweetness of children.

Leticia, Angelina, and Guadalupe Can Change the World—if Given the Chance!
The Story of Casa Matraca and the Advocacy for
Homeless and/or Working Children
Morgan Zo-Callahan

The sight of children working on the streets of Veracruz, Mexico is shocking to most US Americans. The problems of poverty and drug addiction are complicated, but sometimes the solutions seem very straightforward. I had the privilege of learning about one such project, and some of its struggles, from two wonderful, dedicated women, and a girl who was herself homeless. Leticia Alba is a dedicated and highly effective civil servant; Angelina Lopez Cuevas is an ordinary woman who is doing an extraordinary job; Guadalupe Velasco Hernandez is an adolescent girl who has become an advocate for children out of her own experience of homelessness and addiction. I will let them tell their own stories.

■

It's April 23, 2003 and I'm talking with pretty, bespectacled Leticia Alba who works for the Veracruz State Commission for Human Rights. She is the Director of Attention to Women, Vulnerable Groups and Victims. We spoke in her modern office (with the shiniest wood furniture) in Xalapa, Veracruz.

Leticia has a very dignified lightness and brightness about her. She is sharp and compassionate. Both her intelligence and caring for children and vulnerable persons is obvious. I visited Leticia to talk to her specifically about children, but she told me also how important her work was for HIV/AIDS patients and for the elderly. She outlines her job and gives some of the major obstacles she faces.

MZC: Would you talk about your job? What is the purpose of your work?

LTC: The Commission for Human Rights has established this office to represent and give attention to the most vulnerable members of our community: the elderly, those with AIDS, abused women and children. Many children are working in the streets and need to have representation of their human rights.

MZC: I'm aware that there are laws that state children cannot work until the age of fourteen. Yet the needs of many families require children to work at very young ages. Are such laws just overlooked?

LTC: Yes, the parents want the children to work. Our job is to make sure that these working children are treated respectfully, even if not old enough to work legally. They have rights and we are determined to see that they are not exploited. Take the case of children who work in our supermarkets. Perhaps they bag groceries and the like. Well, most of the large supermarkets only accept children who attend school, have good grades, and pay proper attention to cleanliness and appearance. Such jobs are sought out and, to a certain extent, we can say they are being well treated and are accepted and appreciated in our society and economy. Yet, on the other hand, it's sad seeing such working children of eight or nine—even under healthy working conditions. Why? Because they should be playing soccer, having fun with their friends, learning more and so on. But these children are helping the economy of their families and are not as free as other children "to be children."

MZC: Who accepts responsibility for children who work for large companies and may, for example, get hurt or get sick?

LTC: Usually the parents of the children have to sign a letter accepting all the responsibility. We are working to get the companies to share legally in protecting all their workers, including the children. There should be a type of insurance for these children.

MZC: How about the children we see working in the streets and working for small businesses? Isn't there a large contrast between many of these children and the children working in the large supermarkets? Are there any groups in Veracruz that reach out to the children working in the streets?

LTC: Yes, we are most concerned with this group of children who find themselves selling in the streets, washing windshields and the like. We've worked with civil institutes such as Matraca to protect the legal rights of these children who are in the streets and often, too often, have trouble with the police. They may be abused or even find themselves in jail, as you know. We offer assistance to these children. For example, the police have taken away children who help carry bags to taxis in front of hotels. We advocate for those children and make sure the police do not over-step their authority.

MZC: Do you find more consciousness and resources around children's rights? Isn't this protection of children a community responsibility? How about the children of indigenous people?

LTC: That's right. I do find that all of us—including those of us in public service—are growing in awareness of the needs of the most vulnerable in our society, that we can't ignore them. I can't say whether there are more resources to offer better services to children, but there is more knowledge about where the help and service for the most vulnerable children is available. There are five centers in the state of Veracruz that specifically reach out to the indigenous, speaking their languages and so on.

MZC: Are you optimistic about your work? What are your personal aspirations in relation to your admirable efforts?

LTC: Yes, I'm optimistic, but there is so much to do. We have to keep going; this is a most human work and there are many ways to offer a human touch and intervention to the vulnerable of our society. Such problems have always existed and demand both intense, intelligent labor and a sensitive heart.

∎

My Ongoing Conversation with Angelina Lopez Cuevas about Casa Matraca

I first met Angelina in 1998, visiting Casa Matraca, which provides a home for an average of ten girls who find themselves homeless. Angelina has been the loving housemother who has taken care of these children. It's a delight and an inspiration to talk with her. She and her husband Jose along with her daughter Gladis, who was four years old at the time, moved into Casa Matraca in 1998. Gladis is now thirteen years old, and attends junior high school; Jose still works as a waiter; and Angelina continues to be responsible for the Casa.

Angelina was very shy at first. She is a soft person, lovely light caramel brown skin, languid large brown eyes, soft spoken, sometimes wondering what to say. Over the years, I've seen her develop as an articulate and confident communicator of her work. I love the Mexican custom of greeting Mexican women with a kiss on both cheeks, especially with such a lovely lady as Angelina!

The following is a compilation of chats with Angelina, some on audiocassette, one on a DVD, one via intermediary, Octavio Lara, Director of Matraca. My last conversation with Angelina was on March 24, 2008 in the downtown offices of Matraca in Xalapa, Veracruz.

MZC: What is the history of Casa Matraca?

ALC: The first Casa Matraca was opened in 1993 with the purpose of being a refuge for homeless children and adolescents; it was a rented house, called "Refugio," where youngsters could pass the night. We were hoping to start a process where kids had avenues leading away from street life.

We always started directing children to help with getting off drugs, stopping robbing and the like; then we offer a place to live for those who are ready for and need a permanent residence, healthy meals, social assistance, support to attend school, health services, recreation, legal help and defense when necessary. At first, Casa Matraca was only for boys; now it's only for girls. But since the beginning, we've had a few girls who came to us directly from the streets, desperately looking for help.

MZC: I know at first you weren't sure about being involved in this work with homeless girls. It was very new to you. How did you finally become convinced that you wanted to do this service, to have a caring relationship with these girls?

ALC: I was at first afraid of the prospect of taking care of children, living with them. Really I was afraid, seeing the circumstances from which they came and not knowing what to do. As I began learning from the children, really seeing their goodness and need, I wanted to stay with them. I became motivated to love them, so a lot of my fear disappeared. I saw with my own eyes how these children had no future, no hope for education, having a career and a good family life. I experienced at the same time this great potential in the children, this ability to grow to be healthy, happy people. They only needed security, a home, and an opportunity for education. I wanted to provide a stage where children could show and develop their beautiful qualities.

MZC: Why did you change from boys to girls? I think you must have a soft spot for girls, since you, Angelina, have such a lovely daughter, your Gladis?

ALC: Well, it's we women who will change this cold world (laughing). No, you know I love all children the same. It's been almost ten years that Casa Matraca has only offered services for girls who found themselves on the street or who were imminently in danger of being in the street.

MZC: I know Casa Matraca was going to close due to

economic problems. All the boys who were living in Casa Matraca were placed in other apartments with financial help to rent a room, for example, with one of the teachers/teachers' families.

ALC: At this time in the late 90s, all of a sudden more girls were appearing in the streets. As an organization, Matraca reflected about the situation in our town of Xalapa for children who do not have permanent homes. We were aware of the group *DIF Estatal (Desarrollo Integral del Familia) (Integral Development of the Family)* that is run by the state of Veracruz. It offers a home for street boys, but not for girls. The Catholic Church has a house for abandoned children, but not for children coming from the situation of living on the street. A group of Catholic religious has a house for girls, but for abandoned girls only. So we felt we could fill a need—yes in a modest way—for vulnerable girls who were coming to us from street life and whom we felt to suffer the greatest harmful risks.

MZC: What was it like for you when you started to work and live at Casa Matraca with your husband, Jose, and daughter, Gladis?

ALC: It wasn't easy at first. Matraca was broke, barely affording the upkeep of the second Casa Matraca, a house outside of town, donated by the Jesuits. It just sat there for a while with no inhabitants to take care of it. Of course, there was vandalism. Then some homeless youngsters, feeling no alternative just broke into the house, destroying doors, windows. We did our best to help these youngsters, guiding them to others sources of help and also protecting ourselves by having people live in Casa Matraca at night. Before we could open Casa Matraca, we had to fix it up. We put an ad in the paper to have people live in the house and take care of it, pay for water, electricity and so on. That's when I was connected to Matraca, because my husband, Jose, was interviewed by

Octavio (Matraca's director) and we moved into Casa Matraca. That was ten years ago.

We wanted to open again, impelled by many young girls reaching out for a steady refuge and home. The girls just started arriving. We were at first only in Casa Matraca to take care of it, but soon I was taking care of girls. I was doing my service to the Lord, a service I love. *Me encanta mi trabajo.* It's not always easy; sometimes I take a weekend off. But for the most part, I feel, with lots of joy, available twenty-four hours to these girls. Since you've visited Casa Matraca, you know one of our girls has been here for the total nine years and will soon be leaving, with hopes and the intention of going to the university. Her teachers say she will be able to do the university work. That makes me cry with gratitude and pride. We presently are reviewing the cases of five girls who want to live in Casa Matraca.

Let me tell you a little about four other of our girls who are living with us now in Casa Matraca in 2008. This will give you an idea of their supplementary education and also of how they utilize the psychological services available. Some of the older girls may work part-time to help with some of their needs. Matraca, as you know, accepts that child labor is a fact of the unjust Mexican economy, but we make sure the conditions in which our children work are healthy and fair and that the children stay in school.

One little girl came to us when she was six years old and now is in her third year of secondary school. She's had therapy with a psychologist since she was eight years old. She's interested in being a grammar school teacher. She has taken occupational courses in Beauty Shop and in Bakery. She's now enjoying a guitar class, photography class and manual arts, working with clay. She participates on the soccer team in her school.

Another girl began living in Casa Matraca when she was nine years old and is now seventeen years old, in her third year of high school. She dreams of being a professional pianist. She's studied piano since she was five years old and also has taken courses in sewing, dance, theater, photography, drawing, and some arts and crafts. She participated for a few weekends in the winter planting season for vegetables. She's benefited from therapy since she was ten years old.

Our oldest girl is eighteen years old and has lived here for five years. She is finishing her third year of high school and wants to be a businesswoman. She has gone to therapy since she was thirteen years old. She has taken courses in Beauty Shop, painting, making clay masks, drawing, and playing the mandolin.

A seven-year-old girl is completing her first year with us. She's in first grade. She likes to make earrings and bracelets and is interested in the recycling of paper products. All of these girls are concentrating on their studies. I feel that education will give our girls the chance to succeed. Success as a happy person is what they deserve. I love them all and have seen growth in them all. This fuels my enthusiasm to carry on.

Our girls are producing some very beautiful handicrafts; soon we are planning an exhibition of our finest crafts.

MZC: What does being a Catholic mean for you? How does it affect your work?

ALC: My work is just an expression of following Jesus. I feel working in the Casa is my God-given vocation, so it gives me peace and an inner happiness. I work with other groups, not just Catholics. There are Christians who want to support our effort. I encourage the girls to learn from the life of Jesus, to pray and to go to mass. Yet I don't feel I force my ideas on them; I just speak from my heart and desire that the girls are protected and grow in all the ways possible. They must decide for themselves if they want to live as Catholics or not. Some of our girls have sung in choir; others have participated in religious studies at the church.

I think God wants us to care for the homeless. We are the

hands and heart of Jesus here on earth. Didn't Jesus teach us this? I find that the work we do contributes to the nobility of our souls. It doesn't matter what our beliefs are. It's a growing generosity of spirit that I witness in this work and which I want to nurture in myself. Yes, the nobility of our spirits.

MZC: What's a day like in Casa Matraca? What schedule do the girls keep? What challenges do you face?

ALC: Well, first of all, we must provide the girls with security. Some of them have been terribly abused and exploited. We need to give them an environment where they don't feel afraid, where they feel cared for, even if psychological care is needed. We never, of course, leave the girls alone. It's worth all the effort we invest in these lovely girls; we see, we're witnesses to positive changes in their lives. All the girls are required to go to school and they are happy to do so for the most part. At the same time, the girls have the chance to speak with a counselor or therapist, as well as attending various educational workshops which help their growth.

Some of the girls are able to pass some weekends with members of their families; they come back full of stories and some satisfaction of being with their families in peaceful, healthy ways. This maturing of the girls, the growing happiness of most of the girls is the best feeling. Like when my daughter is happy in the real ways.

The hard part for me is when I just get completely blown off the track, in all ways. There are times when I feel "knocked down," but my faith in the good, the divine in each child always keeps me going eventually. I have my bad days. At times the realities that these youngsters present me can just devastate me personally and emotionally. You and I talked once about how we helpers have to take care of ourselves and to get help when we need it. I've come to see how our effort involves many of us together. I want to make our work known to those interested, some of whom will help us to continue this work with a "marginalized population," our children and adolescents who work and live in the streets, here in Xalapa. And, of course, this leads to more consciousness about homelessness in our various communities.

MZC: What's important to you about working at Casa Matraca? What are your goals and intentions in your work with ten homeless girls and adolescents? How do you conceive Casa Matraca?

ALC: Casa Matraca, as you know, started in 1993. We've known each other a bit for the last ten years and you've seen how it's evolved to be a home to take care of, really take care of, to love and nourish and establish conditions where these girls and young adolescents may grow into independent, good people improving their lives and later that of their own children.

We are appreciative of the charitable donations of groups such as the *compañeros* and generous individuals have given us to provide a home for these girls. I'm doing my part and you're doing yours. Of course, Casa Matraca is just a part of Matraca, an integral part. Matraca does work to address the systemic causes that put our girls on the cold, drug-filled streets in the first place. Matraca has volunteers from Europe and the United States. There isn't a culture of volunteerism here in Mexico.

You used to live here in Xalapa so you know how tough it is for our street children and adolescents. Sometimes adolescents get forgotten as supposedly "grown up." To you and me, they are big kids, at the critical time of their lives. Some of the girls here in Casa Matraca have become difficult at times. But I love my very practical work of providing direct help to these girls. I've come to love them as my own daughter, Gladis, and Gladis loves them like sisters and brothers. We work with very poor girls and adolescents who had the traumatic experience of living in the streets or being on the verge of living on the streets. Our focus is to offer up to ten girls, a community full of life, care, and responsibilities to study and to be healthy and morally good. We want to be the base, the ground, the good

191

earth for them. We want their inner shining to come out and bring some peace and goodness into our community. We're doing Jesus' work in a small way.

■

Guadalupe Hernandez lived in Casa Matraca from age seven to fifteen; she took a great interest in her studies and became an excellent student. When she expressed an interest in studying about juvenile justice in her state of Veracruz and in all of Mexico, the director of Matraca, Octavio Lara, encouraged her and invited her to make a public presentation. At the time of her talk, seventeen states of Mexico's thirty-two states had laws that established the penal age at sixteen or fifteen, and the governor of the state of Veracruz, Miguel Aleman Velasco, proposed lowering his state's penal law for children from sixteen to fourteen. Fortunately, in 2007, the Attorney General of Mexico established the penal age at eighteen for all states of Mexico.

A Plea Not to Reduce the Penal Law from Age Sixteen to Age Fourteen in the State of Veracruz

A talk by Guadalupe Velasco Hernandez during the "Forum for Children" at downtown Matraca, Xalapa, Veracruz, 2003.

Good Afternoon, my name is Guadalupe Velasco Hernandez. I'm fifteen years old, and I live in Casa Matraca. Today I'm going to talk about my living circumstance and about the penal age. I'm aware of a movement to reduce the penal age of children to age fourteen.

I was one of a certain kind of girls or adolescents—children who live in the streets, in abandoned houses, in the parks. I'm going to share a small part of my life with you. It all began with family problems when I was seven years old. My grandfather drank and took drugs. My grandmother left each day to work. I never knew my true mother and father. My grandmother left me alone with my abusive grandfather. Under these circumstances, I started to go into the neighborhoods by myself. Then I started hanging out in the streets. I started meeting boys and girls who were taking drugs.

First, I started just visiting my new friends, then I would stay for a day, two days. The first night I slept in the street, I felt a lot of fear. But I was putting on a brave face so I wouldn't seem weak. Inside I was trembling with the fear of being with boys and girls who were high on drugs, who were hallucinating and acting strangely. I felt I was different, that I didn't take drugs, but soon I was staying with them for weeks and months at a time. I became the same as they were; I took drugs; I robbed. I first robbed a small fruit stand, only taking an apple. I did this because I was so hungry. Soon I started stealing other things. I would go to stores downtown and take deodorants or perfumes. But eventually I got caught. And it wasn't a big store, just a stand that sold corn on the cob. The owner called the authorities for that one corn on the cob. I was with three other boys. When we saw the police coming, we ran to the stone walkways around the lakes. You might have thought we were athletes running around the lakes and the police behind, as if we were major criminals. The four of us hid but were found. The police twisted our hands behind us and put us into their patrol van. After, they took us to the other side of the lakes where there aren't people. They took out the three boys and beat them up with kicks and punches. I watched from the side of the police van. Finally they let us go, saying they would punish us severely if we were caught again. Similar experiences happened frequently.

On one occasion, I was taken to San Jose Prison and detained. I was taken from an abandoned house where we were sleeping. We were beaten, including me, despite being a girl. I thought they were going to be easier on me, but they beat me severely, the same as the boys. I felt this wasn't fair. On that occasion, I hadn't robbed or committed any crime. I only was looking for a place to sleep.

So now, with those days behind me, when Matraca invited me to speak about the penal age, I wanted the opportunity to say: "Be fair and help homeless children as well. Make our society more supportive of children. Don't ask children to suffer the same penal consequences as an adult. Try to understand our conditions of living and of not yet being adults. And also I want to advocate directly to you not to lower the penal age here in Veracruz, Mexico.

I don't understand why boys, girls, adolescents who are in the streets are being mistreated if they don't commit a crime or if the nature of the crime is very minor. The homeless children are trying to get food and a place to cover themselves from the cold or from the rain. Seriously, why can't our institutions and organizations do better, create new projects to take care of the situation of homeless children? Why do we feel ignored? Why are we put in jails and holding houses when our only crime is being homeless? Why are we jailed when we are under-aged?

The Constitution of Mexico says we become adult citizens at age eighteen when we are given permission to vote and become able to go to bars or discos, just like all other adults. Granted we aren't all adults, even at age eighteen, as we don't all mature at the same time. Children who are only fifteen or sixteen are being put in jail without respecting their rights. Now there's a movement that wants to make it legal to try and punish fourteen-year-olds as adults. The National Civil Code in Article 450 says that a person who hasn't reached the age of eighteen cannot be submitted to the same adult punishment for a crime; yet many states of Mexico, including our own, do not follow this code. So we have to respect and promote the laws that do protect children and speak against those which do not. We are waiting for change in the laws that will apply to all the states of Mexico.

I do not know so much about the law, but it's one thing

not knowing and another being ignorant of the basic laws we have. I don't believe the thirty-two states of Mexico do not recognize the needs of our laws to make sure that children's rights are respected. It would be a crime in itself to change the law, to lower the penal law. Mexico must respect the human rights of children and adolescents as decreed by the United Nations. I refer you to the Rules of Beijing (the United Nations Standard Minimum Rules for the Administration of Juvenile Justice, adopted by the General Assembly, resolution 40/33, November 29, 1985) which establishes the right of young people to be treated justly, that, from the beginning, they are to be considered innocent (until proof to the contrary) and that the taking away of their liberty must be the last recourse. First and foremost we need to provide alternative programs of rehabilitation and education, combined with effective preventative programs to stop youth from participating in criminal activities.

For these reasons, we should not lower the penal age; further, we must establish the penal age at age eighteen in all the states of Mexico. We must promote the laws, which protect and stand up for children.

Guadalupe now is a struggling single mom and stays in contact with Matraca. She says she is grateful for her years at Casa Matraca.

Being Outside What We Are Inside
Thoughts on Community Organizing
Morgan Zo-Callahan

> *I will no longer act on the outside*
> *in a way that contradicts the truth*
> *that I hold deeply on the inside.*
> *I will no longer act as if I*
> *were less than the whole person*
> *I know myself*
> *inwardly to be*

—Rosa Parks

San Francisco, Spring 1997, A Tribute to Glide Memorial Church

We're visiting Glide Memorial's social services. Some monks have also kindly invited us to the Buddhist center, Spirit Rock, just north of San Francisco. We visited six meal programs for the homeless, including a group that packs up lunch bags and distributes them in public areas where many homeless sleep. We've had a week of full days of talks, discussions, visiting, with the late nights of San Francisco as delicious as ever. We learned from each other and we enjoyed each other's company; we asked lots of questions that meant so much to us.

Question [from a participant]: Can you paraphrase Alinsky's "Rules for Radicals" in light of your organizing tenants who were living in "slum" conditions in Chicago.

MZC: Regarding Saul Alinsky, let me illustrate with an experience during my training as a community organizer. I participated as the community organizer in a project in Chicago, called "POLK-RACINE," where apartment building residents were having trouble with a landlord who refused to spend the money to fix the lead-painted peeling walls, broken plumbing and pest infestation. Some of the kids got lead poisoning from sucking paint chips from the walls.

And "great joy," the landlord was a Catholic! So we organized the people, armed with photographs of slum conditions, to go to the landlord's church, should he refuse to meet with the tenants (he did at first refuse). We came from the solidarity of meetings, educational and artistic presentations, social events, potluck dinners and a dance.

Rules for Radicals

1st rule: Power is not only what you have but also what the "other side" thinks you have.

Even though we were a relatively small group of working poor and welfare tenants, we could present a strong face. The conviction and determination of a small force could make itself "big" in the mind of the landlord we were pressuring to get rid of the lead paint and rats in the apartment building.

2d rule: Don't go outside the experience of the people who want a change. We were clear and emotionally positive about our objective to have a cleaner and safer living environment for our children. Folks would readily volunteer to picket, go to meetings and social events because it was a very down to earth concern that touched them. Mostly Latino, the tenants didn't want to get into political debating, as was common on university campuses. They weren't as anti-establishment as some of the organizers. I found the tenants to be a grounding influence for my overly idealistic ideas of community organizing. They were practical, not ideological.

3d rule: Whenever possible go outside the experience of your opponent. In this case, the landlord was made uncomfortable in his own backyard and within his social and religious group.

4th rule: Make the opponents live up to their own book of rules, e.g. here in this situation we used the Bible.

5th rule: A good tactic is one the people enjoy. If you're

not having fun, feeling alive, something's wrong with your tactics ("having a ball" was Alinsky's phrase). Damn, if it's not fun for all involved, it's not worth it. Not that there aren't challenges, but all are genuinely convinced and enthused about organizing.

6th rule: A tactic that drags on too long becomes a drag. Or, in my words, tactics change with changing conditions. Don't hang on to some worn-out old tactic that might have worked under other societal and cultural circumstances. When the owner agreed to talk, it would have been inappropriate to continue going to his church to show pictures of his deteriorating apartment building. Some of the organizers wanted to go to his church, "to pay him back." But the majority saw this would be applying a tactic when the conditions had changed, which was no longer warranted. At times, we, the organizers, may lose our flexibility to accomplish the change we're focused on or confuse "reform" with "destruction" of an organization or business.

7th rule: Keep the pressure on, adapting and changing your tactics. When you've achieved your realistic goals, move on. Perhaps you may evaluate your goals for a new project, but let's be careful about our hanging on too long. It's healthy for organizations just to disband once it's time and for an individual to separate from an organization once he or she knows it's time.

I hope this gives a flavor of Alinsky's brand of organizing. He was a fireball and a hell-raiser for getting a community's goals accomplished as well as a teacher of aspiring community organizers. He was the genuine product, a community organizer, par excellence. Would the tactics that worked for him, in his times, be helpful in our own times? I don't think so, but his principles of organizing can continue to inspire new and creative tactics appropriate for our own times.

Question: [From a Catholic nun] I feel I'm bored, not having fun (you talked about Alinsky's admonition to the organizer and to the community to have joy and fun). I'm not in that creative process any more. Since I'm a religious, I want to know how I can relate spiritual discernment to my life as a community organizer. I'm not sure what to do and I'd like more security about myself and what I'm doing.

I want to know how to stay close to my own heart which I call God's will, understanding my truest yearnings. I appreciate also those who don't have a personal concept of God. I find myself being confronted with the reality of change. How can I understand and appreciate change and still within that change find the peace and love within my own life, in my own meditation and spiritual practices? I want to have more fun and continue to serve as a community organizer. I just don't know where.

MZC: We all need to be open to change. We have to go past our insecurities. We need to feel free enough to say: "The hell with it. This just isn't fun anymore; it's not fulfilling and satisfying to me anymore." And we all notice your good heart and love for the people you've served. Yet I don't equate living as a begrudging organizer with a strong spiritual life. We respect your inquiry into what are your truest desires as you're evolving, running along with all of us, in this unpredictable curvy stream of life.

It's all changing, isn't it? We have to go with it, without our usual grasping and expectations of what we're supposed to do. Righteousness isn't necessary for being an organizer. We aren't being organizers "to look good." We don't care about that. We are still learning, searching. We admit we don't know. We can let go of the need to "jump on any bandwagon" for any cause. We can keep deciding for ourselves, without fear of changing or being afraid that we're not "politically correct" in the minds of other activists, community organizers.

You say what most of us have gone through as volunteers or full-time workers in our cities and in Mexico and Central America, and a few of us in Asia and Africa also. It's all of us together in this blue-and-white circle of Earth, spinning and floating like a tiny living golden jewel in an infinite universe. It's all evolving, a dynamic living process.

Yet, at times, we've all gone through feeling stuck, out of the flow, stuck in the morass of a life that gets too automatic, repetitive, phony, jammed up. We lose mindfulness in what we're doing; our vitality feels inhibited. So your question is ours: how can we assist each other as volunteers when we lose enthusiasm? Further you mention "spiritual discernment" because you are a religious who dedicates herself to serving the poor. Is it possible, you ask, that I should leave El Salvador? Is my journey there finished? Is some inner current impelling me to move on while conflicting feelings "call" me to stay where I am?

It's not so simple when we speak of changing our work. But we know there are enough disgruntled and sour social workers (even religious ones) to know we want honesty with ourselves. We know we need a process of quiet attentiveness where we recognize our minds and hearts, our intentions and desires.

Somehow we may allow ourselves to be stereotyped social do-gooders, trouble-making liberals, whatever. We've been bent up and out of whack enough to know about self-categorizing and responding to "labels." So we need time to feel and listen to our deep selves, untouched by all that is "expected" from us. And even in the midst of military violence in El Salvador you said you'd find moments of quiet and compassion for yourself and the people you've worked with. Some of us practice meditation, prayer, arts to give us some focus, some ground for our lives, discrimination and heart ("contemplation in action," as St. Ignatius expressed it).

We desire to experience that ground from which discernment and intuition arise and then flow into what we are doing. We don't really feel peaceful if we're not rightly aligned to our talent and work. You know, maybe your work as a community organizer is finished. That is what you're sorting out for yourself. We don't have any definite answers in mind. We just experience as we get older that our regrets are about not following our hearts.

Now it's more settled in El Salvador but you're not. You say if your heart's not into it, why, remote and regretful, force yourself to continue as a volunteer social worker? I really admire your intelligence, guts and religious life, which include service to the poor. You've given so much of yourself. I'm sure your own questions for self-honesty will give you that openness to listen for the "answer." As you've alluded to earlier, you are the answer; just listen, be quiet deeply. Talk with your friends. Jerry Brown right now is very much into making one's intimate friends more a part of the fabric of our daily lives, living more closely together, while at the same time being activists who reach out to genuine needs of the poor and suppressed. So Jerry's into such things as a discussion group about Martin Buber's *I and Thou*. The title says it all.

What is a volunteer? You might say our role and gift is to empower people in need, to help them share in the resources and become self-reliant, to participate in their communities, to add to the harmony of the people's communal life. You respond to an honest need and from your heart. You enjoy it and find it rewarding. You say you want to work side by side with local citizens for solutions not "laid on" them but chosen by the people themselves who are naturally wise and able to express themselves through their own leaders. You have a respect and wonder about your work and you honor the dignity of the individual human spirit.

■

We've been talking mostly about the good work at Glide Memorial here at the corner of Ellis and Taylor in San Francisco, yet each of us gets attracted in our own ways. That's what interesting about our being together, because of all the creative differences. Glide Memorial first began in 1929 when this land was purchased by Methodist Lissie Glide. And how it's exploded with good works since a young Cecil Williams arrived here in 1963. He was innovative and seriously interested in meeting the needs of the immediate community. He created the Council on Religion and Homosexuality in 1964. He was one of the leaders to get ethnic studies at San Francisco State.

In 1969, I was swept up by some of the jazz Christian "whole-body" worship celebrations at the church. When Rev. Cecil shook my hand and gave me a hug, I felt I was touching a giant spiritual man. In the mid 80s, the church addressed the devastating problem of crack cocaine and in 1989, the Glide-Goodlett HIV/AIDS Prevention Program began. We've talked with students and teachers at the high-tech job skills training; some of us volunteered providing meals for homeless sisters and brothers in the Tenderloin. The Meals Program serves up to thirty-five hundred free meals per day, 365 days a year. If you're hungry, eat. Food is available. We are all eating and feeding others on various levels. Part of Glide's motivation is showing a genuine compassion; another aspect is the intention to challenge and stimulate human growth and freedom from over-dependency by making educational, spiritual and work skills providing comprehensive leadership, educational, community improvement, fitness and recreational opportunities, inter-generational youth/senior programs, tutoring, counseling, drug and violence prevention, employment readiness, recycling and gardening projects in programs available. Cf. http://www.glide.org.

Question: Would you speak about PICO as an example of community-based organizing? How did you meet John Baumann, S.J., PICO's director?

MZC: I met John Baumann in 1970 in Chicago. He was a mentor for me in the "Saul Alinsky" school of community organizing. He encouraged me to get out there and organize around strongly felt needs in the community. I've always embraced the principle that the main impetus for change comes from an enthusiasm deeply felt by the people who want to improve their lives. The people are the main energy.

John Baumann had a strong desire to get change going, even if it meant confronting the "big dogs" of power at their work or church. He was and is both a strong and gentle presence He didn't hate the rich or the powerful, not at all. He was a dear friend of Bob Holstein, a Jesuit-influenced attorney, who was well off. Bob Holstein was a special voice and benefactor for the poor and spoke up against the injustices they suffer. It's not being rich that's a problem; it's not sharing. It's not asking and insisting that our governments have a moral conscience, as well as ourselves, as individuals.

(*In 2008, PICO now has an interfaith network of over one thousand local religious congregations organizing for human rights, development, justice, responsibilities in the United States, Central America and Rwanda. Cf.* http://piconetwork.org. *One of the projects I favor heartily is covering medical care for all of America's uninsured children, with the goal of helping states cover all children by 2012. PICO is lobbying to make sure "Congress finalizes an agreement on legislation that grants the full $50 billion needed to fully fund The State Children's Health Insurance Program." PICO's organizers have been successful in being of help to pass legislation in Florida, Colorado, Missouri and Alaska to help reduce the number of uninsured children in their states As we are going to press, PICO is supporting hurricane Gustav's evacuees. PICO recently set up a new fund for the development of community organizers, "The Robert Holstein, Jr. Fund for the Development of Community Organizers."*

Question: Working in Central America, I've seen torture as a political means to control the native population. Mess up, speak up and you get your balls kicked in. What are your reflections on facing the violence, e.g. here in the city where fear also brings a kind of political control?

MZC: You work for human rights, often in an environment of intimidation and elitism. I hope you're careful and don't put yourself in danger. I think it comes down to our wisely resisting human abuse: whether it's a gang terrorizing a neighborhood because they want to sell crack or an abusive army or police. We have to stand up as you do but not to be a "hero" by yourself. Rather together, as you know, we can become an even stronger presence than what threatens the peace of our neighborhoods.

Remember Dr. King's work in the south with other activists, how he faced the prospect of being murdered for his protest against segregation. Supported by all races, Dr. King and his supporters, arm in arm, achieved real political change.

Now those risks for an activist aren't so high but we have to protest, as you say, despite the price we might have to pay. You know I'm not saying be a target out there, least of all when you're in the field. That's why we can align ourselves with avenues of protest such as Amnesty International's strong work against torture in prisons and so forth. But, out there, doing your service I know you're low profile. In a male-dominated oligarchic rule you've seen violence used to inspire fear and obedience even as an abusive husband keeps his wife down. You're wise not to expose yourself unnecessarily or make yourself into a target.

I feel also we have to acknowledge our own violence, our own expressions of anger, our explosiveness, and even our abuse of others and of ourselves. It comes home in our fights and arguments with our loved ones. We know, at times, our own arrogance as social activists can be a way of lording it over others rather than adapting to the work with people. When we're ready to punch somebody out, we can't listen. We all get like that, right? Just as we say an army must be moral and even kind, we need to work on ourselves.

You were in El Salvador in the early 80s when a most tragic example of violence occurred (12/11/1981). El Salvador's Atlacatl Battalion (many trained by our tax money at the School of the Americas mentioned earlier) began a six-day offensive sweep against guerrilla strongholds in Morazon. This was an embattled area. On this day the hamlet of Mozote was wiped out with the exception of one survivor, Rufina Amaya, who hid behind trees while watching troops taking people from their home at about 5 AM. At noon the men were blindfolded and killed in the town center. Early in the afternoon, the women were taken to the hills, raped, killed and burned, totally dehumanized. Lastly the old women were shot. Some of us have listened in person to Rufina's tragic stories.

Question: How do you think Buddhist thought and practice applies to violence? How can you be active when some Buddhists might tell you to be detached from politics, as might some Christians?

MZC: When I protest against the School of the Americas, yes, I am judging it as a US institution whose fruits have been to my discernment, wrong, in particular, having "torture manuals" which are, by the way, against the Geneva Convention, and this school presently has no established Congressional oversight. I don't want to be passive or detached as we might stereotype a Buddhist or a Christian to be. I want to be attached to social justice with the openness also that we can be more aware and change. It's up to each of us to decide what we feel is unjust and learn for ourselves. When such manuals are removed and there is a congressional over-viewing process in place, I'll re-evaluate whether I want to protest or not. Now my goals are for reformation, rather than the closing of the SOA. Yet it may well be necessary to get the school closed. I believe those who protest, insisting on closure of the SOA, perform a useful function of "many eyes" being on a US institution that has produced several well-documented violations of human rights in Latin America.

Just as anger, repressed silence can eat us up as individuals, so globally there's protest against such human abuses as slave labor in China and in other countries. We aren't demonizing any country. The Buddhists encourage practice that softens our anger and hate so we can love, so we, ourselves, are not destroyed by hatred. I don't interpret this to mean we cannot be involved with promoting human rights, even when it gets confrontational. That inner propensity of compassion can be generated out to society, hopefully even in society and politics. We can work for change without being hateful, without anger.

The Buddha says anger is like a forest fire burning down its own support. We start off with good intentions to help out, but we may find ourselves caught in hatred of "the bad guy" and end up hurting others and ourselves. On a political level, murder and torture, all forms of suppression, burn down global humanity.

■

I'm bearing down Leavenworth, leaving the Tenderloin to catch BART for the airport. A bright Indian woman with her young child stops to pose for my last photo in front of a colorful mural of people with signs that say "Respect" and "Organize for the Future." Good-bye, young mother and wide-eyed baby of hope. Organize for the future. You deserve a beautiful one!

Call to Be Transparent
Protesting the School of the Americas/WHINSEC
Morgan Zo-Callahan

In August of 2007, The House of Representatives demanded that the SOA/WHINSEC (Western Hemisphere Institute for Security Cooperation) release to the public the names of instructors and students who attended the school during the fiscal years of 2005 and 2006 and will continue to release names of students and teachers as a routine part of its yearly report. This rule accompanied the FY 2008 Defense Appropriations bill.

This is a small victory for the thousands of protestors of The School of the Americas who demand more responsibility from SOA/WHINSEC in its training of Latin American solders. The question remains whether or not SOA/WHINSEC can really reform or will it be shut down for its impeding the common good both of U.S. interests as well as those of the Latin American countries who send their elite soldiers there. Cf. http://www.soaw.org.

I protested against the School of Americas for four years at Fort Benning, Georgia (1997–2000). Some of us protested for the school to be "transparent," to be accountable for training many human rights abusers in Latin America. Most protested not for reform, but for the complete shutting down of the school. The following is from my record of events and my interviews in 1999.

Our SOA Demonstration on November 19–21, 1999, from my journal

Today's demonstration against SOA is our action to cause the government, and ourselves, to stop and think about the effects of U.S. military training for Latin American soldiers and our obligation to hold our government responsible for human rights violations committed by the solders trained here.

I listen and talk with people of all ages, so many nationalities, including my old friends, Bob and Loretta Holstein, John Baumann, Jerry Lagomarsino, Jim Donovan, Bill Masterson, Jim Straukamp, Bill Bichsel, Larry Castagnola, William O'Connell and others. I'm encouraged to see so many high school and university students interested in being in touch with Latin America and with causes in favor of the poor—the majority here are young people. May we all meet in that place within us where we are one!

I enter a large tent which Loretta and Bob Holstein sponsored to hear several speakers, including many Jesuit school students, present ideas about the School of Americas, and beyond that, the need to reach out to our less fortunate neighbors, to support human rights and dignity, to volunteer where we can, both here and abroad. A banner reads: "When we lament violence, we do not grieve as those without hope.... The life, death, and resurrection of Jesus reveal to us the steadfast love of God."

A young woman laments out loud that she doesn't love the people in her everyday life. I lament my silence against the abuses and unnecessary violence of the country of which I am a citizen. I lament my own violence and abusiveness in relationships. I lament that I do not lift up the poor to the degree I could. Where does the motivation come from? Dorothy Day said in *The Catholic Worker* (April 1964): "The mystery of the poor is this: That they are Jesus, and what you do for them you do for Him.... The mystery of poverty is that by sharing in it, making ourselves poor in giving to others, we increase our knowledge of and belief in love."

A Catholic woman minister speaks of the deep emotion in lamentation as prayer. We sing: "Lord, hear my prayer; come, listen to me"; Psalm 34, "The Lord listens to the cry of the poor ... the Lord hears the cry of the poor"; the song of hope, "O healing river send down new waters upon this land and wash the blood from off the sand ... let the seed of freedom awake and flourish.... "; and finally, "Come live in the Light, shine with the joy and love of the Lord. We are called to love tenderly, to serve, to live in the freedom of the city of the Lord ... to be hope for the hopeless ... to act with justice, to love tenderly.... "

I skip an evening dance organized at the nearby Hilton, and decide to continue visiting and interviewing other participants. I enjoy tape-recording spontaneous conversations. I am stimulated being with students, activists, to shout against the School of the Americas. The energy is just great this evening, lots of music and dance. But Bob had said "Come over. Let's have a few beers, man." So eventually I walk over to the Hilton bar and talk at length with the Southern lawyer who represented Bob Holstein who was jailed for his civil disobedience in demonstrating against the SOA. He tells me there has been a change in consciousness regarding the SOA. He thinks that we shouldn't close the school, but change what they teach. We agree that the military has a rightful function, but should not overstep its principal duty to defend our country first, including helping in emergencies—think Hurricane Katrina in New Orleans. Obviously the recently de-classified torture manual, how to interrogate with physical force the so-called enemy (including many indigenous Latin American people), should not be part of the curriculum. One victory for activists was that they exposed the SOA for teaching torture.

Gene and Jerry take me back to my hotel. I'm feeling a bit tipsy. It's 2 AM. This first evening has been political, prayerful, with serious considerations but also playful, full of stories, jokes, and laughter.

Before sleeping I read two articles from the *Los Angeles Times* (November 18, '99) about two views of the School of Americas. Amelia Simpson is married to army captain Lawrence Rockwell. Rockwell was court-martialed for his actions in defense of human rights in Haiti in 1994, and is appealing his case to the Supreme Court. Amelia writes that since the school now teaches a course in human rights and is starting real reform with more accountability, we should stop calling the school "the school of assassins." While this was accurate in the past, it's an anachronism. It doesn't match what's going on; the school is trying to change, and teaching human rights is not just propaganda. Next year, she says, the curriculum will include a study of the 1968 My Lai massacre in Vietnam, taught by Hugh Thompson, the helicopter pilot who intervened to stop the killing. For a time after Mai Lai, Thompson was considered "a bad guy." Lt. William Calley, convicted of killing innocent villagers, was "a good guy." Robert Brophy, a dear friend, who is demonstrating today against the SOA in Orange County, California, writes in response that we have no business training anyone to participate in the oppression of his or her fellow citizens. He cites ongoing abuses in Mexico and Columbia as evidence that the school should be closed. We all know the past: kidnappings, torture, subversion of civil freedoms, military coups. Bob writes: "The SOA is also lethal simply because it continues to teach skills that will be used not for security from external enemies, but against a nation's own people."

It's a cloudy Saturday afternoon, November 20; I'm walking up to the gates of Fort Benning. I'm going to say a prayer for the six Spanish Jesuits and their two companions who were killed in El Salvador in 1989. I chat with Jerry Lagomarsino already at the gate. He says, "The most impressive thing for me is seeing the young people, from universities and high schools, so enthusiastic. I was moved by John Dear's talk about how we should each strive to be non-violent, that our God is a non-violent God. I'm inspired by listening to the old songs of the 60s here at the gate."

Something about being at the South Gate on Victory Drive stirs my desire to be a drop in the ocean of meaningful activism. The trees are clothed in changing oranges, browns, light and dark greens, reddish brick houses, guys hawking parking spaces for ten bucks. I stop by to say hello to the people in the School of Americas Watch office. It's starting to pour now; I lift up my face to the heavy raindrops. A large banner reads: "Wage Peace." I reflect how much energy is put into waging wars; I remember studying the demanding criteria for a just war at Gonzaga University. I recall how Dorothy Day scoffed at the very idea of a "just war." *Namaste* is written on a small camper of Vedantists who have come to demonstrate: "*Namaste,*" I honor that place that is in you and in me where we are one. A jeep of military folks drives by, looking at us with great curiosity. One of uniformed men gives us the peace sign which we return.

I go to listen to a stirring song, accompanied by lively drums, by a woman from West Africa. We hear flutes and guitars. We listen to North American Indians from Oklahoma and Washington chanting the "Four Directions Song." There's a Mayan blessing from a group from Guatemala. I listen to talks about human rights causes worldwide. I'm stirred and humbled in my heart by meeting and talking with Rufina Amaya, sole survivor of the massacre at El Mozote, El Salvador, December 11, 1981.

I speak with Peggy from Columbus who is a local supporter of the demonstration. "I think this is a good cause. Because I'm in the area and because I've worked at Ft. Benning, I've come to believe we need to clean up the School of Americas. First of all, I'm an American and I care about our boys who serve in the military. If we are teaching any soldiers *uncalled for* violence then I believe we must stop. I support this protest because it is calm. We have a good time. It's peaceful and we're all learning from each other. If the school doesn't become more open to us all, we should close it. Let's make a lot of noise together."

I do a short interview with Alan Nairn. I've met with Alan the last couple years here in Georgia. Alan is an activist hero of mine. His principal cause has been human rights in East

211

Timor, this little country, 90 percent Catholic, at the eastern end of the Indonesian archipelago. Alan wants to see the end of Indonesia's bloody occupation.

East Timor was a colony of Portugal until 1975. It was on December 7, 1975 that the Indonesian military (TNI) occupied East Timor and stayed until this year of 1999; in these years, the military caused the death of one-third of the Timorese population (about two hundred thousand died, killed by Indonesian troops, starvation or disease). The U.S trained much of the Indonesian military and security forces.

Alan went to East Timor to make the public aware of what was going on. On November 12, 1991, while Alan was reporting for *New Yorker* magazine, he ended up in the midst of a massacre at the Santa Cruz Cemetery. He was with Amy Goodman from WBAI/Pacifica radio. They both thought the military would refrain from violence when they saw foreigners. They did not. Alan later testified before the Senate Committee on Foreign Relations on February 17, 1992 "The soldiers rounded the corner, never breaking stride, raised their rifles, and fired in unison into the crowd. Timorese were backpedaling, gasping, trying to flee, but in seconds they were cut down by the hail of fire. People fell, stunned and shivering, bleeding in the road, and the Indonesian solders kept on shooting.… They executed schoolgirls, young men, old Timorese; the street was wet with blood, and the bodies were everywhere … they were beating me and Amy; they took our cameras and our tape recorder and grabbed Amy by the hair and punched and kicked her in the face and stomach. When I put my body over her, they focused on my head. They fractured my skull with butts of their M-16s.… The soldiers seemed impressed when they realized that we were indeed from the States … the soldiers chose to let us live.… This was, purely and simply, a deliberate mass murder, a massacre of unarmed, defenseless people."

The Timorese—about four thousand strong—were at

the cemetery to remember a student, Sebastiao Gomes, who was executed by the viciously suppressive Indonesian army in October 1991, at the Motael Church in Dili. This was a first-ever mass protest by the East Timorese. Sebastiao was shot in the stomach at point-blank range, at the same time that a U.N. delegation (later cancelled) was coming from Portugal to report on conditions in East Timor. About four hundred East Timorese would end up dead. A British cameraman, Max Stahl, videotaped this atrocity and was able to hide the tape inside a grave, eventually smuggling it out later that darkest of nights.

Activists mobilized, ending U.S. support of Indonesia's occupation. In 1996, Bishop Carlos Belo and Jose Ramos-Horta received the Nobel Peace prize for seeking a non-violent solution in East Timor, which gave even more hope to activists such as Alan.

Alan tells me now: "I think the Army has been affected by these demonstrations against the SOA; the Congress is now more involved. My own work in East Timor is finally going well. They are on the brink of freedom; the Indonesian Army has withdrawn. There's a transitional U.N. administration. There's a healthy movement towards independence. There are still thousands of Timorese being held hostage by the Indonesian military. There are bills in Congress that would cut off all U.S. military assistance until those hostages are freed. East Timor won a tremendous victory; they had a referendum sponsored by the U.N. 98 percent of the people turned out and 78 percent of the people voted for independence. After this the Indonesian military burned down much of the country and abducted half the people. But the people won. Activism in this country had a lot to do with this victory."

I'm returning from the mass in the tent, which started at 7 PM, principally celebrated by Fr. Bill Bichsel. The musicians are from Mexico, Peru, and Bolivia. The readings from the mass: one from Ezekiel, that God is our strength and healer;

the gospel says that we must serve the poor, visit the prisoner and that is serving the Lord Himself. "I *am* that lonely prisoner or starving child!"

Tomorrow, almost half of the protestors will cross the line and go onto to the property of the School of America, risking arrest. About four thousand people will go onto the property of the School of Americas. I'm talking with my friend Eric Debode, from the Catholic Worker, who tells me that he plans to get arrested.

It's Sunday, November 21, and I'm interviewing some of the protestors, listening to talks, inter-faith presentations, music, singing, dancing. It's a full, invigorating day.

"My name is Rosena, from El Salvador, and I want us all to live in peace with justice in Latin America. We are poor economically, but rich in spirit. So many of our people have been killed unnecessarily, but this blood is the seed that will regenerate us. The people who died are not only my family members, but also nuns and priests who were working so that life would be different for the poor. We must follow the example of Bishop Romero who gave his life for telling the truth. On March 24, 2000, next year, we will commemorate the twentieth anniversary of the death of Bishop Romero. [He] gives us the courage to seek justice today for those whose human rights are violated."

We listen to Maryknoll priest, Roy Bourgeois, an organizer of the SOA Watch, along with Carol Richardson. Father Roy was an officer in the U.S. Navy and received a purple heart in Vietnam. He was ordained in 1972. "Let's use our voices for our sisters and brothers of Latin America whose voices have too often been silenced. We bring our hopes and dreams, our strong hope for peace and justice. My thoughts turn to Bolivia and to El Salvador where I spent time living for the poor. It was there where I went to serve, to be part of the struggle where I learned about the poor's struggle. This School of Americas is not the starting point; it's the struggle of the poor who just try to survive, who do not receive just wages for their labor, who live in shacks without running water, whose children do not have proper schools and who, when sick, do not have proper care. It's out of this reality of hunger and pain that soldiers come from their countries to our country's School of Americas to learn psychological warfare, insurgency techniques. And, as we looked at that curriculum, we said, 'No, not in our name!' As people of good will, from all faith traditions, we know we are called to be healers in our world, to be peacemakers, to keep the quest for justice alive. This is an expression of our solidarity. This is a sacred moment; we are connecting with our sisters and brothers in Latin America. There are over ten thousand of us here. You can change the name of the School of Americas, but as Representative Joseph Moakley says, 'you can't put perfume on a toxic dump.' It won't work. You do not teach democracy through a barrel of a gun. This school cannot be changed; it can only be closed. We say *nunca mas*. You give us hope."

(Note about Roy: In 2008, Roy publicly supported woman ordination in the Catholic Church; he is facing excommunication from the church.)

Is Roy's goal of closing the school as efficacious as reforming the school, creating open accountability? I'm able to ask him about this; he says he doesn't think the school can be changed.

I'm glad that bright lights are shining on the School of Americas; it's under scrutiny. Whether the school will shut or not, I don't know.

Martin Sheen plays the President of the United States. "I've come to give a decree, as acting President of the United States and thus as Commander in Chief. I decree that the School of Americas at Fort Benning, Georgia cease and desist operations immediately."

Martin Sheen then walks to the back of the stage and

looks out towards Fort Benning and some military brass who are looking out at us protestors.

"Hey, I just closed your school." Martin talks about following the non-violent Jesus, "wherever it may lead me this day. Jesus keeps a lonely vigil costumed in a native lore; there he weeps in Guatemala, Nicaragua, and El Salvador. I'll see you across the line."

We sing "Amazing Grace" together with Pete Seeger. "I once was lost, but now I'm found."

John Dear introduces Dan Berrigan. He reads a short poem, *Some* for "all who brought faith, hope … to all from the inner and outer edges of our lives together." It's a poem I'll also hear him recite in a slightly different form at a Las Vegas protest against nuclear weapons. [Dan kindly gave his permission to reprint his poem in *Meanderings* which you can read earlier in its entirety in Part II.] This is the way he ended the poem at Ft Benning:

They walked the earth; they walked the water; they walked the air.
They were asked,
And why do you stand?
Because of the heart, they said,
and because of the children,
and because of the bread.
Because the cause is the heart's beat
and the children born
and the risen bread.

Adriana Portillo speaks: "Yesterday I was very touched by the expressions of solidarity. I am profoundly grateful. I was moved by Rufina Amaya's story in El Salvador. I held back my tears. I could feel her pain. Rufina and I have two things in common: We are both mothers and have lost children to soldier graduates of The School of Americas.

"On September 11, 1981, my two daughters, Rosaura and Glenda, ages ten and nine, were kidnapped and disappeared by Guatemalan security forces. They were taken with my father, my little sister of eighteen months, my stepmother, my sister-in-law. They have never been seen or heard from since.

"Ten of the leaders and architects of the counter-insurgency in Guatemala in 1981 were trained here. The leader of the feared Guatemalan Intelligence Office was trained here. Last night I had a very painful dream. I dreamed that if we all walked across the line, the road leading to it was covered with the bones and skulls of children. No matter how careful we were, we could not avoid stepping on the bones of the children and crushing them under our feet. We stand here not as individuals, but with all the victims of the School of America's trainees, with the thousands of victims in my own country of Guatemala in the thirty-six years of war, of the thousands in El Salvador, of thousands in other Latin American countries. All the victims are here with us today.

"As human beings, we are all connected. Our children and the children after them deserve to inherit a country [where] all human beings everywhere in the world are equal and where life is precious.… The people of Latin America have seen their rights violated for too many years.… "

A young girl then gets up to speak, representing "the kids." She told the story of Sudaka Sasaki, a twelve-year-old girl who lived in Japan during World War II. She got leukemia from the bomb's radiation. She began to fold paper "peace cranes." There's a tradition in Japan that if you fold a thousand peace cranes, your wish for peace will come true. Sudaka died before she finished, but her classmates finished her project.

We sing a song about Rosa Parks: "No sir, I won't get up. No I won't get up. I'm tired and I want to sit down and I won't get up. I won't get up. You can talk about Martin Luther King and demonstrations, anything; just remember who began was

Rosa Parks.... But she was just like me and you and she did what she could and she said, no Sir I won't get up.... "

At a memorial service led by a Lakota Indian: memory, we experience mindfulness, prayerfulness, encouragement, remorse, lamentation, sorrow, and resolve. We remember our Latin American sisters and brothers. An Indian woman, dressed in ceremonial reds, dances as others chant. Prayers in the Lakota language.

Many people—from Columbia, Nicaragua, El Salvador, Mexico, Argentina, Bolivia, religious, unions, and students—line up, carrying white crosses with the names of victims of soldiers from the School of Americas. Many march in a solemn funeral procession, as an act of civil disobedience, on to the property of Fort Benning, singing "*No mas.*" No more. No more. Companions, we cry out: "No more!"

Witness to Inhumanity
A Short Conversation With a Hero, Rufina Amaya

Rufina emanated an aura of genuine bearing witness to an atrocity, while remaining peaceful and utterly human and humble. I just loved Rufina right away when I first saw her. She had a special beauty, small boned, a round open face, crafted from unbearable suffering met by indomitable spirit. She fixed her hair, pulled back and up into a bun, which stuck straight up. She was slightly chubby; children seemed to be extremely attracted to her. She told us she just wanted to tell her story in quiet, righteous anger, calling for meaningful change. She exuded courage, simplicity and nobility; her voice was strong, as she'd speak before thousands of people at the protests against the School of the Americas.

God saved me because he needed someone to tell the story of what happened.
—Rufina Amaya, New York Times, 1996.

November 20, 1999, Georgia

MZC: Thanks so much, Rufina. I just feel I'd like to be with you. That feeling of sharing this little moment with you and wanting to support you. You're wonderful; I pray for you every day. When the 1981 massacre occurred at El Mozote, with its 809 victims, it was first denied by both the Salvadoran and American governments, despite what many community and church leaders were telling the world. You, being the sole survivor, had the courage to tell what happened in your village of twenty houses facing the community square. You've told this story now for eighteen years. In 1990, you were the first to testify in a criminal complaint against the Atlacatl Battalion (trained by American advisors) by Pedro Chica Romero of La Joya, a nearby hamlet to El Mozote. Pedro was a witness

219

in his little hamlet to another killing of some of his relatives and neighbors by the Atlacatl Battalion. It wasn't until the El Salvador Peace Treaty of 1992 that an Argentine Forensic Anthropology Team was appointed by the United Nations to excavate the zone and finally begin exhumation.

You have our admiration and love, Rufina.

May I ask you about what motivates you to tell your heart-breaking story?

RA: I feel I'm doing what God wants me to do, what I have all my desire to do. It's part of how I practice being a Catholic, not a separate activity. My story telling and speaking with people come from my heart and also from my pain, my suffering the loss of my husband, Domingo Claros, who was twenty-nine; my son, Cristino, nine and my three daughters Maria Dolores, five, Maria Lillian, three; and Maria Isabel, eight months. I can't even cry anymore. It's true: my body produced so many tears that they are all gone. I speak to you; I speak for them, my family, my friends, and my neighbors who cannot speak any more. Even though I'm a simple person, I use my voice so people will not forget what happened at El Mozote.

MZC: Just two more questions would be all right? What's your participation in the organized church? Do you consider yourself an "activist"?

RA: I'm a lay pastor in the Catholic Church in El Salvador; my faith is very important as it gives me love, as do my family and friends. My religion gives me courage not to be afraid to speak out loudly and my religion allows me to get refreshed spiritually. I like to lead "reflection groups," where we talk about the relationship of God to our own lives. I've had so many visitors from all around the world; I truly feel I'm meant to talk and I'm happy and serious to talk. I do practice quiet prayer and have some reflection time also, but I would call myself an activist. I'll never be quiet about what's right and what's wrong, what's unjust abuse, unjust murder against innocent, good people. I'm publicly asking those responsible for the murders to publicly ask our pardon. Yes, I am an activist and also a Catholic. I'm outspoken. I'm not satisfied. Yet, I'm a person of faith too, not only an activist.

Rebel Mentor
A Conversation with Robert Brophy, Ph.D.

Robert Brophy is professor at Cal State University, Long Beach, mentor in activism, theologian, compañero, and great hugger, still teaching university youngsters at a youthful eighty years old.

El Salvador

MZC: Recently I was reading the notes you took when you were an observer of elections in El Salvador several years ago in 1992. What was that experience like for you? Did some of our recent discussion of protesting this year again at The School of Americas remind you of that official excursion to El Salvador?

RB: Yes, it recalled to me my first trip to El Salvador in 1992, that country's initial elections after the civil war. We were international observers in a urine-stinking grade school way out in Huachapan Province, where the temperature and humidity were enough to melt anyone into the floor. Picture me dressed in suit jacket and pants, dress shirt and tie with a camera hanging at my chest. The voters were mostly indigenous, small, and towered-over by the rich ranchers, one of whom got up on a table, pointing to his ballot, yelled out for all to attend: "This is how you are to vote!" Many had come at great trouble and risk. Buses, paid for by some organization, were mysteriously kept from running. The local death-squad, familiar to them all, had just come in as a group to vote and to intimidate, to remind of the thousands of "dissidents' that had to be exterminated in El Salvador's bloody past.

One table that I overlooked had amazingly started to count up and register their vote-tally at noon, due at 5:00 PM; they had already decided who had won! When I reported this to the UN observer, he wouldn't believe it but went and found it was so. He said sadly, "I can do nothing about it; we are here to observe only." It may have been he who pointed out that the voting lists posted by the door contained many of the dead, who had somehow already voted. As the afternoon waned, military aircraft thundered low over the village, not friendly or reassuring—reminding all of the risk they were taking.

That night, while we oversaw the official counting of ballots, an electric switch was tripped, and, when light was restored, a box of votes was missing, one from a rebellious district of the region, it was presumed. The highlight of the night was my discussion with a young member of the ARENA party. He had been educated at Rutgers and spoke English well. When quizzed by my companion, an African-American, and me about the status of El Salvador unions, he went into a tirade. His father had a big business and would never allow such a profit-stifling entity. But the "gem" of the evening was his response to my question of why the ARENA party's Roberto D'Aubuisson had planned and carried off the assassination of Oscar Romero over ten years before: "We never kill anyone who doesn't deserve it." It summed up the whole justification for the SOA—keep the rich in power at all costs; judge morality by its usefulness for keeping the status quo. He was probably a weekly communicant.

The *Spiritual Exercises*

MZC: Broph, it's just so great to be in touch with you and hear what you are doing these years. We've come together at meetings and at SOA protests; we had intimate interchanges on the Internet and conversations at some meetings at Loyola Marymount University.

RB: I especially recall that we prayed and reflected together during a six-month "Nineteenth Annotation" retreat, October 1998-March 1999, that about eight of us made, exchanging reflections ("lumina") by Internet e-mail, progressing through each of the original, intensive four week Ignatian *Exercises*, keeping pace with each other. Don Merrifield was one of the Jesuits who joined us, but we were the "leaders"; that is, we acted as retreat directors for each other. It was a Companions retreat, initiated by Bob Holstein. We used the text *Choosing Christ in the World: Directing the Spiritual Exercises According to Annotations Eighteen and Nineteen: A Handbook* by Joseph A. Tetlow, S.J.

KI: You wrote on 9/18/07 that you were off to a peace and justice meeting where you were to review a book on Ignatian *Exercises* by Dean Brackley, S.J. who teaches at UCA, San Salvador, El Salvador. (Dean and I were at Woodstock together and lived in the same small community with Avery Dulles and Drew Christensen who is now the editor of *America*.) One of the main explorations of "Meanderings" is how we ex-Jesuits who have done the full *Exercises* continue to use the *Exercises* in our lives; most of us would agree that the *SE*, coupled with the strict training at the novitiate, had a major impact in our lives. Would you tell us what you've learned from Dean's book? And how do the Ignatian *Exercises* relate to peace and justice, how do the two enrich each other? There are a several questions in there. Handle them however you like.

RB: It was more than just a review of the book, *The Call to Discernment in Troubled Times: New Perspectives on the Transformative Wisdom of Ignatius of Loyola* (Crossroad 2004). "Micah 6:8," the name of my justice and peace group, made the reading of Brackley, two chapters every two weeks for almost six months, into a new kind of Ignatian retreat. What amaze me are the insights into Ignatius that have arisen in the renewed Society. The retreats that I recall over the years 1946 to 1968 were individual-centered, the sins confronted were personal sins entirely, the evil admitted by the retreatant was undifferentiated, unspecified, not outward-related.

In Brackley's presentation, this concern with sin reflects our complicity in systemic evil. The Foundation's "praise, reverence, and serve" is identified with Jesus' option for the poor. "Indifference" means attaining freedom to choose and undertake justice. There is emphasis on personal sin, but conversion is seen in its social dimensions. Christ's "Call" is to engage the greatest evil of our time, a widespread if not universal poverty that amounts to a criminal "deprivation," enabled and driven by structural sin. That "Call" is embodied in the two "Great Commandments," Love God with your whole heart and your neighbor as yourself" (Luke 10); our neighbor is quintessentially the one who suffers diminishment and injustice, is a pawn in Greed's Chess Game, the world's economic, social and political systems. Conversion is self-transcendence, turning to love as God loves, as imaged in Jesus. This Jesus was concerned about justice. The "Kingdom," called here "The Reign of God," is focused on the social implications of the individual's vocation and quintessentially in the very mission of the Church, a new way to live together in Christ. Choice of vocation asks how do I best collaborate in the Beatitudes. The "Two Standards meditation" opposes riches, honor, and pride with poverty; invited insult, and humility is found in solidarity with the poor, a choice of "downward mobility" for Jesus' sake. The final "week" centers on learning to love like God and in God. The "Contemplation to Obtain Love" is the Pentecostal experience, as always with social implications. Everything is prayer, life permeated with God's ever-fine-focused love. It made one hell of a retreat.

The above is in my shorthand and does not do Father Brackley justice; it was my experience. Brackley, by the way, teaches at the Jesuit University of Central America (UCA), San Salvador, from which Liberation Theology flourished and still flourishes despite the Vatican's frowning.

It strikes me that Pope Benedict's latest warning to the Jesuits' thirty-fifth General Congregation against "aspects of Liberation Theology" (17 Jan 08) evokes the underlying difference in theology between old and the new. For the pope, God intends the poor to be poor and the rich to be rich in a paternalistic world. "Charity" (the old alms-giving) trumps justice. Liberation Theology sees that as the problem. Benedict's world was also Ignatius' world, but Ignatius, according to Brackley at least, was progressively able to see beyond it.

KI: Can you describe the role that your spiritual practice had in your decision to take an activist stance against the Vietnam War? My question is quite close to one that Morgan asks: Could you point to anything from your experience of the *Spiritual Exercises* that made an impact?

RB: Not really. The Ignatian *Exercises* were not for me then the break-through that they are in the Brackley-mirrored approach; maybe in some way they were a time bomb ticking. Dean invites one to meditate on sin as one's own and at the same time as enabling the systemic evil in which we are complicit. He does not deny personal sin but puts it in a larger human context. I did not have that. The "Two Kingdoms" were a medieval military metaphor but actually are the confrontation between the power-hungry profit-at-any-cost machine of the contemporary world, personal and corporate, by Christ's call to a convert mind and stance against poverty, powerlessness, and deprivation. I always had and still keep a small statue of Ignatius on my desk and my vow crucifix. I was not untouched by Ignatius' insights; I have always seen him as an inspiring revolutionary, insisting "nothing counts but the Lord"; the crucified are in Christ the exploited, deprived, degraded poor. The cross says the only way will be the hard way.

MZC: Is there anything from Ignatian *Exercises* that you find most life giving to you, to your life? What do you think are the most important spiritual possibilities for those making/giving the *Exercises* in today's world? How do the *Exercises* relate to our deepest yearnings and desires? Do you find the "Examen" to be helpful? How do you interpret the "Contemplation for Obtaining Love"?

RB: The Foundation is central. The world we live in is not Ignatius' pre-Galileo one, but the one opened by Einstein and Edwin Hubble, cosmos-contexted thirteen billion years from the Big Bang, protons and muons, dark matter and dark energy, NASA's Hubble telescope. But the creator is the same and "indifference" is a goal shared with many faiths. "Contemplation" is changed. If the Gospel is full of metaphor, then I ask meaning rather than topography (though I have been to Palestine and appreciated the metaphor as palpable). I think the *Exercises*' appeal is about getting one's head on straight and one's heart attuned. They help sort-out, correct one's compass, renew. And the Barclay/Liberation Theology reading, that Jesus came to free every human "to be all s/he can be" is a challenge to see new depths, to seek the justice dimension. Yes, I find the Examen helpful for reality-check and reminder that all things are prayer. Prayer unceasing.

Peace and Justice Causes Most Worthy

MZC: Would you describe your work with "conscientious objectors," at Cal State University Long Beach? How do you feel when you are teaching or engaged in peace and justice projects? What do you identify today as "most worthy causes" in peace and justice?

RB: Lacking a military draft the student-body is distracted from war and justice issues, though a campus Progressive Club does focus on them. Yet many students, mostly, but not all, being minorities, cannot achieve a university education because of the costs and ROTC offers a fiscal solution; becoming an Army Reservist offers further financial support. These students usually do not believe that they are being programmed and legally committed to kill other human beings. I suppose that the now-elongated Iraq war should to some extent have changed that, but sometimes the insight comes late. The first student that came to me as the Iraq war began was an ROTC cadet, an Army Reservist and a senior; he confessed that to his consternation and horror he no longer saw a target at the end of his rifle sights, he saw a person.

I let it be known as widely as I can that I am available for counseling. I write guest editorials for the student paper suggesting the problems involved in volunteering for war, any war, and offer help. I keep files documenting the anti-war stance taken by various religions advising conscience versus war, and I have ready many Internet sites for reference. If the student wants to pursue a CO (conscientious objector) stand, I help her/him to work out a personal philosophy. With their permission, I begin a file for each, to attest to the fact that this person has expressed conscience problems at this or that date—as evidence for later military tribunals. I will attach in an appendix below an example of a personal philosophy of conscientious objection.

You ask: how do I experience my teaching as engaging peace and justice? I see my academic vocation as an extension of my priestly one; it is a ministry. Specifically literature, it has always seemed to me, pursues clarification of the human situation in all its aspects. The great writers of the novel, poetry, and drama are the philosophers and theologians of their times; they deal with what it is to have integrity. At both USF and Long Beach I have taught the course "Religious Dimensions of Contemporary Literature." In surveying writers of middle to late twentieth century one finds that they powerfully critique questions of war and peace, justice and evil.

My current "Bible as Literature" course offers a rather direct application. I find, for instance, that the prophets are especially fixated on justice; a few were in their own way conscientious objectors. Happily the section on the prophets comes at the same time in November as the annual protest against the Pentagon's School of the Americas at Fort Benning, Georgia. I confess to the class that I am myself compelled by the prophetic urge to speak and act against militarism, war, torture, and assassination which all are personified in this SOA as arm of the US foreign policy. And I describe my other protests, arrests, and my three days in the LA County jail.

You ask what I identify as the "most worthy cause(s)" for peace and justice today? This, it seems to me, is to be found in the gospel as read by Liberation Theology. As a critique of systemic evil, LT is astounding and compelling. It points out that a real war is at all times and everywhere in progress by the rich against the poor, wealth and power against justice. Profit becomes a ruthless agent of devastating deprivations. NAFTA and CAFTA, in outstanding instances, wipe out the agricultural world of small farmers by dumping subsidized grain on their markets and by expropriating land in huge tracts for mechanized agribusiness farming. Globalization at present *is* the corporate world, blind to the victims, squeezing life from developing countries.

Activism Begun at the University of San Francisco

MZC: Broph, I want to revisit an earlier conversation we had a while ago and learn from your work as an anti-war activist, first as a Jesuit priest as well as a father and esteemed friend of many of us. Would you tell us how you became an activist Jesuit priest at the University of San Francisco?

RB: Returning to San Francisco after graduate school in 1965 and being assigned to USF was one of the highs of my life. San Francisco was my home. It was where my parents lived. I had attended and then taught at St. Ignatius High on Stanyan Street, just below the university 1953 to 1955. I had lived there all my non-Jesuit life. I knew so many in the city, had taught at least some of them. USF hospitality was warm, and I felt privileged from the first. Mine was a fifth-floor room in Xavier Hall overlooking the Golden Gate. I had access to the whole city by three trolley lines heading west to the beach, east to downtown. Two blocks away, Golden Gate Park stretched to the Beach. The Cursillo weekends with the students, organized by Fr. Gerry Phelan, almost immediately immersed me with students—more deeply than anything anywhere I had ever experienced. Together in these especially, we underwent sacramental immersion gathering, praying, and eating together. Those weekends were not political, but they opened the heart, they moved beyond the institutional, they seeded the community. Later the homily at daily Eucharist that I celebrated in Phelan Hall, dormitory and cafeteria, at 5:00 PM, overflowed into the dining room. Eating with the students was a further immersion. I got to know most of the student population, at least the many boarders.

I was brought into the total university early. I had a faculty office in the very middle of campus, upstairs from a student cafeteria/snack bar, within a few steps from classrooms, library, student dormitories, and gymnasium. The English department was small and congenial. Classrooms were always full and enthusiastic.

The student paper, the *Foghorn*, was from liberal to radical. I found friends on the staff and began to write for them, pieces on art exhibitions, campus culture, city life, moral and social issues. When no Jesuit would answer an appeal to join the "Committee for Religion and the Homosexual" at neighboring Glide Memorial Church, I volunteered. When no Jesuit could be found to be faculty advisor for the new Black Student Union, I accepted. When the lay faculty called a press conference to condemn the bombing of Cambodia, I stood with them. When "Urban Renewal" leveled the Black ghetto in the center of San Francisco, heartlessly leaving many of the residents homeless, in order to build a new "Japan Town," tall residences for retirees, and a multi-million-dollar Catholic Cathedral, I spoke against it. I felt these were challenges to the Christian discernment and *a priori* the place of the Catholic/Jesuit clergy.

Your question was: Whence the USF prophetic activism? It had all begun in graduate school, early 1960s, on a weekday afternoon in Chapel Hill, North Carolina, where I was in doctoral studies. I was attacked by a furious local citizen for picketing in Roman collar the town's "Whites Only" prestigious restaurant. The threatened violence was so traumatic (it was as though that moment was framed into my mind forever) that I found myself questioning everything in the political spectrum. I had totally misjudged reality all of my life. I began to participate in marches (it turned out against the local bishop's decree for clergy and religious). From there I moved to my first teaching assignment at USF, where I was visited by a Carolina student friend who was a bombardier in the Air Force. When I asked him his duties, he described leveling towns and villages in Vietnam. His justification was: "As long as they shoot at us it is my duty to bomb them." A logic so skewed drove me to look beyond the current religious rant about saving the world from godless Communism to considerations of conscience regarding war. And it made me look at our USF ROTC officer-factory in a different light. Then my close student friend, Tom Sandborn, took me on a walk to explain to me the direction his newly converted Catholicism was taking him. He opened to me the world of committed non-violence. He was being refused graduation because he could not in conscience take the required ROTC courses. At that point I joined several in suing the Federal government to allow Catholics to use their religious convictions to claim conscientious objection just as Quakers, Brethren, Jehovah Witnesses. Once one begins in these directions, there is no turning back.

As for the morality of cooperation in war, there has been a gigantic leap in the Church's theology of war conscience in the last forty years. When I was at USF in late 1960s, the administration refused to allow draft counseling on campus; evidently no Jesuit was to offer it. That despite the fact that Catholic students were going to federal prison (one spending time on Terminal Island, Long Beach) or fleeing to Canada. Back home, pastors were telling conscience-stricken youth that there was no Catholic tradition of war-resistance. This information was false and suggested culpable ignorance. The Just-War theory was accepted, but the United States presumably would not engage in an unjust war. And defense of one's country under any circumstances was a duty. No matter that for the first three centuries, Christianity embraced non-violence as Jesus' way, as God's will. It was only with fourth century Emperor Constantine, when Christianity was embraced and became the state religion, that Ambrose and Augustine had to work out a theory that would protect the empire by "necessary violence"; thence the Just-War tradition. Wars were blessed ever after. Yet, although some Catholic traditions did oppose wars, one for instance being the Catholic Worker, the main-line presumption was to support wars even when both sides involved Catholics.

Yes, in 1963 came Pope John XXIII's *Peace on Earth* followed by the Second Vatican Council's urging nations to provide for those conscience-harried in time of war. In our time both Popes John Paul II, Benedict XVI, and the Catholic bishops of the United States have judged the present Iraq war unjust. Ironically none of this has been promulgated, preached, or taught. Catholic conscientious objectors have been conspicuously few. Which is another story. Catholic chaplains are notoriously absent in discussions of the morality of wars they oversee. Are they thus chosen and self-chosen for their ministry without confronting key questions. How do they help form the consciences of their men and women? Do they urge them each day to pray for those whom they will kill or maim? How do they settle their vocation with Matthew's picture of Jesus at the Last Judgment 25:31 "As often as you do it to the least of my brethren you do it to me"?

KI: You describe yourself in the USF days as though ending as a desperate rebel. Did you feel isolated? You do suggest there were like minds. Who were they, and what kinds of conversations did you have, if any? Whence came the strength to stand up against the community, the presumed authority of a united, conservative, stance from the old guard. Though younger, I was in the Society in 1966 and was very active in protesting the war, and took a lot of flack from those who were "older and wiser." But somehow I never felt moved to leave at that time. I did have support from some pretty liberal superiors in New England, and the NE Jesuit community in general was probably a bit more liberal than the Californians. At least we thought so. There was a pretty large solid coterie of young anti-war Jesuit activists, inspired by Dan Berrigan whom we knew. He was close, active and very visible to all of us. The superiors could not hide him away, though I suspect that many tried, urged on by Cardinal Spellman.

RB: I never once experienced a "liberal superior" in the Society. Never once. In those times, at least in California, we did not talk to superiors as fellow Jesuits to be questioned and challenged. I certainly did not do it. "Grace of Office" was a wall. In all this I make no judgment on the Society overall or elsewhere. I experienced the California Province as conservative and reactionary. And in the end I presumed that there was nowhere else to go.

In most things I felt alone. Gene Schallert was supportive but waging his own battles. Some nights I would lie on his bed and wait for him to show up so I could talk for a few minutes about my thoughts and current crises. Jim Straukamp was with me on many things, on the Eucharist, ahead of me. But I had no Jesuit confidants on peace and justice issues. Can you imagine a campus in which it was okay to refuse graduation to conscientious objectors to the Vietnam War? As I recall, no one in my time, no Jesuit in California openly objected to the Vietnam War. No one spoke of conscientious objection. I had to learn that from students, with one of whom I am weekly still in touch. Tom Sandborn burned his draft card and fled to Canada. Dan Berrigan was a complete isolate, a pariah when coming to California. I don't know of any community that welcomed him. Certainly not USF.

The Last Turning Point
KI: There is a story that you tell about the treatment of your student at USF, his making campus a poster of Camus's

vilification of the Church's silence during the Nazi horrors, the student court's guilty verdict, the Jesuits' satisfaction—was this the actual event that broke the camel's back, when you knew there was not place for you in the Society? Your language is not that decisive: "Anyway at this time, I decided.... "

RB: On campus in spring of 1968, the *cause célèbre* was a nocturnal lettering of passages from an "Address to the Dominicans" by Albert Camus, who in 1948 had accused the Church, with all its fantastic capacity for authoritative teaching and prophetic voice, of being silent during the Nazi occupation of France. Camus had been part of the underground Resistance, made up mostly of agnostics, confronting each day's heinous crimes against humanity in powerlessness but defiance, attempting, as he said, to keep at least one more child from extinction. The text was being used in my "Religious Themes in Contemporary Literature" class.

USF was into new construction and Phelan Hall was surrounded by an eight-foot plywood wall. One of my students in the dark of night wrote out sections from Camus' indictment on that wall. The Jesuit community was outraged; these scurrilous words were attacking their "holy mother the Church." The student was caught and punished by the student court, a condemnation supported by the Jesuits. So, of course, I argued and advocated for my student and for the doubts and rejections that were surging during this time against the Vietnam War. I challenged the idea of ROTC training at a Jesuit university, training officers to feed this (in the minds of many of us) immoral war. I felt and do today the desire to support students who want to refuse going into military service as "conscientious objectors." I made this option known to my students.

During the last days of my tenure at USF, a Jesuit administrator met me one evening in the hall of the Jesuit residence and came out with this immortal line: "Bob, if we let them question their country [and Church?], they will question everything." This Jesuit friend was denying what a university is supposed to be all about. I knew that he was sincere. And that he was abysmally wrong. That the university was behind him, as were the Jesuit community. Clearly I did not belong.

But the "turning point" wasn't one thing but cumulative. I reached a place where things added up in that spring 1968. I was a leper for the Jesuit community, denounced, avoided, but never addressed. More substantially decisive, I'd say, was my subpoenaed appearance in court for the defense during the "Love Book" obscenity trial. A Presbyterian minister from the Haight-Ashbury district four blocks east of campus was so impressed by the students at our Sunday student liturgy that she invited me to visit a coffee house she and a Methodist minister had opened for the homeless. Complicating that invitation was an added request that I sit in on a panel discussing a book of poetry being locally prosecuted for obscenity. My contribution was that I thought the "Love Book" poem was highly erotic, offensive to some sensitivities, not something for a captive audience, but not pornographic; in fact, could be judged a "paean to human heterosexual love." At that a "plainclothes" person from the audience arose and said to the panel: "You are all under arrest; Father Brophy, would you care to withdraw your last statement." I refused and he backed down, perhaps not wanting to arrest a Jesuit faculty member from USF. But another bridge was crossed and burned.

I will never know whether he was truly from the SF Police Department, but I wrote an editorial the next day for the student paper, detailing the event and describing USF as a circle of wagons shutting out the real world's concerns, in this instance police harassment going on across the park at a Haight bookstore. My editorial was reprinted by the American Civil Liberties Union bulletin without my knowledge or consent, and I was served a subpoena to appear in court for the defense of the clerks who had sold the book to the police. An informer, possibly the police chief who was the brother-in-law of my dean, alerted the administration. Called in by USF president Father Dullea, S.J., I explained what had happened and my decision in conscience to appear. He said my involvement and the prospect of court appearance did not sit well with USF benefactors. He then commanded me not to go within three blocks of the courthouse. I replied that his edict hit deep into my sense of integrity and conscience. He told me I had three days to think it over. I don't know how he intended to fix the subpoena downtown. That is another matter. I appeared in court, was interrogated by the prosecution through morning and afternoon sessions; subsequently another Jesuit was sent to give testimony to contradict me. No Jesuit, including Fr. Dullea, further communicated with me. But the Rubicon was crossed.

In the community "wreck" room I was confronted and abused by Frank Marien, a sweet person, head of a philosophy department that at the time was wrestling with the fact that one of its members had declared himself an atheist. He saw me as an outsider, a fame-monger, publicity-hound, and most un-Jesuit of all. My friend Gene Schallert, a classmate of Frank, stood there and said nothing. It was that insane year of assassinations, when in his death some campus Jesuits openly dishonored and slandered Martin Luther King, when the renewed hope in a Kennedy was snuffed in a hotel in downtown Los Angeles.

Anyway, yes, at this time, I decided to leave the Jesuits, being an un-reformable, somewhat desperate rebel.

Is there a lesson in all this? Had I become a cog in the process of change? I'm afraid not. Ironically I would be no problem at the current 2008 USF that has as president a Liberation theologian, Stephen Privett, S.J., has a Peace Center headed by a world-renowned director, Stephen Zunes, publishes a peace periodical, sends students to Central and South America to witness and work for justice issues. But I see no connection, no role I filled. I wrote to the California provincial and to Pedro Arrupe, the Jesuit general, informing them of my disillusionment and imminent choice to leave. Gene Schallert told me afterward that Fr. Arrupe was saddened by my letter. He didn't elaborate. I don't see myself as a martyr toward bringing those changes. They happened ten or so years later because of an avalanche of other forces. I have admiration for the current Society of Jesus. It is at the cutting-edge for Gospel Justice issues. Where would I be if all this change had come sooner? That's another's lifetime

Church and Fascism, Conservatism

KI: You use the term "all its fantastic capacity" (Camus reference) to describe the power of the Church that was not turned to defeat, or at least discredit, fascism. Of course, that was also the situation in Spain where the preponderance of the hierarchy in the Church actually supported Franco. Do you see something in the organization of the Roman Church that gives a huge weight to conservatism, even fascism, even when it is clearly not in tune with the Jesus Teaching? I suppose that is a position I have come to, especially watching the Vatican close down the great opening of Vatican II. It made me a liberationist in my theology. Any comments about your thinking in the late 60s?

RB: At the time, I found the Church abysmally intractable, untrue to itself. Though we did experience exceptions in John XXIII and the Vatican Council in the 1960s, these were obstructed, especially by Pope John Paul II. Yes, the hierarchical church still appears to be a typical conservative, very human organization intent on damage control, wrapped in sometimes brute, unconditioned power, in many ways corrupt because the power is exercised absolutely. Its modernity is more typical in Pope John Paul II, who will be judged a criminal by many on account of his cold-bloodedly crushing of Latin American Liberation Theology and replacing bishops—those who cared for the poor, deplored dictators and elite-rule, and embraced an option for the poor—with Opus Dei prelates who side with the rich and powerful and do not see justice as a concern. An irony is that the Church has a most revolutionary and lyrical teaching on social issues, war and peace, commutative and distributive justice, human rights, common good, living wage, rights of unions, wealth distribution, and dangers of Capitalism. But these are never preached, too seldom applied.

Typical also is its current dealing with everything from recycling pedophiles to declaring gays unnatural, its dealing with women's place in the priesthood, forbidding contraception, second marriage, condoms for spouses of those with AIDS. Most often egregiously unpastoral, comfortable with power for its own sake, fearing to admit mistakes or missteps, reflecting little humanity, little mercy, allowing few exceptions; intent on keeping an "infallible" system, the hierarchical church becomes in parody an Old Boys' Club. In all its purple head-to-toe garb, pomp, and arcane rituals one finds little holiness, little humility, or even concern because hierarchical loyalties are not to me, you, or us but to their system, to keep it in its every case unquestioned. The lay world at present has no voice, no constitutional rights. They are serfs. Have you ever thought to write to Rome? Write to Santa Claus.

In this latest case of molestation-cover-up, an admission of guilt would/could be healing for all. Stonewalling involves a claim that bishops, cardinals, and pope are the Church not just a skewed, long-outmoded hierarchical structure; they are unresponsive, immune to questions, hostile to challenges. If the Church is to live, the sharing of power might be a first step—as for the acknowledgment of fault. I suspect Vatican and bishops are following lawyers' advice: Admit nothing lest you lose your episcopal palaces, and you lose the loyalty and support of lock-step Opus Dei among whom you are, in all, God speaking and ruling.

Bible as Literature: Genres

MZC: Broph, you teach a course at the university, "The Bible as Literature," beginning with Genesis 1-11, as Myth. What do you convey in your teaching to the students? What kind of questions do your students ask you? How is Literature related to Myth? How do you do the trick of presenting Creation to your students, creation myth as a spiritually rich "deep truth-bearing genre, the dramatizing of a belief system, a creed as told in a story"?

KI: I just read this quote from an e-mail of yours: "One Catholic priest in Orange County I am told (don't know his name) tells his class for converts: 'The Bible is entirely true, and some of it really happened.'" I have heard that there is convincing evidence that the entire Exodus story was made from whole cloth during the Babylonian exile, by I think P (Priest editor). And yet we never, never hear about things like this in the popular press. Instead we get pious documentaries on PBS about following in Moses footsteps or the like? Is there some kind of censorship going on? It can't be conscious? (In my view it is a kind of cultural myopia.)

RB: There is cowardice in not updating the faithful on Bible interpretation; it is true, a kind of pusillanimity, and a fear of undermining faith. But adults can be taught, though it has to be gradual and heart-felt. I teach the Bible as an anthology of genres: myth (story embodying a belief system), fable, legend, epic, covenant, legal and holiness codes, cycle stories, proto-history, oracle, diatribe, vision, allegory, poetic prayer, cautionary tales, revisionist history, melodrama, proverb and diatribe, verse-drama, and so forth. What one seeks is the meaning, the revelation of each pericope. For instance, Genesis 1-11 is a credo in story form (we believe in one god, transcendent and immanent, holy, ethical, forming mankind in his image, creating good and allowing evil, caring but just, forgiving but confrontive; the medium is myth (Greek for "story") turning upside down the polytheistic myths surrounding Israel by using the same story elements (clay potter, tree, serpent, flood, tower) in a new way. Adam and Eve are metaphors of disobedience and infidelity, but no one, not the 1992 New Catholic Catechism, for instance, will breathe such a sentence. We thus ask the wrong questions, listen with prejudiced, preprogrammed ears. We are left as children hugging our stories and oblivious of the meaning they really carry. We want an historic Samaritan with wife and children rather than an extended metaphor demanding that we love and care for our enemies as ourselves, all of them. The result of this prolonged silence and its ignorance is often disastrous for faith. Every year I have five to ten fallen-away Catholic students in class who have not been taught to see beyond fairy stories.

Scholar—Teacher—Activist—with Jeffers as Guru

MZC: Broph, you're a scholar, teacher and activist. How do they relate and complement each other? What projects are calling you, first as a scholar, second as a teacher and third as an activist? And finally, would you say how your appreciation of Robinson Jeffers affects your life? How did you get into his literature? I remember once when we were at a meeting with Bob Holstein at Verbum Dei High School in Watts and you offered to teach the high school boys Robinson Jeffers. I've wondered how Jeffers has captivated you.

RB: Jeffers entered my life almost by chance or was it providence. For my doctoral dissertation I had begun working on the Welsh poet Dylan Thomas. In the summer of 1962, I was back in California and making a retreat at Alma College, the Jesuit school of theology then at Los Gatos. In a break from the *Exercises*, I wandered through the library and looking up to the shelves on American literature, among the poets, I spied the volume *Selected Poems of Robinson Jeffers* and took it down from the shelf recalling that one of my North Carolina professors had done something of a parody of Jeffers in my first year of studies. He assigned Jeffers' two most difficult lyrics—"Night" and "Apology for Bad Dreams,"—probably because he himself did not understand them, and then proceeded to give synopses of Jeffers' long narratives. I was later to think that if anyone had only summaries of Aeschylus and Euripides, he might think that the two playwrights should be in a psychiatric ward—for their fixation on incest, murder, and perverse fate.

My take on Jeffers was quite different; I found him one of the most religious writers of the century. He was obsessed with questions on the nature of God, depth of prayer, meaning of beauty, perversity of mankind, extent of the universe, the beginning and the end. To the consternation of my professor, I found religious awe and austere asceticism in each poem. Here was a man who was obsessed with ultimate questions. He found different answers from mine, but the focus was there. He was a challenge that grabbed, struck deep. He was a determinist and pessimist as regards to mankind, seeing humans as blasphemous, myopic, obsessed with themselves, perverse in their wars and their oblivious destruction of environment. I carried him with me into my growing activism. He was a pessimist and determinist; I argue with him though dead since 1962. He has a saying for me, confronting my activism: "Go out into the Seal Beach surf, hold up your hand for ten minutes, and then come back and tell me how many waves you have stopped." He has kept me honest. He was a mystic; he prayed daily with poems. That was what counted.

I loved to take students on camping weekends to Jeffers Country stretching from Carmel to Big Sur. We went in convoys of five or so cars, launching out from Long Beach at 5:00AM, putting up tents at Big Sur at 11:00, searching through the fantastic stone house and tower he built solely with his own hands in Carmel at 1:00, reading poems to each other from the time we started. Then Point Lobos and down the coast stopping at each turnout to read more poems composed at those spots. It turned out to be the highlight of each student's college years. I found that the two other persons working on RJ were Catholics, the monk Brother Antoninus and the daily communicant Ann Ridgeway.

REDONDO BEACH
A Poem by Robert Brophy

Lines for Matthew Arnold or variations on "Dover Beach"

The sea is calm tonight,
And bleakness full, the fog lies eerie
Upon the shore; toward the pier a car light
Glimmers and is gone; the cliffs off Palos Verdes stand.
Come to the verge, strange is the starless aerie.
Only, from the long line of foam
Where sea meets fog-blanched sand,
Listen! You'll hear those without home
Grieving while the waves draw back, and fling
On their return, up where cold forms stand,
Hiss, then cease, and then again begin,
With tremulous cadence slow, and bring,
Yes, infernal notes of impoverishment in.

Jack Smith not long ago
Heard it by Newport Pier, and it brought
Into his mind that turbid flow
Of Southland misery; we
Find also, in the sound, the selfsame thought,
Hearing it by this the South Bay sea.

Locked restroom stalls
Were once accessible, and round earth's shore
Apartments not burdened with enormous rent,
But now we only hear
The melancholy, long, foreclosing roar
Adjusting to the windfalls
Of new yuppie profits, evictions drear.
Bush safety-net only butt-cold sand has sent.

Ah, love, let us be not austerely continent;
Comfort one another, for the world that seems
To lie, before some, a Disneyland of dreams,
So fireworks-bright, so hospitable, so content,
Hath really neither rooms, nor warmth, nor light,
Nor welcoming Winchell's donut shop with steamy pane,
While vagrant homeless suffuse the darkling plain.
Swept by hawking sheriff and Minute-men, our blight,
Where huddled Ishmaels and Hagars endure the night.

"Trouble Maker"
A Conversation with Harry Wu
San Francisco, August 12, 1997

> *"A barrier to freedom is China's machinery for crushing dissent: the more than 1,100 labor reform camps called the laogai. The laogai is not simply a prison system. It is a political tool for maintaining the Communist Party's totalitarian rule. Many of the laogai's six to eight million inmates are political prisoners."*
>
> —Harry Wu, 1996

Harry Wu was a political prisoner in China for nineteen years, from 1960 to 1979. His personal suffering in the Chinese 'Gulag' or 'Laogai' served his desire to expose cruel injustice. He was a university student in geology. He was born in 1937; Harry's father was a banker and was denounced as a "capitalist" in 1949. Harry was asked to repudiate his father which he couldn't do. His family fell on hard times. Harry went to political meetings with other students. He was imprisoned in 1960 for criticizing the Soviet invasion of Hungary in 1957.

He emigrated to the United States in 1985 and was an associate at the Hoover Institute in 1988 at Stanford University. He started making documentaries for British, Canadian and American TV about human rights violations such as forced labor and the selling of executed prisoners' organs. In 1991, he went back to China to document prisoner abuse with a hidden camera. In 1995, Harry was arrested in China but released, thanks to the heavy pressure by some governments and human rights groups.

My student, Dong Fang, introduced me to his sponsor, Harry Wu. Dong fled China for political reasons, first going one dark evening by boat to Taiwan and then to the United States. Dong continues some activist work and writing, while Harry Wu has dedicated his life to being a human rights activist. I first became aware of Harry Wu when some of my students asked me to support a letter writing campaign for Harry in 1995 when he was being held by the Chinese. After studying about Harry, I gladly wrote: "I wish to express my strong concern over the detention of Hongda Harry Wu on June 19, 1995 and his subsequent arrest. I'm writing to the United States Congress and to President Clinton, urging that the strongest possible measures be used to secure Mr. Wu's release. He is, as Amnesty International states, 'a prisoner of conscience.'" Harry would be under arrest for sixty-six days in 1995, with round-the-clock observance, before being released under massive international pressure. When Harry was arrested as a spy, he said: "The information I was looking for on this trip was not for the intelligence service of the United States I wanted information for the media, to expose where there are human rights violations in China at this time. You must understand that the Chinese Government lies all the time, to its own people, to other governments, that there are no political prisoners in China. They lied about me and to me. Communist Party members lie to themselves. Nobody really believes in communism any longer in China. They just believe in power."

Some of my Chinese students invited me to a discussion of Harry Wu's book, Troublemaker in 1996 *(Also we referred to* Bitter Winds: My Years in China's Gulag: John Wiley and Sons, 1994. *We discussed informally our ideas of community organizing. That also served as background for my questions when Harry agreed to sit with me and record this conversation the following year.*

I found him to be sensitive, outraged, compelling, perceptive, indignant, straight forward in his push for intelligent activism around human rights' issues in China, I was aware of campaign to boycott toys made by prison labor. "China is too big a market for a total boycott and some companies are honest. We want to pinpoint the toy companies where we have evidence that they are making their toys with prison labor."

Since our first meeting we have become friends and stay in touch. What gift and good luck to have a friend and dedicated collaborator. I truly admire his work. I'm also aware some Chinese, especially from the business community, do not support Harry.

MZC: Recently, we read excerpts from *Troublemaker* together. How do you consider yourself now as a troublemaker; in what sense do you consider yourself that?

HW: First of all, the title of "troublemaker" was given to me by the Communist government. In my life, I've received two titles from the Communist government. The first one is so-called "counterrevolutionary rightist." This was in 1957 because my opinion was not acceptable to them: I disagreed with the Soviet invasion of Hungary. I criticized a Communist government for shooting common people who were considered second-class citizens. It seemed to me that this violated international law. I was told that I didn't know about things so naturally I disagreed. The government [stopped using] "counterrevolutionary" in 1979.

Then in 1995 they arrested me; in my interrogation by the chief of police, I said that I had a legal passport and that I didn't violate my visa. I didn't go into China. I was on the border. They took me in. I did no activities inside China that violated their law. If they said, well it's for a couple of years ago, then that's another story. So when they arrested me on the border, I said: According to your law, [show] me your warrant. Give me the reason. Otherwise, you can't arrest me. Because this is your law, right?

And secondly I said, there's an agreement between the United States and China. I'm an American citizen. Within forty-eight hours, you have to notify my consulate. I'm not going to talk to you before I talk to my consulate. This is international law. So I refused to agree to any interrogation. They asked me my name. Nothing. Your address? No. Nothing.

I said I want to call my embassy. And there's my partner, an American female—she also was detained for no reason at all. After about five days, finally, the senior police said, "Harry,

I'll be honest with you, OK? Don't make trouble for me. I can do nothing about that. You know. I have heard from the top, from the chief, and you have to know you have the label of 'troublemaker.' I have heard from Beijing and you are the number one troublemaker."

So I think this is an accomplishment because we do have to make some trouble for this evil part of the regime. Yes, many, many people, especially the Chinese, stand up, become straight, join with me. We fight together; we make trouble for this Communist regime. And then, we try and have a good future.

MZC: Were you frightened to be arrested again in 1995 and then being sentenced to fifteen years in prison? Did you feel support from the American and international community?

HW: I wasn't afraid at all. I know this may sound surprising, but I wasn't. I know these people all too well. I had more than nineteen years of prison life, so I blocked out the memories, didn't think about it. If I dwell on the past I am weak. Of course, I didn't want to lose my freedom, but I was calm.

I felt support both from the international and American communities. I was made an American citizen in 1994. Honestly I didn't feel a part of the United States. I felt somewhat an outsider. But after being released from China, after sixty-six days, I felt that the people of the United States did care for me. When I returned many put up yellow ribbons and that felt very good. They cared about my freedom, my liberty to be who I am.

MZC: Do you feel part of the Chinese character is very reluctant to be a troublemaker? They tend to be politically passive—I'm talking about Chinese from Taiwan and from China—who tend to want not to get involved. Do you think that's changing, especially with younger people?

HW: Yes, you're talking about Chinese tradition. Even when I was young, my father always warned me, don't get involved with politics. Just go ahead, just study, and earn your degree and earn money. You set up a living. This is your life. Don't involve yourself with politics. Because in China, all the time, not only during the Communist regime, politics are dangerous, very dirty. That's why the people are always thinking about not getting involved so they don't get into trouble.

But, we do have to make some trouble for what is evil and hurtful to human dignity and natural rights. Let's consider: what is the trouble I made? First of all I exposed the Chinese gulag system, *laogai* system. Should we turn a blind eye? Should we forget about it? Should we say, we don't know about it? [Though] I was able to survive from the prison system, should I say, Well, OK, that's over? I won't involve myself in politics. To say this is dishonest. So, I exposed it, because this is a dark area in the system.

Today we were talking about Tiananmen, about the Tibetan Repression. Talking about religious suppression—if you want to expose the concentration camp system, under the Hitler Nazi system, if you want to expose the gulag system under Stalin's regime, of course you're going to make trouble.

They don't want you to talk about it, but this is something we have to think about. How many people are unjustly held in China's prison system? Should we turn a blind eye and say, let's do business together because all the people are doing well, and China eventually will get into a democratic society. I hope so. I really wish for a democracy. But, we have no right to turn our back on innocent people. Even today we must in our own [US] democracy, remember things from fifty years ago. You know that there were concentration camps then, but today we overlook that there is a there is today a concentration camp system in China.

If a nation turns a blind eye on its past, and doesn't look at history, then it can never have a good future. Because the Communist government is responsible for a type of holocaust in China, they don't want me to talk about it. They say OK, forget it because they don't want to reveal themselves, their rule of the country, as the power center. Actually they're still doing unjust, inhuman things. That's why I make trouble for them.

MZC: Yes. Do you feel some of the practices you exposed in your book; for example, selling of human organs of executed prisoners, still go on?

HW: In 1996, there, according to Amnesty International, there were 4367 executions [in China]. Organ transplants are an indication of a civilized society. It means, we are able, using our technology, to [donate] our organs for the benefit of other people. I attach a small card to my driver's license that says that I'm going to donate all my organs for the welfare of other people. But to forcibly take and sell the organs of executed prisoners? What is that about? Most Chinese don't understand the concept of organ donation. They want to die with their whole body intact; [that is why] many people today in China don't accept cremation. But we have to get together in a civilized society and have a positive relation to organs.

But, if someone like the Indian or Filipino, sell their organs just to get money, or for food, we see it as a kind of a human tragedy. If someone in Colombia or Mexico murders to get an organ for a millionaire, I think everybody sees this as evil. But today the problem in China is what? Go about your own business, and just mind your own affairs, even if executed prisoners' organs are being sold.

The government, according to their political purpose, the so-called "revolutionary concept," of the legal system in China, is service for Communist party. This is not the law [of] a democratic society. Just like the law under Hitler, the law under Stalin, its purpose is a political purpose. It was about control and power. In the Chinese criminal court, there are sixteen crimes that carry the death sentence; nine of them are political.

The government in accordance with Communist law, arrests the people, prosecutes them, and sentences them to death: everybody knows that in this judicial procedure, nobody has a fair trial. The Communist government just says we sentence such and such to death, according to political necessity. The government arranges the execution, and then claims the right to harvest the organs after the death of prisoners. And lastly the hospital is owned by the Chinese government—the hospital and public security and the court cooperate together to remove the organ.

MZC: There's no international body trying to work some type of a law with that? Not yet?

HW: Not yet, but I think there's more awareness. The government sells your organ in the international market, and that's in recognized international reports. 75 percent [of the world's executions] today happen in China. Every year, several thousand. We don't know exactly. China never gives out that data.

When they sell organs to [people from] a foreign country, the central argument that we are using the waste. Human body becomes a waste? What are you talking about? What is the concept? Second [argument], oh, these people were bad [criminals]. They paid back the damage. What are you talking about? My organ paid back my damage?

MZC: They are taking organs from the political prisoner?

HW: Of course. [Is this really] a pay back to society? If this is really something like that, why do you sell them to foreigners? That's why I argue with the Chinese Communist, the so-called 'nationalists.' They all say China is great; we are helping the Chinese.

China has a lot of diseased patients. Why are you holding back this organ from our Chinese citizens? Why do you sell to the foreigners? Money. Money. This is why, behind the wall, a government is selling human organs. If I murder someone for an organ, for the purpose for making this money, this is crime, this is evil. And the government is doing that today. Yeah. I make trouble for them.

The real troublemaker in this is the Communist Party. They really make big trouble for their own people. They make trouble to me. Deprive my freedom for twenty years. They killed my parents, my mother, and millions of Chinese. They are the real troublemakers. Not me. But, I am honored, to have the title of a "troublemaker" with the Communist regime. We Chinese need the troublemaker to dare to speak out, dare to say no.

MZC: Forced abortions are still going on?

HW: Oh yeah, oh yeah. You can't imagine; there's a government program of fourteen million abortion cases every year. Fourteen million. This is a very conservative number. Actually there's about twenty million. If, we just say that 10 percent are forced, then a million are forced. Actually, so many of them are forced. That is oppression.

MZC: I think it's interesting you use *laogai*; you keep the Chinese name, because that whole system is so important to the government?

HW: Yeah. So the *laogai* is the most salient place for concentrated human rights' abuses. Now some people ask me what are you doing? What is the purpose of the Foundation? I want to see the word *laogai* appear in every dictionary in every language, in every country. What we do know is that before 1974, we didn't have "gulag" as a word. Today "gulag" is a well-known word, and, we acknowledge the past Soviet Union political violence. *Laogai* deserves that kind of exposure. [The word] should be there for all to see.

MZC: "Concentration camp" is part of our vocabulary now.

HW: Yeah. You see. Why are the Chinese so mad about me? Because I'm talking about the *laogai*. In December 1994, the People's Congress passed a resolution to stop using the term of *laogai* because many of us activists are talking about *laogai,*

laogai, laogai. It's infamous because we're raising consciousness in the world community.

In my interrogation in 1995, the secret police asked me why I link together *laogai* and *gulag*? Isn't that too much? He showed me my book. Why do you link them together? Because you know gulag is infamous. It's really terrible. I said well, there's no difference. In the early 1950s, a gulag expert, arranged by Stalin came to China and helped set up Chinese *laogai.* Do you deny that? He cannot deny it. The [Congress] removed the word because they hate it.

Probably 20 to 30 percent of the people in China either themselves, or their parents, or their relatives, or their neighbor or friends, went to *laogai.* A very large number. The Communist government cannot survive without the *laogai.* They need it.

When I went to Geneva to talk to the International Red Cross, I said don't repeat your 1930s mistake. Hitler invited you to see a model concentration camp. Then you wrote a report, saying well, not so bad, not so good. Actually you became a part of their propaganda. They cheated you and you can be cheated like that in China.

MZC: So they can't be just shown one model camp that they can gloss over, with the one thousand they have.

HW: Right. That's right. Now, the other point I will share with you today in 1997 is to go back sixty years.

Today is 1937. German concentration camps. Are you interested? 1937.… Yeah? Many countries blocked the Jewish from escaping. Right? I remember the whole ship loaded with the refugees to go to Louisiana; even Americans at that time turned them back. They didn't know the horror yet. Right? sixty years ago.

How we can upgrade our information? We are not going to say we're 100 percent correct.

But, we are collecting information from different sources; that's why I go back to China. That's why I interviewed many survivors. For example, the priests (former prisoners in China). I went to Los Gatos to interview them. To one I asked how many years? Thirty years. Where you have been? Oh, in this area. There're so many labor camp. (clears throat) I spent nineteen-twenty years in prisons, camps; I've been in twelve camps. But I don't know where else there are other camps. I don't know in the east, that's why we interview the people. That is the resource. See my story in *Bitter Winds* or *Troublemaker.*

It was just a small brick, my being an activist, my organizing. I'm a small part in the effort that will bring more human rights to China.

MZC: What's your feeling about the American policy now? It seems like in our L.A. area, China's the big golden calf today. You know it's the future market.

HW: Today's American policy is to appease, same as the British appeasement policy in 1938. Short term, looking for money. This isn't with everybody, but many are just looking for a promising market, looking for benefit.

I'm very sad Clinton says he admires Kennedy. He wanted to do something like Kennedy. What? For China, he's just looking for money, looking for self-interest. I don't see his courage in speaking against human rights. Yes, sometimes, he speaks out against abuse of human rights, but not as called for by the abuses going on in China.

MZC: We were talking about the possibility of social action, of a boycott against some countries, companies that receive prison-made products.

HW: Particularly for America, it is illegal because since 1930, [there is] a law to not allow in any kind of products made or processed by forced labor. This is not only a human rights issue, it is a legal one. They violate the law.

We are thinking about boycotting Christmas decoration and toys also made by forced labor this coming Christmas. First of all Christmas is a time to deliver our sympathy, our kindness, our love, to other people. When you buy toys that are made by China, or the Christmas decoration made by China, and, if you're thinking they are made by forced labor; then there's a possible involvement of abuses of human rights. Not all Chinese products, of course, are made by forced labor. But when we find that some of the toys/Christmas decorations being sold now by Wal-Mart, let's boycott Wal-Mart until it changes to non-forced-labor products.

When we are thinking about other people, sympathizing with people with sickness and delivering our love, we should now be also thinking about human rights abuses in China. OK? Thinking about the human beings in China. The religious persecution in China is terrible. You know very well how Cardinal Ignatius Kung suffered thirty years in prison for refusing to renounce his religious conviction. He's a brave survivor of the *laogai*.

MZC: I see you are calling for active expressions of solidarity with the men and women who are still in prison and subjected to forced labor.

HW: K-Mart imported seventy-six tons [of products] made by PLA. So we say kick the PLA out of the United States. Please let's be conscious of what we're doing. If we show the evidence, act on it.

MZC: I'd like to end by changing the tone a bit and asking you a more personal question. One of the students, who is Chinese and a Buddhist monk, asked me, if I would ask you about what gave you strength when you were in prison. He said it must have been heartbreaking to be so lonely, to be isolated. We talked about the story when you were beaten and your fellow prisoners caught a frog, cooked it and made a soup and brought you back to health.

This monk has also experienced some very terrible scenes in his native Burma. He wondered if you found any kindness, which helped you get through that time? And what is it from your experience that makes you so sympathetic and compassionate towards the prisoners that still are in that system?

HW: That is why I talk about the most important value and dignity in human beings, in human lives is humanity in its best sense of the word, being civil, being considerate, and being what we can't always define but which we respond to. I like the word "kindness" also. You're being kind even if you get no reward in return. That's being human. Okay? (Harry seems fatigued at this point in the conversation, but his face is brightly animated.)

We were talking about politics, talking about revolution. Talking about injustice. This can make you feel overburdened and out of balance. You have to draw from the best within humanity, its ability to love I would say. Beyond that abuse of human dignity is humanity waiting to emerge. It is natural for human beings to be kind in my opinion. In my book, there's another story when a young lady came to feed me on a regular basis. She never thought about getting some reward or how generous she was. And, she didn't think, maybe in the future we'll become millionaires or famous. Nothing. Just a selfless response to me, at the time, a human being living under horrific conditions in prison.

I was a political prisoner, nobody knows about me. There's no future in it—my family totally got rid of me so they wouldn't be "guilty by association." But this beautiful woman still was like my sister coming to see me. Why? Why? All the time I was in the cell, I really want to know the meaning why? I said this was the Buddha or Jesus coming to me for free, just for love. What's happening? I think it is Humanity—a human being's natural contact and feeling empathy towards another in need. I think this wanting to be good, to express natural human goodness is the fundamental element to life, you know. That's the abiding background to my activist work, which is tough and critical, very activist, calling, along with many others, for China to respect the human rights of others.

I think that when we're talking about religious prosecution, talking about minorities who are persecuted, talking about forced separations due to being political prisoners, about organizing activities and student and workers' movements; we need to remember the human heart and its goodness, joy and humor. That makes us stronger and supported for the fight against injustice in the world

MZC: Thank you, Harry. Many blessings for your loving service to China and to all of us.

Harry Wu was invited to talk at the European Parliament in Brussels, Belgium, November 12, 2003. The forum included members from all the states of the European Union, as well as candidate states and members of national parliaments. Its purpose was to make resolutions regarding the relationship between China and Tibet and, in particular, to promote human rights dialogue. The forum publicly deplored the violations of individual and collective rights of the Tibetan people, especially the right of self-determination. It declared that the government of China was repressing the Tibetan peoples' religious and political rights and encouraged dialogue between the Dalai Lama and the Chinese government.

The Crux of the Tibetan Problem

European Parliament Forum on Tibet: EU Response to Sino-Tibetan Dialogue
Harry Wu, Laogai Research Foundation

It's been almost fifty years since China "liberated" Tibet, crushing its people, government and its religion, and forcing the Dalai Lama into exile. Only thirteen of over six thousand monasteries were left standing after the terror of the mid-1960s. Now about one hundred thirty thousand Tibetans live in exile, mostly in India and Nepal.

Tibetans have fled. However, they have not given up hope. They have not been wiped-out or deemed irrelevant, and I suspect they will never be. To most Han Chinese, Tibetans are an "uncivilized, ignorant, filthy and superstitious" people, who needed to be liberated by the Chinese Communist Party. Yet, all throughout the world, Tibetans stand with pride.

All over the world, exiled Tibetans live together in peace with the local people of their adopted nations, receiving respect and welcome and trust. Tibetans maintain their religion, culture, dress and customs, as well as their own government in-exile, with an unmistakable dignity. Among the younger generation, many obtain high-level academic degrees, and become well-known scholars. They may have lost their land, but they are reaching toward the heavens.

Beijing received a high-level delegation to restart negotiations with His Holiness, the Dalai Lama. Regardless of Beijing's motives for holding these talks, or if the negotiations have any real success, at the very least, the negotiations make one thing clear: despite being exiled for over fifty years, Beijing cannot ignore the Dalai Lama and his people.

Beijing refused to talk with Tibetan delegates for many years; they referred to them as a "Gang of Bandits." Now, Beijing is beginning to accept reality. One of the reasons that brought Beijing back to negotiating table is the fact that the Communist regime is facing a historic crisis. It must change its policies. The exiled Tibetan government does not enjoy any military or any economic power; it does not even have any diplomatic relations. Yet they still matter. As everyone knows, the CCP's political power is always based on physical strength. Yet, the facts prove, although often drowned out by wickedness and greed, justice and truth eventually prevail.

Beijing knows the Dalai Lama and Tibetans are highly respected by peoples and governments of nearly all nations. They know truth is not on their side. Nevertheless, there are two key factors supporting Beijing's Tibet policy: First, most Han Chinese are prejudiced against Tibetans, and believe Tibetans need economic, cultural and other assistance. Second, most Han Chinese believe Tibet was never an independent country, and was always a part of China. As a result, most Han Chinese agree with Beijing's policies. Even many Chinese exiled or domestic dissidents who claim they are fighting for democracy, freedom and human rights. Unfortunately, the sentiment of traditional nationalism is leading them to support and agree with Beijing's Tibet policy.

Many Han Chinese ask: "Isn't Han Chinese culture superior to Tibet's?" Don't Tibetans have an unhealthy, harmful lifestyle? Don't they want a theocracy? Doesn't the Tibetan religion block economic and cultural development, etc.? These questions are important to evaluate and discuss. However, the first thing we should address is this: who has the right to judge right from wrong? Moreover, who has the right to use physical force to implement such a judgment?

If a culture fails to respect another people's right to self-determination, then itself has no right to self-determination. Yet, this is what is happening in China. If Han Chinese are in the process of seeking democracy, freedom and prosperity, then it should respect another culture's right to do the same. Tibetans have the right to seek their own political future, social structure, religious beliefs and culture.

Actually, Han Chinese must appreciate Tibetan's tireless, courageous and consistent fight for its fundamental rights. Their struggle is breaking the power of the Communist autocratic regime in China. Tibet's efforts will eventually benefit all Chinese people.

If most Han Chinese begin believing that they should respect Tibet, and agree that Tibet has freedom of choice, I believe Beijing's current policy would become untenable. When a majority of Han Chinese expresses this type of sentiment, it will represent a significant shift in thought among Han Chinese.

In the last twenty years, the Communist government has hidden its use of force against the Tibetan people under the cover of economic development along with the tens of thousands of Han Chinese migrants pouring into Tibet. The same autocratic government that destroyed Tibetan monasteries now is spending money to rebuild the monasteries. They are building railways, highways, and power stations. Their purpose is to gradually eliminate Tibetan's culture, religion, and people.

I wish Western nations would clearly express their desire to see fruitful negotiations between China and the Dalai Lama.

However, I also hope they will stop investing in Tibet, stop purchasing any products made in Tibet, and never welcome any Beijing-controlled Tibetan delegates, or culture or artistic performances.

The State Department of the United States government has appointed an Under Secretary of State, Ms. Paula Dobriansky, as US Special Coordinator for Tibetan Issues. This is a high level appointment, which highlights that the United States Government is paying serious attention to the non-violent struggle of Tibet. It is time for the European Union to also appoint a senior official to push China to the negotiation table. This is an important and concrete step that the European Union could take. It would show that the European Union does in fact actively defend the rights of the downtrodden and repressed.

The world is changing. In the face of a rising tide of globalization, liberalization, democratization and human rights, the old and tired petty excuses for injustice, such as colonialism, racism, communism and even nationalism, are becoming weak and indefensible. Sooner or later, they will all be thrown into the dustbin of history.

Part III

Section One, Western Approaches

At the center of our being is a point of nothingness
which is untouched by sin and by illusion,
a point of pure truth, a point or spark which belongs
entirely to God,
which is ever at our disposal, from which God disposes
of our lives,
which is inaccessible to the fantasies of our own mind
or the brutalities of our own will.

This little point of nothingness and of absolute poverty
is the pure glory of God in us.

It is like a pure diamond, blazing with the invisible light
of heaven.
It is in everybody, and if we could see it we would see
these
billions of points of light coming together in the face
and blaze of a sun that would make all the darkness and
cruelty
of life vanish completely.

I have no program, for this seeing.
It is only given.

But the gate of heaven is everywhere.
> —Thomas Merton (from *Conjectures of a*
> *Guilty Bystander*, 1966)

"Trans-Traditional Spirituality" and the Tao Te Ching

A Conversation with Eugene C. Bianchi, Ph.D.

> *I surrender to the belief that my knowing is a small part of a wider integrated knowing that knits the entire biosphere or creation.... Mind and Nature form a necessary unity, in which there is no mind separate from body and no god separate from his creation.*
>
> —Gregory Bateson

Gene Bianchi is both a careful, imaginative thinker and a man of heart. I sense he moves from love of the church and continued participation in it, to incisive criticism of it. He works toward a multi-layered, integrative understanding of world religions. He's embarrassed by any assertions that Catholics have the "best" way for all. We learn from and honor several other "best" ways.

He encourages a healthy ecumenism, enticing us with descriptions of spiritual nourishment and understanding from the great religious realizers, within their varying traditions.

He asks us how we might "re-vision our tradition in ways that can speak to a new age, sometimes referred to as post-modern or post-Christian. We should start by realizing that our most basic religious identity isn't Christian or Muslim or Hindu, but rather human ... the transcendent is already immanent and "incarnate" in the natural order whence we sprang.

EB: I see myself as a cosmopolitan and cultural Catholic who is grateful for a long religious education from the Jesuits to the Taoists. I discover spiritual meaning and inspiration from my own tradition: its saints, scholars, scriptures, contemplatives and social justice activists—sometimes even from its liturgies ... but I'm religiously eclectic.

Buddhism has brought me back to the contemplative

western tradition (especially The *Spiritual Exercises* of St. Ignatius), which I got into as a very young man before I had enough life experience to really appreciate them.

My standard poodle, Rhainy, is a constant meditation companion, and she represents a major shift in my spirituality towards what we call the natural world. Nature mysticism has become an ever more important part of my spirituality.

I'm impressed that the Dalai Lama turns to science to complement and correct areas of his theology; he's even questioned whether the succession of Dalai Lamas needs to be done as in the past, holding so tightly to re-birth. We're aware of such studies as in Colorado Rocky Mountain Dharma Center's "Shamantha Project," a ninety-day (2007) careful double-bind scientific study of the effects of meditation, conducted by Alan Wallace. There were thirty-six subjects, thirty-six assistants (cohorts). Eight scientists from UC Santa Barbara, UC Santa Cruz worked full time to conduct this experiment.

MZC: You were talking about the pope recently on line. I like your term "trans-traditional." I feel it respects what is genuine in the great religious traditions, but isn't literalist, fanatical, exclusively proclaiming "whatever religion" as the one true way. Some sections of Pope Benedict's writing on love could be understood this way.

EB: I was encouraged considering the pope's writings on love; yet, to me, contradictory to the spirit of that writing, the pope, while approving the use of the Latin mass (which I think is fine for those who love the Latin mass), also kept a very condescending, arrogant Good Friday liturgy—I must say it reflects prejudice against the Jewish people. Perhaps by now Pope Benedict has corrected this. I can't imagine that happening in 2007.

Pope John Paul extended his arms and theological positions to our great Jewish brothers and sisters. As a Catholic, I can also let be and appreciate the exquisite Jewish expression of their religion (in the very best, genuine, contemplative sense).

Trans-traditional signals to me, both a respectful acceptance of our religious traditions, and sensitivity to other cultural and religious movements. We are enriched by different approaches to finding the spiritual insight and experience. We are blessed to share and grow with each other.

I believe we are deepest and truest in our own religion when we revere other religions and continue to listen … and learn, along our winding, intersecting paths.

MZC: Do you consider that Jesus was an enlightened human being who in the process of his growth became fully united with God? What does scriptural scholarship say about this subject? In recent travels to Central America and Mexico, I've found Jesus in the reaching out to and being with the poor, in the Eucharist shared in small communities, Jesus as a sacramental presence, a spiritual presence of the wonder and sacredness of this life together.

How reliable is religious scripture in regard to Jesus as God? For example, How do we read religious scripture for its spiritual meaning rather than for its literal sense; going only for the literal meaning/literal pronouncements/literal condemnations/heavenly and hellish promises? How can we continue apply teachings to a different time and culture from the one we're presently living, with all our particular problems and resources/advances.…

EB: Within the world of scriptural scholarship, a number of people think that those divinizing statements in the New Testament are later additions, late in the sense of after the time of Jesus' life.

The early faith communities really started Christianity. Jesus was a Jew all the way through his life. The tendency to divinize Jesus in the early church was, in part, a way of competing with other faith groups in the Greco-Roman world, which also claimed divinity for a particular leader. Even Roman emperors were divinized.

The divine Jesus belief was finally set in Hellenistic language at Chalcedon. We might want to say then, rather than "Jesus is God," that God was transparent in Jesus or Jesus was a symbol of God (Cf. Roger Haight). A symbol participates in what it points to; it's not just a sign. Jesus really communicated great spiritual truths that he lived.

Some would argue that Jesus was divine as we are divine, namely that we all have an inward point of contact with the divine, the Kingdom within. We are all Christs.

Jesus had this inner divinity in a very intense, full way. Like the Buddha, Jesus was a great spiritual seeker and teacher who points us toward living a life of love, as well as to fully engage our own mysterious depths within.

MZC: What is an example of how we tend to attach to some idea of "God" or to "no-God"? We tend perhaps to console ourselves as special by saying God/Jesus is totally in love with me personally and is taking care of me? I noticed also in my Eastern spiritual searching in the 60s and 70s that we tended to create cults around some of the teachers.

EB: I always love what Buddha said about not believing something just because it comes from authority, even from the Buddha's authority. Find out for yourself. Be lamps unto yourselves. Of course, a teacher can be very helpful along the path.

The image of God as benevolent sky parent, while supplying some sort of solace, may be our attempt to limit and tame the incomprehensible mystery. The Tao that can be named is not the true Tao, says the Tao Te Ching in the first chapter.

The Jews have been ever wary of naming God.

We also notice with the appearance of the sky god an increasing institutionalization of religion in terms of sacred offices, orthodox beliefs and practices (with sanctions for errant ways). My point is not that this evolution, as seen in Christianity, is wrong or even unusual. It is very human to institutionalize and ritualize. In face of the great insecurities of life on earth, we tend to look to established religion to have the right answers, to direct roads to salvation, to control the means of being saved, to sacrilize offices like pope, bishop and priest, endowing them with supra-human efficacy and meaning.

MZC: Are you against institutional religion?

EB: Not at all. Humans institutionalize in virtually all realms, creating rules, customs, rituals, sacred documents and ethical systems. And they will continue to act in this way. Most of us were introduced to spiritual life through institutions of family and church.

But however significant these beginnings were for us, they do not plumb our most basic spiritual identity, which is that of human beings, immersed in evolutionary nature, beings already spiritual in our quest for meaning and experience in the life of our planet.

Our specific religious tradition is called upon to become porous or permeable to the spiritual signs of the times.

MZC: Speak more about ecumenism and how we can benefit by blending our personal spiritual practice with wisdom from the varying religious traditions.

EB: Trans-traditional spirituality is an attitude or disposition of openness to spiritual wisdom wherever it presents itself. Such insight can come through seemingly secular areas of art, music, biography, science and many other places in human experience where the soul is moved and enriched. It is an attitude of very broad ecumenism in which the religious seeker, either individually or with others, invites and experiences insights and practices from her own and other wisdom movements.

It is helpful to keep in the foreground our primal spirituality of being human, and to hold one's own specific religious tradition (however broadly or narrowly defined) as very valuable but as a partial and culturally relative approach towards truth. We are able to say yes and no to aspects of our own tradition, a process of retrieval and abandonment. A.N.

Whitehead said all religion was "in the making," that is, all religions are products of the human imagination in history; they are all testimonies to the human creativity, individually and in groups, struggling for transcendent meaning and experience.

MZC: I've been eminently helped in my own religious culture by some Eastern teachings/practices especially from Buddhism, sitting meditation and the cultivation of one's heart that is common in all the great traditions. Mastering the Golden Rule in daily life.

I'm hopeful and encouraged by interfaith (and scientific—which include some scientists who are atheists) collaboration. We're happy to be exploring together, with the best we, personally, and our traditions have.

E.B. We can embrace the teaching of eastern and western contemplatives. The title of a very influential book in medieval Christianity, The Cloud of Unknowing, teaches "not-knowing," as does the Tao Te Ching.

MZC: Gene, would you speak about ecological themes as related to Christianity and other religions? We're becoming aware of our Mother Nature's need for loving and wise care?

E.B. Global warming, de-forestation, and other forms of pollution to air, land, and water will continue to expand as the ethos of technology takes over our world. We can learn from such writers like Thomas Berry, Sallie McFague, Jay McDaniel, Rosemary Ruether, and others who have written about this.

The new challenge calls us far beyond recycling or a few prayers for earth at Mass … we have to cultivate a nature spirituality that can permeate into our liturgies and the way we act in life, for the care and cultivation of life. This flows from an experiential conversion in our attitudes toward the rhythms and dynamics of nature.

We are inflicting vast outward damage on the health of the planet and bringing significant psycho-spiritual harm to individuals and groups.

Thomas Berry commented that our fear of death is related to our dissociation from our earthly roots. In Dylan Thomas' words, we 'rage against the dying of the light,' not knowing that our rage is largely based on denying our place on and eventually in the earth. Perhaps the earth-consciousness of the paleontologist, Teilhard de Chardin, led him to pray that he would be able to end well, at peace with his condition in nature.

Certainly, the Taoist master understood this when he taught: "Immersed in the wonder of the Tao/ you can deal with whatever life brings you/ and when death comes, you are ready." The master not only teaches us the virtues of 'non-active action' of living in accord with nature, but helps us sense the deepest mystery of nature, the unnamable Tao, within ourselves and in the natural world.

MZC: Would you tell about your trip to Rome and your reflections about the Catholic Church when you were there? Would mention any thoughts you had about Taoism ("those who say they know the way don't know the way") while rambling like a rolling stone in Rome?

EB: Up early walking along the Janiculum Hill, I stopped to contemplate the striking view of Rome from a parapet near the Finnish embassy to the Holy See. I noticed to my right two lovers doing amorous gyrations on the parapet. They were clothed, of course; no one wants to alert the carabinieri. The sun was hidden behind gray clouds, though most of the sky was bright blue. I think the first chapter of the Tao Te Ching: "The Tao that can be told is not the true Tao. Free from desire, you realize the mystery. Caught in desire, you see only the manifestations. Yet mystery and manifestations arise from the same source. This source is called darkness—the gateway to all understanding."

MZC: How about admitting we just don't have complete answers about such questions as Who is God? Is there an Eternal Life? Is the soul immortal?

EB: I stumbled across a fabulous exhibit on Giordano Bruno at the Casanatense Library just a few steps from the church of St. Ignatius. Bruno was burned at the stake in 1600 at the Campo dei Fiori because the Inquisition was naming the Tao; Giordano didn't name it right. The Inquisition didn't like the darkness, that is, the Taoist "not-knowing," or even his or her own Christian apophatic tradition, which limits our statements about God.

Inclined Toward Love: Notes While Doing the *Spiritual Exercises*
Morgan Zo-Callahan

This essay is dedicated to the memory of two men who played a major role in my understanding the Ignatian exercises: my great friend and mentor, Bob Holstein, dancing away in Peace, still-inspiring-us here on ever-more-connected Earth, and my dear friend, Curtis Bryant, S.J. May they Rest in Peace.

Iñigo was always rather inclined toward love; moreover, he seemed all love, and because of that he was universally loved by all.

> —Luis Gonçalves de Camara,
> a close associate of Ignatius

I might think about a tiny bug or flower, and imagine how many other living and nonliving things conspired to bring it to life and sustain it.... I consider that all the good that I see and know comes to be as a share in the divine good.

> —St. Ignatius, "Contemplation to
> Obtain the Love of God."

We are quite naturally impatient in everything to reach the end without delay. We should like to skip the intermediate stages. We are impatient of being on the way to something unknown, something new. And yet it is the law of all progress that it is made by passing through some stages of instability—and that it may take a very long time. And so I think it is with you, your ideas mature gradually—let them grow; let them shape themselves, without undue haste. Don't try to force them on, as though you could be today what time (that is to

say, grace and circumstances acting on your own good will) will make of you tomorrow.
    —Pierre Teilhard de Chardin, S.J.

This study covers the following topics:
- Nineteenth Annotation retreat
- The Principle and Foundation
- Examen of Conscience (Examination of Consciousness)
- The Call of the Temporal King
- "Application of the Senses"
- "Three Kinds of Humility" and Curtis's story
- The Election and the Discernment of Spirits
- Consolation and Desolation, "Interior Movements"
- *Exercises* that adapt to the needs of each individual

Situating Myself in the Universe
Making the Spiritual Exercises according to the Nineteenth Annotation, 1998

In July of 1998 my dear friend and mentor, Bob Holstein, gathered together a small group of men, most of whom were former Jesuits, to do the *Spiritual Exercises* of St. Ignatius in the long form that is described in the Nineteenth Annotation of Ignatius' final text.

When I read the actual text of the *Exercises*, I am amazed that they have withstood the test of time. This thin volume has been printed more than four and a half million times over more than four centuries, making it one of the most influential works about prayer and meditation in the western world. It is not a self-help book, and Ignatius' directions for the retreat director are as precise, detailed, unembellished, and as dry as any instructions that have ever been written.

Among Jesuit "best practices" have been to create spiritual retreats, sermons, and teaching materials in other languages, for other cultures and times, yet based in the *Exercises*. A good result would be that these adaptations lead to a prayerful, intense, and experiential connection with the Lord Jesus, his life, his death, his resurrection, and his teachings. The Jesuits have met with some success with these projects all over the world. I have attempted to record my own meditations, prayers, and reflections during this nine-month period and final summary weekend at the Loyola Institute of Spirituality in the same open, innovative, and creative spirit. I bow with reverence to Jesus and Ignatius for the life-enhancing principles imparted to me, even though I find myself at this stage of my life more in tune with Buddhist practice informing an Ignatian one.

The intensive thirty-day retreat Ignatius lays out in his manual, requires five hours of spiritual exercises each day in a setting of silence and separation from the day-to-day world. He himself added the Nineteenth Annotation retreat for people who want to do the *Exercises*, but have active lives they cannot leave for such an extended period. It takes thirty-four weeks with at least an hour of prayer and meditation—much listening—and the Examen of Conscience each day. Here's what he himself writes about the Nineteenth Annotation:

> *Nineteenth Annotation: A person of education or ability, who is taken up with public affairs or suitable business, may take an hour and a half daily to exercise himself.*

> *Let the end for which man is created be explained to him, and he can also be given for the space of a half-hour the Particular Examen and then the General and the way to confess and to receive the Blessed Sacrament. Let him, during three days every morning, for the space of an hour, make the meditation on the First, Second and Third Sins, pp. 37, 38; then, three other days at the same hour, the meditation on the statement of Sins, p. 40; then, for three other days at the same hour, on the punishments corresponding to Sins, p. 45. Let him be given in all three meditations the ten Additions, p. 47.*

For the mysteries of Christ our Lord, let the same course be kept, as is explained below and in full in the Exercises themselves.

[All quotes from the *Spiritual Exercises* of St Ignatius cited in this essay are taken from the translation of the Autograph of the *Exercises* prepared by Fr. Elder Mullan, S.J. I have left each section cited exactly as it appears in its entirety.]

Holstein called me, and said, "Come on, take this retreat; I know you're studying a lot of Buddhism, but maybe they can interplay." It had been some thirty-five years since I had undertaken the discipline of an Ignatian retreat, and I had more than a few misgivings about re-emerging in already-rejected ideas of original sin; the guilt that my personal sins caused Jesus to be crucified; absolute, eternal Hells; the put-on "spiritual enthusiasm" of wanting to be a soldier who fights bravely, even fanatically, in the service of the Lord Jesus.

Holstein said that the man who would be "directing" our retreat, Don Merrifield, S.J. had a very open approach to the *Exercises*; Holstein said Merrifield thought that the *Exercises* could be given to Jews, Buddhists, and other religions as well. He was into creating new and relevant expressions of the *Exercises* that weren't to be based primarily in the counter-Reformation theology of Ignatius' time. OK I thought, I'd at least go talk with Merrifield, and read something about his approach.

Merrifield told me that he was "playing around" with Magana's Liberation Theology approach, "Because our times behoove us to enter the politics of oppression, to connect prayer and meditation to the poor." He said that he had been studying nature mysticism, and was very *simpatico* with Pierre Teilhard de Chardin. He assured me I didn't need to take as the truth that I personally caused Jesus' sufferings, or, really, believe all of Ignatius' theology, time bound in the sixteenth century, or from my early training in the post-World War II, 1950s catechism.

We would do the "four weeks" of the *Exercises* over thirty-four actual weeks; we would generally be on our own though some spiritual direction would be available if we requested it; there would also be some group meetings at Loyola Marymount University; and our group inter-e-mailing would serve as a kind of self-generated spiritual direction.

There was to be one final weekend training at Loyola Institute of Spirituality in Orange, California. Holstein and the Loyola Institute of Spirituality wanted to train men and women who had completed the *Exercises* to lead prayer groups, retreats, or counsel using the principles of the *Exercises*. Bob felt that spiritual direction was not only for the ordained—lay people might be equally as gifted spiritual directors as the ordained and should be recognized as such.

Before we actually began the *Exercises*, we each set goals with Don that determined the logistics for our retreat. We each wanted to adapt the experience to our unique selves as well as to our American cultural lives. Some of us, myself included, chose to ask for some spiritual direction.

Each day I would do an Examen of Conscience and a contemplation from the *Exercises*—putting myself into a story or "scene" from Christ's life; for example, Jesus healing the sick and the lame; speaking directly to the abuse of religious power that burdens people, confronting religious leaders and religious hierarchies who create fear, and fall prey to the negative human proclivity to have power and dominate over other humans. I wanted *gustare et sentire res internum,* to taste and feel the inner communications of the Spirit, by making myself present through imagination and fantasy to events in Jesus' life. I would open myself to affections, feelings as I came to know Jesus interiorly, immersing myself in the stories of the New Testament. Then I would let my understanding be applied responsibly and intelligently to how I was living my life. Sometimes, I would just imagine being out in a solitary desert, quietly sitting in meditation and prayer with Jesus, feeling a Presence. I contemplated Jesus' appeal for us to love each other, even the most down and out, contemplating Jesus in prison today, in the hospital, living on the street, among those alone, forgotten and hurting. I would also do *metta* meditations, praying that all of us be happy and without hatred and conflict. (I usually spent almost one to two hours a day doing the *Exercises*, but sometimes there was only enough time to do the Examen of Conscience.)

The eminent scholar of the *Spiritual Exercises*, Joe Tetlow, S.J. says the *Spiritual Exercises* could be fruitfully given to non-Catholics and non-Christians. In many of the great traditions, there are "transcendent" (Impersonal, Unknowable, Uninterested) as well as "immanent" (Loving, Personal) and, according to some sages such as Ramakrishna, one can come to full life by surrender to either a personal God or an impersonal God, or even just to the sense of the wonder of being. So, I was enthused by the possibility of doing the *Exercises* without over-emphasizing its theistic/creator/original sin theology. I told Don Merrifield I'd like to start without any religious preconceptions of what I was supposed to learn and know about Jesus. I'd do exercises to really try to understand who Jesus was, flying in consciousness, in the stark desert, being tempted, fasting, being transformed, being with women, the poor and rich, angry at religious exploitation of people, saying the Father is greater than he, teaching, being fierce, being a son, being a critic of religious tyranny which oppresses people, saying there's no love unless we love ourselves and all others equally.

I'd examine my conscience each day—much like doing a simple observation of mind, body, feelings, emotions, afflictions, joys and "re-ordering" my intentions when I see clearly my "inordinate attachments," usually for money, sex, power, wanting to be popular and rich. I would check in with a spiritual director to talk about and get feedback on what I most truly desire for my life. The director helped me get in touch with my own heart and feelings and how to discern which feelings and yearnings were coming from my connection to my purest mind and heart. So I discriminate between the genuine and a put-on self; I re-order my life as my Buddhist friend, Dr. Eng Moy, so often says to "be a loving, caring, sharing, understanding human being."

The flow of the *Exercises* is moving from disordered, attached, selfish living to seeing in Jesus' life a model of a loving life, and practicing compassion for all, identifying the suffering with Jesus in our world today, and finally to live all as joy and gift, making individual elections, modifications/adaptations in our lives/reformations/personal transformations, as the inevitable changing, suffering, and happiness come and go.

The first week considers the examination of one's conscience, thoughts, words, deeds; our sins and personal hells. We begin the second week with a meditation on the spiritual kingdom of Christ and then move onto contemplate Jesus' life, his infancy and hidden life, his contemplative and prayer life, his public life. We also do meditations about choices we make in our lives based on imitating the qualities of Jesus; in the third week, we contemplate Jesus' suffering and death and consider rules for how we nourish ourselves, how we formulate rules for eating and healthy daily living skills; in the fourth week, we contemplate the resurrection of Jesus, and we make the contemplation to "attain the love of God."

During the nine months, I discovered Ignatian and Buddhist approaches are very complementary. I even reflected on similarities of the individual six year period of spiritual seeking of the prince Buddha, putting on the monk's robe and seeking true happiness and the proud knightly warrior-lover Ignatius, donning coarse clothes of a monk, seeking and finding the true Lover. They both had temptations and mystical experiences, as well as learning that extreme asceticism hurts the body and the spirit. They both completed their spiritual seeking, and founded religious orders based on spiritual practices, which continue to this day.

The Principle and Foundation

The *Exercises* begin with an examination of what Ignatius calls "the Principle and Foundation." These are Ignatius' exact words:

> *Man is created to praise, reverence, and serve God our Lord, and by this means to save his soul.*
>
> *And the other things on the face of the earth are created for man and that they may help him in prosecuting the end for which he is created.*
>
> *From this it follows that man is to use them as much as they help him on to his end, and ought to rid him of them so far as they hinder him as to it.*
>
> *For this it is necessary to make ourselves indifferent to all created things in all that is allowed to the choice of our free will and is not prohibited to it; so that, on our part, we want not health rather than sickness, riches rather than poverty, honor rather than dishonor, long rather than short life, and so in all the rest; desiring and choosing only what is most conducive for us to the end for which we are created.*

The Principle and Foundation is not what Ignatius would call contemplation. It is more a "thought-experiment." Given this principle, what follows? This is not living one's life based on a private revelation but rather on certain principles that are open to discussion, verification, interpretation, disagreement and, even rejection. However Ignatius has also laid the foundation for perhaps the most famous and insightful of his principles: that love is best expressed in deeds and not words.

When for example, Ignatius next says that all on the

"face of the earth" are for men and women to help attaining the goal of saving one's soul, it is open to an understanding that I don't agree with: the implication of a superiority of the human animal and a right, almost an obligation, for us "to subjugate" the natural world. Re-orienting the principle that states our relationship to all the rest of creation is essential to humankind's survival on earth.

We are all part of the natural world; barefooted, grass walks us. We're all the living rain forests in the world, as fellow-retreatant Bob Brophy said. Brophy suggested we be aware that "a clear difference between our present perceptions and those of Ignatius' day is the demand that we de-center mankind—we have lost confidence that humans are the unique purpose of the kind of cosmos that we see through the Hubble telescope. Among the 'many mansions" possible on other planets, there may be races who have reached Teilhard's point of noösphere (the calling forth of evolved mind) long ago.... And in our day of ecological awareness, we are being taught by nature and its God to respect and wonder at the kinds of creatures, at our entire living universe, a humbling of this human-centeredness. All this is God's goodness exploding in beauty.... Finally we have shifted our sin-consciousness or consciousness of "disordered" acts partly from "personal" sins of lust, pride, anger, laziness, etc., to an apprehension of "systemic" sin. It is almost impossible in life not to cooperate in evil by taking advantage of and allowing structures to remain that systematically exploit the poor, the earth, even in rain forest and oceans, air and soil ... this is the world as God gives it to us now."

I'm making these *Exercises* with no emotional feeling that Jesus loves me and cares for me as an individual; I don't think so. I think Jesus just gave us the message to love each other in our present lives. For me God is really ineffable, yet there's a profound presence within life on our earth speeding sixty-seven thousand miles an hour around the Sun. Einstein, like

Spinoza, said God is remote, uninvolved with our human world. Though God isn't necessarily as involved in our world as we like to project, Einstein's idea of God was full of awe and wonder, a deep respect for an impersonal mystery. Some colleagues and friends share a similar view of God.

Three bows to wonderful unknowing! I feel more respect for ambiguity, chaos, imperfection and paradox, obviously as much a factor in life as are clarity and the notion of an ordered universe. I reflected on a Vedic text: "That in which all these worlds are fixed, of which they are, for which they all arise, for which they all exist, because of which they all come into being and which they truly are—That alone is the real, the truth. May we adore That at Heart." Could the *Exercises* be of benefit to me to realize this? Could the *Exercises* make some sense to our contemporary world? My first indications are definitely positive.

And finally in the Principle and Foundation, Ignatius wisely concludes we should give up inordinate, clinging, harmful preferences in the world, whether we're famous or not, rich or not, whether we're enjoying spiritual consolations or not; and concentrate on being who we are, understanding the purpose for which we have been created, and finally to be happy through giving and receiving love within ourselves, for others, and for our world.

I feel that this is not an ontological statement that in order to reach God, a man or a woman ought to be detached from a world that is inherently evil. Rather I think that the entire emphasis here is on spiritual practice. Listen to what Ignatius writes in the twentieth annotation:

From this isolation [imposed by the *Exercises*] three chief benefits, among many others, follow.

The first is that a man, by separating himself from many friends and acquaintances, and likewise from many not well-ordered affairs, to serve and praise God our Lord, merits no little in the sight of His Divine Majesty.

The second is, that being thus isolated, and not having his understanding divided on many things, but concentrating his care on one only, namely, on serving his Creator and benefiting his own soul, he uses with greater freedom his natural powers, in seeking with diligence what he so much desires.

The third: the more our soul finds itself alone and isolated, the more apt it makes itself to approach and to reach its Creator and Lord, and the more it so approaches Him, the more it disposes itself to receive graces and gifts from His Divine and Sovereign Goodness.

Merrifield wrote the following as his adaptation of the "First Principle and Foundation of Ignatius."

"I begin by situating myself, as best I can, in the overall scheme of life. I sense myself alone before the mystery of my existence and the mystery of the existence of the entire universe. Turning from all immediate consideration, all busyness of mind and spirit, I focus on the wonder of it all, even on the wonder of being able to wonder. Reflecting on the Genesis accounts of creation, I find my self, like Adam, newly sprung into being, clay of the earth into which the Shaper of all has breathed spirit and life. I am formed through the clay from which I came, one with the earth and all its wonderful panoply of living things and mountains and seas, rhythms, cycles and beauty. Shaped from the same stuff as all these, over eons, I am amazingly made, a delicate and yet strong bio-system, living in a balance with all else and surviving through all the myriad of interactions with all creation, including of course, my fellow human creatures. But I and my fellows are somehow strange amidst all these other creatures, sprung from the same clay. We have had a life breathed into us from another realm that adds another dimension, spirit. In us this clay becomes open to limitless horizons."

I begin the First Week of the *Exercises*. I agree not to have any expectations about what the process will be about. I agree to let the Spirit lead as she may. I begin to practice my daily Examen of Conscience (some today call Exam of Consciousness) where I pay attention to my thoughts, words, actions, my real, most basic motives.

This is perhaps the right time to say something more about the Examen. Traditionally the "examen" has been used as way of trying to remove the imperfections of character, if not the outright tendency towards sinfulness. Each day, for three periods of approximately fifteen minutes at set intervals, a person doing the *Exercises* or a person who is using the examen outside the context of a retreat, makes a thorough inventory of all his or her thoughts, words, and actions since the time he or she last made the Examine to scrutinize all behaviors in the light of his intention to break a specific bad habit or avoid sin.

I found this form, this context for self-examination, to be less than satisfactory. I borrow from my Buddhist practice of mindfulness. I examine my intentions, thoughts, words and actions and feel them interiorly. First of all I want to be a good human being—free from hurting myself and others—with a primacy of my own conscience and intelligence—not hypnotized by either guru or Pope. I discover that I am an ongoing process towards a brightness-wakefulness based in just the way humans are; negative thoughts lose their power in the face of a joyful spirituality.

And finally I extend the examen of my consciousness to all beings, as a society, as we relate to our environment and to our local and global politics. I "purify" myself, my thoughts, speech and intentions. Thus I minimize emotional distraction, which can overwhelm my particular, unique and undivided expression of a loving life.

The first week deals with our distorted view of the world and the universe. It is often called the "purification" stage of the spiritual process. Much as in Buddhism, *sila,* moral correctness is a foundation of meditation and wisdom. There are certainly hells to confront in ourselves and in our global spinning together. I find the first week to be the opportunity to sit down and be honest with ourselves, inside and out, in our intentions, words, and actions.

For me "sin," is missing the mark of the living heart. There's no need to dwell on guilt and shame, even though there remain emotional negative thoughts about my human nature. As Faulkner says, "the past isn't dead for us; it isn't even past."

The First Week was a call to be brutally honest, and at the same time, not harsh with myself—a time to imbibe my own mortality. Once my dearest friend, Marcus Holly, told me: "Morgan, you make yourself more than you are sometimes, pay attention when you do that. You want others to think you are better than you are." Ignatius suggests we concentrate on what particularly is hanging us up; in my case it was a kind of dishonesty not to present myself just as I am, but wanting to "look good."

My first week was a reflection on the feelings of greed, jealousy, anger, even hatred in myself, to "see it," but also let it go. I had to deal with losses and death, the impermanence of my body. I had to pay more attention to my body. Ignatian retreats may stress that we should want to feel shame, embarrassment, confusion, sorrow that my sins have tortured Jesus. For myself, I no longer find any of that helpful or true. But I feel we do torture the Jesus in our contemporary world by hurting those Jesus said would represent his presence on earth: the oppressed, the poor, the abused children, and the forgotten people.

The culture and theology of Ignatius' time has its own way of expressing sin, hell, impermanence and death; Ignatius' genius, in my opinion, is that essential spiritual insights can come from the *Spiritual Exercises*, even for a non-theistic Buddhist. I've found some First week exercises helpful in counteracting lust and vanity.

◼

Ignatius begins the second week with the famous contemplation of God's kingdom and the Incarnation. It begins with an examination of a personal response to a command from an earthly king and then asks the person who is making the *Exercises* to use those same feelings and listen to the Gospel as a call into the service by the second person of the Holy Trinity.

Here are Ignatius' instructions for beginning the contemplation.

The Call of the Temporal King

> *It helps to contemplate the life of the King Eternal.*
>
> *First Point. The first Point is, to put before me a human king chosen by God our Lord, whom all Christian princes and men reverence and obey.*
>
> *Second Point. The second, to look how this king speaks to all his people, saying: "It is my Will to conquer all the land of unbelievers. Therefore, whoever would like to come with me is to be content to eat as I, and also to drink and dress, etc., as I: likewise he is to labor like me[6] in the day and watch in the night, etc., that so afterwards he may have part with me in the victory, as he has had it in the labors."*
>
> *Third Point. The third, to consider what the good subjects ought to answer to a King so liberal and so kind, and hence, if any one did not accept the appeal of such a king, how deserving he would be of being censured by all the world, and held for a mean-spirited knight.*

As I do this contemplation, I am struck by how much of Ignatius' life experience is reduced to a few words and distilled, allowing me to experience—as much as I can as twentieth century American who cherishes democracy—what Ignatius felt as he underwent his conversion.

In 1491 Ignatius (Iñigo) Loyola was born into a wealthy family, the youngest of thirteen children, in the Basque province of Guipuzcoa in northern Spain. It was the time of discovery, the New World of the Americas, European wars, corruption in the church, and the stirrings of Humanism. As a young man, he was a page for Juan Velazquez, the treasurer of the kingdom of Castille. The free-spirited Iñigo developed a taste for royalty, gambling, swordplay—and, most definitely, the ladies. He was ambitious, romantic, "sinful," vain, anti-religious.

At age thirty, as an officer defending Pamplona against the French, Iñigo was wounded. A cannon ball broke one leg and damaged the other. It was a very serious injury—he would limp for the rest of his life. While recuperating, he read a life of Christ and a book about the saints, it is said, because he was bored and that was the only reading material to be found in the castle. By nature exuberant and whole-hearted, he allowed Jesus' life to deeply penetrate his being. He felt an inner tranquility, as he would lose himself in Jesus, and an equally strong desire to reform himself.

When he could walk again, he set off for Barcelona with the intention of becoming a pilgrim, and going to live in Jerusalem where Jesus had lived. He stopped at the Benedictine shrine of Our Lady of Montserrat to leave his sword and knife at the altar as sign of his intention to change his life. As he prayed there, he began to experience a series of mystical visions and intuitive insights which he knew he had to follow, and he took shelter in a cave along the Cardoner River in the town of Manresa where he stayed for ten months. The principles and practices he created as he underwent his spiritual transformation were the seeds for the *Spiritual Exercises*.

I've often been struck by the similarities between Ignatius and the Buddha. The onset of the Buddha's spiritual crisis is told in a story: the scene, dawn in the palace of Prince Gautama Buddha. After a night of revelry, the rich connoisseur, the admired and accomplished presumptive prince notices the unattractive sleeping poses of the beautiful women who had been dancing for his enjoyment just a few hours earlier, and he sees through the enchantments of the evening. He begins to feel somehow empty living his "perfect" life. All the wonderful entertainments and sumptuous occasions with beautiful women, food, and drink somehow no longer satisfy the Buddha, Ignatius—or me. Both Iñigo and the Buddha begin a quest: I must get to the true Source of life that will bring me peace and happiness.

I can make this contemplation with enormous benefit. I can further expand it into a world where human nature also shows, as I read the *Gospel of Sri Ramakrishna* and his stories, how we all get into "name, fame, and gold." How we love ourselves in a narcissistic way, our eyes/ears wanting always to receive flattery. Our tightening ourselves around our money, power, positions and the contrast between that call and the message of the teachings of Jesus.

The rest of the Second Week is filled with contemplations of the accounts of the earthly ministry of Jesus. Here are two counsels, "preludes" in the language of his manual, that Ignatius gives for beginning these contemplations, the "Application of the Senses" and, then as usual with Ignatius, an inquiry into what actions follow from prayer.

> *First Prelude. The first Prelude is a composition, seeing the place: it will be here to see with the sight of the imagination, the synagogues,[5] villages and towns through which Christ our Lord preached.*

> *Second Prelude. The second, to ask for the grace which I want: it will be here to ask grace of our Lord that I may not be deaf to His call, but ready and diligent to fulfill His most Holy Will.*

Before I begin to share some thoughts about the Application of the senses, however, I would like to point to another place where I found a parallel between the instructions of Ignatius and that of many of my Buddhist teachers. Ignatius writes: "Before entering into prayer, I should rest my mind for a while, either seated or walking; and I will reflect on where I am going and why." (*Spiritual Exercises* [SE], 239) It is about intention, not achieving a particular result. Many people who begin to use the imagination in contemplation question whether they are "doing it right." For Ignatius, the "soul is not satisfied and filled by knowing a lot of facts but by feeling and tasting things in the depths of the heart." (SE 2) When relaxed and focused, Ignatius suggests one's inner Source will communicate directly and intimately with the individual person as "speaking as a friend speaks with his friend." (SE 54). And we know that our friends have different voices. The *Exercises* allow us the necessary time to be in touch with one's own personal, living mind and heart through meditation, contemplation and reflection. Don't even worry what we're supposed to hear. Taking time to listen to one's self in a friendly way is spiritual exercise.

Contemplations, meditations and prayerful reflections using the technique of concentrated imagination have a certain dynamic: Getting in touch with our genuine desire for total freedom and realizing that such freedom for making decisions and taking action requires making ourselves spiritually "indifferent." Ignatius makes his notion of "indifference" clear in the Principle and Foundation. It is not a listless state of not caring, but an active state of being open without as many self-prohibitions and prejudices as possible.

By contemplating Jesus, in the imagination, the mind's eye, one may feel that his or her heart has been opened by "encountering" Jesus, and that his teachings about kindness, fairness, prayer, speaking out against injustices, feel real in a defining way. One of my contemplations was John the Baptist with Jesus. I see how they dress, smell the water; hear the insects buzzing around Jesus' shoulders. I tune into John's preaching; so wild, crazy in his quest for God, in his garment of camel's hair and a leather skirt around his waist, his food of locusts and honey—how sweet that honey must have been. I can taste it. What courage to face up to the Pharisees, while baptizing Jesus: " … the Spirit of God descending like a dove and alighting, alighting on him." I can feel it.

As I contemplate the life of Jesus, I try to place myself as best I can in the living conditions of the time Jesus lived. Even in his parables, I can become the prodigal son welcomed by his father, unconditionally, even after I've messed up and squandered my money and time. I can live this emotionally—my father just loves me; he's not angry or berating me. He enthusiastically wants us to eat and talk and share life with each other, to continue to grow together.

I watch Jesus teaching us to be gentle, peacemakers, to serve everyone but most especially the poor, to value meditation and prayer; before his horrific execution, what we call his "passion." I see him wash the disciples' feet. Though I'm going back in history, applying my senses and imagination, I'm simultaneously exploring what's going on in *my* life, at this time. I'm asking what I desire most deeply for myself. How can I live in the conditions that I find in my life, here and now?

I'm seeing Jesus before any religious authority or organization tells me who Jesus is and what Jesus wants me to do. I'm looking, as best I can, with unbiased "eyes of my imagination" within stories of Jesus. I experience Jesus as a man of unconditional loving, brave activism, a critic of religious authority that is abusive. His humanity is divine.

Such exercises—as a witness or as a participant—of contemplating the life, suffering and death, resurrection of Jesus allow us *to be with* a divine mystery, to participate in a spiritual experience of giving one's heart and energy in response to a deep listening from within. We allow ourselves the space and attention to touch our deepest, most creative desires; to feel and accept our fears, hurting, with gentle embracing; to be with the goodness, energy and wisdom which we are. We are what we wake up to. We have what we most desire.

At this point in the *Exercises*, Ignatius introduces his notion of the "Three Kinds of Humility." This is from the text of the *Exercises*:

> *First Humility. The first manner of Humility is necessary for eternal salvation; namely, that I so lower and so humble myself, as much as is possible to me, that in everything I obey the law of God, so that, even if they made me lord of all the created things in this world, nor for my own temporal life, I would not be in deliberation about breaking a Commandment, whether Divine or human, which binds me under mortal sin.*

> *Second Humility. The second is more perfect Humility than the first; namely, if I find myself at such a stage that I do not want, and feel no inclination to have, riches rather than poverty, to want honor rather than dishonor, to desire a long rather than a short life—the service of God our Lord and the salvation of my soul being equal; and so not for all creation, nor because they would take away my life, would I be in deliberation about committing a venial sin.*

> *Third Humility. The third is most perfect Humility; namely, when—including the first and second, and the praise and glory of the Divine Majesty being equal—in order to imitate and be more actually like Christ our Lord, I want and choose poverty with Christ poor rather than riches, opprobrium with Christ replete with it rather than honors; and to desire to be rated as worthless and a fool for Christ, Who first was held as such, rather than wise or prudent in this world.*

I feel that I didn't benefit much from thinking about, praying over, or meditating on these three kinds of humility. In fact, I had totally rejected self-punishment as a spiritual practice. I would not seek out physical pain, humiliations, or insults to be like Jesus. It had the flavor of masochistic, self-destructive behavior. However, I can reach out to those who are suffering, even to myself, and learn how Jesus forgave and loved even when he was hurt so much, and I would later learn that this spiritual practice is really about how we react, how we respond when we suffer physically or if we are insulted and humiliated.

Knowing Curtis Bryant, S.J., a dearest, sweet friend from high school, and the generosity with which he shared his life struggle finally allowed me to go more deeply and make sense of Ignatius' counsel. Our friendship allowed both of us to grow into this insight. Together we would learn a way to unite our own suffering with that of other people in the world who are suffering, connecting with them and working with the intention that they be happy. [Curtis died from cancer on November 18, 2003 at St. John's Hospital in Santa Monica, California. My telling his story is also my eulogy for a wonderful man. May he be in Peace.]

Curtis was a licensed psychologist. In his fourth year of theology studies, he took a Clinical Pastoral Education course at St. Elizabeth's Hospital, Washington, D.C., and he knew that therapy and counseling would be "the backbone of my life in the future." He went on to earn a Ph.D. at the California School of Professional Psychology, Berkeley, in 1983.

Once Curtis and I talked for a long time about these three levels, traditionally taken as expressions of Christian commitment: the first level, not committing grave, mortal sins, and avoiding evil; the second level, developing indifference to honors, wealth, not even intending to do a minor, venial sin; and finally the third level, seeking to emulate Jesus who was poor, insulted, taken for a fool. Curtis said the notion sin—in the sense of self-condemnation and exaggerated guilt—is both psychologically and theologically unsound, not reflective of our spiritual understanding in the light of what we know about the workings of the human mind, and the church did not have a wise and compassionate perspective in regards to sexuality, sin and guilt.

Curtis lived openly and bravely as a gay celibate priest. We spoke about the prejudice towards gay people and saw that the church's teaching on homosexuality was cruel and ignorantly discriminative. We both felt that the church's people call women to be priests, no longer to be second-class citizens in the church. I'd share stories about Buddhist communities who were facing the same prejudices. We discussed how difficult it was to be gay, how scapegoated gay men and lesbians were in many Muslim and fundamentalist Christian communities.

In 1996 Curtis had landed what he thought would be a tremendous job, working just under the Cardinal as the Assistant Vicar for Clergy for the Archdiocese of Los Angeles. He now had it made. He was proud to show me his posh office, but most of all he shared with me his intention to promote psychosexual development for priests. He also knew that he could help priests who were involved in the terrible sexual abuse scandals that were shaking the Catholic Church to its core, using the best psychotherapy available.

Then in 1998, one imprudent incident, one phone call to the Cardinal and boom! Curtis was shown the door. No longer Assistant Vicar with the cool office and impressive title, Curtis was devastated. But he said he understood for the first time a way to practice the third kind of humility. We could not and should not pray for insults, humiliations to be united with Jesus, but suffering still exists. He didn't deny his suffering, but was able to form more healthy perspectives around it. Once he let go his extreme disappointment in losing a high-ranking job, he felt more compassion toward others who have very hard times. He said his suffering was really minuscule, and he could finally name his pain of going from being a "somebody" at last and then being indecorously dumped. He saw through his attachment to name and fame. He said, "This suffering has helped me grow spiritually, connect to others, and I'm happier."

Curtis began to pray: "Let these feelings of humiliation, and hurt be of benefit to others, as was the life of Jesus." Yes, our suffering unites us to the Christ here today, those suffering loneliness, those misunderstood, those in terrible poverty and violence. We cannot ignore that fourteen thousand children die every day from hunger. We, in some tiny way, take that suffering into ourselves and send out vibrations of loving care to those suffering in such poor, squalid conditions. Curtis and I talked about how we didn't cause Jesus' suffering, even in some remote sense; rather we were inspired to acknowledge how we create so much of our own suffering by refusing to love, by wanting honors and power and also are hurtful to each other in order to achieve such honors and to fulfill our own desires. As in Buddhism, compassion for oneself and others, love is the foundation. We understood Jesus died for his own particular love. We don't need to add to it by making ourselves guilty.

Curtis told me how he felt a freedom from not caring anymore about having the great reputation and enviable position. He said he could be proud and build on the good work he did accomplish during his short stint at Catholic corporate headquarters, L.A.

And what joy he found just going into private practice as a psychologist; we had spectacular lunches together, conversation and good food, at times, wine, but again the open Curtis, spoke freely about his need to abstain from wine. But wine or not, what laughter and freedom from talking to each other without any secrets from each other, with such zest and joy! And some insight, for us at least, into the third degree of humility.

The Election and the Discernment of Spirits

One of the distinctive characteristics of the *Exercises* is what Ignatius calls making an Election, the choice to enter into a deep commitment to a way of living commensurate with what you learn about yourself. God is in the Love. Our love is reflected in our deeds, what we do, not what we say or pretend to do. Love is in the doing.

After the distinction of three levels of humility, Ignatius has a long examination of the kinds of choices that someone on the spiritual path might have to make and gives advice as to how to get to a decision. He counsels the person making the *Exercises* to achieve some degree of indifference so that the soul is free to use "its natural powers freely and tranquilly." [It is the only place in the Autograph, the edition of the *Exercises* which has Ignatius' marginalia, and presumably the copy he used when he gave the *Exercises*, where I note his emphasis: "I said time of quiet.... "]

Here is one section from Instructions on making an Election; the list includes the most distinctive Ignatian methods, "discernment of the spirits," as one of several options:

THREE TIMES FOR MAKING, IN ANY ONE OF THEM, A SOUND AND GOOD ELECTION

First Time. The first time is, when God our Lord so moves and attracts the will, that without doubting, or being able to doubt, such devout soul follows what is shown it, as St. Paul and St. Matthew did in following Christ our Lord.

Second Time. The second, when enough light and knowledge is received by experience of consolations and desolations, and by the experience of the discernment of various spirits.

Third Time. The third time is quiet, when one considers, first, for what man is born—namely, to praise God our Lord and save his soul—and desiring this chooses as means a life or state within the limits of the Church, in order that he may be helped in the service of his Lord and the salvation of his soul.

I said time of quiet, when the soul is not acted on by various spirits, and uses its natural powers freely and tranquilly.

In the first "time," we might be intimately connected to our Source, God, whose nature is to shower gifts continually in the form of our universe together unfolding, evolving, ever changing. The spiritual exercises open our awareness that all of life is gift, and that it is holy in its essence. Through practice, first paying attention, learning to relax ourselves and establishing a modicum of inner peace, spaciousness; reflective wisdom may then arise, an attitude of finding more and more enjoyment in being truly "persons for others."

We see through ourselves, being in our hearts, reflecting about wisdom of Jesus, of Buddha, not "inordinately attaching" to anything, appreciating, not pushing anything away, understanding likes and dislikes, distastes; responding to the yearnings of our heart, making choices from and by our best self, allowing ourselves to be influenced by the life and teachings of Jesus or whatever our religion or flavor of a religion we may live; we begin "finding God in all things," in all people. Ignatius says our first aim is to serve God and that we should not use anything nor deprive ourselves of anything, apart from that natural purpose. Non-theists may change this to say our first aim is to serve, without "inordinate attachments."

I was interested in how the making of an Election fits with my understanding of psychology, but I also wanted to "reform" my expectations in my work and family and friend life; to just pay a bit more attention and caring to them, what Ignatius would call an Election of Reformation of Life. I wanted to take the time to see if I could live more from my heart and intelligence, breathing more life in relationship to being a teacher, a family man, a friend, a volunteer in programs for those less fortunate. I didn't want to change my circumstances of living, but, through an interior effort, to refocus intentions and actions within my daily life as it has already unfolded for me. During this period of making my Election, I find that each day of my very ordinary life feels more full and interesting, with a sense that life—with its "good" and "bad"—is an unexpected gift.

However, if a person needs to make a decision and the methods of "election" are not producing results, Ignatius advises him or her (as any good coach or psychologist might do today) to list the pros and cons of a specific decision in order to gain clarity. There is nothing in Ignatius that hints of neglecting the use of reason or common sense. He even suggests that we consider the examples of men and women we hold as role models. But his unique contribution to the process of election, or decision-making, is the "discernment of various spirits."

"Interior Movements": Consolation and Desolation

Ignatius asks us, as he practiced himself, to use not only our intellects, but also our imaginations, emotions and feelings to discover what we most truly want and desire, what we yearn for and then to find out that those feelings are "God's will" for us, and then to live from those deepest yearnings "without inordinate attachment."

Ignatius observed from his reflective and devotional reading that he was becoming peaceful and felt an inner satisfaction—apart from "worldly" lusts and desires. He was growing within himself. He also noticed when he gave into his thoughts, such as "winning over some noble woman," he would be agitated, restless, and unsatisfied. His "discernment of spirits" would later describe the process of being able to discern/discriminate/understand within oneself, in silent awareness, what brings one a satisfying peace and, in contrast, what is disturbing one's calm. How can we be in touch with our truest needs and desires for happiness? In discernment, Ignatius would recommend that one pay attention to one's feelings, seeing if they bring a sense of calm/satisfaction (as "water filling a sponge") or if they bring conflicting/unsatisfactory states (as "water on a rock") unable to enter us and feed us with spiritual nourishment.

Discernment of spirits leads to an understanding of what is authentic satisfaction, authentic self, and to be aware when we identify with a "false" self.

Consolation and Desolation describe our inner lives. Consolation is great enthusiasm for the love of God. We see everything and everyone as in the context of God; it may include tears of sadness for infidelity to that love. When we find tears of joy or extreme happiness in serving God and just being a loving person, there's a deep peace and satisfaction in living life. It comes naturally and is not merely psychological; it comes from being connected with the Spirit.

Desolation is the spiritual darkness we go through, maybe a terrible heaviness or doubt about the goodness of one's own life; a lack of love felt in our lives, a confused restlessness. We may feel in ourselves emotions of greed, over-selfishness, hatred, dullness of mind, a reluctance to serve others.

Of course, if one is suffering from clinical depression, then this is based in affectivity and in the chemistry of the person and so must be addressed by psychology and medicine rather than by the discerning heart alone.

Desolation is contrasted with depression in that desolation is a spiritual experience (part of a spiritual journey); depression is an affective mental disorder, rooted in our biochemistry and affectivity. Depression can be used for a spiritual effect (such as to understand others). Or depression can negate any taste for spirituality. Desolation isn't as pervasive as depression; it doesn't usually lead to not being able to function which depression can often occasion. Those with desolation don't usually suffer the "somatic" effects of depression, such as not being able to sleep, excessive fatigue, unable to concentrate very well, having to withdraw. One can be desolate spiritually but mostly content in other areas of life. The spiritual desolation is often associated with "an inordinate attachment" the person may recognize, but can't let go, not being spiritually free as yet. The spiritual desolation may be an unexpressed anger toward God, of being abandoned by one's Source. Depression is often described as inwardly turned anger, repressed anger toward others, oneself, and maybe God too. Some depressed people may or may not be into spiritual discovery. Ignatius advises that in desolation, just tell God, acknowledge how you feel, be open to help, to learn, to change, don't just be alone and keep things inside and also be willing to help others, even when you're having a hard time; keep time for prayer and reflection. When you're feeling consolation, be thankful and joyful; also store such experiences in your memories. Such full memories will soften one's inevitable feelings of "being down."

As Buddha also taught, all emotions and feelings and conditions come and go. Ignatius advises when we are feeling the best, in consolation, at peace with ourselves, that's when we should use that energy to devote to our most intimate, deepest desires for our lives. We feel up to the inevitable work, which calls out to the great energy, we're feeling when spiritually happy, in consolation. Ignatius writes about what I might profoundly yearn for in "The Contemplation to Obtain the Love of God": " ... an intimate knowledge of the many blessings received, that filled with gratitude for all, I may in all things love and serve the Divine Majesty." (Louis Puhl, S.J., Second Prelude of Contemplation to Obtain the Love of God)

Finding God in all Faces, finding exercises that adapt to the needs of each individual.

> *For Christ plays in ten thousand places*
> *lovely in limbs*
> *and lovely in eyes not his*
> *to the Father through the features of men's faces.*
> —G.M. Hopkins

It's been ten years since I completed my Nineteenth Annotation Retreat with the fourth week, the *Contemplatio ad Amorem*, "the Contemplation To Attain the Love of God." It is now part of my practice to check my deepest yearnings within and to discover how to translate them into my daily life, living with awareness and joy and a disposition to serve others, attuned to the continuing gifts of God. At times this experience is as bright as the rays of the sun. I try to recognize everyday that we are all part of the universe working together to bring life, God, part of us, "laboring with us" in everything that is. "Consider all blessings and gifts as descending from above." (Louis Puhl, S.J. #237) Love of God is a mutually sharing friendship; I ask "for an intimate knowledge" of all blessings, so that I can be equally grateful. To check to see how I am doing, I ask myself if I can completely embrace my life without greediness, and without fear of enjoying the gifts of life with full gusto.

The last formal part of our work together as a group was a training for prayer/seminar leaders and spiritual directors for the *Exercises* at the Loyola Institute of Spiritual Training in Orange California. The sessions were lead by Sister Jean Schultz and Allan Deck, S.J.

Sister Jean begins our sessions with silence, focusing on the breath, centering our energy in our hearts, listening from the silence within, paying attention to the individuals who were speaking to us in our particular lives at the time, the elderly, the teenager, the person with AIDS, the poor, our families and friends. The practice shares many characteristics with the *Zazen* of Mahayana Buddhism as well as the prayer for the release from suffering that is the aim of the metta meditations in Theravada Buddhism. I sense that enrichment of both my practices, Buddhist and Ignatian, is already beginning to take hold of me.

The first key to her training is to have the "novice" spiritual counselors learn to listen, inner and outer. The process is based on the heart, on feeling. Underneath our anger, disappointments, behind faces we put on for each other, our own hearts yearn to express our selves and engage life.

We explore ourselves, in a non-judgmental way. We ask if we were spiritual directors, how would we be spiritual friends with those we counsel, being able to give guidance when really asked for. The first quality mentioned for a spiritual director was gentleness, a very present enabling quality to let the person express his or her spiritual need, most important questions, deepest cherished desires, afflicting emotions as well, relaxed— but very honest and rich—spiritual conversation. The spiritual director gets out of the way, not imposing, really enabling, encouraging the individual to re-discover and deepen her or his wishes/actions for life, at whatever the changing stage we may be. The truest direction will come from within the person herself or himself. The spiritual counselor helps the person by listening to the learning and experiences going on within the retreatant, answering questions too as best as one can.

The *Exercises* teach me to listen from a peaceful place inside of myself when I am making decisions or am thinking about some important matters. I am still exploring and deepening that practice. Sometimes in meditation, I have the insight that theologies aren't nearly as important as genuine spiritual practice that always includes tolerance and civil kindness— so many views, so many chances to grow, as long as we keep out the preachiness and the combative, religious "either-or" thinking of some communities.

Since completing the Nineteenth Annotation retreat, I notice that I apply some of the practices to my job as a teacher and also to my work in hospice: listening, creating an ambiance for the dying person to connect heart to heart, without judgment, unconditional acceptance with all the good and bad. Buddhists, Christians, Jews, Muslims, and Catholics ask me how they can be more aware, more human, living fully to the end of our lives, and how to face the death of someone in our family and our own coming death. I have seen how religious tradition can be a great solace for individuals in hospice as well as a few unfortunate circumstances when "religion" is forced on a person who doesn't want it. I am able to have conversations with patients and ask what allows them to feel most at peace within themselves, and to recognize what they can do to say goodbye to life, regardless of what others think or even what their religion or philosophy or religious ministers may tell them.

In my early Catholicism, I was taught to avoid Buddhist thought, or Islamic or Hindu spiritual teachings. As I've matured, I find myself admittedly on the fringes of church Catholicism, as I can no longer be Catholic without including my deep love for the teachings of the Buddha, Indian saints such as Ramana Maharshi, Nisargadatta Maharaj, Ramakrishna, Vivekenanda.

Those of us interested in spiritual exercises today can adapt exercises to individuals, to our culture, and to a pluralistic theology. I'm open to do the Ignatian *Exercises*, accepting them as an efficacious way even for those who may not identify with being Catholics or Buddhists or even believe in a personal god such as Jesus. There is a fluid mystical imagination and a rational reflective under-pinning that allow the *Exercises* of the sixteenth century to spill beyond its rich Christian roots. In Iñigo's time, Catholicism would never have permitted the enriching ecumenism and inter-religious dialogue possible for us today, in a way that may alleviate some of the world's problems, sadly many of them coming from religion itself, and its abuses of spirituality and power.

Sometimes spirituality—including the *Exercises*—is used to imply that the human person is not good and divine, but is inherently a sinner, "born bad." Yet the *Exercises*, or any genuine spiritual practice, provide a direct experience of the peace that comes from knowing what's within our hearts, our own most cherished dreams; knowing and realizing for ourselves whether or not we are already that which we're seeking; and knowing, through meditation and The Examen of Consciousness how we ourselves, in our thoughts, intentions, projections and actions somehow "block" and shrink from the love, the life "locked" within us. I'm encouraged to learn that some theologians in the Catholic Church acknowledge the primacy of one's conscience and intelligence, based on the fundamental goodness of the person and respect for varying individual-cultural images of God, personal or impersonal.

We discussed our experience of doing the Examen, which was of great benefit to me personally, to help me pay more attention, ponder carefully, open myself to a "meditative" review and feeling of body, mind, spirit, heart. We particularize whatever afflictive, negative expressions of sin (missing the mark of the heart) were active in us, deflecting the course of our lives away from harmony, balance and a pervasive feeling of gratitude for being alive and a human being too. We share how we "subtly" undermine our own true happiness and discerned the importance of good judgment, good plans for one's life. Meditating helps me release a lot of anger and feelings of lack of success; I also observe how my thinking can fall into the heart, very consciously being grounded in the dynamic circle of life. My friend, Al Duffy, at Rosemead Buddhist Monastery answering a query about whether Buddhism is atheistic, said "I can accept God as being all the Energy, all together, in the Universes."

We meditate on forgiving ourselves for hurting ourselves and others; we accept internally the forgiving of others towards us and we forgive all who hurt us. We give up the idea that "sin" requires "hurting back," even if we have a broken heart. What's really going on in our deepest emotional lives? Feel it, reflect, become aware of the spaciousness around it and let that expansiveness reveal the wisdom we may need at this time of our lives.

When I was struggling with Ignatius' Three Kinds of Humility, I did a Tibetan meditation called *tonglen* (means "giving" and "taking"). On the inhalation, one takes in the suffering of the world, as concretely as possible, the suffering, sickness and death of any human. On exhalation, one breathes out peace, release and joy. The practitioner uses personal suffering, not trying to deny it, but rather to feel compassion for the suffering of others, in our lives together; to unite with the sufferings of others, in order to bring others joy, peace, and happiness.

When I do the Contemplation to Obtain the Love of God, I give up being anything less than what I inherently am. I finally release the guilt of "I'm not good enough" while realizing that I am what I've been searching for so desperately. I am open to giving up theological brainwashing such as "Original Sin," "Eternal Hell," while recognizing that St. Ignatius was living in a theology that matched his particular times. I can give up "literalness." I understand that the meaning of Jesus' teaching on Hell is important; the literal words are helpful, but point to spiritual insight, yet if I cling to literalistic interpretations and push other ideas away—as we see so achingly today—I see the dog days of dogmatism ever-thriving. Let's not miss the joy of Christ playing in "ten thousand places."

May all our intentions, actions, and words be directed to deep understanding, real joy, and unselfish service!

Buddha, S.J.
Ken Ireland

Bro. Tom Marshall, S.J. is one of my cherished teachers, a koan student par excellence, a wily fox, an ordained priest in a Rinzai Zen lineage, a brother in the Society of Jesus and a true son of St. Francis Xavier. Tom directed me to Schurhammer after we spoke about Faure's book, Chan Insights and Oversights, *and then held my hand, or laughed, as I worked my way through the account of Xavier's travels in Japan. Any merit in worlds yet to be discovered that I have generated through my work on this short essay is for you, Tom sensei.*

I want to extend my gratitude to Bonnie Johnson and her husband Daniel Shurman, who, though they might seem to be unlikely members of Ignatius' extended family, brought the Exercises back into my life after I had left them dormant for more than thirty years. May you both experience continued well being and joy. I know that you are already blessed. So do you.

I also have to thank Morgan for giving me the time and space to complete "Buddha, SJ." It is a tribute to those Jesuits who have traveled both the paths pioneered by Ignatius and the Buddha. Morgan, I don't know yet whether it is a mark of completion or beginning for us—perhaps both.

There are conversations you overhear or read in books that are so familiar you feel as if you were a fly on the wall, listening to words you've heard before. The sentences ring with so much immediacy that you have to restrain yourself from finishing them. The tones are as so familiar you think that you are remembering them, not hearing them for the first time.

The conversations that I am going to write about are from the distant past—the case that I am going to discuss was written down in Latin by Francis Xavier more than 450 years ago, sent on an uncertain journey from Japan to Lisbon aboard a Portuguese caravel, then carried onto Rome, and delivered into the hands of Ignatius Loyola. They are the first recorded encounters between Christians and Zen Buddhists, a Jesuit saint and a roshi.

As I read from Xavier's letters in Bernard Faure's *Chan Insights and Oversights*, there were several moments when the hair on the back of my neck stood up—the words, the phrasing, even the jokes seemed to be right out of conversations that I have had with my own Zen teachers. Despite my post-hippie attempts to free myself from all past influences, when I read Xavier's comments, I could hear echoes from my Jesuit training in my responses to my Zen teachers; carefully formulated points of doctrine intended to stem the tide of the Protestant Reformation were still the core of the Jesuit curriculum when I entered the Society of Jesus forty years ago. Among the first seven Jesuits, Xavier was the master of debate, but when he shifts the conversation with the Zen master towards a polemical argument, I was almost embarrassed, realizing how much I had missed when I set out to become a Zen student.

Xavier writes to Ignatius about his conversations with "Ninxit," Ninjitsu who was the abbot of the Zen Temple, Kinryu-zan Fukushoji. "I spoke many times with some of the most learned of these [Zen monks], especially one to whom all in these parts are greatly attached, both because of his learning, life and the dignity which he has, and because of his great age, since he is nearly eighty years old; and he is called Ninxit, which means 'Heart of Truth' in the language of Japan. He is like a bishop among them, and if he were conformed to his name, he would be blessed. In the many conversations which we had, I found him doubtful and unable to decide whether our soul is immortal or whether it dies together with the body; sometimes he agreed with me, and at other times he did not. I am afraid that the other scholars are of the same mind. This Ninxit is such a good friend of mine that it is amazing" (Schurhammer 1982, p. 85).

There is more than enough in the letters to show that what

happened over an extended period in 1549 on Kyushu, the southernmost island of Japan, was a real conversation between friends about what mattered in life. Xavier might have been seeking common ground with Ninjitsu, or, judging by his subsequent actions and recommendations for the missionary effort in Japan, he was looking for the weak points in Buddhist doctrine, the dharma, so he could prove Christianity's superiority. He read the answer "I don't know" as doctrinal blindness and the work of the Devil, but it could also indicate Ninjitsu keeping his mind open in an inquiry.

The historian of religion might see this confrontation simply as the opening salvo of religious infighting that accompanied the civil upheaval in feudal Japan that was to last well into the solidification of the Tokugawa *shogunate*. The Jesuits did become embroiled, taking sides between the warring *daimyos*, tying their missionary success to military victories of lords who converted to Christianity. Daimyo Omura Sumitada and Koteda Saemon used their new religion to undermine the power of the Buddhist establishment, even burning Buddhist temples, images, and statues. These incidents, unfortunately for the Jesuits, were long remembered and bitterly resented (Boxer, p. 47).

In a later letter, Xavier writes, "Among the nine sects, there is one which maintains that the souls of men are mortal like that of beasts.... The followers of this sect are evil. They were impatient when they heard that there is a hell" (Schurhammer 1982, p. 283). Apparently Xavier informed Ninjitsu that he or some of his monks were condemned to hell because they did not hold to the immortality of the soul. Later Xavier began to regard *zazen* as a way of repressing the remorse he believed Zen monks must have felt for immoral behavior. Xavier was particularly offended by the sexual license of some monks and same sex liaisons with the acolytes in the temple.

To place Xavier's arrival in the context of the religious history of medieval Japan, it was only forty-nine years later in 1597, as the Tokugawa shoguns continued to consolidate their rule, that twenty-six Christians, including three Jesuits, two of them Japanese converts, and three young boys, were crucified in Nagasaki. That horrifying event marked the beginning of the savagery of the anti-Catholic campaign that continued until the expulsion of all foreigners in the 1630s, and closed Japan to all but a few trading ships from China and the Netherlands until 1854.

As difficult as it is to recount these events, and as deeply as it touches the central operating myth of Christianity, a term I use with no intended disrespect, that death freely chosen opens the way to salvation, this reading of history is a search for causal events, not a quest for meaning. These few facts connected with some of the actual written reports from the first Jesuit missionaries have located them in the circumstances of sixteenth-century Japan, and I felt that it was important to lay out the context as carefully as I could. Zen is always contained in a specific time and circumstance. But, there is another dimension to these moments that lies in realm of *zazen*, or what Christians call meditation or contemplation.

Now, as much as possible, let's take this unique encounter between Xavier and Ninjitsu out of time and space, and look at it through another lens, or really a pair of lenses, the *Spiritual Exercises* of Saint Ignatius and the tradition of the Zen *koan,* old stories of encounters between teacher and student, mostly of Chinese origin, that are used along with meditation, or *zazen*, to focus and illuminate the mind.

For a moment allow me to use a meditation technique of Saint Ignatius, *the application of the senses*, to recreate this meeting. Allow yourself as much latitude as your imagination requires and enter into this world of long ago.

Imagine that you are a Zen monk with many years of meditation training, living in a fairly remote monastery high above a harbor where you usually see only fishing boats and perhaps, very occasionally, a Chinese junk. You have heard from your followers when they bring you food from the village that there is a dark haired foreigner making inquiries about the local priests. Perhaps you have heard about these barbarians before—Spaniards and Portuguese have been sighted in recent years and have made contact with some people living along the coast. But up to this point, these strangers have been merchants or heavily armed soldiers. The only foreigners you have met hail from Korea and China. You have never met a European.

Perhaps as the abbot of a Zen Temple, you have also heard that this man who wears a simple black robe as unadorned as your own and his Japanese companion have been telling a story about the creation of the world, a great flood, a people who tried to follow a special law given by a god, and a man called Jesus who died and then was returned to life. We know from Xavier's letters that he did craft an oral version of the life and death of Jesus, connected it with some of the stories from the Hebrew bible, had it translated into Japanese, and memorized it syllabically. Why did he come to stand in the middle of the town square and recite in nearly unintelligible Japanese what was, for most Japanese, a bizarre account of the creation and salvation of the world?

In your training you had worked with Jōshū's answer to a monk who asked him, "Why did Bodhidharma come from the West?"—his answer: "the cypress tree in the courtyard," the Chinese answer, "庭前柏樹子," attesting to the origin of the story in the early period of Zen, or Ch'an, (Mumonkan, case 37). Bodhidharma is the mythic remake of an actual monk, or perhaps a group of monks, who traveled to China from India in about the fourth century to plant Buddhism in Chinese culture. He is revered as the first Patriarch of Zen. And now, another bearded barbarian was standing at your Temple Gate with a question about life after death.

At this point in Ignatius' meditation, when you have stepped into your imagination's recreation of the event,

Ignatius introduces another dimension into your meditation, the *discernment*. Simply allow whatever emotions are present to surface, and then examine them. Do they attract you? Do they produce joy and a sense of well being? Or perhaps your gut tells you to stay clear. Examine the meeting between Xavier and the Roshi on an emotional level: what was it that drew them to become the best of friends? Perhaps it was simply intellectual interest. Some (Faure, 1982, p. 18) suggest a certain level of interior inquiry that established a common ground. It might also have been the mutual recognition of a person who meditates, a friend, in the deepest Buddhist sense of the word, a bodhisattva, a Bodhidharma.

I think I can understand from my own Zen training why the Roshi took Xavier seriously. The strange man who stood before him came from the other side of the world, spoke a strange sounding language, wore clothing that seemed somewhat monkish, and asked a question that demanded an answer, not a rote answer, not just a yes or a no, but an answer that revealed a clear grasp of its full dimension coming from his experience in meditation. Many western people today still regard belief in a human immortality as the litmus test for religious faith. From Xavier's reports, I don't think it possible to determine what Ninjitsu actually held about the existence of the soul, but I do know that he considered it important—Xavier asking it made it important.

At the very beginning of a Chinese or Japanese Zen koan, there is usually a terse report of an actual encounter, usually a question and an answer, between teacher and student. Xavier asked Ninjitsu, "Do you believe in the immortality of the soul?"

When I first read the fragments of their conversations that Xavier reported in his letters, I experienced a torrent of thoughts, memories, and explanations, everything incomplete and all lying somewhere in my past, just as what I could either reconstruct or imagine of their encounter also lay in the past,

449 years ago, not as old as the stories of the koan training or the gospel of Jesus, but belonging to a very different world than twenty-first century America.

Their conversation grabbed my imagination in a way that I could not explain to myself, and I found myself wrestling for many months with both the question and my own possible answers. I remembered my last visit with my spiritual director from my Jesuit theology days. He said to me: "I hear that Buddhists don't believe in God." Of course he knew the answer—most Buddhism is non-theistic; it does not entertain the question of divinity, neither affirming nor denying a supreme deity—he is a renowned theologian and high level consultant at the Vatican. He is, like Ninjitsu, "like a bishop among them," and at the time more than eighty years old. But despite our friendship, I still felt as though he was trying to pry an answer out of me that would undermine what he understands of Buddhist beliefs. I didn't have the skill to turn a rhetorical or speculative question into an opening for spiritual discovery, and I didn't know how my friend would take my "turning word," perhaps almost as blasphemy, not that much different than Xavier's response to Ninjitsu?

Despite any difficulties with the translation, I think that Ninjitsu understood perfectly what Xavier meant, and that he might have provided some answer that might have satisfied him given the extensive hells that are available in Buddhist cosmology. But then it occurred to me that Ninjitsu might have been more interested in allowing this man who had arrived improbably at his temple to figure out an answer for himself. Any question in the right hands can serve as a koan, and if a question lies close to a man or woman's heart, summing up the purpose they have given to their lives, it can cut to the quick like a sharp knife. Ninjitsu certainly knew that Xavier didn't risk life and limb to sail into Asia to find out if Buddhists believed in heaven and hell.

We do not know if Xavier attempted to introduce Ninjitsu

to the *Spiritual Exercises*, which might have been a good place to start, but we know for certain that Ninjitsu gave Xavier a critical piece of *zazen* instruction (Ninjitsu to Xavier, quoted in Faure, p. 17). "[W]hen asked what the monks sitting in *zazen* were doing, he ironically replied: 'Some of them are counting up how much they received during the past months from their faithful; others are thinking about their recreations and amusements; in short none of them are thinking about anything that has any meaning at all.'" (Schurhammer 1982, p. 74).

Xavier had been trained in spiritual practice, you might even say "converted," when he did the *Spiritual Exercises* with Ignatius with its rigorous, defined and orderly Four Weeks, the application of the senses, the invocations, colloquies and formal prayer. These are definitely things to do—so many that the mind has little time or space to move undirected. The closest one gets to listing recreations and amusements might be in the first week, which is a prolonged examination of conscience in the light of one's purpose on earth. But it has no random or haphazard quality to it—it is directed. Ninjitsu's comment about what filled the head while meditating had some irony that Xavier didn't find amusing.

Ignatius also included in his *Exercises* instructions on methods of prayer. I have already used the *application of the senses* to recreate the meeting between Xavier and Ninjitsu; Ignatius also recommends invocations and colloquies, which, at least in my experience, are more akin to the prayer of formal ritual. The exercise that comes closest to the practice of *zazen* though is what Ignatius calls the third method of prayer or the *prayer of quiet*. The instructions are quite simple, that one chooses a prayer that is so familiar that it floats in the consciousness with no effort: "Our Father who art in Heaven," and then allow one word to rest on each breath. With the guidance of our spiritual director, over time, perhaps that prayer becomes just a word on a breath until the bell rings to signify the end of meditation.

Here is the exact text from the *Spiritual Exercises*: *Third Method of Prayer. The Third Method of Prayer is that with each breath in or out, one has to pray mentally, saying one word of the Our Father, or of another prayer which is being recited: so that only one word be said between one breath and another, and while the time from one breath to another lasts, let attention be given chiefly to the meaning of such word, or to the person to whom he recites it, or to his own baseness, or to the difference from such great height to his own so great lowness.....* Perhaps Ninjitsu had a similar experience when, as a young monk, he was given *zazen* instruction. I have every reason to believe that his instruction was not much different than the first time I sat in a Zen hall: simply count your breaths from one to ten, and when you lose track, simply redirect your mind back to one and begin again.

Although I had been practicing *zazen* on my own for years, when I officially joined a Zen temple, I asked for meditation instruction. I still recall that meeting vividly. One evening at dusk, after the six o'clock sitting, Zenshin Philip Whalen sat down next to me on the wooden bench overlooking the backyard behind the zendo on Hartford Street. He started by saying that I seemed to sit rather well which he thought indicated that I had done some work—I didn't "wiggle around a lot"—and then he asked me about my meditation. I listed my experience, almost like a spiritual curriculum vitae, *zazen*, *vipassana*, Tibetan initiations and, of course, the *Spiritual Exercises* of St Ignatius. Philip listened quietly and then said that it would be best to put all that aside and to try to begin freshly, but as that in itself was impossible, just the intention to have "beginner's mind" would probably be enough. It was all that most people could do. So I asked, "Well what should I do with my thoughts?" Phil said, "Anything you like. You can't stop your mind. Don't even try."

Over and over in my early meditation interviews with

Phil and Issan Dorsey Roshi, the instruction was clear: leave my mind alone. After perhaps a year or so, I was able to be present to my mind just running on, and I began to notice that the flips and loops of repeated inner conversations seemed linked in a way somewhat akin to the kind of insights that I had had in psychotherapy. Again Phil cautioned me that *zazen* was not psychotherapy; that I shouldn't be satisfied with that insight but continue to sit with an open mind, trying to be in beginner's mind as much as I could.

Learning the Meaning of Eternal Life

From what I can map from the chronology of the letters, Ninjitsu and Xavier met many times over an extended period, at least three but perhaps as long as nine months. It was unlike today's high-level ecumenical gathering, a tightly scripted formal conference negotiated in advance to trumpet straightening out the thread of an old argument—where the parties separated, where they might converge, or where they agree to disagree.

Despite Xavier's dogmatic tone, there are clues that the conversation had elements of spontaneity and laughter. It was also a time to become friends, to learn to deal with the language differences that separated them, and to consider life from a religious or spiritual perspective. Ninjitsu could have answered Xavier's question with the famous, oft quoted response to the question about what happens after death, given by an old Zen Master; "Don't ask me, I'm not dead yet." It has everything that Westerners expect in a Zen answer, trusting the immediacy of experience, the attitude of not presuming to know the answer, and certainly not relying on any doctrine to settle the case. I like it because it makes me laugh, but I remember that Xavier showed very little tolerance for humor when the Roshi talked about what might be passing through his monks' minds as they sat in meditation focused on collection plates and dalliances.

Xavier will eventually find reason enough to condemn the

313

entire Zen sect as the work of the Devil. He was so much the product of his culture and the frayed religious culture that the Reformation left in its wake, he set a confrontational tone for the entire mission of the Jesuits in Japan. Even though a saint, he seemed to love the role of hurtling condemnations like an Old Testament Prophet. That is what spiritual life had come to in Europe and what he expected to find in Asia. I don't know if Ninjitsu would have passed Xavier on his koan work—probably not, but Xavier did come to appreciate the depth and subtlety of the Zen mind, so much so that his recommendations for the Jesuit mission included, besides training in the Japanese language, as complete an understanding as possible of the religious traditions practiced in the kingdom.

For Ninjitsu, I would like to believe that Xavier's question opened a window into his own soul, like a koan. Xavier writes: "I found him [Ninjitsu] doubtful and unable to decide whether our soul is immortal or whether it dies together with the body; sometimes he agreed with me, and at other times he did not" (Schurhammer 1982, 85). What Xavier takes to be wavering and indecision could also indicate Ninjitsu's working with the koan. I can feel some kinship with an attitude that Ninjitsu's answers might have betrayed. I have looked into the eyes of the teacher that I was working with on a koan, and not known what to say, or how to respond, feeling one thing in one moment and something entirely different a split second later. If Xavier's question did not open a new way of viewing the world for the Roshi, it did for me.

If you are inclined, you can find your own answer to Xavier's question. I recommend that you include the practice of *zazen* when you choose some tools to help your search and study. Over time, you can expect that your meditation will reset the language you, and your community, use to describe religious experience. Each time you say "life" on a new breath it will bring that word into the present moment. Each present moment wipes away more traces of the inherited meaning we give to words, the misunderstandings, the exaggerations, the lies and adjustments that we humans make for our precious beliefs, the fairy tales that we were told and believed as children. I won't say that your language will reset to reveal the Truth, but you will certainly be more in touch with your own experience.

Xavier left Japan early in 1551. He died a just over a year later on Sancian, a small island off south China, while waiting for a boat to carry him into the celestial empire. "Ninxit" died in 1565. 1549 or 1550 marked the end of their encounter. It seems from the record that the groundwork for further conversation about religious beliefs between Zen Buddhists and Christians was not very firm. The virtues of friendship, however, cannot be underestimated.

The expression "eternal moment" is more than poetry, but something that can be really experienced in meditation. Lovers, and sometimes friends, can also share this experience. It might also be a lens to open up all of life in every dimension of time and space.

Jesuits enter the Zen hall to sit

Father Enomiya-LaSalle, S.J. is buried in Hiroshima where he was walking on August 6, 1945, only eight miles from the epicenter of atomic explosion that destroyed the city. He survived. He also was a Zen student for the remaining forty-five years of his life, attaining fluency with the practice of *zazen* and a mastery of the *koans* that was fully recognized by his teachers. He wrote about his long work with the practice, but that is the subject of another article. LaSalle led many fellow Jesuits into the sphere of *zazen*, including Pedro Arrupe who was his superior in Japan, and Ignatius' successor as the General of the Society during the time that I was a Jesuit. Arrupe carried his meditation cushion, or *zafu,* with him to the Jesuit Curia in Rome. LaSalle's example and teaching

315

influenced most of the men I mention below who became fully authorized Zen teachers in their own right.

The teaching never ends. The wheel of the dharma, as the Buddhist metaphor is clearly trying to tell us, never stops. I have no evidence that Xavier ever really taught Ninjitsu anything about the Christian way of life, but I have anecdotal evidence that it just might have happened as I imagined it. My friend and teacher, David Weinstein Roshi, was a student of Yamada Koun Roshi during the last years of Father LaSalle's life, and often saw him coming and going at the *zendo* in Kamakura. He worked with his teacher almost until the day he died. David told me this story. One morning after *zazen*, after Yamada had finished seeing students who were working on a *koan*, he was standing next to Yamada as LaSalle was leaving. Yamada turned to David and said, "He is the man who taught me how to apply the *koans* in my life."

There seems to be a way that *koans* enter into our consciousness and change our viewpoint. They can even change a society. After the letters that Xavier sent to Ignatius describing his encounter with the Zen Master Ninjitsu, to my mind, it seemed inevitable that some Jesuits would eventually enter a Zen hall, and, that with the discipline learned from their training under the *Spiritual Exercises*, some would complete their *koan* training and teach Zen. Here are the names of the Jesuits who have followed Xavier and Ninjitsu into that deep meditation. It may be incomplete. I have only used the title "Roshi" for the Jesuits who have publically received "*inka*" which is both recognition of their intimate understanding of the Dharma and a sign of their authority, their seal, as a Zen teacher.

I begin my list with Fr. LaSalle who is the first in this lineage of Jesuit Zen masters. I cannot even guess where their Zen practice will lead; I hope that the work of these men will open and enrich the spiritual lives of many people.

The Jesuit roshis:
Fr. Hugo Enomiya-LaSalle, S.J. (dec. 1990)
Fr. William Thomas Hand, S.J. (dec. 2005)
Fr. Niklaus Brantschen, S.J., Roshi
Ruben Habito, Roshi (a former Jesuit)
Fr. William Johnston, S.J.
Fr. Kakichi Kadowaki, S.J.
Fr. Robert Jinsen Kennedy, S.J., Roshi
Bro. Tom Marshall, S.J.
Fr. Ama Samy, S.J., Roshi

The Verse

In the traditional collections, a commentary on a koan usually ends with a poem, language that points beyond itself. Here are a few lines from Rumi translated by Coleman Barks that I have chosen to close the question of "the immortality of the soul." The words only point to a possible answer, or a way for you to look for your own answer.

Who gets up early to discover the moment light begins?
Who finds us here circling, bewildered, like atoms?
Who comes to a spring thirsty
and sees the moon reflected in it?
Who, like Jacob, blind with grief and age,
smells the shirt of his son and can see again?
Who lets a bucket down
and brings up a flowing prophet?
Or like Moses goes for fire
and finds what burns inside the sunrise?

Jesus slips into a house to escape enemies,
and opens a door to the other world.
Solomon cuts open a fish, and there's a gold ring.
Omar storms in to kill the prophet
and leaves with blessings.

Chase a deer and end up everywhere!
An oyster opens his mouth to swallow one drop.
Now there's a pearl.

A vagrant wanders empty ruins
Suddenly he's wealthy.

But don't be satisfied with stories,
how things have gone with others.
Unfold your own myth,
without complicated explanation,
so everyone will understand the passage,
We have opened you.

Note:
Fukushoji has been alternatively designated as a Soto Temple (Faure), a Rinzai Temple (Kagoshima records), a Sendai Temple (Xavier Memorial Association). Although this encounter was before the 17th century Rinzai revival of Hakuin Ekaku (1685–1768), the instruction has the distinct feel of *shikantaza,* "just sitting," favored by the Soto school, founded by Dōgen Zenji, (1200–53).

References:

Francis Xavier: His Life, His Times, Vol. 4: Japan and China, 1549–1552, Georg Schurhammer, Jesuit Historical Institute, 1973.

Chan Insights and Oversights: An Epistemological Critique of the Chan Tradition, Bernard Faure, Princeton University Press, 1993.

Gateless Barrier: Zen Comments on the Mumonkan, Zenkai Shibayama, Shambhala, 2000.

A Vision Betrayed: The Jesuits in Japan and China, 1542–1742, Andrew C. Ross; Edinburgh University Press, 1994.

Papers on Portuguese, Dutch and Jesuit Influences in 16ᵗʰ and 17ᵗʰ Century Japan, Boxer, C.R., compiled by Michael Moscato. Washington D.C.: University of America, Inc., 1979.

The Spiritual Exercises of St. Ignatius of Loyola, St. Ignatius Loyola and Father Elder Mullan, Cosimo Classics, 2007.

The Essential Rumi, Coleman Barks, translator, Harpercollins, 1995.

Contemplating Out Loud
Presenting the *Spiritual Exercises* for People Like Me
A Conversation with Doug McFerran

On February 21, 2006, I interviewed Doug McFerran. The purpose in my conversation with Doug was to explore some aspects of spirituality: a way to compare Buddhist meditation with the Spiritual Exercises and in how they might complement and enrich each other. It is fascinating how different our experiences can be yet so similar. Our conversation was a meeting of minds and sympathetic hearts.

MZC: What was your first serious exposure to the practice of meditation? What kind of meditation was it? Did you encounter any obstacles? What were its benefits?

DMcF: As a young Jesuit I was taught the specific practices of meditation developed by Ignatius Loyola in the sixteenth century. The concept behind Loyola's *Spiritual Exercises* was simple enough: fully engage the human imagination in a series of vivid recreations that, above all, centered on the events of Jesus' life as told in the Gospels, then allow for a powerful emotional response that, in principle, would make someone a more complete companion of Jesus.

There were two things presupposed in Ignatian spirituality: a visual rather than a verbal mode of intelligence and openness to emotional states. I had neither, and as a consequence the *Exercises* didn't enliven me. The daily morning meditation that was expected to be part of our lives was hardly the spiritual sustenance Loyola intended. However, when visiting the Loyola castle in Basque country some years ago, I saw in one of the displays how the sainted founder of the Jesuits had worried about losing his eyesight because of what was called the gift of tears. It was only then I came to realize what the Long Retreat might have meant for others.

My main obstacle was that the *Exercises* were presented

visually. This distinction of visual from verbal was not really made by psychologists until fairly recently. For someone like myself, who does not readily think in pictures, the *Exercises* were a continuing source of frustration. My knees hurt, the clock seemed to have slowed down, and rather than a heightened sense of dedication I had only a sense of relief when the hour of meditation was over. My meditation didn't have a natural resonance with my personality.

I was a Jesuit for ten years. Perhaps, had I been able to adapt the *Exercises* more to my way of learning and thinking, I might have never left.

MZC: Would you say anything positive came from doing the *Exercises*? Were there any positive aspects of the *Exercises*, such as the Examen, the Contemplation for Obtaining Love, Connecting with what one authentically desires, Degrees of Humility?

DMcF: Sadly, I think I missed the point on all of these when I first did the *Exercises* as a novice, probably because I was constantly trying to work out the preliminary activity called "composition of place." Of course, I was very good at visualization when it just came to any wish-fulfillment type of daydreaming. For instance, I had no problem seeing myself getting some special recognition, and I think had I been asked to imagine being on a date with any of my adolescent fantasies (Maria Montez or Simone Simon, for instance) I could have easily handled it. However, it did not seem to work for what Ignatius had in mind.

The one thing that stuck was the advice Loyola gave not to make changes in a time of desolation. Since I went into a prolonged period of depression well into my first year as a novice, I kept hanging in as a novice and then as a scholastic when by all rights I should have been either getting some straight-out therapy or facing up to the possibility I was just not where I should have been.

The full point of the degrees of humility thing hit home

the year before I left, when I had to admit that in no way would I be willing to invite the kind of suffering Jesus went through just to be more like him.

MZC: How did your study of Buddhism influence your ideas of meditation and how would you re-do the *Exercises* of St. Ignatius in the light of what you've learned about Buddhist practice? Can the *Exercises* be presented to adapt to a person who does not think visually?

DMcF: The irony was that it was because I left and found a new career as a college teacher of philosophy that I discovered that the techniques Loyola presented were paralleled in Buddhist practice, especially in certain techniques of Tibetan meditation. I realized as well that the key was to avoid trying to make my poor brain work in what for me would be a rather unnatural way. Instead of trying to force a prescribed set of images, I could allow a story to tell itself. What I learned about Buddhism was that there are actually two distinct types of meditation we could be talking about. One is Zen, such as the emptying out that the Jesuit William Johnston writes about. The other is the elaborate visualization practices of other Buddhist schools, especially the Tibetan. It was when I became more familiar with the Tibetan approach I was hit with the realization that this was very much like what Loyola had intended. However, thanks to spending time with Carl Jung's take on the *Tibetan Book of the Dead*, I also saw that the point was not to try to somehow "see" the Palestinian world of Jesus as though I were watching a biblical epic. For Jung, a key idea was the Tibetan admonition that the entities seen in the *bardo* experience (the visions of the soul following death) were just projections of oneself and yet real at the same time. Bingo. I could let the images flow without the type of constraint I had felt in the *Exercises*, where I had dutifully and unsuccessfully attempted to "get it right."

If I were to present the *Exercises* to people more like myself, I think I would actually just contemplate out loud and let anyone listening kind of walk along with me, but doing so in such a way that the individual could start a journey in which my suggestions recede into the background. This is actually what I have done with experiments in inducing a hypnotic state, and it is something I have worked with in other situations in which I have used guided meditations

MZC: What is it to "allow a story to tell itself?" What are some of the Tibetan meditation techniques you refer to? What were the fruits of practicing them? How do these techniques parallel Ignatius' *Exercises*?

DMcF: I think it is a kind of method acting done entirely inside your own head, if you want to use such a phrase. Let's imagine we take a snippet of the Gospel narrative. As an example, I'll take the Lazarus story. I'm out there with the grieving relatives. Now maybe I cared about Lazarus, maybe I really did not like the dude at all. Now here comes this preacher type who has him pop back up. What am I thinking about now? How am I handling Lazarus being back? Okay, now how am I handling this weirdo who turned normal things inside out? What's happening, if you think about it, is that I might be getting a better insight into myself by chasing down my reactions.

MZC: Would you say that the way you were given the *Spiritual Exercises* was limited by the notion of historical truth? How has some of the contemporary theologies of interpreting Scriptures as mythical/literary truths, rather than historical facts, influenced you?

DMcF: Yes, a key point to note is that from a Buddhist perspective the notion of historical truth is not the issue as it would be for most Christians. Instead of attempting to relive a set of actual events—being a bystander at the crucifixion of Jesus, for instance—there can be a more free and playful interaction with a rich set of images, a type of self-therapy through which a deeper personal integration becomes possible.

MZC: How does the concept of a "self" impinge on this discussion of the *Exercises* and Buddhist meditation? Don't both include some letting go of the self, especially letting go the egotistical self?

DMcF: At first it might seem that this Buddhist concept of a profound personal integration would be at odds with the traditional Ignatian image of surrendering the self. What we need to remember about Buddhism is that what we think of as a personal self is entirely transitory, and that the goal of Buddhist meditation has been to realize the Buddha within. Personal integration has two aspects: wisdom—going beyond the cravings that are the cause of suffering—and compassion—the readiness to ease others who are in pain. This too is a matter of surrendering the self.

On this basis it makes good sense to imagine how the *Spiritual Exercises* could be presented in a Buddhist context. This is especially the case as the Society of Jesus itself, in the spirit of the Second Vatican Council, has come to include a focus on the issues of peace and justice. Peace, if we think about it, involves wisdom in the Buddhist sense of letting go of the wrong attachments, and justice above all is the attempt to make compassion real.

MZC: What is the importance of "Discernment of Spirits" in The *Spiritual Exercises*? What is its relevance in an age of many non-rational religious enthusiasts?

DMcF: Recently PBS presented the 2006 documentary Jesus Camp about young children brought up in an intense charismatic environment. I found myself very much bothered by it, in part by the "in your face" activism that it encouraged and in part by the comment of one young girl about "dead churches"—those in which congregations were essentially passive—"where God would not want to go." I've been trying to think through my reactions. After all, had I not been raised in the hothouse environment of a Catholic school with as rigid a picture of right and wrong as was shown in the film—and as a young Jesuit had I not been trained in a spirituality intended to be as transforming as the "spiritual exercises" engaged in by these children?

Now, of course, I am looking at things with a far greater sense of moral ambiguity and, I hope, a much better sense of respect for how intelligent and sincere individuals might very well not share the same views I would hold about right and wrong when in fact I am able to decide on such views. The Jesus Camp kids were above all fanatics in the making, and I kept getting an undertone of Christian militancy that provided an unsettling parallel to other bits of film I had seen about young Muslim kids training for *jihad*.

The idea was that through our meditation, above all the intense effort to place oneself at the scene in considerations of the life of Jesus, there would be an appropriate level of response—ideally, a determination to identify with Jesus even to the point of being ready to take up the cross ourselves. However, what this would mean in practice was a readiness to do the ordinary things in what really would be an extraordinary way. It was spirituality then, which has a strong parallel with the training of a Zen monk. Our *satori* would be demonstrated by our actions, not by some emotional display.

Much of the wisdom of Loyola was in the recognition that there could be counterfeits to the action of the Holy Spirit. An important aspect of the Long Retreat was this effort to understand what he called "the discernment of spirits." And it was this that was so markedly absent in what I saw in the documentary. Impressionable children were encouraged to trust their own emotional responses in a highly structured group setting. One thing that was not going to be allowed was that they would begin to think for themselves. As Jesuits, despite all the emphasis in Loyola's *Spiritual Exercises* on "thinking with the church," the very effort at discernment meant that we would be expected to ask questions. With the training that we would then receive as we went through our studies for the priesthood we would find these questions answered. Obviously, since there are so many of us who are no longer Jesuits, this did not always happen, but the importance of the process remains one of the lasting things I took from my years in the Society.

MZC: Would you elaborate on the notion of "self-therapy"? How is therapy related to meditation?

DMcF: Classical therapy—me on the couch rambling on about my dreams and anxieties and whatever—is supposedly going to expose that blockage that keeps me from living up to my potential now. For Freud the idea was to discover a childhood trauma, and it was therapeutic to do so even if the event "uncovered" proves to be entirely fictitious. Scientology plays around with something similar, although the trauma supposed involves past lives.

What impressed me with the Tibetan approach was that the therapeutic aspect involved lay in getting past those emotional states that are the basis of depression. The rich sets of images of Tibetan mythology allow those using them for meditation to explore their own desires and fears and so transcend them. Ideally, the result involves a higher degree of compassion that translates first into an unwillingness to be a source of harm and then actually a readiness to sacrifice for others. I think there is a parallel here with what Loyola wants for the individual who goes through the *Exercises*.

One difference between the traditional Christian outlook and what may be my not altogether orthodox Buddhist one is that there is a constant note of censorship in the Christian model. It would not be okay, for instance, to let myself dwell on some of the things that, in at least one variant of Tibetan meditation, might actually be encouraged (although with full recognition of their danger). I'm not supposed to be getting hot for Mary Magdalene, for instance. I'm not supposed ever to think about Jesus ticking me off. Now the trick is to get through the lust and the anger and whatever else. Force that much of whatever we mean by the self to burn itself out safely rather than keep smoldering with the risk of eruption with actual rape or murder.

On this basis it makes good sense to imagine how the *Spiritual Exercises* could be presented in a Buddhist context. This is especially the case as the Society of Jesus itself, in the spirit of the Second Vatican Council, has come to include a focus on the issues of peace and justice. Peace, if we think about it, involves wisdom in the Buddhist sense of letting go of the wrong attachments, and justice above all is the attempt to make compassion real.

MZC: What do you mean by saying that "the goal of Buddhist meditation is to realize the Buddha within?" Does this relate to Jesus' "the kingdom of heaven is within you"?

DMcF: Realizing the Buddha within can mean the recognition that the energy that allows consciousness itself to function is not determined by any specific form. It is like white light in that sense—the potential for all colors depending on how it is reflected. Getting to a recognition of this at a deep enough level means not worrying about some next stage of existence—the end of rebirth, then. On a Buddhist basis, I can then say I should not fear death as an end, but it is definitely not being tired of living. I would like to think it means discovering a capacity for joy in existence that wants to share itself by easing the suffering of others.

Now what Jesus talks about in the theology we were all taught does seem to presuppose us all being around in the great beyond, only with lots of us burning away with unfulfilled desire for something that had been rejected and others getting off to some extent, as Aquinas suggested, by watching this. So I think I do have to scratch this. A much less orthodox version of the idea of the kingdom of heaven being within us would be more like what my Buddhist musings suggest. In that reading, it is a call to not look for a Messiah who makes everything right again (get rid of those damn Romans) but instead to find

327

a sense of righteousness that does mean feeding the hungry and clothing the naked and all the rest—being Messiah-like in our own limited spheres of influence.

MZC: Can you relate meditation to the life of activism? Does "Contemplation in Action" have significance for you?

DMcF: Meditation above all means stopping the continuing dialogue we carry on inside our own heads. In the silence there is some chance for a more honest recognition of the actual dynamics of the situations in which we are involved (wisdom). That means letting go of the scripts dictated by our egos, and this opens the possibility for both a better identification with the suffering of others (compassion) and sometimes, then, seeing what may in fact move things forward to a more positive resolution.

I'm often skeptical of activism. I've seen it promoted for its own sake, as though individuals need to prove their identities by learning certain prescribed scripts and carefully adhering to them. That's not really Buddhist, and it's not Ignatian, either. The real trick of changing things is looking at them—or better, letting them be revealed—from unexpected angles. Meditation can help with this, and it is what comes to mind when I hear that phrase "contemplation in action."

Becoming Whole: *Spiritual Exercises* and Therapy
Ed, Ph.D.

[Note: While we feel that Ed's description of his personal experience, his course of therapy and his prayer life contain nothing but an example of the most responsible and human way of handing a situation that has become a source of major scandal in the Roman Catholic Church, we have agreed to respect the anonymity that Ed requests. So much harm would have been avoided if other religious superiors and members of the hierarchy had acted with the honesty, love and professionalism of his Jesuit superiors who will also remain anonymous.—editor]

I am no master of the spiritual life, but I have accepted Morgan's request to set down something of my own experience of St. Ignatius' *Spiritual Exercises* and how that might relate to my personal psychotherapy, which took seven years, during the first two years of which I still functioned as a Jesuit. I do so with no motive to defend or persuade but rather simply to communicate something of one man's journey.

When I look back on my therapy, my prayer life, and the *Exercises*, nothing turned out exactly as I expected, or, living in the Society of that era, as it was supposed to. But, over time, a sort of synthesis has developed, which permeates my life on a daily basis. I don't recommend the path I took to anyone else—they couldn't take it even if they wanted to—but perhaps the benevolent reader may find my experiences helpful in working out a prayer life of his or her own.

I was born in the Western United States, to a mother and father who had both married relatively late for those days, and who therefore looked forward with great anticipation to the birth of their first child. They subsequently had two more children, a son and a daughter. I was bright, healthy, and good-looking. I did well in school. We had hard times during the Great Depression, but we were never in actual want.

I started parochial school a generation before Vatican II. I found many of the sisters who taught me quite loving and supportive, though the code tended to be strict and inflexible. The prevailing theology was one of crime and punishment, and it left in me an intense awareness of the pervasiveness and evil of sin, as well as the severity of the corresponding divine punishment.

I was an intelligent and sensitive child and intensely aware of my emotional and sexual needs well before I started school. I was also aware that any overt expression of them was not only socially unacceptable but was also considered mortally sinful. Looking back from my experience now as a mature man, I can also see that I was precociously aware that it never could be otherwise, given my "natural" preference. Puberty was an emotional explosion. It seemed that, especially for a boy, it made it just that much easier to damn oneself.

High school with the Jesuits was, in many ways, a new and wonderful world for me. I was "aptissimus" (most apt) for the Jesuit plan of studies. I loved history and literature and language, and I enjoyed public speaking. I greatly admired the combination of youth, enthusiasm, learning and dedication of the Jesuit scholastics (i.e. Jesuits in training), which taught us.

The prevailing spirituality, however, was still one of sin and guilt. The *Spiritual Exercises*, as we experienced them in our annual retreats, consisted almost entirely of material from the First Week of the *Exercises*, with its emphasis on sin and its consequence, hell. The Sacraments were the primary means of salvation. They worked automatically, given the required dispositions, and you hoped that you might one day die in the "state of grace," possibly by being hit by an automobile walking home from church, just after you had gone to confession

In the case of a three-day retreat for adolescent boys almost the entire period was often taken up with this process. The goal was to lead them to repentance for sin and reconciliation with God by means of the Sacrament of Penance. Retreat Masters with a gift for rhetorical flair, presenting this part of the *Exercises* to hundreds of students at a time could become extremely formidable and downright scary.

Within this context, I began to think, "Why not become a Jesuit, where I would be able to put to use my talents as a humanist as a way of "going in the door" of my students and forming them to a sacramental Christian life?" It seemed for me the best way of being of service to them, while hopefully saving my own soul at the same time. Accordingly, upon my graduation from high school, I entered the Jesuit Novitiate and began the long training required to become a Jesuit priest.

The spiritual formation of the Jesuit novice is in the hands of an experienced priest, who is called the Master of Novices; "Master" in the sense of "Magister," teacher, not "Dominus," lord. I had two novice masters. That meant that I experienced two different thirty-day retreats during which we made the full *Spiritual Exercises*. I undertook the *Exercises* generously, though I am not sure I made them well, as I'll discuss later.

My second novice master gave me a number of opportunities to get to know the *Exercises* even better. The first and most obvious one was that he appointed me "Archangel" for all the incoming novices. That meant that I oversaw the other second-year novices, each of whom was assigned an incoming novice, whom he would instruct in the customs and rules of the house. This assignment became more important than it previously had been for a couple of reasons. First of all, it was customary for the new novices to make a three-day retreat shortly after their entrance. This retreat had previously been given by a young priest, the assistant to the Master of Novices, called Father "Socius" (The Latin word means "companion"). In this case the new assistant had only recently arrived, and Fr. Master informed me that I would be giving the retreat(s) for all incoming novices instead of Fr. Socius. I was initially dismayed but also flattered that he thought I could do it. I began to have fantasies of becoming a Master of Novices myself one day.

The assignment proved to be much more strenuous than it initially sounded, because there were multiple dates of entry that year. One was in early July, another in mid-August, and then there were several novices who entered individually during the course of the year. The result was that I had occasion to give the *Exercises* (mostly the First Week) six or seven times during my second year as a novice. I mention this only as history. I'm not at all sure than I acquired any special insight into what the *Exercises* are or could be.

After the two years of Novitiate, Jesuits in training normally made an eight-day version of the *Exercises* each year. During the years that followed I had a number of highly regarded retreat masters: one who became Superior of all the Chinese missionaries in exile, another who was president of a University, a third who was in charge of the final year of spiritual training for Jesuits, called *tertianship* and who was much venerated by his *tertians*, another, a returned Chinese missionary, was bent over with arthritis but full of holy fire, and finally, a former Assistant to Fr. General. In later years I even made this annual retreat in French and German.

My thirty-day retreat during *tertianship*, a final year of spiritual formation placed at the very end of a Jesuit's training, was certainly one of the most memorable events of my life. Our *Tertian* Master had previously been a Provincial in France and this was his first year as *Tertian* Master. He was a rather distant, stiff and austere person; some of the *tertians* referred to him as "the Colonel."

His manner of giving the *Exercises* was quite extraordinary and challenging. He met with us as a group once a day, in the evening, for about twenty minutes, to give us "points" for meditation. He would tell us where we were in the *Exercises* and what the spiritual fruit was that we should be seeking in our prayer. He might suggest a passage or two from Scripture for us to meditate upon, and then indicate that, after that, we were to make two repetitions and an application of the senses, and that he would see us all again tomorrow evening. He was available to any of us at any time during the day and he met with each of us individually every third day, to see how we were doing.

I have never felt so utterly alone! It was up to each of us when he got up, when he said Mass, the Divine Office and the rosary and when he made his meditations four or five times a day. I think only five or six bells rang during the whole day, and three of them were for meals. I had never had such an experience of silence and solitude! At first I wasn't sure I could do it, but, after a few days, the silence became kind of comforting. I would not have traded that experience for anything now, but it was a really stressful month.

I still have my journal of those days, with an entry for every single meditation, with detailed descriptions of subject matter, desolation, consolation, discernment of spirits, doubts, distractions, resolutions etc.

And … what? I'm not sure what. In most of my experience with the *Exercises* I would give myself an A for effort, but I'm not sure I ever really made them correctly. And the difficulties I encountered were pretty much the same, whether it was eight days or thirty days, alone or with others, in English or in other languages.

I think my most basic difficulty was that I never made the *Exercises* to make a real Election, i.e. to truly make a decision on my state in life. We were told that we had already made that decision by entering the novitiate, and that our vocation was settled, as long as superiors found us "apt." The result for me was that my "elections" were invariably limited to recommitting myself to my vows and the rules. Often in my case that led to an increased rigidity in the observance of the rules, which I think must have annoyed some of my companions. So each year, for me, the spiritual effort of the *Exercises* resulted in what seemed like Horace's proverbial "ridiculous mouse".

Election wasn't the only problem I had, however. Contemplation, as proposed by St. Ignatius, was a skill I just never mastered. Perhaps I'm too cerebral. Part of my difficulty was a deep-seated mistrust of the imagination. It seemed to me that you could make it up any way you wanted and then decide that that was the way of imitating Christ.

I remember hearing one retreat master say, in reference to Jesus, "He smiled, but He never laughed." Give me a break! And as I became mistrustful of the individual retreat master, even of men with great reputations, I became equally mistrustful of my own ability to imagine the situations any more authentically. I tried again and again, but I don't think I ever felt at ease or at home in Ignatian contemplation, as I have heard other men describe their experiences.

A third basic problem I had with the *Exercises* is closely related to the previous one. It might just be a variant of the same thing. It has to do with the "discernment of spirits." Over the years, while I respect the honesty and sincerity of the men I have listened to talk about their process in this regard, I have often had the impression that they had gone through a very long, elaborate process to come to the conclusion that they themselves wanted in the first place. One very saintly Jesuit, a man I greatly revered, was quoted as having said, "Our capacity to deceive ourselves is infinite!" I don't think he could have meant that literally since that would make any effort pointless, but I think it expresses something close to what I think, with the possible addition of the qualifier "almost" infinite.

In my case, it meant that I was mistrustful of my own conclusions. My way of handling the situation concretely was to take very little initiative and to rely passively on obedience to make the major decisions in my life.

I can trace the results out in my life as a Jesuit. At the

end of my first year of Classical Studies, which followed the novitiate, I was asked by the Province Prefect of Studies what I was interested in specializing in. I answered that I enjoyed all my studies but particularly liked history, literature and language. He enthusiastically approved and told me to get some direction from my history professor and do some reading on the side in history during the year to come.

I did that during the year that followed, and, when he came by again at the end of second year and asked me how things were going, I told him, "Fine!" He paused and then, out of the blue, asked if I had every thought of specializing in philosophy. I honestly answered that I didn't even know what it was. He replied that "they" were thinking of having someone in my class specialize in philosophy, "and your name has been mentioned."

What I realized almost immediately was that this put an end to my dreams of ever returning to high school as a scholastic or as a priest to teach the juniors or seniors Cicero or Shakespeare or Ancient History.

That was it! I don't know who "mentioned my name" or why. I had no further direction than that. During my three years of studying philosophy which followed, I felt rudderless. Some of the teachers I had were sincere and devoted but woefully unable to inspire or elicit enthusiasm in their students, and I developed no passion for philosophy at all. I faithfully went though all the requirements. In the third year, I successfully defended certain propositions of Natural Law in oral arguments for what are called the "Disputations," one of the famous hurdles in Jesuit philosophical training. I was considered by some to be a sort of "Golden Boy", but I certainly didn't feel that way.

Fast forward to the *Tertianship,* my last year of regular Jesuit training, when I received word from the same Prefect of Studies that it had been decided that I should subsequently get a doctorate in philosophy. I had no enthusiasm for the assignment, but holy obedience had spoken. I discussed the news with a companion of mine, who had been with me through theology and *tertianship* and who was very perceptive. He was scheduled to go on to get a Ph.D. in English. He had a way of being very direct. He said to me, "You know, if you go on to get a doctorate in Philosophy and go on to teach at one of our universities, you'll be a great teacher, the kids will love you, you'll be someone they'll come back to visit with etc., but your gifts will be wasted. That will be nothing to what you could do in comparative languages! Your ability at languages is remarkable. You could teach a class comparing Cervantes, Racine, Goethe, Dante and Shakespeare. Think about it!"

What he had said really hit me. I got up my courage and wrote a letter back to the Prefect of Studies, simply telling him what my classmate had said and wondering if he thought it had any merit. I soon received a reply. It was friendly and understanding and full of reasonable cold water. Father pointed out to me that, although I was fluent in several languages, I had no graduate credits in foreign languages. He estimated that a doctorate in comparative languages would take about five years to obtain. Then he raised a couple of practical points: supposing that I got such a degree and offered such a course, "Who would be able to take it? You would end up teaching Intermediate German".

At this point I felt I had correctly manifested to my superiors the alternative "spirits" that were moving me, and they had authoritatively replied that the spirits were misleading or at least impractical. And I could not argue with their reasoning. Maybe if I had said something earlier, back in classical studies, and told the Prefect that when I thought about majoring in philosophy I found myself feeling uneasy, unhappy and depressed, and that when I thought about history or literature or language I felt joyous and eager and enthused, there might have been some possibility to making different plans. But I was too mistrustful of my own "spirits" at that point. Being in that state, I could only resolve my mistrust of my own judgment by always choosing what was least appealing (to avoid self-deception) or by doing what I did, which was to leave it all in the hands of obedience. I was clinically depressed during my doctoral classes in philosophy at the University. I completed my thesis, however, during the following year and returned to the Province to teach philosophy. Again, I seemed to some a "Golden Boy". There was one father in the community, not that many years older than I, who never failed to say, as he passed me in the corridor, "There's the man who has it made!" I felt it as a taunt, and it never failed to sadden me.

So, where have we gotten so far? I've spoken at length about the influence of the *Exercises* in my life as a Jesuit. I can't really offer my experiences as any special insight into them. It's really more a description of the difficulties that one well-intentioned individual had in making use of them.

■

This is the point in my story at which I will begin to say something about therapy and its effects in my life. As my life progressed in the Society, through my years of teaching, theology, *tertianship*, graduate studies and thereafter, it became obvious that I had a core problem; I tended to fall in love with my students. I attempted to sublimate or spiritualize the attraction, and the sublimation was successful to a considerable extent, but it was undeniable that, at the core, there was an erotic dimension to it.

Its manifestation was not gross or obvious, or at least so I thought, but I experienced an overpowering curiosity about the sexual lives of some of my students or friends. I wanted to know what their sexual feelings and histories were like. I wanted to know what they looked like naked. The result over time was that I became involved in a number of situations that were not overtly and or grossly sexual but definitely sexualized and certainly might be interpreted as inappropriate if they came to public notice. I was now teaching at a university and was very successful as a teacher, a valuable addition to any faculty, one might have thought.

In these circumstances I was transferred to a different university. There I experienced extraordinary friendship and support from the man who was my religious superior. He made arrangements for me to get into therapy. And I don't mean he simply referred me to someone. I later had a very close and talented friend, who was a psychoanalyst. He used to say that it was dangerous to go shopping for a therapist on one's own, because one would be likely to unconsciously choose a therapist who was not likely to explore one's core issues. He said the best way to do it was to seek the counsel of someone who knew you very well and who had your best interests at heart.

I thought that this superior was the person to take that role for me. When we were discussing choosing a therapist, he told me that several members of the community were or had been in therapy. One therapist had seen several of them, but he felt the therapist was getting old, and recent outcomes had not been very satisfactory. There was another possibility, a younger man, whom he thought was much more promising, but he added that he didn't think he would be right for me because he thought I was smarter than the prospective therapist was and I might be likely to discount him or work around him. Instead, he said, there was a third possibility; a man whom he had never actually met but whom he had heard speak a couple of times and had been very much impressed by what he had to say.

I accepted his suggestion. I was happy to get any help I could but was not very hopeful or enthusiastic, having had a very disappointing experience with a very inadequate attempt at "therapy" the year before.

Both my passive attitude and my prospective therapist's

acuity were manifest in our very first contact. The superior had given me his number, and I phoned him. I identified myself and said, "I'm supposed to meet with you." "Supposed to?" he asked. "Do you want to meet with me?" I immediately realized what I had said and corrected myself. "Yes, I want to meet with you." "Well," he said, in his broad Texas accent, "That's just dandy!"

My intake interview with him occurred on the following Saturday. My superior, ever faithful, accompanied me to the meeting. The doctor asked him to wait in the waiting room, while he assessed my suitability for treatment. My superior assented without demur. And he waited for eight hours! That's how long my intake interview lasted.

On the basis of what I told him, the doctor suggested an initial interpretation, which really impressed me and which was to be pivotal in all my subsequent therapy. He said, "A man of your intelligence could be the most sexually active clergyman in the state, and no one would need to know anything about it. But you repeatedly set up situations in which you get a minimum of actual sexual satisfaction but have the potential for enormous amounts of scandal". He further suggested that, although I externally and consciously embraced the celibate life, I was, at a deeper, unconscious level, furious against my parents, my teachers, the Church and the Society, all of whom told me effectively that I had no right to fulfill my deepest sexual desires.

Finally he asked the superior to come in. "I think Father needs treatment," he said. "I think he is treatable, but I offer no guarantees of outcome. Things could get worse before they get better. But I would not touch this case with a ten-foot pole, unless the Society commits itself to completing the therapy, no matter what happens." The superior didn't bat an eye. "Of course," he said, and that was the beginning of my therapy. That reply really made an impression on me, and it cemented the superior and me for life. I can still remember the two of us walking out afterwards and going down the block to an International House of Pancakes to get some dinner.

The therapy went on for seven years, at times at a frequency of five times a week. During the first year and a half, I was still teaching at the university. Then, as my therapist judged that my reaction to the exploration of the material was making it likely that I might act out my resentment and thus both hurt my family, the Church and the Society, while at the same time punishing myself in the process, he suggested to my superiors that I seek a leave of absence from religious life, "So that, if Father actually acts out his urges, he and he alone will suffer the consequences." He was obviously trying to deprive me of those motivations to act out. My superiors jumped at the suggestion.

So, that fall, I started living as a layperson. The only request I made of the Provincial was that I be allowed to pursue my therapy with the same therapist, and he agreed.

The next six months were extremely painful, as I sought to find some suitable way of supporting myself. I calculate that I had eighteen interviews as I was looking for work, without any favorable outcome. A friendly and helpful young lady at the employment office told me, "You are over qualified and under experienced. The Bank of America doesn't want to hire as a teller a man who has a Ph.D." There were nights when I cried myself to sleep.

I was living within walking distance of a local university and started taking some evening courses in psychology. Eventually I applied for a post-doctoral fellowship, and that was the beginning of five years there as a Visiting Lecturer. By the end of my tenure, I passed the examination for licensure as a psychologist.

At this point I had been on leave for five years. The Provincial, whom I had known since high school, wrote to me and said that he didn't want in any way to pressure me, but that he had to write a yearly letter to the General, updating him on my status. He asked me to provide some material.

I thought it over carefully. I had been in therapy seven years. I had grown in many ways, especially psychologically. I loved and was loyal to the Society, but, on the basis of my experience, I did not think that I could promise that I would not be a likely cause of possible scandal and damage to the Society and the Church. Accordingly, I asked for dismissal.

That was in September. I was on the staff at the university but in a temporary capacity. I had received my license as a psychologist by then and began looking for a permanent position. I got a lot of support in my efforts from the faculty with whom I had worked during the previous five years. I considered several possible positions. Then, unexpectedly, I was offered a position at a university close to where I had grown up. I would spend the rest of my professional career there.

What to say of therapy, then? Therapy did not change my sexual orientation; much less eliminate my sexual needs. Nor did it make it possible for me to return to the Society, toward which I still felt strong loyalty and love. What it did make possible, I think, was what I think of as a friendly divorce. I didn't have to break the furniture in order to leave. No one suffered great harm. We respected each other, but recognized that we just didn't belong together.

In some ways I think my experience might serve as a paradigm for the way in which religious superiors might handle parallel cases involving danger of grave scandal due to sexual issues. My family, the university, the Society, the Church and I myself were spared the scandal and shame of my having gotten involved in forms of sexual expression that might have harmed them, as well as the students who might potentially have been involved.

My life since then has been what it has been. I still have a dozen or so former students who have remained close friends,

341

but I have never established a lasting intimate relationship. But I still love a lot of people and have a lot of people who love me. The Following of Christ says that saint differs from saint as star from star in glory. I did it my way (per *forza!*), but I think it has turned out a lot better than it might have, had I not had the support of the Society and the help of my therapist.

The psychologist Eric Erikson says that the developmental task of old age is integration vs. despair. With all the ups and downs I have known, I feel remarkably whole.

Prayer

Having discussed the roles that the *Exercises* of St. Ignatius and psychoanalytic psychotherapy have played in my life, it may be worthwhile to add an account of the form that prayer takes in my daily life.

I am at this point an old man, and the ways in which I have prayed over the years have undergone development. I cannot describe the whole process, but I can perhaps give an idea of the form prayer takes in my life at present.

My prayer does not take just one form. It is rather a collection of methods of prayer, which I have found useful over time. The first part of my morning prayer is a collection of short prayers in Latin, which speak to my past and which I personally find very expressive.

I rise early in the morning, and one of the first things I do is take my dog for a walk. My home is located on a rather steep driveway, and, as I close the gate and first step out onto the driveway and look across to a long redwood covered ridge, I make the sign of the cross on my lips and quietly murmur the prayers with which I was accustomed to preface my praying of the Divine Office, as a priest, asking God to open my mouth that I may bless His Holy Name. I then ask Him to help me focus my thoughts and feelings, so that my prayer may be worthy of His attention. *Aperi, Yahweh, os meum ad benedicendum nomen sanctum tuum. Munda quoque cor meum ab omnibus vanis, perversis et alienis cogitationibus. Intellectum illumina, affectum inflamma, ut digne, attente ac devote has preces tibi offeram et exaudire mereamur ante conspectum divinae majestatis tuae.*

By this time my dog and I have reached the bottom of the driveway and step out onto the street that leads to the Green Spaces. I lift up my hands and recite the prayer that accompanies the offering of incense in the old Latin liturgy. "May my prayer rise as incense in your sight, *Yahweh*, the lifting up of my hands a morning sacrifice." *Dirigatur oratio mea sicut incensum in conspectu tuo, Yahweh, elevatio manuum mearum sacrificium matutinum.*

Then, as we proceed on down the road among the oak trees, I recite several more short Latin prayers.

The first comes from the old Office of Prime, which I used to recite each day as part of my thanksgiving after Mass. I ask the omnipotent God, who has brought me to the beginning of this day, to sustain me, so that I may avoid any offense against Him and do what is right in His sight. Actually, this prayer is framed in the plural, so that I am including in my prayer all my human brothers and sisters. *Yahweh, Deus omnipotens, qui ad principium hujus diei nos pervenire fecisti, tua nos hodie salva virtute, ut in hoc die ad nullum declinemus peccatum, sed semper ad tuam justitiam faciendam nostra precedant eloquia, dirigantur cogitationes et opera. Per Christum Dominum Nostrum.*

Then I recite a favorite prayer, which, I used to recite in English before all my classes, when I was teaching. In it I ask God to both inspire my actions and assist me in carrying them out.

At this point we generally break out of the oaks, which line the road, and step into the open from where I see across a narrow valley a series of tree covered ridges, usually bathed in early morning sunlight. My heart lifts up at the sight, and I pair it with a line from the psalms, "To You, O *Yahweh*, I have lifted up my soul. In You, I trust. I shall not be put to shame.… " *Ad Te, Yahweh, levavi animam meam. Deus meus, in Te confido, non erubescam.*

And, as we now cross into the green space and slowly begin the ascent of the mountain, I recite another verse from the Psalms, originally used by pilgrims beginning the ascent to the Temple of Jerusalem. "Who shall go unto the mountain of Yahweh, or who shall stand in His Holy Place? The man with clean hands and a pure heart, who has not received his life in vain, nor sworn deceitfully to his neighbor." *Quis ascendet in montem Yahweh, aut quis stabit in loco sancto ejus? Innocens manibus et mundo corde, qui non accepit in vanum animam suam nec juravit in dolo proximo suo.*

Up until this point my prayers have been formal and traditional. But, now, as we proceed on our walk up the road, I make a shift from a fixed form to a freer form. It starts with an adaptation of parts of the traditional Sanctus and Gloria of the Mass in English. For me it is the most important part of my prayer, and to give you an understanding of its significance I must digress a bit.

I begin by slowly and quietly murmuring, "Holy … Holy … Holy … *Yahweh*, God Almighty, Heaven and earth are full of Your Glory.… "

These words are loaded for me. My professor of Old Testament Scripture, the best teacher I ever had, used to insist that, while the Hebrew idea of the Holiness of God doubtless contained an element of moral righteousness, its most basic, root meaning contained an important element of distance, of being apart, separate, different, what the great protestant, Karl Barth, meant when he referred to God as "the Wholly Other". I thus try to begin with an attitude of awe and adoration.

The next essential element is that of God's glory, which I fear is often misunderstood. My second Master of Novices taught us that God's essential glory is identified with His essence. But His glory "ad extra" consists of His essential goodness as manifested in the goodness of all that He creates. This relates to what I said earlier about St. Ignatius' Contemplation for Obtaining Divine Love, which invites us to see God present and active in all creation.

As I breathe in the pure and cool morning air and look across the valley to the ridges of oak and redwood bathed in morning sunlight, or look up to the soaring red-tailed hawk, or watch my dog prancing through the high grass, I am filled with awe. Sometimes I extend this movement out into the universe, beyond the planets, to the stars and the galaxies and beyond. At other times I turn it inward and become aware of God's presence within me, in my ability to breathe and walk and think and digest, all the way down to the subatomic level. Either way it is a marvel.

My prayer then expresses itself with elements from the Gloria, "I praise You.... I thank you.... I adore You....

And there follows what may be the most important part, as I add, " ... and I am silent in the awareness of Your presence."

The term "silent" has many variations for me. Sometimes I substitute "I am speechless", sometimes, "struck dumb", or "without words" or "put my hand on my mouth."

This invocation of silence has two aspects to it. One is that God's perfection exceeds my ability to express it. Another is that, along with all this perfection, I am aware of elements in creation and in history, which I cannot explain. "God's ways are not our ways." When I was a young man, I used to rashly attempt to justify to my fellow human beings the existence of human suffering. Maybe it was because I had not really suffered enough myself. But I gave that up. I have no answer, and I acknowledge that daily in my prayers. I acknowledge that both God's existence and His Ways are beyond me. And I shut my mouth!

At this point I recall another verse of Scripture, "Be silent and know that I am God!" and I proceed on my walk in silence. This is not easy for me, because I am by disposition talkative, even to God. But these are moments that I cherish. Personally I have no doubts about the existence of God, but I am clueless as to what "He" is like. For me, the basic act of religious faith is the affirmation that the Creator and Sustainer of the Universe is benign. And I can't prove it. On the contrary, I am surrounded by indications that call it into question.

After this period of silence, I integrate into my prayer what might otherwise be distractions: thoughts, feelings, memories, that course through my mind. They may be related to family members or dear friends or even to world events. For the happy thoughts and memories, I thank God; a recently born great grandnephew, for instance, or a friend I spoke to on the phone last evening. For the potentially unhappy ones, of illness or suffering or death, I voice my concerns. I do not, however, ask God to do anything. I have difficulty with the traditional forms of the prayer of petition. I remember, when I was a novice, asking my beloved second Master how the prayer of petition was compatible with the immutability of God. His reply was something I never forgot. "We do not pray to change God's will, Brother. We pray to change our own!" My efforts, then, are to accept whatever happens, but by verbally expressing my concerns I sometimes realize that there are things that I can do to ameliorate the situation, and thus God, acting in me, may effect some change.

I would say that prayer of adoration, praise, thanksgiving, acceptance, abandonment, surrender and silence all make sense to me, but I do not ask God to change the world to the way I want it.

When these "prayers" are completed, I usually engage in an abbreviated form of examen for the previous day. It is not nearly as formal as that taught in the *Exercises*. Basically, I simply ask myself, out loud, "What did I do yesterday?" At this stage in my life what I do on one day does not greatly differ from what I do on the next, but sometimes I realize that in my contacts with friends or neighbors or family I have been insensitive or non-responsive or selfish and I can regret that and resolve to act differently. In line with what I said above about God's acting in me in relation to others' needs, I can become more effective, or so I hope.

An extension of this attitude occurs whenever I encounter other people out on their early morning walks, many of them also with dogs. I try to consider meeting them not as an interruption in my prayer but as an extension of it, to the extent that I can contribute to their early morning enjoyment. And that is the way I begin each day spiritually.

There is another form of relatively silent prayer, which I practice and which it might be worthwhile to describe. It is much more dependent on external circumstances and does not occur as regularly as what I have described above. I experience it mostly during the warmer months of the year, usually after dinner in the evening out on the back deck of my home. It occurs during the hours of sunset and twilight as I'm gazing out toward the Northwest. Even my dog seems to sense that the time is special, for he comes and lays himself down on the deck beside my chair. The prayer is mostly wordless, though some phrases from the Psalms or the liturgy may spontaneously rise to my lips. The affects I experience then are mostly those of awe, thanksgiving, adoration and surrender, but they are much less structured and focused than my morning prayers. Their duration is variable, but they usually last longer than the morning prayers. They don't have an easily defined end. I just know when it's time to go inside.

In closing I would like to repeat what I said earlier—that I am not proposing "my way" for anyone else to follow. The Spanish have a saying, *Caminante, no hay camino. Se hace camino al andar.* "Wayfarer, there is no way. The way is made by walking". I think that is true for all of us but for each of us in a different way, and that the ways to God are as various as the infinitely varied circumstances of our individual lives.

Gabriel Whispers to Muhammad:
Be a Prophet of Peace
Morgan Zo-Callahan and Ken Ireland

In the Name of Allah, the Compassionate One, the Merciful, Praise be to Allah. And we add, "Praise Compassion, Praise true Love for ourselves, others, the environment, and the poor."

This joint piece began as a reflection about Morgan's real face-to-face meeting with three American Muslims at the Rosemead Buddhist Temple where he practices. That was a very interesting story and so characteristic of the way in which he approaches his interior life—always seeking and always looking for an outer expression of interior work. I recalled that John Lounibos in his essay here, My Path to Islam, *made the observation that most Americans are uneducated about religion, including "their own." Suddenly, a new focus for the article about Morgan's experience began to take shape: How to begin a conversation among ordinary believers from any religious community and the followers of the Prophet, religious people, who after 9/11 had real questions for one another? What resources would you try to have on hand as everyone was grappling for his or her own answers? What are good ways to frame questions? And finally, what, if any, results you might be able to expect? – ed.*

This paper will cover these topics:
- Talking with real Muslims
- Poets and Sufis, Rumi and Hafiz
- The Five Pillars
- Ordinary Muslims and Christians and reform
- The Shari'a and the roots of radical Islam
- Antidote to extremist interpretation: View the entire life of the Prophet.
- New voices! Support the best spokespersons for Islam
- Muhammad's Dream of Gabriel

The events of 9/11 shocked our political sensibilities as liberal Americans with some religious sensibility; we'd always assumed that religion, at least the kind of core beliefs in the Deism of the founding fathers, was good, even essential, for our democracy. That day, radical Muslim fundamentalists claimed their god was pleased that they drove two aircraft into New York City's twin towers killing a huge number of innocent people.

Those horrible events, plus the actions-reactions that followed, left most of us feeling helpless. Morgan and I shared the impulse to do something, but visceral reactions to what we read in the press open very few possibilities other than attack and reprisal. Given our education and, especially, our shared Jesuit and Buddhist training, we knew that any course of action we chose had to involve a deeper understanding of Islam as a religious expression of living a life dedicated to God. Although neither of us was completely ignorant about the teaching and history of Islam, there was some blind spot, and the worst part was that there was no strategy to guide action, study and prayer.

At an inter-faith conference at Rosemead Buddhist Monastery, Hindus, Buddhists, Catholics, Protestants, Jews, Jains, Sikhs, and Muslims held talks and discussions, prayers and meditations; there was also sharing about various programs that serve the poor and promises of mutual support. At the conclusion of the meeting, as people mingled in small groups, continuing conversations from the formal part of the gathering and saying good-bye, Morgan found himself talking with three Muslims and a Buddhist monk from Thailand.

Morgan had read Karen Armstrong's warning: "To cultivate a distorted image of Islam, to view it as inherently the enemy of democracy and decent values, and to revert to the bigoted views of the medieval Crusades would be a catastrophe.... Be kind to everybody. It doesn't matter what tradition you belong to. "Though he knew it wouldn't be easy, he had to say what he

349

felt in his heart: "Why aren't there more protests from Muslims against violent terrorism, against intolerance towards women and gays?" he asked animatedly. The Muslims were calm and direct saying Muhammad was a prophet of peace; the Thai monk commented that he seemed angry, that this interfaith conference *is* all about espousing peace.

There was an insight in that moment, and the beginnings of a real conversation: Morgan knew he had both to look inside for the source of his feelings, and talk to real Muslims, not some impressions that he carried from his reading or the press. And he began a conscious effort to clarify and deepen his understanding of Islam. Some of his feelings were deeply angry, but the monk, just by his comment and presence, helped Morgan see that he could engage in conversation without *being* angry. At the same time, this encounter in an atmosphere where shared humanity felt more important than any particular religion, stimulated a desire to go deeper into Islam and the mind set of Muslims, especially those who are our fellow citizens. Morgan was talking sincerely and directly with Muslims; he did not hide his anger; and he asked some difficult questions.

The Muslims that Morgan encountered that day wanted to answer his questions as honestly they could. They pointed out that in many of the fifty-three Muslim countries being a moderate could be a ticket to jail or, even, to beheading. So we have to consider the circumstances and conditions of the one who is speaking out. But "we are American Muslims," they said. "We want to live in a pluralistic democracy."

They had a fairly long, friendly conversation, first connecting as humans, some attitude adjustment, some levity and laughter, which allowed for meaningful interchange. Morgan felt he was listening to real people, not from Rumi's thirteenth century, not in an idealized or merely intellectual way, but now, talking with believers who embrace Islam as a religion of peace and tolerance.

These Muslims told Morgan that the Islam they follow and were taught is fundamentally rational and human which translates as being peaceful and non-violent. "No rational person is a suicide bomber." The majority of Muslims are not radicals or terrorists. They reminded everyone that all prejudice is wrong. They related personal incidents that happened to them in the milieu of the heightened emotions after 9/11. One related an experience of racial and religious hatred directed at her, just for being a Muslim. She was yelled at, pushed, called names. She said she felt as if the frustration of 9/11 was being screamed and spat upon her. She added with a smile, that she had plenty of understanding American friends who comforted her.

Since 9/11 many Muslims complain that they have been stereotyped, automatically considered fanatical; compared with other religious traditions, inferior and, compared with other people culturally, as not quite human. They say other Americans assume that they must be silently in favor of terrorism; they're called "brainwashed," afraid to speak up for tolerance, civility, and mutual understanding. This is a very harsh indictment of prejudice. Muslims make up less than 1 percent of the total US population (2.3 million). Sixty-five percent are immigrants who hail from India, Pakistan, and Bangladesh, not Arabia (most Arab immigrants are Christians). So the numbers are small enough in this country that their complaint can be overlooked.

However, it is not an American tradition to allow racial and religious prejudice to remain unchallenged. The Iranian-born American writer and scholar of religions, Reza Aslan says, "There are millions of Muslim Americans who have fully reconciled their Islamic and American identities and who are solidly middle-class and integrated into every level of American society. They're our doctors, our lawyers. Sixty percent of them own their own homes. They're the most educated ethnic minority in this country. And they're living proof that this idea that there is one fundamental clash between Islam and the West is absurd. Here is Islam in the West, and it's doing just fine. They are working diligently to provide a counterweight to these ideologies of fanaticism and Puritanism and violence and extremism, but they're being ignored." (*Sun* magazine, December 2006)

Such interfaith conferences have stimulated Morgan's interest in continuing to learn and become friendlier towards Islam and Muslims, to develop a sense of what Muslims are about in a most genuine sense. This has to happen before we can all open our hearts, while at the same time being vigilant against violence in Islam, or in any religion, or in ourselves. We cannot change Islam to suit our expectations, but we can educate ourselves, and experience ourselves as equals, whatever our religion or spiritual practice, believer, atheist or agnostic, man or woman, gay or straight. Our study and conversations have helped us see that American Muslims are people of good heart, who have no intention to follow blindly tribal norms of their ancestors or their native lands, and it is only a small number of radical Muslims worldwide who hold "ideologies of fanaticism and Puritanism and violence and extremism."

We would like to encourage the kind of dialogue that Morgan experienced at the interfaith dialogue at the Rosemead monastery, and the rest of the paper will be suggestions about the conditions that encourage these kinds of exchange. We both hope that this produces a balanced image of Islam and the followers of the Prophet.

صــوفــيّة

In the late 70s, Morgan began a Ph.D program in Comparative Religion under Professor Haridas Chaudhuri at the California Institute of Integral Studies in San Francisco. His work included Arabic, and comparative religion—Islam, Buddhism, Christianity, Hinduism—but his first real encounter with

Islam was reading about Sri Ramakrisha's three-day retreat of worship, meditation, prayer, based on the teachings of Muhammad. During the retreat, Ramakrishna said he felt no attraction to do his Hindu rituals. He immersed himself in Islam and would go on to praise and honor Islam as a true way to know the Eternal.

Muhammad, as Karen Armstrong writes: "made a distinctive and valuable contribution to the spiritual experience of humanity." Our minds may immediately go to the heart-felt wisdom of the Islamic poets, Hafiz and Rumi whose wonderful human touch expresses a most exquisitely true religion as lived and practiced. Genuine teachers and teachings point the individual to life and joy within one's own being.

Reading Rumi and Hafiz has been a continued habit, but after 9/11, Morgan wanted to go back to deeper study, and if possible, some conversations about Islam. He says: "I've been learning that my own level of human maturity and understanding has a lot to do with how I relate to someone else and how I talk to them about the two most interesting but taboo subjects: religion & politics. How do we each live in a religiously plural society? Can this pluralism, with welcoming conversations, be enriching for us all?"

Rumi and Hafiz can open our eyes to spiritual dimensions never seen before. "The word Sufi comes from the Arabic *suf,* wool, for the simple coarse, woolen garments worn by early mystics. Sufis were concerned about the new wealth and excesses that accompanied imperial expansion and rule…. They emphasized the importance of a spiritual life of piety, fasting, and prayer. Sufis stressed the spirit over the letter, seeking to experience enlightenment or the presence of God. In place of intellectual or legal understanding, they followed a more mystical path." (*The Geography of Religion,* p. 359)

Poetry is also a way to begin to read scriptures of the great religions as literature, rather than as historic or literal fact. We value them as evoking imaginative and poetic modes of consciousness that point the way and encourage us to be better human beings. Every religious tradition is given much of its heart and inspiration from its particular forms of mysticism and from its highest moral values for the individual who requires respect, rights and dignity. This mysticism promotes a feeling of connectedness to all others. Gary Schouborg, who is a scholar and contributor to *Meanderings*, says that this kind of knowledge is esoteric rather then exoteric understanding, expanding in a useful way the meaning of esoteric understanding beyond some specialized, ritualized secret knowledge.

What a marvel Rumi is! He inspired the Mawlawyiwah order, better known as the Whirling Dervishes. We have both witnessed their sacred dance, twirling elegantly, chanting Koranic verses, tall red cone hats, thick black belts cinching their flowing white skirts—spinning yet focused, centered, graceful, swinging in ecstasy. This is art, poetry, dance, and prayer all together. As young seekers in the late 1970s, disillusioned by our own Catholic religion as the only, true faith, Rumi taught us to look for a faith behind all faiths, the inner confidence of goodness and genuine joy, and pointed a real path to the heart of real religion through the cultivation of the interior life.

Rumi is now well known in the United States, but perhaps Hafiz is not. Morgan only became aware of him when his friend, Lily Hsu, gave him a copy of *The Gift, poems by Hafiz, The Great Sufi Master*. Born around 1320 in Shiraz, Iran, Hafiz (Shamseddin Muhammad) is a phenomenon of insight, poetry, intelligence, love that can arise in any human. Can such a revered poet offer the world, in the present circumstances of religious fanaticism, an artistic call for the respect for human freedoms and one's *own* deepest desires? Goethe wrote of Hafiz that he "has inscribed undeniable truth indelibly, a madness I

354

know well." And Emerson said of him, "He fears nothing; he sees too far; he sees throughout; such is the only man I wish to be."

In one poem Hafiz asks,

What
Do sad people have in
Common?
It seems
They have all built a shrine
To the past
And often go there
And do a strange wail and
Worship.
What is the beginning of
Happiness?
It is to stop being
So religious
Like
That.

Our religion can either be fresh, friendly, and of service, or it can become just a stale shrine for worshipping past religious expressions or, even worse, it can inspire violence. A tentative answer is also found in his poetry:

How
Do I
Listen to others?
As if everyone were my Master
Speaking to me
His
Cherished
Last
Words …
(*The Gift*, p. 99, translated by Ladinsky)

This is how we might listen to Americans who are Muslim if we are courageous and able to be completely open to the religious expression of another. It has some of the feeling as Merton's description of listening in *The Hidden Ground of Love,* 1985: "By being attentive, by learning to listen (or recovering the natural capacity to listen which cannot be learned any more than breathing), we can find ourselves engulfed in such happiness that it cannot be explained: the happiness of being at one with everything in that hidden ground of love for which there can be no explanations."

The great periods in Islamic history when Muslims scholars inter-mingled peacefully with other religious scholars could serve as models, and provide possible remedies to stop destructive conflicts and wars. Political, civil and religious freedoms allow for creativity to flourish. To extend true inner happiness into our own intimately inter-related world, these conditions have to be encouraged.

By the eighth century, it took one year to get from one end of the vast Muslim empire to the other. Yet Baghdad's House of Wisdom invited scholars who were Hindu, Christian, Jewish, as well as Muslim, to think collaboratively, to do art, philosophy and science. In medicine, the first study of germs began, as well as the hospital system; mental illness was addressed. Western medicine would use their anatomical descriptions for six hundred years. The Muslims developed Arabic numerals; trigonometry; algebra; astronomy; engineering. It was a period of respect for the various cultural and religious sources of knowledge. The Muslims made a gift of Greek writings by first translating them into Arabic. From the eighth to the thirteenth centuries, there were more religious, philosophical, medical, geographical, historical, and astronomical works in Arabic than in any other language.

In Cordova, Spain, this ninth and tenth century Muslim "City of Light," was filled with libraries, open tranquil streets, large homes, running water, when in Paris people lived in shacks, along the sides of the river. Viewing the *Alhambra* in Granada, Spain, when he visited, Morgan felt imbued by lovely textures, space, light, water fountains, marble pillars, artful designs and curves, inter-playing to delight and facilitate the flowering of human hearts.

صوفية

It also seems, before any real conversation can begin, that there ought to be some understanding of the basis of Islam and the Five Pillars: faith in one God; charity; prayer; fasting at Ramadan; if possible, pilgrimage to Mecca.

The first pillar, *shahada,* is "bearing witness" to Gabriel's message to Muhammad: *There is no god but Allah and Muhammad is His messenger.* There's also a bearing witness to all the great teachers and prophets who preceded Muhammad in both the Hebrew Scriptures and the gospels of Jesus.

The second pillar is *salat*, group prayer and worship, most commonly five times a day (dawn, noon, mid-afternoon, sunset, evening). Muslims prepare by cleaning their space of worship and by ritual washing with water or with sand if water is unavailable, bowing to the knees, making prostrations, and finally sitting or kneeling for recitations and meditation.

The third pillar is *zakat,* meaning "to purify," "to bless," "to increase." It consists of tithing, alms giving—both of which I consider forms of activism—for the poor, for worthy causes. "Alms are for the poor and the needy.… " (Qur'an 9:60) "By paying it, one is aspiring to attain blessing, purification and the cultivation of good deeds." Muslims contribute 2.5 percent of their annual income as a compassionate practice. (*Islamic Free Market Institute*, Vol. V, No. 1, Dec. 10, 2002)

The fourth pillar is *sawm,* fasting during the month of Ramadan, the ninth month; continuing the purification, the practitioner examines his or her thoughts, actions, intentions, relationships, much like in the Examen of St. Ignatius or

Buddhist mindfulness meditation. One releases such rocky emotions as jealousy, greed, excessive lusting. We're encouraged to let go the emotions which torture us, into the spaciousness created by meditation. *Eid-al-Fitr* is the happy celebration of breaking the fast and cleansing introspection. It's time to play and be happy, to socialize, to give and receive gifts.

The fifth pillar is the *hajj*, the holy pilgrimage to Mecca, usually about sixty days after Ramadan. Mecca is sacred to Muslims. Ali Sharitate writes in *The Geography of Religion:* "As you circumambulate and move closer to the Ka'aba, you feel like a small stream merging with a big river." Morgan had that same feeling of awe when, many years ago, he entered the sinking cathedral in Mexico City to see paintings of St. Ignatius and other saints. Pilgrims spend five days in Mecca, worshipping, meditating, visiting various holy sites, such as Medina where one can touch the tomb of the Prophet, just as in Vatican City, Morgan was able to "touch" the tomb of St. Peter.

صــوفـيّة

If we look for nourishment and wisdom within what's best in the great religious traditions, as lived and taught by seasoned, accomplished practitioners who are sensitive to contemporary culture, this is the place to begin a conversation. Muslims can turn to the Five Pillars to find a way of peace and happiness. For Buddhists the way out of inner and outer violence is through the Four Noble Truths and practice.

Several years ago, Morgan heard the Dalai Lama speak at the University of California Irvine. While struck by his good humor, and lack of anger, his really listening and refraining from the blaming of others, Morgan couldn't help thinking about the sufferings of Tibet. Here was a man full of joy and intelligence. What could be a better 'advertisement' for Buddhism? One woman, a Roman Catholic, asked him if she should convert to Buddhism to find "liberation." The Dalai Lama said all religions can lead to liberation, and laughing said "perhaps no official religion at all." He said it's usually best to stick to your own religion and really live it—study other religions, so you can practice your own religion even better! "I reverence all the religions," he said. "And I reverence each person."

The dark side of human nature, however, can be a stronger force than any religious ideas. Not all Buddhists conduct themselves with the non-violence and poise of a Dalai Lama; not all Buddhists are free from using violence as a tool for control and domination. In Korea Morgan watched mobs of Buddhist monks hurling bottles and fists at other monks, fighting over who would control the largest temple in Seoul. He had a sinking feeling, but also saw a lesson of how strong a force our attachment to power can be. What conditions all conspired together to bring about this bloody conflict? We can appreciate that this angry confrontation doesn't exemplify the rich ground of Buddhism.

More recently we saw the attempted uprising in Burma (Myanmar). The military oligarchy there claims to be Buddhist, yet they kill and imprison Buddhist monks. They also have a dreadful history of forcing children to be soldiers. As American Buddhist practitioners, and to most of the world, this is totally contrary to Buddhist practice.

The limitations of both ordinary Muslims and Christians with regard to real, widespread reform are apparent. If we cannot cause real reform in our own religions, how can we ask Muslims to clean up their own houses? "Ordinary believers" are not so encumbered by theology and tradition as the higher level within churches and mosques, we can begin to have real conversations with real people, working on our own prejudices and feelings. Not entirely wed to the past, this is the only possible course of action.

It is unfair to use Pope Benedict's apparent *faux pas* in a public lecture (September 2006) at the University of Regensburg where he once taught, to denigrate the authority of his position as a teacher of the Gospel message, but it might be an example of how *not* to set up a useful conversation. It does not seem possible for believers of various religious faiths to speak to one another if the past keeps getting in the way?

The Pope quoted a 1301 work attributed to Manuel II Paleogus, who was one of the last Byzantine emperors of Constantinople before its fall to the Ottoman Empire: "Show me just what Muhammad brought that was new and there you will find things only evil and inhuman, such as his command to spread by the sword the faith he preached." Very few people heard anything other than the quote, and didn't care that it was taken out of context.

The Pope's staff was perhaps unaware of modern Islamic scholarship that contradicted the Pope's implied objection to Islam. Mustafa Akyol, a Muslim journalist from Turkey, observes: "Pope Benedict said that the Koranic verse 'There is no compulsion in religion' is 'of the suras of the early period, when Mohammed was still powerless and under threat.' However, that verse, numbered 2:286 is actually a very late verse. The traditional Islamic consensus was that this verse was revealed in the Medinan period, when Prophet Muhammad and Muslims were not powerless, but in fact, were the rulers of their own state. This is one reason why the great majority of Muslim scholars accept that forced conversion is against Islam."

History shows that violence is possible within all religious traditions, at various times and to varying degrees. The Church of the early Middle Ages actively promoted warfare and violence against Muslims; the Pope organized armies and lobbied with kings and princes to recapture Jerusalem. Plenary indulgences combined with looting and plunder seemed to be a winning combination. And to be fair, the Pope ought to have acknowledged that "forced" conversions were practiced by the clergy who followed Portuguese and Spanish armies to the new world and India.

It also seems that the Pope's remarks have to be seen in light of a very different situation in Europe. As distinct from the United States, the population of immigrant Muslims into the EU is substantial and gaining in political power. The European press is filled with anecdotal reports that seem to reinforce the prejudice that Muslims will not and cannot integrate into the culture of western democracies.

But as one Muslim critic of the Pope's remarks, Mohammed Mahdi Akef, said: "most westerners don't listen to him anyway, so why should we?" (MSNBC Sept. 17, 2006). After examining the situation carefully, Thomas Haidon, of the Free Muslim Coalition (http://www.frontpagemag.com; 1/18/08) makes an insightful criticism: "The current model of interfaith dialogue which superficially focuses on general high level and common traits of faiths has failed. An effective meaningful framework for "safe" dialogue must be developed which also focuses on the "difficult" issues in Islam that Muslims have failed to address." And, from the perspective of Roman Catholics, the top-heavy authority within the Church either is unable to address these issues or refuses to see them outside ancient history.

What might a "framework for 'safe' dialogue" look like? This would be a good beginning: if your words inflame the person or persons you're talking with, quickly acknowledge it, and then try to see where you were misunderstood, or what in you seems to be blind to the other person's point of view. You may have been wrong in your assumptions.

صـوفـيـة

The Shari'a and the roots of radical Islam

Wahhabism (from Saudi Arabia, eighteenth century) and Salafiyya (late nineteenth, early twentyieth century in various countries) are usually puritanical, extremist, intolerant, homophobic, militant, and violent. Since 9/11, we've paid more attention to religious extremists coming from these two movements. Wahhabism is a form of Sunni Islam, coming from Muhammad bin Abd al Wahhab (1703–91) who called for a "pure" practice of Islam. Followers of Wahhabism have fought with other Sunnis, as well as Shiites and non-Muslims. In the 1920s, Wahhabi-trained warriors, Bedouins, allied with the founder of the modern Saudi kingdom, Abd al Aziz ibn Saud, attacking fellow Sunnis in Arabia (western part) and also Shiites in Iraq. So Wahhabis became, and remain, a politically powerful faction in Saudi Arabia and within the Saud family.

Salafiyya, sometimes used interchangeably with Wahhabism, became very strong during the Afghan resistance to Soviet occupation in the 1980s. During that period, the fighters would be indoctrinated in large numbers in mosques. Al Qaeda comes from elements of this movement.

Power and dogmatic religion do not combine gracefully. So when there's no separation of church and state, there's power and money available to back up violence, to provide *madrasas,* mosques, which indoctrinate young people into intolerance and militancy. Studies show that there are some tolerant Saudi school textbooks, but many which are not. Students are forced to conform to Wahhabi beliefs. Law and belief are mostly undifferentiated in Saudi Arabia. Radical Islam lacks the freedom of thought based in reasonable discourse, at least by western standards.

Islam is dangerous when viewed and lived as a religio-political dogmatic ideology of authoritative Shari'a, which calls for violent imposition of *jihad* as war, waged against "infidels" and also against Westernized Muslims who are considered "apostates." Such radical Islam wants to control and impose its dogmatic interpretation of the Shari'a on others.

We feel that even dealing with the terror of this fundamentalist interpretation of *jihad*, there is an opportunity to understand Islam more deeply. We are still faced with the question what can I do? I want to change my own attitude to be *jihadist* in a spiritual, inner way, rather than in violent, destructive ways. There is an inner, spiritual meaning of *jihad* within the heart of Islam. We have had to face our own confusion about Islam. Muhammad said that it is wrong to take one's own life, so how can terrorism be justified? Professor Carl Slawski comments: "It is important to emphasize the theological difference between greater (or primary) *jihad* (work to perfect oneself) and lesser (or secondary) *jihad* (converting unbelievers, which via individual extremist textual interpretation, gets morphed into violence unto death of the infidel)."

صوـفـيـة

Faith demands that we acknowledge the absolute accountability of each individual before God, and that communal solidarity should never impede honest self-criticism, nor should it lead to injustice against other groups.

–Ingrid Matteson

As Americans we find great wisdom in the U.S. Constitution to protect freedom of religion, religious expression and to ban government from dictating what the people must believe. But this tradition, and its common law roots, are not something that are shared with the Muslim code of law, the Shari'a, where the basis is that entire polity, the *Ummah*, be in accord with God's will as envisioned in the Qu'ran. Although there is still concern for what we would call "human rights" in the west, there is not the same legal recourse as in the United States for those who are suffering oppression, even if it were in the name of religion.

Muhammad says: "A person should help his brother,

whether he is an oppressor or is being oppressed. If he is the oppressor, he should prevent him from continuing his oppression, for that is helping him. If he is being oppressed, he should be helped to stop the oppression against him." Does this mean that contemporary Islam encourages more individual personal expression and choice? Will Islam protect human rights or stop oppression, because it is truly a serious Islamic obligation? Reza Aslan says, "If we are going to talk about human rights, we have to discuss them on a country-by-country basis. Nobody in their right mind would say that the Muslim world is free of human-rights violations, but to say that human rights and Islam are incompatible is ludicrous."

Doug McFerran, another contributor to *Meanderings*, writes privately: "Just as Muslim businessmen have managed to work around the Islamic prohibition against lending or borrowing money at interest, Muslim citizens, in the United States at least, have accepted democratic values without feeling they have betrayed their religion. Islam today is going through a difficult time of adaptation; the fundamentalism found in such places as Saudi Arabia and in Bin Laden's movement will be seen for the anachronisms they are, rather than as the wave of the future." The Islamic fundamentalists would like the Sahari's to be seen as set in their efforts to purify within Islam. Yet history again shows that the system was developed over several centuries after the death of Muhammad and his early followers.

Within a Western context, it's certainly legitimate to challenge Islam's religious and societal leaders, just as Catholics question and criticize their pope and bishops. Our contemporary circumstances force us to fiercely criticize crimes, even if they are supported by religious leaders and their followers. It does not seem acceptable to allow the Vatican or fundamentalist Christians to meddle in U.S. elections or in same sex marriage debates just as much as it does not allow the justice system here or in Europe to turn a blind eye to honor killings.

We need to be clear what is acceptable behavior in affluent, tolerant democracies and what is unacceptable: homophobia, abuse of women, honor killings, what is called euphemistically "family law" in some western countries (i.e. that a Muslim household stand outside the rule of law and is allowed to continue practices of "tribal" justice which often contravene western notions of individual rights). We do not and will not condone slavery—Muhammad had slaves and slavery still exists in parts of the Islamic world—yet slavery remains unacceptable in a civilized world. The practice of polygamy, common in Arab culture at Muhammad's time, will not find wide acceptance in modern western cultures. The execution of women for a variety of offenses by stoning or the beheading of homosexuals cannot be tolerated by the international community. This is barbarism.

صوفيّة

Antidote to extremist interpretation: View the entire life of the Prophet.

There are many qualities that make Muhammad a compelling spiritual figure for our times. He is the only major religious founder who was a family man, not a celibate, throughout his entire career—he fathered six children and was totally devoted to his wife, Khadijah; he was a successful merchant who conducted his affairs in an ethical, admirable and profitable way and did not withdraw from the world after his experience of the Transcendent; he was a mystic who spoke very personally about his inner turmoil—he went through a genuine spiritual transformation, rooted in his whole-hearted devotion to the one God, the Compassionate. He was also a reformer and innovative spiritual leader. He wasn't always a man of peace—he lead armies and killed in battle, but by the end of his life, he actively sought peace, and we will argue, by extension, would have no part of today's terrorist actions or fanatical interpretation of the Qu'ran.

The story of Muhammad's life has been told by biographers and historians with more knowledge and skill than we have. We will consider in broad strokes a few incidents that tell of the times when Muslims lived in peace and inspired diversity and acceptance of others, a story that we as non-Muslims have to consider.

When he was forty years old, Muhammad retreated to a cave, questioning the materialistic aspects in the Meccan market places. We have heard the story of how he heard a voice telling him to "Recite ... recite in the name of your Lord who created; he created man from a clot. Recite, by your Most Generous Lord, Who taught by the pen; He taught man what he did not know." At first Muhammad fled to the lap of Khadijah, terrified by the voice, confused, but impelled irrevocably into a deep spiritual life in response to Gabriel's message. As he gained in his confidence as a messenger of God, however, he preached against greed, materialism, and covetousness.

Over the period of twenty-two years during which Muhammad 'recited' the 114 chapters of the Qu'ran, he proclaimed there was only one God and that surrender to God brings true peace. After he had finished writing down the last verses of the Qu'ran, he is reported to have said, "It was as if the scripture were written on my heart."

Islamic scholars have noted the differences between the verses of the Qu'ran that date from the early, Meccan period and later Medinan verses. The verses can be viewed as either contradictory, or evolving in wisdom, and in some cases abrogating the earlier verses. This type of textual analysis is now widely accepted by most Christian scholars and theologians, though not in the most fundamentalist readings. And that is certainly reflected in the range of Muslim understanding of the Qu'ran. Muhammad grew in his understanding over the span of his life, just as we all change, adapt, and grow in our own practice.

Muhammad insisted that Christians have the right to practice their religion without fear. After he was established in Medina, a community of Christians lived at Najran was under his care and protection: "If anyone infringes upon their rights, I myself will be their advocate." He also wrote one of the world's first constitutions, the Covenant of Medina. He promoted rights and privileges to women in his early community. Muhammad was married to Khadijah for twenty-two years, giving them two boys who died in childhood and four girls who survived. Khadijah and Fatima, his youngest daughter, were said to have best exemplified his teachings. Muhammad defended the rights of orphans, widows, and the poor.

Muhammad challenged the conventional, age-old society of many tribes, many gods. During Muhammad's early life as a community leader, when the Ka'aba fell into disrepair and the sacred black stone fell (Abraham was said to have founded the Ka'aba and the black stone to have fallen from the heavens), the chiefs of four clans argued bitterly about who should return the black rock to its proper place. Muhammad suggested that all four carry the black symbol reverentially, each holding a corner of a rug on which the rock was placed.

He asked his disciples to be accepting and understanding, even when confronted. He taught by example: in Mecca, he was constantly berated and taunted by an opponent to his teachings. This "protester" would throw garbage and obstacles in Muhammad's path, and his disciples urged him to retaliate, but Muhammad refrained. When he noticed no trash or obstructions in his path, he inquired about his "adversary." It seems he was deathly ill, confined to his bed. Muhammad then went to the man's home to ask after his health, to wish him well and to say that he missed the encounters on the road.

After Muhammad and his followers were in control of Mecca, he gave up warring and made a treaty with tribes who had been adversaries. He did not demand that his religious title as "Prophet" be put on the document, which horrified some of his followers. He signed as "Muhammad, the son of Abdulla" to the treaty that brought an extended time of peace. Peace. Why won't we let it last?

Muhammad's farewell teaching, "to regard life and property of every Muslim as a sacred trust," ended long held customs of raiding and vendettas. "Hurt no one so that no one may hurt you.... Remember that you will indeed meet your Lord ... it is true that you have certain rights with regard to your women but they also have rights over you ... an Arab has no superiority over a non-Arab nor a non-Arab has any superiority over an Arab, also a white person has no superiority over a black person nor a black has any superiority over a white—except by piety and good action" (*The Geography of Religion,* pgs. 350-1*).*

صوفية

New voices! Support the best spokespersons for Islam
If this is to be a conversation, and it has to be, at least in Europe and the United States, how does one enter in without prejudice and without dictating?

Writers like Reza Aslan and Karen Armstrong and scholars-activists such as Ingrid Mattson point out one possible direction. Movements for reform are growing within Islam; inter-religious dialogue and learning are increasing. There are dedicated activists and dedicated thinkers arising within Islam. Let's listen to each other.

In October of 2007, prominent Christian, Jewish and Muslim scholars, clergy and laity met in Los Angeles to discuss scriptural passages that are "hostile" to other religions (Cf. *Los Angeles Times*, October 20, 2007). Similar conferences are planned in 2008 and 2009 in Germany and in Israel, respectively. Muzammil Siddiqui, chairman of the Islamic Law Council of North America, spoke of a "troublesome" passage in the Qu'ran (5.51) which says: "You who believe, do not take the Jews and Christians as allies; they are allies only to each other. Anyone who takes them as an ally becomes one of them—God does not guide such wrongdoers." Siddiqui explains that it is only extremists who use such texts to promote distrust of other religions. "The idea behind this verse is not that Muslims should shun Jews and Christians, but that they should stand up on their own feet and do their best." It was written at a time when Muslims of Medina were a minority and some Muslims wanted to ally themselves—from fear—with Jews or Christians for protection. It was saying if you really are into what I'm saying as a prophet, then strap on your balls and engage the practice, even if we're not popular or influential. Don't run to religion just for its security. This is an important step in the direction that faces the "difficult" differences within religion. These conferences are being given to implement what Thomas Haidon recommends: inter-religious talking about important, serious, "difficult" topics, to really ask each other our most burning questions.

On October 13, 2006, thirty-eight Islamic authorities, leader and scholars—with differing denominations—from all around the world delivered a letter to Pope Benedict XVI by the Royal Academy of The Toyal Aal al-Bayt Institute for Islamic Thought in Jordan. They proposed offering the true teaching of Islam to affirm the common ground between Muslims and Christians: to be in love of God and of our neighbor, the two great commandments (http://www.acommonword.com).

Muslim women will be at the heart of the leadership for a renewed generation of Islam. Author Ayaan Hirsi Ali (*Infidel*, Free Press) calls for a reform, "Enlightenment," within Islam to overcome the inequality, the fundamentalism, the abuse of women in the name of religion, in particular, in Africa.

Irshad Manji is a thirty-eight year old Canadian Muslim, a self-declared "mouthy chick" and "out" lesbian. She wrote *The Trouble with Islam Today: A Muslim's Call for Reform in Her Faith* (http://www.irshadmanji.com). "Through our screaming self-pity and our conspicuous silences, we Muslims are conspiring against ourselves.… Will we move past the superstition that we can't question the Koran? By openly asking where its verses come from, why they're contradictory, and how they can be differently interpreted, we're not violating anything more that tribal totalitarianism.… "

Mohja Kahf (author of *The Girl in the Tangerine Scarf*) encourages respect for all religions despite differing customs and beliefs. "Does wearing a veil make you less American than wearing a yarmulke or a Mennonite bonnet?" Mohja also criticizes her own Islamic religion. "The egalitarianism that the prophet Muhammad (peace be upon him) preached never much budged Arab tribalism. The Qu'ran's sexual ethic, enjoining chaste behavior and personal responsibility was for both men and women, not tribal ownership of women's sexuality."

The Pakistani-American writer Munawar Anees was nominated for the Nobel Peace Prize in 2002 for his work encouraging cultural and religious pluralism. Munawar Anees received his Ph.D in biology (Indiana University) and has dedicated his life to the study and teaching of Muslim religion and science. He's written six books, including *Islam and Biological Futures* and *Guide to Sira and Hadith Literature in Western Language.* He founded the journal *Periodica Islam;* he's religious editor of the online encyclopedia, *Nupedia. He* co-founded the *Journal of Islamic Philosophy* which can be found on the scholarly and extensive Web site http://www.muslimphilosophy.com. Anees calls for reform—intellectual, economic and cultural. He says "a strategy of change in the Muslim world is one of the crying needs of the hour … how to revive the *culture* of learning, how to revive the *culture* of tolerance, how to revive the *culture* of liberalism." (Cf. *What is Enlightenment* magazine, May-July 2004) Anees wants to get at the roots of why an "ossification" has happened in Muslim thought and behavior, why "an inward-looking attitude" has led to literalism, fundamentalism and the rejections of others' opinions and ways of living. Muslims must learn "the magnanimity of critical self-analysis." Anees points out that Muhammad in the later part of his life allowed Jews and Christians to live as they pleased, without trying to force conversion. In fact, Anees says that this openness to other schools of thought is inherent in Islam: "According to the teaching of the Prophet, one's cognizance of the Almighty is inseparable from the cognizance of the Muslim tradition of liberalism and tolerance."

Muhammad's Dream of Gabriel

Once Muhammad dozed off after evening prostrations and found himself in the angel Gabriel's company, riding on horseback from heaven to Jerusalem. "Muhammad alighted on the Temple Mount, the Temple of the Israelites, where Abraham, Moses, Jesus, and other prophets welcomed him into the circle. Offered goblets containing wine, water, and milk, Muhammad selected the one with milk—a sign of the middle way of Islam, neither indulgent nor austere.... From that spot, Gabriel led Muhammad up a ladder into heaven, where God greeted him and told him that the devout must pray fifty times a day. On the way down the ladder, Moses advised him that daily prostrations could number as few as five but still fulfill God's wishes," (*The Geography of Religion*, p. 344). How interesting that Moses trimmed down God's demands by 90 percent! And that some of the greatest prophets from Judaism and Christianity are together in this communication.

This is a dream of unity and cooperation among the great religious traditions of Judaism, Christianity, and Islam. Muhammad finally fully drank from the milk of a "middle way," a balance to promote harmonious living, that we all together "have life more abundantly."

A final story shows a human, light and wise Muhammad.

Muhammad goes out late at night to pray in the desert. And his young wife, Aisha, thinks he's going to meet another woman. So as he's going out into the silence of the desert (as Jesus would do), Aisha, full of anger and condemnation, stomps out to confront him. Muhammad looks at her enraged face and says, "Oh, Aisha, Lovely, have you brought your little Satan with you?"

"What little Satan?" she answers, calming down in his serene presence.

"Every human being has a little devilish part, their *nafs*."

And she, softly now, roundly open-eyed, asks sweetly: "Even you, O prophet of God?"

"Yes, even me. However, I made mine a Muslim."

صوفيـة

My Path to Islam
John Lounibos, Ph.D.

It is an honor to have John Lounibos write an essay about his discovery of Islam through the life and work of Al-Ghazali. At seventy-five years old, he is a marvel of energy and unceasing academic accomplishments.

John's insightful article highlights one aspect of religious scholarship: that study of our religious heritage can heal our souls and deepen our understanding of who we are as humans. Close examination of these materials may reveal that the religious tenets which seem, on the surface, to divide may actually be the source that unites.

After teaching at Dominican College in Blauvelt, New York, for thirty-six years, I have concluded that the vast majority of U.S. students, and by extension, the general population of this country, is ignorant of religion. We cannot assume that anyone knows, or bothers to ask, about the major differences as well as similarities between Christian and Muslim beliefs. Years ago one of my Catholic students in the course in which I teach Jewish, Christian and Muslim authors, asked me why we don't study "our own religion". Even though the majority of my students have Christian backgrounds, most are as unfamiliar with the history of Christianity, the Catholic Church, or historical and literary biblical study, as they are with the history of Islam.

The attitudes toward Islam in the United States have severely polarized since 9/11/01. Now as our political leaders and some portion of the population have learned the differences between the Sunni and Shia sects, I see some hope that we will see the necessity of exploring Islam's history and theology with curiosity and openness as well as a sharpened awareness of what is at stake.

Biblical Abraham was promised many descendants. Islam

traces its heritage to Abraham. In the spirit of Abraham, and other biblical persons who figure in Muslim traditions, I offer the following personal reflections and accounts of some research I have conducted on my way to understanding Islam. My remarks are a summary of what my students and I have learned about Islam through my encounter with Al-Ghazali and his path to Sufism. I see Ghazali as representative of the non-violent greater *jihad*, the warrior who is an "athlete for God", the role of an advocate for the good. My intent in this essay is to immerse myself in Ghazali's world and retrieve his methods and content. I believe there is enormous value in this for the twenty-first century world citizen.

A Starting Point: Aristotle's Agent Intellect

My journey to Islam began at Gonzaga University in Spokane, Washington. Fr. Edmund W. Morton, S.J., the president of Gonzaga when I was a student there in 1960, offered a tutorial course on the Agent Intellect. I was required to access and interpret the medieval Latin texts of Aristotle (384–332 BC), Avicenna or Ibn-Sina (980–1037), Averroes or Ibn Rushd (1126–98), and Aquinas (1225–74) on the agent intellect.

In his work on psychology, called the *de Anima* in Latin, Aristotle divided the mind into passive and active functions. Passively the mind is a power to become all things. Actively, the mind, when it thinks, is capable of making all things, like light that makes potential colors become actually all colors, said "The Philosopher".

Thomas Aquinas, who studied Aristotle from Latin translations in Naples, Paris and Rome, interpreted the powers of the active and passive intellect as functions and capabilities inherent in the intellect of each human being. Avicenna in Baghdad and Averroes in Cordova, with minor variations, interpreted the agent intellect as the world mind that activates the world soul. Plotinus (205–270), who taught in Rome, was considered the greatest teacher of Plato in late ancient society by his disciple, Porphyry (232–303). Plotinus taught that ideas in our human minds participate in the thoughts of a cosmic or universal mind, *nous,* through our participation in a cosmic world soul. Who we are and what we know originates from the universal soul and mind. The superior powers of a cosmic soul/*psyche* and mind/*nous*, emanate from the original and originating One. The knot that cinched this ancient story of soul and mind, was philosophy. For Plotinus, Porphyry, and other neo-Platonists, philosophy was the pathway that leads the thoughtful human soul to return back to its true origins in the great world Soul and world Mind, toward the One.

As a result of my work with Morton, I saw that Aquinas interpreted the active and passive intellect in Aristotle's *de Anima* in a personal, integral, and humanist sense as an active power each person has the ability to engage while the two famous Muslim philosophers, Avicenna and Averroes, interpreted Aristotle's agent intellect in a Neo-platonic context, as part of the world soul and world mind. At that time I did not consider what impact this world-soul doctrine had on Islamic views regarding the relative value of the individual person or the view of the community of Islam. It was my study of Ghazali, which eventually led me a fuller understanding of the Islamic worldview. Now I think that many advocates of a universal Islamic civilization, whether violent *jihadist* or peaceful Muslim, often seem to be drafting their notion of world Islam from the ontology of the world soul and world mind.

Mystical Experience and Islam

Before I even began to grapple with the work of Al-Ghazali, called Algazali or Algazel in Latin, I plunged into the history and nature of Islamic religion and culture, the basic known facts about the life of Muhammad (570–632), the founder of Islam, information on the spread of Islam, the composition and development of the Qur'an/Koran, and the three great Caliphates.

I attended presentations on Islam by John Renard of St. Louis University. I purchased two English translations of the Qur'an and began to collect syllabi for courses that taught Islam. I read Renard's studies and the work by his Harvard mentor, Annemarie Schimmel (1922–2003), *Mystical Dimensions of Islam* (1975). Then in 1984 I met Arthur Hyman, and the world changed for the better.

I was awarded a National Endowment for the Humanities to study with Hyman on "Virtues, State and Law in Medieval Philosophy" at Columbia and Yeshiva Universities in 1984. Arthur Hyman and James J. Walsh were co-editors of an anthology of medieval philosophy, *Philosophy in the Middle Ages, The Christian, Islamic, and Jewish Traditions* (2d ed. 1983). It was Dr. Hyman who introduced me to the study of Maimonides (1135–1204), his *Guide of the Perplexed* in the Shlomo Pines translation, and modern debates about the interpretation of Maimonides since Leo Strauss. Hyman, fluent in Hebrew and Arabic, wrote introductions and notes to the five Jewish and four Muslim philosophers in the textbook above.

After that seminar I searched for a Muslim author who would complement my teaching that included not only Maimonides' *Guide,* but also Augustine's *Confessions,* Julian of Norwich's *Revelations,* and Dante's *Inferno.* Then I happily discovered Al-Ghazali's *The Inner Dimensions of Islamic Worship,* 1983, translated by Muhtar Holland. A few years later I found the autobiography of Al-Ghazali, 1980, translated by Richard J. McCarthy, S.J. In 1983 I discovered Huston Smith's film "The Sufi Way" which helps one understand Sufism. And finally, the poetry of Jalaluddin Rumi (1207–73), the founder of the Mevlevi order rounded out my reading.

Before I drag the reader, screaming and wailing, to Baghdad and the eleventh century world of Ghazali and medieval Persia, let me explain a few things about medieval and classical readings, which create a context for the encounter with Ghazali. Let me also share something about the way in which I read ancient, classical literature.

I am no therapist, but I read and ask my students to read every text as therapy. Why read the classics for therapy? Because most of them were written with some intent to heal the soul. So I read the Bible for therapy. I read Julian of Norwich (1342–1420?), Augustine (354–430), Al-Ghazali (1058–1111), Maimonides (1135–1204), Dante (1265–1321), and Ignatius of Loyola (1491–1556) as therapy; then I read them for history, for social, political values, for critical thinking, for poetry, for creative thinking. Then I read them for windows on the catastrophes of their time and apply lessons for our own contemporary times. I also read them for meditation.

Reading authors in this way can provide plausible links and insights from the past to the challenges of present day living and engage interdisciplinary and global conversations, for example, to construct contexts for Jewish, Christian and Muslim dialogue, and promote a respectful, healthy conversation among the great religious traditions. We can read them and explore divine communication or revelation, in human language and experience, and at the same time encourage in-depth reflection on one's own religious and human experience, connecting the past with similar contemporary experiences, distinguishing what liberates humans from what destroys human values and relationships, in personal and social life.

The Encounter with Al-Ghazali

I invite you—as mutual explorers for meaning—back into the life and time of Al-Ghazali. I approach Ghazali's life and presentation of Islam under the themes of pilgrim, mystic, mentor, and warrior.

He was born in 1058* to a Sunni family in Tus, modern Mashad, on the northeastern border of Persia close to western

Afghanistan. Arthur Hyman says Ghazali was orphaned at an early age. Ghazali began his studies in Tus. At age fifteen he studied at Jurjan/Gorgan on the southeast corner of the Caspian Sea. At age nineteen he studied with Al-Juwayni, a great theologian, in Nishapur. After that, at the invitation of the powerful vizier, Nizam al-Mulk, Al-Ghazali worked in the court of the Seljuk Sultans. At age thirty-three, in 1091 he taught for four years at the prestigious Nizamiya College in Baghdad, a leading position in the Sunni world. Early in the "conversion", or *Da'wah*, of Persia to Islam, Baghdad, founded in AD 726, was the center of major trade routes through Mesopotamia on the banks of the Tigris River amid fertile irrigation canals.

Ghazali was a contemporary of Omar Khayyam (d. 1123), the Persian poet and mathematician, who was born in Nishapur at the highpoint of the Seljuk era. Though Khayyam's poem, the *Rubaiyat*, has been made famous in English translations, he is best known in Islam as a mathematician. In the west, Ghazali was a contemporary of Anselm of Canterbury (1033–1109), Bernard of Clairvaux (1090–1153), Abelard (1079–1142), and Heloise (1100–63).

A century after Ghazali, the grandeur of the Persian-Muslim caliphate collapsed under the crush of the Mongol invasions. Tus and Nishapur, cities on the perennial "silk route" which, through various pathways, supported mercantile trade and exchange among eastern and western societies, were targets of the brutal Mongol massacres of men, women, and children under Genghis Kahn (1206–27).

*(I use Montgomery Watt (1963) for the chronology of Ghazali's life and follow Watt's spelling of the name).

Ghazali on The Pillars of Islam

A portion of Ghazali's *Ihya'* was translated as *Inner Dimensions of Islamic Worship* by Muhtar Holland (1983, 138 pp.)

Holland is a British-born convert to Islam. The "Revival of the Religious Sciences" is considered the greatest work by Ghazali. There we find Ghazali's teaching on four of the five pillars or duties of Islam, with chapters on: Prayer (*Salat*), Almsgiving (*Zakat*), Fasting (*Sawm*), Pilgrimage (*Hajj*), followed by three brief sections on devotional practices of Islam, the "Night Vigil", "Invoking Blessings upon God's Messenger", and the "Merit of Seeking Forgiveness."

On the first pillar or duty of Islam, the *Shahadah*, or profession of faith in the one God, Allah, and Muhammad the messenger of God, the Dominican College librarian, Harbhajan Arneja, a Punjabi Sikh, told me that Muslims say that if you recite these words of faith-witness three times, you will become a Muslim. The words testify to the unity (*tawhid*) of God, and the belief in Muhammad as God's last and final prophet.

An example from the *Inner Dimensions* will illustrate Ghazali's method. He divides the Pilgrimage or *Hajj* into an introduction with quotations from the Qur'an and Hadith of Muhammed, then comments on the merit of the pilgrimage, the excellence of the Ka'aba and Mecca/Makka, the merit and demerit of residing in Mecca, the superiority of Medina the Radiant over other towns. He then adds ten points for proper internal conduct of the pilgrim: 1. purity of intention and means, 2. shunning unlawful taxes, 3. moderation in expenditure, 4. forsaking evil conduct, 5. going on foot, 6. modesty and simplicity of transport, 7. shabbiness in dress and appearance, 8. kindness to beasts of burden, 9. sacrificing animals, 10. equanimity. Finally he presents "inner states" for each stage of the Hajj, subtitled as: understanding, yearning, resolve, severing ties, provisions, transport, purchase of a shroud, leaving home, crossing the desert, putting on the shroud and crying "Labbayk", to "rid yourself of your power and strength, and rely on the grace and generosity of God" (111), entering Mecca, circumambulating the house, touching the black stone, standing at *multaza,* the draped wall of the Ka'aba, running between *Al-Safa* and *Al Marwa,* standing at Arafat, casting pebbles, sacrificing animals, visiting Medina, visiting God's Messenger, with a conclusion for these "duties of the heart". Ghazali gives similar inner and outer advice and counsel for proper conduct in each of the other three major practices of Islam. Holland's book represents less than one quarter of Ghazali's "Revival", which is filled with the spiritual advice Ghazali composed for living the authentic Muslim life.

In his effort to explain to Muslims the motives for making the pilgrimage, Ghazali quotes the Qur'an (5:82) about priests and monks who were not arrogant, and then comments.

> *But when all that had vanished, and people had become interested only in chasing their desires, shunning exclusive devotion to God, Great and Glorious is He, and getting lax about it, then God, Great and Glorious is He, sent his Messenger Mohammed, on him be peace, to revive the way of the Hereafter and to renew the method of traveling along it in accordance with the practice of God's Envoys.*

> *Members of the earlier religious communities asked God's Messenger, on him be peace, if the ways of the monks and anchorites were followed in his religion and he replied: "God has replaced them for us with the Jihad and the declaration of His supremacy on every elevated place" (alluding to the Pilgrimage). When asked about the anchorites, God's Messenger, on him be peace, said: "They are the ones who Fast." [I suspect "hermits" might be better here than "anchorites".]*

> *So God, Great and Glorious is He, has favored this Community by making the Pilgrimage its form of monasticism and has honored the Ka'aba, the Ancient House, by calling it His own, Exalted is He (105).*

Muhammad had met many Jews and Christians who traded or lived in late sixth century Mecca and early seventh century Medina. He knew Christian and Jewish stories some of which have Arabian counterparts in the Qu'ran. Jewish and Christian practices of daily prayer, fasting, tithing, and pilgrimage are incorporated into the pillars of Islam. Christians find the spiritual teaching of Jesus on prayer, almsgiving, and fasting collected in one section of Matthew's sermon on the mount (Mt 6:1-18). Passover was a pilgrimage festival in ancient Israel. For many centuries Christians made pilgrimages to Jerusalem and the Holy Land.

Thus if a Christian or Jew reads Ghazali on prayer, almsgiving, fasting, and pilgrimage, they are on familiar grounds. Except for the Arabic and Muslim context, these practices are part of the heritage of the three religions of Abraham.

Spiritualities of Al-Ghazali and Ignatius of Loyola (1491–1556)

Some contemporary Jesuits claim that Sufis, who were among the Moors of Spain, may have been known by Iñigo of Loyola and thus directly or indirectly influenced Ignatian spirituality. I also see many similarities between Ghazali and the *Spiritual Exercises* of St. Ignatius Loyola. Scholars of Spanish History, Catholicism, Sufism in Andalusia, comparative studies of Catholic and Muslim practices, and those with better knowledge of Iñigo of Loyola than I have, may draw different conclusions than I do here. With that in mind, here are a few comparisons I see between Ghazali and Ignatius on the exercise of their particular religions.

Both men are deeply committed believers who appeal to mystical experience; they create meditations and contemplations out of their scriptures; they teach one how to pray and serve God, by right intention, by appeals to understanding when possible, by example of the saints. Both add colloquies with angels and with God to end their prayer sessions. Both Ghazali and Ignatius composed rules and duties for proper observance of their respective traditions. Both teach discernment of spirits, modesty in conduct. Both lived their personal lives as models of the revival and renewal of their respective faiths, something needed and characteristic of their times. Both lived during times of renewal. Ignatius lived during the European Reformation and Ghazali at the turn of the new century, AH 500, when renewal was expected in Islam.

One purpose of these reflections is to show a non-violent trend in Islamic Sufism and its role as the "greater *Jihad*" in Ghazali. Ignatius and Ghazali each exhibit their unique kind of "spiritual *jihad*". Ignatius was a convert from the life-style of a Spanish hidalgo, a career of soldiering and courtly self-promotion. In his *Spiritual Exercises* he asks his spiritual follower to compare and contrast the call of an earthly king to a good knight with the call of Christ to be a dedicated disciple. Ignatius' imaginary earthly king says to a generous, gallant, chivalrous "warrior-servant":

> *It is my will to conquer all the land of the infidel. Therefore whoever wishes to join with me in this enterprise must be content with the same food, drink, clothing, etc. as mine. So, too, he must work with me by day, and watch with me by night, etc., that as he has had a share in the toil with me, afterwards, he may share in the victory with me (tr. L.J. Puhl, S.J., 1960, 43).*

Ignatius then contrasts the crusader-like military call with the spiritual call of Christ: " … to conquer the whole world and all my enemies, and thus enter into the glory of my Father.… " (44). The labor and sufferings in service of the heavenly king that leads to glory and eternal reward are put in the form of a prayer: " … to imitate Thee in bearing all wrongs and all abuse and all poverty, both actual and spiritual.… " (45). This meditation is placed by Ignatius as the introduction for the spiritual follower to the calls of Christ that echo through meditations on the Gospel accounts of his life, death, and resurrection.

On almsgiving, *Zakat*, what the Bible knows as a tax or tithe, Ghazali cites the Qur'an on renunciation of attachments to ego and belongings (9:111). Ghazali paraphrases the sura:

> *This concerns Jihad, the struggle in the way of God, which entails a readiness to sacrifice even life itself to meet God, Great and Glorious is He. The renunciation of wealth is trivial by comparison (54).*

The Qur'anic text cited by Ghazali goes on to assert that the *Jihad* demonstrated by prayer and alms-giving stems from the notion of fidelity to the covenant recognized "in the Torah, and the Gospel, and the Koran" (9:112), which has the eschatological promise of "the gift of paradise" (9:112). The importance of *Jihad* in the rhetoric of Islam since the Muslim terrorists attacks of 9/11 on U.S. targets, is one reason I propose reading Ghazali. It is clear that Ghazali has in mind and advocates the inner or greater *jihad*. Military *jihad* texts in the Qur'an, called the lesser *jihad*, were composed during the Medina wars with the Meccans for the most part.

At several junctures St. Ignatius of Loyola's *Spiritual Exercises* appeal to the rhetorical device of divisions of three. He describes "three classes of men" and "three degrees of humility". His "Letter on Obedience" (1553) outlines three degrees of obedience, of execution, of understanding, and finally with will and judgment. When reading Ghazali on the three groups who respond to *zakat*, I thought of similarities with the experience of Ignatius of Loyola. I found A. Hilary Armstrong, the classical scholar, identified classical Greek writers who employed the division of people into three different groups based on their degree of response to social or cultural initiatives. By contrast, Jesus' parable of the sower of the seed, a key parable in all three synoptic Gospels, divides the response to the seed of God's word into four types of soil or circumstance that illustrate the various intensities or seriousness of human responses. At least we observe that the classification of people by degrees of response to initiatives from others has a long history of discerning differences.

Out of knowledge of human character, Ghazali finds three classes of people who respond to the practice of *zakat*. The first group gives alms most generously. The second group gives but more sporadically. Group three of ordinary people give the bare minimum and lack detachment from money and property. Ghazali analyzes motives by discerning spirits. He advocates gratitude for God's gifts and ways to break the hold of deadly sins and reform the habits of greed and miserliness, which come by way of demonic suggestion. One cure recommends selection from three possible months for a fixed time for the distribution of alms, either the first of the year, or Ramadan, or the Hajj month.

On giving in secret Ghazali writes, give "without his left hand knowing what his right hand has given" (59). This is a paraphrase of Jesus in Mt 6:3. It is typical of Qur'anic stylistic borrowings from Jewish and Christian scriptures, a feature of pedagogical imitation, common to people who lived in oral, memory cultures. Muslims often say that the only miracle of Islam is the writing of the Qur'an, because Muhammed is considered to have been illiterate. The lack of reading and writing skills increases the importance of oral memorization and recitation habits in Islam. The Arabic word Qur'an/Koran means "recitations". On almsgiving, Ghazali gives some of the best advice for true altruism and philanthropy in his treatment of the free and humble surrender of wealth and property to the poor, something that is "actually His property all along ... all wealth belongs to God" (60-1).

On prayer I find another set of similarities between the teachings of Ghazali, the Muslim Sufi, and Ignatius, the Christian mystic. Both reflect with psychological sensitivity to guide the practitioner how to manage external and internal distractions and movements, including the proper time and place for prayer, modesty of the eyes, and placing oneself in the presence of God with our eschatological destiny always in the balance. Both advocate a kind of mindfulness, to examine what disturbs the mind and imagination at prayer, discern emotional movements and desires, something Ghazali sometimes calls a "review of your heart" (44). Ignatius called for reflection on how one's prayer went, taught daily examinations of conscience. Ghazali ends his lengthy study on prayer with salutations, *salam*, to Muhammed the "prophet", to God's servants, the angels, others present, with supplications for your parents and other believers. The practice of *dikhr*, "remembrance" in Islamic prayer might be stretched to incorporate the practice of mindfulness in Buddhism. They are not the same, but they touch on similar experiences. The way Ghazali closes his prayer with "salutations", reminds me of Ignatius who closes meditations in his *Spiritual Exercises* with colloquies or conversations with divine and human interlocutors. Like Ghazali, Ignatius often identifies parties with whom one is to converse in the colloquy.

Al-Ghazali's Autobiography

In Ghazali's last years teaching in Nishapur, a city in eastern Iran, he composed his autobiography, *Munqidh min al-dalal*, often translated as *Deliverance From Error (DHE)*. He completed *DHE* just before he finished his great summa of Islamic religion, "The Revival of the Religious Sciences", *Ihya' 'ulum al-din*, at Tus in the last month of his life Dec, 1111 (AH 505), at age fifty-three.

Ghazali's autobiography is a valuable and timely work. I have used it to introduce Muslim spirituality, Sufism, to U.S. students whose media perceptions of Islam are shadowed by contemporary "*jihadist*" terrorists, the "Great Satan" or adversary of our time. I add to two modern titles of the translations of *Munqidh min al-Dalal*, to call it "My non-violent *Jihad*". Richard J. McCarthy's (1913–81) translation, introduction, and notes are classics in themselves; he writes about Al-Ghazali in *Freedom and Fulfillment* (1980), republished under the title *Deliverance From Error* by Fons Vitae in 1999, abbreviated as *DFE*. I use the page numbers in the short edition by Fons Vitae called Al-Ghazali's *Path to Sufism* (2000). This new edition is abbreviated *GPS*. (McCarthy was a Jesuit priest who, with several other Jesuits, founded Baghdad College in the 1930s. He taught at Al-Hikma University, Baghdad, and was its last president when Saddam Hussein expelled the Jesuits from their Baghdad schools and confiscated their property in 1968. I met some of these expelled Jesuit companions at a Thanksgiving dinner at the Gregorian University, Rome, in 1968).

Ghazali's life is presented by McCarthy as an adventure and quest. The reader joins him to visit four major movements within eleventh century Islam, one of which, Sufism, wins Ghazali's critical commitment and allegiance as the proper path to achieve Islam's great aim of achieving unity in diversity. In a general way, Ghazali's narrative of social inquiries, critical thinking, exclusion of competing pathways, and commitment to Sufism has four moments or movements similar to Augustine. The major difference besides time frame and the social-political-religious context is that Augustine, although a Catechumen, was not a believing Christian until his mid-career change of mind, *metanoia*, at age thirty-two. Ghazali made a mid-career, life-style change to dedicate his life to Sufi practices at age thirty-seven. But Ghazali was always a Muslim believer. Unlike Augustine, who moved dramatically from "outside" to "inside" the Christian faith, Ghazali moved dramatically from "inside" to "deeper inside" the Muslim faith.

Ghazali begins his life story by explaining that the starting point for radical freedom on his path to Sufism required overcoming "servile conformism," *Al-taqlid*, literally, living like a "roped animal", as McCarthy notes (2, 18, also 25). (Again paragraph numbers are from McCarthy, followed by page numbers from *GPS*.) Ghazali compared the confusion concerning Islamic teachings to a deep sea where many flounder from insecurity, while some uncritically proclaim they have the true way. Augustine also used the stormy sea metaphor for his times (*Conf* I xvi 25.18). Ghazali says, "from the time I reached puberty before I was twenty until now, when I am over fifty, I have constantly been diving daringly into the depths of this profound sea.... " (4, 18-19). His method was critical inquiry. He cites the Muslim tradition that "Every infant is born endowed with the *fitra*: then his parents make him Jew or Christian or Magian" (6, 19-20). I understand *fitra* to mean something like the natural desire to know or seek God, an idea found in St. Paul's letter to the *Romans* and turned into a Catholic dogma that emphasized the ability of human reason to know God at Vatican Council I (1870). (Cf. Revelation chpt. 2, canon 1. It is not *fitra,* but it is part of a similar claim of basic human orientation.)

Ghazali then describes the search of the young mind for certitude with scientific examples how this creates doubts for sense perceptions. He allegorizes a debate between "sense-data" and "reason" which knows primary truths. This leads him to a major thesis of his education: "The mere fact of the nonappearance of that further perception does not prove the impossibility of its existence" (12, 22, also pp. 76-77). This principle operates today in debates between science and faith. Ghazali cites dreams and the after-life to imagine altered states of consciousness beyond "rational beliefs", something claimed by Sufis. The "sense-reason" debate put Ghazali into two months of teenage skepticism. It was resolved by means of an enlightenment, " ... the effect of a light which God Most High cast into my breast" (15, 23). At this point Ghazali says revelation of truth is from God who "dilates his breast for submission to Himself" (i.e. to embrace Islam) [Qur'an] 6:125 (16, 23). He then adds "Your Lord, in the days of your lifetime, sends forth gusts of grace: so then put your selves in the way of them" (16, 24). Later on Ghazali defines the heart as "the essence of man's spirit which is the seat of the knowledge of God, not the flesh which man has in common with corpse and beast.... " (121, 64-5). Nakamura thinks Ghazali had met Sufi teachers in his youth. The source of Nakamura's inference about Ghazali meeting Sufis when he was young may arise from this discussion about a grace that broke through his youthful skepticism. Ghazali concludes the section on his youth saying his purpose is to emphasize that one should be "most diligent in seeking the truth ... [but] ... primary truths are unseekable, because they are present in the mind.... "(17, 24).

Arthur Hyman informed me that Moses Maimonides (1135–1204) read Ghazali's *Munqidh*. One thing the *Guide of the Perplexed* has in common with Ghazali's *Munqidh*, besides the search to overcome error, is arguments against Mutakallimin, Muslim apologetes for orthodoxy and polemical defenders of Kalam, theology. Ghazali admits the Mutakallimin tried to defend orthodox Islam against innovators, but " ... their discussion was not thorough-going; therefore it did not provide an effective means of dispelling entirely the darkness due to the bewilderment about the differences dividing men" (24, 26-7). The Mutakallimin remind me of Catholics who quote the catechism, theologians who quote Denzinger, or evangelists who quote the Bible as the last word and end of discussion. It is notable that Ghazali's deeper search is to find remedies for unhealthy divisions in Islam.

On philosophy Ghazali uses his critical thinking. Muslim philosophy reached its apex in Baghdad in the east and Spain in the west. Persian Muslim scholars provided Arabic translations of the Greek texts of Plato and Aristotle that had circulated in Syria in previous centuries. Eventually Western Christian scholars like Thomas Aquinas benefited from these texts. The Muslim philosophers Al-Farabi and Avicenna helped make Baghdad a center of lively thought. Philosophers clarified ideas about God and man that the two great schools of Mutakallimim, the Mu'tasilites and Ash'arites had debated. Therefore it is not surprising that Al-Ghazali, a master of *Fiqh*, Muslim jurisprudence, when appointed to teach at Nizamiya college on the banks of the Tigris River in Baghdad in 1091, composed two works on philosophy, *The Intentions (Opinions) of the Philosophers, Maqasid al-Falasifah,* (1094) and *The Incoherence of the Philosophers, Tahafut al-Falasifah,* (1095). Over a century later Averroes wrote a refutation of the *Tahafut,* calling it *The Incoherence of the Incoherence.*

The section on philosophy in the autobiography revisits some of Ghazali's earlier Baghdad studies. He reminds his readers what he wrote in his *"Incoherence"*, that Aristotle as received by Muslim philosophers had twenty dangerous teachings, seventeen innovations or heresies and three of unbelief or apostasy. McCarthy lists the twenty errors in fn 103, *(GPS,* 97-8). The three propositions that contradict Muslim faith, and Jewish and Christian faith as well, are: 1) the eternity of the world—contrary to belief in creation; 2) God knows only universals, not particulars—contrary to belief in divine providence for each person; and 3) the soul alone lives after death—contrary to faith in the resurrection of the body and a final reward and punishment. Similar theses return again to a Christian condemnation of thirteen propositions attributed to Latin Averroism by Stephen Tempier, bishop of Paris in 1270.

The Politics of Aristotle were translated into Arabic but were not taught. Government by secular constitutions was not permitted because Islam wanted Qur'anic law, Sunna traditions, and Hadith sayings with Sharia, religious law, to govern Muslim people. Plato's ideal state and the practice of virtue in Plato and Aristotle provided sufficient political-moral guidelines. Ghazali says philosophers took their moral teachings " … from the sayings of the Sufis"(50, 37). This anachronism is partly due to centuries of confusion regarding textual transmission and false attributions of texts of Aristotle.

389

A similar confusion follows in Ghazali's remark about "the Companions of the Cave" Qur'an sura 18, which McCarthy notes is "a borrowing from the legend of the Seven Sleepers of Ephesus" (fn 115, 99). There is an abundance of Neoplatonic thought in Ghazali as found in almost all medieval Christian and Muslim writers. I have already mentioned how the great chain of world soul, world mind, and the One affects the ideal of world Islam. Each individual is oriented to global Islam like all humans were believed to be linked in the Neoplatonic cosmic vision.

Al-Ghazali thinks some errors arose when Muslim philosophers mixed scriptural or Qur'anic texts with Sufi views and their own views. Clarification requires each view be examined on its own merit (52, 38). We are also susceptible to error when we are swayed by the opinions of others. Then we are like those "who know the truth by men, and not men by the truth" (53, 38). The intelligent person discovers the truth and then evaluates a speaker or teacher not by his or her institutional authority, rhetorical power, or emotional appeal, but by criteria of true and false, right and wrong. Pundits with "an overweening opinion of their own competence and cleverness.... "(54, 39), will often convince the gullible hearer to accept as total, a view of which only one part is correct. Ghazali's examples are from a culture of snake charmers, counterfeiters, and deceivers in a society of open marketplaces where the buyer must learn to beware, *caveat emptor.*

The Batinites or Talimites of Ghazali's day remind me of some Shia in our time. They held secret teachings that came from an invisible Imam. This authoritative teacher was "master of truth" which was hidden, *batin,* having an interior, inner, or esoteric meaning. The twelfth and last infallible Imam died in 941, but his followers said they still secretly communicated with him. Ghazali answers that there is only one infallible teacher in Islam, Muhammad (64, 44). In uncertain cases of law, "the prophets and religious leaders referred men to the exercise of personal judgment" (67, 46). This teaching is similar to the catholic moral doctrine that an informed conscience is the proximate norm of morality. For Islam it applies to religious practice. Ghazali says " … judge according to the most probable opinion.… "(66, 46). To answer the objections of the three groups, Talimites, philosophers, and Mutakallim, Ghazali composed *The Book of the Correct Balance* to guide the perplexed person to learn how to discern the truth "by weighing the matter with the five scales" (75, 48). This little book is translated with notes by McCarthy as "Appendix III" in DFE (1999, 245-283). Without good norms for discerning judgment no one will be saved "from the darkness of conflicting opinions" (77, 50). In my view, the Shia are more prone to this Muslim school of Gnostic authoritarianism than the Sunni.

Sufism takes up the longest section of Ghazali's autobiography. His account is illustrated by a dramatic personal narrative of the deep emotional crisis that became manifest in a psycho-somatic illness that accompanied his decision to stop teaching and depart from Baghdad, to practice with Sufis in Damascus and Jerusalem, before making the Hajj. He gave up fame, fortune, and attachments in Baghdad and by means of this detachment took up Sufi practices that brought him deep spiritual profit which he designates with the phrase, "fruitional experience." In one place he praises Sufism by saying:

> *[Sufis] … uniquely follow the way to God Most Holy; their mode of life is the best of all; their way the most direct of ways, and their ethic the purest. Indeed, were one to combine the insights of the intellectuals, the wisdom of the wise, and the lore of scholars versed in the mysteries of revelation in order to change a single item of sufi conduct and ethic and to replace it with something better, no way to do so would be found! For all their notions and quiescences, exterior and interior, are learned from the light of the niche of prophecy. And beyond the light of prophecy there is no light on earth from which illumination can be obtained (94, 56-7).*

Ghazali presents the Sufi path or way, *tariq,* as a synthesis of theory and practice, what we in the west might call contemplation and action. Sufis aim " … to lop off the obstacles present in the soul and to rid oneself of its reprehensible habits and vicious qualities in order to attain thereby a heart empty of all save God and adorned with the constant remembrance of God" (80,51). Ghazali says the most "distinctive characteristic" of Sufis is that they learn "not by study but by fruitional experience, and the state of ecstasy and the exchange of qualities" (82, 52). The Sufi appeal to a lived, felt experience, compared to taste, *al-dhawq,* reminded McCarthy of Ps 34:8, "Taste and see that the Lord is good". This "taste" means a "savoring, or relishing, and enjoyment.… " (McCarthy fn 162, 103), a sense of general inner well-being. "Ecstasy" is a term commonly used for a mystical experience because it "stands out", *ex stasis,* from normal experiences. The "exchange of qualities" "refers to a moral change" (McCarthy fn 164, 103) a moral conversion, the acquisition of virtuous habits that replace bad habits.

Ghazali then narrates the circumstances of his personal, critical decision to turn away from his attachments to fame, honor, wealth, and prestige as the "greatest" teacher in Baghdad, (he had three-hundred students), to begin "a long journey" (86, 53-4) dedicated to the practices of Sufism. I think it more than historical irony that the same year that Ghazali resigned from teaching in Baghdad and under went his psychosomatic illness of loss of speech and appetite as he struggled with an anxiety ridden, heart rending decision, was 1095, the year that western Christians organized and launched the first crusade, which slaughtered Muslims and Jews in the holy land. This tragic irony is strongest if we compare and contrast teachings and actual practice on war and peace in the history of Christianity and Islam.

Ghazali distributed his wealth, provided for his children and his associates, arranged for a brother to teach in his absence and left Baghdad and the Iraqi leaders "firmly resolved never to return.… " (89, 155). He went to Damascus, then Jerusalem, then made the Hajj to Mecca and Medina. He returned to his native Iran ten years later when "certain concerns and the appeals of my children drew me.… " (93, 56).

Ghazali was fifty-years old when he finished his autobiography. Muslims believe God plans a renewal for Islam at the beginning of each century (137, 71), so as the year AH 500 approached, Ghazali began to compose his *Revival of the Religious Sciences.*

Ghazali closes this work with comments on prophecy or revelation and discernment of true and false in religion. Here I close with the gem of folk religion buried in the last section of his book. Alex Trebek once used the mathematical riddle called "Ghazali's square" on a televised quiz program. Ghazali learned that midwives used two pieces of cloth never touched by water to assist in difficult childbirths. One piece was visible for the pregnant woman to fix her eyes on, the other placed under her feet, "and forthwith the child hastens to come out" (145, 75). Each cloth had nine Arabic letters written on them in a square form such that the mathematical sum of each letter, which stands for a number, "in any one line, read straight or diagonally, is fifteen" (145, 74-5).

4	9	2	D	T	B
3	5	7	J	H	Z
8	1	6	*H*	A	W

The number fifteen was related to a myth of moon power and sacred to the goddess Ishtar in ancient Nineveh and Babylonia. McCarthy notes what a scholar wrote to him, that fifteen "is reminiscent of (or influenced by) the Jewish shunning of the letters *yodh* and *he,* the two Hebrew letters that represent Yah (God-Yahweh); *yodh =ten* and *he =five*. The Arabic letters, too, have the same numerical equivalents of the

Hebrew letters. God's help may be invoked symbolically by this talisman" (fn 248, 114). Thus religious folklore contains popular practices that belong in the domain of faith and revelation whose heritage may have begun when writing first appeared in ancient Sumer.

"With the time came the man" begins McCarthy's "Introduction" quoting Macdonald on Ghazali (*DFE*, 1999, 9). McCarthy concluded his forty-three pages of "Introduction" saying, "The time is gone; but the man remains, and will remain, for you, for me, and for all men [sic]" (*DFE*, 1999, 52). He imagines meeting Ghazali in heaven to continue the conversation and to thank him and his co-religionists for sharing their immense learning with us.

I thank Al-Ghazali and Richard McCarthy, both of whom have shared the wonders and achievements of their rich educations, made learning and understanding a delight, and while celebrating learning, reveal steps in the world's pathways to Islam.

Can One Be Muslim and Christian?
Robert Blair Kaiser

I went in search of a man I had been hearing about for some time, a Jesuit named Paolo Dall'Oglio, who was following Matteo Ricci's path.

In 1601, after spending twenty-one years studying the language, history and culture of China, Jesuit father Matteo Ricci landed in the court of Beijing and put his Western learning at the disposal of the emperor Wanli. For almost a decade Ricci became the most important link between East and West, between the ancient Chinese civilization and the world of Europe. He was reined in by Church authorities in Rome for using secular Chinese rites to honor the dead in Catholic requiem masses.

On October 24, 2001, Ricci's memory was rehabilitated by Pope John Paul II who hailed him as the very model of a modern missionary. The pope said Ricci brought "the Christian revelation of the mystery of God" to China in a way that "did not destroy Chinese culture" and pursued the "patient and farsighted work of enculturating the faith in China, in the constant search for a common ground of understanding with the intellectuals of that great land."

In 2001, I met Paolo Dall'Oglio, who was following Matteo Ricci's path--not in China, but in Islam. In 1991, Dall'Oglio had founded a Christian community called Deir Mar Musa, the Community of St. Moses the Ethiopian, high on a cliff in the Syrian desert. His goal: to further a greater rapprochement with Islam by "reinventing the positive relationship that existed between the first Muslims and the Christian monks on the borders of the Arabian deserts." He was twenty-five years into a project mandated by the visionary Jesuit general Pedro Arrupe, who saw a new world taking shape in the early 1970s. It was a world the various religions had to stop fighting over, and start fighting for. That called for new kinds of missionaries who would go forth not to convert the heathens, but to listen and learn from those often more spiritual than they.

I wondered if Dall'Oglio was a man who could make himself over as completely as Ricci did, when he "became Chinese." I wondered if Dall'Oglio, too, was a syncretist? I also wondered if he was the kind of Catholic link to Islam envisioned by General Fr. Pedro Arrupe after Vatican II? Paolo Dall'Oglio became one of this new breed. In 1977, Arrupe dispatched him to Lebanon to learn Arabic and Islamic culture--to begin, at age twenty-three, the kind of deep cultural transformation epitomized by the giant Matteo Ricci.

At the time we met, some twenty-five years later, Dall'Oglio at age forty-eight did not consider himself a giant. But he did think of himself as a Muslim–"because Jesus loves Muslims, the same Jesus who is alive in me. In a sense, I cannot but be a Muslim--by way of the Spirit and not the letter." He said he is also a syncretist--"culturally and theologically–without losing my faithfulness to the mystery of the Church of Jesus Christ."

Though he claimed to be a Muslim, in spirit at least, and a syncretist as well, Dall'Oglio looked and talked very much like a twenty-first century Jesuit, as I quickly learned when I met him in a parlor at the Gregorian University in Rome where he was visiting. He was a tall, animated man-on-the-move with flashing eyes, wearing Nikes, a ski jacket and a backpack–and coughing through a very full salt-and-pepper beard. "I am sorry," he said, "I have the flu, or something." His English was good--a great deal better, at least, I told him, than my Italian. "Or," he joshed, "your Arabic."

I asked him about his immersion in Islam. "As soon as I arrived in Lebanon in 1977," he explained, "I tried to start thinking in Arabic." Among other things, he learned the Heart Prayer in Arabic (Lord Jesus Christ, be merciful to me, a sinner) and made it as habitual as his own breathing. He came back to Rome for his seven years of philosophy and theology, but he spent every summer somewhere in the Arab world. And he not only learned what Islam was, he learned to love it, too, not least from the writings of Catholic Islamic monk, Charles de Foucauld (1858–1916) and the Catholic Islamic scholar, Louis Massignon (1883–1962).

Dall'Oglio produced a doctoral dissertation in theology at Rome's Gregorian University called "Hope in Islam." He was ordained a priest in the Syriac Catholic Rite, and then moved to his first assignment–to Islam, to Syria, where he eventually came upon his future monastery. Dall'Oglio dug into his backpack to find a picture of Deir Mar Musa, a long-shot of a white, fortress-like complex built on top of a cliff. It was first constructed, he said, in the sixth century, frescoed in the eleventh century, and abandoned in the nineteenth century, then given to him by the Catholic Antiochian bishop of Homs, Hama and Nebek in 1991. The frescoes in its chapel are priceless.

When Dall'Oglio spoke to me in Rome, the Community of Deir Mar Musa had an international cast of monks and nuns in their thirties, plus some lay collaborators, including two married couples, and some novices, too. After four years, those who are approved take perpetual vows of poverty, chastity and obedience, plus promises of contemplation, work, hospitality and loving Islam. They wear gray woolen habits, cinched with a leather belt. They do not follow any special dietary restrictions but do not eat pork or drink wine when they have Muslim guests. Shoeless, their heads covered with prayer shawls, kneeling on fine Oriental carpets, the community shares an hour of prayer every morning, starting at 7:30, followed by a talk with Dall'Oglio. After breakfast, they work until 2:30 PM, milking their goats, making cheese, tending their gardens and constructing a new building for the nuns and female guests. (They have already remodeled a series of ancient caves north of the monastery, for the monks and male guests.) After lunch, they take a siesta when they can, they study, they go on the Internet, creating a virtual monastery in cyberspace at http://www.deirmarmusa.org .In the evening at seven, they have an hour of silent prayer in their ancient chapel. Then they celebrate their Eucharist.

Dall'Oglio said, "We practice an Abrahamitic hospitality." In fact, hospitality was the whole point of their existence. They wanted to bridge the tremendous gap between the followers of Jesus and the followers of Mohammad, and they felt they could do this best by meeting with all who came--for a day, or for a week--answering their questions, inviting them to join in their prayers, building on their mountain a people's park with and for them, joining in their fasts for peace.

In the beginning, they had problems – with both Muslims and Christians who did not understand what Dall'Oglio was up to. He was approached one day by a group of four middle-aged men, who charged him with being a spy. "This," he recalls, "was hard to refute. The more I look okay and sound okay, the more I prove how effective a spy I really am. Finally, I tell them, 'All right. Look in my eyes. If you see something that is not sincere, you have every right to beat me. And I am honor bound to let you do it.'"

They withdrew, conferred together, then re-approached him and looked into his deep brown eyes and saw--something good. They did not beat him. "Today," Dall'Oglio says, "they're among my best friends."

The library at Mar Musa contains all the classic Christian texts ("we have to sink roots deep into our own tradition") and the Qur'an and some of the classic commentaries on Islam's sacred book. "Our monks and nuns know the Qur'an almost as well as many Moslems," said Dall'Oglio.

Dall'Oglio said he saw his work of reconciliation with Islam extending in the future toward some kind of mediation between all the warring parties in the Middle East. "This is very delicate," he says, "but everyone knows that we cannot continue to use religion as an excuse for violence of all kinds.

We have to find a way to break through the infernal circle of fear that we feel, all of us."

Where put the focus? Dall'Oglio said it was clear that the people in every religion have to dig deep into their own roots to find the rationales for dealing with everyone in justice and peace. He had found those roots in both the Old and New Testament. He had found them in the Qur'an. People who don't go to their roots, but follow only the letter (of whatever sacred text), he said, are the real troublemakers in this world. "Follow them and we are doomed."

In the spring of 2005, the Holy Office in Rome launched an investigation of Dall'Oglio for his views on syncretism.

Jesus: Beloved Disciple, But Not the Belovedest
David W. Van Etten

"I recently picked up the Pope's latest book about the historical Jesus, Jesus of Nazareth, while I was recovering from knee surgery. At the time I was holed-up for a week in my girlfriend Abby's apartment with my leg entombed in bandages and a machine-generated ice sleeve and a dramatic black brace. I was entirely dependent upon Abby's care, which she gave generously. The room smelled like a bored invalid. I don't know if it was the pain pills or the underlying pain, but I was ready for a sparring match with the theologian formerly known as Cardinal Ratzinger."

I didn't intend to instigate another tussle with Abby.

"He knows each sheep by name, and they recognize the sound of his voice," I shared with her, explicating a passage and elaborating on the Pope's theory of love. The shepherd comes through the gate, while the robber hops the fence. The shepherd is responsible for the sheep, while the robber possesses the sheep like property. Benedict's theory of love is a theory of belonging. I was actually quite taken with Benedict's reflections—surprisingly so.

Abby responded, "What I fear about with all this talk of sheep is the blind following. I don't see how Jesus' sheep are any different than a dictator's sheep."

She was right, of course. Scriptural passages would usually raise the same interpretive suspicion in me.

But I was irritated that she wouldn't join me on my afternoon reverie and enjoy the fleshiness of the particular passage: a shepherd naming his sheep and genuinely knowing the personality of each sheep; the sheep recognizing the sound of the shepherd's voice when he calls their names. The shepherd hoisting the fleecy body of a stray across his shoulder, and carrying the weighty animal back to the fold.

"I feel like you are criticizing the way that I love again," she said.

My irritation transitioned to mild fury, and I barked at Abby. Barked—that term appropriately fits the series of curt warnings with raised tenor that passed through my teeth. Why does my afternoon reading have to lead to our problems? Why can't I just muse about Love-with-a-capital-L out loud and express my rare appreciation for something Benedict has to say? Why does it always have to be about us?

Of course, she was right again.

The last time I waxed philosophic about love, I directly criticized what I see, in these off moments, only as neediness. On that occasion, she had jokingly said to me, "Dave, do you love me?"—mimicking the way a stereotypical high-schooler might say, "Do you think I'm pretty?" But her joke didn't seem entirely in jest—her attention was focused intensely on my response—not my verbal answer, but my exaggerated swoon. Then I stood on my soapbox, and informed her that our exchange made me feel a little awkward and sad. Why couldn't she just love, without the constant reassurance of being loved?

■

The lover's quarrel echoes a familiar theme in my life. My close relationships eternally return to the same impasse: we are special friends, but how special are we? I resist anyone trying to ascend too high in the intimacy ranks. I tell myself that I'd much prefer that everyone remained intimacy-equals, more or less, rather than creating separate classes of officers and grunts.

Perhaps I might flesh out the intimacy impasse by contrasting Benedict's reflections on the Twelve Apostles with my own reflections on the Twelve Kids at my parents' home-daycare business.

Pope Benedict makes an interesting move in *Jesus of Nazareth*: he argues that the Gospel of John is more historically authentic than the Synoptic Gospels because the Gospel of John is more beloved. He flips conventional wisdom—at least when "conventional" refers to my Jesuit-shepherded studies—on its head.

In my college religious studies classes at Santa Clara University, the Synoptic Gospels—Mark, Matthew, and Luke—were considered more historically authentic, in part, because they were composed closer to the events of Jesus' life and death. Since they were written only a couple of generations after the events they describe, the accounts were more reliable. One is reminded of the childhood game of "Telephone," whispering a long phrase into the ear next to you and watching the message whispered around the room. By the time the message returns to you, the words and the meaning of the message have changed amusingly. The Gospel of John, written a generation later than the Synoptic Gospels, must have morphed similarly, according to critical historicism.

Further, the Synoptic Gospels seem more authentic, more Jewish, more folkish, less contrived, and the Synoptic Gospels agree overwhelmingly with each other. Meanwhile, the Gospel of John seems more Greek and theological and different, with all of its talk of Logos and its redaction of Synoptic events. Teachers often explained the Gospel of John as a hybrid account, marrying the simple Synoptic story with something philosophically interesting but alien—something Neo-Platonic and Gnostic.

Benedict, in contrast, asserts that the Gospel of John is actually more authentic because it carries the wisdom of Jesus' beloved disciple, John. Essentially, John was party to more late-night conversations with Jesus, and held a closer confidence and intimacy with Jesus than the other Eleven Apostles. The Apostles John and James were sons of Zebedee, who owned the Jerusalem apartment in which the Last Supper was held.

John sat at Jesus' side, the place reserved for the host or the host's eldest son. Thus, John was not only closer to Jesus, he was also Jesus' host.

What does this matter? Benedict argues that John was a better eyewitness to the events of Jesus' life: his intimacy and his customary relationship made John privy to more of Jesus' public and private works. John had ordinary conversations with Jesus, if any conversation with Jesus was ordinary, and better understood Jesus' internal debates.

Further, Benedict argues that the apparent "Greekness" of the Gospel of John can actually be understood as a combination of two authentic factors, rather than evidence of foreign influence. First, John came from a very learned and priestly class. We should not be confused by John's fisherman occupation. His father, according to Benedict was also a Galilean fisherman who employed many other subordinates; and his father was also a priest who regularly attended his ministerial duties in Jerusalem, like many other prominent priests. Thus, the learnedness of the Gospel of John isn't necessarily "Greekness," but instead high-priestly Jewishness. Second, the philosophical lyricism of the Gospel of John may be understood as containing genuine vestiges of the late-night conversations held between Jesus and John. Rather than alien thought transposed onto the Jesus narrative, the flights of Logos may actually be Jesus talk and Jesus thought interspersed with the Jesus narrative.

Although the Apostle John did not write the Gospel of John, Benedict argues that Apostle John's intimate wisdom was carried intact to publication. Apostle John's own beloved disciple, John the Presbyter, acted as a trustee to the special eyewitness account until that account was written and broadcast to the world. One is reminded of the genealogical relationship between Socrates and Plato and Aristotle. Don't we accept that Aristotle has an authentic understanding of the Socratic theory of knowledge, even though Aristotle's writings are different from and temporally distant from Socrates? Similarly, can't we posit that the Gospel of John has an authentic relationship to the historical Jesus and his theory of love, despite the generational differences and distances?

My response to Benedict's reflections about John, the beloved disciple, cut two ways. On the one hand, I really like the idea of beloved discipleship. It is a wonderful way to re-read the New Testament and re-relate to each other.

On the other hand, I really don't like the Pope's recurrent need to highlight "belovedest" relationships. Benedict doesn't use the term "belovedest," but I think it aptly fits the awkward tendency toward superlatives in the Pope's thought. Jesus is not only the new Moses, but he is also the most Moses-est man in all human history. John is not only the beloved disciple, but he is also the beloved-est disciple—logically diminishing the beloved quality of everyone else who came into contact with Jesus.

It's as though Benedict just doesn't get it. Obsessing about superlatives and specialness reveals an uncertainty about the underlying relationship. When I need to be the most loved I am concerned about being loved at all. One feels that the Pope protesteth too much.

When Jesus was asked if he was the Son of God, what was his response? He said his Father was the greater; he washed his disciples' feet, saying we should do the same.

■

My sister and I were raised in a home-daycare center, the family business that my parents called the Van Etten Zoo. We were licensed to care for twelve children; and over the past three decades, we have cared for an ever-rotating group of twelve. Some children arrive at six in the morning and leave the house at six at night. Some arrive as infants and don't leave until junior high school.

My sister and I never harbored any doubt of our parents' love. That said, my parents tried very hard not to give us any special treatment or mark us out as different. I am sure this was difficult at times, and only varyingly successful. The Twelve Kids knew that my sister and I remained in the house, even after they left in the evenings. They knew the rooms they napped in were "Mary Grace's room" or "David's room."

But I also feel in my heart of hearts that the Twelve Kids did not belong differently than my sister and I. There were not two classes of beloved and belovedest in the household.

My mom knows each of us by name.

She literally remembers names. A few years ago, a woman named Denise Bissonnette contacted my mom out of the blue, saying my mom was her teacher in Kankakee, Illinois forty years ago when my mom was still a nun with the Sisters of Loretto. My mom's immediate response: "Oh yes, Denise, you had an older brother named Andy, and an older sister named Mary, and two more older brothers named Tommy and Eddy, and a younger sister named Michelle."

More metaphorically, my mom genuinely knows our names. She knows each child's personality and routine. She knows the parents or the creative family that raise the child at home. She knows the teachers' temperaments and the seasonal swings of each school year. She knows each trouble, each comfort, each joy. My mom strikes me as the very hub of neighborhood life, the person who anchors a thousand different lives. It defies description. My mom understands how each child loves differently and how each child needs to be loved differently in turn.

We recognize the sound of my dad's voice.

We literally recognize his voice. When my dad sneezes it's like the firmament of the house shakes: "Yaaaah-HOO." And when my dad calls your name, because its lunchtime, or because your parent just arrived to pick you up—I don't care

405

if you're playing in the farthest reaches of the backyard, busy on a swing—you come running to that voice.

More metaphorically, we genuinely recognize the sound of my dad's voice. He guides the Twelve, in form and in substance. Formally, my dad is a father figure to the kids, sometimes the primary male role model in their lives. Substantially, the kids listen for and respond to his guidance. I watch it and marvel. The way the kids relate to my dad reminds one of pack dynamics in the wild. They gravitate toward him when he walks in the room. Some kids butt heads with my dad because they are not sure how to relate to a caring man they respect. When my dad unexpectedly laughs, or sings a line from a song, or cheers enthusiastically for a sporting triumph, the room quickly fills with looks of wonder.

There was only one instance in the history of the Van Etten Zoo when we contemplated expelling a child from our services—many, many years ago. The boy was about as disruptive as you can imagine. The energy of the household tightened when he entered the room. He yelled at the other kids. He yelled at my parents. His mom and step-dad were distant even when they were standing in front of you. My parents told them they simply couldn't do it any longer. My parents said they just couldn't take care of the boy.

Later that summer evening, as night fell, my parents walked over to the boy's house and asked his mom if she would bring the boy back to the daycare. He returned the next day. Every few years that boy returns to our house and visits for a couple hours. Each visit he submits a new photograph of himself—and more recently, of himself and his wife and his baby—to place on the wall of photographs in the kitchen, replacing the photograph submitted during his previous visit.

■

My parents sat and listened as I described my lover's quarrel with Abby, my perception that she always needs to be the belovedest. Love was not a quid pro quo, I complained. I didn't know how to continue maintaining her well-being indefinitely.

We all want to experience unconditional love, said my dad. We all want the self to disappear from the way that we love and the way that we are loved. But life only gives us a little taste of unconditional love every now and then. "Like appetizers," said my mom.

And then the two of them opened up about their own relationship and the daily work that goes into its maintenance. I knew my parents had disagreements. But I was rarely privy to the internal dynamics of their relationship: how they communicated with each other; how they addressed the differences that could be addressed, and accepted the differences that needed to be accepted. Their late-night conversations always took place out of earshot, so to speak. But now, understanding my relationship challenges, they shared more about their own.

People have different ways of loving and being loved. Even one's parents.

What I realized was that the differences between Abby and I could not be wholly attributed to our family backgrounds. Some were universal differences between men and women. Some were unique differences between the two of us, each of us strange, each of us alone.

What I realized was we are each stray hearts—insecure, stubborn, lost. Your loved ones call you by name, nudge you back to the fold, and remind you that you belong. You get hoisted onto a shoulder and carried back through the gates.

Unconditional Well-Being, Allowing Gestation in Mind and Soul

A Conversation with Gary Schouborg, Ph.D.

More than any other philosopher, Gary Schouborg has shown me how valuable are subtle distinctions, patience and rational, tolerant attention to what's being discussed. He encourages us all to pay attention to our experience and to add the balanced rational gift of incisive intellect to understand our complex/multi-variegated lives and to extend that rationality to our philosophies and theologies.

GS: I reread Claudio Naranjo's *How to Be: Meditation in Spirit and Practice* (Jeremy P. Tarcher, Los Angeles, 1990). Naranjo sees meditation as a triadic dialectic of concentrative, expressive and the *via negativa.*

In the concentrative, the meditator loosens himself from his ordinary habits of thinking by becoming absorbed in some object of contemplation. In the expressive, the meditator loosens herself from her ordinary habit of thinking and control by yielding to her deeper impulses, such as "speaking in tongues," going into ecstasies. In the *via negativa*, the meditator aims toward a stillness and peace within by practicing techniques such as Vipassana (insight meditation) where we let go of anything that arises, letting go and thereby creating a space around whatever we think.

MZC: How do these processes inter-relate? How do meditative practices fit individual differences, inclinations, needs?

GS: These three methods can be given greater attention according to individual need, but they still are dialectically related, implicating one another. I can't be absorbed by something (concentration) without following a spontaneous impulse to move beyond habitual patterns (expression). And if I follow my deeper impulses (expression) I do so toward something (concentration). Either concentration or expression is also a *via negativa* insofar as it enables me to let go of habitual thinking that possesses me. I can slow down and see what I am doing mentally and emotionally that brings me suffering. This ability to meditate leads me to the stillness of not being pushed and pulled by my habitual ways of thinking and acting.

By radically letting go of my habitual ways, the *via negativa* allows me to be aware and present even in the midst of painful emotions, without reacting, without getting lost in thinking. Being in the space of just being there, just sitting, I free myself to be absorbed by the reality around me (concentration) and to awaken to my deeper impulses-yearnings (expression).

MZC: Another Buddhist meditation technique I've found nourishing is *Metta* practice of wise compassion and prayerful good wishes towards us, our intimates, and our fellow citizens of the world. Even to those who have caused us hurt and resentment. In the Buddhist Monastery we chant: "May all of us be happy.… May I be free from affliction and hatred" and then we try to remember to practice in our daily lives, sending out blessing feelings, even to the guy who cuts us off on the freeway, rather than cursing, souring up our faces and pumping up our blood pressure. We can let go of hostilities, irritations in the daily challenges of living together. Hell, the guy on the freeway is in a hurry just as we are. I understand that. I should also slow down and I wish him the opportunity to give up his unnecessary rushing around also.

GS: I can appreciate Metta as a helpful practice, which is based, in our natural empathy with others.

The operative word in your comment is *wise* compassion, which knows the difference between inherent and unnecessary vulnerability. Any sentient being is *inherently* vulnerable to death and the unfortunate vicissitudes of life. However, we humans make ourselves *unnecessarily* vulnerable when we over-identify with our desires by assuming that our happiness necessarily depends on achieving them.

Over-identification distracts us from where our true happiness lies—an elemental contentment in living provided by our body independently of achieving our desires. By distracting us from this sense of unconditional well-being, over-identification leaves us strangely dissatisfied even when we achieve our desires. And when we fail to achieve them, it increases our suffering by exaggerating the importance of our loss. In short, over-identification simultaneously intensifies our suffering while depriving us of any consolation we might derive from an elemental contentment in living.

Unwise compassion is caught up in this maelstrom of over-identification. Both the sufferer and the unwisely compassionate individual are captives in the exaggerated drama of the moment. If we're unwisely compassionate, we only reinforce any illusions of those suffering. Yes, misery loves company. There have certainly been times when I've been consoled by the sympathy of another who shared in my illusions and suffering. But when it's aware of options, misery prefers company that alleviates rather than merely shares its suffering. A wisely compassionate friend—one who experiences my suffering from the perspective of an elemental contentment in living—can be an embodied, unstated testament for me that there is happiness to be had beyond my current pain.

A final clarification. Although we tend to frame our understanding of compassion in terms of one person feeling it for another, it's essential to realize that wise compassion includes oneself as well as others. To paraphrase Tolstoy's line about marriage, individuals differ in the unnecessary vulnerability they create for themselves, but they all share the vulnerability that is inherent in the human condition. When it comes to our inherent vulnerability we're all in it together, so that we awaken to one another's and our own vulnerability simultaneously. But the more we over-identify with our desires the more we see ourselves as separate individuals with unrelated needs. Only to that extent do we see ourselves as forced to choose between ourselves and others.

MZC: Some theologians say nothing is certain about God; that God is ultimately ineffable, beyond even our most refined thinking and our "enthusiastic" translations of spiritual experiences into theological certainties. You recently commented: "We can attribute nothing to God literally, only analogously. Superstition and idolatry come from missing this point. In the end there is only silence, so the wise theist and the wise atheist are unable to be distinguished."

Such writings as *The Cloud of Unknowing* communicate that God is ultimately ineffable. Buddhists might hint at Nirvana, the "deathless," but say it is not helpful to speak of it. Theists may develop a more Personal approach, but admit of only glimpses before a Mystery. Can we engage in theology, reasonably and civilly, with clarifying language as to what we can know and what we can never know?

GS: It can sometimes be legitimate to hypothesize about personal as well as impersonal Gods or Ultimate Realities. The Buddha only cautioned against taking such speculation too seriously. His point was that our elemental contentment in living cannot be derived from our beliefs, however true they may be. Expecting any belief to be our *primary* source of happiness is like expecting a color to taste sweet. It's simply looking in the wrong place for what we're after.

Beliefs are complex, involving commitment, content, and function.

Commitment is how we hold a belief. When we over-identify with a belief, we overly commit to it, taking it as having too much importance for our happiness. This was the Buddha's primary concern: that we understand that no belief—no matter how profound, incisive, or true—is a substitute for the elemental satisfaction in living that our body naturally provides us.

Content is what we believe. It can be complex. Some of us

may say that God exists and others may deny it. Yet perhaps only our words differ and we are pointing to the same reality. Perhaps both sides can agree that people are good, the golden rule should be followed, and life is worth living. Or perhaps the realities to which we're referring are surprisingly different. Perhaps the theist is affirming a dark God and a pessimistic view of human nature, whereas the atheist is more optimistic and in many ways agrees more with some theists than we might have suspected initially.

Function is how a belief functions in our life. Belief in God may serve a defensive function by assuring us that our opinions are divinely inspired, so we don't have to listen to opposing views. By the same token, denial of God may serve a defensive function as well by assuring us that there are no mysteries in life beyond the limits of our understanding. On the other hand, belief in God may serve an expansive function by reminding us of our ignorance and of how much we might benefit from listening to others. Similarly, denial of God may function expansively by helping us work with others to understand the world around us rather than depending on God to magically answer our questions.

In short, rather than treat words as though they have a life of their own, we should listen carefully to speakers' real meaning and understand how their words are actually functioning in their lives.

MZC: You say do not confuse "apodictic"—certain-absolute faith—with "heuristic" faith which is provisional, ongoing. The beliefs of true apodictic faith cannot be tested (such as Jesus is Divine, There is an Unborn, Eternal). Yet belief can be rational and full of conviction, even if you can't prove it. One can be irrational in his/her apodictic faith if it's applied dogmatically (as if it were *proven*) or applied to empirical issues (which can be tested). Too often Islamic, Catholic, Buddhist, Hindu followers propagate certain, absolute knowledge which keep others shut out, which can even lead to destructive violence and hatred. How can we promote more ecumenical and respectful dialogue?

GS. The difference between apodictic (dogmatic) and heuristic faith is where we attach our commitment. Dogmatic faith attaches it to content, whereas heuristic faith attaches it to function.

Dogmatic faith in God is committed to the *content* of the proposition that God exists. The commitment here is to what one believes, which then colors one's personal experience. Faith in God is taken to be a true belief that results in a desirable way of seeing and experiencing life, whereas denial of God is taken to be a false belief that results in an undesirable way of seeing and experiencing life.

A heuristic is a guide to inquiry. *Heuristic* faith is a guide for inquiring into one's personal experience. The experience is more fundamental than the belief itself, which imperfectly expresses the experience. The proposition that God exists expresses a deep, mysterious, personal experience that one spends a lifetime trying to understand and articulate. While the belief itself remains fixed, the understanding of its ramifications in one's life evolves. In this spirit, one might interpret St. Anselm's *fides quaerens intellectum* (faith seeking understanding) as the classic expression of heuristic faith.

The dogmatic theist necessarily clashes with the dogmatic atheist, since the contents to which they're committed (God exists v. God doesn't exist) are incompatible. But the heuristic faiths of the theist and the atheist may lead them in overlapping directions, depending on how their understandings evolve from their different starting points.

MZC: Do you have any definition of enlightenment? How do you relate enlightenment to "process" theory? What place do our varying religious symbols, rituals, icons and theologies have?

GS: To say that process is our innermost reality is to say that each of us is a river (process) of consciousness in which patterns (sensations and meanings) emerge and disappear constantly. Enlightenment is an awakening to ourselves as river; it's not a process of reasoning. It's realizing our sense of unconditional well-being. What enlightens us is not understanding fascinating (and even important) theories, such as what is the "self," but rather understanding *anicca* (changing), *anatta* (no self), and *dukkha* (anguish). To understand these three fundamental aspects of our personal experience is to understand that our elemental contentment in living cannot reside in static beliefs—however useful they are for practical, everyday living—but only in the ever-changing reality that we are.

Concrete symbols, icons, rituals and theologies serve to apply spirituality in diverse contexts and in practical ways; but we shouldn't fixate on them. When we do, we cling, which keeps us from flowing.

We need to awaken to the transitory nature of experience, the fact that no concept or set of concepts captures all that "I" am. When we fail to grasp change and "no self," we suffer unnecessarily. We are victims of our own mental anguish.

MZC: To me, the idea of "no self" is often misunderstood as trying to somehow "get rid of the ego" or "killing the ego." As I understand it, Buddhism doesn't deny the existence and importance of a wholesome personality in an empirical sense. Rather it denies it as a permanent entity. The individual is *santati*, a psycho-physical flux or continuity. We may be "no self," but we are all co-being, inter-connected, with intrinsic value and dignity.

GS: Sure an integrated, healthy ego is important. It takes a healthy ego to reflect on itself and see its ever-changing nature, and through that insight to discern that the happiness that it experiences through pursuing the desires of the ego is secondary to the elemental satisfaction in living that the body naturally provides independent of whether the ego succeeds or fails in that pursuit.

Clinging arises when "me" or "mine" are taken absolutely. Non-clinging arises when they are understood within the framework of *anicca, anatta*, and *dukkha*. "Mine" and "yours" are not absolute, but rather interrelated and constantly evolving realities. Having a felt understanding of this is to "be in the flow" of what we are, in which experience provides its own inherent contentment and happiness.

MZC: Paradox: How can there be no self and yet re-birth? How can one explain in down-to-earth terms how re-birth is not a series of successive lives connected by a substantial soul or self; but rather that it is just the impersonal flowing on of a process, yet influenced by our very personal, volitional actions of body, speech and mind? And what did Buddha mean in practice that there is a process to free one from the cycle of re-birth?

GS: We can resolve the paradox once we understand the difference between describing our experience and explaining it.

The notions of "self" and "no self" can *describe* our experience. On this descriptive level of discussion, "self" is merely a verbal rack on which I hang all my attributes. For example, when I say that I myself am writing this paragraph, I'm merely pointing to a unique address in the universe called Gary, the son of Bob and Lucille. And I'm saying that at that address the writing of this paragraph is going on. On the other hand, "no self" refers to the fact that no description or set of descriptions ever adequately captures that address. No matter how rich the description, I'm more complex than it can say. And even if a description were rich enough to describe me completely at any moment, I'd have changed in the immediately following one, making that description instantly incomplete. On this descriptive level, there is no paradox and not even any controversy. On this descriptive level, reincarnation merely refers to the fact that appearances come and go, that this moment's self dies and a new moment's self is born in a constant cycle of death and rebirth.

Puzzles arise only when notions of "self" and "no self" *explain* our experience. At this level of discussion, there is considerable controversy. Some argue that there must be a self behind the descriptions in order to explain why all the attributes cohere, referring to the same entity. For example, there must be a self that explains why we say that the same Gary who's writing this is also the son of Bob and Lucille. On the other hand, others argue that no such explanation is necessary, any more than we must argue for a marital soul to explain why a married couple remains together.

The paradox of how no self is compatible with reincarnation arises only when we confuse the two levels of discussion. On the level of explanation, reincarnation clearly requires that there be a self behind the appearances, since reincarnation is the movement of a self behind one set of appearances in this life to another set of appearances in a future one. If there is no self, then reincarnation is impossible. However, the Buddha never denied that explanatory self. His words were descriptive. They were concerned with our immediate experience, in particular with our realizing that our life can never be adequately captured by words and beliefs, so that we should look elsewhere for our elemental contentment in living.

MZC: What is the pleasure and joy associated with living in the flow of our immediate and natural waking state? How is it related to our desires and our goals?

We've spoken before about how Buddhism rightfully criticizes attachment to "consumerist" desires, but often doesn't develop—or rather distinguish—"creative" desires. Without this distinction, Buddhism can be seen as rather bland and stoical, apart from our deepest inner yearnings. What is the difference between passive happiness (passive fulfillment = being passively filled = consuming objects of desire) and vital happiness (having a dynamic sense of vitality)?

GS: We can understand vital happiness by adapting Aristotle's notion of *eudaimonia*, being "well-souled."

There are two levels of being well-souled.

The first is what Aristotle had in mind: *eudaimonia* as the exercise of one's abilities. This is happiness at the ego-level—that is, happiness dependent on executive (ego) functions. The difference between this and passive happiness is parallel to what Alfred North Whitehead had in mind when he said that the role of the teacher is to make himself dispensable. The continually indispensable teacher is the one who fills the student with knowledge, a task that's never finished and keeps the student dependent (passive). The teacher who makes himself dispensable teaches the student how to learn—that is, stimulates and nourishes the student's learning powers (vital). It's a parallel point to the difference between giving someone fish (passive) and teaching him how to fish (vital).

Beyond that ego-level vital happiness (vital ego) is what I've called the sense of unconditional well-being, which is supplied by the body independently of any ego-level achievement. It's a sense of elemental wholeness, of unconditional vitality. Without this sense of unconditional well-being, even the optimal exercise of one's powers has a hollow ring to it.

We can talk about this in terms of pleasure in relationship to our goals. We have at least three forms of pleasure: a) from achieving a goal; b) from pursuing that goal; and c) an abiding somatic pleasure (a basic, elemental contentment) that is natural to our waking state—that is, independent of whether we are successful or not in achieving our goals, fulfilling our desires.

Basic contentment is a primal somatic pleasure that is present whatever our goal. It's independent of our specific goals, our pursuit of them, and our success or failure in achieving them. Basic contentment abides. We lose awareness of it by overly focusing on achieving our goals. Letting go of this insistence on success, we may reawaken to the satisfactions inherent in what we do in pursuing goals. Letting go of obsessing over our destination, we allow ourselves to enjoy the trip along the way.

MZC. How can our meditation practice relate to this realization of natural contentedness?

GS: Having quiet times of meditation can be useful for some to awaken to this equanimity.

Buddhists refer to a "passive/receptive" heart, which gets to a fundamentally important point. It is in an inner quiet that we realize that our innermost happiness does not depend on satisfying any of our desires. It is already here. At this point, we have no need for the metaphysical scaffolding that hopes in God's salvation or in higher reincarnations or in life after death. What we have at this moment is self-justifying, if you will. We are unconditionally gratified in being alive. We can experience this happiness even in the midst of intense daily activity. When we do, we experience that daily activity as part of life with all its joys and suffering. From that *felt* perspective, we take none of our daily life's joys or sufferings as essential to our happiness.

MZC: What is the value of prayer? We often see how prayer is profoundly comforting for the individual. Perhaps we don't share the same belief system of the person who prayers, but don't you think genuine, heart-felt prayer is both human and valuable?

GS: In the final analysis, the value of any method of prayer is how it functions in the individual's personal experience.

Shortly after 9/11, one of the TV magazine shows was interviewing a woman, seemingly of modest means, who had lost a twelve-year-old daughter on the plane that crashed into the Pentagon. The daughter had been picked to attend a three-week school in California for talented children interested in biological sea science. The mother spoke of her child as being God's gift, whom God had taken back. She said that she was truly content to have enjoyed her daughter for the twelve years she had her, and she was genuinely happy to know that the daughter was now blessedly in God's bosom.

Philosophically, what the mother said is problematic. Human beings have debated for centuries, with no end in sight, about whether God exists and whether a loving God would allow such suffering. One can ask whether what the woman said makes any real sense.

Psychologically, however, she seemed to be feeling genuinely and deeply what she was expressing, not just mouthing words she thought she ought to say. The clear *functional* value of her beliefs was in making her able to turn away from the useless negative thought that she no longer had her child with her, and instead turn her daughter into a fond, salutary memory, a current presence in her heart. Rightly employed, that is what any prayer can do, however it is dressed. In the face of her warm wisdom, who cares about the philosophical issues of whether to take her beliefs literally or not?

The Old Man and the War
A true story as told by Rev. Sam Haycraft

A tropical afternoon rain thrummed a persistent patter on the thatched roof. The American lowered his head as he followed his companion through the doorway of a small country cottage in the verdant Mekong Delta.

In the dim interior, a small figure in black pajamas waited to greet his guests. One of them, his son, wearing the uniform of a South Vietnamese army officer, addressed him respectfully. The soldier then introduced the American, who was married to the old man's daughter. This was their first-ever meeting.

The wizened farmer merely nodded at the introduction and gestured toward two small stools for them to sit. In silence, he carefully poured steaming tea into three tiny blue porcelain cups. The room was permeated by a pleasant fragrance emanating from a small altar where burning incense sent a small curl of smoke upwards. A statue of the Buddha between two small candles and faded black and white photos of departed family members defined the spirituality and familial respect of the occupants.

"You are American," he said, "I don't know where America is, but I hear from my son that it is a rich country, very different and far from here. How do you like my country?"

The American answered: "Oh, very much." He fumbled for words to express his appreciation for the hospitality and for the opportunity of this meeting. The old man's dark eyes glowed behind the mask of his weathered face. The power of his gaze was in stark contrast to his small body. He began to speak again.

"I was born here and have lived my whole life here on this land. We are ordinary farmers. My son tells me that you want to know about our life … true?"

"Yes, my baby is your granddaughter and someday I want to be able to tell her about meeting you."

The old man closed his dark eyes, pondering his reply.

"Well, my father had only two sons. This was a French colony and sometimes we were treated very severely. When I was young, French soldiers came and took my older brother away to work for them. We never saw or heard from him again. Later they took my father to forced labor, because he had angered one of the tax collectors. When he came home, he was never able to work again. Within a year he died.

"One day the French Army was gone. I thought we could live happily, but soon Japanese soldiers arrived, the 'Sons of Heaven.' They swept through this land many times, always taking chickens, fruit and ordering us to show them our stores of rice. They were extremely cruel.

"Then some of our people (the 'Viet Minh') began to organize secretly to fight the Japanese. They would ask for our livestock and whatever they needed. Finally we heard the Japanese had lost their war, but we still did not have freedom. The French returned, so the Viet Minh continued their guerrilla war, asking for our support, including our young people to fight in their army. French airplanes would shoot at us and drop bombs, hoping to kill Viet Minh, but many innocent farmers were also killed. I remember holding my baby daughter, your wife, in water up to my neck, hiding for the whole day.

"One day, the French accused me and I was made to kneel while they tied my hands behind me. They put a nail in my ear, promising to put it through my brain if I would not identify Viet Minh who were secretly living around us At the same time, my wife and children were hiding for two days without food in a small cave I had dug. Luckily, the French soldiers finally gave up and after beating me with bamboo canes, released me.

"I have another piece of land a few kilometers from here.

On that land were some wonderful mango trees, and because it is remote, I could always go there and bring some fruit to sell for a little money to feed my family. We survived better than many others.

"In 1954, there was news that Ho Chi Minh and the Viet Minh had finally driven the French from our country. Everyone was celebrating, thinking the worst was over. But no, soon Vietnamese began to fight their own Vietnamese brothers and sisters. Both sides would come to our homes to demand our help and loyalty; but to help one was to betray the other. They wanted our sons and daughters to join them. Many did.

"So both of my sons became soldiers, one in the South Vietnamese Army and the other in the Viet Cong, as the Viet Minh is now called. They are brothers who cannot talk to each other."

The old man's son looked away.

The American's thoughts raced for some appropriate comment. He was married to the old man's daughter, but she feared coming to this home of her childhood because of her marriage to an American. His brother-in-law, the old man's son, had brought him to this lush countryside of rice paddies and palms. The placid beauty and apparent serenity of the surroundings gave no hint of the suffering of its people.

The American expressed his gratitude for the meeting and his admiration for the old man's ability to withstand a lifetime of hardship. He felt embarrassed by the hollowness of his words.

The old man looked directly into the eyes of his son-in-law and said, "I have never had a choice ... now I am old and tired; I will never see my mangoes again. Go, live safely and take care of your daughter ... and mine."

When they stood, the American was again aware of his father-in-law's small stature; yet he felt himself to be the smaller of the two. He felt ashamed of the comfort and luxury to which he was accustomed and wanted to somehow lessen the burden of the old man's unhappy years. But he merely took the old man's limp hand and said "Goodbye, Father, thank you."

There were no other words.

The memory of this brief visit which occurred in 1970 haunted the American many times in the thirty-seven years since it took place.

The cruelty of humans to each other in the names of politics and religion has caused untold suffering. This evil is fueled, as Buddha taught, by the three poisons of ignorance; anger and hate; and selfish greed and desires.

Violence seems to only create more violence.

The old man of this story died in 1973 without seeing his children, or his mangoes, again.

Section Two, Eastern Influences

Big Dog Chews the Fat: Just Sit
A Conversation with Ken Ireland

In 1997 I first met Ken Ireland in the Central YMCA in San Francisco's tenderloin where I was staying while visiting the social programs of Glide Memorial Church. A photocopied flyer announced Zen style meditation at 7 PM on Tuesdays. A dozen or so black cushions on the floor of a small room normally used for yoga practice (and chairs for those who could not sit on the floor), no bells, no incense, no chanting, just sitting with some brief instructions about breath and posture, then walking meditation. During the informal question period following two periods of meditation, I arranged to meet with him later, and I recorded our conversation. Just this year, when Ken agreed to edit Meanderings, we had the chance to revisit and explore some of the questions that we had opened during that first meeting.

The two interviews and some conversations for clarification in between have been combined. Ken says: "In many ways, I was sad to edit out things that I said, and sometimes believed, almost ten years ago. It might have been better to just stick a date on them and let them stand. But in the interests of holding the reader's attention, I did some editing, heavy at times. So it looks a lot better than it was. And there's some danger in that: I don't want to leave you with the impression that questions about practice have to be really good, well thought out questions. They don't. Your questions are important because they're yours, not some expert's. They matter to you and that's what counts."

424

The journey into the inner self is not just the important one; it is the only one. We need to listen to the sound beyond the silence.

—W.B. Yeats

Mr. Bloom lived a short distance from his body.

—James Joyce

MZC: We're in San Francisco with Ken Ireland. Tell me a little about this practice group.

KI: Here in the Tenderloin there are lots of street folks, hookers, homeless, drug addicts, ex-cons, pensioners and really poor folks on very meager fixed incomes, immigrants getting a toehold in one of America's most expensive cities. In the group there are queers, transsexuals, great enthusiastic young people from the Volunteer Corps of America, men and women in twelve-step programs; even a Japanese cab driver comes to sit, something he says he can't do back home. It is a small group, but there we have a higher proportion of African Americans than most meditation halls. American Buddhism, the kind that is separate from the temples of immigrant Asian communities, is largely a white middle class phenomenon. Tenderloin folks just do not feel comfortable in a hall where everyone comes in nice clothes from the Gap. And someone at the San Francisco Zen Center is not going to feel comfortable sitting next to someone who hasn't showered in a week.

But I didn't start the Tender Zendo because these folks are not being served by the larger Buddhist communities, though they aren't. And I didn't come here because I'm some goody two shoes, though I might have some traces of that in me too, but because an ex-con I met in an elevator told me he had been a student of Kennet Roshi and had no place to sit near his SRO hotel. He asked me to come and start a meditation group, and then someone gave me a thousand dollars to buy the cushions and pay the first year's rent; that was an invitation I couldn't refuse.

I love it here. It is a very rich experience. I am learning so much.

MZC: What can you tell us about your background, Ken, and how that led you to become deeply involved in Buddhist practice?

KI: First can I say that I've been really blessed? I think about the number of gifted, dedicated people I've met over thirty years of Buddhist practice. I've encountered some really wonderful teachers, had the luck to talk with them, to ask questions, to listen, to practice with them. I can't, and don't, discount or minimize my training as a Jesuit either, the practice of religious life, the intellectual rigor and the _Spiritual Exercises_. I started my Buddhist meditation practice when I was a Jesuit studying theology.

My first Buddhist teacher was Yogi C. M. Chen (1906–87), and he was a Master of meditation. He practiced all three vehicles, Hinayana, Mahayana and Vajrayana. He practiced many forms of tantric Buddhism in Tibet and Xikham. After he had been in Tibet more than forty years, the army of the People's Republic invaded, and he fled with the Karmapa who was a kind of spiritual mentor. That was before the Dalai Lama fled. Safely over the Himalayas, he lived in one room for many years in Kalimpong, India until, after a series of fortuitous circumstances, he received an invitation to come to the United States.

In 1972 Chen wound up in a little studio apartment near the University of California, Berkeley where he stayed until his death in 1987. I was doing theology at the JSTB at the time and was in one of Claudio Naranjo's groups. I met Master Chen on one of Claudio's retreats.

I would walk over, climb the stairs, sit with him, and listen to him or I would take him shopping or drive him to the cemetery for _puja_. I have never meet anyone so accessible who had his credentials: he had lived and practiced in Tibet for almost forty years; he knew Mao when they were both in normal school; he meditated in Chinese ch'an monasteries as they were just after the end of Qing dynasty. I knew that he was an "adept," not just from his spiritual c.v. but by the way he was with me and others. He had grace, humor, and a focused attention that was extraordinary. He could, and did, talk about anything with real equanimity. He had real feelings about Mao and the way that the Tibetans were being treated, but there was never a hint of hatred. When he heard something new, he had real curiosity. When I spoke to him about my homosexuality, there was never a hint of negative judgment. I did a Nineteenth Annotation version of the *Spiritual Exercises* while I was seeing him frequently and he was genuinely interested in my experience in meditation, and actually was very helpful.

One day I asked him for meditation instruction and he said, "Meditate on Impermanence!"

"What you mean?"

"You are going to die, you are already dying." Then he went on to describe what happened when people died in China, including professional mourners who set the right tone, and how that helped meditation. I thought that I had already done this meditation, particularly the first week of the *Exercises*, but gradually I came to see that the meditation on death Chen gave me was not the same as when you imagine yourself at death's door and look back over your life with regret and sorrow for your sins. Impermanence is like a fullness of the present moment that only lasts for the blink of an eye. You have a great quote from Chen—you always come prepared.

MZC: He wrote "all is changing; minute to minute … impermanence applies both to subject and object. It is impossible to speak definitely of either … life is a continuous process of traces with nothing that can be held onto."

KI: There! That's more than a meditation on death. That's

like a koan. But at that time, back in the early 70s, I discovered that before I could meditate and not hold on, before I was able to sit for longer periods of time, I needed to do some psychological work with myself. Apparently when some of us begin to sit (certainly in my case), parts of our mind, our "past," are very troubling and when they pop up, our mind wants to jump up and run away, find some wonderful distraction. So I spent a few years just handling the "negative" aspects of my mind and heart in a responsible way. Psychotherapy helped me a lot. Gradually, I was able to sit with some presence, depth, and became comfortable with my practice.

MZC: What have you been telling beginning meditators?

KI: I try to just be as honest and transparent as I can be about my own Meditation 101: get comfortable with your self, sit as still as possible, follow your breath, and see what happens.

When you begin, you just sit and find any way you can to convince yourself that sitting is a good idea. If you can do that, you will eventually get beyond the resistance, and your body and your mind will get it—the posture, following your breath. Don't bully or criticize yourself, if you can stop yourself. Good luck with that. If your body tells you to sit in a chair, that's fine. After that, you will probably want to find someone to talk to about your experience.

MZC: How did your teachers from China and Japan convey a Buddhism which could be applied here in America?

KI: Yes, we're Americans who are Buddhists. When legendary heroes, like Bodhidharma, carried Buddhism to China, like the great Japanese monks who brought Zen back across the Sea of Japan from China, or the Korean patriarchs who brought the teachings back home, they all transformed the Teaching into the language of their culture. Parts of any Asian Buddhist traditions are just expressions of that culture.

Chen was very aware of the process of Buddhism taking root in a new culture. He tried as much as he could to help things along. All his ceremonies were in English. He wrote a Buddhist ceremony for the birthday of Jesus and Easter. He became a US citizen. I tutored him for the citizenship exam. He was sworn in the year that Jerry Brown ran for president and Chen registered as a Democrat so he could vote for Jerry (as I recall Jerry withdrew before the California primary). How American is that? To let religion dictate your vote.

I am sure that as we Americans deepen our practice in any of the forms that have been handed to us, we'll grow into our own sense of what dharma is, living in the conditions that are uniquely American. Most American teachers are, as far as I have experienced them, moving very slowly, afraid to throw the baby out with the bath water. I think they are just unsure of themselves. John Tarrant is an exception. Of course as his student, I think he is really onto something.

MZC: You have performed, officiated, is that the right word, at Buddhist ceremonies? How did that come about?

KI: It was almost entirely circumstantial. I had been working for several years to establish humane care for my friends, gay men with HIV, so that they could live full lives and die with dignity. In the late 80s and early 90s, I was directing Maitri AIDS Hospice. Issan Dorsey, the founder and guiding light, was a Soto monk, so we tried as best we could to follow the traditional Zen rituals of death, washing and sitting with the body, cremation, services with food offerings, chanting. It was not like going to a seminary and learning the proper rituals for each occasion. Nearly eighty people died while I was at Maitri. In most cases we had talked with the person about his final wishes, read the manuals for ceremonies and cremations, and then we figured out what we could do and what was simply not possible. I worked out an arrangement with one of the funeral homes, that the body would not be carried out immediately after death, but left for three days so that we could sit with it, and there would be no embalming. One of the three priests who lived at Hartford Street might chant. When Issan died, his teacher, Richard Baker, officiated and Kobun Chino roshi, who had been a kind of Master of Ceremonies at the main Soto training Temple in Japan, called Eiheiji, supplied some very elaborate ritual and chant for someone of Issan's stature and he was celebrated with full honors. As one of his wealthy benefactors said after the ceremony, "That was more impressive than the last Bishop's funeral I went to." Usually our rituals were more by the seat of our pants.

Over those four years at the Hospice, I learned several really important things about ritual: Buddhist ceremony grows out of the meditation practice—a cremation ceremony is a meditation on Impermanence—and ceremonies teach dharma in a profound way. But equally important, that there are deep human feelings that have to honored and taken care of when a person dies (or is at any of life's important moments?). I got high marks for my understanding of the tone of a ceremony and my ability to assemble the various pieces and relatively low marks for my ability to accurately reproduce the Japanese monastic ritual, the chanting and bowing. Reminds me of a joke I once heard from a Benedictine monk: At a Jesuit ceremony it's every man for himself. Some parts of mind never change.

In 1995, I was in Hawaii on a seven-day retreat with Aitken roshi to celebrate the Buddha's Enlightenment. I had carried the ashes of one of my best friends, Dan Dunning, with me to fulfill his wish that I scatter them on the waters off Queen's Surf. At the end of the sitting, I told the roshi what I was going to do, and he said that, yes, he remembered Dan from a previous visit, that he was sad to hear of his death, and he asked what he could do. I asked him about hiring a boat to navigate to Queen's Surf. He filled me in on the protocol of beach boys and canoes. Then he asked what I planned for the ceremony. I told him that I had planned nothing; just dump the ashes and cry. He said: "A few words would be appropriate for the occasion." And I did not take those words as a casual "suggestion."

And so a few days after sesshin, dressed in aloha shirts and leis, two friends and I carried Dan's ashes down Kalakaua in a kind of procession. We got in the outrigger canoe and were taken out swiftly beyond the surf. We brought flowers to throw on the water after I poured out Dan's ashes; we spoke tributes and kind words of remembrance; we banged the gunwale of the outrigger, like a drum, singing the praises of the Bodhisattva, Quan Yin, as we rode the surf to shore. We took pictures to send to Dan's mother. It was perfect. I will remember it always. It felt almost spontaneous though we had planned carefully. Too much form and religious language gets too close to magical thinking for my non-theistic prejudice in the presence of the great mysteries.

Being present when a person seeks a presence outside the narrow confines of this life at the end, when another human asks forgiveness, when he or she promises love, commitment and friendship with a lover or partner, yes, I think at those times a few words are appropriate. I make myself available for these occasions, if asked. I am non-sectarian. I do not charge money. The beach boys at Queen's Surf did not charge any money for the outrigger either, but they allowed me to contribute to the Beach Boys' Benevolent Association. I follow that style of *dana*.

Over the years, I've created welcoming ceremonies for babies, adoption ceremonies for gay couples and their families. I think I was the only Buddhist "minister" to officially marry a same sex couple during the short period those unions were legal in San Francisco. My teacher John Tarrant was thrilled when I told him I had done that.

MZC: You mentioned Vipassana practice where teachers speak of posture and breath, paying attention, noticing. But they always add: do it mindfully. In other words, that just posture in itself and just breathing in itself isn't useful if you don't relate it to your consciousness in the moment.

KI: Right and wrong. What is being "mindful"? A friend of mine had been sitting for a long time at Hartford Street. When we did a retreat there, after we ate *orioki* style, some of us would have to go back to the kitchen and wash up. We'd pick up the dishes carefully, slowly. Then we'd put them in the water slowly. We'd follow our breath and we'd carry on like that, you know, that was what we thought of as "mindful." This same friend went on retreat with a Tibetan lama, a teacher. There were about eighty people there and he was assigned to the kitchen after dinner. My friend walked into the kitchen and started his tasks *very mindfully.* The lama came in and said rather loudly, "What are you doing? "Well," he said, "I'm trying to be mindful as I wash these dishes." The teacher said, "We have eighty people to feed and take care of. Speed it up mindfully."

Mindfulness is paying attention in a particular way. It is training, like sitting and following your breath.

MZC: I have heard it described as "an aware and loving quality of attention that you can bring to the changing conditions you encounter."

KI: That's what the Buddhist catechism will tell you. Lovely words, but in my view it is the attention training that counts. The rest, that loving quality, will appear on its own. It is like falling in love with your life—you really can't get in through training though you might be able lay some groundwork, create some favorable conditions. It just happens when it happens.

MZC: You've had the experience of studying the life of Jesus and being involved with Catholic rituals such as the Mass. As you know, Thich Nhat Hanh places images of both Buddha and Jesus on his altar. Do you relate to Jesus as well as to Buddha as human examples of great spiritual genius? I know you participate in Zen rituals and lead some. Do you still find spiritual nourishment in the Catholic Mass?

KI: I've been attending Mass for some time now, owing entirely to a romantic involvement. I like the music. I really like singing. The preaching is usually not related to the Gospel and real life, even tangentially. I have not found the feeling of the liturgy or the sermons, as Karl Barth said, easily transferable into people's real lives (which he attributed to the celibacy of the clergy). After I began directing the *Exercises* with Bonnie, which I will talk about at more length later, I went to All Saints in Palo Alto with her. I have to say that the presence of women priests softened the liturgy and brought lots of heart. Both the priests in Palo Alto had remarkable singing voices; so the sung mass had an extremely lovely quality.

MZC: There're various expressions of Buddhism available to us today, with its great panoply of genuine teachers/teachings/compassion, in Mahayana, Theravadin, Zen, Vajrayana from the Tibetans. For me they all have added flavor to insight and the opening of my heart.

Would you say there's a common thread in all these traditions? I've asked other teachers, who most commonly say that it's in the Four Noble Truths: suffering (feeling dissatisfied, anguish); its foundation in inordinate desire and attachments; the truth of liberation from being enslaved by our desires/attachments/clinging; the practical way in living to know what's true and to be of loving, wise service to others, decent, kind behavior, acceptance of others and oneself in gratitude and taking the time to relax, reflect, meditate to cultivate both wisdom and one's own heart.

Also would you comment on how the teacher communicates with the student so he or she can "get" the Four Noble Truths? We acknowledge that the student-teacher relationship is—to avoid harm to ourselves and others—respectful of each one's human integrity. The teacher is a servant, not exploitive, as we've unfortunately seen in some Buddhist communities.

Catholic priests sexually-abusing kids also comes to mind. But dogmatic Buddhists, arrogant in their "rightness" are as much a pain in the ass (and dangerous) as dogmatic Muslims (gratefully, more dialoguing Muslims are speaking up) or dogmatic Catholics, Christians.

Luckily, as you say, Ken, we've had the opportunity to have had contact with some genuine articles, both in their practice of Buddhism and the ability to bring out our potential to begin understanding ourselves, most profoundly. And we can also, from our experience, say we've encountered true Muslim, Jewish, Christian and Catholic teachers. Would you tell us any stories with your teachers, Ken? Do you follow a particular school?

KI: I just met a woman teacher who is not well known at all. She said to me, "I have the stick." And she showed me, the symbol of her personal realization, which was recognized by her teacher in a venerable tradition. Yet she doesn't have a zendo—she talks to people who come and sit in her living room. She doesn't ask them whether or not they're Buddhists, whether they believe or not. She asks questions about their lives—not always the most comfortable questions, but they're good questions. They come from her experience, her love and, in particular, her practice dealing with her daughter's death and her own cancer.

She's really a wonderful woman who doesn't put much importance on "being Buddhist." But it's Buddhism, the real thing. Her teacher was a recognized Buddhist teacher and that "thread of something genuine" you mention is deeply felt. She approaches her life and the problems of life with a delicacy, full of the joy of living and taking each breath carefully, practicing meditation. She's able to express herself in a direct way, and you understand, stand in your own life more fully.

I don't know if she's teaching Zen, practicing Vipassana or whatever (well I do have some clues), although she can tell you a lot about various practices that she has personally done over the years. She's not coming from a dogmatic or institutional place. She's not trying to squeeze you into a particular practice. She's coming from the place of authentically living her life in such a way that's selfless. She is very willing to share that if one wants to ask her questions and talk, and then work with her. That's the way she's a guide and teacher. I like her way much more than any churchy Buddhism.

MZC: You know I teach in the public schools, so I'd like your advice as to what's important with working with young people. I've found that we all have some troubles and lose our ways. This can be observed in some of the students who have lost confidence and may even become bitter and self-destructive.

Yet in the midst of it, I'm usually blessed to see the goodness of the person of each student. Sometimes I can feel that these students don't see that basic goodness. You know, they don't see it. They feel they aren't good enough, smart enough, whatever. So—because I can truly feel their goodness crying to come out—I encourage them to experience their goodness and strength and potential within themselves, not to give up on themselves.

Chogyam Trunpa was the first Buddhist teacher I heard speaking about our basic goodness, "the primordial dot, that spark of goodness that exists even before you think." He would describe how one could overcome our habitual tendencies, which keep us from experiencing an "unconditioned possibility of cheerfulness."

KI: I've never had your good luck to teach youngsters, so I have no idea what you really face. But I'm reminded of the title of one of Bob Aitkin's books, *Encouraging Words*. As teachers, hell, as humans, we need to get past the judgmental, critical, overly comparing attitudes with our students. Kids are great. That inner enthusiasm is evident. A general observation: I see many people, the professionals, trying to overly specialize, direct the innate drive to learn, or stultify it or correct it or channel it to someone else's goals. Just encourage it. I hear folks my age saying that young people are failing in this way or another, the same as, I'm sure, the parents-teachers of young people said in the time of Buddha and Jesus.

MZC: So the heart and soul of meditation is in the *practice* of it, in that vital, personal place. In what way do you think that a teacher is important in your practice and do you think it is possible to practice Buddhism without a teacher?

KI: I don't know for certain, but I think we need a teacher. I do. Maybe the community, the *sangha*, can also function as a teacher. The teacher prevents you from entering into a solipsistic world where your own thoughts justify your obsessions, attachments and prejudices.

Part of being in conversation with someone about your meditation comes from the basic understanding that we are not separate. You're entering deeply into yourself in meditation only to enter into communication with the world in a completely different way. The teacher is your feedback, to point to the questions that are behind your questions. I've tried to invite my teachers into my life so I can ask questions which mean the world to me, which unlock my life, which make me an open and caring human being, which allow the Dharma to come alive in me. It's not so the teacher or *sangha* can give you a truth that exists outside of yourself. It's not so they can hand a dogma to you. It's to enter into a real conversation, so that you can begin to explore for yourself at a completely different level.

MZC: Ken, would you say something about your work in the hospice and with dying people?

KI: I think I started off trying to work with dying people, but they ended up working on me. You know the first thing that you become aware of when you work with people who have a grave diagnosis, and who are close to death, is that metaphysical considerations tend to fall away. Am I going to be around as a spirit in another world? What is going to happen to me after death? When that kind of thinking fades out, the real selves and the real concerns start to surface. "I want to clean up my relationship with my family before I die. I want to make peace with my bitchy old boyfriend; I want to die in clean sheets."

Dying is natural; we can't fight it, although medicine tries. The process of nature takes over, and the body begins to shut down. You just help someone deal with the physical pain and circumstances that he or she can't control any longer. Physiological mechanisms that govern the functions of living are shutting down so you assist others to give up trying to control it or stop it. I found that I really have to be present without any of my own agendas.

What's the question behind our questions about dying? Does it mean: how can I do something of value in my life? I will struggle with that until my time comes. For me it seems that I never think I do enough and certainly not do it well enough. I will probably be dealing with that in some form all my life.

MZC: How do you relate our deepest desires with our spiritual practice? Some Buddhists, like all of us, seem to confuse being stoical with being non-attached. I like the way St. Ignatius phrases it, "inordinate attachment." I personally think desires are good, wholesome, but get "off the mark" when we are clinging too much, inordinately wanting, hanging on to some pleasure or experience. Isn't part of meditation's possible fruit, the revelation of what we truly desire? Jesus said he came to make life full, to be full of life. Buddha too is presented as full, energetic, happy, and humorous. Yet how is it some Buddhists teach a negation of desire?

KI: Morgan, you'll have to ask them (laughing). Oh, I've read the texts too, and the word that I see often is "extinguish" as in put out a fire. I don't know the Sanskrit or Pali that is being translated, but I get the idea of putting out a fire before it burns you and destroys all you hold close to your heart.

But in my own practice, I think it was important for me to get away from treating, for example, my sexuality as something that I had to negate. It gets a little sticky here—it just might be me, or my penis, not wanting to take a back seat.

I too really think that Ignatius expresses more closely in English what I think is meant by non-attachment. It was that puritanical Irish Catholic training that I had to distance myself from in order to begin to see my sexuality for what it is, not something evil that had to be negated.

I have one last comment here, and that is that in my experience "extinguishing" is more like disappearing. One day I might be in a situation that might have fanned the flames of desire a while back and this time nothing happens. I didn't consciously try to negate or suppress anything, yet something is very different and I can't explain it. I don't feel trapped or confined or driven. That is just a suggestion of a place to begin to look after you've been meditating for a while.

MZC: It seems our expectations of how it's all supposed to be (including Buddhism) gets us into clinging and "inordinate" attachments. Suzuki roshi writes: "If your mind is empty, it is always ready for anything. It is open to everything. The beginner's mind is always appropriate. In the beginner's mind there are many possibilities. In the expert's mind, there are few. When your mind become demanding, when you long for something too much, you will end up violating your own precepts, not to tell lies, not to steal, not to kill, not to be immoral and so forth. Yet if you keep your original mind, the precepts will keep themselves."

KI: This is so simple and direct. Suzuki expressed a key Buddhist teaching in beginner's mind. It became the heart of Suzuki's teaching, at least in popular culture, and Issan learned it well—just to see what's so and then open to infinite possibilities.

MZC: The last three nights I've stayed up late to read *Street Zen*, which moved me to tears and an appreciation for the life and work of Issan Dorsey. I never met Issan, though I heard so much about him. Your taking me, Ken, to Maitri Hospice in San Francisco was all the more meaningful to me, knowing that Issan was the founder of Maitri. What did you learn from Issan and how did he manage to be such a genuine teacher amidst such a wild life?

Reading about Issan recalled to mind, Suzuki roshi and Baker roshi from the San Francisco Zen Center. My first superficial Zen was from '69 to '71 while a teacher at Bellarmine High School in San Jose. I met Suzuki roshi, sat a few times and listened to talks. I read his book, *Beginner's Mind*.

I did meet Baker roshi later on; a friend went through the crisis time with Baker. She was very upset with Baker—"Roshi was secretive." I'm afraid I was a bit judgmental towards some of the teachers' sexual improprieties. But I feel some of the criticisms of Baker and other Dharma teachers were warranted. The few times I did see Baker and his entourage, I felt there was a cultic quality to the "theater." Also I felt some of the members were burnt out doing Temple business projects. It was too damned organized and harried for me.

KI: Of course the criticism was warranted and necessary. I don't know whether or not Baker lied about his affairs, but he gave the impression he did, and you don't harm the Three Treasures of the Teaching, the Community, the Buddha. But when is enough enough?

I have various opinions about the dalliances of various teachers at various times. Nothing is set in stone, but at least I hope we can get away from our puritanical upbringing. There are few real saints and most of them are suspect anyway. Nomination for sainthood, as you know, has a very political side anyway. So we have teachers who do their best and are human beings. Most that I've known have functioning sexual apparatus. Certainly Issan did.

Phil Whalen always urged me to go practice with Dick

Baker. And I tried, doing several sesshins at Crestone in the San Luis Valley. He is a formidable guy. The continuing life of scandal surrounding Dick is really, I think, a kind of smoke screen that hinders people from engaging life as it presents itself.

MZC: I was aware Jerry Brown was friends with Baker. Jerry was all over the place, an intense spiritual seeker, even when he was the governor. Jerry once went to Adi Da's commune; I saw him at a seminar with Thich Nhat Hanh.

KI: Jerry Brown used to sit sometimes with John Tarrant's group; he even opened his home in Oakland to the group. He worked with Yamada Roshi in Kamakura. Kamakura was where most of the Jesuits who practiced Zen did their work: LaSalle, Johnston, Hand, Kennedy, Kadawaki, even Arrupe.

MZC: Would you expand upon why you like Rinzai practice?

KI: The particular school that I practice with at the moment, Robert Aitken is the American source, is a combination of Rinzai and Soto practice. His Japanese teachers received *inka*, transmission, in both the Soto tradition and the Rinzai tradition. Soto is known for practicing *shikantaza*, sitting, just sitting. The great teachers of the Rinzai school—at least the modern version of it in Japan—felt people needed some grit for meditation, the "something" of koan practice. In Rinzai you sit with a koan and work with a teacher in terms of understanding and demonstrating the answer to the koan.

But the Soto sect uses koans also. They're just not as close to the surface and you may work on them from time to time with your teacher. The connection and communication with your teacher during *sesshin,* or the long sittings, is not as intense in Soto practice as it is in Rinzai practice where you'll see the teacher as many as two or three times during the day; in Soto, we may see a teacher once or twice during seven days.

MZC: What have you been learning lately from John Tarrant? I just finished reading John's article for *Shambala Sun*

(July 2007) magazine and he writes about how powerful it can be to work with a koan, to let the koan be with you all through the day. What's your experience with working with a koan? I imagine that using a koan might be helpful for some and not as fruitful for others. What do you find useful in having a koan?

KI: You like to hear the teaching stories of Jesus either read or meditated on? As if you are hearing them for the first time. Or maybe you don't. I did at one time and then it became just about the commentaries and Biblical scholarship that took all the juice out of them. Koans are juicy teaching stories that point to some aspect of Buddha mind. The word koan means something like "public case," an encounter between teacher and student, Buddha and student, Buddha and Bodhisattva that became a teaching tool, and has traveled a written and oral path to an encounter between you and your teacher in one moment of present time. There is commentary, poetry or more stories or another teacher's notes. Only sometimes helpful in terms of getting a right answer. That, getting a right answer, just leads me to more mind numbing encounters with the questions that I had had all my life. John and the people he trained, Rachel Howlett, Daniel Terrango, David Weinstein, started to show me a different way to use them. Tom Marshall, a Jesuit brother whom we both know, had a big influence on my use of koans. The stories themselves are not, as they are sometimes portrayed, puzzles or mind numbing mental gymnastics designed to cut off normal discursive thinking and open up Buddha mind. Well they may do that, but I have found them to be a source of really experiencing the Teaching of the Buddha and the ancestors right here and now.

MZC: You recently gave the *Spiritual Exercises* of St. Ignatius. What was that like? Can you compare Ignatian and Zen meditation? What's the difference between Ignatian "inordinate attachment" and Buddhist "non-clinging, non-attachment"?

KI: Daniel Shurman, an old friend from Claudio Naranjo's group, called me and asked what book he should get for his wife, Bonnie Johnson, who wanted to do the *Exercises* when she went into the isolation ward at Stanford Medical Center for chemotherapy. She had just received a very grave diagnosis of leukemia. I told him that of course I would recommend a text but that usually one had a director for the *Exercises*. His response was very straightforward: "When can you begin?"

Bonnie had a total miracle when we did the *Exercises* (I still don't really believe it). I hadn't even really looked at them in fifteen years or longer. But when she asked to do the *Exercises*, I made a decision that I would give her the *Exercises* exactly as Ignatius wrote them. Everything, the fire of Hell in the first week right though. If she had any problems with what was presented, and she did, it always took place in what Ignatius calls a state of recollection. What resulted was her understanding. I don't think that I am skilled enough to accomplish that simply by changing the language. I wouldn't know where to begin actually, and why would I be that arrogant to rewrite Ignatius. But after years of meditation, I can talk to someone about his or her inner experience. That was basically what I did, leave my opinions at the door, present the *Exercises* as exactly as I could, and listen to what Bonnie (and I, and her husband) experienced.

MZC: I admire—as you—the Japanese teacher, Nyogen Senzaki (1876–1958), a painter and poet also. He came here to Los Angeles, Japantown and was one of Robert Aitken's teachers. Two of my favorite poems are his:

early in the morning
in the western sky
one star blinks at me
I love its green light.

~

As a wanderer in this strange land forty-two years,
I commemorate my teacher each autumn.
Now, on the sixth floor of this hotel,
He gazes at me as severely as ever
"How is the work, Awkward One?" He might be saying
to me.
"America has Zen all the time, why, my Teacher, should
I meddle?"

KI: God, that's so fabulous (weeping). I'm incredibly moved by this man's life. Think of him, teaching *zazen* after work as a dishwasher in a little walk up apartment in Los Angeles.

Robert Aitken told me Nyogen Senzaki started practicing seriously in the '40s. Bob was in a concentration camp in Japan and Senzaki was in a US internment camp for Americans of Japanese ancestry. After Bob went back to Hawaii, he started working with Senzaki in Los Angeles. When Senzaki got home at the end of the day after washing dishes in a Japanese restaurant, he'd set up folding chairs and he'd give basic meditation instruction. I think that he also worked with some people on the koans. It was a beginning of the *dharma* opening up in our country. He did many jobs in America, a caretaker and a housekeeper, unfolding chairs three flights up in Los Angeles. God bless him.

MZC: Maybe this is a good place to end, for now.

KI: Yes, and thank you Morgan.

Zen Is Eternal Life
A Conversation with Jiyu-Kennett Roshi
1983: Santa Barbara, California

I was lucky that Jiyu-Kennet Roshi agreed to an interview after one of her talks at the Santa Barbara Zen Priory where she was leading a weekend of recollection, talks and meditation, specifically for Catholics interested in Buddhism. She spoke from time to time and we practiced sitting meditation, zazen. We followed our breath and were encouraged to surrender to the moment. She took most of her talks from her book, Zen is Eternal Life, *which urges us "to be with," and to practice meditation and a loving life, which leads to touching the "Eternal."*

She was a large presence, on the surface a bit grouchy, but underneath I found a twinkly wisdom and a heart, loving and warm. She had this harrumphety demeanor and a somewhat cool response to me when I asked to sit down with her. I kidded her about the loud construction that was going on during her lectures, which annoyed her ("I wish they'd stop that loud noise," she said a few times. "It's interesting that they asked us to be quiet, that's all.") She softened and she agreed to an interview. During lectures, she was at times exasperated, saying "I can never read my own writing," as she was writing on the chalkboard. I liked the way that she laughed out loud which seemed to bring her face to life. Also I sensed some deep sadness in her (as if her heart were irrevocably broken as with perhaps all of us).

She said: "O.K. Begin your questions." Her complaints about noise during her talks were minor compared to her intense inquiry about Zen. She communicated a dedicated commitment to Zen teachings as she interpreted them from her own teachers. She was at the same time, strong and imposing, and also imbued with vulnerability and a hard-won wisdom. Kennet Roshi was a sincere teacher with a "no nonsense" presence. I was able finally to be relaxed with her, which I appreciate to this day.

MZC: What is Buddhism for you? What was its attraction

for you, a young lady in England, who would later go to the Japanese Soto Zen Soji-ji Monastery ('62-'68) to study and practice with your teacher Koho Zenji for whom you have such admiration and affection, and then founded Mount Shasta Monastery in '71 in Northern California?

How did you come to understand the Buddhist teachings regarding the cultivation of insight and wisdom, founded in moral and character development, heart-connected in compassion? And secondly, you are offering this retreat for Catholics and many Catholics tend to shy away from Buddhism as "atheist."

Would you clarify for us Buddhism's purpose and heart, which you said in your talk, is "to find the Eternal," an aspiration appreciated by us Catholics who are theists? This idea of the Eternal is consoling to my sense of a deep Presence in life, what Einstein called "a benign, intelligence within the Wonder of the universe."

KR: Yes, it is the being intimate with the Eternal that both attracts me and puts my own practice into perspective, even with the incredibly varying expressions of Buddhism. I acknowledge that some Buddhists teachers don't agree with me.

When I was first studying Buddhism, I was the "lady in white tennis shoes" who was always asking "dumb" questions. Yet I discovered they were questions everyone wanted to ask. I really wanted to understand what it's all about. I continue to have that attitude of not getting attached to Buddhist doctrine by asking questions that have some element of challenging the status quo. I'm a bit of a rebel still, but I don't need to be convinced any more of the basic teachings.

You are a Catholic, yet there are significant places where we can meet in our two traditions, as well as acknowledge our theological-philosophical-ritual differences. So I will start by quoting an ancient *sutra*, attributed to Buddha shortly after his own experiential finding of the Eternal: "O monks, there is an Unborn, Undying, Unchanging, Uncreated. If this were not true, there would be no point to life and no point to our training and practice." This is the nearest Buddhism comes to God; it is the "apophatic" way of stating that there *is* something, as opposed to the "cataphatic" way which gives specifics of what that Reality is. You can find these verses in the earliest Pali Canon; its English translation can be found on page 33 of *The Buddhist Bible* by Dwight Goddard.

Negatively, we say that the great Reality is not changing, not dying, not being born, not being created; so we are far from being atheists. Some Buddhists call it "the deathless." Zen just refuses to say what it doesn't know for sure and encourages people to find out for themselves rather than rely on doctrine, including Buddhist doctrine. I don't like the word enlightenment; I like the phrase, "finding the Eternal." I call this the beginning point of Soto Zen. We don't take refuge in some personal deity, but rather in the Eternal, in what the Eternal teaches us, in those who know the Eternal.

MZC: Yes, thanks for conveying that we are in this together, as Buddhists and Catholics; I appreciate being with you here in Santa Barbara.

I've been adjusting my own notion of sin, both original and personal, from observing the possibility that we can experience great potential for love in ourselves and others, by not covering up this potential with all our thinking and hurtfulness. I know you speak of moral precepts, which we, Catholics, also try to embrace as essential to spiritual practice, along with our prayer, worship, meditation, reflection, service.

May I review meditatively with you the Five Precepts? Don't kill; don't steal; don't practice hurtful sexual practices; don't lie; don't abuse intoxicants—expressed positively as, may I practice compassion, generosity, sexual responsibility, truthfulness and listening, and mindful consumption? How do the Buddhist precepts relate to meditation? What is the purpose of meditation?

KR: Yes. There's a famous Buddhist scripture, which says that the most important human challenge is to understand birth, life and death completely. Life and death should not be avoided but embraced, lived, met completely; being detached does not mean being disinterested, above it all, not caring. We usually turn to religion because of our fear of death and our fear of life, of living vibrantly. As I often say, I feel we are more afraid of living than of dying. We contract and cut ourselves off from feeling the life within us. The purpose of meditation is to find the Eternal in both life and death. We then taste the freedom of being free from those fears. We become full of life. We meditate in the tradition of the Buddha to become one with the Eternal. Buddha's teaching can be used by any religion, including by Catholics. We practice the precepts in order to have the peacefulness necessary to actually sit down and have meaningful meditations. We then get glimpses of the Eternal, what Daisetz Suzuki Roshi called "the little moments that make one dance."

MZC: You relate all the precepts to eliminating violence. Would you expand upon this admirable reason for keeping the precepts?

KR: You teach yourself to refrain from killing, stealing, lying, abusing intoxicants, and misbehaving sexually. We do this for our own peace of mind, which is a necessary condition for us to realize the Eternal, which I've sometimes called "Cosmic Buddha." If we break the precepts, we cut ourselves off from our own peace of mind. We steal our own inner tranquility. We keep and honor the precepts not to judge ourselves; it's not moralistic. Each precept is truly against violence to others and ourselves. We avoid the causes of our fears by honoring the precepts in our daily living. I told you the story of how when I was studying in Japan, I told my teacher I thought the precepts should be about "others and self" rather than about "self and others." My teacher told me to go sit and think about it. I hadn't fully grasped that I couldn't help others without "refraining from" all forms of violence to myself. I would learn that we have to create peace with ourselves, to love ourselves if you will, and then we would not be afraid to act, to speak, to be of help to others. But the starting point isn't "others."

MZC: Catholics also might say: "Love your neighbor as yourself." We can't love others without a reverence and cherishing of our own selves. I also think the purpose of practicing my religion is to understand life and death.

KR: Life and death themselves will be found to be *Nirvana*, with your sincere involvement. Practice and taste for yourself. If we find the Eternal in life and death, then we are no longer so afraid. Even death is another moment in the Now. Life becomes a sharing in the Eternal and that's why we meditate—to stay in that beautiful, peaceful place with the Eternal. That's why we strengthen our ability to concentrate and to discipline ourselves to be morally straight. The kingdom of heaven is within each of us. Since we've found this peace beyond our inner terror, we can help address the problems we face as a human community.

This teaching can be used by you, as a Catholic, or by one from any religion or without a religion, because we're talking essences of what great religion is, rather than all the "isms" themselves. Buddhism does not require any doctrine. Prove it true for your self.

Your questioning of sin is an instructive example. In Buddhism we say, "Refrain from," not "You shall not." Your unskillful intentions, speech, and actions are covering up the original ability to discover the Undying for yourself. You do not, in our view, have some outside God giving you a commandment, but you find out that if you do good, refrain from being hurtful, greedy, jealous and mean, you will then know a peace and happiness.

You only let yourself and others down if you break a precept; but you don't feel shame and guilt before a God. You just dust yourself off and start to practice again; you don't feel a fear of a supreme being who will condemn and punish and judge you. You yourself carry the consequences. That's the meaning of karma.

MZC: Would you summarize some of the practical instructions you've been giving about meditation? In our hectic lives, we don't seem to always be able to do a daily meditation practice.

KR: None of us seems to be able to always follow an exact schedule for meditation. However, we can do our best to have a regular practice. When I was in Japan, we could not always stick to our meditation schedule. We just do our best, with the intention to keep at it, to cultivate the practice of meditation.

I was telling you all that meditation is just "properly done prayer." You hold your mind still; you want to be one with the Eternal. You wash your face before you sit, as it's important to have a sense of freshness. You choose a quiet room or place. You don't want to be in too small a room, as you want the feeling "I can expand." You allow your eyes to naturally focus on a point on the floor or wall. If you wear glasses, you can keep them on. You want to be as normal as possible. We usually sit about one meter from the wall; we find that sixty-five to seventy degrees is an agreeable temperature and that early morning or early evening are the best times. We use a candle or an electric candle in a carpeted room, which should not be too dark or too bright. I suggest you don't give yourself an unpleasant experience of meditation as a beginner. We don't want you shouting "ouch!" Later, you'll be able to adapt to all sort of conditions, which in your beginning practice would be intolerable.

You choose an appropriate sitting cushion (*zafu*), adapted to your weight and height. The bigger you are, the smaller and better stuffed your cushion should be. All these instructions should not be taken as absolute blueprints. What's right for one is not right for another. We want to find the Eternal. This is not an endurance test. We want to find that which makes us lose our fear from being full of life. Usually we sit cross-legged with our spines straight, but not ramrod. Feel your head as weightless as possible. Let your head sit naturally on your shoulders and your hands and arms relaxed. There is no one way. Some sit on chairs, also erect, but not rigid and tense. Some need to even lie down on the floor and that can be perfectly legitimate. I've known elderly people who do very well with this lying, "corpse" pose.

You take two or three deep breaths to clear the passages and then you breathe naturally. You sit in the peaceful feeling of being with the Eternal. We keep our eyes partially open, because when our eyes are shut, we might get caught up in shapes that form in our imagination. At a later time, roughly after three or four years of meditating, visions might come that are genuine. Of course, again, all of us are different. When your eyes are partially open, such visions can't be imagined on the back of your eyelids. But even visions, yogic experiences and the like are not what are important. Zen is the touching of Eternal Life. Read *Zen Is Eternal Life* to get a deeper feeling of my meaning.

MZC: Would you say something about what characterizes Soto Zen?

KR: Soto Zen is the oldest school of Zen. Rinzai and Obaku Zen broke off from Soto around the tenth century. Soto was founded by Bodhidharma who brought Buddhism to China from India. Soto was founded in Japan by Dogen and propagated by Kaizan. That's the lineage we are following in our temple in Mount Shasta. I suggest you read about these on your own if you are interested. Although the actions and rituals in Soto and Rinzai may differ, their aims are the same, namely to gain the liberation of all fear of life and death by realizing the Unborn, Undying within life and death themselves.

Soto says that if given a koan, we can share it with others, so we can help each other. Rinzai says only share your koan with your Master. I personally believe the great teachers were artists and, whether Soto or Rinzai, they'd adapt what's best for their individual students.

Let's stop. Hope I've answered some of your questions. Come visit us at Mount Shasta.

MZC: Thanks. Many blessings to you and your students in Mount Shasta. Yes, your words are very helpful and also inspirational for me to practice meditating more earnestly.

The Path of No-seeking
My Five Years Working with Franklin Jones
Morgan Zo-Callahan

> *Death is utterly acceptable to consciousness and life.*
> *There has been endless time of numberless deaths, but*
> *neither consciousness nor life has ceased to arise. The felt*
> *quantity and cycle to death has not modified the fragility*
> *of flowers, even the flowers within our human body.*
> *Therefore, our understanding of consciousness and life*
> *must be turned to the utter, inclusive quality, that clarity*
> *and wisdom, that power and untouchable gracefulness*
> *this evidence suggests.*
>
> —Franklin Jones, *The Knee of Listening*

In 1972 I became aware of Franklin Jones, and by 1973, I was his student. I was graced with, or maybe just lucked into, an intense five-year relationship with Franklin as my spiritual teacher. (Franklin was later known as Bubba Free John, and, by the last time I saw him in 1979, Master Adi Da). He died on November 27, 2008. I was, and remain, truly grateful for this gift. This is the story of my experience as his student, my leave-taking and re-visiting, some reflections of what later happened within Master Da's community, and what my experience taught me about the relationship of a spiritual seeker to his or her teacher. I am certain that my life today is quite different than it might have been because of my experience with Da, and I will conclude by trying to say how and why that is so.

It was the late 60s and early 70s, and so many of us were searching like crazy to be in touch with what our lives were about and how we might bring our fullest life to the world community. For me it was a time of great turmoil, both personally and socially. All of us were being torn apart over the war in Vietnam. The answers proclaimed by the religions of our fathers and mothers no longer satisfied. This was the age of Be Here Now, Black Power, Women's Rights, Gay Rights, Brown Rights, and Native American Spirit based religion. Theologies of "Preference for the Poor," and Latin American "Liberation Theology" were emerging.

I had been in the Jesuits for nine years, from 1962 to 1971, mostly great years, meaningful, fruitful, not-without-shadows, ever-continually-influencing-me. The Jesuits had made my life fuller, offered me opportunities and challenges to grow spiritually, to serve the poor, to learn meditation, to receive a wonderful education, and to enjoy the company of my fellow Jesuits, a very bright, varied and dedicated group of men.

I'd never been entirely separated from the Jesuits since I was an adolescent, yet by 1971, I didn't want to be a Jesuit any longer. They would have to find their way without me. I felt that Catholic groups, including the Jesuits, were falling apart, doubting them. I was very put off by the body-sex negativity in the Catholic Church, the teaching that human beings are born in original sin that we're naturally bad. (Of course, the church increases its power through the rituals of forgiveness to erase that inherent sinfulness—forgiveness for something we aren't in the first place). Some Jesuits lived "double lives," being sexually intimate while putting on a celibate face. Others, including myself, were suffering the "horny celibate" syndrome.

At age 26, I left the Jesuits, and became a community organizer with the Jesuit Volunteer Corp to Xalapa, Mexico. Living with the American Jesuits there for a year allowed me a healthy separation from the Order and showed me a way to stay fully involved with activist projects without being a Jesuit. After this year, I decided to slow down and respond to the exploding echoes coming from the 60s–70s Eastern infiltration. I decided to "drop out" for as long as it took, be a hippie and spiritual seeker outside the Catholic tradition.

There were so many drums calling me. It was time for me

to tap into other resources for spiritual growth. I was being pulled from the warring West to the blissed-out East.

■

In 1972, I was teaching a course at New College in Sausalito, California, on Comparative Religion: The *Spiritual Exercises* of St. Ignatius, Buddhism and Indian meditation. Alan Watt's "rockin'" houseboat was also moored in Sausalito, and, through a fortuitous series of circumstances, I met Alan. We liked each other immediately. He invited me to his parties, and later, I became part of the group that would gather on the houseboat or in his forest retreat at the foot of Mount Tamalpais. It was a time of incredible conversation, meandering all over the spiritual landscape, plus lots of shenanigans.

Alan was the greatest lecturer and most entertaining speaker I ever encountered. I went to as many of his lectures as I could. He told fantastic stories of leading tours to Japanese Buddhist temples and monasteries. He was fascinating, alive, and quick, with roaring humor and a sharp mind and twinkling eyes; he was an artistic, sensual person and "popular" scholar, conversant in so many areas, including Tai Chi, architecture, music, art; but it was Zen that he (along with Suzuki Roshi) introduced to me, in a rudimentary though very meaningful way.

Alan introduced me to the concept of "non-effort" in spiritual practice. He said that the release of all our spiritual seeking is an experiential realization in the Zen tradition. He would tell, with great pizzazz, stories of Zen teachers who would frustrate students into giving up all their effort and just surrender to the moment. They would ask the student "to figure out who you are, before you were somebody." "Just get up and dance. Stop thinking so much."

Alan insisted on some irreverence to counter-balance our precious methods and teachers of the spiritual life. We can appreciate our teachers, our rituals, our prayer and meditation without getting so attached to them that we forget to find our true selves. He had a quality of being a wise rascal who sometimes enjoyed the bawdy aspects of life, excessive, yet in the midst of that, still a teacher. There was a time to celebrate and a time to be sober. In the year I knew him, Alan always seemed to be partying and without any regrets. He had a very generous heart and also, like all of us, his own "demons." I loved being with Alan.

Alan taught that you can't even try to let go, as we if could decide, "OK, I'm going to completely surrender to life." He was like a pied piper trying to get us to see the realty of our situation, to have a meditation practice. He said meditation would lead to deep intuitions that we are not separate from one another or from our world; that we don't need to go anywhere or achieve anything to attain what we think we want or need to be enlightened. He taught us about Vipassana insight meditation where we grasp the implications of change and death, "nothing to attain." No need for seeking. Alan said that the opening of one's heart and intelligence, already experienced within an individual with deep confidence, undermines the search from the beginning. It's all right, all of it; no need to chase spiritual snake oil.

Alan asked us to try different forms of meditation, but he seemed most partial to Zen. It was a time, even more seriously than when I was in the Jesuits, where I began looking at the reality of my personal situation, my way of living, my intentions, my deepest desires, even my deep-rooted "hang ups." He taught that with intuition, understanding, with the opening of one's heart, we would see there's no need to search beyond our personal situations. We are presently living. We are full within ourselves, ever-co-related with others. Alan quoted what Ramana Maharshi said: devotions to spiritual teachers or traditions, practices, recitations, meditations, readings, serve their purpose when you don't need them anymore.

As Wei Wu Wei says: "Disciples and devotees.... What are most of them doing? Worshipping the teapot instead of drinking the tea!"

Alan was a great academic teacher, but I was looking for a practical spiritual Master. I heard Alan speak of Franklin Jones' *The Knee of Listening*, as an excellent presentation of the idea that all our seeking outside of ourselves is unsatisfactory because "it's already the case that you are living in God." Alan often said that we all tended to think we weren't already all right, already enlightened, and that it was our seeking, our sometimes anguished, scattered effort, that kept us separated from who we are, if we would just be ourselves. Later I would hear Franklin quote Ramana Maharshi, "Liberation is getting rid of non-existent misery and attaining the Bliss which is always there ... in the Heart."

Alan wanted to check out Franklin Jones for himself, which I think would have been mutually enriching for them, but Alan died on November 16, 1973 and never had that opportunity.

■

I visited a bookstore on Melrose Avenue in Hollywood, run by Franklin's community, to buy the book that Alan had recommended. There was a big picture of Franklin in the front of the bookstore, which was a turn off, but I found Franklin's autobiography and initial teachings about meditation and Eastern and Western religious wisdom, very compelling. Alan wrote in his introduction to a later edition: "To say what Franklin Jones is trying to say is like drawing an asymptotic curve, a curve which is always getting nearer to a straight line, but only touches it at infinity ... he has simply realized that he himself as he is, like a star, like a dolphin, like an iris, is a perfect and authentic manifestation of the eternal energy of the universe, and thus is no longer disposed to be in conflict with himself."

From Franklin's book, and from some of his unpublished notes, I found out about Franklin's background and his own seeking for the "removal of internal contradictions or the mutual alternatives that enforce kinds of experience, the pattern of seeking and of conflict." (*The Knee of Listening*, p. 17). His personal journey fascinated me and called to me. He had spoken out in the 50s and 60s against the injustice towards African Americans in America. In 1962, he had been a volunteer for psychedelic drug experiment at the Veteran's Administration Hospital in Mountain View, California. During a six-week period, he ingested mescaline, psilocybin, and LSD, separately for three sessions and one session combining the three hallucinogens. Alan Watts similarly in the late 50s experienced LSD*; when asked about LSD, Alan said: "When you've got the message, hang up the phone." After ingesting the drugs, Franklin had various *kundalini* experiences, which made him feel more conscious, alive and loving. The force of energies moved upwards from the base of his spine through the "centers" (*chakras*) exactly as described in ancient Kundalini Yoga texts. When Franklin felt this intensely tangible energy in his heart, he was overcome with emotion and wept. Franklin said he also re-connected with some experiences he had in childhood seizures resulting from illness.

As Alan, Franklin would leave hallucinogens. "Like any other stage in my life, it came to the end of its serviceable use, and at that point I abandoned it." (*The Knee of Listening*, p. 22) Later, he would be convinced by Jung that a part of our consciousness is free from death, an awareness, a spirit, free from the limitations of body, a disembodied, yet aware soul that was immortal. He was struck by Jung's reports of out-of-body, conscious experiences that happened to some of his patients. Such patients reported looking down on their bodies and being aware of what was happening in the room.

Franklin would write: "This passage from Jung signified in me a liberation from mortal philosophy and all bondage to the form of death" (*The Knee of Listening*, p. 34). [Recent scientific research has shown that "out of body" experiences can be induced by running a current through a part of the brain, as well as arising from other conditions, and doesn't imply a spirit apart from the body.]

In 1964, Franklin started a three and a half year practice of Sidda Yoga with Rudi, Swami Rudrananda, who taught Kundalini Yoga out of his Asian antique store in New York's Greenwich Village as well as a retreat center in the Catskills. Rudi had worked with both Swami Nityananda and Swami Muktananda, and continued their practice of discipline and self-surrender by concentrating on the form of the guru (a method Franklin would give his own students, but one I didn't always find helpful). Rudi encouraged Franklin to enter a Christian seminary where he studied theology and biblical languages. Franklin also worked with the methodology of Scientology before going to India to be Swami Muktananda's disciple.

After reading *The Knee of Listening*, I started to think that I wanted to become Franklin's student later on, if the conditions were right. I continued the rest of 1972 learning from Alan and also from the seminars of Ram Dass. I would sometimes visit the Zen Center in San Francisco, but I missed Suzuki Roshi, and no longer felt that it was my practice place.

* Alan was initially introduced to mescaline by Dr. Oscar Janiger. He experimented with hallucinogens several times with Drs. Keith Ditman, Sterling Bunnell, and Michael Agron.

■

Franklin Jones accepted me as his student in 1973, and I began a five-year period of work and study with him. I felt a natural connection with Franklin, yet it was with some fear and trepidation that I immersed myself in a student-teacher relationship and in living communally. There was some sense of struggle on this quest for "no struggle" and "no seeking," but the early years with Franklin were, for me, a spectacular time of learning, observing myself, becoming aware of my own distracting mind and clenched heart, and being able to touch "inner goodness."

When I say, "being accepted as Franklin's student," I mean I accepted him as a mutual relationship, as my spiritual master in a most human sense, one who is psychologically mature as well as spiritually adept. I can say I was never Franklin's devotee, though I was a serious student, in what I considered an adult though vulnerable relationship. I refused to become subservient to a spiritual master who makes himself or herself a god and whose followers say, "We're the only ones who know the answer," and I never felt that Franklin demanded that of me in order to be his student.

My time with Franklin was a long spiritual retreat, not completely calm, also a chaotic whirlwind of trying out new ways of thinking and living in a community. I was fully and happily involved during my time with Franklin, and yet I felt Franklin's community was "nothing special." He taught hatha, pranayama and Sidda yoga, and communicated this Eastern wisdom in Western terms. He stimulated the light within us. I accepted his authority to teach, passed to him through Swami Nityananda and Swami Muktananda, and I felt fortunate to work in an authentic Siddha Yoga tradition. He revered and respected his teachers, but didn't make them an object of worship.

There were long hours in the meditation hall, many spontaneous periods of meditation, both in the company of Franklin and alone. It was a time for late night spiritual conversations about God, about health, diet, sex, community living, children, education, and learning from the various great religious traditions. We, as a community, allowed ourselves to grow into an intimate relationship. There were sumptuous meals, but also fasts, times for detoxifying. And there were times when we mingled in the baths and pools, fooled around in the water, singing, listening to Stevie Wonder music, smoking cigarettes and drinking beer. But I also remember many more times during this period of meditating in the steaming mineral waters, giving each other massages, doing various yoga practices, including tantric yoga; being naked, both physically and psychologically, with intimate friends.

Even if at times we were all, including Franklin, drunken fools, Franklin always taught. He was having a ball, laughing and joking, but also engaging individuals very directly, stimulating our intelligence as well as our hearts, intensifying the student's native ability to conduct the life-force and to rest the mind in the heart, as Pantanjali taught: "Let your mind fall into your heart," breathing that realization, breathing the deepest peace within us, bringing life and love to oneself, extending that outwards to all others and to our environment.

Most important to me were my conversations with Franklin. They were direct and personal. I'd enjoy their free flow. Eventually I'd come to know and call Franklin "Bubba" or brother. It was a very engaging friendship, with lots of give and take. He had an ability to inquire in conversation, in a non-dogmatic way, and was adept at getting to the questions behind the questions, addressing my real needs.

In the beginning, Franklin would say, "no beads, no bowing, no incense … just relationship." He asked his students to be free of drugs, to work, to study and meditate, and to live responsibly in their relationships. For my part I focused on staying in relationship to him. I was also very fond of him and enjoyed his company which made that very easy. Franklin was always open to answer my real questions at the time. Since I had a physiotherapy license, Franklin invited me to be with him many times, to give him massages or to do some "body work" techniques with him, such as from the Alexander technique, or movements from Dr. Rudolph Stone and Dr. Robert Hall.

I feel so fortunate Franklin allowed me to learn with him. I felt Franklin's whole agenda was to wake me up, to push me to pay attention to my heart, to be intelligent and actively find out what's important to me, as I live my tiny-timed life. He was a Mr. Gurdjieff who shook up my "programmed" way of living.

Bubba would sit in meditation with us, much as in the Indian-guru tradition of sitting with a teacher whose presence is "felt-in-the-heart" and who communicates directly—with grace, not effort—to the student. Bubba's meditation hall was spiritually and tangibly charged, and I could easily enter into deep states and spontaneously relax in graceful conductivity generated in the company of the teacher. Some people had *kriyas* (spontaneous shaking, movements of the body), blisses, crying, screaming, moaning, talking in tongues; some had "out of body" experiences and visions. (Yoga describes these as manifestations of descending and ascending life force within and permeating us).

He might consciously "regard" those sitting with him, looking into our eyes, and, it seemed, communicating unconditional love. If asked to contemplate the human guru, I rather felt more comfortable just sitting in meditation with Bubba, "being with the teacher." He might ask us to examine how we were "contracting," tightening ourselves—he'd make a fist to show how we unconsciously do this ourselves, inquiring "avoiding relationship?" Tight throats, heads, chests, hearts, stomachs just seemed to loosen and fill in the intensified, expansive field of energy that he generated. For me, I found that meditation is where the life force is energized and an understanding of the self begins.

Bubba would listen carefully to our questions, upsets, and doubts. He would try to help the questioner directly, as

Ramana Maharshi suggested: first question; observe yourself, the questioner; ask, "Who am I?" Inquire into "the avoidance of relationship" in our lives, as reflected in stiff body and contracted feeling. As in Buddhist meditation, we wouldn't avoid what we were feeling but allow expansiveness around whatever was occurring in us.

He tried to communicate his own realizations to us. He said his spiritual influences were Jesus, Buddha, Krishna, Ramakrishna, and Ramana Maharshi. He wrote after a time of meditation at the Vedanta Temple in 1970: "All paths pursue some special state or goal as spiritual truth. But in fact reality is not identical to such things. They only amount to identification with some body, realm or experience, high or low, subtle or gross. But the knowledge that is reality, which is consciousness itself, which is not separate from anything, is always already the case."

I was totally taken by Ramana Maharshi—his teaching to be just as you are. "Give up the notion, 'I am impure'. The Self you are, authentic self is ever pure ... If you get at the basis of the mind, all these wrong notions disappear." Studying Maharshi began to open up the path of no seeking; that realization is already here echoed the Buddhist Heart Sutra, "there is nothing to attain." We only have to give up seeking for an authentic self and just realize for ourselves that we don't need to seek so desperately or to suppress what's manifesting in our own particular lives. This process wasn't some kind of killing the personality and individuality of the student. As Franklin said, "You are not invited to annihilation, but rather to the fullness of God that is happy and free. There is no murder involved in such an event."

■

Wendy became my first wife. We met in 1973 when we were both Franklin's students. I fell in love with her the first time

I saw her—she was sweet, energetic, sharp and a wonderful listener. Three months later, I asked her to marry me. She accepted and asked me to go with her to Maumee, Ohio, to meet her parents and ask for their blessing, which we did. Her parents and I hit it off right away. Bubba later officiated at our religious wedding ceremony on the land, witnessed by the community, friends, and a few relatives. It was a memorable, fun day. I had the feeling: "The world is charged with the splendor of God" (G.M. Hopkins).

My only sadness was that my mother would not attend the ceremony. I tried to understand her. She had been upset and distant for a few years by this time, because I had stopped going to the Catholic Church; I had left the Jesuits; and now I was involved with "hippies and gurus and leftists." She would have been so much happier if I had gone to law school.

Wendy and I felt no demand "from on high" to conform to any particular social norms. We wanted to be "as free as the wind." The fact that Wendy and I agreed to experiment sexually was very important to the authenticity of our experience together. As difficult as it was at times, as even dangerous as it could be, Wendy and I agreed not to lock each other up psychologically, letting each other be free to engage with other people. It was a form of discipline to get along in a happy and mature way with others and to live and sleep together as a couple.

While Wendy and I were living on the land, one night, March 23, 1974, Franklin discussed our responsibility to live more communally, without clinging to our own relationships, to our wives or husbands or lovers or our "few friends." This would test our intention.

Bubba said don't let fear of losing what we think is "ours" (even if nothing is just "ours") keep us trapped in our conventional arrangements. If we had agreed to an open marriage, then don't be afraid to let your spouse enjoy others, including sexually. "Be a community of free persons …

touch one another, love one another, deal with one another as intimately as you please, not like gangsters, rapists, and whores, but in that radical freedom … approach each other directly, the more you understand, the less you feel the form of inner suffering necessarily created when you feel your contracts are violated … so allow this self-purifying responsibility and privilege to love and be free and happy."

When Wendy slept with a friend, Sal, Wendy had wanted to see what it was like to make love with another man; she wanted to allow herself the experience of being seduced and to learn and grow from that experience as several in the community had already done. What's it like to have more than one lover?

Sometimes, my meditation and yoga helped me be more aware that all movements were the life force of my breathing-flexing-stretching body. At other times, if I was boiling with jealousy, anger, or self-doubt, I spent my meditation time just feeling rotten, just breathing. But that night how I screamed and howled in grief, pounding the walls of the wooden cabins on the grounds until I exhausted myself. I had occasionally made love with other women, but I wanted Wendy only for myself. Somehow the whole incident combined with practicing meditation allowed me to let go of holding onto Wendy in that way. The next day I spoke with Sal and, after some words, some forgiveness, some sorrow, I spontaneously hugged him and Wendy. I realized that I had changed. Both Wendy and I had changed; we discovered our playing around was hurtful to the other and we were naturally faithful to each other for as long as we were married.

At some point in 1976, Wendy became uncomfortable and doubtful about continuing to live in the commune. She said to me "I don't know whether Bubba is God or the Devil, or maybe both." We had a long of conversation and in the end, both of us felt all right about leaving each other, grateful for the three years we were together. There's nothing worse than pretending to do spiritual practice or uphold a false allegiance. It was time for Wendy to go, and she felt totally free to leave. I was in tears; Wendy was crying too; we held each other for a long time. I told Wendy that I wanted to continue studying with Bubba, even though I knew I would also be leaving soon. Then Wendy and I made love one last time.

I feel gratitude and appreciation of the incredible time we had together. And I also regret that I wasn't more mature, that sometimes my bad temper surfaced, fueled by jealousy. Wendy taught me how to love someone without being possessive, angry when not "being loved." She taught me love is a very sudden gift—not to be taken for granted or clung to. A love relationship suffers many changes, and doesn't have to be "forever."

Wendy was so sweet and wise—how can I ever forget her? We have never spoken or seen each other since, though I still feel her. After we split up, she returned to her relationship with a man who had never forgotten her or given up on getting her back. She asked me not to contact her, and I have respected that, but a clean break doesn't mean you no longer love someone.

■

Like many of the first generation of western gurus, Master Da would make all too human mistakes around the perennial issues of power, sex, money, relationships, organizational politics, marketing, and excessive spiritual claims. Certainly not a fraud, not an exploiter, and, in my opinion, truly genuine without any ill will, yet still Master Da is subject to human frailty. I realize Franklin may have had an entirely different public image than what I experienced as his student in the early years of his teaching. But I knew even then that Franklin Jones "is not for everyone," as Ram Dass would say to me. "He does have a lot of personal charisma and power." Franklin and

Ram Dass knew each other and knew each other as "human beings," with some of the particular "shortcomings" we all share.

I had been away from Da for several years when I when read charges in the newspapers that some of his former students felt manipulated, "traumatized," by the excesses and the sexual experimentation. I know some of those close to Franklin in the period 1973–76 who were angry and upset with "teaching theater." They felt that Franklin was intimidating his students. One has to find for oneself what is genuine and what is the "play" in teaching theater. I also know that some serious allegations against Adi Da would later surface in 1985–86, and some of his students would harshly, perhaps justifiably, criticize him. In my experience, however, I never saw any imprisonment, sexual abuse, assault, brainwashing or involuntary servitude with Da, as he would later be accused of and then sued in 1985 and 1986. (Let me be clear: I support anyone who was intentionally and illegally abused by any spiritual teacher to take appropriate action and allow his or her grievance to be judged in a court of law.)

The heart of the student-teacher relationship is engaging in a process with the teacher that he or she has mastered. Whether living in healthy human community or alone, it requires direct face-to-face encounter with the teacher. When someone comes as a sincere, curious, questioning student, it's a very down-to-earth sacred relationship. This relationship can never be beneficial, however, if there isn't a chance for the student to challenge the teacher and vice-versa—that "clicking" can't be forced. A relationship with a spiritual teacher is then exquisite play, a kind of art, and entrance into an understanding of ways to pray and meditate that is potentially more powerful than pure academic study. But this power can also be dangerous. There is always a possibility of indoctrination, brainwashing, religious sloganeering, or being manipulated by a remote authority.

Franklin possessed a genuine yogic power which was tangible to me. He taught that all yogic and meditative experiences, absorptions, mystical visions just happen. Benefit and learn from them, but let them come and go. The Buddha taught that there's a profound peace beyond even the greatest of the *jhanas* (absorptions), however useful they may be and integrated to the meditative path. Although I never had any dramatic spiritual experiences in the meditation hall, many around me did. I found also some people exaggerated their experiences, seeking public approval from Franklin. That is another instance of the darker side of a spiritual community, based in the fear that we need to kiss the teacher's ass. The teacher, if he or she is worth his salt, wants to see who you really are and what you're really about. False ingratiating faces are really a hindrance.

The spiritual Master is sometimes tough, but he or she will never intentionally harm any one. I found Franklin Jones a loving human being, a spiritual teacher of integrity and—most importantly—a teacher who embodied a priceless teaching. At one of Franklin's first public talks, a young man became angry and said that Franklin was full of it, that he wasn't making any important communication, that he wasn't answering his questions. After some interchange, the man left the room pissed off. Franklin said, "I appreciate the challenging questions, the confrontation."

It was fine that the man walked out of Franklin's talk and in the future many would do the same. Everyone in the community had the opportunity (sometimes it did take some courage to speak up and reveal yourself) to get his or her most vital questions and communications across. Franklin appreciated the passion in the man, and Franklin had just wanted the chance to get the man to see for himself why he was so angry. Franklin wanted to engage the individual on a sincere and deep level, mutually respectful, but no bullshit; let's deeply enter a consideration of divine worlds, beckoning us to its realization, in kind and wise actions, while we're all breathing the world together. Through our work with one another, I, the community, many of us came to see how some of our questions have deep emotions behind them, hidden in anger and self-centeredness.

No spiritual teacher ever has the right to abuse his or her student; such abuse violates the mutual condition of love, which is the basis of the master-student relationship. I understand how vulnerable a person can be who is in a concentrated teacher-student relationship. However, I always felt free to express what I wanted to say to Franklin and I also felt free to ignore institutional dictates. Franklin didn't give me the feeling he wanted anything from me. He loved Indian scripture: "Whenever there is an 'other,' there is fear." The true teacher always communicates—even if being tough on the student—that what a spiritual master has realized is exactly the same as what the student already is. I never slowed down as much during this time and at the same time, never ran so fast, "accelerated," enthused to try a new life style. I never had so much leisure to study and meditate, listening to talks by a Spiritual Master and occasionally, being with other teachers such as Krishnamurti, Chogyam Trungpa, and Ram Dass.

Teachers such as Chogyam Trungpa were also accused of being of abusive, sexually inappropriate and addicted to alcohol and power. I'd met with Trungpa a few times when I was studying with Master Da and learned a bit about his Tibetan Buddhism. Trungpa was a heavy drinker and, as was Da, sexually very liberated. I didn't particularly like the organizational-cultural setting around Trungpa and the attitude of "kingly" and elegant circumstance. It was too much of a separation from the world I'd seen in our inner cities and in Mexico. Though it appeared elitist to me, it was not without benefit. Trungpa was certainly a good teacher and I enjoyed hearing him speak and engaging in conversation.

I never was comfortable with guru-worship even though

Franklin's approach later emulated much of his teacher's, Swami Muktananda's, Hindu rituals, bowing, pujas, incense. I looked at these rituals—though focusing and engaging—in the same way as we burn incense at the Buddhist monastery and Catholic Church. They are not worth getting hung up about. Leave all rafts on the other side of seeking. It is "mass mind" that makes gurus and monks into gods. No matter how gifted, the teacher is in a mutually respectful relationship with the student. A student is free to leave a teacher, to criticize, to put light on the "shadows." (I include Franklin's community and Franklin himself). It's only foolish cultism that wants to make a teacher into the only font of wisdom, to make dogma which stifles the ability to think for oneself or to come and go following the stream of one's most authentic life.

Ken Wilber was one of the first important writers (Watts was the first) to appreciate Da's spiritual writing. Wilber, along with Georg Fuerstein, Ph.D., would praise the wisdom of Da's teaching, but criticize his dealing with the perennial problems of power, control, sex, and money. Wilber said that Da was fully developed spiritually, but morally and socially immature. As a teacher, Wilber thought that Da should be willing to meet with other teachers and adepts; that he should enter the public forum of spiritual conversation, and be challenged in the world. "The great difficulty is that, no matter how enlightened you might be, it takes a certain amount of practical wisdom to gauge the effects of your teaching work on the world at large."

Master Da is not the public personality that Watts was, and so be it, if he wants to teach privately, leaving religious inquiry to others, such as Wilber. Da is an able theoretician and keen thinker as well as an avid reader of spiritual literature. He is interested in serious and enlightened conversations, but he apparently doesn't want a very public life which is his right. If he chooses to live and teach privately with a few students, free to explore with them the particular fruits of his own realization, does this limit his ability as a religious teacher? Of course not. It might be healthy and mutually beneficial for Da and his community to have a more public conversation, but not necessarily so. However his emerging voice might soften the nasty attitude that "we're the only ones with any Truth" that seems prevalent in religious practice.

I think his contributions lie in other areas, which will inevitably find their way in the more public conversation. They already have. Why should Da have to be like the wonderful Dalai Lama or Thich Nhat Hanh? But who knows? Master Da may show up at an important public forum in the future.

"Realize it's what we already are," said Ramana Maharshi. The purpose of sitting with the spiritual Master is to enjoy one's own enlightenment, not adore an individual teacher. The spiritual Master is a teacher and a servant. Franklin encouraged me to find the Divine within myself. "We're supposed to be cool and hip and straight, oriented toward our survival, worldly and wise. But to be simply alive in God and happy, and to speak about it and act that way and think that way, is absolutely unwanted and not allowed. A cult object is allowed to be Divine in this world, a conventional guru is allowed to be Divine, a God in a book is allowed to be Divine, all kinds of fetishes are allowed to be Divine, but you are not allowed to be Divine. It is taboo to be already happy. You must seek happiness."

■

In 1973 when I was first Franklin's student, I lived a short while in L.A. with my friend, Billy Tsiknas, who amazed me by being able to sit in the full lotus position. We painted the exteriors of houses while we did interior work with our teacher. This was a beautiful time, full of joy, and also a strict time of doing deep personal examination (which for me included the Ignatian examen). Besides our strict vegetarian diet, we followed a steady schedule of study and service, learning and acknowledging through meditation and conversation, where our hearts were closed, and changing some destructive habits.

When two old Jesuit friends dropped by to visit, and saw that I had a photo of Franklin in my meditation corner, along with images of Jesus, and Buddha, I felt embarrassed. I worried that they might have felt that I was worshipping and bowing to a man in a weird cult. My friends' reactions were understandable. They did not share my relationship with Franklin. (My mistake was not to keep my meditation area private. Jesus says: "Close the door and then meditate and pray." To this day, I keep a few photos of Master Da.

Most of my Jesuit friends didn't take my involvement with Franklin seriously. Yet during most of the time I was in Franklin's community, I continued to have a Jesuit spiritual director, Father Francis Rouleau. "Let's talk from my heart to yours, yours to mine," Francis would say. He was a very skilled and mature spiritual director—he recognized that there were very powerful practices that I was learning and he took me seriously. He was never judgmental about me; he really did understand.

Despite his strong theological and moral convictions, which were contrary to those I was developing for myself, our personal relationship and his commitment to my spiritual growth was what really mattered to him. He was very human and down to earth, not at all "condescending" as so many priests and teachers and I loved him for that. For example when I discussed the sexual ethos of Franklin's community with him, and my no-guilt sexual exploration outside traditional Catholic morality, he was genuinely interested, speaking himself about those still living in the Society of Jesus who fall in love, some having sex. He also asked my feelings about homosexuality, as my best friend Marcus Holly was openly bi-sexual. (Sometimes Marcus and I would visit Francis together).

I was integrating my Buddhist meditation, the *Spiritual*

Exercises' "Examination of Conscience," and self-observation, observation of our lives, in conversation with Franklin Jones and in the company of community. Franklin writes: "I do not recommend that you meditate. There is only understanding— therefore, understand. When understanding becomes observation, reflection, insight and radical cognition, then the state of consciousness itself is meditation." What is radically cognized? One experiences an inclusive connection with all, a joy of being alive, "to consider," as St. Ignatius encourages, "all blessings, all life, as descending from above, from the supreme and infinite power ... descending as the rays of light descend form the sun, and as the waters flow from their fountains." Franklin continues: "Understanding arises when there are true hearing and self-observation in relationship.... Observe yourself in life. Observe yourself when you suffer to any degree. Observe your motives. Observe the activity of identification. Observe the activity of differentiation. Observe the activity of desire. Observe the patterns of your existence." (*The Knee of Listening*, p.171)

I felt the energy and love in Father Francis' presence much like in the presence of Franklin, though Francis was not as "demanding" as Franklin nor was his teaching complicated by a community of followers. Both he and Franklin embraced mysticism, though in their own particular way. Francis said: "We are never God, only God's servants." Bubba would agree we are truly all God's servants, while declaring himself—in his Eastern religious vocabulary—to have been enlightened, to have 'realized the Self, as understood in genuine Eastern thought and practice. "I am That."

Bubba, like Francis, was personally charismatic, an intense teacher. Unlike Francis, Franklin was not always gentlemanly. Sometimes he was just a drunken laughing fool. He might have been, as the Jesuits say, finding God in all things. Francis was self-effacing whereas Franklin wasn't given to humble expressions, saying "I am God; you are God," which was very eastern, and later, accepting the bows of his disciples, just as he had bowed before his teacher Swami Muktananda.

Neither man was perfect. I thought that Father Francis was a saint; Franklin didn't pretend to be a saint, and he isn't. And I always tended to distrust some of the religious trappings around him. I did experience Franklin as a loving person, a tremendous hugger, a person with a remarkable sense of humor and an insightful, penetrating teacher who could be shy and withdrawn.

Francis was pleased when I left Master Da, but he still considered it an extremely important learning time for me, as do I. Da is still a great teacher to me, initiating me in his tradition from his teachers, still helping me now, just practicing at the Rosemead Buddhist Monastery, my daily meditation, and my practice of service at the Jesuit Dolores Mission—just living my life.

■

When I fall in love with someone, I say it's forever. I don't mean just the sexual falling in love, but the love that can happen between friends, or even between a student and teacher or a teacher with his or her student. This kind of love has a natural component—a very human, warm appreciative reverence that can last beyond any interaction with the person. Love doesn't always mean life-long contact, as in the case of Da and of my first wife, Wendy, but its influence is for life.

The interval after leaving the community and integrating back into ordinary life was awkward. I had somewhat the same confusing time as when I left the Jesuits. I was for a while a fish out of water on both occasions. Because my family was ashamed of my leaving the Jesuits, there was a feeling of failure. And the Jesuits, without conscious intent, made leaving a matter of disgrace. But I was confident in wanting a different kind of life for myself apart from the Jesuits. Just as clearly when I knew for certain that a life of celibacy wasn't for me as a Jesuit, I knew when living in Bubba Free John's community wasn't right for me any longer.

From 1977 to 1979, I worked at a special education junior high school on the corner of Geary and Franklin, called Fairfield School around the corner from the Unitarian Church. I stayed in touch with some of the community members, some of whom chastised me for leaving the community and for criticizing Bubba, even though my criticism was respectful and sincere. Marcus Holly and I went to workshops on therapeutic body/movement work, as well as going to parties or volunteering for campaigns with César Chavez and Dolores Huerta.

I felt some emotional raggedness after leaving Free John and the community. Working and being with these children, many of them tough kids with deep emotional challenges, was a kind of therapy for the "fallout." I look at some of their pictures even today with profound tenderness. Joyce Roberts was the amazing principal who encouraged me be creative and make San Francisco part of my classroom—the wharf, the museums, fire and police stations, the sea. Various businesses opened their doors to us. The students set up a small business where they sold jewelry and art they made or was donated. Our business profits paid for lunch, and I began to feel totally connected to the ordinary world again.

The last time I saw Bubba Free John, by then known as Master Da, was September 16, 1979 on the land in Northern California. I had been away from the community for two years, but we were together again to celebrate his spiritual "awakening" at the Vedanta Temple in Hollywood nine years earlier (September 10, 1970), the same place I had visited when I was in high school. He had included many of us from early years who were no longer involved with the community on the guest list. Dressed in white, wearing a tall white hat and using a cane with an ornate metal handle, Da seemed very peaceful and full. He said: "This is the most beautiful occasion that has ever taken place here." I'm not sure exactly what he meant, but, as I watched him walk back to his home, I too felt that it was a beautiful occasion. I bowed and said my final good-bye.

Celebrating Master Da's realization at the Hollywood Vedanta Temple, I felt I had come full circle. In '61 when I was a junior at Loyola High School, I had visited the Vedanta Temple—the gardens, rooms, and bookstore with Christian, Hindu, Buddhist, and Muslim literature—just above the frenetic Hollywood freeway. Inside I had been attracted to the serene images of Buddha's round face and the tender face of Jesus from the Shroud of Turin. At first, repelled by the shrine with a picture of Sri Ramakrishna, I hurried away feeling that real altars and shrines and rituals were for Jesus alone. But soon I found myself drawn back, just to sit in the temple and explore books or sometimes to have lunch with the Indian swamis who would invite me to talks. I was totally confused in 1961, but interested. By 1979, having studied with Master Da for almost five years, I had a real taste of an ancient and powerful spiritual tradition.

■

The understanding that my study and work with Franklin began in me thirty-five years ago continues to this day. I have a way of pursuing my own religious quest that Franklin taught me in the deepest part of my being: No one can give us happiness or freedom—we have to realize it for ourselves. That's the current in his teaching that most touched me and the one that I most explored and continue to explore.

My experience with Master Da, in what was at root a Hindu tradition, would be my only experience of Siddha Yoga, the relationship of teacher to student as the centerpiece of spiritual practice. Yoga is a general term for practices from

India, which tune body-mind abilities to be in union with the Divine Source. A Siddha is someone who has "fallen into the Heart," a "completed one." The Siddha comes from a living tradition, having been initiated, going through a process of understanding her or his life through the practice of yoga and meditation, finally completely surrendering to Life itself and being recognized by that accomplishment. In my case, that relationship was also a friendship. Many joyful experiences and insights arose spontaneously, without effort. It was a rare opportunity for me to learn some ancient wisdom from a wild, loving, Siddha Yoga teacher

Master Da taught that we must bravely allow our "hanging on" to loosen. He said that our natural state of being happy and peaceful becomes obvious when we can observe how our mind and heart work; when we pay attention to how we separate ourselves, how our bodies and hearts become hard or weak. My most "prior" being is whole, creative, and not contained only in my ego. We are all continually changing, and yet the "I" wants to attach to feeling good, even to mystical experiences, all of which just come and go. Da taught me to embrace all of life, including parts of myself that I have disowned, whether I am honest about the disowning or not. I learned to be sensitive to when I'm being self-indulgent, as well as when I'm refusing the invitation to drink deeply from life's gifts.

The person of understanding is someone filled with joy and pleasure, of love and knowledge, the ability to help, as well as detachment, calm, energy, clarity and force. To this day, Da inspires me to meditate and pay attention to the heart of no-seeking—that it is already 'enough' to be living from the heart, in wonder and not-knowing-it-all, being fully alive. I continue a daily meditation practice with both Buddhist and Ignatian flavors. After Suzuki Roshi introduced me to Zen meditation, my practice with Da gave the experience of meditation, not suppressing feelings, whether "self-loving" or "self-hating," to observe my breath and feel the tightness in my belly, around my heart and in my throat, and allow myself to be present to what's going on, now in this moment.

Once I quoted Ramana Maharshi at a meeting of activists who were bickering at the time: "Trying to help the world without knowing yourself will be just like a blind man trying to treat the diseases in the eyes of others. First, clear your own eyes. If you do this you will see the eyes of all others as your own. Then, if you see the eyes of all others as your own, how can you exist without helping them?" (*Ramana Maharshi Answers 100 Questions*, p.6) Several of the activists got this message enthusiastically.

Master Da was iconoclastic, even regarding his own teachers. I have learned that we, as humans, want to create an exclusive God, an "idol." Today, as a teacher and sometimes organizer, I discover that I have a sixth sense for this "us against them" attitude. Our organizations lose the human touch, get stuck in power, money, and they become cults, whether Da's community, the Catholic Church, or a Buddhist Monastery. No religious organization is off the hook! There are organizational abuses of power, which I've seen in most spiritual communities, and churches with which I've had varying degrees of contact. True spiritual communities—I'm discounting the ones that are out and out hoaxes—are growing up, evolving positively and encouraging mature relationships, including being critical of each other in a loving, supportive way. There is wisdom in the Buddha's promoting consensus and the sharing of power and responsibilities within a community.

Alan Watts spoke about the possibility of doing one's spiritual practice in relationship to a teacher. He told stories of Marpa and Milarepa in Tibet, where the guru seemed to be absolutely demanding and the disciple had to be completely dedicated. And yet there was a feeling of love between them. True spiritual relationships of teacher to student can happen and do happen, even if there are limitations. First and foremost it's important to remember both the spiritual director and spiritual master are human beings, perhaps very evolved in different aspects of their being, with varying levels of capacity and maturity, but human beings. Anyone who lives or works with a master or spiritual teacher should be free from any fear to speak up, to have personal and intimate boundaries while living in community, and always to refer to one's own heart and mind and conscience rather than any kind of organization "group-think" or "group-pressure" that force conformity with the self-appointed authorities.

I also learned from both Alan and Franklin that the spiritual life is not a dreary matter. There is no need to walk around with lowered head and serious frown. We have not been assembled to witness an execution. Life is joyous. The raucous parties, both with Alan and Franklin—still remarkable and appreciated—are long past. Alan's extravagance may have shortened his life; Franklin used intoxicants, partied like crazy, but for both men spiritual life was always the focus. And the joy I experienced with both stays with me.

All true gurus, both Alan and Master Da insisted, have submitted to the Eternal Siddha-Guru who is God. I still hear Da telling me to be awake, the Heart, just be what I am. I hear Fr. Francis saying: "Touch the Eternal Heart of God in our every day life." What a way to live!

A Disciple of Satya Sai Baba
A Conversation with Dilip Trasi

We want to take a particular medicine, then we have to follow the directions written on the label. We cannot take the medicine according to our own whim or the direction of a friend. It must be taken according to the directions on the label or the directions given by a physician. Similarly, Bhagavad-gita should be taken or accepted as it is directed by the speaker Himself. The speaker of Bhagavad-gita is Lord Sri Krishna.

—Swami Prabhupada

MZC: Dilip, we were discussing Andrew Cohen's article in his magazine, "What is Enlightenment?" which features Ken Wilber. Andrew talks about his own realization as an experience of cosmic consciousness. Is the experience of "cosmic consciousness" equivalent to enlightenment? Some Buddhists seem to say that "cosmic consciousness"—though a high mystical experience—doesn't guarantee spiritual liberation.

The oldest school of Buddhist meditation, the Theravadin, the one that I am most familiar with, teaches that the *jhanas,* deep absorptions in meditation, as meaningful as they can be, fall away. They say that the Buddha taught that mystical levels of consciousness are not enlightenment—both those who are enlightened and those who are not can experience such states. What is your view about this? Isn't it about the cultivation of wisdom and compassion, rather than acquiring such experiences?

DT: Many of the gurus we meet today are persons who have experienced some heightened states of consciousness that they are unable to explain. They then look for similar experiences in others and find a few who are ready to corroborate their experience as one of enlightenment. However, not all such cases are experiences of cosmic consciousness. The next step would be a sincere investigation to find out where the experience leads, what knowledge and freedom is gained from such an experience and whether, when repeatedly experienced, it leads to higher and higher states of consciousness finally culminating in genuine cosmic consciousness. Just a one-time feeling of euphoria cannot be considered as experience of cosmic consciousness.

An experience of cosmic consciousness is also an experienced phenomenon and as such is temporary and hence not reality. It is only when your individual consciousness merges in the cosmic consciousness that it becomes real and permanent. A genuine experience of cosmic consciousness is characterized by the absence of oneself as the experiencer-- the individual ego dissolves in the cosmic consciousness and is reinstated after the experience ends. The reinstated ego no longer causes attachment and clinging and so is akin to a snake with the fangs removed. During his so-called experience of cosmic consciousness, Andrew was reported to have heard a voice, which said "Surrender yourself to Me". Andrew was disturbed when he heard the voice and could no longer continue with the experience. The surrender did not take place and so there was no mergence. Hence his experience did not result in an altered ego as was expected.

For some, cosmic consciousness may constitute an intermediary stage prior to realizing freedom from suffering. Buddha's meditation included mystical states, powers deep in the mind. But Buddha still wasn't free until, under the Bodhi Tree, he completely comprehended the cause and cure of our suffering. Christ's statement "Search and thou shall find" implies that you find what you seek. Buddha started his search with the intention of finding a way out of misery. Hence for him the seeking ended when he found a way out of it.

MZC: We can see in others, and ourselves including in monks, priests, how much we cherish our spiritual experiences.

We get attached to such experiences, craving them. And when we have such experiences, we may start blowing ourselves up; making ourselves more important than we really are. Choygyam Trungpa called it "spiritual materialism." We're motivated to get high, to be lifted up in ecstasies. Of course, it's such a gift! But with freedom and lack of clinging, we let ecstasies and high-expansive states go, learn from them and be energized by them, yet not to be greedy for them.

What do you think about the article by Ken Wilber, "A Spirituality that Transforms," which also appeared in *What Is Enlightenment?* Magazine. Wilber says: "Nobody was ready for Chogyam's or Da's ultimate no practice of always-already Spirit and non-separate, non-dual Consciousness." Students weren't ready to give up the great search; they wanted to make great efforts to find something outside themselves, apart from what they already were.

Chogyam Trungpa and Adi Da called for practices, for spiritual effort that "made the body-mind more susceptible to radical, already-accomplished enlightenment.... You are enlightened Spirit; it is only seeking Spirit that prevents realization. Adi Da originally taught nothing but the path of understanding, not a way to attain enlightenment, but an inquiry into why you want to attain enlightenment in the first place ... your own eternal and timeless condition is totally present from the start." What is your experience with Satya Sai Baba? Does he also teach the way of "non-seeking"? What does the guru relationship mean to you?

DT: In India the word guru stands for teacher or preceptor. A sat-guru is an accomplished spiritual master 'sat' meaning truth. My guru, Satya Sai Baba, who is an avatar and a Sat-guru, knows, and is able to assist, aspirants at all levels in various ways. For the majority, his speeches, books and publications describe the methods to be adopted for one's spiritual journey. For spiritually advanced pupils his approach is different. He telepathically guides those who are at higher levels.

Baba says, as Master Adi Da, that seeking is inherent in all and ends only when the subject realizes that the object of his seeking is his own inner self. This is known as self-realization. Thereafter, the subject realizes that the same inner self pervades all life, and that in its primordial form the same self constitutes matter as well. With this he gains knowledge about matter and energy and the means to control them. He gets a taste of cosmic consciousness. In due course, he gains supernatural powers over matter and energy. This is known as God-realization. There are various degrees of god realization leading towards omniscience, omnipresence and omnipotence.

Regarding non-seeking, Baba does not agree with the idea that it can lead to enlightenment, but accepts that intensive seeking is a desire that, like any other desire, can hamper one's final emancipation. Intensive seeking is necessary in the early stages of spiritual development, when one is required to put in effort to calm the mind and keep it free from worldly attractions, which tend to disturb it. Once practice becomes steady and we recognize the path most suited to us, the desire for liberation is of secondary importance.

MZC: Would you speak about the difference between a cultic relationship to a guru and an authentic, liberating one? Isn't the relationship to a guru a mature relationship between two mutually respectful human beings? In the earliest times of his teaching, Master Da led the student into self-inquiry and criticized all forms of exclusive worship of any guru. Da would often quote Indian theology: "The Guru and the Self are one." The true guru or spiritual teacher, in my opinion, gets out of way, such that the disciple realizes what's important, what's real for herself or himself. No one can be for us what we already are. The guru is only the way to our most profound inner self. Our own self-freedom is to understand and judge and choose for ourselves—based on our own lights. I reject any "blind obedience" to any guru/religious leader/political leader. Would you agree with this?

Just as in Mahayana sutra of the Great Heart Wisdom: "There is nothing to attain." Would you speak about the process of having a spiritual Master, both in your own case and in the rich Indian tradition? And what are the pitfalls one must be conscious of?

DT: A guru is not supposed to force his ideas on the disciple but only show the way. There should be no stereotyping either. There can be many variations to the techniques of spiritual practice. Freedom to try other variations should be encouraged in a spirit of research. In this way the disciple finds the means most suited to his nature. Cultic worship is uncalled for.

Before I met Satya Sai Baba I was devoted to Anandashram Swamiji, who was an accomplished yogi and a sage par excellence. After his *mahasamadhi* in September 1966, I turned my attention to Satya Sai Baba. I was a novice then and thought that I could gain self-realization through yoga and spiritual effort, and I imagined that Baba would take me into his room and teach me meditation. After meeting him in October of 1966 and talking to him, a great change came about—I became my own guru. The need to have a guru to teach me was obviated. A few months later, I had a dream in which his appearance coincided with a certain sensation, a vibration inside my body, centered behind my neck. I dwelled upon that experience and thought to myself that maybe he wants me to practice it voluntarily. It took me a week or so to recreate that feeling of vibration, which I came to know many years later as *vipassana*, a kind of meditation prescribed by Buddha. Though Baba's guidance continues, or so I think, he never makes me feel that the guidance is coming from a source external to myself. He does it ever so subtly that it's hard to tell for sure. In the ultimate analysis we have to realize that God, guru and one's own inner self are the same reality.

The modern world is filled with opportunists who try to pose as gurus and attract gullible, rich and unsuspecting disciples and induce them to part with their wealth in exchange for spiritual favors. There are just a few genuine gurus who shun wealth for themselves and if they accept it, use it only for the good of humanity.

MZC: How do you describe meditation? How does meditation carry on into your every day life?

DT: Before meditation can begin, one has to sit silently for some time like a witness and watch the mind spinning thoughts, without getting involved in them. In case we do get involved and start spinning new connected thoughts and detect it, we have to immediately discontinue the involvement. After a while, the mind becomes silent and peaceful. Rhythmic breathing can be used effectively as a tool for slowing down the mind There can be total focus on the present without disturbance from our experienced past or imagined future, our sorrows and fears, our desires for something not achieved, or fear of losing. Actions become automatic. Attachments fall away. We prevail as witnesses only and not as actors. This is a preliminary stage of pure witnessing. Witnessing ends when there is nothing to witness. This is a state known as *nirvikalpa*—a state of non-being. Beyond that is a state which is neither being nor non-being. That is the ultimate state! The last two states cannot be acquired but happen automatically when the witnessing state is transcended, but the probability of occurrence depends on certain conductive factors.

MZC: Would you tell us more about your own spiritual journey? Who were the teachers who influenced you? We've both experienced that intense spiritual dialogue with Jiddhu Krishnamurti. I found him at times a bit severe and overly serious, yet also penetrating, enlivening. He always spoke on the great topics: meditation, enlightenment, being present, phony spiritual teachers, education, politics, personal responsibility, inner capacity to know for ourselves. Again, most useful for me was the admonition to find out for myself.

DT: I was living in New York in 1980 and went to hear many different teachers speak, a Zen master, swamis, Tibetan lamas, a Sufi sheikh, a rabbi, and even Christian faith healers. I remember a talk by Swami Chidananda, disciple of the legendary Sivananda: "When someone asks what you do, say: 'I meditate … and I also live!'

It was also in 1980 I went to hear J. Krishnamurti teach in Switzerland. I was at the time sure of the classical Indian yogic path; yet here I was no longer so sure where I was going or how. Now there was room for that real inquiry, this unexpected space suddenly emerging within my mind, just through listening and considering with this great man.

MZC: What was your experience with other forms of meditation?

DT: My first experience of Buddhist meditation was the *vipassana* experience conferred by Satya Sai Baba on me in a dream. It was the lantern that helped me to navigate through the rough waters of spiritual practice. I later read and practiced Sufi meditation techniques as taught by Osho Rajneesh and had several wonderful experiences. The cathartic processes taught by him, though not free of physical side effects, are capable of taking one to the highest pinnacle of experiential understanding of the greatest esoteric truths. I also studied and practiced "the Course" Goenka taught at Igatpuri, a wonderful place with idyllic surroundings that harbor peace and goodwill. The meditation rooms are specifically designed for advanced practitioners. In retreat environments, I was able to meditate for long periods of time. The profound peace and intense clarity that resulted from such Buddhist practice is awe-inspiring. The Buddha dharma taught me a lot about the mind and how it works. I also attended J. Krishnamurti's lectures. I felt that his emphasis was on understanding deeply and analyzing one's thought processes, a technique more suited to the intellectual elites and not to the masses. His philosophy and denial of spiritual tutorship through a guru can be understood from his own life history.

I met Nisargadatta Maharaj (1897–1981) during some

of his conversations with visitors in the living room of his house in Mumbai. [His book, five hundred pages plus of conversations, *I Am That* (published in 1973), is considered a classic of Advaita philosophy.] I also met Haidakhandi Yogi (d. 1984) who was believed to be one of the forms of the legendary Mahavatar Babaji mentioned in the Book *An Autobiography of a Yogi*. [He also taught his followers to chant *Om Namah Shivaya*, "Lord, Thy Will be done."] Another teacher I met was Dada Bhagwan (1908–88). [He taught that spiritual knowledge does not bring about enlightenment. "A conclusion comes from knowledge that is experienced."] I always viewed all the masters I met later in the light of my experience with Satya Sai Baba. Hence I never clung to any of them, though I learned a lot from each.

In 1987, I visited USA. I found some differences in the spiritual environment there as compared to India. In India, I felt a much greater freedom to give myself in to my longing for liberation. The atmosphere in India is conducive to spiritual practice and growth. Life in America, on the other hand is orientated towards materialism and good for business and accumulating wealth. I felt spiritually inhibited in America, in some way or another and unable to meditate for long intervals.

In India, I found the confidence to abandon myself completely to the wish to become a liberated human being. I spent over sixteen and a half years, meditating and studying yoga. When I was thirty I got married and a new spiritual journey began with my wife, Anjali, as a spiritual co-partner in the search for liberation. She was equally interested in spirituality and we complemented each other. So that's how I proceeded further on my spiritual adventure. At the age of thirty-two, I experienced the highest state that I described earlier.

Spirituality is an attempt to understand the mind-body instrument we are equipped with and purify and control it. In the process we realize ourselves as independent of them and as ever free and filled with knowledge and power. The mind is a bundle of desires. It is like a mirror that reflects whatever is placed before it. It weighs the pros and cons of that object—whether it is desirable or repugnant. Accordingly it directs the body to perform actions that either aim to acquire the object or to cast it away. It can be in various states—attenuated, as in sleep,—expanded, as in waking,—overpowering, as in infatuation,—dejected, when faced with losses—frustrated when deprived of the desired object—etc. etc. The list is endless.

MZC: Ken Ireland said that many religious scholars think that the emergence of the Bhagavad Gita (its actual composition is usually dated several hundred years after the Buddha) is what halted the spread of Buddhism in India. It personalized and applied so much of what we call Hinduism to life situations, putting it into the voices of heroes and gods. Do you have any thoughts about this?

DT: I don't agree with those scholars. Krishna's birth predated Buddha's. The Gita was told on the battlefield in a condensed form by Krishna to Arjuna, to help him overcome the feeling of dejection when faced with the prospect of vanquishing his own brethren and elders. Buddhism lost its punch in India after Adi Shankaracharya expounded the Vedantic teachings and organized debates with contemporary leaders of other religions, vanquishing them on their own grounds with his logical argumentation.

The Hindus treat the Bhagavad Gita as a summary of the Vedanta—Essences of the Vedas, known as the Upanishads. It is a science of Brahma (the Absolute) and a scripture on Yoga, as the means to enlightenment. It is hard to say what is more important in it. The Vedanta comprises the essence of the Vedas, whereas the Gita is the essence of Vedanta itself. That makes it the essence of essences. To tell what in it is important is to point out the essence of such an essence.

MZC: We were discussing that it may not be so appropriate to call Buddhists "atheists." I quoted what for me has become a koan over the years: "There is an Unborn, a Not-Becoming, a Not-Created, a Not-compounded. If there were not, this Unborn Not-becoming, not-created, not -compounded, there could not be any escape from the changing.... There is a path out from what is born, become, made, and compounded." I say a kind of "koan" only in the sense that it's a rich source of inquiry for me, not that's it's a formal koan I use in dialogue with a teacher.

I'm aware Buddha denied the existence of a personal God, but seems to allow what Hindus call Nirguna Brahman, which Hindus believe is primary to everything, including the idea of a personal God. Brahman is immanent, vast, beyond concepts. Why do we see such differences of a personal God, an impersonal God and so on? Why do Hindus firmly believe in atma, and Buddhists not?

DT: Concepts such as these are not the truth but a means or attempt to understand the truth. They differ from person to person, time to time. You might be aware that the Old Testament and [some] early Christians believed in the doctrine of rebirth. Both Christ and John the Baptist were portrayed as reborn prophets of an earlier era. The rebirth theory was later abandoned during the time of Emperor Constantine. Buddha himself had developed distaste for the dogmatic views of the Hindus of his day—the dogmatism, rituals and caste system. He criticized the Hindu scriptures.

Actually, if we study deeply the highest common factors in all major religions, they are similar. Followers later came and modified (and continue to modify even to this day) their religion to suit their individual tastes. Ultimately, little of the original religion survived. Hence there is a need for an in depth study before jumping to conclusions.

The subject itself is such that it is about entities that are not clearly defined and various viewpoints are possible. For example, if we take up rebirth for study, the question can be asked, "What, or who, is being reborn?" If you say, "The soul," one can argue, "When was the soul ever born, that it may be reborn?"

The most important point is that religions and doctrines have something great to be realized or experienced. We have to see for ourselves, within our selves and actions, what the Hindu concepts of freedom (*swarajya*); independence (*kaivalya*), self-realization (*atma sakshatkara*), God-realization (*brahma sakshatkar*), merging (*saayujya*) are truly all about.

All religions have such concepts that are necessarily limited; I just happen to be talking more about Hinduism with you. God exists in the same way as nature his creation exists. There are many connotations for God. God as Brahma, the creator, has a limited life period. When one Brahma's existence ends, another takes his place. In fact, there are many Brahamas coexisting. It is a field of existence called *Brahmaloka*. A person who nearly attains perfection and fails to reach the final goal attains this *loka* (region). His existence (individuality) lasts till the Big Crunch. Thereafter everything dissolves into Parabrahma, the originator that exists before during and after the Big Bang and continues even after the Big Crunch. To quote your favorite so called koan, "There is an Unborn, a Not-Becoming, a Not-Created, a Not-compounded. If there were not, this Unborn Not-becoming, not-created, not-compounded, there could not be any escape from that which is born etc."

MZC: Would you tell us about the roots of Hinduism?

DT: The Hindu religion has no founder. Rama and Krishna are Avatars (which is also how the Buddha is considered by the Hindus). They speak and act for its philosophy and Dharma, but are not its inventors. The philosophy is based on the discoveries made by Rishis (Seers) through deep meditation and reasoning, ceaselessly, for years on end. The rishis are also not its inventors. They have only discovered it for humanity, out of their own desire to know the truth. Knowledge is inherent in man and comes from the source—the Self—that is all knowing, but which through ignorance or limitations of the untrained mind believes itself to be limited. Systematic training and sharpening of the intellect part of the mind through meditation is all that is necessary to know the truth.

Relative knowledge comes from God and his creation. Beyond and above the knowledge of God and the Vedas is the knowledge of one's true nature—unborn, a not-become, not-made, not-compounded. Yet Buddha said concepts of such are incapable, in themselves, of liberating us from the sorrows of the world. Concepts are useful only as pointers to the truth. So the Buddha warns us against rote and dogmatic learning; he asks us to take up spiritual practice for the purpose of actually experiencing these truths.

MZC: What are your spiritual practices these days? What areas of spiritual inquiry interest you now?

DT: As I said earlier realization came at age thirty-two of this body. Thereafter the search ended. However, today relative existence continues as a part of the phenomenal world. I still practice *vipassana* and *kriya* yoga as they give me physical strength and mental well-being. When we do *vipassana*, we experience a great amount of rest and relaxation resulting in physical well-being, as well as peace and tranquility of the mind. This happens both before as well as after realization. Realization is something way beyond the mind and body. It is permanent and does not depend on any of these factors. Even then, the health of body and mind is an important factor, which contributes towards guiding others in the spiritual line. It helps to set an example. Your youthfulness, presence of mind, your intuition, ability to give sound advice etc. are the qualities that people look for in a realized person. So this serves as an inspiration to others. After complete relaxation through *vipassana*, the body/mind have to be reconditioned or reshaped to the required form as explained above. This is achieved through *kriya* yoga. They are mild exercises of mind and body, which help circulation, oxygenation, and re-energizing of the cells of the body and brain. The body & mind are like clay, which is kneaded and reshaped to something better each time. The sense of oneself being the body or mind is lost and the two are seen to be just instruments in the hands of the realized soul to be used for a noble cause. Some useful *kriyas* and *bandhas*, which can be got from any book on hatha yoga are *Moolabandha, Janandhara bandha, Uddiyana bandha, Nauli kriya, Jal neti* and so on.

Signals are brought in to the brain as before by the five senses, but their effects on the brain and mind have changed. They no longer hold the mind in sway and capture it. It is seen as a passing show. However, I still wish to maintain an interest in the spiritual knowledge of the phenomenal world known as *tatva jnana* or elemental knowledge. It helps to understand better the world in which I live and use this knowledge effectively to combat odds. In this way I can help others reduce their suffering and assist them in their quest for spiritual knowledge and freedom. For the past twenty-five years I have been acquiring such knowledge and disbursing it through discussion with interested persons. Relatively recently, since the past five years, I have been using the "*atmadnyana*" group site for sharing this knowledge with several other interested persons.

MZC: Just a last question. We've discussed that activism can be deluded and even harmful if the activist does not connect to the true sources of happiness and intelligence herself or himself. I would say activism is very important to help heal and empower all the people in our world, with fairness, equality for women, for homosexuals, for religion, for race. Sometimes there's a need to speak up strongly. If we look at all "as a passing show," we might be tempted to stoicism and non-involvement. How does the activist get in touch with the knowledge of what is truly good for all of us as a living community?

DT: I find there is the need to understand what good is and what not. Good and its opposite are the obverse and the converse of the same coin. You either take both or you take none. To do something believing that to be good for the world is a myth. You are actually doing good to yourself—soothing the pain you feel when you see someone suffering. A person who does good with this attitude never feels he is great or allows his ego to bloat. Even to think that one is God's chosen instrument to do good to others is egocentric. A truly enlightened person may be an activist, of course. He or she sees the law of cause and effect taking its course, perhaps in cultural prejudices against women and feels that the right approach would be to put an end to the causes of what's causing misery for these women, to eliminate the root causes, once and for all.

MZC: We can agree that "aggressive" can be viewed positively or negatively—that we don't want to do violence to others and ourselves as a way to achieve our activist goals. We intend to minimize the suffering both to ourselves and in the world as it presents itself to us. But this doesn't preclude forms of activism. My own view is that activism can be inspired by the best in religion, as well as inspired by the worst, fanatical, fundamentalist currents in all the religions, or by no religion at all. But the human heart still shines brighter than religion; we see "hometown" activism at its best all around us—helping ourselves and others to more independent and healthful.

How about saying let's do good both for each other and us. They go together; they are the "golden rule." Thanks a lot, Dilip. Let's keep exploring, growing, and evolving in goodness and life! Many blessings to our friends in India!

DT: Thanks to Morgan and Ken, for having stimulated such an enlightening discussion. I think it will be useful to all of us.

"I Meditate … and I also Live!"
Vipassana: Insight into Non-Self through Mindfulness
A Conversation with Nitin Trasi, M.D.

> *As darkness of night, even were it to last a thousand years, could not conceal the rising sun, so countless ages of conflict and suffering cannot conceal the innate radiance of Mind-Heart.*
>
> —Tilopa

MZC: Two principal forms of meditation are "concentration" meditation where we focus on one object or thought. Its purpose is serenity and has been practiced in many forms in India, long before the Buddha taught. Buddha's contribution to meditation practice is *vipassana* (insight) practice, or at least a new flavor of insight meditation; its purpose is to see through, with clear wisdom, all forms of the clinging that bind us, how we go from craving to that clingingness, that holding on and squeezing of our own minds and hearts. To see the way it is—that it's all changing, that there's suffering and distress, that we're not some solid selves, separated somehow from all else. We see how evanescent our sense of self becomes.

In the Theravadin School, where the name *vipassana* comes from, meditation practice must be based solidly on being human and compassionate to others and ourselves. How can one be present to the process within one's self while we observe and note our thoughts, feelings and consciousness itself? Can we notice our intentions? Can we allow (by gently witnessing) disturbing feelings just to be without added reactions? How does concentration meditation create a calm, quiet mental space wherein "insight" is said to intuitively arise?

NT: I would define the *vipassana* technique as the volitional practice of mindfulness (to be clearly distinguished from the occurrence of spontaneous, detached mindfulness or *vipassana* after enlightenment).

This pre-enlightenment *vipassana* technique is the meditative art or way of passive, alert, non-judgmental self-observation; all the "good" and "bad" that arises in your consciousness is simply witnessed. It is "passive" as contrasted with most Hindu meditative techniques, which teach active concentration on a single object, and it is non-judgmental as contrasted with Western psychoanalytic techniques. The result of intuitive wisdom which may then arise is a profound inner peace and in Buddhist terms, lasting insight into "non-self" (interconnectedness); the ever-changing nature of reality; and the "non-satisfactoriness" of clinging to self and permanence.

MZC: Does even this witnessing and subtle noticing fall away and weaken with the arising of intuitive wisdom?

NT: Some degree of tranquility seems to be a pre-condition for real understanding and insight. Concentration and insight are complementary. The process does become more and more spontaneous; and then techniques fall away.

The thirteenth century Japanese Zen master Dogen writes: "No mind, no body." No subject-no object. Identification (or attachment) arises when we are being overly concerned with the feeling of "me" and "mine." Therefore, who is to observe what? Observation happens. Your sense of separation, even as a witness, begins to dissolve.

MZC: Would you discuss the varying ways we refer to "I"? What is the ego and how does our relationship to the ego affect our spiritual lives? How can we understand the psychology of the "I"?

Sometimes, the process of meditation is described in terms of the ending of the ego. How are we able to function in the world if we don't have a healthy ego? How would you describe this "loss of ego"?

We might enrich our description of meditation with respect to the function of the healthy ego, rather than exclusively in its demise. Of course, ego is sometimes only considered in its negative, exclusively selfish aspect. We can also understand the ego in a positive sense, as our center of consciousness, worthy of self-love and appreciation, whose highest function is to serve and love, the ego as our bodies with perception, motor control, memory, ability to access what is preconscious, our affective life and affective memory from our earliest significant relationships to the present? We go to work or talk with our friends and children; our ego, given fresh and joyful perspective, engages life intelligently and with gusto.

In meditation and understanding, perhaps we could say we "lose our ego," but this "doer" is still available to us in our every day activities. This ego isn't eliminated.

NT: Alice, in Lewis Carroll's *Alice's Adventures in Wonderland*, exclaims: "Who in the world am I? Ah, that's the great puzzle!" The faculty of human thought is extremely complex, and the "I" of the average man or woman is much more than just a label for referring to his or herself. It is a complex conglomerate of several things. In Indian spiritual literature, the complex mechanism of the "I" (Sanskrit: *aham*) has been referred to as the "ego" (*ahamkara*), and it is said to be lost upon spiritual awakening or enlightenment.

But this is not easy to understand. As you say, how can a person function without the "I"? How will one act effectively in this intensely competitive world? Will he function in ordinary everyday activities and satisfy the demands of professional life or will he have to retire to the seclusion of the mountains, forest, or monastery? In other words, if spiritual awakening is tantamount to loss of the "I," how is this compatible with daily life?

The "I" is, of course, a label to refer to a particular living unit, but also consider "I" as the following: the "executive unit," making decisions; the "mental image" of ourselves, past memories included; and finally, "the soul (*jivatman*)," a belief that the "I" is somehow a separate entity that will survive death and go on to an afterlife or be reincarnated in another body.

Even if a person does not believe in the soul or afterlife,

there is still the conscious or unconscious belief in, and identification with, a "me" which exists during life, and which passes from birth to youth to old age to death, a continuity of a "me" which is seen as going through time in a linear fashion.

The mental image "I" is spiritually significant, because it is the cause of self-centered thinking and expectations and consequently of much avoidable suffering. So in spiritual teachings, this is the "ego" referred to, rather than the ego of Freudian psychology, which you rightly refer to as being able to be positive and healthy in human living and which, of course, should not be "destroyed."

The process of living and decision-making happens more efficiently, when untrammeled by unnecessary fears and anxiety about personal credit or risk, exaggerated self-pride or blame. Whereas the average man or woman may feel exalted by perceiving "himself" or "herself" as crushed by perceiving oneself as a "failure," the liberated person may be pleased and disappointed, but such pleasures or disappointments do not affect his happiness.

So enlightenment is not incompatible with a notion of "myself" as apparently continuous with time, but not where this valuation is taken so seriously that it affects one's happiness, and not where there is clinging to past or future in a way that rips away attention from the present.

The proper understanding of the entire psychology of the "I" ultimately leads to seeing "non-self," "non-soul." The "I-ness" and the otherness of the "you" are lost and there is therefore no basis for alienation, enmity, blame, envy. This isn't contradictory to your wanting a healthy human personality that grows into an authentic character or "self."

MZC: How do you describe "self-inquiry"? I am most familiar with Ramana Maharshi's teaching, but which I'm aware was in ancient Hindu spiritual literature such as in the Sri *Vasistha Sangraha* II, 44-6. In the West, "Know yourself and know for yourself," goes back to Socrates.

NT: Self-enquiry is not a method of sitting meditation. It refers rather to an inner attitude of constant introspective investigation or "looking inward" to see into one's own mental processes and understand the psychological composition of the "me" or "self" within. Whereas all other methods assume a "doer" of those respective methods, self-enquiry strikes at the very root of "doer-ship" by questioning "who" is the "doer" of any method—or the "thinker" of any thoughts! The object of self-enquiry is thus not to get an answer (say like "I am pure awareness") but rather to feel the absence of a superimposed entity (self) whatsoever. This very absence being the "finding" of "pure presence." Self-enquiry is a method to end all methods.

MZC: Would you describe the term *samadhi* which has several meanings when we speak of meditation?

NT: One *samadhi* is a state of temporary bliss which can be reached in meditation. The technical terms *kevala savikalpa samadhi* and *kevala nirvikalpa samadhi* in Sanskrit denote the two successive stages in temporary, blissful states achieved through forms of meditation. However, the state of the awakened person has also been referred to as *samadhi*, and this is a different state altogether, the actual term being *sahaja Samadhi,* meaning "natural," "spontaneous." This is the state in which the awakened person finds himself or herself and which is permanent or rather his or her "default" state. This is a state whose basic feature is contentment.

MZC: Yes, Buddhist meditation is sometimes describing falling away of bliss, finally resolving in a deep, untouchable sense of inner peace.

NT: Bliss is a temporary, pleasurable state, the opposite of misery. On the other hand, contentment here is taken to mean not the opposite of any unhappy state, but rather the basic nature of our essential awareness, "who" we really essentially are, beneath the layer of who we think we are, which is said to be contentment. This state doesn't need anything from the outside to achieve it. It is already always there. The enlightened one may experience other modes of mind including bliss, but even here the bliss will be temporary. There may also be sadness or disappointment. This sounds strange, for how can anyone be contented and sad at the same time? But remember that sadness here is a superficial emotion, and is recognized as such, and the person remains a basically contented individual who does not change. Our very nature is this happy peacefulness. This consciousness is always already here for us and does not need anything to bring it "on." This is so in all people, right here, right now.

MZC: And what about our ordinary human pleasures? Why do you think religion often equates naturally beautiful sexual expression with somehow being anti-God inspired?

NT: The daily pleasures are felt and enjoyed even more keenly, because they are enjoyed fully, wholly and whole-heartedly. But there is no clinging to them as in the average person. And the reason why there is no clinging is that there is constantly the intuitive understanding, insight or sensing that it is the primal consciousness and its inherent taste, bliss (*ananda*) that abides and is the necessary condition for all our human pleasures as they come and go. This causeless contentment of being is awakened in us and gives us an abiding peace; thus the need to cling to pleasures and desires is released naturally.

The difference in the enlightened is not in the manner of daily living, but in the inner silence that enables him or her to be keenly alive to this primal awareness, which animates the body and which, is the core and basis of his or her very being.

So the strong egocentric perspective of the average person changes to a softer, broader perspective which allows many more points of view and possibilities. This changed perspective leads to a process of de-conditioning from the effects of the earlier egocentric conditioning which had built up throughout life.

MZC: Would you comment on the different levels of individual responsibility as we encounter both our responsibilities in our lives, as well as meditation experiences?

NT: Perhaps, very simplistically, we can speak of three levels of spiritual teaching: first, there is the level where each individual is responsible for his or her own actions and is expected to follow moral laws; second, there is the level where the individual surrenders to God or whatever power he or she believes in. Here the individual is seen to have no ultimate volition different from "God's will." This devotional quality can be sincere and is known in all the great religious traditions. In India, such an individual is called a *bhakta*; third, on the ultimate mystical level, there is no separate individual to have any separate volition.

Of course, these levels are not exclusive of each other and are complementary.

MZC: Can a "neurotic" or "emotionally-disturbed" individual bypass therapy and begin to meditate?

NT: He or she may first need psychotherapy, depending on the individual case. The path to enlightenment through *vipassana* is most commonly for the well balanced, for the psychologically mature individual. It requires a focused, open presence.

In the context of enlightenment, all techniques, all therapies serve to bring one to a certain preliminary stage from which one could perhaps, if one is so inclined, whole-heartedly take up meditation as a path to full spiritual growth. Meditation is not for everyone. And not everyone who takes up meditation necessarily needs therapy.

MZC: Are you aware of any empirical studies comparing the usual psychotherapies with mindfulness meditation applied to clinical cases?

NT: Two of my colleagues, both psychiatrists, one also

a senior *vipassana* teacher at the Igatpuri Institute, have done research on this. *Vipassana* can be a useful adjunct to treatment in minor neuroses, in receptive clients. It may be used to give the practitioner an insight into her or his own neurosis. *Vipassana* has also been tried in more severe cases. An experiment was also conducted in Tihar Jail in India where some hardened convicts gave *vipassana* meditation an honest try and had excellent results. Again, what works for one may not work for another.

MZC: How do you feel about activism? Are there some activist causes that attract your attention and interest? What are they? What's the positive and negative about activism?

NT: Most issues where activism exists today are complex issues. I am interested in many of these issues, but I can see both, or even several, points of view, and so find that I cannot take sides. In fact, as one matures, one's viewpoint broadens and one begins to see many more points of view of these complex situations. So it is difficult for such a person to take a strong view on them in any one particular direction. In fact, in a complex issue, there may be more than one correct point of view.

This is how activism is defined:

> *A doctrine or practice that emphasizes direct vigorous action especially in support of or opposition to one side of a controversial issue (Webster).*

> *The use of direct and noticeable action to achieve a result, usually a political or social one (Cambridge).*

As you can see, the very meaning of the word implies the use of force to achieve an end, or to convert people to one's own point of view. I don't see this as the best way to do that anyway, even presuming that one's particular point of view is definitely the only correct one, which of course there is no real way of deciding to everyone's satisfaction.

The activist approach appears to oversimplify these issues

and see them only as black or white questions, which they are not.

Moreover, most activists, even if they start off with basically good intentions (and not all do), are eventually carried away by their own arguments and enthusiasm and often end up doing more harm than good.

MZC: Well, that's very helpful, Nitin. Yes, I must agree—I wouldn't say most—but some activists can be carried away by their own self-importance. And there are many levels of "violent" and "non-violent" activism. Activism doesn't have to imply violence and I feel there is a deep non-violent peaceful definition of being activist. For me the simplest, most practical and peaceful activist projects catch my heart, but also larger issues involve my support, my taking sides if you will, such as in the past, the civil rights movement in the United States and the present struggle in Myanmar for political freedom— activist in the sense of achieving social result, and sometimes, a political result. I've been inspired by people who advocate for the poor, the homeless, for AIDS and many good causes. Wasn't that what Jesus was about?

Thanks again, that was very informative and enlightening, Nitin.

Taking the Next Step
A Note on Activism as a Spiritual Practice
Ken Ireland

> *The Blessed Lord said: Time I am, destroyer of the worlds,*
> *and I have come to engage all people. With the exception*
> *of you, all the soldiers here on both sides will be slain."*
>
> Bhagavad-Gita 11:32

Dilip Trasi and Nitin Trasi are committed and skilled practitioners who speak out of their own experience of meditation. Both have a deep understanding of the Hindu meditation tradition and both have worked with authentic teachers. They are also both laymen, not Brahmins, gurus or clergy, who set themselves apart by claiming special knowledge and this, in my view, allows for a freer exchange of ideas as well as a search for a common language in which we can share our experience. However, when questioned about activism and practice, we entered a territory where they felt that they had to offer cautions and reservations. Not that their reservations might not be valid in some cases, but I hope to show if the heart of the spiritual activists' motivation and practice is of the simple "do-gooder" variety, it does not work as a spiritual practice and much less as effective community organizing.

One argument against activism runs like this: when faced with a choice between several courses of action, or taking no action whatsoever, we cannot say with certainty which one is the better, and, even if we practice some form of meditation, given that maturity in practice seems to sharpen our ability to discern the shades of grey, we cannot favor one position over another. This caution halts us in out tracks. The idea is not exclusively Eastern. Albert Camus said; "The evil that is in the world almost always comes from ignorance, and good intentions may do as much harm as malevolence if they lack understanding." (*The Plague*)

However, in all cases, no matter what our motivation or position, in any situation, in any relationship, in any community, country, tradition, or time, all actions produce results. Religious precepts, as they are called in Buddhism, recognize that living our lives leaves a trail of consequences. The possibility of making a mistake does not relieve the obligation to try to act responsibly; rather it imposes a further, perhaps more difficult obligation to remain open and test your experience, examine the results, and then change course if you find yourself embarked on an unproductive or negative course of action.

There is a second argument: that the desire to relieve universal suffering really stems from a desire to relieve one's own suffering, that it is a myth to believe that we actually help others. From a Buddhist point of view, we are all intimately interconnected in a world that is always in flux. Most practitioners recognize that the source of suffering is not outside ourselves, that we are ultimately responsible for the conditions that cause suffering. That is in fact one of the reasons why we act. Activism is not reserved for enlightened beings. Submitting to moral obligation is for both ordinary and "enlightened" people. Besides, the conservative position—don't act unless you are certain that your actions will have no harmful consequences—presupposes that omniscience, being able to foresee all the consequences of our actions, is available to humans. I have seen no evidence that such awareness is possible, even in supposedly enlightened beings.

And finally, what I would like to call the "conservative position" asserts that the strain on the social order caused by righting a wrong, causes far more pain, confusion and upset than any possible benefit of the actions. I do not buy into the argument that activists are wrong headed, self-indulgent and create harm because they upset the status quo.

The only part of that analysis that I can support is that some consequences of our actions will be unforeseen. But what is wrong with that? It will not stop me from trying to prevent women and children from being sold into sexual slavery or help innocents caught in the crossfire of the civil strife in Iraq. I will say more about any strain on the social fabric when I touch on the practice of non-violence.

Take ending of the enslavement of Africans in America or stopping the holocaust of the Jewish people that came with the Allied victory over Germany in 1945. These were patent evils engrained in the fabric of a society, or the programs of a powerful single party fascist regime. They had to be eradicated by whatever force necessary though we may have to sort out the consequences of both the American Civil War and World War II for several more generations.

Morgan, who is deeply involved in the activist world, said that he too regretted that some activists, though relatively very few, get carried away by their own self-importance. When I questioned Morgan, his objection was that "full fledged" activists who had a lot of unexamined personal motivations made organizing difficult, not that they, with few exceptions, were prone to mistakes that would cause harm in the outcome. But even this is not my experience. Perhaps my position is biased because my sample of activists comes largely from a group that creates effective actions in support of a cause as spiritual practice, not an add-on, or something to do during the rainy season when you don't feel like meditating. Practice does more than keep an activist focused. It is the source of their action.

Nitin Trasi used this definition of activism in his analysis: *A doctrine or practice that emphasizes direct vigorous action especially in support of or opposition to one side of a controversial issue* (Webster). I want to suggest that this definition is not broad enough to include cases in which spiritual practice is the real operative factor.

The greatest modern proponent of the spiritual practice of activism was Mahatma Gandhi, and the traditions from which he derived *Satyagraha,* Sanskrit for "truth force," were mostly Indian—Hindu, Buddhist and Jain. He also read the gospels of Jesus and was undoubtedly influenced by the saying: "whatever you do for the least of my brothers, you do also to me." In the Western monotheistic traditions, taking care of the world, *tikkun* in Hebrew, caring for the least fortunate of society, *charitas* in Latin, has always been part of religious practice, much more so than in Hinduism. When we talk or write about the practice of non-violence as Gandhi developed and practiced it, we are translating the Sanskrit, *Ahimsa*, which means literally "the avoidance of violence," but it is impossible not to see the influence of his western education.

Gandhi himself, Martin Luther King, Dick Gregory, as well as the Dalai Lama in his efforts to free Tibet from the oppression of Han Chinese overlords, have all undertaken practice to quell selfish motivation and focus on the goals of clearing a path to justice and equality. Many of the Jesuits and ex-Jesuits represented here in *Meanderings* use the discernment of spirits outlined in the "*Spiritual Exercises* of St. Ignatius" to weigh their activism. The American abolitionists of the nineteenth century were for the most part inspired by their religious convictions, transcendentalism or Quakerism, worldviews that hold all the created, visible world to be intricately connected and their practice had the flavor of the Great Awakening, with all its limitations—preaching and conversion.

Without humans, aggression, hatred, anger are not a perpetual motion machine. They need our energy to keep the pendulum swinging. A problem arises when, by applying a force strong enough to counteract the prevailing intransigence of a social order which supports evil, inequality and social injustice, we perpetuate the underlying mechanism that holds those structures in place. Halting that engine also has side effects— what will fill the void?

There are always far-reaching effects accompanying any action, violent or non-violent. For example, World War II, which was to be the war that ended war, has not marked the end of aggression and killing. It was not enough to defeat Hitler just as winning the US Civil War was not sufficient to cause the complete freedom of African slaves. (Though there is some evidence that the amount of armed conflict has been reduced since the defeat of Germany and Japan). In the ending of the British rule over India, the Mahatma struggled with the immediate consequences of partition and the bloodshed between Hindu and Muslim. The fast he undertook in an attempt to halt the violence nearly cost his life. He says in *The Story of My Experiments with Truth*, "When I despair, I remember that all through history the way of truth and love has always won. There have been tyrants and murderers and for a time they seem invincible, but in the end, they always fall—think of it, always." It's just simplistic to think that any one action can end injustice or suffering. It is more a continuing struggle in which humans must engage. The birth of modern India, the largest functioning democracy on earth, has increased wealth and opportunities for Indians of all social strata. This is neither a myth nor inconsequential.

Whether or not one holds to some vague concept "progress" or the endless repetition of karma due to the consequences of our actions, it seems that the world has changed and continues to change. That all life is impermanent, always being born and passing out of existence seems almost self-evident. Though I have never studied all the ways that the Hindu point of view differs from the Buddhist view, in Buddhism lived experience opens the door to religious practice.

Those who have some taste for practice seem to have chosen the path that was begun by Mohandas Gandhi. As with any practice, *Ahimsa* takes practice. It is not a theory. Though solidly based on the most ancient understanding of man's place in the universe, it launches us into the unknown territory of caring for all of humanity, the entire earth in a new way. It requires the most courageous action and deep meditation. It requires that our spiritual practice take on a wider goal than our own salvation or enlightenment.

We are in the middle of such a revolution. The aims of the revolution seem to be clear clean the environment, curtail the destructive power of our weapons, find new ways of resolving conflict, create universal recognition of human rights. They also include what Jesus taught as 'charity'—to feed the hungry, care for the sick, clothe the naked, visit the prisoners. What is not clear is the path we chose to follow to achieve those goals. The old institutions have failed or are crumbling. What will emerge? Where do we place our bets and focus time and resources? Those who are in the middle of a revolution are least likely to recognize it. They are certainly among the last to appreciate it—they are way too busy tending to immediate concerns of Right Now! We don't even know if we will succeed.

It will also demand new myths, and I mean myth in the most powerful sense, not fantasy, but images that capture the imagination in a powerful way. And it seems that one of those myths will be the story of the *Bhagavad-gita,* which has inspired Hindus and fascinated Westerners. In Philip Glass's *Satyagraha, An Opera in Three Acts* (2001), huge chariots for Arjuna and Krishna with larger than life puppet figures are drawn up on the stage; the prologue is verses from the *Gita* sung, chanted in Sanskrit. On the Kuru Field of Justice, Lord Krishna tells the warrior Arjuna to put aside pain and pleasure, that action is his moral duty: "Be unconcerned with consequences, with victory or defeat, but act with the world's welfare as your intention" (*LA Times*, April 2008). Then when the figure of Gandhi walks onto the stage, small and clothed simply in a loincloth as he appears in later pictures; it is a powerful statement of "Truth Force." But the performance is not left in some reverential version of Indian history—in the third act, Martin Luther King appears behind Gandhi, superimposed in a TV clip of his famous "I have a Dream" speech which electrified a generation of civil rights activists.

I would like to quote what J. Robert Oppenheimer said about his experience at the first test explosion of the atomic bomb, July 16, 1945. "We knew the world would not be the same. A few people laughed, a few people cried. Most people were silent. I remembered the line from the Hindu scripture, the *Bhagavad-gita;* Vishnu is trying to persuade the Prince that he should do his duty, and to impress him, takes on his multi-armed form and says, 'Now I am become Death, the destroyer of worlds.' I suppose we all thought that, one way or another."

There may be some exaggeration in his statement. By the time he said it on TV in the 50s, Oppenheimer had already become an activist working to stop the "Arms Race" and curtail the use of both nuclear fission and fusion in the manufacture of weapons.

Man now has developed a technology powerful enough to destroy himself, certainly to visit unfathomable pain and destruction on his fellow beings. The usual political balance for checking power, aggression and greed do not seem to be adequate to the task. It is not surprising to see that creativity, coupled with the spiritual dimension of reverence for all life, have shown up as potential sources for finding a way, not just to remedy injustice and relieve suffering, but to ensure human survival.

Because Dilip or Nitin didn't have the opportunity to read and respond to my argument, I will give Dilip the (almost) last word on the subject.

"Let me investigate the useful side of [activism]. Activism in a beneficent sense can be defined as aggressive action towards a specific goal. We always find that in nature there exist thresholds. Right from the atom onwards, we find that a minimum energy barrier has to be crossed to overcome the forces of nature, which is called the threshold force. For example to get free of the force of gravity of the earth, a minimum velocity called escape velocity has to be exceeded (approximately seven miles per second).

"Applying activism to inventiveness, we find that many of the great inventers were intoxicated with only thoughts concerning their invention. Scientists were considered as absent-minded people. But this is the kind of aggressiveness and activism that is necessary to break the thought barrier.

"Finally, applying activism to spirituality, we find that a paradigm change in understanding is necessary, like the quantum jump of an electron, freeing from the influence of the nucleus. Maya is like the intra-atomic force that binds the electron to the nucleus. To overcome the influence of Maya or ignorance, one has to be intoxicated with *Atma*-consciousness or God-consciousness. Ramakrishna Paramahansa and Ramana Maharshi were typical examples of such persons."

In the last analysis, any call to action for the spiritually centered person is an act of faith, in the deepest sense—that he or she is called to participate in the action of God loving, caring for our world, that the easing of suffering is part of the dynamic of God's love. To close, I am not going to quote scripture or give a sermon, but rather quote one of my heroes, the visionary architect, Bucky Fuller (from *No More Secondhand God* by R. Buckminster Fuller):

> Yes, God is a verb,
> the most active,
> connoting the vast harmonic
> reordering of the universe
> from unleashed chaos of energy.
> And there is born unheralded
> a great natural peace,
> not out of exclusive
> pseudo-static security
> but out of including, refining, dynamic balancing.
> Naught is lost.
> Only the false and nonexistent are dispelled.

509

Unlocking Inner Peace
Vipassana Meditation in Prisons
Rebecca Shepard

From *The Land Of Plenty* by Leonard Cohen

For the millions in a prison,
That wealth has set apart,
For the Christ who has not risen,
From the caverns of the heart.

For the innermost decision,
That we cannot but obey,
For what's left of our religion,
I lift my voice and pray:
May the lights in the land of plenty
Shine on the truth some day.

Cohen's lyrics may be about all the kinds of personal prisons that we create for ourselves, but it is a startling fact that of any western democracy, the United States incarcerates the most people. There are many causes. One is that prison itself is a cause of creating, not rehabilitating prisoners—more than one half will return after they are released. A June 2006 U.S. prison study by a bipartisan commission on Safety and Abuse in America's Prisons reports that the United States has about two million incarcerated. African Americans are imprisoned at a seven times higher rate than whites and Hispanics at a three times higher rate. Within three years, 67 percent are re-arrested and 52 percent are re-incarcerated. The commission says that even small improvements in medical care could reduce recidivism. There is, perhaps, at least a suggestion of a way towards a solution to this problem in a modern adaptation of one of the oldest forms of Buddhist meditation, Vipassana.

The Web site http://www.prison.dhamma.org is a wonderful complementary resource to Rebecca's article and provides contact information if you know of an opportunity to expand the program. Its topics include Vipassana; S.N. Goenka; Code of Discipline for Prison Classes; Interviews with a director of a Seattle prison; research documentation and a link to the International Vipassana Meditation Web site. Vipassana is taught by S.N. Goenka in the tradition of Sayagi U Ba Khin, http://www.dhamma.org. *The book,* Letters from The Dhamma Brothers *(Pariyatti Press) by Jenny Phillips, takes us into a maximum-security Alabama prison where we meet men " who form a brotherhood" after taking a ten-day Vipassana meditation retreat.*

My friend Don Foran suggested this article about Vipassana and Prison by his former student, Rebecca Shepard. He says that Rebecca was the very rare student, a practitioner of meditation, who is both self-motivated and imaginative in bringing her passion for prison reform into her classroom communication.

S.N. Goenka writes: "Our task is to eradicate suffering by eradicating its causes: ignorance, craving, and aversion. … Vipassana, the development of insight into one's own nature, is observation of the reality within oneself … taking as the object of attention one's own physical sensations. … [I]n order to develop experiential wisdom, … we must develop awareness of sensations … whereby we also observe the mind."

In recent years, a new type of prison rehabilitation has been introduced. It is called Vipassana meditation, and, when integrated into prison reform, it can aid the prisoner in overcoming behavioral addictions and facilitate healthy change in the prisoner's life.

In a July/August 1999 article "Vipassana Meditation at the North Rehabilitation Facility" published in the *American Jails Magazine,* Lucia Meijer describes Vipassana meditation as "a mental discipline and ethical practice taught over two thousand years ago by the historic Buddha. Although Vipassana contains the core of what later has been called Buddhism, it is not an organized religion, requires no conversion, and is practiced by people of many different faiths and nationalities."

Vipassana literally means "to see things as they really are." It is a logical manner through which one eradicates impurities by means of self-observation. One observes the physical sensations throughout the body. This attentive introspection, in turn, starts uprooting the foundation for such impurities as craving, aversion, anger and ignorance. Once the roots of suffering in the prisoner begin to be removed, one starts to purify the mind/heart and begins the long process of liberating oneself from the bondage of bad habits, being uncontrollably reactive.

S.N. Goenka Vipassana courses, whether inside or outside of a prison, are taught during a ten-day silent retreat. Students undertake a rigorous daily schedule from 4 AM to 9 PM. They are asked to follow a simple code of moral conduct: not to steal, lie or kill and to refrain from intoxicants and sexual misconduct. The students' minds become calmer which aids them in their journey. Goenka, and his trained assistants, teach the courses. They are taught in over one hundred different centers worldwide. Recently, courses have been integrated into prisons as an alternative and complement to traditional prison rehabilitation. More than ten thousand prisoners have attended ten-day Vipassana retreats around the world.

The students learn to observe their breath—by focusing on breathing at the nostrils—for the first three days. In doing this simple—yet difficult—task, the mind starts to become more concentrated and begins to quiet. The student calms down. This is the first step in learning how to have control over the mind. On the fourth day, students learn to observe sensations in/on the body—such as heat and cold, pain or tingling, itching or even numbness and to try not to react to them. This simple attitude of non-reaction begins to change the habits of the mind.

Alan Marlatt (*Mindfulness and Acceptance*, Guilford Press, N.Y., 2004): "People may go through life thinking they are addicted to alcohol or drugs and always needing more and more to satisfy their craving. But in actuality, they are not addicted to these outside cravings or aversions—they are actually addicted to the sensations created on the body by these substances…. If one can learn to observe and not react, one starts to come out of the circle of always reacting. In the end, this gives the person the opportunity to make real choices, not based on blind reactions but on inner wisdom … to assist inmates to change long-standing habitual behavioral problems such as addictive behavior, relapse and recidivism."

I've studied three particular prisons, which have used the Vipassana model: Tihar Jail in India; North Rehabilitation Facility in Washington; and W.E. Donaldson Correctional Facility in Alabama. The results were very similar in that prisoners gained a sense of clarity, responsibility and self-worth, tremendous help in changing their lives from the inside out. Once offered a retreat and then accepting this opportunity to change through meditation, prisoners realize that they *themselves* can alter habit patterns. They can live and act, not by automatic reactions, but from conscious, "life-giving" choices.

Tihar Jail

In the *New York Times*, an article written by Stephen Holden was published titled "Prisoners Finding Hope in the Art of Spiritual Bliss." This was a review done on an award-winning documentary film title *Doing Time, Doing Vipassana*. The documentary was filmed in 1997 and told the story of the early Vipassana courses in Tihar, India's largest jail in New Delhi. Holden claims that in 1993, "When Kiran Bedi became Inspector General, Tihar was a violent overcrowded hellhole … the idealistic reformer introduced Vipassana … to Tihar that year in a course offered to one hundred prisoners. It was so successful that the next year enrollment was expanded to one thousand. Ms. Bedi was determined, she says, not only to improve living conditions in Tihar, but also to make prisoners 'better people.'"

In taking this step of faith, Ms. Bedi not only helped to create a better jail system at Tihar, but the courses proved to be so beneficial to the inmates that a Vipassana Prison Center was established in the jail itself offering courses to inmates year round for anyone who chooses them.

Two detailed studies were conducted based on the results that directly followed a ten-day meditation course at the Tihar Jail. In *Psychological Effects of Vipassana on Tihar Jail Inmates* (Igatpuri, India) Kishore Chandiramani asserts that after the Vipassana courses, inmates were found to be significantly less hostile towards others and felt less helpless as well as noted improvement in those who suffered with anxiety and depression. The inmates who meditated emanated a sense of well-being and had a positive outlook for their future. The overall results of these two studies were encouraging which suggests that Vipassana was a good source of prison reform. Chandiramani reports "the prisoners engage themselves in more productive work and have a sense of achievement."

The limitations of the studies are pointed out as well. "A major limitation of any scientific investigation is that it tests only that which can be objectified and experimentally measured. The unique characteristics of each individual and the finer human aspects of change process are often ignored. It is therefore essential that the scientific information gathered through inventories and scales be supplemented with individual based, in-depth experiential accounts and the qualitative assessments by the jail supervisors."

The first study in January 1994 had 120 subjects. Well being, hostility, hope, helplessness, personality, psychopathology, and, for those suffering psychological disorders, anxiety and depression were the dimensions studied. The second study was in April 1994 with 150 subjects. It consisted of two groups, eighty-five subjects who attended the Vipassana course and a group of sixty-five who did not. Here the dimensions were anomie, "attitude" towards the law, personality and psychiatric illness.

The subjects were found to be less hostile and felt less helpless. Among the 23 percent of patients with psychological disorders, there was improvement in their anxiety and depressive symptoms. The studies used questionnaires and, for the impact of Vipassana on personality, the Personality Trait Inventory and Draw a Person test were used. Drawing a Person test is administered such that "the drawing of a person represents the expression of the self or of the body in the environment," thus representing the self-image or body image of the person who draws. There were positive changes in the study group, such as a more holistic balanced picture of self. "Subjects without any psychological symptoms reported improvement in the form of enhanced well being and a sense of hope for the future. Their sense of alienation from the mainstream life, though unchanged immediately after the course, was found to be lower after three months. The follow-up evaluation at three and six month intervals revealed further improvement on many of these dimensions, although the initial improvement in hope and hostility was not sustained. The change process thus initiated can be strengthened by eliminating the factors working against the impact of Vipassana and by encouraging the regularity of practice."

Tihar jail has about nine thousand prisoners. Introducing Vipassana is part of the effort to shift from a custodial to a rehabilitative approach, "a more humane approach in dealing with prisoners." More than two thousand prisoners have learnt Vipassana and it's also been offered in other Indian prisons, such as in Baroda, Hyderabad, Ahmedadbad, Bagalore, Patna.

Once given the opportunity to really change, some of the prisoners realize that the only thing stopping them from leading more positive lives is the lack of the ability to free

515

themselves from old habitual patterns. Once the prisoners begin to break down their inner walls, they have the chance to rebuild them with more wholesome actions based not on plain reactions but on conscious choices.

North Rehabilitation Facility, King County, Washington

Recidivism rates are alarmingly high in American prisons, with about 67.5 percent within three years of release according to a 1994 U.S. Department of Justice in a study of just under three hundred thousand prisoners. Vipassana can be a way to create an opportunity whereby prisoners can take the responsibility to change from within. By putting Vipassana into action, prisoners begin to take charge of their lives and work towards improving themselves to become better people and therefore better citizens in the community.

In November 1997, the North Rehabilitation Facility became the first jail in the United States to hold a Vipassana course inside its compound, as well as the only jail to have repeating courses. Many of the institutional staff believed that the inmates could not endure the difficult 10-day course of silence, long hours of sitting and a challenging schedule. After eleven men completed the first course, friends, family, staff and other inmates greeted them at a reception in the gymnasium. As the men walked in, other inmates and staff stood up and cheered. One of the observing inmates cheered, not just because of those eleven men who completed the course, but also for the opportunity of hope and change that these individuals represented.

The jail staff noticed changes in the students. Staff enthusiasm and support increased after seeing the results of the first course. They said that the students participated more in other prison programs, got along better with each other and with the staff, followed rules with less resistance, and had improved relationships with their families.

The *Vipassana Newsletter* published a statement from one of the former residents of North Rehabilitation Facility: "I had been drunk all my life before taking the first Vipassana course at NRF in 1997. Since then, I've not had a fight, not a drink. I have a family life. My family appreciates you, the people who facilitated the course, so much." A sense of gratitude is a tremendous quality to develop and this shows how inmates coming from all walks of life embrace this simple yet ethical truth of gratefulness. This is a large part of becoming a good person starting from the inside out.

In 2002, Dave Murphy, the programs manager at NRF, completed a Vipassana recidivism study that was published on the Vipassana Prison Trust Web site with data from the initial eight Vipassana courses at NRF. Murphy's study showed that within two years, three out of four NRF inmates were re-incarcerated, while only two out of four Vipassana inmates were re-incarcerated. Moreover, the average number of bookings declined from 2.9 pre-Vipassana to 1.5 post-Vipassana/post-NRF releases.

In 2002, NRF closed after twenty-one years as an "alternative detention center. It hosted twenty Vipassana courses over five years. However, since then, there have been courses in California, Alabama, Texas, Massachusetts, Vermont, Taiwan, Israel, New Zealand, U.K. and Mexico.

W.E. Donaldson Correctional Facility, Bessemer, Alabama

A column was written in the *Vipassana Newsletter* about a prison course that took place in January 2002 at the W.E. Donaldson Correctional Facility with its barbed-wire walls and heavily armed grounds. "Donaldson State Prison is the highest security-level prison in Alabama and has a history of being Alabama's most violent and brutal prison.... Approximately half of the twenty inmates taking the course were under a life-sentence, some with the possibility of parole, others without hope of parole." A guard says: "This is where they send all the screw-ups."

The second course took place in May of 2002. One of the inmates who had completed the course said, as he wiped away tears of gratitude: "I've always been angry, I've always been angry. I've took (sic) anger management, stress management. But anger management is showing me how to conceal the anger and stress management is teaching me basically the same. When I took Vipassana and sat on that cushion for ten days, that showed me how to let it come up and deal with it, don't ... suppress it ... I've made a mistake and everyone can change ... and I can say I can change and it feels good." (Jenny Philips, Ph.D., Lionheart Foundation, from a 12-minute preview of the documentary, *Freedom Behind Bars*)

Another prisoner writes: "I must say that Vipassana had the most profound effect I have ever witnessed on a group of inmates. The changes I've noticed within myself have made a remarkable difference in the way I view things ... equanimity. I'm able to deal with situations more calmly than before because now I can see everything in a better perspective.... It has brought about tremendous changes in my life." (See *Vipassana Newsletter*, Vol. 30, No. 1, May 2003)

Conclusion

When prisoners practice this type of meditation, it begins to work at the root of problems; it opens the prisoner up to realizing that every action they have taken in their lives was influenced by their own decision. They begin to see they have some responsibility for the actions that they have done in the past. More importantly, an understanding develops that they have the ability to choose all their future actions. They have tools that can be applied to their daily lives, daily decisions. Of course, taking the ten-day course is just a beginning. Prisoners are encouraged to continue to meditate one or two times a day, if possible, to help in strengthening the benefits from their meditation practice. This should help the prisoners prepare for life in society.

Vipassana is not rewarding prisoners for their crimes, but giving back what first belonged to them: their inner freedom and the choice to make rational decisions based on their human sense of morals. In his book about the effects of Vipassana, Chandiramani reports that the key to Vipassana is within the individual herself or himself. "He or she must be treated with love and compassion; he must be trained to improve himself, not by exhortations to follow moral precepts, but by being instilled with the authentic desire to change. He must be taught to explore himself, to initiate a process which can bring about transformation and lead to purification of mind. This is a change that will be enduring. Vipassana has the capacity to transform the human mind and character. The opportunity is awaiting all who sincerely wish to make the effort." (p. 44)

This meditation is not magic nor is it an escape route from life. It is a plain and simple technique that once practiced and applied, gives enormous benefits to the one who is practicing. It reveals a person's inner truth and gives heart to that person in living a happier and healthier life attuned to the person's inner will to change for the better.

Bathing Baby Buddha
Studying the Vinaya in the Twenty-first Century
Morgan Zo-Callahan

> *"We're kind of a communist outfit, spiritual communists! All the real property of the community is owned by the community. Things that affect the whole community are most often discussed and decided on by the whole community. And decisions are ideally made by consensus. According to the Vinaya, the monastic discipline, everyone has an equal say. Occasionally, if things cannot be decided by consensus, they'll be decided by majority vote."*
>
> —Ajahn Amaro, speaking about
> his Buddhist community

In many Asian countries, the Sangha, the community of Buddhist monks and nuns, is one of the most visible symbols of the spiritual world of Buddhism, and their influence in these societies stretches over long periods of time, much longer than religious communities have even existed in the West. Buddhist monastic communities trace back their lineage twenty-five centuries to the Buddha himself who abandoned lay life, became a seeker and, after his Enlightenment, gathered other like-minded people, both men and women over the course of his long teaching career, to learn from him and practice together.

The rules and norms for community life and the conduct of ordained monks and nuns are found in the Vinaya. The Vinaya fills the entire third section of the Buddhist Canon, the Tripitaka. Ancient texts in both Pali and Sanskrit have been passed down to this generation. The version that is most widely observed in the monastic communities called the Theravada, "the elder school" in English, includes 227 major rules for *bhikkhus* and 311 major rules for *bhikkhunis*, specific regulations that cover almost every activity from mealtime to toilette etiquette. This is the Pali version of the Patimokkha.

"The Vibhanga section(s) of Vinaya Pitaka gives a commentary on these rules, along with the origin stories for each rule. The Khandhaka/Skandhaka sections give numerous supplementary rules grouped by subject, again with origin stories. The Buddha called his teaching the "Dhamma-Vinaya", emphasizing both the philosophical teachings of Buddhism as well as the training in virtue that embodies that philosophy. In the collected Chinese editions of the Scriptures the Vinaya pitaka has a broader sense, including all four Chinese *vinayas* listed above, parts of others, non-canonical *vinaya* literature, lay *vinaya* and bodhisattva *vinaya*." (Wikipedia)

There is a venerable ancient tradition of careful Vinaya study by all followers, lay and ordained. It is an indispensable foundation for some aspects of the Buddha's teachings, inseparable from the Dharma. I will try to make a case that our conversations, discussions and practice of the Vinaya, both as it applies to the ordained monks and nuns as well as lay people who take the precepts. Our study is turning the Dharma wheel, an indispensable part of living as Buddhists in our day-to-day lives here and now. But, if made into a dogmatic, literalistic scripture, it becomes, not liberating, but a heavy restraint, as we venture into this our flowing journey.

And it is no surprise that there are great differences in the interpretation of monastic rules between countries and sects, some groups dogmatically insisting that their ways are the best, the only, the most authentic, the usual list of exclusive modifiers. Jack Kornfield says: "The roots of this conflict [about the interpretation of the Vinaya] can be traced to the moment before the Buddha died, when he said to Ananda, 'When I die, you may abolish the minor rules.… ' there is a tension between those who would like to adapt the teachings and those who would conserve things the way they believe they were. But meanwhile, everything is changing."

I take this saying to be authentic and the tension within communities is real. This is my interpretation of the Buddha's instruction to Ananda: please, minor rules aren't absolute, as they are meant to address particular conditions in life that are always changing. Work out your own rules to live as communities. The Buddha also said a community should be run by the consensus of the people living in them, not from an outside authority. This requires ongoing dialogue, open discussions and, in a term from modern organizational development, "consensus building." I feel that Buddhists should follow the great inquisitive and "common sense" spirit that the Buddha himself conveyed, to accept that there are varying interpretations and beliefs and, while following one's own best lights, to appreciate the richness that comes from authentic diversity.

In 2006, I assisted the abbot at our temple, Bhante Chao Chu, on a paper regarding monastic rules that he presented in Thailand for the consideration by the clergy there. Bhante tells me how confused many in the Sangha are in an age of cell phones and emerging new approaches to Buddhism around the world. Bhante has a gracious mind. He is always inviting different approaches to our one large table for Buddhist celebrations and practices, and he also hosts regular inter-religious forums and discussions. He himself supports a non-literalist approach to the Vinaya which he respects, but is not indiscriminately wed to every tradition, practice, rule, or ritual. The views expressed here are mine, though I hope informed by my conversations with Bhante

As Buddhism takes root in the west and becomes increasingly prominent in the worldwide religious landscape, to turn the dharma wheel, I think it needs to adapt to modern society. I'm most interested in seeing the evolution of American Buddhism where we don't recreate Eastern cultural rites and practices if they don't fit us. Certain aspects of the traditions need thoughtful review and modification to better enable monastics to travel and perform their duties in this contemporary world of air travel, time changes, technology, communication, and financial matters. Stephen Batchelor writes (*Buddhadharma* magazine, Summer 2007): ".... I suspect the Buddha wanted his legacy to be a set of principles, an interpersonal set of guidelines, that would govern the life of the community through consensus. He did not want an autocratic system of governance ... the Buddha told Kashyapa that the Vinaya rules should be applied according to the country, the time, and the situation, which gives us a lot of room."

The nature of the Sangha is different in Western cultures, and will continue to develop in its own unique way. The participation of lay people in practice is different and requires a different way of organizing the community.

At the Rosemead Buddhist Monastery where I practice, the members are very diverse. The majority are ethnic Chinese, but there are also numerous other Asians, as well as western born Asians and westerners who are not culturally Buddhist. Our abbot, Bhante Chao Chu, is from Sri Lanka.

My own family and other Chinese friends visit the temple on certain holy and important days, and pray for good fortune during the New Year; they come to burn incense and make offerings of food and flowers before their ancestors' shrine, to arrange ceremonies for the dead, and to give alms; some visit the abbot when they are presented with great difficulties in their lives. Most of the Westerners, as well as some Chinese and other Asians, also want a steady and consistent practice for personal transformation. We come to meditate, to study, discuss and practice the pure precepts; we have conversations about what we're noticing in our lives through sitting on a regular basis, individually and in groups, and we talk with the abbot or other monks about our personal practice.

The entire Rosemead Monastery community supports the work of a project in Sri Lanka, *Bosath Children's Educational*

Foundation, which provides computer training and English courses for poor children at ten different centers.

These are just different approaches; one way is not better than any of the others.

Our community at Rosemead Monastery is adapting to Western ways. We still have a ways to go, but our awareness of different needs is growing. We are preserving the opportunity for different Asian cultures to continue to practice as they do and we all participate together for celebrations. I've taken on a practice of offering respect to Papa Fu at the temple where our ancestors are venerated, and we are developing programs which are directed at developing a spiritual practice, with guidance and advice from the abbot and other teachers.

■

Someone once asked the Buddha: "How can you call yourself a monk when the king invites you to the palace and you eat at banquets? A seven-story building was built for you. How can you accept such a thing?" The Buddha answered: "Of all the monks who live in this seven-story mansion, none of them consider that they 'own' it or that it is their 'right.' They all look upon it as a roof over their heads for a night. They didn't ask or maneuver for it. So it is blameless." The Buddha didn't teach us to avoid life, just not to be craving and then clinging on to rules, chanting, theologies, techniques, and celebrations.

The monastic way of life and its disciplinary codes—in general, called precepts—began during the Buddha's lifetime. The Vinaya Pitaka, the third section of the Tripitaka, was codified within a generation after the Buddha's death. It defines a way of life and social structure for harmonious relationships to help the community progress in its spiritual practice. In the Buddha's own lifetime, as the Sangha grew and became more complex, the Buddha found it necessary to address conflicts that occurred when members behaved in unskillful ways, for example when a monk asked for money to get special food he wanted. In some cases, rules were laid down to discourage future misconduct. These rules, responses to actual situations, were codified and called the Pratimoksha. The Pratimoksha was never meant to be static. Rather, it was a dynamic guideline, subject to change by the Buddha. The penalties for violating the rules varied, from expulsion, to required expression of regret, confession and apology. They were grouped as to type of offense, severity and penalty. I don't believe spiritual communities have to follow this model to the letter, yet all communities need ways to address problems that inevitably arise when more than one of us are gathered together.

The Buddha was not inflexible when new or changing circumstances challenged the practicality of the code. The Buddha would sometimes modify or make the rules stricter so the life of monastics would be more gracefully focused on spiritual development. The Buddha was always aware of different climatic and social conditions. The community was encouraged by Buddha to make its own rules of living together as a monastic community. But our human tendency is to do the opposite of what Buddha taught: we rigidify ourselves into rules that don't allow us to breathe; we overly cater to the spiritual teachers to the point of not being critical of hierarchical religious cults† that focus power on themselves as gurus, not sharing power and open communication among all the members of the community.

The Second Council was convened about one hundred years after Buddha's death. The subject of monastic rule was again raised. Some of the monks felt that certain rules were obsolete; other rules were being ignored or misinterpreted. Some monks said certain rules should be changed. Their petition was debated and the majority again concurred that the original rules should apply, with some of the monks continuing to disagree.

Occasional changes have been made informally within

varying groups to accommodate needs of practicality. Certainly, conditions that existed twenty-five hundred years ago differ from the world of today. Many of the rules—depending on monastic conditions—appear to us now as impractical or even impossible. Let's look at two Buddhist scriptures.

Should any bhikshu take gold and silver, or have it taken, or consent to its being deposited (near him), it is to be forfeited and confessed. (Nissaggiya Passitiiya18)

This precept brings into focus our contrasting modern society for a teaching monk, living in the world: money, banks, ATMs, credit cards, cell phones, laptops, all of which are necessary for travel and ordinary, efficient daily life … all of which are a forms of power, the ability to exchange information in order to promote the life of the entire community, both of monks and of lay people. Some monks, who have the mission of educating and serving the community today, cannot live practically under such a restriction about money. Rules for monks living in relative solitude can practice not taking "gold and silver." But the point always is to practice the inner spiritual attitude of non-attachment, whether in the world or in a cave.

Should any bhikshu bathe at intervals of less than half a month, except at the proper occasions, it is to be confessed. Here the proper occasions are these: the last month and a half of the hot season, the first month of the rains, these two and a half months being a time of heat, a time of fever; (also) a time of illness; a time of work; a time of going on a journey; a time of wind or rain. These are the proper times here. (Pasittiya 57)

Such a precept in our contemporary times applies only to monks who now live a secluded monastic life.

The Buddha voiced rejection of authoritarianism, even to any kind of blind obedience to the Buddha himself. The precepts of the Pratimoksha for monastics are more explicit and confined in nature to specific behaviors. The basic precepts for monks, or training rules, are broad in scope and require a great deal more interpretation.

Bhante Chao Chu offers two stories to illuminate the need for flexibility regarding rules. "I recall years back, in Korea, during an International Conference, travel conditions interfered with eating arrangements, i.e. 'time of eating' rules. This resulted in confusion among some of the monks as to where to eat. Some resorted to eating in buses without tables, some missing lunch altogether, while others ignored the Rule. This problem should not have occurred, and could have avoided by a better understanding of the meaning and intention of the Rule, rather than rote obedience to the letter of the Rule."

Bhante cites another example of a situation that occurred at a United Nations Conference in Paris; the organizers were unfamiliar with Rules regarding the appropriate time for monks to eat. During one of the speaker's presentation, some of the monks attending left the hall before noon to eat. This caused the speaker and sponsors to interpret their untimely departure as a protest against the message being delivered. (In Zen monasteries, a Mahayana School, the evening meal is light, but it is still a meal taken after noon. However, it is called "medicine" so as to not break the letter of the Vinaya.)

Ven. Dr. Havanpola Ratanasara writes: "Monks are not like stones … they are living creatures; they have to face changing conditions in the society. So, according to certain conditions, things are continually changing." "Furthermore," Ratanasara asked rhetorically, "Who can go and make a petition to the Buddha these days?" He added, "Buddha has given permission to the Sangha … therefore it is with the Sangha to tackle the problem."

Understanding deeply that Buddhism is a living tradition, the Ven. Thich Nhat Hanh and the Council of Plum Village wrote: "Like a tree, dead branches need to be pruned in order for new shoots to grow. New shoots are the teachings and practices that respond to the need of our present time and culture. Technological developments, mass media, and the speed of modern life have all influenced the life of monastic communities. Degradation of the monastic lifestyle is evident in places all over the world, in both Buddhist and non-Buddhist communities. To respond to the (present) situation a revised Pratimoksha is urgently needed." The revision they developed was released in 2003 and addresses many contemporary issues such as use of cars, computers, television, cell phones, e-mail.

The Revision was a compromise, creating and substituting new training rules which work in modern day conditions, but not eliminating any. The classical version of the Vinaya would not be discarded, but kept to be studied and learned parallel to the Revision. Thus, a modern adaptation can be practiced concurrent with the classical Vinaya, insuring that the original purposes are not lost. Some monks living in isolated conditions, for the most part, can still follow the original Vinaya if they choose.

Further, the Revision itself is to be reviewed and updated every twenty years by an appropriate Council. Adaptations will be made gracefully and with common sense, in the spirit of Buddha's call for us to develop moral perfection, compassion and wisdom. I realize that even in such communities as Thich Nhat Hanh's, there are the difficulties that arise in just about all the communities around power, authority, sharing work and resources, being communicative and supportive of community members. All rules and rituals should support the monk's growth into the spirit of the Buddhist Vinaya where all have an equal say. In my opinion, too many Buddhist communities perpetuate the worn out Eastern hierarchy: men monks in front, women monks behind, then laymen, with laywomen in the back. Attachment, therefore, to such rules, can cause problems and misunderstandings. Many of the original rules cannot be forced upon modern day circumstances. Stubborn adherence to archaic rules is not in the best interest of Buddhism.

One of our goals is to be decent, considerate human beings in our modern society. It should be noted, that in the present world, there are issues not covered by the Vinaya, but which should certainly be considered and addressed. By updating rules in a way consistent with technology, the use of cell phones, credit cards, air travel, automobiles, will only serve to enhance the ability of monks and nuns to serve the community and accomplish their mission. All of us must continue to practice detachment, non-greediness in the use of these modern conveniences. The public does not benefit when monks and nuns cling to impractical, out-of-date customs that impede growth and communication.

Of course Buddhism has a cultural, historical, even a national form wherever it has been long established, but one of its most significant features is the ability to adapt itself to many societies, new soil where the seeds of the teaching have taken root. It is important that practitioners and teachers be flexible in adapting to modern times and evolving technology, with life, energy, curiosity, and joy.

■

One afternoon several years ago, during the ancient ceremony of Bathing the Buddha's statue to celebrate his birthday, I noticed in myself something like "spiritual materialism," a feeling that I was missing the inner values of the ritual by distracting myself with the externals. The celebrations at our Rosemead Temple are usually a great joy for me—the problem was being distracted by my "attachment to" ritual, my "attachment to" the showiness of it, and my judgments about others as being just mechanical worshippers.

I wrote a poem to express my feeling that I was overly caught up in the externals and in my own self-importance.

529

Bathing Baby Buddha

Yellow, gray robes
swishing all over the place
flowing orange, maroon,
brown, black, too, all busy-walking.
I hear chants, groaning
"nothing to attain"
"no dying, no end to dying,"
We shiny devotees wrapped in merit-gaining.
I smell incense, amber-peach-sweet-blowing,
scratching my darting-doubting eyes,
lingering smoke; fluffy gray-purple traces, tickling scrunched faces,
I'm avoiding textures, colors, vast violet-green skies.
I'm pouring bathing waters on Buddha's bare shoulder,
running away from essential crystal rose waters
beckoning me inside; liturgical spreads,
quickly munching tasty veggie tarts.
I'm still hungry, speculating,
ah, such self-made insipid festivities.
Where are you, Beloved golden hearts?
Where are you, lovely Baby Buddha hearts?

What an opportunity for me to understand what the Buddha meant when he described how we get attached to rituals and rules. In the context of my study of the Vinaya and adapting the ancient teaching to present circumstances, my friend and editor Ken Ireland reminded me of the old proverb: Don't throw the baby out with the bathwater.

Taking a fresh look at the rules, the precepts, is not a bad thing, as long as we sincerely search look for the original intention and are not just interested in creating debate. Ken said: "Washing the baby with respect and love, here and now, is our practice, not arguing about where the water came from, how to pour it, what kind of soap is appropriate because it's what was used at Varanasi, what to wear, or what kind of songs to sing while soaping, rising and drying."

And I will let that be the last word—for now.

Golden Paper Mercedes-Benz
Reflections on Rituals, Chanting, Burning and Sacred
Dance
Morgan Zo-Callahan

> *The old religion said that he who does not believe in God*
> *was an atheist. The new religion says he is the atheist who*
> *does not believe in his fundamental opportunity to find*
> *deep goodness within that capacity to love.*
>
> —Vivekenanda

Several years ago, I asked a Chinese friend at the Rosemead
Buddhist Monastery why he was burning a paper Mercedes-
Benz, along with incense, paper money, gold, and a food
offering, for a departed, beloved grandfather. He said it was
simply a gesture of respect, common in Chinese culture,
acknowledging a life now ended. "Grandpa would have loved
to have had a Benz; I'm not being literal; it's our thoughts for
him as we perform the ritual, it's our remembering him that
matters for us, his family."

This gesture at first seemed almost entirely superstitious
to me. I've never heard this kind of 'puja' or ritual mentioned
in any *sutta*.

Paper Gold Mercedes-Benzes

Buddha's Nirvana burns up inner turmoil,
his, mine, or yours, Grandfather?
Gate, gate, parasamgate! Bodhi Svaha!
gone, gone, completely gone, poof!
Suffering's sizzling, I boil.
Will it be extinguished
when the paper Mercedes is in ashes?
Light more fires? It's me I rue.
May we flower in rich inner soil;

may we see with our own eyes,
and cry real tears for all our lost loves
like you, Grandfather.

But it was after a deep reconnection with my own Roman Catholic religious tradition that I began to feel a deep empathy with this practice.

When I enter the Monastery, I'm often captivated by the feeling of serenity emanating from the white statue of Quan Yin. The statue isn't an idol representing some being "out there"; it's art that points to an all-embracing consciousness, a human gesture that encourages us to be compassionate to ourselves. I have a similar opening to compassion, when I view art of the Virgin of Guadalupe.

In Mexico City and in San Miguel de Allende, I have seen the Black Mother honored with a procession—her statue dressed up gaily for her day out in the excited streets with the people. Mother passed by with much decorum, songs, music, and offerings of flowers.

The variety of "Black Mothers" is invoked to come graciously into our every day lives as loving Mother, the Black Madonna in Europe, Kali for Hindus, Tara in Tibetan Buddhism and Crow Mother among the Hopi. Wise Mother balances masculine and feminine, rich and poor, within the dynamic vibrancy of "opposites." She inspires pilgrims, and marchers, protestors who seek freedom from oppression.

Closer to home, several years ago I arrived early at Our Lady of Lourdes, in East Los Angeles, for the Festival for Black Madonna, the Dark Mother, *Madre Morena*, Lover of the poor, the Compassionate One. I wanted to watch Alessandra Belloni* and her ensemble from Southern Italy practice the hour or so before the sacred rite began.

Alessandra sang and danced and played the *tamburello*, a white framed drum; tambourines, frame drums, and percussion instruments accompanied her. Melodies were vibrating through the room, soul-fully: *Canto della Madona di Montevergine*, reverencing the Mother Earth goddess; *Ave Maria* from Montserrat, powerful rhythms of a jubilant and plaintive song; a Brazilian Yoruba processional chant honoring the Goddess of Love; the *Ritmo e Danza,* from Calabria, where it was sung in the Middle Ages as protection from the plague and to free those whose listened from their fear of death.

Alessandra was then perhaps sixty years old, with a supple body, and a haunting, powerful voice. She wore a white gauze dress embroidered with pink blossoms on deep black, like her long hair. She performed a wild ecstatic dance, a healing trance, called the *tarantella* in southern Italy by women who worked the fields. Often exploited and abused, the women danced to overcome the "bite of the tarantula," or the "bite of love," and release any feelings of anger and resentment, as well as repressed sexual frustrations and desires. This is another side, the darker side, of the bright Quan Yin in our Temple, but most definitely bore the marks of deep Compassion.

After her heart-opening performance, Alessandra was at the entrance saying good-bye. I felt I wanted to hug and kiss her, but people were so tightly crowed around her, I waved and cheered from a distance. In my mind's eye, I sent her the chocolate and roses that a star deserves and I whisked her back to her hotel in a shiny gold Mercedes.

In the distance, I could see smoke in the San Gabriel Valley—houses and forest were burning in wind-blown blazes. Our Mother can be fierce and merciless as well, with a mind of Her own.

*Alessandra is the artist-in-residence at the Cathedral of St. John the Divine. You can visit her Web site to see her play, chant, and dance in a video clip: http://www.alessandrabelloni.com.

I was the Male Swan in *Swan Lake*
Joyce C. Sin

The experience Joyce describes here is such a beautiful, elegant, and moving account of a moment of sudden enlightenment; we are honored to include it. We think that Hui Neng, the sixth Patriarch, is smiling.

> *And the day came when the risk it took to remain tightly closed in a bud was more painful that the risk it took to bloom.*

—Anais Nin

Over the years, I have seen various productions of the marvelous ballet, *Swan Lake*. The images of delicate swan ballerinas leaping across the stage were deeply imprinted in my mind. So I was not prepared to see Matthew Bourne's version of *Swan Lake* at the Ahmanson Theatre in Los Angeles, March 2006. All the swans were danced by bare-chested male dancers!

As the curtain went up, I found myself very critical of everything that happened on stage. I did not like the "clumsy" movements of muscular swans, their repetitive formations, and the comic act of the Prince's girl friend. Why would Mr. Bourne want to spoil Tchaikovsky's classical work?

Then during intermission, a subtle shift occurred in my consciousness. I re-examined my opinion towards this dance. I lessened my distance from it. I caught myself using a preconceived idea to view the dance. I was seeing "a supposed-to-be" presentation. My judgment was based on what I had known before and what was familiar to me. I was not fully present; I was too much in my head. I was not giving myself the chance to experience something entirely new. I was viewing the performance with intellect alone, not experiencing with my heart as well. I was wasting my time there.

As I re-entered the theater for Act II, I also readjusted

my attitude. I would go see the ballet, as if for the first time. I envisioned myself as the principal character, as the Male Swan on stage. I flapped my long wings to show my strength; I pecked and hissed at my fellow swans to gain dominance; I swooped down from the sky to rescue my Prince. I embraced him and let his weary body cling closely to mine. I danced with love, with pain in my soul and loneliness in my flesh. Finally, through liberating death, came the joyous rebirth.

As the curtain came down, I sighed, a heavy relieved, grateful sigh. I was moved beyond words. For the first time in my life, I had experienced a glimpse of what "non-duality" must be like. I felt the unified sense of life. Because I was— through refreshing metamorphosis—the Male Swan in *Swan Lake*.

Like Buddha, We Are Human Beings Trying to Understand and End Suffering

A Conversation with Eng Moy, M.D.

MZC: We're here with Dr. Eng Moy to talk about Buddhism. We also want to talk about spiritual wisdom as applied to our lives and this, of course, can come from any of the great religious traditions or other humanistic sources.

Dr. Moy, would you tell us about your background in terms of your contact with Buddhism? You were born in the Buddhist country of Burma. What experiences brought you to a deeper understanding of Buddhism?

Dr. Eng Moy: In my case, yes, I was born in Burma of Chinese descent. We called ourselves Chinese Buddhists, but in the real practice, local Burmese practiced differently.

In our family we mostly followed our ancestors' traditions. It was my mother who went to the temple where she would pray for good luck and to be successful in business. I only went to the temple for ceremonies or when friends called me to eat there. I went to a Catholic school.

In the Burmese culture, you must speak to the Buddhist monks in a certain deferential way which I didn't like. I tended to avoid the temple. It wasn't until I came to the United States that I became involved with Buddhism on a more meaningful level. A friend asked me to help a monk start a temple here. When I spoke with the monk, I realized the true practice is different from what I knew before. The monk told me about meditation and so I read Buddhist literature in English. Unfortunately the monk was killed, but we built the temple and got Ven. Chao Chu to help us.

I then started to come to the Rosemead Monastery every Sunday, as I liked the emphasis on meditation practice, along with study, discussion. I'm not so interested in the tradition of just praying and taking what the teacher says without analysis.

MZC: What more specifically didn't you like about the way you were supposed to speak with Buddhist monks in Burma?

EM: The monks had to be addressed like a god. There was an over emphasis on being respectful. This is part of my character. I didn't want to focus on the individual monk but on the Dharma, the real teaching of the Buddha. You were supposed to pray to the monk, whether he was good or bad.

Early on, I knew that the practice by each individual person is most important. It wasn't just Buddhist monks; the Catholic school brothers were overly strict and traditional, so I wanted to avoid them too. Respect is fine, but I felt Buddhist monks and Catholic brothers should be like spiritual friends, without all the "superior-inferior" attitudes.

MZC: You've traveled extensively after you took on Buddhist practice here in the States. What are your reflections about your travels to Buddhist temples and talks with Buddhist lay people and monks in other countries?

EM: I've been to Thailand. There they tend to just burn incense and seek fortunetellers. I say this knowing there are some good teachers in the East, including in Thailand and Burma.

I went with Ven. Chao Chu to India to visit where the Buddha was born. Most of my approach has been to look at the history and find the principles of the practice. This has been helpful. However, many of the temples in India have again over-used prayer and asking for merit, rather than on personal spiritual growth and transformation.

That's why when I go back to Burma I don't usually visit the temples. They have become tourist attractions, with their myths about how Buddha was born, unrealistic stories.

Buddha was a real human being who went through the process of ending his own unnecessary suffering. We, ourselves, can realize what Buddha taught.

I visited a small town in Burma with a large monastery.

The head monk invited me to visit, so I asked him about whether they taught the local children; he said they only had ceremonies such as weddings. I felt very sad that the monastery wasn't reaching out more to the local community.

I continue to do my own practice and study here in Rosemead where I concentrate on what is the essential practice. I did have a good experience in Kuala Lumpur for the Buddhist Council where they were more serious about what Buddhism truly means and how it is a practical way of life, being present, mindful, loving, sharing, caring about ourselves and others.

This is much more important that all your questions about the Eternal, Nirvana, what happens after death to the enlightened one, is there a soul or something which survives death? The Buddha wanted us to concentrate on this life and how we are living it.

MZC: As a doctor, you're faced with physical, mental and spiritual suffering. How does spiritual health relate to physical health?

EM: Most people know they have a body, mind, and spirit. It's like a cycle; we need health on all these levels and they support each other.

The Buddha talked about spiritual wholesomeness and health, how to learn what is right and wrong, how to be conscious and aware, to be caring. So I'm interested in one's spiritual health history as well as his or her physical/mental health history. Buddha always taught about suffering and how to get rid of it; how to look profoundly at cause and effect. So I regard Buddhism not so much in terms of a tradition, but what the Buddha was trying to teach, no matter what particular religious or cultural ideas we may have. When a person is sick, I try to get the person to be aware of what he or she can and cannot do in order to be fully healthy.

MZC: You must have patients who mostly come from Christian traditions. How do you apply and impart this practical help that you are learning from Buddhism? How do you lessen suffering in your patients?

EM: I never say, "this is what Buddha says." I just encourage good moral behavior, being more aware and loving. People from all religions can realize what the Buddha taught.

In fact, some of my patients say I should be a preacher. I say that spiritual health comes from talking and considering, and then truly practicing what you learn. There's no pill for this kind of inner health.

We have to go through the process of waking up. The beauty of Buddha's teaching is in its life application, in each one's individual life, how you do what is wholesome or not.

When everything goes well, then praying is good; when things are bad, then one questions prayer. When business is good, then Feng Shui is always good; when bad, then it's lousy. Not that prayer and Feng Shui are totally bad, but the reality is that a good life is in how one chooses and is mindful in one's own circumstances.

The right way isn't right because the Buddha says it or I say it; the way is the principle of good living.

I tell my Christian patients I compare God with food, available for everyone, be it Chinese or Mexican food. Likewise, you can say there is God or not God, but the practice is to develop your mind and practice good, wholesome living, being peaceful and mindful.

MZC: How do you relate to your terminally ill patients?

EM: My approach is to accept whatever one believes. I've told Christians to pray, even though that may not be for me. One Christian patient told me she didn't feel praying would help her and complained that she had to die. "Why me?"

In Buddhism we try to take away the suffering that comes when we don't accept that all changes. I know it is difficult to gain insight when one is in pain. So it's important now to prepare spiritually for our death, rather than be confused when one is in the process of dying.

I do try to be mindful with terminal patients and not to annoy them. I communicate: "Do what you need to do."

MZC: Buddhism tries to cultivate ethics, a meditative-contemplative life and understanding and insight. All these go together. Do you feel there's a progress of this process in your own life?

EM: My approach is scientific, rather than to believe in this or that. We investigate the teaching in an open approach to life. We listen, but we don't just accept what a teacher may say. We need to know what is good for us, as individuals, how we use our own minds, to be present.

I focus on the five precepts as guidance to do what is right. I try to see cause and effect, looking at conditions and what happens from them. I find I then have less anger and less hate. Meditation helps me develop, but after that, I'm exposed to daily challenges where the approach is the same: be mindful, open, doing the best, correcting one's errors. I always remind myself to apply what I learn to daily living.

MZC: You also have mentioned that the heart is essential to Buddhist practice that we need sharing, loving, caring and compassion.

People may think of Buddhism as only a solitary, intellectual-meditative pursuit, even to the point of a stoic indifference, not full of life and kindness.

EM: People in the West and in other religions may misunderstand Buddhism by saying that Buddhists simply don't believe in God and further that Buddhism is selfish, concerned only with individual liberation. Yes, there can be too much focus on practice only for one's self, so one may not get involved with social concerns.

I talk about sharing, loving, caring and compassion to help people know the meaning of God. We may talk about God or even Nirvana and not treat others well; yet God *is* love and compassion. Whether God created everything or not is not so important; what is important are how you understand yourself, how you practice sharing, loving, caring, and compassion.

So this can help us not to argue about whether there is a God or not. Anyone who has any understanding of God has no anger or hate. If someone uses the name of God to hate and kill, then the meaning of God is not being understood.

The final point is that each human being can attain what Buddha himself attained. You don't have to be a monk. Create conditions where you can focus and be aware of how you create your own suffering. Then, you can become free of it.

MZC: Thanks and blessings to you.

"We Inter-Are"
Contemplating Virtue from my Hospital Bed, 1989, Hollywood
Morgan Zo-Callahan

> *In a sense human flesh is made of stardust. Every atom in the human body (excluding only the primordial hydrogen atom) was fashioned in stars that formed, grew old and exploded most violently before the Sun and Earth came into being.*
> —Nigel Calder

> *Dependent co-arising fits right into Ecology. People who are sensitive to the interrelationship of all things are into Dharma lore. There isn't a more certain path into enlightenment than that of the realized capacity for being wide-eyed in the Cosmos, being totally alive, right now, with no separation between he who is aware and that of which he is aware. Yes. Just look at It All!*
> —Tom Marshall, S.J.

The other darkest blue-black night, I was looking up at the moon, bright pearly silver, inviting wonder. I took a deep breath, viewing golden-lighted stars with spontaneous seconds of delight and submission to being alive, aware, somehow being consciously a part of spacious skies; 14.6 billion years of creating itself, the universe is changing, ever-evolving, all being, causes and effects of each other, all continually inter-acting. You and I are related so closely in this luminescent, mysterious process, beyond what we can fully know, bringing joys as well as disasters that we cannot control. I'm a tiny participant, along with you, in this dance of stars. I was shaken into this humbling realization of Thich Nhat Hanh: "We inter-are."

A very shocking experience taught me on the deepest level how inter-dependent we are in life and how I'm connected even with those I consider hostile people. That which is in all people is likewise to some degree in myself.

I was walking out of a 7-Eleven in Hollywood, just before dark, when six gang bangers attacked me. The police would later say I must have looked like a rival gang member. They did not go for my wallet—they wanted to kick the shit out of me. I fought back as best as I could. I was punched, head butted and finally one of the guys sneaked a long gray blade into my stomach, severing my renal vein and cutting my left kidney in half. There was blood all over the place. The guys disappeared into my twilight zone of being between life and death. I experienced the thin line of passing out and somehow willfully hanging onto consciousness. For a few seconds of expansive consciousness, a "part" of me went up into the sky, looking down at my body below and my immediate surroundings. My body expanded. I don't interpret this experience as a disconnected spirit or immortal soul *(atma)* looking down on me. I don't know if there's any separate-non-physical eternal consciousness; yet, there's no doubt, as many have related, this remarkable psychic process happens. I was, if only quickly, floating above my body, quite a crumbling, bleeding mess.

I pressed the wound in my stomach to stop some of the blood from coming out.

The doctors told me I was the first one to save my life by putting pressure on my wound. But to live I needed to be saved by the Good Samaritan. Later I would need expert surgeons. How we need each other! Passersby ran by the desperate scene, frightened. Cars slowed down and then screeched away, ignoring my "*Please* take me to the hospital!" A few cars stopped, opened their doors and then changed their minds and took off. Me alone now for perhaps twenty minutes, holding my guts as tightly as I could, telling myself to keep breathing, keep awake; don't give in to that fainting feeling. If I pass out, I joke, I'll die in front of a 7-Eleven, instead of in front of the Grauman's Chinese Theater? Not this way! Not by fellow Latinos, so many of whom in my life I love.

Finally, my good, lovely Samaritan, a Christian named Mike Bunnell, passed, stopped, opened but didn't shut his car door, and took me to the emergency room of Kaiser Hospital on Sunset Blvd., just a few blocks from where I was stabbed. I was in for a long surgery, my lungs collapsing, more than a month in the hospital.

What a strange and wonderful experience for my growing as a human being: sensing the "inter-being" of the attackers, a hero who saved my life, the surgeons-nurses-therapists who healed me, police, friends, family visiting me in the hospital and myself: all together. This unexpected, difficult trauma also allowed me to feel forgiveness, as well as blaming, being angry. Luckily it was mostly an occasion of gratitude for life, for resolve to live well, to improve myself in the areas of virtues such as mindfulness, being peaceful, releasing my anger, jealousies.

I had some hours of quiet and many hours of social interaction. Sometimes pain wouldn't allow for social contact or the presence required for meditation and reflection As police showed me pictures of gang members, I would think how much they looked like some of my students, dark, Latin, handsome, looking older-more hardened than their ages; and my rage somehow melted before it could start. My heart went out to them, understanding that they are finding acceptance and some personal power by being in gangs; some of them are seriously addicted to crack, to meth, to heroin.

You hurt me, dear *hermanos*, but I truly forgive you, by which I mean I still wish that you be happy and that I intend no revenge or payback. Even though I cannot like you right now, I won't close my heart to you. I wish you find what will really make you feel peaceful and full. I agree to cooperate with the police to find you young men who pulled off this payback on the "wrong man." You need to face the consequences of your harmful actions—not a payback though you might interpret it that way. Believe me it's not. [I could identify two of the six gang members, but the police gave up after a year of searching for them. No witnesses came forward.]

And how close I still feel to you, Mike Bunnell!—though we're totally off into our own worlds—we stay in touch. I would later visit the doctors, therapists and nurses to personally thank them and give them small gifts. A lady therapist once asked me "if I wanted to talk about it?" I just cried for about the entire hour with her; she facilitated lots of healing just by her warm, open and understanding presence. How dependent I was on that kind, lovely woman. Without the air of the skies and the warmth of the sun, we would perish. Without Mike's generosity, my good luck and preparedness of expert medical care, I wouldn't have made it.

I spoke extensively with the policemen and policewomen on a few occasions. They talked about their frustrations with the huge gang problems in L.A. They related how a different gang that same day had stabbed an elderly man in the spine, taking his wallet and watch. The man is now paralyzed from the waist down. We talked about the gangs from El Salvador, from Mexico, from East L.A. and South L.A. We talked about the work of Dolores Mission in Boyle Heights. I told them about my Mexican and Salvadoran students and how I went to funerals for a few them, murdered in drive-by shootings. Sometimes we talked about our personal lives. I had never felt such closeness with people in law enforcement and never thought much about how tough their jobs are, in often-hostile surroundings. How is it that we ended up speaking with each other for so long? I learned so much about lives I knew very little about. It's crazy to say it, but here we were also enjoying ourselves in our conversations about "good" and "bad" guys. We were making more of the occasion than just looking at mug shots and my groaning in pain from the after-effects of a long surgical wound, stapled together from my stomach to the bottom of my chest.

The violence in my attackers, the kindness in my hero, the dedication in my nurses and doctors, the encouraging thoughtfulness and visiting of my friends and family, the struggle of the great police officers: I was finding all these people and these qualities in myself. I am the Samaritan. I am the therapist and the patient. I am the gangbanger and the policewoman. We have all the different so-called "positive" and "negative" qualities. This terrible experience was an opportunity to cultivate virtues, *Paramitas*, in myself.

All Buddhist traditions, just as other religious traditions, include teachings and practices regarding virtue. In the Mahayana tradition, the ideal and the consciousness of the Bodhisattva, the super-generous, self-sacrificing spiritual attitude of compassion, is held in high esteem. This consciousness is described as luminescent wisdom, heart-full. Swimming deeply in the inner heart, it is expressed as love and impartial acceptance of all others, wishing all to be in touch with the inner heart-goodness within each person, meeting that same "place" within ourselves. We include ourselves, even though we are last. The Theravadin Arahant concentrates on inner liberation, which of course, includes the metta practice of wishing that all be happy and insisting on a moral practice, leading to a strong and kind character. The Vajrayana Siddha Tradition of realized masters also includes teachings of virtue and vice. It offers its own methods for becoming strong in virtue, especially through the relationship to the Spiritual Master.

I tried to name and consider the "Seven Deadly Sins" (pride, lust, covetousness, envy, anger, laziness, gluttony) and the corresponding Life-giving virtues, which eliminate the deadening result of living principally for ourselves, alone. Jesuits are fond of saying to live as "women and men for others." I made it my meditation to think about what qualities

I could engender in myself to live a better life. There are virtues the Buddha extolled and those who follow him attempt to cultivate. *Paramita* is Sanskrit for "perfection," "reaching the other shore of the eternal." The idea of "reaching the other shore" marks the end of seeking. Six virtues (sometimes ten) are mentioned: generosity or charity (*Dana*); discipline, integrity (*Sila*); patience, non-expectation (*Khanti*); energy, joy (*Viriya*); meditation, attention (*Dhyana*); wisdom (*Panna*).

Our English word "virtue" comes from the Latin word *virtus* meaning strength and vigor to refrain from collapsing under the weight of afflictive emotions such as anger, pride, laziness, and addictive pleasures. In Buddhist traditions, such collapses result from not letting go and clinging to selfish desire. Due to our seemingly overwhelming genetic and social, conditioning, it's difficult to first be honest about ourselves and then to continue our personal practice of developing our insight into the "interrelatedness" of all things and the accompanying compassionate action that flows from this insight.

It is our cordial, friendly intention, our kind actions, which greatly influence our present consciousness and circumstances; therefore, a major factor in developing generosity is letting go of being overly attached to our time and schedule, to slow down, to take breathing breaks for ourselves, even in the midst of busy days. Be generous to let ourselves be human. I used to give the finger to people who cut me off on our chaotic L.A. freeways, sometimes adding a "*Fuck You*"; now I say, "May you be happy whatever your day may bring you; I wish you good fortune."

Generosity is sharing, being a charitable giver and a gracious receiver. It's exemplified in my Good Samaritan, Mike Bunnell, who just gave to me, just for the giving. In my own life, it is opening up to communication, going beyond irritations and rushing. Be a generous listener. It's being truly present with the Right Effort to serve others, rather than being preoccupied with our own obsessive thoughts or the dualistic thinking of "looking down on" or "looking up to" others. A few friends said to me that the gang should just get blown away by Uzis, that they were trash. No such idea ever entered my mind. It's a practical concern for the poor as well as for the affluent, to share money for really good causes. It's being grateful for the warm sun, for beauty, for being loved and connected to the whole of life. We are all a part of each other, so why not give with gusto and generosity?

Discipline is—even in the midst of our mistakes and difficulties—to keep the moral precepts, practice compassion, cause no harm. It is being authentic; living with integrity, not necessarily what society says is the right way for us to live. Our lives are ours. Who else can live them but we ourselves? I felt somehow renewed and resolved to try and be a better human being from my time in the hospital, some healing of body, mind and spirit. I felt I could overcome my negative habits and conditioning, and cultivate inner strength and understanding. I have to do it for the young women and men down at Homeboy's Industries and Homegirl's Cafe who are doing such great jobs.

Patience is the cultivation of serenity, not trying so much to change others, but rather, to pay attention to changing ourselves. It is the skillful means not to be overly reactive to our complex emotions, which arise in our daily interactions. It's knowing that our happiness does not have to depend on the fulfillment of our expectations. I was happy to be alive at the hospital, so I could handle the very laborious therapy required just to be able to walk. I wasn't a "difficult" patient; though I would express my needs respectfully.

I tend to repress my emotions when I'm hurt and angry. The practice of meditation and self-observation allows me to breathe, feel and be mindful of the turbulent emotions I may have. It creates an atmosphere of patience within me. Our awareness will embrace our emotions and gently allow them to subside. In the process we let go of our need for others to be as we want them to be and of our anxiousness to be overly critical of others and ourselves.

Joyful energy is the result of our genuine interest in what is most real and vibrant for us; we also are happy for another's success when we know that we share our lives together. I felt this speaking especially with Los Angeles police officers at the hospital; we were so energized by sharing our joys as well as cultivating sympathy in our sorrow. Before this time, I had some fear of the police. When sincerely interested in others, we are happy when they are happy. This interest, appreciation for, celebrating with others overcomes my jealousy, my prejudices, my envy for what others have, any feeling that I'm better than or lower than anyone else. Getting banged up, ending in the hospital brought lots of pain and anxiety and fear. Yet joy was present! I also reflected how we can be content with enough in our lives. I like what Nisargadatta says: "We don't want what we have and we want what we don't have. Reverse the attitude and intention. Want what you have and don't want what you don't have."

Meditation is the practice of being still, quiet, attentive, and mindful. We just observe and breathe. Be here in the moment. We do not seek experience or push any away, whether bliss, deep "absorptions" or "negative" emotions. We are awake to whatever arises in consciousness, to see for ourselves what is unfolding within. In the hospital, I had no experience of bliss; I could barely follow my breath most of the time. Yet the practice helped me deal with physical pain, by being able sometimes to "creating a space around the pain."

Wisdom supports every virtue. It is integral to our practice of loving-kindness. Wisdom cuts through separating of people, including ourselves, into "us" and "them," "I" and "you." I learned this thanks to a wide array of people at the hospital and even to the gang members. Wisdom discriminates, allowing us to understand the conditions of all actions. I thought about my activism, realizing that when "I'm being nice," I am sometimes just protecting my own image. That does not serve anyone. Appropriate social actions arise from wise compassion, intelligent organizing to help others be more free and independent.

At least now, my meditation is not even "work." I no longer supplicate some energy or force or godhead outside myself. It's natural for me to sit down and check in with my thoughts, to see what's in my heart. I pay attention to myself, and make efforts to be kinder, especially to those closest to me, gentler, vigilant not to cause harm to others and myself intentionally.

I'm most grateful just to be able to follow the course of my breath and my life's yearnings. I'm calling life's curves and turns "meanderings" because there's no sure path; it's so windy and unexpected; we're being fired into the Unknown; but somehow subtly able to be connected to the whole of living, in peace, bliss, mental discernment and understanding. We can create circumstances where intuitive insights "loosen" us from severe uptightness. I experience happiness when living at peace within and letting others live, without any need to control or exploit others or myself.

Ryokan, a Zen monk in eighteenth century Japan, lived in a little hut, leading an ordinary monastic life with few possessions. One night he returned home and found a thief had stolen all his belongings. In response he wrote the following haiku poem:

> *"The moon at the window,*
> *the thief left it behind."*

Such is the wisdom and freedom from clinging! May all of us be happy and strengthened in our practice of virtue!

Sun. Orange-Yellow burning orb, eating forty million tons of material per second, sustaining us, exploding as one of four hundred billion stars in our local Galaxy, Milky Way, just one of the one hundred forty billion galaxies in our universe. Here we are—small, yet with precious opportunity—with a sincere intention that all beings be happy and strengthened in our practice of virtue and understanding. Ven. Dao Yuan sometimes recites at Sunday morning meditation: "The Earth is our support.... " We inter-be—no separate self—the stars, moon, sun and earth inter-mingle, the whole vibrating mesh of life courses through us in every breath.

Appendix I
Web Sites & Resources of Interest
Death, Dying, Living Fully
Morgan Zo-Callahan and Ken Ireland, eds.

Hospice, living wills & advance directives, spiritual resources, support, training for caregivers, and last wishes.

> *When death comes, as it must, how would you face it? Could you smile yet, and say: "Hello Death, Goodbye Life"?*
>
> —Visuddacara

Over the past several decades, talking with people who are in the last stages of their life's journey, their family and friends, we have come to realize that no one has to take this journey alone. The Web sites we have chosen for our list reflect a shift away from a strictly medical model for the care of people with a grave diagnosis to a more integrated approach.

There is wide diversity of resources now available. People have been drawn to the modern hospice movement from the heart, not from a profit motive. Most materials are free of charge. Some sites offer books, trainings and other services for a fee. Some, like this one, offer an opportunity to make a donation to support their ongoing work.

Traditionally, the term, "The Last Things," refers to the soul's transition to the afterlife. In the more ancient, traditional forms of Christianity, the phrase signifies the expectations of the end of time.

We use the term in a more humble, this-worldly sense to indicate the concrete, real issues that confront most people at the end of human life, as we know it:

- The decisions that you can make about your medical care, how you want to be treated, when faced with a grave diagnosis.

- Access to the kind of support you, your family, or your friends, might need or want.
- Specific legal issues and documents that have to do with death and dying.
- The spiritual and religious considerations that come up during this period.

Our intention is to create quick and easy reference to various Internet resources that address these specific concerns. We have chosen them carefully with the intention that they are of use to caregivers, nursing home staff, family and friends and, perhaps most importantly, persons who want to be as fully informed as possible in order to make specific decisions and have confidence that they will be honored.

There are many Internet sites with such information, good people with good programs and good counsel. Direct access to hospice care is also far more available across the United States than it was twenty years ago.

However, most of us put off making these decisions until the moment is upon us, and we may want to turn to a trusted friend to help.

Both of us, Ken Ireland and Morgan Zo-Callahan, have taken the role of spiritual adviser to people who are dying, and their friends and families on numerous occasions. It is daunting. It is our kind intention to make our personal experience available to any one who asks for it.

We have both worked with people who have had a wide range of religious beliefs and perspectives, as well as those with none at all. All humans have a point of view. So that you know ours, we have listed the simple, clear and straightforward guidelines we base our recommendations on:

- We reverence life itself, all of life and all the stages of human life. By reverence we mean that we honor the life experience of each individual, and treat it with the utmost care.

We try not to interfere with life's natural course.

- We are dedicated to reducing the suffering of people when confronted with the end of human life, as we know it—here and now.
- We honor the sacred traditions that have been handed down to us, knowing that each generation has to enliven them in their own experience and make them their own.
- We respect the right of every individual to make informed choices about his or her own life, and have the best information about resources and help available.

The Web sites we chose reflect the shift away from a strictly medical model for the care of people with a grave diagnosis to a more integrated approach. We tried to include as many faith-based projects and perspectives as possible. Please alert us if we have missed resources that you, your friends, or your community have found valuable.

People from many disciplines have been drawn to the modern hospice movement for reasons of the heart, not from a profit motive. Most materials on the Web are free. Some sites offer books, trainings and other services for a fee. Others provide a way to make a donation to support their ongoing work. We hope to keep our own Web site, http://thelastthings.com, up to date and welcome suggestions.

Hospice

Caring Connections, http://www.caringinfo.org, a program of the National Hospice and Palliative Care Organization (NHPCO), is a national consumer and community initiative to improve care at the end of life. The Web site provides free resources and information to help people make decisions about end-of-life care and services before a crisis. HelpLine: 800-658-8898; Spanish HelpLine: 877-658-8896

Familydoctor.org, http://familydoctor.org/online/famdocen/home.html is a section of American Academy of Family Physicians site. It contains comprehensive explanations of various hospice options, disease specific, palliative care, and advance directives. It is simple, well written and specific, providing an explanation of the spectrum of care options for terminal illness. I would recommend it to any family who has a member who is dying. It is a good source of some factual information about what to expect.

Growth House, Inc., http://www.growthhouse.org is an international portal to resources for life-threatening illness and end of life care. Their primary mission is to improve the quality of compassionate care for people who are dying through public education and global professional collaboration. Their search engine is an easy to use tool to find up-to-date, reliable resources for end-of-life care.

Living Wills and Advance directives; Patients' Rights

American Bar Association: ABA Commission on Law and Aging http://www.abanet.org/aging/home.html Provides information about advance directives and links to publications and other information about health care decision-making. Search engine to find information on living wills and advance directives.

California Secretary of State, http://www.ag.ca.gov/consumers/general/adv_hc_dir.htm. Explains California law regarding Advance Health Care Directives, and provides links to sample forms, which comply with that law.

Compassion and Choices, http://www.compassionandchoices.org, focuses on the broad issues regarding a grave diagnosis, and advocates a person's right to specify treatment. Some physicians and health practitioners are not well trained or skilled in managing pain; C&C provides assistance to survivors of a terminally ill patient who did not receive adequate pain and symptom management. Besides state specific living wills and advances directives, C&C also has a downloadable form that authorizes hospital visiting rights for unmarried partners. I do not know if this directive has been court-tested in any state. http://www.compassionandchoices.org/pdfs/hospital_visitation.pdf. Toll free number: 800-247-7421

Caring Connections, http://www.caringinfo.org, provides free advance directives or medical power of attorney forms for each state. The packet for each State includes thorough directions for completing and filing the forms correctly. This is extremely important. The documents are opened as a PDF (Portable Document Format) file and printed out. It is, in our opinion, the best resource for the information online.

If you wish to continue aggressive medical treatment till the end of life or only restricted under limited circumstances, the National Right to Life, http://www.nrlc.org/default.html, publishes the Will to Live, "a Pro-Life" living will.

There are state specific forms available for download http://www.nrlc.org/euthanasia/willtolive/StatesList.html

The Five Wishes document http://www.agingwithdignity.org/ helps you express how you want to be treated if you are seriously ill and unable to speak for yourself. It looks to all of a person's needs: medical, personal, emotional and spiritual. Five Wishes also encourages discussing your wishes with your family and physician. You specify: 1. Who do I want to make care decisions for me when I can't? 2. What kind of medical treatment do I want toward the end? 3. What would help me feel comfortable while I'm dying? 4. How do I want people to treat me? 5. What do I want my loved ones to know about my feeling and me after I'm gone? (This document has the force of law in forty states).

Simply completing and signing an advance directive or living will does not guarantee that your wishes will be honored. Make sure you choose a person as "health care representative" or "attorney-in-fact" who will follow your instructions and insist that your wishes be respected. You should also have copies of these documents on hand in an easy to place. Without a hard copy of a "do not resuscitate order," hospital or emergency medical personnel will use aggressive treatment. They are legally obliged to do so.

When considering your end of life wishes, here are some points to keep in mind:

- An advance directive is only as good as your family's willingness to honor it.
- Having a conversation with family about end-of-life wishes and reasons for them gives you the best chance of getting a directive honored.
- If you live in more than one state, it is advisable to have a directive from each state.
- You may need a pre-hospital "do not resuscitate" order separate from the client's advance directive. Your lawyer or hospital caseworker can advise you about the specific procedures for a particular state or facility.
- For any case manager, hospital administrator, or hospice worker, who is concerned that a person's wishes might not be followed, we recommend talking with the person directly and, if need be, with appropriate legal counsel. To prepare for that conversation, you might read "Advance Directives: Ten Topics to Discuss with Client", http://www.abanet .org/genpractice/magazine/2002/jul-aug/flemingmorgan.html, from the American Bar Association.

Spiritual Resources

http://www.supportivecarecoalition.org Catholic healthcare organizations; supportive care of the dying.

http://www.shiraruskay.org/doula.html The Jewish Family Consultation on Care Near Life's End, Shira Ruskay Center of New York

Utne Reader, January-February 2005 has a blurb on the work of Phyllis Farley (80-year-old New Yorker) who has a program to train people to assist and be with others who are terminally ill. The volunteers take an eight-week course, which teaches how to relate to the dying and such practicalities as helping others make a living will. "Most people have enormous resistance to considering death … you can't let your own feeling get in the way … it is a very selfish act to help the dying … helping ease someone's passing is wonderfully satisfying."

Support for Family, Friends and Caregivers
http://www.compassionatefriends.org
The purpose of Compassionate Friends is to offer bereavement support to families that have experienced the death of a child. There are more than 550 volunteer-run chapters around the United States. Printed materials are available.

Training for Caregivers (Buddhist)
Being with Dying," http://www.upaya.org/programs/event.php?id=184, a course created by Joan Halifax, PhD. a Teacher in the Zen Peacemaker Order, combines contemplative practices and teachings. It explores such subjects as perspectives on impermanence; dying in community; the eight-fold path in relation to dying; preparing for death; mindfulness and loving-kindness meditation; "the Native American Elders Council"; "the wounded healer"; guided meditations.

Roshi Halifax created the Project on Being with Dying in 1994. Joan: ".… Dying people were basically ignored in hospital settings because they were a 'lost cause'. I was inspired to be with people who were facing extreme situations.… Mostly my work is listening … not doing guided visualizations, not applying fancy meditative technologies, not giving advice or doing psychotherapy … we are being present."

The Center for Contemplative End of Life Care at Naropa University takes a spirit-centered approach to facilitating those in need of palliative care. Through both its Certificate Program, http://www.naropa.edu/extend/contemplativecare/certificate.cfm, and Annual

Conference, Naropa aims to bring a mindful approach to improving the quality of life of patients and their families.

The Zen Hospice Project http://www.zenhospice.org has begun to create a national network of end-of-life counselors, in which caregivers and medical professionals learn to become midwives to the dying. They operate a five-bed hospice in a Victorian home and also help with a twenty-eight-bed hospice at the Laguna Honda Hospital. One of the volunteers told me their "slogan" is: "Stay close, do nothing." I'm reminded of John Wooden: "Be quick, but don't hurry."

Frank Ostaseski is the Founder of the Zen Hospice Project. To quote Frank: "We see why every spiritual tradition speaks to us of keeping death as our adviser, our mentor in opening fully to life. Five precepts to develop practical presence at the bedside: 1. Welcome everything. Push nothing away; 2. Bring your whole self to the experience; 3. Don't wait; 4. Find a place of rest in the middle of things; 5. Cultivate "don't know" mind."

Last Wishes, Memorials & Funerals
http://www.ethicalwill.com
http://www.personalhistorians.org

An "Ethical Will" leaves an account of what's most important to you, expressing your cherished wisdom. Dr. Barry Baines, author of *Ethical Wills: Putting Your Values on Paper* (Perseus Publishing, 2002), calls the ethical will "a documentation of your values, beliefs, life lessons, hopes, love and forgiveness for family, friends and community."
http://www.finalpassages.org

Based in Sebastopol, California, Final Passages holds seminars on home funerals.
http://www.mylastemail.com
If we wish, we can send a final, after death e-mail, videos, photos, and messages of adios to your e-mail buddies.

General
http://www.dyingwell.org
The Web site of Ira Byock, M.D., http://www.dyingwell.com, provides written resources and referrals to organizations, Web sites and books to empower persons with life threatening illness and their families to live fully. Dr. Byock is a long time palliative care physician and advocate for improved end-of-life care. He is also a past president of the American Academy of Hospice and Palliative Medicine. I found the section of frequently asked questions to be very well done, touching very delicate and difficult issues with intelligence, sensitivity and care
http://www.travel.state.gov (Click "Family Issues" & choose "Death of U.S. Citizens Abroad").
Medical evacuation services for those who travel abroad (first two sites). Services are by yearly memberships or by the trip. In 2005, more than six thousand Americans died abroad. It is suggested that the traveler carry emergency contacts, next of kin, durable-power-of -attorney, any instructions regarding what you want done with your remains. Travel insurance may help with transportation costs for the deceased.
http://www.unos.org (888-894-6361)
Organ donors are matched to waiting recipients, 24 hours a day. http://www.va.gov
   Department of Veterans Affairs; provides a wide range of services for eligible veterans.

Appendix II
Section One, Resources for the World of Islam
Compiled by Morgan Zo-Callahan, Ken Ireland

MZC: I have criticized and will continue to criticize terrorism and violation of human rights done in the name of Islam, but I also realize that ultimately I cannot change others; I can only change myself. I can also seek "good company" with Muslims who reflect some depth of understanding of our shared human life and insight into the life and teaching of Muhammad as a man of peace and wisdom.

And in any conversation, I find myself most aligned with promising inter-religious connections for healthy change. In the process of uncovering these voices, I found the following resources to be helpful.

Hartley Film Foundation (*Jihad for Love*)
Interfaith Alliance
International Forum for Islamic Dialogue
Islam Online
Islamic Society of North America
Muslim Women Lawyers for Human Rights
Sufi Order of Austin

The Hartley Film Foundation
http://www.hartleyfoundation.org
The Hartley Film Foundation claims to produce, cultivate, support and distribute excellent documentaries and audio meditations on world religions, spirituality, ethics, and well-being. They have several resources, some promoting inter-religious peace.

Jihad for Love (2007), produced by Sandi DuBowski, is the first-ever feature-length documentary to explore the complex global intersections of Islam and homosexuality. With unprecedented access and depth, the film brings to light the hidden lives of gay, lesbian, bisexual and transgender Muslims and goes where the silence has been loudest, to countries such as Iran, Iraq, Pakistan, Egypt, Saudi Arabia, Egypt, as well as to Turkey, France, South Africa, Bangladesh, India, the United States. Some Islamic nations monitor, imprison, beat, levy fines, torture and even execute homosexuals. Since 1979, in Iran more than four thousand homosexuals have been murdered by the government because of homosexual acts. Turkey is the most tolerant of Muslim countries.

Jihad's Director Parvez Sharma, quoted in the September 6 issue of *The Guardian*: "All the people in my film are coming out as Muslims. Islam is the heart of this film. They are proud to be gay, but fundamentally they're coming out as Muslims and saying they're as Muslim as anybody else, and their Islam is as true and fundamental as anybody else's." How can these gay people reconcile their intimate faith in Islam with their very nature of being homosexual? Sharma spent six years to make his film: "I felt a tremendous sense of responsibility to start a discussion of Islam that hadn't been heard before. This was very necessary for my being a Muslim and a gay man."

In the film, an Islamic lesbian couple, Maha and Maryam ask: "Why can't we be together and be with G_d at the same time?" Payam is a gay Iranian who seeks asylum in Canada and says his Islamic community has a "deep problem with acknowledging homosexuality. Quasim, a homosexual in India, is told to pray more intensely and if necessary to go to a psychologist to be cured of his sickness. Kiymet is a lesbian living in Turkey with Ferda. She talks about her love for and deep faith in Islam. There's the moving scene of Mazen in Egypt who has been persecuted as a homosexual, but is seen reverently reciting the Shahadah (Muslim profession of faith). Amir fled Iran after being sentenced to one hundred lashes. Mushin Hendricks is a South African Islamic scholar who speaks of being both gay and a devout Muslim. Hendricks organized a Muslim gay organization called the "Inner Circle."

In his previous work, Sandi DuBowski, who directed and produced the award winning and groundbreaking film *Trembling Before G_d* (2001), which Hartley sub-distributes. Go to http://hartleyfoundation.org/trembling-g-d for a review. I am very moved by the lived experience of these gay people. I hope their voices will be heard and that the showing of this film will encourage discussions and more openness, acceptance, understanding and integration for all of us.

Hartley also distributes Mystic Iran, a woman's mystical journey into the heart of her native country Iran, to search for spiritual rites and rituals. There's an interview with its writer/director/producer, Aryana Farshad on the rich bog: http://www.mysticsaint.blogspot.com, which has a link to the Mystic Iran official site, http://www.mysticiran.com. Farshad comments: "My spiritual journey had taken me from the land of Ahuramazda to the realm of Allah. I came to believe there is only one god, the god of light, goodness and joy. A god who abides not on the mountains or in the oceans, nor the cities or the sanctuaries, But in the human souls who worship there." Ahura Mazda is the ancient "wise Lord" of the Persians.

Islamic Network Group http://www.ing.org

Maha ElGenaidi is the founder and president of Islamic Networks Group based in San Francisco. On February 23, 2008, Islamic Networks Group sponsored Karen Armstrong's seminar "Interfaith" at the California Institute of Integral Studies.

Armstrong wrote in *The Guardian*, Saturday, July 21, 2007: "When I arrived in Kuala Lumpur (June 2007), I found that the Malysian government had banned three of my books as 'incompatible with peace and social harmony.' This was surprising because the government had invited me to Malaysia." And, of course, in this electronic age, plenty of Malaysians read Karen Armstrong. Armstrong talks about how free speech can expose "double standards" on both sides between the West and the Muslim world.

Armstrong starts with a story of Mulla Sadra. "In the 17th century, when some Iranian mullahs were trying to limit freedom of expression, Mulla Sadra, the great mystical philosopher of Isfahan, insisted that all Muslims were perfectly capable of thinking for themselves and that any religiosity based on intellectual repression and inquisitorial coercion was 'polluted.' Mulla Sadra exerted a profound influence on generations of Iranians, but it is ironic that his most famous disciple was probably Ayatollah Khomeini, author of the fatwa against Salman Rushdie." Armstrong points out how, contrasting with pre-modern society, "liberty of expression … has become a sacred value in our secular world … free speech is embroiled in the bumpy process whereby groups at different stages of modernization learn to accommodate one another."

Armstrong concludes: "Our inability to tolerate Islam not only contradicts our western values; it could also become a major security risk."

Fundamental to Civilizational Islam is civility, based on respect for different cultures and religions. The twelve Danish cartoons, caricaturizing Muhammad, certainly were offensive to Muslims. The U.S. press did not publish these cartoons. Maha ElGenaidi writes in the *San Jose Mercury News* of February 8, 2006, Offensive Caricatures Tantamount to Shouting 'Fire' in Crowded Theater: "As a Muslim American I am proud of the responsibility that the American press has generally shown in respecting Muslim sentiments regarding the caricatures.… As a Muslim American, I am deeply grieved by the irrational overreactions of extremist Muslims abroad."

The Interfaith Alliance http://www.interfaithalliance.org
The Interfaith Alliance has the mission of promoting interfaith

cooperation around shared religious values to strengthen the public's commitment to the American values of civic participation, freedom of religion, diversity, and civility in public discourse. The Honorary Chairman, Walter Cronkite writes: "I am deeply disturbed by the growing influence of people like Pat Robertson and James Dobson on our nation's political leaders ... to further intolerant political agendas."

This is a nonpartisan organization with about one hundred eighty-five thousand members from about seventy-five faith traditions. Founded in 1994 in Washington D.C., there are forty-seven local activist groups in the United States which can be contacted through this Web site.

They claim to be a grassroots organization "dedicated to promoting the positive and healing role of religion in the life of the nation and challenging those who manipulate religion to promote a narrow, divisive agenda." They champion mutual respect for human dignity in our conversation, acknowledging both the sanctity of religion and the integrity of government. How do they justify calling themselves "grassroots"? This alliance organizes community forums to promote legislation such as End Racial Profiling bill which would provide funds for data collecting reporting; rules of compliance, rights of plaintiffs to sue (sponsored by Sen. Russ Feingold, D-WI; Rep. John Conyer (D-MI), Rep. Christopher Shay, R-CT); being on school boards; organizing against government funds going to religious organizations.

Interfaith Alliance sponsors LEADD (Leadership Education Advancing Democracy & Diversity). Each year thirty high school students go to Washington D.C. for a week of camping, education, community with the purpose of sharing and celebrating diverse faith backgrounds and then implementing what is learned in local community projects. There's a short video on the site, which talks about the program. A boy: "I'm a Muslim so I guess people tend to judge me. Here I can explain who I am." A girl: "Putting this into reality is the hardest part." The young people speak of being "inspirational activists."

Here are three examples of projects that show a practical activism arising from the week in D.C. for high school students. Cameron K. in Kailua, HI from the Junior Young Buddhist Association in 2007 organized a statewide "Peace Day" to understand what pluralism is and how we can implement the benefit of pluralism in our daily lives. Aishwarya C. and Tanya B. in Tampa Bay, Florida, started LEAP (Leadership, Empathy, Acceptance, Pluralism) to bring different people together for meetings, coffeehouses, movies, discussions. Katie G. in Chappaqua, New York, gathers small groups to go to different places of worship and/or discussion (such as to mosques, Buddhist temples), "everything from different sects of Christianity to atheists and non-affiliated." The idea is not to convert others, but for educational and tolerance purposes.

The Alliance gives local activism awards (started in 2001) in the name of Maryland Bishop P. Francis Murphy (RIP, 1999), a founding member of the Interfaith Alliance Board of Directors. I am familiar with Bishop Murphy's work on the bishops' initiative regarding nuclear weapons and his founding in 1989 of Interfaith Housing of Western Maryland, which has provided safe housing for Western Maryland's rural poor.

The Alliance produces the radio show "State of Belief" with Rev. Dr. C. Welton Gaddy through Air America Radio Network. Show archives can be searched. I searched for Dr. Ingrid Mattson (president of Islamic Society of North America) and found she was on the show on January 12–13, 2008 where she spoke about "unprecedented dialogue between Jews and Muslims" which does not avoid the topic of Israel-Palestinian relations and which is the first organized venture of its kind on a national level.

Press Releases are available for viewing such as April 20, 2007 "Interfaith Panel Discusses Virginia Tech Shootings" (Bishop, Imam, Rabbi); The Alliance's newsletter, "The Light,

One Nation, Many Faiths" can be read online. The summer 2007 issue talks about the Hate Crimes Bill, citing that in 2005, the FBI documented 7,163 hate crimes because of race, religion, sexual orientation, national origins or disability.

Some Resources referred to are: The Pluralism Project at Harvard University http://www.pluralism.org; Teaching Tolerance http://www.tolerance.org; and The Center for Church-State

Islam Online http://www.islamonline.net/english/index.shtml
Islam Online is a unique, global Islamic Web site that provides services to Muslims and non-Muslims in several languages. Its stated goal is to be a reference for everything that deals with Islam, its sciences, civilization and to have credibility in content, distinction in design, and a sharp and balanced vision of humanity and current events.

We can judge for ourselves to see if we find "a sharp and balanced vision of humanity and current events." There's a lot to explore on the site. I find it inviting both inquiry and discussion. There are many areas to pick from such as: News, Health & Science, Muslim Affairs, Reading Islam, Family & Culture, Euro-Muslims, Living Islam, In-Depth Studies, Muhammad, and Islam. I first visited "Ask the Scholar," but the Scholar was full of questions for at least the next few days. In "Ask the Scholar," I explored such pieces as "Playing Music at Weddings," "Does the Qur'an Disrespect Women?" and "Continuous Thinking of Death."

I opened an article, "Muhammad the Feminist" by Professor Shahul Hameed. He defines a feminist as one who always stands for the rights of women. He praises Muhammad for his speaking out for women, at a time when baby girls were burned alive, when being a woman meant being property. The Prophet "always listened to women with consideration and respect." He valued their views and opinion not only about domestic matters but matters "of wider significance." Muhammad helped his wives with chores such as mending clothes, repairing shoes, sweeping the floor, caring for the animals. "Islam, unlike Christianity, does not view the woman as the cause of the fall of man!"

Under the curious "Arts & Culture," I found three different poems on love: Shakespeare's Sonnet 116 ("Love is not love which alters when it alteration finds."); Robert Burns' A Red, Red Rose; and Khalil Gibran from The Prophet ("When love beckons to you, follow him, though his ways are hard and steep. And when his ways enfold yours, yield to him, though the sword hidden among his opinions may wound you.") The reader can read the full poems online and then share their favorite love poems.

A very moving piece on the site, under "Multimedia" was "From Inside Guantanamo Bay," from a radio show (with a psychedelic laser show on the screen) in which a Pakistani man, who was born and raised in England, told his story of being imprisoned, first in Afghanistan and then for two years in Guantanamo Bay. He claims he was held without any trial, denied his human rights. He told of his experience working with poor children in Afghanistan and then being detained in a Russian built detention Center where he saw atrocities against fellow Muslims. He was sentenced then to two years of solitary confinement in Guantanamo, which he said wasn't as terrible as in Afghanistan, but that he was being held for crimes without any evidence. Some guards were sympathetic, but the guards were not allowed to protest. He saw the Qur'an abused, with obscenities written on Islam's holy book. He was never sentenced and finally released to the U.K. He works now in the U.K. for a group called "Caged Prisoners" which lobbies for the release of prisoners where the organization finds there is no evidence of crimes. He said they also protest abuses about questionable arrests of Muslims in the U.K. He says he's not full of anger or self-pity and that he has met many decent Americans, including soldiers from Guantanamo.

Islamic Society of North America

http://www.isna.com/home.aspx

> *Faith demands that we acknowledge the absolute
> accountability of each individual before God, and that
> communal solidarity should never impede honest self-
> criticism, nor should it lead to injustice against other
> groups.*

—Ingrid Mattson

Ingrid Mattson Ph.D, a professor of Islamic Studies at Macdonald Center for Islamic Studies and Christian-Muslim Relations at Hartford Seminary in Hartford, Connecticut, is the president of the Islamic Society of North America. Matteson was a convert from Catholicism in her twenties. From 1987 to 1988, Mattson lived in Pakistan where she worked with Afghan refugees. She received her Ph.D. in Islamic Studies in 1999 at the University of Chicago. Ingrid Mattson defines religion as "our human attempt to implement the prophetic message and to approach the divine. As in all human endeavors, sometimes we do things well, and sometimes we do things poorly. Islam emphasizes the dignity of women and their complete equality with men. Unfortunately, some Muslim men have not gotten the message."

"In the summer of 1987, I was riding the train out to British Columbia to start a tree-planting job in the mountains. I had just finished my undergraduate degree in Philosophy and had only recently begun my personal study of Islam. I came across Fazlur Rahman's Islam in a bookstore a few days before my trip. Reading that book as I traveled across the Canadian prairies, I made the decision to apply to graduate school in Islamic Studies. His book sparked in me a keen desire to study the classical heritage of Islamic theology and law. Going a step further, I wrote a letter to Rahman (this was before we all used e-mail) describing my situation and inquiring if I might be able to study with him. I dropped the letter in a post box somewhere in the Rockies and forgot

570

about it until I returned east in August. There I found a hand-written note from him, inviting me to come to the University of Chicago to study with him. Rahman died before I arrived in Chicago, but it was his book and his encouragement that inspired me to start on the path to scholarship that I have found so rewarding." (http://macdonald.hartsem.edu/mattson.htm).

Mattson is a strong voice urging Islam to stop Muslims within their own communities from committing oppression against others. She says "the first duty of Muslims in America is to help shape American policies so they are in harmony with the essential values of this country.… Muslims need to address injustice when it is committed in the name of Islam." I'm impressed with her efforts to involve Muslims in community service, to go beyond just theology and discussion groups by embracing humanitarian projects.

ISNA has been around for more than forty years. Presently, Mattson has spoken about going more global, as well as national, not only to work with state/civic structures regarding Muslim issues, but to embrace causes to stop the tragedy in Darfur and to alleviate the plight of those who suffered from the tsunami in SE Asia.

Michelle Boorstein, Washington Post staff writer, writes about this "activist" side to inter-religious dialogue in "News" on this site: "Interfaith Movement in America Digs Deeper, Efforts Shifting to Intimate Dialogues, Service Projects." Interfaith movements are growing, but "participators and experts say a new credo is changing the movement: Go deeper." Boorstein gives examples of the movement to go past "feeling good" about each others' religions to participating in concrete, effective small groups who are willing to ask questions such as a Jewish man who emigrated from Eastern Europe who asked at a interfaith group: "How do you bond with people who believe when they destroy you, they will go to heaven?" She talks about interfaith anti-gun violence programs, education trips. ISNA has sponsored trips to Oman, Jordan, and Qatar to learn about Islam. They have initiated with the Reform Movement a pilot program with an extensive curriculum, including Israel-Palestinian issues. Rabbi Robert Nosanchuk (Reform Temple in Reston) has initiated dialogue with the All Dulles Muslim Society (in Sterling) using this curriculum. At St. Stephen's Episcopal Church in Richmond Virginia, Rev. William Sachs runs interfaith groups of Muslims and Christians who work together on local projects, such as the downtown renovation.

Under the Section "Services": Domestic Violence Forum; Aging and Counseling; Addiction Prevention

Domestic Violence Forum: Purports to reach out and embrace those in need in the Muslim community, after suffering domestic abuse, 92 percent that is male on female. "Abuse is a pattern of behavior used to establish power and control over another person through fear and intimidation, often including the threat or use of violence." Referrals are made to the many agencies that work in this field, such as NOW Legal Defense & Educational Fund. There is counseling offered to abuse among immigrant women who are more afraid to come forward for fear of deportation. Includes a Guide for Non-Muslims. The National Domestic Violence Hot-line is 1-800-799-7233.

Aging and Counseling: Gives a summary of Burial/Funeral Regulation in Islam. "It is important that the reflection of death should be ever present in the minds of men and women … to hanker for something which is transitory is the highest of folly." There is a Guide for a Muslim Funeral (with a focus on a natural release to the Earth). There is a listing of the six-fold process: 1. Contact your Muslim Community Center which usually has a Chairman of the Burial Committee; 2. Washing the body; 3 Wrapping the Body; 4. Prayer; 5. Funeral; 6. Burial. Different state regulations are posted.

Addiction Prevention: Education awareness programs; referral assistance; recovery support; addiction prevention. Works with the Hazelden Foundation, which is a nondenominational organization to prevent and heal addictions. http://www.hazelden.org.

Under "Islam": 1. The *Qur'an* translated into English, Spanish, French, German. 2. *Hadith* (meaning "sayings," reports of words or actions of Muhammad or his companions, oral tradition relating to words and deeds of Muhammad meant to supplement the Qur'an. These two sections allow the reader to get to these two principal Islamic source texts.

There are several articles available on this site such as: "Islam in Prisons"; "A Muslim's Anguish in the Midst of the Attack on America"; "Ethics of Intervention Roles in Community Disputes"; "Strength Through Diversity"; "Ending Domestic Violence in Muslim Families"

Muslim Women Lawyers for Human Rights
http://www.karamah.org

> *We have given dignity to the children of Adam*
> —Holy Qur'an, 17:70

This charitable and educational organization was conceived and founded by Professor Azizah al-Hibri and a handful of women Muslim lawyers who worked on Wall Street. It took shape in the late 80s and early 90s with the purpose of uplifting the status of Muslim women past "patriarchal" prejudices, with the empathetic point of view of women helping other women.

After 9/11, the organization, called Karamah, focused more on domestic issues of human rights for Muslim, though still addressing global challenges. It is dedicated to research, education and advocacy work in matters pertaining to Muslim women. Members continue to meet with International Muslim delegations about challenging topics/problems for women Muslims around the world. Karamah applies both Islamic jurisprudential perspectives as well as American perspectives in its practice of the law.

Karamah offers:

- Legal outreach
- Referring poor clients to pro bono or reduced fee attorneys throughout the United States.
- Peaceful conflict resolution
- Divorce consultation
- Assistance with immigration problems/ immigration laws
- Help in civil rights cases
- Referrals to culturally sensitive mental health services

There are articles on the site about Religious Freedom and about Women's Rights, including in North Africa, Algeria and Morocco. One of the pieces traces the "Qu'ranic Foundations of Rights of Muslim Women in the 21st Century." This article presents Muhammad as a spokesperson on behalf of women in a time full of discrimination against women.

Karamah means "dignity" in Arabic. It sponsors forums and research to stimulate "positive and constructive" communication to "bridge communities and individuals" from different schools of thought. On December 4, 2007, Dr. Condoleezza Rice attended an evening of prayer, speeches, and conversation at the Karamah Washington D.C. headquarters. You can read Dr. Rice's remarks on the Web site.

Press Releases are available to view. From July 2007, in Washington D.C.: "Muslim Women from Around the World to Discuss Human Rights on Capitol Hill" which recounts Karamah hosting its fifth annual Law & Leadership Summer Program for Muslim Women. Seyyed Hossein Nasr, renowned Islamic scholar, gave a speech on Human Rights. Invited delegates from Belgian, Holland, Saudi Arabia, Syria, Senegal, Canada and the United States attended for three weeks of "thought-provoking" programs.

Sufi Order of Austin http://www.towardtheone.com

The Sufi "acknowledges and celebrates the thread of unity throughout all religious paths and philosophies, the message of Love, Harmony and Beauty."

Sufism is defined as "seeing God in the heart of humanity, to recognize the divine in everyone and to be considerate in thought, word and action ... that love is a divine spark in one's heart, to blow that spark until a flame may rise to illuminate the path of one's life."

Sufi roots are in Islam. Yet the Sufi Order International seeks to respect and honor all the religions, and to find the thread of truth in varying religious expressions. This Web site presents the first three leaders of the Sufi International Movement, of which the Sufi Order of Austin is a part. My own introduction to Sufi philosophy was principally from the teachings of Hazrat Inayat Khan. Much like Vedanta philosophy as taught by Sri Ramakrishna and by Vivekenanda, I found an embrace of all the great religious traditions.

Pir (meaning "spiritual leader") Hazrat Inayat Khan (1882–1927) is the founder of the Sufi Order International. He was born in Vadodara, Gujerat, India, into a Muslim family of musicians. His family was open-minded and some were Hindus. Inayat was proficient at music and taught at his grandfather's music school as a teenager. He sang and accompanied himself on the ancient Indian instrument, the vina. You can hear his sacred music/singing on the site: http://wahiduddin.net/index.html which lists Inayat Khan's books, papers, music and photos as well as other pertinent materials related to Sufism.

In 1910, Hazrat Inayat Khan sailed from Bombay to the United States, after studying with his teacher, Abu Hashim Mudani. His grandson, Pir Zia Khan, the third and present leader of the Sufi Order International, writes that the "transmission of the esoteric school of Sufism is passed on from heart to heart, from teacher to student.... When my grandfather first took initiation with his mushid (teacher), for months they would sit together and speak about the most ordinary things.... It was only after many months that his teacher began to speak about esoteric subjects using the terminology of the Sufis. When my grandfather heard this, his curiosity was piqued, and he took out his notepad. And seeing this, his mushid just as quickly changed the subject back to mundane topics ... grandfather learned that the teaching must be dictated upon the tablet of the heart.... " (Cf. *Religion & Ethics News Weekly,* November 8, 2002).

In 1912, Inayat married Ora Ray Baker from New Mexico; she was the cousin of Mary Baker Eddy, founder of Christian Science.

Inayat Khan writes: "There is one religion and there are many covers. Each of these covers is called 'Christianity,' 'Buddhism,' 'Judaisim,' 'Islam,' etc., and when you take off these covers, you will find there is one religion of the Sufi (or you can keep it nameless if you dare....) And at the same time a Sufi does not condemn a church or creed or a certain form of worship. He says it is the world of variety."

Pir Vilayat Inayat Khan (1916–2004), son of Hazrat Inayat Khan, was the second leader of the Sufi Order International. He studied with various masters from different traditions in India and found the "Abode of the Message, a community in the Berkshires for more than thirty years, as well as the Omega Institute, a learning center. He wrote many books, his last being In Search of the Hidden Treasure ('03) where he got together an imagined group of Sufi mystics to converse on contemporary and universal themes.

Pir Zia Inayat Khan, Vilayat's son, received a Ph.D in Religion from Duke University and continues to teach in the Sufi tradition, which he calls "fundamentally experiential." He says, "The path exists within. And along the way, all of the resistances, all of the fears, all of the feelings of inadequacy, all of the desires--these are not extraneous to the path. These are the very substance of the work."

At the site, http://www.sufiorder.org, one can explore more about Sufism.

Section Two, Bibliographies on Islam

Reference Resources on Islam from University of Virginia Library

http://guides.lib.virginia.edu/middleeaststudies

Library Religious Studies Reference Resources, 2004 Summer

The Encyclopaedia of Islam, new edition. Index of proper names to volumes I-X (fascicules 1-178) and the supplement, fascicules 1-6 / compiled and edited by E. van Donzel. Edition: [7th ed.] Leiden: Boston: Brill, 2002. Call numbers for Alderman Reference: DS37 .E5192 2002. The Supplement, DS 37. E5194, has a Subject Index, see under Women.

The Oxford Dictionary of Islam, John L. Esposito, editor in chief. New York: Oxford University Press, 2003. Call numbers Alderman Reference: BP40 .O95 2003. Women and Islam, p. 339-40.

A Basic Dictionary of Islam, Ruqaiyyah Waris Maqsood. Lahore: Talha Publication: [Distributor] Progressive Books, 2001. 239 p. Alderman Reference: BP40 .M35 2001

An Historical Atlas of Islam = Atlas historique de l'Islam / edited by Hugh Kennedy. Edition: 2d, rev. ed. Leiden; Boston: Brill, 2002. Alderman and Clemons Reference. G1786 .S1 H57 2002. Regional and historical maps.

Historical Dictionary of Islam, Ludwig W. Adamec. Lanham, Md.: Scarecrow Press, 2001. 417 p. Alderman Reference: BP50 .A33 2001. Such as Hadd, p. 275-76.

The Muslim Almanac: a reference work on the history, faith, culture, and peoples of Islam, Azim A. Nanji, editor. Detroit: Gale Research, c1996. Alderman Reference: BP 40 M83 1996. See women in the index, and especially Part IX: Women and their contribution to Islam (24 pages)

The Oxford Encyclopedia of the Modern Islamic World, John L. Esposito, editor in chief. New York: Oxford University Press, 1995. Four volumes. Alderman and Clemons Reference. DS 35.53 .O95 1995 v.1-4. (See volume 4, "Women and Islam," p. 322-331, and more following that essay.) [Note: John L. Esposito is also the editor of Geography of Religion, along with Susan T. Hitchcock]

Islamic Desk Reference, compiled from *The Encyclopedia of Islam* by E. Van Donzel. Leiden; New York : E.J. Brill, 1994. Clemons Reference: Alderman Reference: DS 35.53 .I83 1994

A Popular Dictionary of Islam, Ian Richard Netton. Atlantic Highlands, NJ: Humanities Press International, Inc., 1992. 279 p. Alderman and Clemons Reference. BP 40 .N48 1992

The Contemporary Islamic Revival: a critical survey and bibliography, Yvonne Yazbeck Haddad, John Obert Voll, and John L. Esposito ; with Kathleen Moore and David Sawan. New York : Greenwood Press, c1991. 230 p. Alderman Reference: Z 7835 .M6 H23 1991. Focus on Islamic revival, with bibliographic essays and lists by geographic area. Women titles listed on p. 76-83

The Concise Encyclopedia of Islam, Cyril Glassé ; introduction by Huston Smith. San Francisco: Harper & Row, 1989. 472 p. Alderman Reference: BP40 .G42 1989. (Women, p. 419-421)

Guide to Reference Books for Islamic Studies, C.L. Geddes. Denver, Colo.: American Institute of Islamic Studies, 1985. 429 p. Z7835.M6 A54 no.9

Women and Islam:

Routledge International Encyclopedia of Women: global women's issues and knowledge, Cheris Kramarae, Dale Spender, general editors. New York: Routledge, 2000, 4 volumes. Alderman Reference: HQ1115 R69 2000 v.1-4. (see

"Islam" article, v. 3, p. 1158-1162; with see also references, and "Politics and the State")

Encyclopedia of Women and Islamic Cultures, First of six volumes published 2003 / Suad Joseph; Afsaneh Najmabadi. Leiden; Boston, Mass.: Brill, 2003- ; ISBN: 9004132473 (set) 9004113800 (vol. 1) English Book v. 1: ill. ; 28 cm. Contents: v. 1. Methodologies, paradigms and sources. On Order LC call number: HQ1170. http://www.brill.nl/m_catalogue_sub6_id11342.htm

Women in the Third World: an encyclopedia of contemporary issues, editor, Nelly P. Stromquist; assistant editor, Karen Monkman. New York: Garland Pub., 1998. 683 p. Alderman Reference: HQ 1870.9.W6548 1998 (see "Islam and Women's Roles," by G. Mehran, p. 115-124, and "Women in Some Liberal Modernizing Islamic Countries," by N. El-Sanabary, p. 513-523.)

Women's Issues, consulting editor, Margaret McFadden. Pasadena, Calif.: Salem Press, 1997. Three volumes. Alderman Reference: HQ1115.W6425 1997 v. 1-3. (see volume 2, p. 465-468, entry for "Islam and Women")

Women's Studies Encyclopedia, edited by Helen Tierney. Westport, Conn.: Greenwood Press, 1999. Three volumes. Call numbers for Alderman Reference: HQ1115 .W645 1999 v.1-3. (see "Arab Women," v. 1: p. 99-103; "Islamic Law," v. 2: p. 747-750)

Selected Readings on Islam
John B. Lounibos, Ph.D.

Al-Ghazali, *Deliverance From Error, An Annotated Translation of al-Munqidh min al Dalal and other relevant works of Al-Ghazali trans. by Joseph McCarthy, S.J.,* Louisville KY: Fons Vitae, 2000 (1980). A shorter version of McCarthy's translation of Al-Ghazali's autobiography without the extensive introduction is *Al-Ghazali's Path to Sufism,* Louisville: Fons Vitae, 2000.

_____ *Inner Dimensions of Islamic Worship.* Translated by Muhtar Holland. Leicester UK: The Islamic Foundation, 1983.

_____ *The Duties of Brotherhood in Islam.* Translated by Muhtar Holland. Leicester UK: The Islamic Foundation, 1980 (1975).

_____ *Al-Ghazali on the Ninety-Nine Beautiful Names of God.* Translated with Notes by
David B. Burrell and Nazih Daher. Cambridge: The Islamic Texts Society, 1992.

Arberry, A. J., A Translation. *The Koran Interpreted.* New York: Simon & Schuster, 1996 (1955).

Armstrong, Karen. *Islam, A Short History,* rev. updated, New York: The Modern Library, 2002.

Augustine, *Confessions.* Translated with introduction and notes by Henry Chadwick, New York, Oxford University Press, 1991.

Barazangi, Nimat Hafez, Zaman, M. Raquibuz, Afzal, Omar, eds. *Islamic Identity and the Struggle for Justice.* Gainsville: U. Press of Florida, 1996.

Bogle, Emory C. *Islam, Origin and Belief.* Univ. of TX Press, 1998.

Bormans, Maurice. *Guidelines for Dialogue between Christians and Muslims; Pontifical
Council for Interreligious Dialogue.* Tr. R. Barston Speight. NY: Paulist Pr. 1990.

Clark, Peter B. *West Africa and Islam.* London: Edward Arnold, 1982.

Cook, Michael. *Muhammad.* New York: Oxford U. Press, Past Masters, 1983.

Cragg, Kenneth. *Readings in the Qur'an*, Selected and translated with an Introduction, London: Collins Liturgical Publications, 1988.

_____*Muhammad And the Christian; A Question of Response.* Orbis, 1984.

_____ and Speight, R. Marston. *The House of Islam.* Third ed. Wadsworth, 1988.

_____ *Islam from Within; Anthology of a Religion.* Wadsworth, 1980.

Cunneen, Sally. *In Search of Mary, The Woman and the Symbol.* NY: Ballantine Books 1996.

Dante Alighieri. *The Inferno.* Translated by Robert Pinsky, bilingual ed., New York: Farrar, Straus and Giroux, 1994.

Dodds, E. R. *Pagan and Christian in an Age of Anxiety, Some Aspects of Religious Experience From Marcus Aurelius to Constantine.* New York: W.W. Norton, 1965.

Eck, Diana L. *A New Religious America, How a "Christian Country" Has Become the World's Most Religiously Diverse Nation.* HarperSanFranciso, 2001.

Enright, Robert D., and Joanna North, eds. *Exploring Forgiveness.* Madison: The University of Wisconsin Press, 1998.

Esposito, John L. *Islam: The Straight Path* third ed. New York: Oxford U. Pr., 1998.

_____ *The Islamic Threat: Myth or Reality?* rev. ed. New York: Oxford U. Pr., 1995.

Fisher, Mary Pat. *Living Religions.* Fifth ed. Upper Saddle River: Prentice-Hall, 2002.

Fisher, Robert B. *West African Religious Traditions: Focus on the Akan of Ghana.* Maryknoll: Orbis Press, 1998.

Fitzmyer, Joseph A, S.J. *Spiritual Exercises Based on Paul's Epistle to the Romans.* Grand Rapids: William B. Eerdmans Publishing Company, 2004 (1995).

Guillaume, Alfred. *Islam.* New York: Penguin Books, 1954.

Hashmi, Sohail H. "Interpreting the Islamic Ethics of War and Peace" in S. H. Hashmi, ed.

Islamic Political Ethics: Civil Society, Pluralism, and Conflict. Princeton: Princeton University Press, 2001 chpt 10; also in "The Journal of Lutheran Ethics".

Hiskett, Mervyn. *The Development of Islam in West Africa.* NY: Longman, 1984.

Hyman, Arthur and James J. Walsh, eds. *Philosophy in the Middle Ages, The Christian, Islamic, and Jewish Traditions.* Indianapolis: Hackett Publ. Co. 1983 (1973).

Jackson, Sherman A. *On the Boundaries of Theological Tolerance. Abu Hamid al-Ghazali Faysal al-Tafriqa.* New York: Oxford U. Press 2002.

Johnson, Elizabeth A. *Truly Our Sister, A Theology of Mary in the Communion of Saints.*
NY: Continuum, 2003.

Julian of Norwich. *Revelations of Divine Love* (Short and Long Text). Translated by Elisabeth Spearing with notes and introduction by A.C. Spearing, London: Penguin Books, 1998.

Kelsay, John. *Islam and War; A Study in Comparative Ethics.* Louisville: Westminster John Knox, 1993.

Leon-Dufour, Xavier, "Peace" trans. by Patrick H. McNamara, in *Dictionary of Biblical Theology*, rev. ed. New York: The Seabury Press, 1973 (1967).

Maimonides, Moses. *The Guide of the Perplexed.* Vol. I and II, Translated with Introduction and Notes by Shlomo Pines with essay by Leo Strauss. Chicago: University of Chicago Press, 1963.

Martin, Richard C. *Islam, A Cultural Perspective.* Englewood Cliffs: Prentice-Hall, 1982.

Moosa, Ebrahim. *Ghazali and the Poetics of Imagination.* Chapel Hill: University of North Carolina Press, 2005.

Morewedge, Parviz, ed. *Neoplatonism and Islamic Thought.* Albany: SUNY Press, 1992.

Muslim Christian Research Group, *The Challenge of the Scriptures; The Bible and the Qur'an,* Orbis, 1998

Nasr, Seyyed Hossein, ed. *Islamic Spirituality: Foundations.* NY: Crossroad, 1991.

_____ *The Heart of Islam, Enduring Values for Humanity.* HarperSanFrancisco, 2002.

_____ *Islam, Religion, History, and Civilization.* HarperSanFrancisco, 2003.

Nizam Ad-Din Awliya, Morals For The Heart. Translated and annotated by Bruce B. Lawrence. New York: Paulist Press, 1992.

Poston, Larry. *Islamic Da'wah in the West, Muslim Missionary Activity and the Dynamics of Conversion in Islam.* New York: Oxford U. Press, 1992.

Renard, John. *In the Footsteps of Muhammad; Understanding the Islamic Experience.* Paulist Pr. 1992.

_____ *Islam and the Heroic Image, Themes in Literature and the Visual Arts.* Columbia:
University of South Carolina Press, 1993.

_____ *Ibn Abbad of Ronda, Letters on the Sufi Path.* Translated and Introduction by John Renard, S. J. New York: Paulist Press, 1986.

Roy, Leon. "Reconciliation" tr. By Joseph A. Bracken, in *Dictionary of Biblical Theology.* Rev. ed. New York: The Seabury Press, 1973 (1967).

Schimmel, Anne Marie. *Islam, An Introduction.* Albany: SUNY P., 1992.

_____. *Mystical Dimensions of Islam.* Chapel Hill: Univ. NC Pr., 1975.

_____. *The Mystery of Numbers.* New York: Oxford University Press, 1993.

Schmitt, Robert C, and Lounibos, John, eds. *Pagan and Christian Anxiety, A Response to E.R. Dodds.* Lanham, MD: University Press of America, 1984.

Schreiter, Robert J. "Mediating Repentance, Forgiveness, and Reconciliation" What is the Church's Role? In *The Spirit in the Church and the World* ed. Bradford E. Hinze, NY: Orbis Books, the CTS Vol. 49, 2004.

Schuon, Frithjof. *Sufism: Veil and Quintessence.* Translated by William Stoddard. Bloomington: World Wisdom Books, 1981 (1979).

Simon, Yves. *Work, Society, and Culture.* Ed. Vukan Kuic, New York: Fordham University Press, 1971.

The Challenge of the Scriptures, The Bible and the Qur'an. Muslim-Christian Research Group, translated by Stuart E. Brown, Maryknoll: Orbis Books, 1989.

Watt, Montgomery. *Muslim Intellectual-A Study of Al-Ghazali.* Edinburgh: University of Edinburgh Press, 1963.

Weaver, Andrew J. and Monica Furlong, eds. *Reflections on Forgiveness and Spiritual Growth.* Nashville: Abingdon Press, 2001.

Williams, John Alden, ed. *The Word of Islam.* Austin: University of TX P., 1994

Appendix III
Web Sites and Resources for the *Spiritual Exercises*
Compiled by Morgan Zo-Callahan, Ken Ireland

W hat inspires us. *Morgan Zo-Callahan*

Ignatius underwent an interior transformation, which changed his life and would inspire and establish the Jesuit Order. We still experience the impact of his mystical awakenings nearly five hundred years after his personal journey at Manresa. The exploration of this experience—what we can know and learn from Ignatius' experience as well as what we can experience for ourselves when we "do" his *Exercises*—motivates the work that both Ken and I have put into this compilation of Ignatian resources.

Ignatius surrendered his sword and dagger as a way of life at the altar of the Black Madonna at the Benedictine monastery on Monteserrat, and was on his way to Jerusalem to surrender his life into the service of Jesus as a pilgrim. Yet, before he would walk the earth as Jesus had before him, he would have to undertake a long, unplanned spiritual retreat. He spent eleven months in a cave in Manresa on the banks of the river Cardoner, about forty miles west of Barcelona. Norman O'Neal, S.J. says of this period: "Ignatius seemed to be on an encounter with God, as He really is, so that all creation was seen in a new light and acquired a new meaning and relevance, an experience that enabled Ignatius to find God in all things."

He prayed and meditated seven hours a day. He experienced doubts, illuminations, visions, spiritual joys, scruples, temptations, inner battles, even struggling against a mad impulse to kill himself. He recorded his experiences in journals. Later he wrote in his autobiography of a vision, an enlightenment experience, in which "I learned more on that one occasion than during the rest of my life." He said of this mystical sojourn that he was "awakened from a drugged sleep."

During those eleven months of prayer and meditation, which included begging for himself and for the poor as well as working as a volunteer in a hospital, he learned that he needed to balance his ascetic practices with a wise consideration of his well-being. He would later say that Jesuits needed no fixed hours for prayer, no sung Office that had been a practice in consecrated communities for many centuries, because any time was appropriate for prayer.

We hope that these resource pages contribute to wider appreciation and understanding of the gift that Ignatius so graciously gave us in his *Exercises*.

A few notes about our resources. *Ken Ireland*

The nice thing about a bibliography is that we can list any book that we like, for whatever reason we choose. Most bibliographies tend to be conservative and limit recommends only to books entirely on point. Our point of view is far more liberal. We are seeking new and fresh ideas as well as what focused study can provide. There are books here that only reference *The Spiritual Exercises* obliquely or are further explorations of ideas that and areas of concern that we or other readers and practitioners of the *Exercises* have pointed to.

For book lovers this is great—most people who are captivated by prayer or meditation usually spend as much time as they can reading about it. The proviso is of course that reading is no substitute for religious practice, and that the reader will have to rely on his or her own resources when choosing what to read. This can also be considered great groundwork for doing the *Exercises*.

Our list is a compilation from many sources, our own reading as well as that of friends and colleagues. Most of the recent titles should be available through your local bookseller or online. When luck and grace align, you might be able to find copies of books that out of print and others which had a limited audience when they were published through several online second hand services such as http://www.alibris.com.

Lists can be deceiving. What looks like a simple presentation hides points of view, even prejudices that the complier wants to propagandize. I make no bones about having a point of view, even some prejudices, but I want to let the reader know what they are, at least in so far as I can understand them myself.

The *Spiritual Exercises* belong to the world. They are not the exclusive property of the Jesuits or even Catholic Christianity. I have not restricted the list to writers and practitioners who are Roman Catholic. Non-Catholic use of the exercises, particularly among the separate Anglican/Episcopal communities is increasing.

Ignatius' *Exercises*, though a unique contribution, belong to a long line of mystical tradition, which in the West extends back before the destruction of the first Temple in 586 B. C. E. Though it is very difficult to trace those influences in a precise historical manner, I have included several books that might open that exploration.

Psychology and prayer are separate and distinct, but there are also areas of overlap. I have included some work that deals with the confusion, which dilutes both endeavors. There are places of intersection where both psychological practice and the specific kind of contemplation that Ignatius developed work well together. I have tired to include work, which might help to see synchronicity as well avoid potentially serious harm.

Every human has the ability to make the *Exercises* if the spirit is leading them in that direction. Several groups of people within the Church face hostility and prejudice. I have included some books devoted to opening inner, spiritual work for gays and lesbians.

Ignatius was a religious genius and he was also very much a man of a particular time and culture. Today there are many women who are directing the *Exercises*. I have included many women's voices, and specifically those that address the difficulties that women face when they have to deal with the patriarchal mindset of Ignatius and those who followed him.

Any person who meditates is already doing a great service to him or herself and to the communities in which they participate. Many people who are not Christian practice meditation, and in many cases, have longer history and experience with meditative states. I have included some work on meditation instruction from Asian and Buddhist traditions. Because there are space limitations, I have only sought work that makes the explicit connection between Christian prayer and meditation.

The sharing of books on the spiritual life has always been an activity among friends. This is a different universe than the marketed literature of mass culture. During Ignatius' life, there is some evidence that a group know as the "Friends of God" might have even circulated the writing of Julian of Norwich from her native England deep into continental Europe. We are deeply grateful to all the contributors though we cannot mention them all. As a tribute to that kind of prayerful, thoughtful sharing, we have included a conversation among friends about the compilation of Bernard Lonergan's thoughts on the *Exercises*, *The Dynamism of Desire*. All the books recommended have contributed to our understanding and use of the *Exercises* as a method of prayer and discernment.

We have included only a few articles about the *Exercises*, which were published in journals or periodicals. If you have a good Catholic University or a Christian theological school nearby and can gain access to their library, you will discover a wealth of shorter articles about specific issues or areas of interest for a person who is a spiritual director or anyone interested in the *Exercises*.

As a continuing project, we intend to update this online bibliography, at http://spiritual-direction-papers.blogspot.com/2007/05/ignatian-bibliography.html, as well as our bibliography, "The Last

Things," http://thelastthings.com, resources concerning the end of life, as we know it now. This is a major undertaking for people without church or academic support. Trying to be both useful and frugal, we will certainly include ways that you can add books that you have found useful, even inspirational, perhaps we may even design the site's architecture to allow you to add titles yourself and include a few sentences about your recommendation.

A bibliography for the *Spiritual Exercises* of Saint Ignatius.

The titles we have not read ourselves were found in the bibliographies in work by an author whom we have read and admired. The books and articles are arranged alphabetically by the author's last name with two exceptions: 1) translations of Ignatius' own work, the Spiritual Exercises or his autobiography, are listed under "St. Ignatius" and the translator or editor's name has been placed after the title; 2) strictly biographical work contains his name as the first words of the title. We placed these titles first so that all these books would be grouped together.

Ambruzzi, Aloysius & Lepicier, Cardinal Alexis-Henri-Marie, *Companion to the Spiritual Exercises of Saint Ignatius.* Kessinger Publishing, LLC, 2003

Amis, Robin, *A Different Christianity: Early Christian Esotericism and Modern Thought* (S U N Y Series in Western Esoteric Traditions). State University of New York Press, 1995

Aschenbrenner, George A., *Stretched for Greater Glory: What to Expect from the Spiritual Exercises.* Loyola Press, 2004

Barry, William A., *A Friendship Like No Other: Experiencing God's Amazing Embrace.* Loyola Press, 2008

Barry, William A., *Finding God In All Things A Companion To The Spiritual Exercises Of St. Ignatius.* Notre Dame, IL, Ave Maria Press. 1991

Barry, William A., *God and You: Prayer As a Personal Relationship*. Paulist Press, 1987

Barry, William A., *Letting God Come Close: An Approach to the Ignatian Spiritual Exercises*. Loyola Press, 2001

Barry, William A., *The Practice of Spiritual Direction*. Harper & Row, 1986

Becker, Kenneth L., *Unlikely Companions: C. G. Jung on the Spiritual Exercises of Ignatius of Loyola*. Gracewing, 2002

Boisvert, Donald L., *Sanctity And Male Desire: A Gay Reading Of Saints*. Pilgrim Press, 2004

Borg, Marcus J., and N.T.Wright, *The Meaning of Jesus: Two Visions*. San Francisco, Harpers, 1999

Brackley, Dean, *The Call to Discernment in Troubled Times: New Perspectives on the Transformative Wisdom of Ignatius*. The Crossroad Publishing Company, 2004

Buechner, Frederich, *Listening to Your Life: Daily Meditation with Frederich Buechner.* Compiled by George Connor, San Francisco, HarperSanFrancisco, 1992

Chilton, Bruce & Neusner, Jacob, *The Brother of Jesus: James the Just and His Mission*. Westminster John Knox Press, first edition, 2001

Chilton, Bruce, *Mary Magdalene: A Biography*, Doubleday, 2005

Classics), 2003

Coelho, Paulo, *The Pilgrimage: A Contemporary Quest for Ancient Wisdom*. HarperOne, 1995

Coles, Robert; Herbert, C. M., nar., *Dorothy Day: A Radical Devotion, Library Edition*. Blackstone Audiobooks; Unabridged edition, 2000

Cowan, Marian and Futrell, John, *The Spiritual Exercises of St Ignatius of Loyola: a handbook for direction.* Denver, Ministry Training Services, 1981

Cusson, Gilles, *Biblical Theology and the Spiritual Exercises*, Mary Angela Roduit and George E. Ganss, trans. St Louis, Institute of Jesuit Sources, 1988

Cusson, Gilles, *Pédagogie de l'expérience spirituelle personnelle: Bible et Exercices spirituels* (Broché). Bellarmin, Édition: troisiéme triage, 1986 (this, the original Cusson book that Roduit and Ganss translated, is out of print).

Cusson, Gilles, *The Spiritual Exercises Made in Everyday Life: A Method and a Biblical Interpretation.* Mary Angela Roduit and George E. Ganss, trans. St Louis, Institute of Jesuit Sources, 1989. This is an authorized translation of Cusson's *Conduis-mois sur le chemin d'éternité.*

de Guibert, Joseph, *The Jesuits: their spiritual doctrine and practice.* ET. St. Louis, Institute of Jesuit Sources, 1972

de Montoya, Antonio Ruis, The Spiritual Conquest. Trans., McNaspy, C.J., St. Louis: Institute of Jesuit Sources, 1993

Donohue, John W., S.J., Jesuit Education. New York: Fordham, 1963

Dozier, Verna J., *The Dream of God: A Call to Return.* Seabury Classics, 2006

Dyckman, Katherine, et al. *The Spiritual Exercises Reclaimed: Uncovering Liberating Possibilities for Women.* Paulist Press, 2001

Eckhart, *Wandering Joy: Meister Eckhart's Mystical Philosophy.* Schurmann, Reiner, trans., Lindisfarne Books, 2001

Empereur, James L., *Spiritual Direction and the Gay Person.* Continuum International Publishing Group; first edition, 1998

Endean, Philip, "Who do you say Ignatius is? Jesuit fundamentalism and beyond", Studies in the Spirituality of Jesuits 19, 5. Nov. 1987

English, John, *Spiritual Freedom.* Guelph, Loyola House, 1982

Fleming, David L., (ed.), "Notes on the *Spiritual Exercises* of St Ignatius of Loyola". St Louis, Review for Religious, 1981

Fleming, David L., Modern *Spiritual Exercises.* New York: Doubleday, 1982

Fülöp-Miller, René, The Power and the Secret of the Jesuits. New York: Viking, 1930

Gallagher, Timothy M., *Discernment of Spirits: The Ignatian Guide for Everyday Living.* The Crossroad Publishing Company, 2005

Green, Joel B. *The Theology of the Gospel of Luke* (New Testament Theology). Cambridge University Press, 1995

Green, Thomas H., S.J., *Weeds Among the Wheat Discernment: Where Prayer and Action Meet.* Ave Maria Press, Inc., 1984

Green, Thomas H., S.J., *When the Well Runs Dry - Prayer Beyond Beginnings.* Ave Maria Press, Inc.; Revised edition, 1979

Habito, Ruben L.F. (2004) *Living Zen, Loving God.* Wisdom Publications

Haight, Roger, "Foundational issues in Jesuit spirituality", Studies in the Spirituality of Jesuits 19, 4. September 1987

Hebblethwaite, Margaret, *Finding God in All Things.* London, Collins, 1987

Himes, Michael J., *Finding God In All Things: Essays in Honor of Michael J. Buckley. S.J.* Herder & Herder, 1996

Holloway, J. B., "Godfriends: The Continental Medieval Mystics". http://www.umilta.net/godfrien.html. 1997

Holloway, J. B., The Westminster Cathedral/Abbey Manuscript of Julian of Norwich's *Showing of Love.* http://www.umilta.net/westmins.html. 1996

Ignatius of Loyola, founder of the Jesuits, his life and work, Candido de Dalmases. ET. St Louis, Institute of Jesuit Sources, 1985

Ignatius of Loyola, Karl Rahner and Paul Imhof. ET. London, Collins, 1979

Ignatius of Loyola and the Founding of the Society of Jesus, Andre Ravier. ET. San Francisco, Ignatius Press, 1987

Ignatius of Loyola, Philip Caraman. London, Collins, 1990

Ivens, Michael, *Understanding the Spiritual Exercises.* Gracewing, 2000

Johnston, William, *Christian Zen.* San Francisco, Harper & Row, 1979

Jordan, Merle, *Reclaiming your story.* Westminster John Knox Press, 1999

Julian of Norwich, *Revelations of Divine Love.* Grand Rapids, Christian Classics Ethereal Library. 2002

Keating, Thomas, *Active Meditations for Contemplative Prayer.* Continuum, 1997

Kung, Hans, *My Struggle for Freedom: Memoirs.* Wm. B. Eerdmans Publishing Company, 2003

Lonergan, Bernard, *The Dynamism of Desire, Bernard J F. Lonergan, SJ on the Spiritual Exercises of St. Ignatius of Loyola.* The Institute of Jesuit Sources in St. Louis, 2006.

Lonsdale, David, *Dance to the Music of the Spirit.* Darton, Longman & Todd Lt, 1992

Lonsdale, David, *Eyes to See, Ears to Hear: An Introduction to Ignatian Spirituality (Traditions of Christian Spirituality).* Orbis Books; Revised edition, 2000

Lonsdale, David, *Listening to the Music of the Spirit: The Art of Discernment.* Ave Maria Press, 1993

Louth, Andrew, *The Origins of the Christian Mystical Tradition: From Plato to Denys.* Oxford University Press, USA; second edition, 2007

Lowney, Chris, *Heroic Leadership: Best Practices from a 450-Year-Old Company That Changed the World.* Loyola Press, 2005

Lucas, Thomas, S.J. Ignatius, Rome and Jesuit Urbanism. Vatican, Biblioteca Apostolica, 1990

Meissner, William W., S.J., *Ignatius of Loyola, The Psychology of a Saint.* Yale, 1992

Merton, Thomas, *Contemplation in a World of Action.* Garden City, N.Y., Image Books, 1973

Michael, Chester P. and Norrisey, Marie C., *Prayer and*

Temperament: Different Prayer Forms for Different Personality Types. Charlottesville, Virginia. The Open Door, 1991

Modras, Ronald, *Ignatian Humanism: A Dynamic Spirituality for the 21st Century.* Jesuit Way Loyola Press, 2004

Modras, Ronald, "The Spiritual Humanism of the Jesuits." America, 1995, 172, (3)

Muldoon, Tim, *The Ignatian Workout: Daily Spiritual Exercises for a Healthy Faith.* Loyola University Press, 2004

Needleman, Jacob, *Lost Christianity.* Tarcher, 2003

Neusner, Jacob, *First century Judaism in crisis: Yohanan ben Zakkai and the renaissance of Torah.* Abingdon Press, 1975

O'Malley, John W. S.J. The First Jesuits. Cambridge: Harvard University Press, 1993

Peters, William A.M., *The Spiritual Exercises of St Ignatius: exposition and interpretation.* Rome, Centrum Ignatianum Spiritualitatis, 1978

Rahner, Hugo, Ignatius' Letters to Women. New York: Herder & Herder, 1960

Scroggs, Robin et al., *Putting Body & Soul Together: Essays in Honor of Robin Scroggs.* Trinity Press International, 1997

Segundo, Juan Luis, *The Christ of the Ignatian Exercises.* ET. London, Sheed & Ward, 1988

Sheldrake, Philip (ed.), *The Way of Ignatius Loyola: Contemporary Approaches to The Spiritual Exercises.* St. Louis, Institute of Jesuit Sources, 1991

Silf, Margaret, *Inner Compass: An Invitation to Ignatian Spirituality.* Loyola Press; Rev Sub edition, 1999

Skehan, James W., *Place Me With Your Son: Ignatian Spirituality in Everyday Life: The Spiritual Exercises Arranged As a 24-Week Retreat in 4 Phases.* Georgetown University Press; third sub-edition, 1991

Smith, Carol Ann; Merz, Eugene F., *Moment by Moment: A Retreat in Everyday Life.* Ave Maria Press, 2000

Spence, Jonathan D., *The Memory Palace of Matteo Ricci*. Penguin (Non-Classics), 1985

St. Ignatius of Loyola, George E. Ganss, *Ignatius of Loyola: The Spiritual Exercises and Selected Works* (Classics of Western Spirituality). Paulist Press, 1991

St. Ignatius of Loyola, *The Spiritual Exercises and Selected Works*. George E. Ganss, ed. New York, Paulist Press, 1991

St. Ignatius, *Iñigo: original testament*. William Yeomans, trans. London, Inigo Enterprises, 1985

St. Ignatius, *St Ignatius' Own Story*. William J. Young, trans. Chicago, Loyola University Press, 1980

St. Ignatius, *Spiritual Exercises and Selected Works*. Malatesta, Edward J., S.J.; Divarkar, Parmananda, S.J., ed., N.Y., Paulist Press, 1991.

[Note about this work by Morgan: This book was difficult to locate. Catholic Library was able to supply information about the publisher. I met Edward Malatesta in 1965, and remember him fondly as a wonderful scholar with enthusiastic energy. He worked with my mentor, Fr. Francis Rouleau. Edward would later take Francis' work to the Matteo Ricci Institute at USF, one of the largest collections of books in Chinese in North America. Edward died in 1998 in his beloved China.]

St. Ignatius, *The Spiritual Exercises of St. Ignatius*. John F. Thornton, ed., Avery Dulles, preface, Louis J. Puhl, trans., Vintage; first edition, 2000

St. Ignatius, *The Spiritual Exercises*. Louis J. Puhl, trans., Chicago, Loyola University Press, 1950

St. Ignatius, *The Spiritual Exercises of St Ignatius: a literal translation a contemporary reading*. David L. Fleming, trans. St Louis, Institute of Jesuit Sources, 1979

Stanley, David M., S.J., *A Modern Scriptural Approach to the Spiritual Exercises*. St. Loius, The Institute of Jesuit Sources, 1971

Taylor, Charles, *The Ethics of Authenticity*. Harvard University Press; first edition, 1992

Tetlow, Joseph A., *Choosing Christ in the World: Directing the Spiritual Exercises of St Ignatius Loyola According to Annotations Eighteen and Nineteen: A Handbook*. The Institute of Jesuit Sources; 2d edition, 2000

Tetlow, Joseph A., *Ignatius Loyola: Spiritual Exercises* (Crossroad Spiritual Legacy Series). The Crossroad Publishing Company, 1992

Tetlow, Joseph, S.J., "The Lay Ministry of the *Spiritual Exercises*." National Jesuit News, 1994, 24, (3)

Tickle, Phyllis, *The Night Offices: Prayers for the Hours from Sunset to Sunrise*. Oxford University Press, USA, 2006

Toner, Jules J., *A Commentary on St Ignatius' Rules for the Discernment of Spirits*. St. Louis, Institute of Jesuit Sources, 1981
Toner, Jules J., *Discerning God's Will: Ignatius of Loyola's Teaching on Christian Decision Making*. St. Louis, Institute of Jesuit Sources, 1991

Van Beeck, Frans Jozef, *Christ Proclaimed: Christology As Rhetoric* (Theological Inquiries). Paulist Press, 1979

Veltri, John, *Orientations, volumes 1 & 2*. Guelph, Loyola House, 1979 & 1981

Walsh, R., *Friends of God*. The Catholic Encyclopedia, online Edition. K. Knight. 6. 1909

Ward, Keith, *Pascal's Fire: Scientific Faith and Religious Understanding*. Oneworld Publications, 2006

Wills, Gary, *Chesterton*. Image; Revised edition, 2001

Wolff, Pierre, *Discernment: The Art of Choosing Well: Based on Ignatian Spirituality*. Liguori Publications, revised ed., 2003

Online resources for the *Spiritual Exercises*

There are several sites in English dedicated to Ignatius' *Exercises* set-up and maintained by American Jesuits or Jesuit

Universities. While the usual bibliography is not aimed at critique, and certainly when aimed at spirituality, it might even be frowned on, we want to encourage full use of the interactive capabilities of the net. Retreats are full of participation and exchange. We would like to encourage the people who create sites be able to fully use the potential of the net.

Although there will inevitably be duplication and overlap, a site devoted to retreat work has to create some background without having to click all over the internet to get oriented. But we wonder why in the nearly instantaneous online world, every site feels compelled to cover every inch of the same ground, slowly, ponderously. It is waste of resources. There are, however, a few very good sites with wonderful innovations and initiatives. We will highlight those.

This information is current at the end of the calendar 2008. We expect that there will be more online resources and hope to keep our information up to date. We have also only considered sites that are US based. As sites become more interactive and less advertisements for local retreat services, we intend to include them.

The sites:

The full text of *Spiritual Exercises of St Ignatius*, the translation of the Autograph of the *Exercises* prepared by Fr. Elder Mullan, S.J. is available in PDF format at the Web site of the **Jesuit Conference of the United States**. http://www.jesuit.org/Spirituality/Spiritual+Exercises/default.aspx. Knowing what Ignatius thought and how he informed the Jesuits who directed the *Exercises* is pretty basic. This site is just the translation, not interpretation or commentary, with no search capability.

The Web site of the Conference also includes a page listing the contact information for all their retreat houses and "retreat opportunities" in the US: http://www.jesuit.org/ParishesRetreatCenters/RetreatOppsCenters/default.aspx.

The Web site of the Creighton University Online Ministries, http://www.creighton.edu/CollaborativeMinistry/online.htm, has been highly recommended by many people. We also like the format and the functionality. The heart of this work is an innovative thirty-four-week retreat, an adaptation of the format that Ignatius counseled. The creators call it a "retreat for everyday life." There is an interactive function on the site. You can make your retreat with or without a director. You also have the option of joining a group that is doing a retreat at the same time, and can share your experiences as a kind of peer direction. Of all the online presentations, Creighton University had by far the most real-time human support.

Loyola Marymount, Los Angeles http://www.lmu.edu/Page965.aspx. The California Jesuits offer the *Exercises* to individuals/small groups to make the *Exercises*, "with an emphasis adapting to the individual retreatant." Morgan did a Nineteenth Annotation Retreat here which he writes about here in "Inclined Toward Love: Notes while doing the *Spiritual Exercises*." The Web site promotes that retreat work.

We would like to point to an innovation of the Institute for Ignatian Spirituality that is outlined with some very clear instructions: An Awareness Examination of Conscience.

Ignatius' examen seems to emphasize the gap that exists between humankind and God and our failures to respond to God's love. Thus you look back over the recent part of your day to check on the number of times a fault that you are guarding against occurred in thought or deed. The Awareness Examination asks that you pay attention to "feelings, moods, thoughts, desires to get a sense of what is going on in one's life; praying for healing and forgiveness," and that as you end you period of reflection, you consider "the immediate future and paying attention to the feelings that spontaneously arise."

The Jesuit Collaborative, http://www.jesuit-collaborative.org. The Jesuit provinces of the Northeast have initiated "a professional association of Jesuits, laypersons, clergy, and religious who share in common the spiritual tradition of St. Ignatius" to carry on and promote the work of the *Exercises*. Though not a site with much information about the *Exercises* themselves, it appears to be a portal for information about a broad range of opportunities.

A Book Conversation

The following conversation about The Dynamism of Desire, Bernard J. F. Lonergan, S.J. *on the* Spiritual Exercises *of St. Ignatius of Loyola was recreated from several e-mails. The participants are Morgan Zo-Callahan (MZC), Robert Rahl (RRR), Joe Mitchell (JM), John Lounibos (JL), Don Maloney (DM), Gene Bianchi (GB).*

All but Mitchell and Maloney are contributors to Meanderings and some personal information is in the first pages of the book. By way of introduction Joe Mitchell is an enthusiastic student and facilitator for Non-Violent Communication (Marshall Rosenberg). He was a Jesuit from 1962–71. Don Maloney lives in Okinawa, Japan, where he teaches for the University of Maryland Asian Division. He was a Jesuit from 1952–83.

MZC: I'm encouraged by Lonergan's thesis that we humans "can learn and know well," and that this learning and knowing leads to loving well, which then governs how we act as responsible human beings, aware of our being inter-connected. We're, so to speak, "maturing" our ability to make decisions from our deepest hearts and well-informed intelligence.

RRR: Yes, for Lonergan Dynamism is the process of realizing potential, moving from experience through understanding to judgment and, in the practical order, taking action based on judgment. Desire is what motivates the process, what kick-starts the dynamism. By nature we all desire to know and we all desire to be fulfilled.

JM: I have a juicy quote from the book: "Bernard Lonergan's analysis is to help one understand the inbuilt dynamic of the human subject and so to reach authenticity and self-transcendence..… Authentic human living, then, consists in self-transcendence. Achieving human authenticity is a matter of following the built-in and self-transcending laws of the human spirit."

MZC: Robert, you have outlined the steps that are included in the process: experiencing, understanding, judging, choosing, and intending to live those joyful values with the zest of free flowing life. Say more.

RRR: Insight summarizes Lonergan's three-step program for human cognition (knowing): experiencing, understanding, and judging. There is a fourth step when the subject moves from cognition to volition (choosing): being attentive to experience (experiencing), posing questions in pursuit of understanding those experiences (reflecting), evaluating those understandings (judging), and making decisions or taking action (deciding).

MZC: How does Lonergan get from "Insight" to the *Spiritual Exercises*? I think that I can see that it will not be hard to locate *discernment* because of the fourth step, volition or choosing.

JM: Another quote: "The primary role of the *Exercises* is to foster the dynamism of desire, what Lonergan calls "the eros of the human spirit." Desire is the most powerful dynamic in any aspect of life—human life or divine. The dynamism of desire is at work in God, not just in us. And the most wonderful moment in our connection with God is when we finally realize that the passion and desiring of God is in fact our own deepest most precious desiring for ourselves. That is the ultimate dynamism of desire!

GB: I like your focus on one of the points in the book: that religious goals, when they are not corrupted, bring out the best in the human; that there's an innate human spirituality to be cultivated. And you lifted up the ecumenical aspect of all this, that non-Christian spiritualities move in the same direction.

JM: To quote: "Lonergan's ideas can be helpful to other religions besides Christianity. Today whether one is a Christian or not isn't essential as to the possible efficacy of doing the *Exercises*."

DM: Another way of saying that might be that "seeking of God in all things" is the true impetus of Jesuit spirituality, which is none other than Christian spirituality, and which includes Hindu and Buddhist spiritualities, even if they do not "name" what they seek as we do.

GB: I would like to return to the idea of desire. I wasn't going to comment on the *Dynamism of Desire* since I haven't read the book, and maybe the word "desire" is handled nicely in the book. But there is a further and maybe ultimate stage of getting beyond our personal desires, our "me-drama" of fears and wants to be at peace in the moment, in the now (without getting passive about world suffering). Desire, frequently driven by fear, pitches us toward the future and often becomes excessive (this word is important.... I'm not saying that all desire is bad). Let me illustrate this from the Good Samaritan narrative and some eastern stuff. The Samaritan is plunged into the now of the bleeding guy on the road. He was riding along with sweet thoughts about his girlfriend in Jericho, the candle-lit supper of roast lamb and her soft bed. He doesn't even have a cell phone to call and explain. The now moment pulls him out of his "me drama." In Christian language, it's beyond his desires to what is called unselfishness, unconditional care.

DM: Many moons ago, I heard Bernard Lonergan speak at Georgetown, or was it at LMU? He seemed stiff and uncomfortable and delivered his wisdom in a monotone. I never did worship at his altar, although I knew many who underwent the epistemological "conversion" experience that Lonergan's thought seemed to trigger. However, when I read that "achieving human authenticity is ... following the in-built and self-transcending laws of the human spirit," and the "eros of desire," I am reminded of Karl Rahner's view of man, outlined in "*Hoerer des Wortes*." Of course, Karl had his followers, too, (I am admittedly one of them)--and he, too, delivered his convoluted German in a monotone. But neither Bernard nor Karl could or would claim to be a prophet.

GB: I agree with you, Don, about the "sanctifying" well, almost, of old texts like the *Exercises*, and even the Gospels, as if they had to be beyond critique (any nay-saying) and were always adaptable to any century. I don't hear a word of harder criticism about trying to adapt a sixteenth century mind to today. I had the same feeling during the five-hundredth-year honoring of Ignatius, Xavier and Faber. All fine men, to be sure, but we don't entertain any nay-saying about them on virtually anything. It's like an older habit of holding that Aquinas said it all and better than subsequent philosophers.

DM: Of course, and I assume that you can still do the *Exercises* without having read or been converted to Lonerganism. This new book, according to some, finally gives us the "key" to what Ignatius really meant. I am skeptical, first, about the "deification" of Ignatius and his writings. I doubt he would claim for himself what we are making of him. He was as limited in perspective and theology as any good man in his century and asking "what Ignatius would do today" is as futile as asking what any of us would do if inserted into sixteenth-century life as a sixteenth-century person?

JL: I suggest Jesuits or former Jesuits may be the worst judges of Ignatius and his exercises due to the duress of circumstances when we made them or the particular retreat director(s) one had. My unforgettable one was an Alaskan missionary of the Oregon province, (I met many remarkable Alaskan missionaries) who compared the call of Christ the King to the lead sled dogs you depended on to survive in the Arctic.

As for Ignatius and the *Exercises*, I cannot speak to them without mentioning Bill Meissner, S. J.'s work, *Ignatius of Loyola, The Psychology of a Saint,* on the psychology of Ignatius and the psychology of the *Exercises*. Consider the times Ignatius lived through. Consider his spiritual exercises as the work of layperson. Consider how many unique personal leaders followed him.

DM: Ignatius' exercises are, to me, sometimes lifted to the level of the New Testament, that is, as a special "latter day revelation of God" good for all times and all peoples, if only their true meaning can be plumbed.

JL: The Christian test of the *Exercises* should be whether they lead a person to closer and more joyful service of Christ. I still think the four-week structure of the exercises and the contemplation on love to be works of genius for Iñigo. For Iñigo, after all, the director of the person making the retreat was the Holy Spirit, as little as that may be apparent to the literalist reading of his text or the rationalists who taught us how to mediate. That is clearly the point of the discernment of spirits.

MZC: Thank you all. So I think we can conclude that Lonergan's work is useful to help us examine the *Exercises*, and I have to say that most of us still look back into the experience itself rather than a theory. And on that note, I am going to give the last word about spiritual experience, at least for the conversation, to Gene who has a quote from an American Zen master.

GB: This is from Toni Packer's *The Silent Question*: "What unfolds in awareness is a new, subtle listening that may not ever have been experienced before, because most of the time it has been drowned out by all the other noises (desires/fears) taking place in the bodymind.... Can all the rush of wanting, the silent ambition underneath it, the neediness hiding behind it-- can all of that reveal itself in quiet listening and looking.... That is why it's so very important to come to a place of silence, stillness and wondering.... where one can enter into an almost motionless not-knowing." Finally, here's how she describes the now experience: "Awareness replaces thinking and fantasizing about myself with simply being here-- computer humming, keyboard clicking, wind rattling, snowmelt dripping, heart beating, back paining, breathing in and out, in and out -- one moment at a time."

Lonergan, Bernard, *The Dynamism of Desire, Bernard J F. Lonergan, SJ on the Spiritual Exercises of St. Ignatius of Loyola.* (The Institute of Jesuit Sources in St. Louis, 2006)

Robert Doran, SJ, has been at the forefront of publishing Lonergan's Collected Works. You can view his Web site, or register and dive into the seas charted by Lonergan at http://www.bernardlonergan.com.

Boston College's Lonergan Institute:
http://www.bc.edu/bc_org/avp/cas/lonergan/institute/about_institute.html